MAKING DRY BONES LIVE

A Practical Approach to Church History

by Robert C. Walton

Planters Press ™
Brookhaven, PA

Other works by Robert C. Walton

Chronological and Background Charts of Church History
Zondervan, 1986; revised and expanded, 2005

Eternal Values for a Valueless Age
Planters Press, 2011

Faith Reformed Baptist Church Sunday School Curriculum Project
Editor and Principal Author
www.rcwalton.com

Notes on Classic Literature for the Christian High School Teacher
www.rcwalton.com/Literature.htm

MAKING DRY BONES LIVE
Copyright © 2011 by Robert C. Walton. All rights reserved.
ISBN 978-0615539492

Charts taken from CHRONOLOGICAL AND BACKGROUND CHARTS OF CHURCH HISTORY by Robert C. Walton. Copyright © 1986 by The Zondervan Corporation. Used by permission of Zondervan Publishing House. All rights reserved.

MAKING DRY BONES LIVE
A Practical Approach to Church History

TABLE OF CONTENTS	i
LIST OF CHARTS	iii
PREFACE - WHY STUDY CHURCH HISTORY?	iv
PART ONE - THE ANCIENT CHURCH (to 476)	1
1. THE NEW TESTAMENT CHURCH (The First Century)	3
2. THE NEXT GENERATIONS (Post-Apostolic Leaders)	11
3. A GROWING CHURCH FACES COMPETITION (Pagan Religions and Early Heresies)	21
4. THE SEED OF THE CHURCH (The Roman Persecutions and the Edict of Milan)	31
5. BISHOPS AND BAPTISMS (Church Organization and Practice)	41
6. MEN OF IRON WITH FEET OF CLAY (Fourth and Fifth Century Church Leaders)	55
7. THE WORD, THE LORD, AND THE WORK (Doctrinal Controversy)	67
8. OUT OF THIS WORLD (The Development of Monasticism)	83
PART TWO - THE MEDIEVAL CHURCH (476-1517)	95
9. THE CLASH WITH THE INFIDEL (The Rise of Islam)	97
10. THE FALL AND RISE OF THE ROMAN EMPIRE (The Development of the Papacy)	105
11. EARLY MEDIEVAL THEOLOGY (Early Medieval Theology)	113
12. FROM THE DEPTHS TO THE HEIGHTS (Church and State in the Middle Ages)	121
13. RENDING THE SEAMLESS ROBE (The Great Schism of 1054)	131
14. GOD WILLS IT (The Crusades)	139
15. CATHEDRALS OF THE MIND (Scholasticism)	153
16. THE POOR IN SPIRIT (Medieval Monasticism)	165
17. FINANCIERS AND HUMANISTS (Schism and Reform)	179
PART THREE - THE PROTESTANT REFORMATION (1517-1648)	193
18. REFORM EFFORTS THAT FAILED (Forerunners of the Reformation)	195
19. A WILD BOAR IN THE VINEYARD (The Reformation in Germany)	205
20. THE SCHOOLS OF CHRIST (The Reformation in Switzerland)	217
21. REFORMING THE REFORMERS (The Radical Reformation)	231
22. GENEVA'S CHILDREN (The Reformation in France, Scotland, and the Netherlands)	241
23. THE MIDDLE WAY (The Reformation in England)	253
24. THE HOLY COMMONWEALTH (England Under the Stuarts)	265
25. REFORM, REACTION, AND RENEWAL (The Counterreformation)	275
PART FOUR - EUROPE AFTER THE REFORMATION (from 1648)	289
26. GOD, MAN, AND MONKEYS (The Scientific Revolution)	291
27. MEN OF THE COVENANT (The Scottish Covenanters)	301
28. BABEL REVISITED (Theological Collapse in England)	307

29. THE DEEP LONGINGS OF THE HEART (German Pietism)	317
30. THE WORLD FOR A PARISH (The Methodist Revival)	327
31. GOD'S ORPHANS (German Liberal Criticism)	339
32. ESTABLISHMENT AND DISESTABLISHMENT (Decline and Dissent in England)	351
33. THE REFORMED CHURCHES OF EUROPE (Continental Protestantism)	363
34. THE WORLD IN THEIR HANDS (The Golden Age of European Missions)	371
PART FIVE - THE AMERICAN CHURCH (from 1607)	381
35. A CITY SET ON A HILL (Early Colonial Settlements)	383
36. THE SURPRISING WORK OF GOD (The First Great Awakening)	397
37. BROTHER AGAINST BROTHER (The Revolution and the Churches)	405
38. FIRE ON THE MOUNTAINS (The Second Great Awakening)	415
39. ONWARD, CHRISTIAN SOLDIERS (Evangelical Social Reform)	425
40. THE INVISIBLE CHURCH (The Black Church in America)	435
41. WEEDS IN FERTILE GROUND (Utopian Communities and Heterodox Cults)	445
42. ROOTS OF AMERICAN FUNDAMENTALISM (Princeton Theology and the Growth of Dispensationalism)	459
43. THE BATTLE FOR THE BIBLE (Liberals Versus Fundamentalists)	467
44. THAT THEY MAY BE ONE (The Ecumenical Movement)	479
45. TODAY'S NEWS, TOMORROW'S HISTORY (Contemporary American Evangelicalism)	489
APPENDIX - The Popes of the Catholic Church	499
BIBLIOGRAPHY	501
INDEX OF NAMES	505
INDEX OF PLACES	517
INDEX OF EVENTS, MOVEMENTS, ORGANIZATIONS, BOOKS, AND TERMS	523

LIST OF CHARTS

THE ARGUMENTS OF THE APOLOGISTS	14
ROMAN PERSECUTIONS OF CHRISTIANS	33
DEVELOPMENT OF EPISCOPACY IN THE FIRST FIVE CENTURIES	43
FACTORS CONTRIBUTING TO THE SUPREMACY OF THE BISHOP OF ROME	47
THE DEVELOPMENT OF THE NEW TESTAMENT CANON	69
MAJOR ANCIENT CHURCH DOCTRINAL CONTROVERSIES	71
THE ECUMENICAL COUNCILS OF THE EARLY CHURCH	75
THE PRIMARY CAUSES OF THE EAST-WEST SCHISM OF 1054	133
THE CRUSADES	145
THE MUSLIM CONQUEST AND THE CRUSADES - A COMPARISON	147
THE GREAT SCHISM OF THE PAPACY (1378-1417)	183
MEDIEVAL ECUMENICAL COUNCILS	187
THEOLOGICAL ISSUES - LUTHERAN VERSUS REFORMED	227
THEOLOGICAL ISSUES - CALVINIST VERSUS ARMINIAN	249
THEOLOGICAL ISSUES - PROTESTANT VERSUS CATHOLIC	281
MODERN ROMAN CATHOLIC ECUMENICAL COUNCILS	284
GERMAN PIETISM AND ENGLISH METHODISM - A COMPARISON	329
JOHN WESLEY AND GEORGE WHITEFIELD - A CONTRAST	331
RELIGION IN THE THIRTEEN COLONIES	391
MAJOR NINETEENTH-CENTURY AMERICAN CULTS	450-51
A COMPARISON OF HISTORIC COVENANT AND HISTORIC DISPENSATIONAL THEOLOGY	463
DENOMINATIONAL DIVISIONS OVER THE MODERNIST-FUNDAMENTALIST CONTROVERSY	474

WHY STUDY CHURCH HISTORY?

The hand of the Lord was upon me, and he brought me out by the Spirit of the Lord and set me in the middle of a valley; it was full of bones. He led me back and forth among them, and I saw a great many bones on the floor of the valley, bones that were very dry. He asked me, "Son of man, can these bones live?" I said, "O Sovereign Lord, you alone know." (Ezekiel 37:1-3)

Many students approaching the study of Church History have felt a certain kinship with Ezekiel. They have looked around them and seen nothing but dead men's bones - and exceedingly dry ones, at that. What good does it do to study the lives and writings of men who lived hundreds or even thousands of years ago? Will such information help me to get better SAT scores, or find a better job? The answer, of course, is no. But those who study Church History with open eyes and open minds will find much that will make them better servants of Christ, both in their churches and in their communities. What are some of the things that you as a student should expect to gain as a result of this course?

First of all, Christians should expect to benefit from the examples of those who have gone before them. Such benefits can come in a number of ways. To begin with, history is filled with fine Christian men and women whose examples should inspire us to follow in their footsteps. On the other hand, there is much to learn by observing the failures and mistakes of others - as George Santayana said, "Those who fail to learn from history are doomed to repeat it." Furthermore, Church History is able to teach us humility, as we observe the sins and blind spots that plagued even the greatest of God's servants. If men like Augustine, Luther, Calvin, and Whitefield had their flaws, both in their understanding of Scripture and in their way of living, how much more must we, who lack their gifts and zeal, be on guard against those sins that make our own service to God less than perfect?

Secondly, Christians should be able to gain a better understanding of how God works through the study of the history of the church. If Paul told the Corinthians that the incidents of the wilderness wanderings happened to the Israelites "as examples for us," the same is true of the more recent history of God's people. The same God is at work carrying out the same purposes, though admittedly we lack the inspired interpretation of more recent events that the Bible supplies for the events of the Old Testament.

Thirdly, the study of Church History gives life to Christian doctrine. Doctrine makes more sense if we realize how and why the church came to believe what it does. Furthermore, understanding differences among the beliefs and practices of various churches will help us to be more tolerant of those differences, while at the same time developing the kind of discernment that will allow us to distinguish between truth and error, between legitimate differences and outright heresies. Furthermore, realizing how false teachings develop will enable us to be on guard against such teachings in our own lives, in our churches, and in the Christian world at large.

Finally, the study of Church History helps the student to develop a global perspective. We can serve Christ much more effectively if we understand that the church goes far beyond the boundaries of our congregation, our denomination, and our country. A vision for the world comes only through a greater understanding of that world. The study of Church History not only serves the purpose of drawing Christians together as they see their common heritage, but it also motivates believers to care about and participate in the big picture - the Kingdom of God as it advances, around the world and throughout the centuries until Jesus comes.

Part One

THE ANCIENT CHURCH
(to 476)

1

THE NEW TESTAMENT CHURCH

Unlike the famous tale by Charles Dickens, the story of the church in New Testament times could be entitled "A Tale of Three Cities." The center of the church that grew by the power of the Holy Spirit through the work of the followers of Jesus of Nazareth moved successively in the first century from Jerusalem to Antioch to Rome. As it did so, it encountered many of the issues that Christians have faced ever since those early days. The most important questions faced by the church in its early years, however, concerned the relationship between Jews and Gentiles. This matter went to the very heart of the nature of the church and the Gospel, and the ramifications of the Jewish-Gentile question were felt in almost every area of the church's life.

JERUSALEM (A.D. 33-44)
THE JEWISH CHURCH

The Christian Church in its early years consisted largely of Jews. This was the case from its very inception, on the Day of Pentecost, when Jews from all over the Roman world were gathered in Jerusalem for one of the three major Jewish feasts held each year. When Peter preached the good news of Jesus Christ to the crowd assembled that day, over three thousand responded, and the church was off to a good start.

From the very beginning, the church was thought to be a sect within Judaism by both Christians and Jews. The former considered themselves true Jews because they worshipped the promised Messiah, while the latter cast a wary eye at this dangerous heresy being taught by the followers of the Galilean rabbi, Jesus of Nazareth. In fact, it was because of the identification of Christianity with Judaism that the early church faced persecution from the Jewish leaders in Jerusalem. The Jewish leaders would have had no reason to move against a pagan sect, but they felt it their duty to stamp out any attempt to pervert the true religion handed down by God through Moses.

Despite the opposition of the Jewish leadership, however, the church continued to grow by leaps and bounds. From the account given in the early chapters of the book of Acts, five reasons for this growth can be established. The first of these reasons was the spectacular popular impact of the miracles performed by the apostles. Though these were by no means public relations stunts, they served to gather large crowds on several occasions, and the preaching that followed led to the conversion of many. The miracles of the apostles, as with those of Jesus Himself, were the Holy Spirit's way of putting the obvious mark of God upon the preaching of the early church. Having seen such clearly supernatural works, who could doubt that these men had been sent from God with a very important message?

The second factor used by God to bring about the growth of the church was the persecution initiated by the Jewish leaders. It may be difficult to imagine persecution as a cause of growth, but the New Testament makes it clear that growth was the result of the persecution recorded there. The persecution faced by the church in Jerusalem came largely from the Sanhedrin, which was the religious ruling body of Judaism. It consisted of seventy men, almost evenly divided between Pharisees and Sadducees, and wielded considerable authority in both religious and political matters (remember the effective way they blackmailed

Pilate into crucifying Jesus by threatening to report him to the emperor if he didn't do things their way?). The Sanhedrin felt that it was their responsibility to serve as a sort of watchdog over Judaism, and take action against any undesirable deviations from the norm. They were hopeful that the followers of the Way (the earliest term used to describe Christians) would die out quickly after the death of their leader, but that did not turn out to be the case. At first, the persecution took the form of arrests, stern warnings, and brief imprisonments of the apostles. This only resulted in greater enthusiasm on their part, however, since they seemed to cherish the peculiar idea that it was a privilege to suffer for the sake of their Master. After several incidents in which official opposition did nothing to hinder the spread of the Gospel, the venerable rabbi Gamaliel finally advised the Sanhedrin to stop the persecution, reasoning that, if this new movement were of God, nothing could stop it, and if it were not, it would die out on its own without any help from them. Obviously, not many members of the Sanhedrin listened to Gamaliel's advice, as the later experience of Stephen and the early career of Saul of Tarsus clearly attest.

The third factor that contributed to the growth of the Jerusalem church was fellowship. The loving spirit of the early believers, and the way in which they shared their material goods freely with one another, made a strong impression on the local population. It was not so much the power of the preaching that attracted people to the church (though it was the preaching that was used by the Holy Spirit to convert them), as it was the strong fellowship that existed among the body of believers.

The fourth attribute of the early church that contributed to its growth was the discipline exercised by the leaders within the church. The clearest example of this is the account of Ananias and Sapphira given in Acts 5. The result of this disciplinary action was that "great fear seized the whole church and all who heard about these events." People both inside and outside the church were impressed by the evident seriousness of what Christians were doing. This was no social club or intellectual curiosity, but was clearly a matter of life and death.

The last factor given in the book of Acts that contributed to the growth of the church in Jerusalem was the steps taken by the apostles to provide organization for the infant church. Even among the Jews who made up the early church, there were factions, consisting of the Jews who had clung firmly to the traditions of the Jewish religion on the one hand, and those who had largely adapted themselves to the prevalent culture of the Graeco-Roman world in which they lived on the other. This division was a long-standing one, going back to the days of Alexander the Great in the fourth century B.C. Since the church had begun in the midst of a Jewish festival, the converts in Jerusalem were a mixture of local Jews (largely traditional) and Hellenistic Jews (those who adopted Greek ways). It did not take long for the two groups to start fighting. The conflict arose over the distribution of the food donated to the church. The Hellenistic Jews were concerned that the needy among them were being short-changed (after all, the apostles were all traditional Jews), and protested to the apostles. The church resolved the issue when they appointed seven men to oversee the entire food-distribution process, all of whom were chosen by the Hellenists and approved by the entire congregation. This distribution of labor foreshadowed the later establishment of church offices, and led not only to greater peace within the church, but opened a door of ministry to several men who went on to do great work for the Lord (including Stephen and Philip).

Even when the church began expanding outside the city of Jerusalem through the preaching of Philip and Peter, Jerusalem remained the center of church activity. It was in Jerusalem that the apostles stayed, and to Jerusalem that Christians in other places sent when questions arose (as did Philip in Acts 8). It was not until persecution became so severe, with the execution of James the son of Zebedee and the imprisonment of Peter around A.D. 44, that the focus of attention moved from Jerusalem to Antioch. From this time on, though the

Jerusalem church was highly respected, it was on the receiving end of much activity in the church (including the famine relief that was such a matter of concern to the Apostle Paul).

ANTIOCH (A.D. 44-68)
THE JEWISH-GENTILE CHURCH

It was about the time of this severe persecution under the leadership of Herod Agrippa I that the character of the church began to undergo an important change. God had always said that it was His purpose that all the world should be brought under His dominion and should give Him the worship He deserved. Many Jews had lost sight of this important Old Testament truth, however, and had begun to think of themselves as God's people in a way that shut out the rest of the world. Jesus, in His own ministry, had shown that God's Kingdom is open to Gentiles as well as Jews (in His encounters with the Roman centurion and the Syrophoenician woman, for instance), though His disciples had never clearly grasped the point.

God finally found it necessary to spread His truth to the Gentiles in a way that left no question with regard to His intentions. Peter, generally recognized as a leader and spokesman among the Twelve, received a vision from God, directing him to go and preach the Gospel to a Roman centurion by the name of Cornelius, a God-fearer (a term used to describe those who worshipped the true God, but had never been circumcised). When Peter preached to Cornelius and his household, the Holy Spirit fell upon those assembled while Peter was still preaching (he hadn't even gotten to his challenge or application yet!), and the power of God became evident in their midst. How could Peter doubt that God intended to incorporate the Gentiles into His church?

The impression was strengthened by the enormous blessing given by God to the preaching of Paul among the Gentiles on his first missionary journey. Many came to Christ through his preaching, though this occurred amid severe Jewish opposition. Paul quickly discovered that many of the Jews in the church were not at all impressed with the idea of opening the membership to Gentiles. They saw this as a threat to the divinely-given Law of Moses, and accused Paul of perverting the truth for the sake of getting more converts.

All during this time, the center of the church had been shifting from Jerusalem to Antioch in Syria. While Jerusalem was a relatively small city in the vast Roman Empire, not even recognized as the administrative capital of the province in which it was located, Antioch, "The Queen of the East," was the empire's third-largest city, behind Rome and Alexandria. The city had a large Gentile population along with a sizable Jewish minority. The Jews in the city were mostly Hellenistic, and had learned to get along with their Gentile neighbors rather well. When Christianity was brought to the city, many were converted, and the church soon became large and well-established, largely under the leadership of Barnabas and Saul. It was in Antioch that the followers of Jesus were first called Christians, and it was the church in Antioch that sent Barnabas and Saul out on the first missionary journey. According to Paul's account in Galatians 2, the church in Antioch did not struggle significantly with the differences between Jews and Gentiles until the church at Jerusalem interfered, at which time many of the Jewish Christians, including Peter and even Barnabas, were intimidated into separating themselves from the Gentile Christians at meals (it should be noted that meals were a particular problem because of the dietary laws of the Old Testament). The Jewish-Gentile issue was causing so much trouble that everyone realized that something needed to be done. A council was called in A.D. 49, to be held in the city of Jerusalem.

The council, described in Acts 15, heard testimony from those who had had direct contact with God's work among the Gentiles, including Peter and Paul. They spoke in glowing terms of the clear work of the Holy Spirit, insisting that the church should not oppose what God was doing in the world. After much discussion, James, the highly-respected brother of Jesus (said by early sources to have knees like those of a camel because of the untold hours he spent in prayer), expressed the conclusion of the council by affirming that the Old Testament had indeed predicted the spread of the worship of God among the Gentiles, and that consequently it was not necessary for Gentiles to become Jews in order to become Christians. He did insist, though, that in the spirit of brotherly love for the Jewish Christians, Gentiles should be careful not to cause offense in the areas of diet and sexual ethics (in which the Roman world was notoriously lacking).

From this point on, despite persistent opposition from a few remaining "Judaizers," the Gospel spread rapidly among the Gentiles, until soon the Jews were a distinct minority within the church. Paul was not the only apostle who was traveling around and evangelizing during this time. Though the Bible does not tell us anything about their labors, the records of the early church indicate that the apostles of Jesus traveled far and wide preaching the Gospel. Though many of the traditions are unreliable, we know that the disciples scattered in all directions, both inside and outside the Roman Empire. For example, the thriving church in Alexandria is said to have been founded by John Mark, while Thaddaeus supposedly went as far east as Edessa (in present-day Turkey). Thomas is even said to have gone as far as India with the message of the Gospel.

The spread of the Gospel was made easier by several characteristics of the Roman world that God had providentially prepared for the geographical growth of His church. The vast expanse of the Roman Empire made travel easy all around the Mediterranean. Not only were all the nations around the Great Sea at peace with one another as part of the Pax Romana, but they also were linked by the finest system of roads that the world had seen up to that point in history. The Mediterranean world not only shared a common government, but also a common language. The conquests of Alexander the Great had spread the culture and language of the Greeks, and Greek had become the trade language of the Western world. The Old Testament had been translated into Greek several centuries before the time of Christ, and the access to that book (the Septuagint) thus gained by many helped to pave the way for the spread of the Gospel anticipated by the Old Testament prophets. In addition, social conditions in the Empire contributed to the ready acceptance of the Gospel by many. Exposure to various religions had made the Roman world skeptical about many of their beliefs. Gods who had been trusted had failed to deliver their people from the Roman conquerors; Roman gods were increasingly seen as immoral copies of immoral men; even the Greek and Roman philosophers had been able to see that the truth must lie in a realm beyond the material, and that the polytheism of the Greek and Roman gods was a philosophical absurdity.

As we know from the book of Acts, the most prominent ministers of the Gospel continued to be Peter and Paul, the former as the Apostle to the Jews and the latter as the Apostle to the Gentiles. Their success was such that, within a matter of two short decades, a religion unknown to the majority of the Roman world could be described as having "turned the world upside-down."

The shift of the church from Jewish to Gentile brought with it its own set of problems, however. While the Jewish persecutions soon became insignificant, both because of the growing distinction between Christians and Jews and because of the waning power of the Sanhedrin (they were being overwhelmed by the growing popularity of the violently anti-Roman Zealot party in Palestine), the stage was being set for the great Roman persecutions that would dominate the next two and a half centuries.

As long as the Christian church was recognized as a Jewish sect, it enjoyed the protection of the Roman Empire. Judaism had since the days of Herod the Great been recognized as a legal religion, and had even had the privilege of being exempt from the idolatrous rituals associated with many Roman public affairs. The connection with Judaism now began to be questioned, both by Jews and Romans. The Jews had no desire to see the Christians protected by a privilege to which they had no right, but the differences that to the Jews so clearly marked Christianity as a separate religion were of little consequence to the Romans. As a result, when Paul was brought before Gallio in Corinth, for instance, the proconsul refused to rule on the case, insisting that it was an internal Jewish affair that was none of his business (Acts 18:12-17). This case and others like it had much the same effect as when the Supreme Court of the United States refuses to hear a case presented to it today. If the Supreme Court passes on a case, the ruling of the lower court is allowed to stand. Similarly, Gallio's refusal to hear the Jewish charges meant that he affirmed the precedent that placed Christianity under the protective umbrella of Judaism.

Conditions in Rome soon began to change, however. Jews began to come into increasing disfavor in the capital. Claudius had expelled the Jews from Rome in A.D. 49. Conditions in Palestine turned the emperors more and more against Judaism, as corrupt Roman officials did nothing to answer the protests of the Jews, resulting in ever-growing support for the Zealots and their revolutionary ideas. Finally a full-scale revolt broke out in A.D. 66, lasting until the conquest of Masada in A.D. 73. Roman troops were sent to Palestine. In the struggle that followed, Jerusalem was destroyed and thousands upon thousands of Jews were killed. The destruction of Jerusalem ended the Jewish-Gentile conflict in the church, largely because the entire ceremonial system that had been at the heart of the Judaizers' protest had been destroyed with the loss of the Temple. It also ended the threat earlier faced by the church of persecution from the Jewish leadership. It did not, however, end the church's persecution, since it also destroyed the protective umbrella that the church had enjoyed by means of its association with Judaism.

A situation that would eventually pose great danger for Christians had begun to develop in Rome. The rulers in the East had traditionally been treated as gods, and the same honor had been accorded to Western conquerors from the time of Alexander the Great. Few Roman emperors had taken these honors to heart, though they had appreciated the gestures of support thus rendered by their subjects. The first emperor to take the idea of emperor-worship seriously was the madman Caligula (A.D. 37-41; the same emperor who made his horse a consul of Rome and sent his army to attack the sea). Rather than waiting to be declared a god by the Senate after his death, as had been customary since the time of Augustus, Caligula decided that he wanted to enjoy the privileges of deity while he was alive. While this made things uncomfortable for those around him, it set the stage for an intolerable situation for monotheistic Jews and Christians. Only the assassination of the emperor kept him from carrying out his plan to set up a statue of himself in the Temple in Jerusalem, for instance. While emperors after Caligula rarely took this notion of divinity seriously, they continued to follow his precedent and had themselves declared gods by the Senate.

It was this linking of patriotism and worship that ultimately caused trouble for the church. Any who refused to offer incense to the genius of the emperor were thought to be disloyal. As long as Christians were considered Jews, they were exempt from this requirement. But when the legal bond between Christianity and Judaism was severed, Christians were left unprotected against the wrath of a long series of insecure rulers.

The first of these persecutors was Nero, who ruled from 54-68. Though he started off well, his popularity declined rapidly after the deaths of his two chief advisers, Seneca (the brother of the aforementioned Gallio) and Burrus. When a great fire broke out in Rome in A.D. 64, rumors began to circulate that the unpopular Nero had started the fire himself in order to have the opportunity to rebuild the city, including the construction of a golden palace and an enormous statue of himself. Nero needed a scapegoat. He turned to the Christians, who were generally disliked anyway. Most of the Romans disliked Jews because of their peculiar customs, and the Christians were thought to be even worse. The Christians were sour spoilsports who refused to participate in the Roman festivals, looked down their noses at the gladiatorial games in the arenas, and worshipped a god who was so doubtful that they couldn't even make a statue of him!

Thus when Nero announced that the Christians were to blame for the disastrous fire, few came to their defense. The persecution that followed was brief but brutal, and was restricted to the vicinity of Rome itself. The methods used by Nero have been chronicled often, including the practice of sewing Christians up in the skins of animals so they could be torn to pieces by dogs, and taking others and covering their bodies with pitch before burning them to illuminate his gardens at night. This bestial treatment of Christians eventually turned even the sated Roman public against Nero's excesses. But the precedent had been established for the treatment of Christianity as a religion in its own right, and the protection of Judaism had been lost forever.

ROME (A.D. 68-95)
THE GENTILE CHURCH

The persecution under Nero affected the church in several ways. Between the time of the Great Fire and the suicide of Nero, the church lost its two most prominent leaders, Peter and Paul, both of whom were executed in Rome between 64 and 68. It was also during this time that the church in Rome grew to be the largest in the empire. The population of the empire's largest city had been exposed to the preaching of Paul as well as Peter. The large Jewish community in Rome had responded favorably to the Gospel. Furthermore, the persecution had produced a backlash that had gained, not only sympathy for the Christians, but also many conversions as a result of the testimonies of the martyrs. The center of the church thus shifted from Antioch to the capital city of Rome. The church by this time was largely Gentile, with Jews making up only a small minority.

For the thirty years following the end of Nero's persecution, the main challenges faced by the church came from within. Heresies arose that were to be repeated over and over again in the history of the church. Many of these heresies appear in seminal form in the epistles of the New Testament. The most familiar source of such difficulties, of course, is the church at Corinth, which was mired in conflict because of idolizing human leaders, showed a tendency to accept uncritically the morality of the secular world, overemphasized the miraculous gifts of the Spirit, and made adaptations to Greek philosophy that caused them to question the reality of the bodily resurrection of Jesus. The church in Colosse apparently was exposed to some incipient form of Gnosticism, a heresy that would plague the second-century church. They had been taught to worship some sort of angelic hierarchy, and had been seduced by the conflicting temptations of asceticism (denial of the flesh) and moral looseness. The epistles of John reflect the fact that the Greek denial of the permanence of matter had infiltrated the church, causing some to deny the truth of the Incarnation. All of these heresies would appear again, often in many forms, in the centuries to follow.

The years after the destruction of Jerusalem also brought challenges to the leadership of the church. It is obvious from the New Testament that not all accepted the authority of the apostles. Not only did Paul face constant questions about the legitimacy of his apostolic office, but even John, the beloved disciple, was haughtily ignored by men such as Diotrephes. Cerinthus, who taught an early form of Gnostic doctrine (he may have been one of those John had in mind when he penned I John 4:1-3), brazenly asserted his false teachings right in the city of Ephesus, where John was ministering. In fact, the late second-century church father Irenaeus tells a story about John fleeing from a bath-house in Ephesus upon hearing that Cerinthus was in the building. These disputes over what constituted legitimate church leadership were to become a major point of controversy in the second century.

The century closed with another period of persecution, this time at the hands of the emperor Domitian. Ironically, Christians were persecuted at this time because of Domitian's failure to distinguish between Christians and Jews. It was really not until the beginning of the second century that Christians were specifically singled out for persecution by the empire. Domitian sent the Apostle John into exile on the island of Patmos off the coast of Asia Minor, and it was there that he saw the visions that became the basis for the book of Revelation. With the completion of the canon of Scripture (though that canon was not formally recognized until the fourth century), the church was ready to meet the challenges of the post-apostolic period.

MAKING DRY BONES LIVE

The church of the first century has much to teach us that is of value for the church in the twenty-first century. The factors that God used in bringing about the growth of the early church are still important for the church today. Let us consider them, one at a time:

Apostolic miracle-workers no longer exist today, yet the miracles done by the apostles in the first century may serve as evidence of the work of God through the medium of the Scriptures. The miracles recorded in the Bible show to men today that Christianity is no mere philosophy among philosophies, nor is it merely an ethical system that tells men how to live. It is no less than the power of God, and we in the church today would do well to realize that it is that same power that is at work today, changing the lives of men and women.

The persecution faced by the church was a blessing, not a curse. The history of the church has shown again and again that the church thrives when men oppose it most vehemently. Persecution causes God's people to depend on Him rather than themselves, it discourages those who have no genuine commitment to Christ from identifying themselves with the church, and it produces the powerful witness of those martyrs who give their lives for Christ. On the other hand, the church that faces little opposition often has little power or commitment. Does our church today lack power because we comfortably depend on ourselves rather than God?

The early church was known far and wide for the love Christians showed to one another. As a visible demonstration of the power of God to change lives, few things reveal the Gospel to the world more clearly than love shown by Christians to Christian brothers and sisters of different races, cultures, and backgrounds. The church today will only grow under the blessing of God if we show a supernatural love that goes beyond the boundaries of those with whom we would normally associate.

Discipline has never been terribly popular in the church (or anywhere else, for that matter). We think that discipline will turn people away, so we have a tendency to tolerate almost anything in the spirit of open acceptance. It should not surprise us, however, that in our own day many people are attracted to various cults simply because of the strict discipline to be found in such authoritarian groups. Discipline is only undesirable when it is cut off from the twin principles of truth and love. When administered according to truth rather than whim, and carried out in love with the goal of reconciliation, discipline can be a positive force in the growth of the church. A church without discipline cannot long adhere to the truth.

The organization of the church is not some sort of imposed human structure, but rather a recognition of the diversity of gifts given by the Holy Spirit to the Body of Christ. When people in the church are properly organized, they minister, not only to one another, but also to the world in which the church is to be salt and light. Therefore it is important that our churches be organized, not arbitrarily, but according to the guidelines established in Scripture.

FOR REVIEW AND FURTHER THOUGHT

1. Indicate the role played by each of the following men in the growth of the church in the first century: Peter, Paul, John Mark, Thaddaeus, Thomas.

2. What do the opposition (or lack thereof) given to the church by Gamaliel, Gallio, Diotrephes, and Cerinthus indicate about the conflicts faced by the first-century church?

3. Why did the Jewish leadership persecute the early church?

4. Why did the Roman emperors in the first century oppose Christianity? What were the specific reasons for the opposition of Caligula, Nero, and Domitian?

5. What was the original name by which Christians were known? Where were they first called Christians?

6. What three cities were the early centers of Christianity, and what made each one important in the first-century church?

7. Why was the Jerusalem Council of A.D. 49 important in the development of Christianity?

8. What were some of the ways in which God prepared the Roman world to facilitate the spread of the Gospel?

9. Name and describe early heresies that appear in the writings of the New Testament?

10. Define the following terms in one sentence each: Sanhedrin, God-fearer, Judaizers, Pax Romana, Septuagint, Zealots.

11. What do the five factors used by God to bring about the growth of the early church teach us about what is required to keep the church strong today?

2

THE NEXT GENERATIONS

It is a rare thing in the history of the church when a revival lasts more than a single generation. As we will see in the chapters to come, the second generation tends to take for granted the battles won by the first, and as a result often becomes complacent, allowing the "letter" of external observances to replace the "spirit" of true religion. One of the most notable exceptions to this trend was the generation following that of the apostles. Increased persecution forced them to fight the good fight for themselves rather than depending on the deeds of those who had gone before them. The result was a succession of men of God who provided strong leadership for the church during times of great trouble.

In this chapter, we will be looking at three generations of post-apostolic leaders. These men are generally referred to as the Apostolic Fathers, the Apologists, and the Church Fathers, and they provided leadership to the church for the first one hundred and fifty years after the death of the last of the apostles.

THE APOSTOLIC FATHERS

The Apostolic Fathers were the men who led the church in the early part of the second century. They are called Apostolic Fathers because most of them were believed to have had contact with the apostles early in their lives. We will begin by looking briefly at the men and their writings, and then evaluate their importance in the history of the church.

The earliest of the Apostolic Fathers was Clement of Rome (c.30-c.100). We know little of his life, although some suggest he could be the same Clement mentioned by Paul in Philippians 4:3. He was a leader of the church in Rome, and around 95 A.D. he wrote a letter to the church in Corinth, usually referred to as *I Clement*. Things apparently hadn't improved very much since the time Paul had written to the Corinthians over forty years before, because the younger members of the congregation had just staged a minor revolt against the church leadership. Clement wrote to warn them about the seriousness of such an action, and to emphasize the authority of the God-ordained leaders in the church, who had themselves been appointed by apostles.

A contemporary of Clement was Ignatius (d.117), the bishop of Antioch in Syria. About the only things we know about this man come from his own writings, which consist of seven letters written as he was being taken to Rome to be executed. As he traveled through Asia Minor, he wrote letters to six churches, and one to his friend Polycarp, the bishop of Smyrna. These letters encourage the churches to obey their leaders, whom Ignatius designates as bishops, elders, and deacons (the first recorded distinction between bishops and elders). He also warns against the heresy popular at the time that denied the reality of Christ's physical body (Docetism). Perhaps the most striking thing about the letters of Ignatius is the eagerness with which he looks forward to martyrdom. In his letter to the church at Rome, he warns them not to interfere or do anything to prevent his death, using language that to our ears seems peculiarly graphic:

"Let me be food for the wild beasts, through which I can attain to God. I am the wheat of God and I am ground by the teeth of wild beasts so that I may be found the pure bread of Christ ... I would enjoy the beasts that have been prepared for me, and I pray that they will be found prompt for me ... Even if they are unwilling, I will force them ... Fire and cross, packs of wild beasts, cuttings, rendings, crushing of bones, mangling of limbs, grinding of my whole body, wicked torture of the devil - let them come upon me if only I may attain to Jesus Christ."

A third Apostolic Father was Hermas, a Jewish convert in the city of Rome who gained his freedom from slavery, became wealthy, then lost both his family and his wealth under tragic circumstances. He wrote a book called *The Shepherd*, which consists of a series of visions, moral exhortations, and parables. It taught, among other things, that baptism forgave sins previously committed, but that one could repent of serious sin after baptism only once, after which no further repentance was possible. This book was so highly respected in the early church that some even thought it should be given consideration for inclusion in the New Testament.

Another man from this period of whom we know little was a citizen of Alexandria who wrote a letter circulated under the name of Barnabas. Though some in the early years of the church thought this letter to have been written by the companion of Paul, we now realize that it was written from Alexandria in the early part of the second century. Since it was a fairly common, though dishonest, practice in those days to write letters in the name of some famous person in order to gain acceptance for their contents, we cannot even be sure that Barnabas was indeed the author's real name. Whoever wrote the letter, though, we know that he had a good knowledge of the Old Testament, and used that knowledge to try to advance the cause of Christianity. He sought to find Christian truth in the Old Testament by a process called allegorizing, which involves looking for hidden symbolic meanings in passages of Scripture. Though the *Epistle of Barnabas* made little impact in its own right, the use of allegory continued for many years to be popular in the church in Alexandria, and produced many doctrinal distortions.

The next of the Apostolic Fathers, Papias (c.60-c.130), is a bit of a mystery man. We know little of his life except that he was a bishop in the church in Hierapolis in Asia Minor. The tradition that he studied under the Apostle John was accepted by some of the later church leaders, but rejected by others. His writings, too, are mysterious, because none have survived intact over the centuries. All that remains are a few scattered quotations in the writings of other men. These come largely from a work by Papias on the Gospels, and give us the information that Mark wrote his Gospel based on information given him by Peter, and that Matthew originally wrote his Gospel in Hebrew. He also spoke of a future earthly kingdom of Christ, though the man who mentions this, the church historian Eusebius, took a dim view of this particular teaching. It would certainly be fascinating to have in their entirety these works from which we know only such tantalizing tidbits of information!

The last of the Apostolic Fathers was Polycarp (c.69-160), the bishop of Smyrna to whom Ignatius wrote one of his letters. Our knowledge of Polycarp comes from three sources - the letter of Ignatius, a letter written by Polycarp himself to the church at Philippi early in the second century, and an account of the death of Polycarp written by an eyewitness. Polycarp had known the Apostle John in his youth, and grew to become a beloved and respected pastor in Asia Minor. When Ignatius died, he entrusted Polycarp with the responsibility of finding a successor for him. Polycarp himself tried to help the church at Philippi deal with a dispute by writing a letter to them that consists almost entirely of quotations from the books of the Old and New Testaments. The Roman persecutors eventually hunted down this beloved pastor and brought him to the arena, where a large crowd had gathered to witness his execution. The Roman governor begged Polycarp to offer incense to the gods, but he refused. The governor offered to release him if he would merely say, "Away with the atheists!" (Christians were considered atheists because they worshipped no visible gods). Polycarp obligingly pointed to the eager crowd surrounding him in the stands and said, "Away with the atheists!" After further pleading, Polycarp stood firm, saying, "I have served him eighty-six years and in no way has he dealt unjustly with me; so how can I blaspheme my king who saved me?" He was then burned at the stake, much to the delight of the jeering crowd.

Before evaluating the Apostolic Fathers, one other writing deserves mention, an anonymous work called the *Didache*, or *The Teaching of the Twelve Apostles*. This manual of church practice was compiled early in the second century. It contains a section contrasting the way of life and the way of death, gives instruction for receiving members into the church, talks about how to deal with traveling preachers, and closes with warnings in connection with the Second Coming of Christ. It gives considerable insight into the church practices of the day, telling us, for instance, that baptism of believing adults by immersion was considered the norm, but that pouring was acceptable if necessary; that fasting was to be practiced twice weekly, not "on the same days as the hypocrites, who fast on Monday and Thursday" (a reference to the Jewish practice), but "you should fast on Wednesday and Friday"; and that a false prophet could be recognized if he asked for money, or if he took advantage of the church's hospitality for more than two days.

The major value of the Apostolic Fathers to us today is the picture they give us of the life of the church in the early part of the second century. They reveal to us godly men who were dedicated to the Lord and concerned for the churches over which God had given them oversight. They did not shrink from following their Lord to the point of death, and as such are examples to us all. The voluminous quotations from Scripture to be found in the writings of these men demonstrate that, long before any official decisions were made on the subject, the writings that now make up our New Testament were recognized by the church as having equal authority with the books of the Old Testament.

The Apostolic Fathers also made some negative contributions to the life of the church, and these must be recognized, as well. Though their willingness to give their lives for the sake of Christ is praiseworthy, the sort of obsession shown by Ignatius was to bear bad fruit in the life of the church. The glory associated with dying for Christ led ultimately to the lifting up of the martyrs as "saints," a distinction that has led to numerous abuses in the church's history.

The distinction made by Ignatius between elders and bishops, coupled with the emphasis placed on the authority of the bishop by many of these men, turned out to be "the camel's nose under the tent" (according to an old proverb, if a camel puts his nose under your tent, the rest of him will soon follow!). As we will see later, this was the first step in the long process that was eventually to produce the Roman Catholic doctrine of the papacy, in which the pope is seen as the head of a great hierarchy of church leaders.

The final negative contribution of the Apostolic Fathers was the practice of allegorical interpretation introduced in Alexandria. This approach to Scripture, which divorced the Word of God from the intentions of its authors and left it to the whim of the "spiritual" interpreter, was much abused in the generations that followed.

THE APOLOGISTS

As the persecution of the church by the emperors of Rome became increasingly more severe, two things happened - the rationalizations used by the rulers to excuse their attacks against Christians became more and more far-fetched, and the church began to respond to these arguments in ways that unbelievers could understand. The men who undertook the responsibility of defending the Christian faith against its unbelieving attackers were called Apologists. Most of these men were educated men who had become Christians in adulthood. They knew the ideas that were popular in the Roman world, and they used those same ideas to defend Christianity. They were particularly active in the second half of the second century, beginning with the reign of Marcus Aurelius (161-180).

The greatest of these was Justin (c.100-165), known as Justin Martyr because he was beheaded for his faith. He had grown up in Palestine, the son of pagan parents, and had

THE ARGUMENTS OF THE APOLOGISTS

JEWISH ARGUMENTS VS. CHRISTIANITY	RESPONSES OF APOLOGISTS
Christianity is a deviant form of Judaism.	The Jewish law is by nature temporary and points to the New Covenant.
The humble carpenter who died on a cross does not correspond to the Messiah prophesied in the Old Testament.	The Old Testament predicted both the sufferings and the glory of the Messiah.
The deity of Christ contradicts the unity of God.	The Old Testament indicates a plurality of persons within the unity of the Godhead.

APOLOGISTS' ARGUMENTS AGAINST JUDAISM

Old Testament prophecy is fulfilled in Christ.
Old Testament types point to Christ.
The destruction of Jerusalem showed God's condemnation of Judaism and vindication of Christianity.

PAGAN ARGUMENTS VS. CHRISTIANITY	RESPONSES OF APOLOGISTS
The doctrine of the Resurrection is absurd.	There were eyewitnesses in the Gospels. The effect on the disciples was profound. There are analogies in natural cycles (e.g., seasons).
There are contradictions in the Scriptures.	Harmonies like Tatian's *Diatessaron* answer contradictions.
Atheism is widely held.	Even Plato favored an unseen god.
Christianity is the worship of a criminal.	Jesus' trial violated both Jewish and Roman law.
Christianity is a novelty.	Christianity had been in preparation for all eternity. Moses antedated pagan philosophers.
Christianity evidences a lack of patriotism.	Christians obey all laws that do not violate conscience.
Christians practice incest and cannibalism.	Observe the lifestyles of Christians, particularly the examples of the martyrs.
Christianity leads to the destruction of society.	Natural calamities are really the true God's judgment against false worship.

APOLOGISTS' ARGUMENTS AGAINST PAGANISM

Pagan philosophers plagiarized, stealing their best ideas from Moses and the prophets.
Polytheism is a philosophical absurdity and a moral disaster.
Pagan philosophers contradict one another and even themselves.

APOLOGISTS' ARGUMENTS FOR CHRISTIANITY

All truth found in pagan philosophers anticipates Christianity and is brought together by it.
Miracles performed by Christ, the apostles, and other Christians prove its truth.
The spread of Christianity despite overwhelming obstacles shows it to be true.
Christianity alone is suited to meet the deepest needs of human beings.

studied philosophy, though his training left him with the impression that most philosophers cared more than anything else about the amount of money they could make from their teaching. After a conversation with an old man in Ephesus, he became a Christian, and settled in Rome to teach his newly-found philosophy. His major surviving works include two Apologies and a book called *Dialogue with Trypho the Jew*. In the Apologies, he argued that Christianity was superior to all other philosophies because it brought together the truth to be found in all that pagan philosophers had discovered. In the *Dialogue with Trypho*, he argued for the truth of Christianity on the basis of fulfilled prophecy from the Old Testament.

Another noted apologist was Tatian (110-172) who, unlike Justin, saw nothing of redeeming value in the secular philosophies of the age. He attacked the pagan religions as immoral and absurd, and defended Christianity against the charge that the Gospel writers contradicted one another by compiling the *Diatessaron*, the first harmony of the Gospels. Toward the end of his life, however, he went off the deep end into allegorical interpretation, and associated himself with the Gnostic heresy.

The apologists found themselves defending the Christian faith in the face of incredible prejudice and misunderstanding. Christians were accused of being atheists because they worshipped no visible god; of being cannibals because they ate the body and drank the blood of a dead Jew; of incest because they married those whom they had earlier called "brother" or "sister"; of destroying society, and other equally absurd charges. The apologists encouraged their pagan critics to observe the lives of Christians so they could see that these charges were false; in particular, they held up the example set by the martyrs to demonstrate the sincerity and commitment of Christians. They also attacked pagan philosophies, claiming that Christianity had been around much longer, and that people like Plato had really gotten all of their good ideas from Moses. They even turned around the charge about the destruction of society, insisting that earthquakes, floods, and other such natural disasters were not caused by Christians, but were the result of God's judgments against pagan Rome.

The apologists certainly did not succeed in putting a halt to the persecution, and it is questionable how many people were converted to Christianity by their arguments. In fact, their tendency to picture the Christian faith as bringing together the best of worldly philosophies may have contributed in some measure to the later practice in the church of using pagan philosophies to deal with doctrinal questions. There can be no question, however, that the lives of these men made an impact at least as large as their writings. The deaths of the martyrs provided perhaps the most convincing argument for the truth of Christianity, and many turned to Christ because of the example of these dedicated believers.

THE CHURCH FATHERS

The third group of church leaders in the period before us is the men known as the Church Fathers. They provided leadership for the church in the first half of the third century. Among these men, there are five to whom we must give our attention.

Irenaeus, who lived in the last part of the second century, sat at the feet of Polycarp as a young man growing up in Smyrna, then later went to the Roman province of Gaul, where he did extensive missionary work and eventually became the bishop of Lyons. In addition to his missionary work, he is known best for his work *Against Heresies*, in which he defends orthodox Christian doctrine against the various forms of false teaching prevalent in his day, especially Gnosticism. Though a fuller treatment of Gnosticism appears in the next chapter, it would be useful to note at this point that the Gnostics believed that they had access to special insight into the Scriptures that came from allegorical interpretation, and that was only available to the elite few. Irenaeus argued that the true teachings of Scripture (the "rule of faith") had been passed down from the apostles through the leaders of the church (for example, from Jesus to John to Polycarp to Irenaeus), and that those who claimed insight into the teachings of Jesus by means of some mystical process were deceiving themselves and the church.

Another leader in the western part of the empire was Tertullian (c.160-c.220), a skillful lawyer from Carthage who never accepted an official position in the church. Though he was not converted until middle age, his powerful arguments made him one of the church's greatest weapons against pagans and heretics alike. He argued against the persecution of the church on legal grounds, and opposed false teachers with devastating logic. He also was the first to use the Latin term from which we get our word *Trinity* to describe the Godhead. His personal discipline caused him to detest those who lived less consistent lives than himself, and he eventually joined a group known as the Montanists, who sought a higher level of spirituality through lives of strict holiness.

A third western representative of the Church Fathers is Cyprian (c.200-258), who served for the last eleven years of his life as bishop of Carthage. He, like Tertullian, studied law and became a Christian relatively late in life. When he came to Christ in 245, he gave himself diligently to the study of the Scriptures. He made such a good impression on the people of Carthage that he became the bishop of the church only two years after his conversion. In the year 250, the emperor Decius initiated a major persecution of Christians. Cyprian himself went into hiding, believing that the church would be better off with him alive rather than dead. When the persecution ended a year later with the death of Decius, Cyprian returned to find that some had denied the faith in order to avoid persecution, either by offering incense willingly or after torture, or by bribing a friendly official to say that they had. These people now wanted to repent and be restored to the fellowship of the church. Cyprian took a hard-line position, insisting that those who had offered incense willingly or who had bribed officials could never be restored to the church, but must pray to God alone for forgiveness. He allowed those who had given in under torture to return, on condition that they do penance for a designated period. The resulting controversy, coupled with a similar one in Rome, almost split the church to the point that two different sets of congregations and leaders existed, each refusing to recognize the validity of the other. This dispute, eventually called the Donatist Controversy, continued to get worse until the days of Augustine in the early fifth century, when it was resolved to the satisfaction of most of the parties involved. Cyprian also insisted firmly on his own authority as bishop, requiring obedience from his own people, but maintaining that no other bishops could tell him what to do (he said that, though the bishop of Rome may have a primacy of honor, he has no right to claim authority over other bishops). He also opened the door for the Roman Catholic doctrine of transubstantiation (the teaching that the bread and wine of the Lord's Supper actually become the body and blood of Christ) by teaching that clergy were sacrificing priests, offering the body of Christ on the altar of the church. He ultimately died a martyr's death, though his influence in the church opened the door to much trouble for many years thereafter.

While the Latin Church Fathers in the west were concerning themselves with matters of doctrine and practice in the church, the Greek Church Fathers in the east were much more involved in philosophical considerations. The two most notable of these were Clement of Alexandria (c.150-c.215) and his famous pupil, Origen (c.185-c.254). Clement, not to be confused with the Clement of Rome mentioned earlier, was trained in philosophy and was converted as an adult. In about 190, he became the instructor in the school in Alexandria founded by Pantaenus. He perpetuated the allegorical interpretation that had been popular in Alexandria since at least the time of Christ, and passed this approach on to his pupils. He brought together the philosophy of the Greeks and the teachings of Scripture by emphasizing Christ as the *logos*, the divine reason that had been such a matter of concern to Plato and others. The fruit of his allegorical approach to Scripture was not fully seen, however, until the time of Origen.

Origen was born into a Christian family in Alexandria. He was a brilliant and dedicated young man, committed to Christ and to his studies. When his father, Leonidas, was arrested in 202, Origen, though still in his teens, was insistent upon joining his father in the arena. His mother pleaded with him to remain at home and save his life, but the young man would not hear of it. Finally, his mother kept him from martyrdom by hiding all of his clothing so he would be unable to leave the house. The following year, Clement left the school in Alexandria, and Origen was named to replace him. He took the allegorical approach developed by Clement and applied it to many different areas of Christian thought. He wrote commentaries on Scripture that contained three levels of interpretation, the literal, ethical, and allegorical, which he said corresponded to the body, soul, and spirit of man. He wrote one of the church's first systematic theologies, in which he tried to bring together all Christian truth. He also wrote *Against Celsus*, a response to one of the more philosophical attacks against Christianity to be published in the third century.

Origen's life was one of unquestioned piety. He lived very simply, and according to Eusebius he took literally the admonition to make himself a eunuch for the sake of the kingdom of heaven. Despite his brilliance and his piety, however, his doctrine did much to damage the church. He adopted the Greek distinction between matter and spirit, maintaining that the former was evil while the latter was good. He taught that all eventually would be saved, even the demons, and that matter would be destroyed and all absorbed into God. He died a martyr after torture by the Romans, but was declared a heretic by the Synod of Constantinople in 543.

The contributions of the Church Fathers consist largely in their amplification of our understanding of Christian doctrine, largely in relation to the deity of Christ and the doctrine of the Trinity, and their opposition to the heresies of their day, particularly Gnosticism. They did contribute much to the movement of Christian doctrine away from the Scriptures in other areas, however. There are two major ways in which this occurred.

The first involves the prevalence of allegorical interpretation, particularly in Alexandria. There is no question that the use of allegory paved the way for theologians in the church to interpret the Scriptures in any way they pleased, and often very fancifully at that. The most significant departure to come from this practice was the combining of Greek philosophy and Christian theology, which produced many doctrines in the church that were not even remotely connected with Scripture. One example of this is the role assigned to Mary, who was seen as the Second Eve, fulfilling a similar role in redemption to that Eve had played in the Fall.

The second relates to the authority of the church in general and the bishop in particular, a matter of concern largely in the west. The authority ascribed to the bishop involved both seeing him as a representative of Christ because he was a successor of the apostles, and seeing him as presiding over the sacrifice of Christ, as a successor of the Old Testament priests. As the authority of the clergy grew, so did the emphasis on the role of works in salvation. The sacraments grew in importance, leading men to believe that they could be right with God if they only participated faithfully in the ritual of the church.

MAKING DRY BONES LIVE

What can be learned of practical importance from the church leaders in the first century and a half after the apostles? We could easily focus on the importance of interpreting the Bible according to its grammatical and historical contexts instead of spinning off some allegorical fantasy. We could center our attention on the significance of keeping the authority of church leaders within the bounds designated by Scripture. Certainly both of these issues play a major role in the period of time before us. I would like to reserve these matters for later consideration, however, since we have seen the beginnings of the departures from the Word of God in these areas, but have not yet had the opportunity to see the full fruit of such departures. Consequently, we will return to these questions when their results in the life of the church have become more obvious.

The issue I would like us to consider does involve church leadership, however. Paul told Timothy that an elder "must not be a recent convert, or he may become conceited and fall under the same judgment as the devil" (I Timothy 3:6, NIV). A perfect example of the wisdom of Paul's warning may be seen in the life of Cyprian. This brilliant and dedicated man must have been a real "prize convert" for the church in Carthage. How they must have rejoiced when they heard that the great lawyer had come to Christ! They assumed, as we often tend to do today, that great talent will make a man a great servant of God. In some ways, Cyprian turned out to be exactly what the people in Carthage expected. He was a great administrator, and met crises decisively and with assurance. Yet his lack of humility in dealing with other church leaders, with those with whom he differed, and with those who had lapsed into sin led the church in North Africa to the brink of ruin. He promoted schism in the church because he refused to accept the fact that he could be wrong, or that those who differed with him could be a legitimate part of the church.

How often do Christians today fall victim to the same mentality that led the Christians of Carthage to choose Cyprian as their leader? We may not often ordain new converts as bishops, but how often do we expect newly-converted "celebrities" to act as spokesmen for the Christian faith, whether they be athletes, musicians, or politicians? Should it surprise us when many such new converts turn out to be dismal failures and terrible disappointments, or should we instead be surprised when such a person occasionally, by the grace of God, succeeds in accomplishing much good for the kingdom?

The qualification discussed here is only one of many listed by Paul in I Timothy 3, of course. If we learn nothing else from this period of church history, we must remember the importance of taking seriously the Bible's teaching concerning qualifications for church leadership. Whenever the church chooses its leaders according to the world's standards of ability rather than those given by God, the church will suffer, not only in the lifetime of that leader, but often for generations to come.

The Next Generations

FOR REVIEW AND FURTHER THOUGHT

1. When did the Apostolic Fathers live? Why are they called Apostolic Fathers?

2. What does the *Didache* tell us about the practice of baptism in the early church?

3. What is allegorical interpretation, and why is it dangerous?

4. Why is it important that the Apostolic Fathers quoted many of the books of the New Testament?

5. What was the attitude of the early Christians toward persecution? Do you think this attitude was a proper one? Why or why not?

6. What were some of the charges directed against Christians by the Romans? How did the apologists respond to these charges?

7. Why is Tatian's *Diatessaron* considered a work in defense of the Christian faith?

8. Do you think that the attempt by the apologists to use philosophy, and thus meet the critics of Christianity on their own terms, was a good idea? Why or why not?

9. For what good reason did Irenaeus emphasize the fact that the bishops of the church were the successors of the apostles?

10. Do you think that Irenaeus' argument that the true doctrine of the church is that which has been passed down through the leaders of the church would be effective today? Why or why not?

11. Identify the following people and the role each played in this unit: Marcus Aurelius, Eusebius, Decius, Leonidas.

12. Define the following terms in one sentence each: martyr, Docetism, *The Shepherd*, allegory, *logos*, rule of faith, transubstantiation, Synod of Constantinople.

13. How is Cyprian's career a warning against ignoring Paul's teaching that new converts are not to be made leaders in the church?

3

A GROWING CHURCH FACES COMPETITION

The spectacular events surrounding the life and ministry of Jesus elicited little more than a yawn from the Roman world at large. Few seem to have known anything of the events taking place in the obscure border province of Palestine, and those who did know saw little importance in them. Within a century, however, all that had changed. Christianity quickly became the fastest-growing religion in the empire, a force none could afford to ignore. Though they did not give ground easily, the decadent religions of the Greeks and Romans simply could not compete with the spiritual energy and lofty ethics of Christianity.

Growth produces its own troubles, of course, and the growth of the church was no exception. At the same time that Christianity was threatening to overwhelm the empire, there were forces at work threatening to tear it apart from the inside. These forces are what we call heresies. The word "heresy" comes from a word meaning "choice," but it usually refers to a religious teaching that differs from the commonly-accepted norm. The heresies of the second and third centuries had the potential to change the character of Christianity drastically. The extent to which they failed is a mark of God's sovereign protection of His church; the extent to which they succeeded should serve as a warning to any who would become complacent of the continual tendency of the human heart to follow the wisdom of men.

COMPETITORS FOR THE SOUL OF THE EMPIRE

The secular state is a modern phenomenon. The idea that politics and religion should be divorced from one another never occurred to the ancients. To them, religion was central to life. Even if rulers themselves sometimes put little stock in the religion of their people, they nonetheless realized that religion could be a powerful tool for manipulating the population.

In the Roman Empire of the first three centuries after Christ, religion was indeed everywhere one might look. When Paul commented on the extreme religiosity of the Athenians, he was not describing something unique to the city of Athens. The vast Roman Empire contained religions of all sorts. The Romans themselves had a long history of nature religion, to which they had appended the traditional mythology of the Greeks. Other conquered peoples within the Empire had brought their own religions with them, and were allowed to practice them freely, as long as it did not interfere with the stability of the state.

To all outward appearances, the worship of the traditional gods and goddesses was flourishing in Rome. Vast crowds filled the temples on festival days, and pagan priests thrived on the contributions of the people. The emperors themselves consulted astrologers and oracles before making major decisions, and outwardly supported the temples of their favorite deities. But under the surface, all was not well. Despite the wide participation in the worship of the pagan gods, few really believed. Philosophers had long ago realized that the gods were inferior in their behavior to many good men, and had even asserted the philosophical absurdity of polytheism. Most treated the stories of the gods as myths, often attempting to avoid the blatant immorality of many of the stories by the use of allegory. While cynicism about the gods provided considerable fodder for the entertainers of the day, the widespread unbelief in the traditional religions left a moral and spiritual vacuum in the lives of the people. They needed more than entertainment when faced with the suffering of life and the prospect of death.

One solution to this religious vacuum was to substitute political loyalty for spiritual comfort. As historian Will Durant has noted, "The deification of the emperors revealed not how much the upper classes thought of their rulers, but how little they thought of their gods." The emperors recognized that religion could be a powerful tool for holding the empire together. It was this desire to unify the diverse peoples of the empire that caused the emperors, though at first reluctantly, to support the spread of emperor worship. Though this attempt to bring the peoples of the empire together on a political basis failed, it was the main cause for the vicious persecutions of Christians during the second and third centuries. Ironically, what the emperors were unable to accomplish through the cult of emperor worship was eventually done successfully by Constantine and those who followed him. Christianity itself became the force around which the empire coalesced.

Before Christianity became the tool of emperors, however, other religions rushed into the vacuum created by the laughable traditional religions and the sterile philosophies of the Stoics and Epicureans. Most of these aggressive new religions came from the East, by way of traders, captives, and the Roman soldiers who had occupied posts for many years on the eastern borders of the empire. These new religions are known collectively as mystery cults, largely because of the close secrecy surrounding their rites. The mystery cults resulted from the transplantation of eastern religions into the Roman world. In general, the mystery cults were dualistic and incorporated fertility rites of some sort. Older versions included the Baal-Astarte fertility religion of the Canaanites, the Dionysian and Orphic cults among the Greeks, and the Isis-Osiris myth of the Egyptians.

By far the biggest competitor to Christianity for the soul of the Roman Empire, however, was a mystery religion called Mithraism. Though it appealed to a different segment of the population than did Christianity (Mithraism, open only to men, flourished in the macho world of the Roman army, which at this point contained few Christians, largely because participation involved offering incense to the emperor), there was a time in the late second century when it was growing almost as fast.

Mithraism had its roots in the Persian religion of Zoroastrianism, which grew out of the teachings of the Persian prophet Zarathustra, who lived in the fifth or sixth century B.C. Zoroastrianism was dualistic, teaching that the universe was caught up in a great battle between the good god Ahura-Mazda and the evil god Ahriman. The followers of the religion believed that by living lives of purity they contributed to the eventual victory of Ahura-Mazda and the overthrow of Ahriman. Mithraism incorporated the dualistic view of the universe taught by the Zoroastrians, but focused its attention on the Persian god Mithra, a sun god who was thought to play a mediatorial role between good and evil. The cult also incorporated the fertility idea, as Mithra was usually pictured riding astride a bull. The god is shown killing the bull, and from the wound in the bull sprout various kinds of grain. Bull-slaying rites were common to many of the fertility cults. Mithraism borrowed a ceremony known as the taurobolium from the cult of the Great Mother (*Magna Mater*). The taurobolium was an initiation ceremony in which the initiate would be lowered into a pit, which was then covered with an iron grate. A bull was led onto the grate, then was slaughtered, effectively baptizing the initiate in the steaming blood of the bull. It is easy to see why such a religion would appeal to the men of the Roman army. But Mithraism also had certain characteristics that set it apart from the other mystery cults, and contributed significantly to its growth. Unlike the other mystery religions, which were notorious for the immorality of their fertility rituals, Mithraism advocated an austere and ascetic lifestyle, and upheld high moral standards that attracted many who were fed up with the debauchery all around them.

Though the mystery cults eventually faded from the scene, they left their mark on both the empire and the church. Their rapid growth briefly filled the spiritual vacuum that Christianity was eventually to occupy. But their greatest impact was through attempts to bring the teachings and practices of the mystery cults into Christianity itself.

COMPETITORS FOR THE HEART OF THE CHURCH

Christians have always had difficulty dealing with the tension of being in the world but not of it. It is important for Christians to meet the world on its own ground in order to preach the Gospel effectively, yet remain apart from the world in order to maintain its distinctiveness. The church has always found it very difficult to do both of these at the same time. Either they have isolated themselves from the world in order to maintain their difference, or have become too much like the world in order to communicate the truth to unbelievers. Such imbalances strike at the very heart of Christianity. The message of the Gospel is both incarnation and redemption - God became what man is in order to make man other than what he is. To deny either is to undermine the Christian Gospel.

In the second and third centuries, several variations of Christian teaching arose to compete for the heart of the church. Because they failed, we know them as heresies. In one way or another, each struck at the foundation of the Gospel, and were subsequently rejected. The three most important of these heresies were Ebionism, Gnosticism, and Montanism.

A.   EBIONISM

The Ebionites were a group of Jewish Christians in the region east of the Jordan River in Palestine. Their name means "the poor," and despite the conviction of their critics that the name referred to their theology, it is most likely derived from Jesus' reference to "the poor in spirit" in the Sermon on the Mount. They were in many ways survivors of the "Judaizers" opposed by Paul throughout his ministry. They taught that the Jewish law was necessary for salvation, practiced circumcision, and used only an altered version of the Gospel of Matthew in Hebrew. They elevated James the brother of Jesus, along with the apostle Peter, while denying the legitimacy of Paul's apostleship. They denied the incarnation of Christ, teaching instead that Jesus was a prophet upon whom the Holy Spirit came at His baptism. Because of His obedience to the law, God the Father later adopted Jesus as His Son. They anticipated that the Messiah would soon return to earth to set up His millennial Kingdom with its capital at Jerusalem. The Ebionites rejected the Jewish sacrificial system, but maintained the purification rituals and dietary restrictions. In this, they were somewhat similar to the Essenes, the writers of the Dead Sea Scrolls who lived in the same general area. They saw themselves as the true bridge between Christianity and Judaism, hoping ultimately to reunite the two religions in the truth as they saw it. In reality, they were rejected by Jews as innovators and by Christians as legalists. They survived into the fourth century, but are known to us today largely through a group of third-century writings falsely ascribed to Clement of Rome, along with descriptions written by their opponents among the orthodox theologians of the church.

B.   GNOSTICISM

Gnosticism was not a single movement, but a group of diverse movements connected by the idea of a hidden knowledge (Greek *gnosis*). The numerous variations of Gnosticism had certain elements in common. All were dualistic, borrowing from the Greeks the belief that spirit was good and matter evil. As a result of their assertion that matter was evil, they denied many of the fundamental teachings of Christianity, including the biblical doctrines of creation, incarnation, and redemption. Since matter was evil, God, who is good, could not have created it, so some other explanation had to be devised. Since matter was evil, God could not have taken on human flesh, so the Gnostics denied the humanity of Christ. If Christ was not man, he could not have died, so redemption was tied, not to the death and resurrection of Christ, but to the impartation of a secret knowledge that was available only to the chosen few. Gnostics drew widely divergent ethical conclusions from their denial of the importance of matter. Most were ascetics, teaching that involvement with the flesh was involvement with evil. A few, though, taught that since goodness was in the mind, what people did with their bodies made little difference. They thus engaged in lives of unbridled indulgence, including sexual orgies of the most disreputable sort, which they claimed elevated their minds to ecstasies of enlightenment.

The origins of Gnosticism are shrouded in contradictory evidence. The early church almost universally ascribed the Gnostic heresy to the work of Simon Magus, the Samaritan sorcerer who was soundly condemned by Peter for trying to buy the power of the Holy Spirit in Acts 8. According to early traditions, he claimed that he was the incarnation of the divine principle, and that salvation consisted in knowledge of himself. Traveling with him was a prostitute named Helena, who he said was the incarnation of divine intelligence. Simon allegedly dogged the steps of Peter from town to town, opposing the Gospel with his own magic arts. One version of the story claims that Simon finally reached Rome, where he sought to bring down the claims of Christ once and for all by instructing his followers to bury him, so that he, too, could rise from the dead on the third day. Needless to say, this (or some similar calamity) ended the career of Simon Magus. While most today would doubt that Simon was the founder of Gnosticism, recognizing that Gnosticism developed from a wide range of religious influences both inside and outside of Christianity, the evidence of Simon's involvement as an early teacher of heresy is too strong to ignore. In order to understand something of the variety of Gnostic teachings, we now turn to a consideration of three major versions of Gnosticism - the sects that grew from the teachings of Valentinus, Marcion, and Mani.

1. VALENTINUS

Valentinus was an Alexandrian whose exposition of Gnosticism was the most influential and best known version of the heresy. He traveled widely and spread his views in North Africa and Rome, and his personal magnetism was such that he narrowly missed election as the bishop of Rome. Before he died in about 160, however, he had been excommunicated by the church, and with good reason. For many years, our knowledge of his teachings came only from the writings of his opponents, such as Irenaeus and Tertullian, but in 1946, a group of documents was discovered at Nag Hammadi in Upper Egypt that contained numerous Gnostic writings, including *The Gospel of Truth*, probably written by Valentinus himself.

His version of Gnosticism begins with the Greek assumption that matter is evil, and then seeks to explain the problem of how evil can exist in a universe ruled by a good God. The problem is not a new one, nor one that the church has found easy to solve, but Valentinus' approach to it was certainly unique. He asserted that God originally existed alone. Of this God we can know nothing. Because he did not wish to remain alone, he produced two spirit-beings called aeons. These in turn produced others, who then produced more, until there were a total of thirty aeons, who were as a group known as the *Pleroma* (the Greek word for "fullness"). As these aeons were created, each successive pair became weaker as they got further from the Unknown Father. The last of the aeons was a female named Wisdom, who desired to know the Unknown Father. Because God is unknowable, she was unsuccessful, and in her sorrow produced another female aeon called Achamoth. This created an unthinkable situation in the Pleroma -imbalance. As a result, Achamoth was ejected. Other aeons in the Pleroma attempted to restore the balance by creating more aeons called Christ, Jesus (both male), and Holy Spirit (female). Unfortunately, the damage had already been done. Achamoth gave birth to another aeon called Demiurge. In cooperation with her son, the disreputable Achamoth created matter; her son then gave it form. He created not only the bodies of men, but also their souls. Through the influence of Wisdom, however, Demiurge infused the souls of men with varying sparks of divine intelligence. It was the task of the aeon Jesus to come to earth and teach those men with sparks of divinity in their souls the secret knowledge they needed to shake off the evil bodies in which they had been imprisoned. Most men have no spark of divinity, and thus are impervious to spiritual things. Others contain so little that, though they may be said to have souls, the best they can hope for is to live by faith. The chosen few, however, can live by knowledge - that hidden *gnosis* passed on from Jesus to His disciples, and from them to the teachers of Gnosticism. They alone will be able to escape their bodies at death and make their way through the heavenly spheres to be reunited with the Unknown Father.

2. MARCION

A far more dangerous version of Gnosticism was taught by a wealthy ship builder from Sinope in Asia Minor named Marcion. His teachings were far more dangerous to the church than those of Valentinus because they were far closer to Christianity. Anyone looking at the scheme of Valentinus would immediately recognize that it was very different from orthodox Christianity. Marcion, however, was able to incorporate a certain internal logic into his teaching that enabled him to draw many sincere Christians after him.

Marcion grew up in a Christian family in the region of Pontus, and his father was the bishop of Sinope. He left his home around 140 A.D., and came to Rome, where he came under the influence of a Gnostic teacher named Cerdo. The brand of Gnosticism taught by Marcion was a thinly-veiled form of anti-Semitism (something in which the church has rarely needed encouragement). While rejecting the Pleroma myth of Valentinus, Marcion taught that the God of the Old Testament was really the Demiurge, the creator of matter. It was this God who chose the Jews and harshly destroyed all others. It was the Unknown Father who sent His Son Jesus into the world, not the Jehovah of the Old Testament. Jesus was not born of a virgin, but suddenly appeared in the synagogue of Capernaum in 29 A.D. His body was not real, nor was His death or resurrection. He came to save the souls of men, but not their bodies. His true message was preached by the Apostle Paul, but corrupted by His other followers. Marcion consequently rejected the entire Old Testament, as well as any books in the New Testament (which had not yet been formally defined) that smacked of Judaism. He accepted only ten epistles of Paul (minus the pastorals; even the ones he accepted were edited to remove references to the Old Testament) and a severely reduced version of the Gospel of Luke. Though he rejected the validity of the law, he advocated a life of strict asceticism. Like Valentinus, he was excommunicated by the church in Rome, but his teachings forced the church to answer two key questions: What are the books of the New Testament, and how do they relate to the Old Testament of the Jews?

3. MANI

While some scholars do not consider Marcion a Gnostic because his teaching was too close to Christianity, others do not consider Mani a Gnostic because his ideas are too far away. Mani is the best example we have of what happened when the ideas of the mystery cults were combined with Christianity. His teachings were a combination of Zoroastrian dualism, Gnostic Christianity, and some would suggest even Buddhism.

Mani was born in Ctesiphon in Persia in the year 215. His father belonged to a group known as the Mandaeans, who professed to be followers of John the Baptist. He left this sect when he began to have visions, and began to spread what he saw as a universal religion. The

Magi (Zoroastrian priests) exiled him from Persia, and he traveled to India, where he gathered followers and also probably had some contact with the teachings of Buddha. Upon returning to Persia, he was imprisoned and executed (some versions say he was beheaded, others that he was crucified, still others that he was flayed alive), and his skin was stuffed and hung from the city walls as a grisly reminder of what happened to those who opposed the established religion.

Mani taught that there were two eternal principles, light and darkness. Earth was the focus of their struggle, and though it was under the control of the forces of darkness, men had within their souls a spark of light. Even women, who were Satan's masterpieces to seduce men to create more bodies in which to imprison the light of the soul, had a spark of light within them, however small. All great religious teachers, including Buddha, Jesus, and Mani, have been sent by the Light to liberate the light in men's souls from the evil of their bodies. The soul can only attain freedom by extreme asceticism. This included abstinence from meat and wine, renunciation of property and manual labor, and total celibacy. Not everyone could accomplish these great austerities, of course, so the "hearers" could only hope to gain liberation by waiting on the "elect" hand and foot. Even then, it might require several lifetimes (Mani believed in reincarnation) to achieve deliverance from this material world. When deliverance was accomplished, the soul would travel through the heavens on the moon (this source of light gradually darkened each month as it filled up with the souls of the righteous), avoiding the planetary spheres controlled by demons on the way to the kingdom of light, which, like the Buddhist Nirvana, is impossible to describe.

Strangely enough, Manichaeism was the most tenacious of the Gnostic heresies. It attracted intelligent men like the young Augustine, and continued to plague the church with its combination of many religious ideas for several centuries. Though the church succeeded in stamping out Manichaeism by the sixth century, it reappeared in later heresies known successively as the Paulicians (in Armenia in the seventh through twelfth centuries), the Bogomils (in Bulgaria and the Balkans in the tenth through twelfth centuries), and the Cathari or Albigensians (in southern France and Northern Italy in the twelfth through fourteenth centuries).

C. MONTANISM

If Ebionism represented an attempt to tie Christianity to its past, Montanism was an effort to turn its eyes to the future. If Gnosticism sought to make the Gospel attractive to the pagan by making it unnecessarily broad, Montanism tried to close the doors of the church to the insincere by making it unnecessarily narrow. Montanism was not a heresy in the same sense as the other two groups we have examined so far. Their beliefs about God and Christ were completely orthodox. Yet they posed a challenge about the nature of Scripture and the nature of the church that forced the church to make some hard decisions.

Montanism arose in the region of Phrygia in Asia Minor in the middle of the second century. The church had been free from all but sporadic persecution for more than a generation, and some in the church were becoming lax. In particular, the growth of the church was bringing into it many who lived lives of less than pristine holiness, foreshadowing what was to happen to an alarming degree after the Edict of Milan at the beginning of the fourth century. Montanism was a reaction against this laxity in the church, as well as against the rationalism of the Gnostics.

The movement began with a man named Montanus, who according to tradition was a former priest of the pagan mystery cult of Cybele. This Montanus practiced religious ecstasies, and ascribed these to the work of the Holy Spirit. In fact, he proclaimed that he was the channel through whom the promised Paraclete spoke. He taught that, while the Old Testament had been the Age of the Father, and Jesus had inaugurated the Age of the Son, the Age of the Spirit was about to begin. This new age would involve the prophesying predicted by the prophet Joel and foreshadowed at Pentecost, and would soon see the return of Christ to set up His kingdom on earth. This kingdom, according to Montanus, would descend in the form of the New Jerusalem in the Phrygian town of Pepuza. His "gift of prophecy" soon spread to others, most notably two wealthy women named Priscilla and Maximilla, who left their husbands to help Montanus spread his gospel of the New Age. They, along with hordes of followers, descended on Pepuza to await Christ's return, which was sure to occur at any moment. The church leaders in Asia Minor considered them to be demon possessed, and tried to exorcise the demons, but to no avail. Christ did not return, of course, and though the movement lost many followers as a result, it did not disappear.

Montanism soon settled down into an ascetic community of the super-spiritual. They lived simply, fasted often, and married only as a way of preventing lust (second marriages, however, were forbidden as an example of excess). The men and women alike practiced the gifts of the Spirit, including prophesying and speaking in tongues, and considered all others in the church to be carnal. They eagerly sought martyrdom as a final badge of commitment. In fact, when persecution came to Phrygia in 190, Montanists flocked into the Roman court, begging to be executed. The Roman governor was so flabbergasted, he is said to have blurted out, "Miserable creatures! If you wish to die are there not ropes and precipices?"

The church at first tolerated Montanism as a somewhat extreme but permissible departure from the mainstream. Eventually, however, the Montanists were excommunicated from the church, although this did not occur until the year 230, long after the death of Montanus himself. The reasons for their excommunication were twofold. They insisted that the true mark of spiritual authority was prophesying, not ordination. This undercut the authority of the church and its leaders to an unacceptable degree. Secondly, the teaching that the miraculous gifts of the Spirit continued the revelation of God to man undermined the sufficiency of Scripture.

Before their condemnation by the church, however, the Montanists won one major victory. In the year 207, the great Latin church father Tertullian became a Montanist, attracted largely by the spirituality and commitment of these sincere people, while at the same time rebelling against the laxity in the church at large. In his later writings, Tertullian staunchly defended the Montanists and argued that the church rejected their teaching because their example was too convicting to the leadership. In his work *On Fasting*, Tertullian asserted that, "the New Prophecy is rejected because Montanus, Maximilla, and Priscilla plainly teach more frequent fasting than marrying."

Though Montanism died out not long after its condemnation by the church, many similar movements have followed it in the church's history. The millennial enthusiasm of the Montanists is similar to that of the Millerites in the 1840's. The emphasis on the gifts of the Spirit puts the Montanists at the beginning of a long line that includes the Irvingites in England and the Pentecostals and charismatics in America. Their desire to define Christianity by a dedicated lifestyle and to reform from within a church that they saw as dead also connects them with the Pietists and Moravians in Germany and the Methodists in England.

MAKING DRY BONES LIVE

There is no question that false teaching has the potential to do great harm to the church, and has been very destructive over the years. It is also true, however, that God can use heresy to help the church. The main value of heresy in the church is that it forces the church to define its doctrine more carefully. In the second century, the church believed and used the New Testament, but it never would have defined it had not Marcion begun spreading his truncated canon. Heresy, in short, forces the church to say not only what it believes, but what it does not believe, and the result is a more thorough understanding of Christianity. Thus whether the heretics were sincere or destructive in their approach to the church, they produced growth because they made the church think.

Though the Gnostics and the Montanists were totally opposed to one another, both forced the church to define doctrines in the same two areas. One of these was the area of Scripture. The Gnostics forced the church to define a list of the New Testament books, and the Montanists forced the church to close it by asserting that God has given the church all that it needs in His Word.

The other area in which the church was required to think and define its position was that of authority. Both Gnosticism and Montanism encouraged the church's emphasis on the authority of the bishop. The Gnostics brought this about because of their reliance on secret *gnosis*, against which the church asserted a continuity of tradition from the apostles to the bishops. The Montanists claimed a spiritual authority by virtue of their holy lives and gifts of prophecy and tongues, and the church insisted that God worked through the orderly process of ordination.

It should surprise no one to see that the church's reaction against heresy was not always helpful. Most would agree that the definition and closure of the New Testament canon was a good thing. The authority invested in the bishops, however, ultimately was taken to extremes, and wound up undermining the sufficiency of Scripture by entrusting to the bishop full power to interpret that Word through the traditions of the church. Furthermore, the rejection of Montanism also caused the church to turn away from any real expectation of the imminent coming of Christ. Such overreaction may be termed the Pendulum Effect, and will be the subject of consideration at the end of a later chapter.

FOR REVIEW AND FURTHER THOUGHT

1. What is a heresy?

2. How was religion used as political tool by the Roman emperors?

3. What were the mystery cults? How did they come to be called that?

4. What were the principal beliefs of Mithraism?

5. Identify the following terms associated with the mystery cults: Ahura-Mazda, Ahriman, *Magna Mater*, taurobolium, Zarathustra.

6. What were the principal beliefs of the Ebionites? To what movement in the New Testament were they similar?

7. What is dualism? Why did belief in dualism cause the Gnostics to deny most of the major teachings of Christianity?

8. What are the differences among the three major Gnostic groups discussed in the chapter?

9. Identify the following terms and names associated with Gnosticism: *gnosis*, asceticism, Nag Hammadi, *The Gospel of Truth*, aeon, Pleroma, Ctesiphon, Mandaeans, Albigensians.

10. Identify the following names associated with Gnosticism: Simon Magus, Helena, Achamoth, Demiurge, Cerdo.

11. What made Montanism different from the other heresies discussed in the chapter?

12. Identify the following names and terms associated with Montanism: Cybele, Paraclete, Pepuza, Priscilla and Maximilla, Tertullian.

13. What about Montanism makes it similar to modern Pentecostalism?

14. In what ways can God use heresy to help the church to grow and advance?

4

THE SEED OF THE CHURCH

In the latter half of the second century, the Christian apologist Minucius Felix wrote a dialogue called *Octavius* in which he defended Christianity against the ridiculous charges that were being leveled against it. The unbeliever in the dialogue voiced the common opinion about Christians in the following words:

"They form a rabble of profane conspiracy. Their alliance consists of meetings at night with solemn rituals and inhuman revelries. They replace holy rites with inexpiable crimes. They despise temples as if they were tombs. They disparage the gods and ridicule our sacred rites. They look down on our priests although they are pitiable themselves. They despise titles of honor and the purple robe of high government office though hardly able to cover their nakedness.

"Just like a rank growth of weeds, the abominable haunts where this impious confederacy meet are multiplying all over the world, due to the daily increase of immorality.... They recognize each other by secret signs and symbols.... Everywhere they practice a kind of religious cult of lust, calling one another `brother' and `sister' indiscriminately. Thus, under the cover of these hallowed names, ordinary fornication becomes incest.

"They consecrate and worship the head of a donkey.... To venerate an executed criminal and the gallows, the wooden cross on which he was executed, is to erect altars which befit lost and depraved wretches. The blood of the infant ... they lap up greedily, they distribute its limbs with passionate eagerness.

"Their feastings are notorious.... After a surfeit of feasting, when the blood is heated and drinking has inflamed impure passions, a dog which has been tied to the lamppost upsets and extinguishes the tale-telling light. Darkness covers their shamelessness, and lustful embraces are indiscriminately exchanged.... Otherwise why do they have no altars, no temples, no images? Why do they not speak in public? Why do they never meet in the open? Is it not simply because what they worship and conceal is criminal and shameful?"

How did Christians come to be perceived this way? How did the prejudice against them grow so great that they became scapegoats for any misfortune that befell the Roman Empire? Why were Christians viewed as enemies of society?

THE REASONS BEHIND THE PERSECUTIONS

There could be no doubt about it. Christians were different. It's not as though the Roman Empire did not contain within it a varied population, including people from all sorts of ethnic and religious backgrounds. The problem was simply that the Christians insisted on teaching that they were right and everybody else was wrong. How intolerant! As has happened often throughout the history of mankind, difference spawned prejudice, and prejudice led to persecution. What was it that set the Christians apart from the society around them and marked them as targets of persecution?

In the political realm, Rome constantly faced the problem of holding a vast and diverse empire together. The emperors needed ways of monitoring political loyalty. And since separation of church and state would have been unthinkable to the men of the second and third centuries, the logical way to monitor loyalty and hold the empire together was through the imperial cult. At first, emperor worship involved offering incense to the genius of the emperor, or to the goddess Roma, the personification of the state. Even when the emperors later demanded recognition as gods, most citizens viewed this as little more than symbolic patriotism. Christians, however, were not free to take such an easy way out. Whether the incense was being offered to the personification of the state, the genius of the emperor, or an image of the emperor himself, it was idolatry, and Christians were forbidden to participate. Jews were exempted from the requirement, but with the severing of ties between Christianity and Judaism late in the first century, Christians lost their umbrella of protection. Emperors were convinced that anyone who was so stubborn as to refuse the simple act of offering incense must be up to no good, and must be concealing some underlying disloyalty to the state. Such people were dangerous. Suspicions about the political loyalty of Christians were made worse by the fact that many Christians refused to serve in the armed forces because of the emperor worship involved in swearing loyalty to the state. And as the church grew, its leadership structure was viewed as a threat to the security of the empire. The emperors saw that not only might these people be disloyal, but they were also very well-organized, and thus in a position to undermine the unity and peace of Rome.

Socially, the pagan populace viewed Christians with suspicion because of their unwillingness to participate in many of the normal aspects of life in the Roman Empire. They avoided holiday celebrations in the pagan temples; they loudly criticized the gladiatorial games; they refused to attend the theater because of the immoral content of most of the plays. On the other hand, their refusal to participate in anything that smacked of idolatry shut them out of certain legitimate social endeavors. There were some jobs that Christians couldn't hold because the trade organizations paid homage to some patron deity. They were even reluctant to send their children to the available schools because of the pagan religion that was part of the curriculum.

From a religious standpoint, Christians generated suspicion largely because of their secrecy. This was a sort of catch-22 situation - they were driven into secrecy by persecution, and stirred up opposition because of the rumors surrounding what went on in their secret meetings! While the rumors of cannibalism and incest reflected in the quotation with which the chapter began were clearly based on misunderstandings of basic Christian practices, it was Christian exclusivism that really irked many of their neighbors. Romans, like Americans today, were very open about religion. A person could believe or practice just about anything, as long as he allowed the same privilege to others. While Christians did not seek to interfere with the worship of others, their entire attitude and lifestyle proclaimed loudly and clearly, "We're right and everyone else is wrong." Like Americans today, the Romans responded by telling the Christians, "We don't know who's right, but you're wrong!" A society that believes that truth is relative can tolerate anything except the teaching that truth is absolute. Such intolerance eventually led to massive paranoia. Every calamity that befell the Empire, whether foreign invasion, flood, or famine, was blamed on the Christians. As Tertullian complained in his *Apology*, "If the Tiber floods the city, or if the Nile refuses to rise, or if the sky withholds its rain, if there is an earthquake, a famine, a pestilence, at once the cry is raised, `Christians to the lion.'"

THE NATURE AND EXTENT OF THE PERSECUTIONS

The period of the Roman persecutions of the church extends from the reign of Nero to the early part of the fourth century. The persecutions during this time were by no means uniform in extent or intensity, however. Traditionally, ten persecuting emperors are singled out in the period of two hundred and fifty years during which the persecutions occurred. Sources differ as to which ten should

The Seed of the Church

ROMAN PERSECUTIONS OF CHRISTIANS

DATES	EMPEROR	NATURE AND EXTENT OF PERSECUTION	NOTABLE MARTYRS
64	Nero	Took place in Rome and vicinity only. Christians were made scapegoats for burning Rome. Sadistic measures included burning Christians alive to illuminate Nero's gardens.	Paul Peter
c.90-96	Domitian	Capricious, sporadic, centered in Rome and Asia Minor. Christians persecuted for refusal to offer incense to genius of emperor.	Clement of Rome John (exiled to Patmos)
98-117	Trajan	Sporadically enforced. Christians were lumped with other groups whose patriotism was considered suspect. Christians were to be executed when found, but not sought out.	Ignatius Symeon Zozimus Rufus
117-138	Hadrian	Sporadically enforced. Continued policies of Trajan. Any who brought false witness against Christians were to be punished.	Telesphorus
138-161	Antoninus Pius	Sporadically enforced. Continued policies of Trajan and Hadrian.	Polycarp
161-180	Marcus Aurelius	Emperor was Stoic who opposed Christianity on philosophical grounds. Christians blamed for natural disasters.	Justin Martyr Pothinus Blandina
202-211	Septimus Severus	Conversion to Christianity forbidden.	Leonidas Irenaeus Perpetua
235-236	Maximinus the Thracian	Christian clergy ordered executed. Christians opposed because they had supported emperor's predecessor, whom he had assassinated.	Ursula Hippolytus
249-251	Decius	First empire-wide persecution. Offering of incense to genius of emperor demanded. Enthusiastic return to paganism required utter extermination of Christianity.	Fabianus Alexander of Jerusalem
257-260	Valerian	Christians' property confiscated. Christians prohibited right of assembly.	Origen Cyprian Sixtus II
274	Aurelian	Required sun worship as official state religion, but died before it could be implemented.	
303-311	Diocletian Galerius	Worst persecution of all. Churches destroyed, Bibles burned, civil rights of Christians suspended, sacrifice to gods required.	Mauritius Alban

be included, however, and a compilation of all those who are alleged at one time or another to have persecuted the church comes closer to an even dozen. It is much more helpful to view the persecutions as falling into three general time periods. In the first century, Christianity was persecuted almost as an extension of Judaism; from about 100-250, the church was officially an outlaw organization, but the persecutions tended to be sporadic and restricted to certain localities. From 250 to the end, persecutions were relatively brief, but severe and empire-wide.

A. THE FIRST CENTURY

The persecutions of the first century were already described briefly in chapter one. The first, under Nero (A.D. 64), was brief and restricted to the city of Rome itself. In it Christians were made scapegoats for the great fire that swept through Rome in that year. The persecution may have been brief and localized, but it left significant scars. Not only did the church lose its two most visible leaders, Peter and Paul, between the outbreak of persecution and the death of Nero in A.D. 68, but the severity of the persecution was such that many Christians were convinced that Nero would rise from the dead and become the Antichrist whose brutal reign would precede the return of Christ in glory.

At the end of the century, the emperor Domitian ascended the throne. He followed his brother Titus in the imperial chair, and was terribly jealous of the success his brother had enjoyed. Like Herod the Great a century before, he was afraid that all those around him were trying to plot against him and remove him from the throne. He particularly hated the Jews, and determined that the line of David should be exterminated in order to prevent any future Jewish monarchy. According to the church historian Eusebius, Domitian summoned to Rome the grandsons of Jude, the brother of Jesus, because they were from the line of David. After finding them to be simple peasants who spoke only of a heavenly kingdom, he recognized that they were no threat to his reign and dismissed them. Domitian took the idea of emperor worship seriously, and demanded to be called "Lord and God." Though the Jews were exempt from such a requirement by law, he attempted to find another excuse to persecute them by levying a tax for Jupiter Capitolinus, which they refused to pay. In the ensuing persecution, Christians were included, though the emperor had some in his own family. His cousin Flavius Clemens was executed, and the apostle John was sent into exile on Patmos. Clement of Rome is also said to have perished at this time, though it is possible the early sources could have gotten him confused with the emperor's cousin. The persecution ended when Domitian was assassinated in A.D. 96.

B. CHRISTIANS AS THE ENEMIES OF THE STATE

By the second century, it became increasingly obvious that Christians were distinct from Jews, both because of the denials by the Jews and the increasingly Gentile makeup of the church. The church thus lost its legal protection, and was lumped with a large number of other organizations that were refused legal recognition because they were suspected of subversive activities.

The first emperor to set forth this policy was Trajan (98-117), one of the most capable emperors in the history of Rome. An interesting exchange of letters has survived from the reign of Trajan. In it, Pliny the Younger, governor of Bithynia, writes to the emperor to find out how he should deal with this puzzling group of Christians in his jurisdiction. Though they were guilty of no overt crime, their teachings were spreading like wildfire, so that the pagan temples were empty and the animals for sacrifice remained unsold in the marketplace. Pliny had taken two young women and had them tortured, but the information they produced was of no value. He therefore asked the emperor to what extent these Christians were to be persecuted. Were they to be hunted down? What if they admitted to being Christians, but agreed to sacrifice to the emperor? What of the old, the young, and the infirm? Trajan responded that Christians were not to be sought out, but that if they were brought before the court, they were to be punished unless they recanted by offering incense to the emperor. In no case were anonymous charges against anyone to be accepted. While this policy was humane in comparison with many of those that followed, it drew justifiable criticism from the apologists for being inconsistent. How, they asked, could Christianity be called a crime on the one hand, and on the other hand the emperors instruct their governors to leave Christians alone unless they committed some crime?

Inconsistent or not, the policy of Trajan stood during his reign and that of the two emperors who followed him. In fact, Trajan's successor Hadrian (117-138) extended the protection of Christians even further by instructing that those who brought false accusations against them should themselves receive punishment. This, of course, did nothing to help those who overtly proclaimed their faith. Christians were officially criminals, but prosecution of their crimes was left to the regional governors, who were strict or lax according to their whim. Martyrs during these years were relatively scarce, though several notable examples have been recorded, including the deaths of Ignatius, who was thrown to the lions in Rome during the reign of Trajan, and Polycarp, who was burned at the stake in Asia Minor during the reign of Antoninus Pius (138-161).

With the accession of the Stoic philosopher Marcus Aurelius the situation became considerably worse. He found Christianity philosophically distasteful, and was convinced that it was undermining the virtues that made Rome great. He consequently stepped up the persecution, principally by decreeing that the property of those executed as Christians should be given to those who had brought the charges against them. Needless to say, this brought tremendous hardship on the church, and much suffering in those regions where the magistrates were inclined to encourage the anti-Christian enthusiasm generated by the imperial decrees. The apologist Justin gained the death that has made him known to history as Justin Martyr when he was brought up before the magistrate on accusations presented by the Cynic philosopher Crescens, who had been defeated in debates by Justin many times. The worst incidents of Marcus Aurelius' reign occurred in the cities of Lyons and Vienne in Gaul in the year 177. A mob uprising against Christians generated a situation where it was not even safe for Christians to poke their heads outside their doors. Many were slaughtered in the streets and their bodies left there to rot. Others were taken to the arena and tortured to the delight of the jeering crowds. Included in this number were Pothinus, the ninety-year-old bishop of Lyons, and a slave girl named Blandina, who survived numerous tortures and was finally killed by being tied up in a net and bound to the horns of a bull.

A long succession of weak emperors followed Marcus Aurelius, most of whom either favored Christianity or ignored it. It was a period of great confusion in Rome, and emperors rarely were allowed to die natural deaths. Most of the emperors from Marcus Aurelius to Constantine died by assassination. The only two significant persecutions in the first half of the third century were brief and politically motivated. Septimus Severus (193-211) favored Christians early in his reign, but was later frightened by the rapid growth of the church. In about the year 202, he forbade conversion to Christianity or Judaism (no hardship for the Jews) to try to slow down the spread of these anti-imperial religions. Enforcement again varied from place to place, but seems to have been most severe in North Africa. It was in Alexandria that Leonidas, the father of Origen, was beheaded, and Clement of Alexandria was forced to flee the city. Eusebius tells of a beautiful young woman named Potamiaena who remained steadfast despite tortures, and was eventually killed by being boiled in pitch; the soldier who led her to execution, Basilides, was shortly thereafter converted and himself suffered martyrdom. In Carthage, two young Montanists, a noblewoman named Perpetua and her slave girl Felicitas, though one was nursing a young child and the other delivered a baby in prison, refused the entreaties of the authorities and their families, and were executed after undergoing horrible tortures.

The other period of persecution occurred during the reign of Maximinus the Thracian (235-238). This brutal peasant had risen through the ranks of the army, eventually gaining the imperial throne by means of the assassination of his predecessor, Alexander Severus. Alexander had been pro-Christian, and Maximinus wanted to be sure that none of the slain emperor's supporters were in a position to undermine his rule. Consequently, his persecution of the church was directed largely against the clergy. Mercifully, his reign was a brief one.

C. FINAL ATTEMPTS TO DESTROY THE CHURCH

The year 247 was a year of great celebration. In that year, the city of Rome celebrated its millennium - one thousand years of glory. The emperor at the time, Philip the Arabian, is reported by some to have been a Christian himself, but there is no question that he participated enthusiastically in the pagan rituals surrounding the millennial celebration. Though the rejoicing at 1000 years of Roman history was great, it also produced sorrow and concern in the eyes of the people and their leaders. There could be no doubt in people's minds that the glory of Rome was a thing of the past. The empire was crumbling. Goths harassed the northern and western frontiers, while Persians threatened in the East. The emperors provided no security or sense of continuity, since most of them came to power through violence, and no dynasty lasted very long. The people of Rome began to ask themselves the crucial question - Why? The easy answer, one that came readily to Roman pagans in the third century and secular historians in recent years as well, was to blame the collapse of the empire on those who refused to support it - the Christians.

In the year 249, an emperor came to the throne who was determined to restore the "good old days" of the empire's power and glory. Decius believed that the imperial cult was the only way of bringing the empire back together. Since Christians were the only ones who refused to support the imperial cult, Christians had to be stamped out. He directed his early efforts at converting Christians, not killing them. He made one very simple requirement. All citizens of the empire had to offer a pinch of incense to the genius of the emperor once a year, and receive a certificate called a *libellus* stating that they had done so. The Christians, of course, were the only ones who objected. In the years preceding, however, the church had grown so much that many within it had never faced serious opposition. Enormous numbers of Christians, faced with the choice of offering a meaningless pinch of incense or losing their lives, rationalized the offering as a political act that had no religious significance. Others bribed friendly officials to obtain false *libelli*, while still others agreed to offer incense after undergoing tortures. Some remained steadfast, and suffered death as a result. It appeared as if Decius was succeeding in destroying the church. Those who offered incense or bribed officials to say they had done so were summarily excommunicated by their churches. Meanwhile, thousands of the faithful were suffering imprisonment, torture, and death. Only the mercy of God cut this persecution short when Decius died in battle in the year 251.

Two years later, in 253, Valerian came to the throne. Initially he was favorable to Christianity. But a Persian invasion in 257 made him decide that unity in the empire was a necessity, and he began to persecute the church. At first, he tried to avoid executions, which he knew from the experience of Decius only made the church grow faster and increased public sympathy. He threatened exile, confiscation of goods, and slavery for those who refused to renounce their faith. These threats, however, did little, and he had to resort to execution of those who were so stubborn as to refuse to support the empire. He first targeted the bishops and other leading clergy, which resulted in the deaths of Cyprian, bishop of Carthage, and Sixtus, bishop of Rome, who was caught teaching in the catacombs outside Rome and was killed with four of his deacons. Valerian forbade public assembly by Christians (actually, this was already illegal, but he saw that it was enforced), and even made it illegal to visit a Christian cemetery (not only were the underground tombs favorite meeting places for Christians, but as was often true in communist countries in the twentieth century, funerals provided an acceptable rationalization for Christians to meet in public and worship). This persecution, as well, was mercifully short-lived, as Valerian was captured in 260 in a battle against the Persians and never was heard from again.

For the next forty years, the church enjoyed unprecedented freedom. Many emperors openly favored the Christians, who they were finally realizing made good and loyal subjects because of their reputation for honesty and integrity. The only attempt at persecution was made by the emperor Aurelian, who in 274 issued an edict attempting to unify the empire by requiring sun-worship. However, he was assassinated before the edict could be put into effect.

The worst persecution of all was the last, which began under the reign of Diocletian in 303. Diocletian came to the throne in 283, and was the most capable emperor the empire had seen since Marcus Aurelius. He completely reorganized the administration of the empire, dividing it in half, with each half ruled by an Augustus, who was assisted by a Caesar. Diocletian himself became the Augustus in the East, while maintaining final authority over the other rulers. For twenty years, Diocletian left Christians in peace. However, his Caesar, Galerius, bitterly opposed the Christians, and finally succeeded in convincing Diocletian to try to wipe them out. In 303, the emperor issued a decree closing all churches and ordering all sacred books to be burned. Shortly thereafter, another decree suspended the civil rights of Christians and ordered all clergy imprisoned if they refused to sacrifice to the gods. Though Constantius Chlorus, the father of Constantine, the Caesar in the West, generally ignored these edicts, they caused severe hardship in the rest of the empire. Churches were destroyed, Bibles were burned, and thousands of Christians died. In 304, matters got even worse when a decree was published requiring universal sacrifice, even by children, which added many young martyrs to the rapidly swelling ranks of those who had given their lives for the sake of Christ. In 305, Diocletian abdicated the throne, but this only made Galerius, who was now the Augustus, more vicious. He even decreed that all the food in the marketplaces throughout the empire had to be sprinkled with ceremonial wine from the pagan temples, thus making it difficult for Christians of good conscience even to find food to eat. Finally, in 311, on his deathbed, Galerius ended the persecution, realizing that his policy had been a failure. In the battle of empire against church, the church had won, not by fighting, but by yielding the blood of the saints.

THE RESULTS OF THE PERSECUTIONS

The persecutions had a number of effects on the church, both positive and negative. On the positive side, while the persecutions obviously cost the church some of its most influential and capable leaders, the testimony of the martyrs was probably the most powerful apologetic the church had in the years of trial. Many became Christians through the witness of those who suffered, unable to deny the reality of what was enabling these weak, flesh-and-blood people to suffer terrible torments with seemingly superhuman strength and courage.

Two negative effects of the persecutions can also be discerned, one stemming from those who died in the persecutions, and the other from those who gave in under the intense pressure exerted by the Roman officials. Those who died were held in great esteem by the church, but this esteem quickly degenerated into a martyr cult, in which the possessions and remains of those who died were venerated, and those who had suffered were thought capable of interceding with God for those who remained. Thus the great persecutions planted the seed of the veneration of saints and relics in the Catholic Church.

Those who gave in under pressure also presented problems for the church. Most later sought restoration, but the church had trouble agreeing about what policy to follow. Some believed that the lapsed should be readmitted to the church if they repented. Others said that only those who gave in under torture could be restored, while some thought that no one who had compromised his faith in any way could ever be part of the church again. This dispute, which involved large numbers of people, especially in the last fifty years of the persecutions, caused a major split in the church known as the Donatist controversy, which we will study in chapter seven.

THE CONVERSION OF CONSTANTINE AND ITS IMPACT

Constantine, the son of Constantius Chlorus, was proclaimed emperor in the West by the Roman legions upon the death of his father in 306. His leading challenger was Maxentius, the son of the former Augustus in the West, Maximian, who gained the support of the army in Rome. Constantine marched toward Rome to meet his rival. In 312, at the Battle of Milvian Bridge, the forces of Constantine soundly defeated Maxentius. On the eve of the battle, Constantine allegedly saw a vision of the cross in the sky along with the words, *In This Sign Conquer*. He thus undertook the battle in the name of the Christian God, and declared himself to be a Christian as a result of his resounding victory. A similar power struggle occurred in the East, where Licinius eventually won out over the vicious Maximin Daia, who had attempted to continue the persecution of Christians even after Galerius had called it off. In 313, in Milan, Italy, Constantine and Licinius met and officially put a stop to the persecution of Christians. In the Edict of Milan, Christianity was added to the list of legal religions of the empire, Christians were released from prison, their property was returned to them, churches were reopened, and the government paid for repairs to the churches that had been damaged during the persecutions. Licinius later tried to initiate further persecutions in the East, but Constantine defeated him in battle and became master of the entire empire in 323.

Like the persecutions, the Edict of Milan had both positive and negative effects on the church. On the positive side, the church now was free from the fear of persecution. The stigma of being an outlaw organization had hung over the church even in the years when there had been no active persecution. Now Christians could live and worship freely and openly. Furthermore, they could give much greater attention to evangelism, not only within the empire, but beyond its borders as well. Evangelism was now encouraged, often with support from imperial coffers, rather than being looked upon with suspicion. As a result of this, the church grew rapidly.

On the negative side, tremendous growth brought serious dilution to the level of spirituality and commitment in the church. If nominal commitment had been a problem during the relative prosperity preceding the persecution of Diocletian, how much more so was that the case once the church became the favored religion of the emperor himself! Converts flooded in, many with political and social motives that had little to do with Christ. Pagans brought with them their superstitions and low morals, and the church declined as a result.

The other major problem was that imperial favor brought imperial interference. Constantine had legitimate concerns about the peace of the church, and this led him to step in whenever he felt it was necessary to try to solve doctrinal problems that arose. This injected an element of politics into the doctrinal deliberations of the church that muddied the waters, to say the least. As we will see in chapter seven, interference in doctrinal questions by the emperors seriously harmed the church.

MAKING DRY BONES LIVE

Jesus assured Peter in Matthew 16:18 that the gates of hell would never prevail against the church of God. Like the rose petal that releases its most beautiful fragrance when crushed, the church is at its best when facing opposition from the world. Conversely, the favor of the world can be a deadly poison to the church. Those who are "at ease in Zion" often lose their commitment, leaving the church as just one more social club in a society that is full of them.

Should Christians today then pray for persecution? Certainly the eagerness for martyrdom expressed by men like Ignatius is neither biblical nor healthy. Yet we must recognize that the fundamental character of the church is to be different. In the same way that the early Christians simply did not fit in the world in which they lived, so Christians today should be marked by that same distinctiveness. Whether we are talking about family life, morality, the relationship to government, employment, education, or entertainment, the Christian is to be different because he looks at life from a different perspective. He cannot accept the relativism espoused by the rest of the world, but must show in everything he does that Jesus Christ is the only Way, the only Truth, and the only source of Life, and that He died to redeem sinful man in every area of his sin. Any Christian who puts this into practice will face persecution. He may not have to stand before lions in the Colosseum, but he will have to live before his friends and neighbors in a way that says, "I am different because I belong to Jesus Christ."

FOR REVIEW AND FURTHER THOUGHT

1. The church father Tertullian said, "The blood of the martyrs is seed." What did he mean by that statement?

2. From the quotation from Minucius Felix with which the chapter opens, list as many different reasons as you can find for why Christians were disliked.

3. Why were Christians considered political threats by the Roman emperors?

4. Why did Christians stick out in Roman society as being different from their neighbors?

5. How could Roman officials be so tolerant of all kinds of religious practices and yet persecute Christianity?

6. What made the persecutions of the first century different from those that followed?

7. Describe the policy for dealing with Christians that was first set forth by Trajan.

8. How did Marcus Aurelius make life harder for Christians than his predecessors had done?

9. What motivated Maximinus the Thracian to oppose Christianity?

10. Is it fair to say that the persecutions of Decius, Valerian, and Diocletian were motivated by desperation? Why or why not?

11. What is a *libellus*? How was it used to persecute Christians?

12. Name the emperor under which each of the following martyrs died: Basilides, Blandina, Cyprian, Flavius Clemens, Ignatius, Justin Martyr, Leonidas, Paul, Peter, Polycarp, Potamiaena, Pothinus, Sixtus.

13. In what ways did the persecutions harm the church? In what ways were they beneficial?

14. In what ways did the Edict of Milan help the church? In what ways was it harmful?

15. What attitude should Christians today take toward persecution?

5

BISHOPS AND BAPTISMS

In 445, Emperor Valentinian III proclaimed the following:

"... Since therefore the merit of St. Peter, who is the prince of the episcopal crown, the dignity of the city of Rome and the authority of a holy synod have established the primacy of the Apostolic See, let not presumption attempt to carry out anything contrary to the authority of that See; for then at last the peace of the church will be preserved everywhere, if the whole body recognizes its ruler.... We decree by this perpetual Edict that it will not be lawful for the bishops of Gaul or of other provinces to attempt anything contrary to ancient custom without the authority of that venerable man the Pope of the Eternal City. But let whatever the authority of the Apostolic See decrees or shall decree, be accepted as law by all."

Clearly, what had been in the first century a Spirit-filled community of followers of the Way had by the fifth century become an imperial hierarchy, full of pomp and ritual. What happened in the years between Peter and Leo I (the pope mentioned in the decree quoted above) to bring about these changes? How did the organization and practice of the church develop during the first five hundred years of its history? These are the questions with which we will concern ourselves in this chapter.

CHURCH ORGANIZATION

The New Testament says relatively little about the organization of the church. Most of what the New Testament records occurred in the first generation of the church's history, and thus most churches really hadn't had the opportunity to get settled and establish a pattern of organization. The apostles, of course, exercised direct oversight of the churches, but it is only in the Pastoral Epistles that we are given any concrete teaching about the permanent pattern for authority in the church. The Pastoral Epistles specify two types of officers. The overseers, called bishops or elders, are entrusted with the spiritual leadership of the congregation. That the two terms are synonyms can be seen by comparing verses 17 and 28 of Acts 20, where the Ephesian elders are called bishops or overseers. Similarly, both terms appear in Titus 1:5-7. Deacons, based on the precedent established in Acts 6, are to supervise the material affairs of the church in order to free the spiritual leaders to concentrate on their tasks. Each congregation was led by a group of elders and a group of deacons. There is no indication that anyone except the apostles had authority outside the realm of his own congregation. How, then, did this simple structure evolve into the hierarchy of the Catholic Church? The development of the episcopal structure in the early church can be traced as a step-by-step process, though we don't know as much about these changes as we might wish.

A. THE MONARCHICAL BISHOP

Rule by committee is not easy. Committees tend to have difficulty arriving at decisions, and often important matters seem to slip through the cracks. When everyone is responsible for something getting done, too often no one does it. Furthermore, different men have different gifts. Some excel in the area of personal ministry, while others do their best work in front of a large group. In any small group, it is inevitable that a leader will emerge to take charge when necessary, at least on the informal level. In the churches of the first century, it appears that such leaders emerged in many of the Christian congregations. Whether because of natural ability or ambitious self-assertion (compare the obnoxious Diotrephes rebuked in III John), many congregations came to recognize one man as their leader. He was still one of the body of elders, but he was seen as first among equals. Before long, however, this distinction began to be formalized through the use of a title. The chief elder came to be called the bishop - a title previously used for all elders, but now reserved for the leader of the congregation. The church now had three offices rather than two.

The three-office structure first appears in the writings of Ignatius. As he traveled from Antioch to Rome to suffer martyrdom around 117, he wrote to several churches in Asia Minor, along with the church in Rome. These letters place great stress on the role of the bishop, who is distinguished from the elders and deacons. Ignatius himself was the bishop of Antioch. He speaks of bishops in most of the churches to whom he writes, though he mentions none in Rome. He places the sacraments under the authority of the bishop, stating that baptism and the Lord's Supper may only validly be performed by the bishop or one designated by him.

Such a three-office structure was by no means universal in the second century, however. When Clement wrote a letter from Rome to Corinth at the end of the first century, he speaks only of two offices, not three. The confusion of early writers as to the order of succession of bishops in Rome confirms what Ignatius' letter to Rome indicates by its silence - that the Roman church did not at this time have a bishop, but was ruled by a group of elders. The *Didache*, probably written early in the second century, mentions only two offices, and speaks of a group of bishops and a group of deacons in each church. When Polycarp wrote to the church at Philippi in the middle of the second century, they were led by a group of elders. The church in Alexandria, until late in the second century, was under the supervision of a group of twelve elders who would elect a president from among themselves. By the time we get to the fourth century, however, the church historian Eusebius is trying to list single bishops for major churches back to the time of the apostles, and leading theologians are comparing the bishop, elders, and deacons to the high priest, priests, and Levites of Old Testament Israel. The three-office view had not only become firmly entrenched, it had also picked up both historical and theological justification along the way. But this was not by any means the end of the changes that were to be introduced into the organization of the church.

B. DIOCESAN BISHOPS AND SACRIFICING PRIESTS

The rapid expansion of the church during the second and third centuries necessitated further organizational changes. These changes were enhanced by the threats posed to the church by heresy and schism during the years of persecution.

1. EXPANSION

The amazing growth of the church may have posed a challenge to the Roman officials who looked askance at this threatening new cult, but it also required some creativity on the part of the church itself. New converts needed to be discipled, not just evangelized and ignored. The bishops of the churches tended to be among the most active evangelists. After all, they had been set aside in the first place because of their spiritual gifts, and were paid by the church so that they could devote all of their energies to spiritual endeavors. Many of these bishops were not only successful evangelists, but also church planters, setting up new congregations in the countryside around the towns where they lived and worked. These new churches, having no experienced leaders of their own, naturally looked to the man who had won them to Christ for oversight. Thus gradually there developed the idea of the diocesan bishop - the notion that the bishop is not the head of a single congregation, but rather the supervisor of all the

DEVELOPMENT OF EPISCOPACY IN THE FIRST FIVE CENTURIES

PERIOD	SOURCES	DESCRIPTION
1st century	New Testament	Elder-bishops and deacons in each church were under the supervision of the apostles.
Early 2nd century	Ignatius	Elders and bishops differentiated. Each congregation governed by a bishop, elders, and deacons.
Late 2nd century	Irenaeus Tertullian	Diocesan bishops - a bishop now oversaw a group of congregations in a geographical area; they were thought to be successors of the apostles.
Mid-3rd century	Cyprian	Priesthood and sacrifice - elders (*presbuteros*) come to be seen as sacrificing priests. Primacy of bishop of Rome asserted.
Early 4th century	Council of Nicea	Metropolitan bishops (archbishops) by virtue of their location in population centers gain ascendancy over *chorepiscopi* (country bishops)
Late 4th century	Council of Constantinople	Patriarchs - special honor given to bishops of Rome, Alexandria, Antioch, Constantinople, and Jerusalem. Patriarch of Constantinople given primacy next to the Bishop of Rome.
Mid-5th century	Leo I Council of Chalcedon	The supremacy of Rome - Leo I claimed authority over the whole church on the basis of succession from Peter.

congregations within a specific geographical area. As the role of the bishop expanded, so too did the role of the elders. They were often assigned to give direct guidance to the newly-formed congregations, thus taking over the role performed by the bishop a century earlier. These elders who supervised their own congregations eventually came to be called "priests," from *presbuteros*, the Greek word for "elder." Like the priests in the Old Testament (and the priests in the pagan religions with which the Roman Empire was filled), these men were believed to be offering sacrifices - the body and blood of Christ - when they officiated at the Lord's Supper.

2. HERESY AND SCHISM

As we saw in the previous chapter, the Gnostics and Montanists both threatened the authority of the church by designating as authoritative a special group of "spiritual" people who rarely corresponded to the leadership of the church. The Gnostics did so by claiming a secret knowledge that set the "spiritual" apart from the "carnal." The Montanists saw the gift of prophecy as the distinguishing factor that set apart the spiritual man. In addition to these threats, the persecutions of the middle of the third century almost split the church over the issue of readmitting those who had lapsed. The church was faced on many fronts with the question of defining itself and its authority. What ultimately determines the true church in opposition to all those impostors out there? For the church of the third century, there could only be one answer - the bishop.

Our three best sources for this development are the writings of Irenaeus, Tertullian, and Cyprian. Irenaeus lived in Gaul in the latter part of the second century. He argued strongly and convincingly against the Gnostic heresy, and one of the main building blocks of his argument had to do with the continuity of bishops from the time of the apostles to his own day. The Gnostics argued that Jesus had passed secret knowledge on to His disciples, who had then communicated it to Gnostic teachers through the years. Irenaeus argued that the apostles had not passed down their knowledge to obscure teachers, but to the men they had put in leadership positions in the churches. At that time, of course, the line was a rather short one. For instance, Irenaeus himself had known Polycarp as he was growing up in Asia Minor, and Polycarp had as a young man known the apostle John. The unbroken succession of bishops from the time of the apostles thus becomes the guarantee that the doctrine of the church is that taught by Christ. Irenaeus does not argue for the personal authority of the bishop, but for the authoritative nature of the doctrine he teaches. Tertullian makes much the same point, insisting that no congregation may truly call itself a church unless it conforms in its teaching to what has been passed down from the apostles through the churches they founded. Thus for these men the role of the bishop lay not in the perpetuation of apostolic authority, but in the preservation of apostolic teaching.

The man who more than any other contributed to the growth of the role of the bishop was Cyprian, the bishop of Carthage in the middle of the third century. He taught that the bishops were the successors of the apostles, not only in their teaching, but also in their authority. In fact, he maintained that in a sense the bishop was the church, so that a person's relationship to the church, and thus to Christ, depended upon his relationship to the bishop. He boldly taught that, "He cannot have God as his Father who has not the church as his mother." And for Cyprian, having the church as one's mother meant being in fellowship with the bishop. What drove him to these conclusions? For the most part, it was the controversy over restoring those who had lapsed during the persecutions that stimulated his teaching on this subject. Cyprian found himself caught in the middle between those who maintained that all those who had given in under persecution should be forgiven and restored and those who taught that salvation for such was impossible. Though he asserted his authority as bishop against those who sought to admit the lapsed too easily, he believed that the real troublemakers were the separationists who not only refused to readmit the lapsed, but also would not recognize as legitimate those bishops who did so, nor even other bishops ordained by such men. To Cyprian, this was a clear case of rebellion against God-ordained authority that demonstrated that the rebels were not Christians at all. He thus pronounced that no man could be saved except by submission to the bishop - a doctrine that has continued, with considerable expansion, in the Catholic Church to the present day.

C. METROPOLITAN BISHOPS AND PATRIARCHS

Once the persecutions ended, the organization of the church took on flow-chart proportions. The Council of Nicea in 325 formally recognized the authority of priests to perform the sacraments, which were believed to convey the grace of God to the recipient. Bishops were said to be the visible manifestation of the church of Christ on earth, and bearers of apostolic authority. When the emperor Theodosius made Christianity the official religion of the empire in 381, the church did officially what it had been moving toward for a long time unofficially - it adapted its own organization to the political structure of the empire. Thus the bishops in large cities supervised those in the surrounding countryside, while those in the provincial capitals came to be recognized as exercising authority over all the churches in their province. The latter were called metropolitan bishops, known today as archbishops. At an even higher level of authority were the patriarchs, the bishops of the leading cities of the empire. The Council of Nicea recognized the bishops of Rome, Alexandria, and Antioch as patriarchs of the church. The Council of

Constantinople, held in 381, not only added the bishop of Constantinople to the list of patriarchs, but also designated him as next in primacy after the bishop of Rome due to the fact that Constantinople then served as the Eastern capital of the empire. The Council of Chalcedon in 451 also recognized the bishop of Jerusalem as a patriarch, but this was more a matter of honor than influence; Jerusalem had long before ceased to be an important city in the empire, and was singled out only because it was the birthplace of Christianity.

The bishops were now administrators, carrying on the authority of the apostles over the church at large. The elders had now become priests, offering the sacrifice of the Mass and supervising their own congregations. Deacons also gained a larger role, becoming administrative assistants to the bishops. As the church hierarchy became more complex, other offices began to develop at the lower end of the organizational chart to fill the void left by those who had gained wider responsibilities. Priests were now assisted in congregational work by readers, who helped in leading the worship services, and exorcists, who not only cast out demons but also participated in all baptismal services. Bishops were aided by acolytes, who served as personal secretaries, while deacons had sub-deacons to help them in their work. As is usually the case in hierarchies, offices were filled from the bottom up. Lower clergy were eligible to become deacons when they reached the age of thirty, deacons could become priests at thirty-five, and priests could become bishops at forty-five. Vacancies among archbishops and patriarchs were filled from the ranks of the bishops. This increasingly complex hierarchy was not yet complete, however. The final step was the development of a pecking order among the patriarchs themselves. While the patriarch of the church at Rome eventually gained supremacy, the process through which this occurred produced divisions in the church that have never been healed.

D. THE SUPREMACY OF ROME

The church at Rome has a long and glorious history, but its origins are lost in obscurity. The claim that the church was founded by Peter and Paul, made by Irenaeus, cannot be true. When Paul wrote to the church, it was already a flourishing congregation, yet he makes no mention of Peter, nor had he ever visited the church himself. The connection of the church with Peter and Paul is more because they were martyred there than because they founded or even led the congregation. Yet the church had apostolic associations from its early years.

The Roman church gained further prominence because of its suffering, not only during the Neronian persecution, but also the many that followed. Martyrs received great honor from the church at large, and Rome certainly could boast of many, among them such prominent men as Peter, Paul, Ignatius, and Justin Martyr. Thus the church at Rome was held in high esteem by many throughout the empire.

Prior to the Edict of Milan, the Roman church held a high place of honor in the minds of many, but exercised no special authority in the church at large, though some of its leaders tried to do so occasionally. Some would cite the letter written by Clement of Rome to the church at Corinth as an early example of the authority of the Roman church, but Clement makes no such claims, either for himself or his church. The first clear example of a Roman bishop trying to exert authority outside Rome is that of Victor, bishop of Rome from 189 to 199. In the year 190, he attempted to settle a dispute about the date of Easter by excommunicating all bishops who would not conform to his view. Though his view of the date of Easter eventually prevailed in the church, his attempted excommunications were widely criticized and never carried out. At about the same time, Irenaeus, in arguing against the Gnostic heresy, spoke of the church in Rome as the one with which, "on account of its greater authority, every church must agree." He did not mean by this that the church in Rome had authority over all others (after all, he had been one of the most vocal critics of the action taken by Victor), but rather that the church in Rome preserved the true doctrine passed down from the apostles, and therefore those who taught any other doctrine were outside the realm of the true faith.

In the time following the persecution of Decius, when the church was in turmoil over what to do about those who had given in, the role of Rome again was the object of considerable attention. Stephen, bishop of Rome from 254 to 257, insisted that all who repented should be restored, and attempted to impose his views on the North African churches. In doing so, he was the first to use Matthew 16:18 as the basis for his authority, though his position was hardly well thought out. Cyprian argued that while the primacy of Rome was essential to the unity of the church, this gave the bishop of Rome no authority over other bishops. He said that Peter had received the keys first, and the other apostles later, so that the unity of the church could be focused in a single individual. This did not allow Peter to tell the other apostles what to do, however. Consequently Cyprian refused to allow Stephen to interfere in any way with his administration of his own church in Carthage.

After the Edict of Milan, the authority of Rome grew rapidly. It gained prestige as the empire's largest church in the empire's largest city. The emperor himself often sought out the bishop of Rome for advice on church matters. As the only patriarch in the West, the bishop of Rome supervised much more territory than the other patriarchs. In later centuries, that territory would expand through missionary outreach, while that of the Eastern patriarchs would shrink because of the Muslim Conquest. Ironically, while the prestige of being in the capital city had enhanced the authority of the Roman bishop, so did the later shift of the capital to Constantinople. With the emperor spending most of his time elsewhere, the bishop of Rome became the most powerful man in the city. This became even more true when the administrative capital in the West was moved from Rome to Ravenna in 404. Eventually the bishop of Rome would assume the title Pontifex Maximus, which had originally been used by the high priest of Neptune in ancient Rome, and was later adopted by the emperors as heads of the imperial cult.

Thus we find the bishops of Rome in the centuries following the Edict of Milan becoming increasingly assertive. In 341, the Roman bishop Julius wrote to Antioch, objecting that they had tried several prominent bishops without consulting him first. He maintained that all disputes between bishops should be mediated by the bishop of Rome. Two years later, the Council of Sardica affirmed this procedure. When the Council of Constantinople in 381 declared that the bishop of Constantinople, as leader of the church in the New Rome, had "primacy next after Rome," Damasus of Rome objected that spiritual authority came from Jesus Christ, and had nothing to do with imperial politics. He claimed sole authority in the church, referring to Rome as the Apostolic See, and addressing fellow bishops as "sons" rather than "brothers." Around the year 417, Innocent I told the Council of Carthage that they were right to check with him before condemning the Pelagian heresy, asserting that no doctrinal rulings were final until they had received confirmation from the bishop of Rome. Though Rome produced no outstanding theologians in the fourth century, the church played a major role in settling theological disputes. Some have speculated that language differences contributed to Rome's success in this area. Most of the hottest disputes were in the East, and were carried on in the Greek language, which is capable of expressing infinitely complex shades of meaning. When the disputes were brought to the bishop of Rome, they were translated into Latin, a much simpler language in which many of the points of dispute simply ceased to exist. The bishops of Rome thus gained a reputation for being theological arbitrators of the highest rank.

The man who did the most to establish the authority of the bishop of Rome, however, was Leo I (440-461). He broadened and deepened the theological justification for Roman supremacy and asserted his authority in church disputes from Asia Minor to North Africa to

FACTORS CONTRIBUTING TO THE SUPREMACY OF THE BISHOP OF ROME

FACTOR	RESULT
MATTHEW 16:17-19	Papal claims rest on the assertion that Peter was given authority by Jesus over the entire church. This claim was first officially recognized during the papacy of Leo I.
APOSTOLIC SUCCESSION	The teaching that the apostles passed on their authority to their successors led to the conclusion that Peter's supreme authority had been perpetuated in the bishops of Rome.
MARTYRDOM OF PETER AND PAUL	With the rise of the veneration of martyred saints, Rome gained prestige as the site of the deaths of the two principal apostles. The persecution under Nero also gave to the Roman church a special prominence by virtue of its suffering.
POPULATION OF ROME	Both the size of the city and the size of the church contributed to the authority of the bishop.
IMPERIAL CAPITAL	After the Edict of Milan, the emperors often sought advice on religious matters from the bishops of Rome.
LANGUAGE	The Latin-speaking West, led by the bishop of Rome, was often able to cut through the knotty theological dilemmas that incapacitated the Greek-speaking East, because of the lesser ability of the Latin language to express subtle shades of meaning.
LOCATION	Of the five patriarchal cities, only Rome was in the West; thus the bishop of Rome exercised authority over much more territory than did the other patriarchs.
MISSIONARY OUTREACH	The bishops of Rome, such as Gregory the Great, encouraged successful missionary work among the barbarian tribes, who then looked to Rome with great respect. The Eastern patriarchs were much less successful in evangelizing the Persians and later the Muslims.
BARBARIAN INVASIONS	The collapse of the Western Empire under the barbarian invasions left the church as the major integrating force in society - in the empire as well as among the "Christian" barbarians.
MUSLIM CONQUEST	The loss of the territories of the patriarchs of Antioch, Alexandria, and Jerusalem to Islam and the continual pressure exerted against Constantinople also increased the authority of the bishop of Rome.
LEADERSHIP	Leo I played major role in resolving Christological Controversy. Gregory I acted to protect Rome against Lombards, encouraged mission to England, contributed pastoral and theological writings.

Gaul. He also was not afraid to call on the power of the emperor to back up his claims, as the quotation with which the chapter began demonstrates. When the Council of Chalcedon met in 451 to decide the issue of the relationship between the humanity and the deity of Christ, Leo's doctrinal pronouncement was accepted as the ruling of the council, the members of which lauded the document as "Peter speaking through Leo." Chalcedon also gave Leo some setbacks, however, since it recognized the patriarch of Constantinople as having equal honor with Rome, and rejected the theological basis for Leo's claims to supremacy. The council did, however, allow Leo and his successors sole claim to the title of Pope, derived from the Latin word for "father." Leo bolstered his authority even further through his diplomacy as he was instrumental in turning away two barbarian invaders from the gates of Rome, including the feared Attila the Hun.

Other factors also contributed to the authority of the pope, as the bishop of Rome was now known. The destruction of the Western part of the empire by the barbarians and the conversion of those same barbarians created a situation where the pope was viewed as the integrating focus of society. He came to exert political as well as religious leadership. When, after the fall of Rome, the Eastern emperor dared to interfere in church matters, Pope Gelasius I wrote to inform him that even the emperor, as a member of the church, ought to submit to the authority of the Pope.

CHURCH WORSHIP

We turn now from the organization of the church to its practice, where the changes were every bit as radical. Again, the movement is from simplicity to complexity, and from freedom to ritual. Churches originally met in the homes of members of the congregation. The first church buildings were converted synagogues, used in situations where whole communities of Jews turned to Christ. During the worst of the persecutions, Christians met often in underground caves used for burial that came to be known as catacombs. In the long interval between the persecution of Valerian and that of Diocletian, the churches began to build structures specifically designed for congregational worship. This practice only became universal after the Edict of Milan, when the church not only had freedom to worship publicly, but often had government funds to help in church construction.

The New Testament tells us relatively little about the worship of the early church. It seems to have been rather open and flexible, with participation by many as described in I Corinthians 14. Since many of the early Christians were Jews, the worship of the church borrowed heavily from that of the synagogue, incorporating the same practices of Scripture reading, prayer, and exhortation. The church also sang when it met together, using both the Psalms and hymns with specifically Christian content, some of which may be recorded in our New Testament (e.g., Philippians 2:6-11). As the authority of the bishop grew, the worship became more and more leader-centered rather than congregation-centered, more formal and less spontaneous, and the laymen became passive observers of the clergy's worship, involved only to the extent that they received the grace of God through the sacraments. The following special elements of the church's worship deserve our consideration.

A.   BAPTISM

Even those whose practices differ today generally agree that the New Testament church practiced believer's baptism by immersion. Why, then, by the sixth century do we find the almost universal practice of infant baptism by sprinkling?

In the second century, baptism was a very serious matter indeed. When it was a crime to be a Christian, one did not approach baptism lightly. The church of that day consequently focused on the meaning of baptism, but was necessarily flexible about how it was done. The *Didache* insists that baptism is only for believers, but maintains that pouring is permissible, though immersion is the preferred mode. After all, the catacombs were not often equipped with baptismal pools! Justin Martyr describes baptism as "being born again," thus foreshadowing the later idea that baptism actually communicates saving grace to the one baptized. Baptism also became a tool to be used against heresy, as lengthy instructional periods were required prior to baptism, and the candidate was asked to affirm agreement to the Rule of Faith, the basic beliefs of the church that evolved into the first creeds (the Apostles' Creed probably came into existence as a baptismal formula).

In the third century, two opposing tendencies surfaced in the practice of baptism. Some moved toward infant baptism, both by analogy with circumcision in the Old Testament and because of the increasingly widespread belief that baptism washed away original sin. Others encouraged people to postpone baptism until immediately prior to death, since they believed that serious sins committed after baptism could not be forgiven (Constantine himself was not baptized into the church until he was on his deathbed). Still others actively sought martyrdom because they believed that it served as a "second baptism," washing away all sins committed since one had been baptized in water. The conflict was resolved by institutionalizing the practice of penance, another area where Cyprian led the way. Infants, he believed, should be baptized to bring them into the church; any serious sins committed after baptism could be forgiven through acts of penance. Thus a third sacrament began to make its way into the practice of the church.

With the end of the persecution and the advent of a "Christian society," infant baptism gradually became the dominant practice. The only ones baptized in adulthood were those remaining few, often barbarians outside the empire, who had not been born into Christian families.

B.   THE LORD'S SUPPER

In the first century, the celebration of the Lord's Supper was often preceded by a communal meal called the *agape*, or "love feast," the abuses of which were criticized by Paul in I Corinthians 11. The practice continued into the second century, though the persecutions gradually forced the church to discontinue such celebrations. From the beginning, the Lord's Supper was open only to those who had been baptized. During the persecutions, the observance was driven underground, sometimes literally, and it became a sort of secret ritual open only to "initiates." Such secrecy helped to spawn many of the ridiculous rumors that plagued the church during the years of persecution. Those going through pre-baptismal instruction, called *catechumens*, were allowed to attend the early part of the service, but were required to leave before the celebration of the Lord's Supper. Participation was considered so important that the deacons had the responsibility of taking the elements to those who were sick or in prison after the service was over. It was only after the persecutions had ended and the church dominated the empire that the Lord's Supper became a public observance, though participation continued to be open only to those who had been baptized.

The observance of the Lord's Supper became associated with more and more superstition over the years. The imagery used by Jesus about eating His flesh and drinking His blood was taken increasingly literally by the church. When Cyprian introduced the idea of clergy as sacrificing priests, all the parts were in place for the eventual construction of the doctrine of transubstantiation, the teaching that the bread and wine in the Lord's Supper actually become the body and blood of Christ. And since only the priest has the power to effect such a transformation, he holds the means of salvation, which may be obtained by the congregation only through him.

In the centuries following the Edict of Milan, other practices began taking on a sacramental character. To baptism and the Lord's Supper were added penance, confirmation (necessitated by the growth of infant baptism; it originally was the rite performed by the exorcist at the time of adult baptism), last rites (needed to remove any sins not covered by penance), ordination (it was the grace of God that set the clergy apart), and marriage. Ambrose, bishop of Milan, also advocated the inclusion of foot-washing, though this never gained wide acceptance in the church. Thus by the end of the seventh century, all the practices that were later to be recognized by the Catholic Church as sacraments were in common use, though they were not formally designated as such until the twelfth century.

C. THE CHURCH YEAR

It was also during this period of time that the special annual celebrations of the church developed. The oldest annual festival of the church is Easter, which we know was observed by the middle of the second century, and probably much earlier. The church originally commemorated the resurrection of Christ by changing the day of worship from Saturday, the Jewish sabbath, to Sunday, although many of the early Jewish Christian congregations continued to observe both days. As the church became predominantly Gentile, Sunday worship became the rule, and Constantine made Sunday an official holiday shortly after his accession to power. The annual celebration of the resurrection first comes to our attention because of a dispute concerning its date. Apparently the churches in Asia Minor celebrated Easter on the fourteenth day of the Jewish month Nisan, the beginning of the Jewish passover, no matter what day of the week this happened to be, and claimed that such a practice had been initiated by the apostle John. The churches in the rest of the empire celebrated Easter on the following Sunday, insisting that Jesus had risen on a Sunday, and therefore Easter should be observed on a Sunday. The two observances survived side by side until Victor, the bishop of Rome, tried to assert his authority and force the churches of Asia Minor to do things his way. This dispute, known as the Quartodeciman Controversy (from the Latin word for "fourteen"), was, as we saw earlier, the first instance in which the bishop of Rome tried to exercise authority over other churches. Though his position eventually became that of the church at large, he was strongly rebuffed for his efforts to throw his weight around.

Easter early became the time of year in which people were baptized into the church, since baptism symbolizes the death and resurrection of Christ. It was preceded by a period of intense instruction, and often by fasting. The whole congregation would generally join the catechumens in their fast to demonstrate the unity of the people of God. Gradually this practice of pre-baptismal fasting developed into the observance of Lent. Other practices and symbols associated with Easter came to the church by way of the barbarian tribes who were converted to Christianity. They brought with them fertility symbols such as eggs and rabbits that were quickly adapted to the Christian festival.

Later other festivals grew up in connection with Easter. One of the earliest was Pentecost or Whitsun, the celebration of the coming of the Holy Spirit fifty days after the Jewish Passover. Forty days after the resurrection was the feast of Ascension, remembering when Christ was taken up into heaven. By the fourth century, the church in Jerusalem had begun to celebrate Palm Sunday the week before Easter, and that practice soon spread as well.

The celebration of the birth of Christ was a later development. No one in the early church ever claimed to know when Christ was born, which made it a little difficult to celebrate the event. Accuracy was eventually overcome by more pressing issues, however, and the church gradually began to celebrate Jesus' birth. Again there was a dispute over the date. The Eastern church celebrated Epiphany on January 6th, which was something of a catch-all, used to commemorate Christ's birth and baptism as well as the visit of the wise men. In the West, the date of December 25th was chosen to coincide with the pagan *Saturnalia*, the birthday of the Immortal Sun. Near the end of the fourth century the church settled on the December date, while reserving Epiphany for the wise men. As with Easter, the celebration gradually became encumbered with all sorts of pagan elements, including the giving of gifts, borrowed from the Saturnalia but justified by the gifts of the wise men.

Thus developed what came to be known as the church year, during which the worship of the church reenacts the major events of the life of Christ. To this were added numerous other festival days to honor the saints, but we will consider these when we look at the development of monasticism in chapter eight.

MAKING DRY BONES LIVE

What are we to say about change in the church? In this chapter we saw the church develop from a simple organization with local leadership to a vast hierarchy, and saw an informal worship grow into a complex maze of ritual. How are we to evaluate these developments? Must we conclude that the church must change to fit changing conditions in society in order to survive, or do we view these changes as deviations from the Scriptures that led the church astray?

In the Gospels, Jesus criticized the Pharisees repeatedly for nullifying the Word of God by adding to it the traditions of men. When men such as Irenaeus and Tertullian spoke of the tradition that served as the basis for the faith, they were not referring to extra-biblical truth, but to the truth of the Word of God itself. They emphasized the fact that it had been entrusted to men only because the content of the New Testament had not yet been universally recognized. The question about the validity of the changes we have observed boils down ultimately to the issue of the sufficiency of Scripture. If God has given us all we need in His Word, to add to that Word is to distort it. If, on the other hand, God intended for the leaders of the church to continue the work of the apostles and serve as an ongoing channel of divine revelation, then we should expect that many church practices that have no biblical foundation would be acceptable as God exercises His wisdom through His ordained representatives on earth.

It was this very issue that stimulated the Protestant Reformation. Martin Luther taught the principle *Sola Scriptura* -that the Bible alone is the Christian's authority for what he should believe and do. All things are to be judged by God's Word. If we believe that the Word of God is truly sufficient for all of life, we not only need to measure things like church government, baptismal practices, and Christian holidays against the Bible, but also many of the other things that we do in our churches today that are not found in Scripture. Any church that elevates the teachings of men to the level of the Word of God is sowing the seeds of its own destruction. We must continue to evaluate everything we do in the light of Scripture.

FOR REVIEW AND FURTHER THOUGHT

1. What are the two church officers specified in the New Testament, and what are their duties?

2. What factors might have caused the early church to separate the offices of elder and bishop?

3. Why did bishops eventually gain jurisdiction over a group of churches rather than a single congregation?

4. How was the role of the elder changed when the bishop began to supervise a diocese?

5. Why did Irenaeus and Tertullian emphasize the bishop as the successor of the apostles?

6. What role did Cyprian play in the growth of the power of the bishop? In the way in which the authority of the bishop of Rome was viewed by the church? In the church's views of baptism and the Lord's Supper?

7. What church offices developed because the church adopted the organizational structure of the Roman Empire?

8. How did the bishops of Rome come to be known as theological problem solvers despite the fact that Rome produced few great theologians?

9. What political and geographical factors contributed to the rise to prominence of the bishop of Rome?

10. Identify the roles played by the following bishops of Rome in the growth of papal power: Victor, Stephen, Julius, Damasus, Innocent I, Leo I, and Gelasius.

11. How did the following councils contribute to the development of the church hierarchy: Nicea, Sardica, Constantinople, and Chalcedon?

12. Identify the following terms used in the chapter in one sentence each: priest, archbishop, patriarch, exorcist, acolyte, Pontifex Maximus, pope.

13. When and why did the church begin to build its own buildings in which to worship?

14. What worship practices did the early church borrow from the Jewish synagogue?

15. What factors caused the church to change from baptism by immersion to pouring or sprinkling? What factors contributed to the change from believer's baptism to infant baptism?

16. How did the Lord's Supper come to be associated with a sacrifice performed by a priest?

17. How did the changes in baptism and the Lord's Supper produce a group of new sacraments for the church?

18. How did pagan practices become associated with the church's celebrations of Christmas and Easter?

19. Identify the following in one sentence each: catechumens, *agape*, Quartodeciman controversy, Lent, Epiphany, *Saturnalia*.

20. To what extent do you believe that the church is free to modify its organization and practice to meet the needs of a changing society? Support your answer.

6

MEN OF IRON WITH FEET OF CLAY

The period of time between the conversion of Constantine and the fall of Rome was a time of great ideas, great conflicts, and great men. In chapter five, we saw some of the changes that occurred in the organization and practice of the church during this era of prosperity. In chapter seven, we will be looking at the great doctrinal controversies of the Ancient Church. But these changes in organization and practice and these great doctrinal debates were carried out by influential men to whom the church owes a great deal. They are known to history as the Nicene and post-Nicene Fathers (because they lived during and after the Council of Nicea, which will be discussed in the next chapter), and fathers they truly are. Among these influential fourth and fifth century teachers could be included the names of Eusebius of Caesarea, Hilary of Poitiers, Athanasius, the three Cappadocian Fathers (Basil the Great, Gregory of Nyssa, and Gregory of Nazianzus), Ambrose, John Chrysostom, Jerome, Theodore of Mopsuestia, Cyril of Alexandria, and Augustine of Hippo. Catholics and Protestants alike share the doctrinal foundation that these men helped to establish. Though their contributions were great, they were men who had faults and weaknesses like any others, of course. They had their sins and blind spots, and their positive contributions to the church were often counterbalanced by the unbiblical practices they helped to foster and encourage. Rather than devoting a paragraph each to a long list of influential teachers, we will concentrate our attention on the giants. This chapter will therefore focus on the lives and contributions of six men, three from the East and three from the West - Eusebius, Athanasius, Chrysostom, Ambrose, Jerome, and Augustine. Their names will appear frequently in the discussion of doctrinal controversies in the next chapter, and knowing something about them should help the reader to see those doctrinal controversies in the light of the men who debated them.

FATHERS OF THE EASTERN CHURCH

A. EUSEBIUS OF CAESAREA (c.263-c.339)

In the years following the conversion of Constantine, some of the leaders of the church rose to places of great influence in the Roman Empire. It should not surprise us that Constantine, after professing the Christian faith, should seek out Christian leaders to advise him on religious affairs. One of the first to rise to prominence under the imperial favor was Eusebius of Caesarea.

Eusebius was born in Palestine, possibly in Caesarea itself, and studied under a presbyter and scholar named Pamphilus, who was the caretaker of the immense library compiled by Origen before his death, and ran a theological school in Caesarea. Eusebius became a teacher in the school of Pamphilus, and his years of study stimulated a life-long love for scholarly research, which prepared him for the historical work that was to be the basis of his lasting reputation in the church. When Pamphilus was martyred in the last great persecution of the church in 310, Eusebius took the name Eusebius Pamphilius in honor of his teacher and friend. After the death of Pamphilus, Eusebius traveled to Tyre, where he saw for himself the brutal persecution being experienced by the Christians there, and later to Alexandria, where he was briefly imprisoned. In about the year 315, he was appointed bishop of Caesarea, in which post he served until his death.

It was during the years immediately following the conversion of Constantine that Eusebius produced the work for which he is best known today. For many years he had been collecting records of the events from the Christian era, and he compiled these records into a book called *Ecclesiastical History*, which traced the history of Christianity from the birth of Christ to the conversion of Constantine. This book is by far our best source of information about the second and third centuries, and has earned for Eusebius the title, "Father of Church History." Eusebius' work contains references to many ancient writings that have long been lost, and gives us access to people and events that would otherwise be unknown. Eusebius made a genuine effort to evaluate his sources and to sift out superstition and legend, though he was not entirely successful in this. The *Ecclesiastical History* is little more than a list of facts, with no effort to determine causes of the events recorded, and is written in a rather laborious style, but is an irreplaceable resource for an era about which we know relatively little.

No one knows how Eusebius came to know Constantine, but he turned out to have the ideal temperament for an imperial advisor. Like many historians, he had seen enough of different sides of arguments to incline him to moderation, and his research gave him a certain degree of objectivity that allowed him to distance himself from any dispute that may have been going on at the time. These qualities put him right in the middle of the first doctrinal dispute to arise during the reign of Constantine, the Arian Controversy. Arius was a popular Alexandrian preacher who, fearing that referring to Christ as God would drag Christians into the same polytheism that dominated the pagan religions, taught instead that Christ was the first and greatest of the beings created by God. While other Christians, most notably Athanasius, were condemning this teaching as heresy, Eusebius, who knew Arius personally and understood where he was coming from, though not agreeing with his conclusions, sought some kind of compromise. This led many to accuse Eusebius himself of heresy. When Constantine called the Council of Nicea to resolve the Arian Controversy, Eusebius was given a place of honor at the side of the emperor and cleared of all accusations. He proposed a compromise doctrinal statement that was used by the council in preparing its eventual findings. When the council condemned Arius, Eusebius went along, though with some reservations.

Eusebius' ability to compromise made him a favorite with Constantine, who wanted peace in the church above all else, but it brought him nothing but suspicion from other leaders in the church. Though he was unwilling to accept the radical teaching of Arius, he thought that Athanasius went too far in the other direction, and thus opposed that greatest defender of the doctrine of the Trinity. To his credit, Eusebius recognized his shortcomings as a theologian, and when offered the patriarchate of Antioch in 331, he politely declined.

His other contributions to the church were mostly in the literary realm, including his *Chronicle*, which was a history of the world from the time of Abraham to his own day, and a *Life of Constantine*, which, though giving an incredibly rosy picture of the first Christian emperor of Rome, provides valuable information to modern scholars about this critical period in church history.

B. ATHANASIUS (c.296-373)

"Athanasius against the world!" Never in the history of the church has there been a better example of the fact that biblical truth is not determined by the vote of the majority. Athanasius, the greatest defender of the deity of Christ and the doctrine of the Trinity, spent his entire life fleeing from and fighting opposition, and often had to stand alone in his support of the truth.

According to one rather unreliable tradition, Alexander, the bishop of Alexandria, was walking through his city one day shortly after the end of the great persecution, and saw a group of children playing church. The young man playing the bishop was carrying out his role with such obvious sincerity that Alexander determined to take him under his wing. That young man was Athanasius. He grew up in a wealthy family in Alexandria, and studied at and later taught in the catechetical school made famous many years before by Clement and Origen. He had contact early in life with Anthony of Thebes, credited with being the first monk, and later wrote a biography of that saintly ascetic. He became a deacon in the Alexandrian church, and the secretary of the bishop Alexander. When Constantine summoned the Council of Nicea in 325, Athanasius accompanied his bishop to the council. At that council, he became the most outspoken voice in favor of the full deity of Christ, which position the council finally adopted, with only two negative votes out of several hundred delegates. It would seem that Athanasius had become the spokesman for the official doctrinal position of the church. In fact, his popularity at the time was so great that, when Alexander died in 328, Athanasius was chosen as bishop despite the fact that he was only in his early thirties. There was trouble on the horizon, however. Politics soon intruded even further on the debate, and when Constantine insisted that Arius be restored and Athanasius refused to do so, Constantine sent him into exile. Because of political maneuverings that will be detailed in the next chapter, Athanasius wound up being exiled from his church on five separate occasions. Out of the forty-five years he served as bishop of Alexandria, he spent seventeen in exile, though in some of those he was hidden in and around Alexandria by his people, who loved him dearly, and thus was able to continue to lead the church. His last ten years were spent in peace, and he lived long enough to see his teaching gain ascendancy in the church, though he died before it was officially accepted by the Council of Constantinople in 381.

The theological position of Athanasius concerning the deity of Christ has become that of orthodox Christians everywhere, and his understanding of salvation still dominates the Eastern Church. His view of salvation was, very simply, that Christ was made man so that man might be made divine. If Christ were not God, man would have no hope of overcoming his corruption. In addition to his defense of the doctrine of the Trinity, Athanasius also did much to stimulate monasticism, not only through his biography of Anthony, but also through his own life. It was also his Easter letter to his congregation in 367 that gave us the first list of the books of the New Testament as we know them today.

C. JOHN CHRYSOSTOM (c.347-407)

The greatest preacher of the Ancient Church was John of Antioch, given the name Chrysostom ("Golden Mouth") more than a century after his death because of the eloquence and power of the more than six hundred sermons from his pen that have survived the years. A fearless preacher whose holy life backed up his words, John was loved, respected, but eventually hounded to death by those who could not hope to measure up to his spiritual attainments.

John was born into a wealthy Christian family in Antioch. His father was a Roman military officer, and died shortly after John's birth. His mother, Anthusa, was a godly woman who was determined that her son should serve the Lord. The prosperity of his family enabled him to have a fine education, and he studied rhetoric and law under the pagan tutor Libanius, who had also taught the emperor Julian. John was so successful in his studies that, when Libanius died, he expressed the desire that John should take his place, "but the Christians have stolen him from us." When he was baptized into the church in his early twenties, John gave up the practice of law to become a monk. His mother begged him not to leave her alone, and he consented, remaining with her until her death in 374, though during that time he lived the life of an ascetic in his own home. After his mother's death, he went to live as a monk in the Syrian wilderness. During these years, he met Theodore of Mopsuestia, whose radical ideas about interpreting Scripture had a major influence on him. In opposition to the allegorical interpretation of Scripture that was so popular in those days, Theodore insisted that any passage of Scripture should be interpreted according to its literary and historical context. This approach to biblical exegesis was to give to the preaching of Chrysostom a solid substance to go along with the power of his rhetoric.

The years in the wilderness may have helped to form his thought, but they ruined his health. He ate and slept so little that he almost died, and was forced to return to Antioch in 380. His gifts were quickly recognized by Flavian, the bishop of Antioch, who made John a deacon in 381 and ordained him to the priesthood in 386. For the next eleven years, Chrysostom was the most powerful preacher in the Christian world. He filled his people's ears with the Scriptures, day after day and week after week, preaching through many of the books of the Bible, using illustrations and applications that have made him a model for preachers ever since. But John became a victim of the Peter Principle, that maxim that states that, in any hierarchy, men tend to be promoted to their level of incompetence. After eleven years in Antioch, Chrysostom was called to become the bishop of Constantinople, the capital of the Eastern Empire. Though he was an enormously gifted man, John was ill-equipped to handle the politics and petty jealousies that abound in any imperial court. He was too honest and forthright, and refused to flatter those in power around him. These noble characteristics soon brought him to grief in the capital.

Antioch was a big city, but the open immorality in Constantinople was unlike anything John had ever seen before. He hadn't wanted the job in the first place, but now that he had it, he was determined to execute his office faithfully. He spoke out boldly against the moral abuses he saw, both in the city and in the church. He soon made some very powerful enemies. The Empress Eudoxia, who dominated her wishy-washy husband Arcadius, disliked his pointed sermons. The members of the imperial court were miffed when John refused to host lavish banquets in his home as previous bishops had done, choosing instead to live simply and give his money to the poor. The bishops and priests under him chafed under his strict discipline; it was fine for John to live as an ascetic if he chose, but he had no right to impose his lifestyle on them!

The man who really initiated John's troubles, however, was Theophilus, the bishop of Alexandria. The cities of Antioch and Alexandria had long been rivals for influence in the Eastern Church, and Theophilus was enraged when John was given the second most powerful position in Christendom. In his jealousy, he determined to bring about John's downfall. His opportunity came in 403 when John assisted a group of monks who followed the teachings of Origen, whose teachings by this time had been condemned as heretical. Theophilus quickly scurried to Constantinople on the pretext of a courtesy visit, and stirred up the movers and shakers in the city against their bishop. He found in the Empress Eudoxia a particularly willing ear. When John heard about the plot, he preached a sermon on the persecution of Elijah by Jezebel. This was too much for Eudoxia. She talked her husband into sending John into exile. Before he was out of the country, however, the people of the city were ready to riot in support of their bishop, and a sudden earthquake that seemed particularly potent in the bedroom of Eudoxia forced Arcadius to reconsider. John was quickly brought back and restored to his office.

Trouble broke out again a few months later when John's preaching was interrupted by the noise of workmen erecting a statue of Eudoxia near the cathedral. When John responded by saying, "Again Herodias rages; again she is confounded; again she dances; again she demands the head of John on a charger," he had signed his death warrant. Encouraged by prompting from Theophilus, the emperor had John arrested by soldiers in the middle of a baptismal ceremony and exiled to Armenia. Even there, crowds from Antioch and Constantinople flocked to hear him preach, and he kept in touch with his beloved churches. Eudoxia decided that Armenia wasn't far enough, and ordered John to be sent to Pityus, beyond the Black Sea. Forced to travel far too fast for an old man, John died before reaching his destination.

The treatment John had received so enraged the church at large that the bishop of Rome, among others, refused to have anything to do with anyone who had taken part in the disgraceful fiasco. Finally, the son of Arcadius and Eudoxia was forced to do public penance for the sins of his parents, who by then were deceased.

John Chrysostom is remembered as a great preacher and advocate of monasticism, but his career also set the tone for the relationship between church and state in the East. While in the West, church and state struggled for dominance for over a thousand years, in the East the issue was settled quickly - the church was dominated by the state, and became an arm of imperial rule. The same pattern has persisted for the last fifteen hundred years in the Eastern Orthodox churches, whether the state be the Byzantine Empire or the Union of Soviet Socialist Republics.

FATHERS OF THE WESTERN CHURCH

A.   AMBROSE (c.340-397)

In chapter two, we looked at the career of Cyprian, and noted how his premature elevation to the office of bishop had done great harm to the church. In Ambrose, we have an example of the fact that God's mercy often overcomes man's foolishness. The circumstances under which Ambrose became bishop of Milan are hardly what one would call biblically sound, but God used the man tremendously despite his lack of preparation for the job he was coerced into doing.

Ambrose was born to Christian parents in the city of Trier in Gaul, where his father was the Roman governor. His father died when he was thirteen, and his mother prepared him to follow in his father's footsteps. He studied law in the city of Rome, and the combination of his well-placed family ties and his own exceptional ability earned him a position as governor of Northern Italy by the age of thirty. Though Ambrose professed to be a Christian at this time, he was not yet baptized into the church. Milan, the capital city of the province governed by Ambrose, was caught in the middle of the Arian Controversy. The population of the city was evenly divided between Arians and Trinitarians, and when the Arian bishop of Milan died, it looked like a riot might break out between the two factions over who would succeed him. Ambrose was quickly summoned to the cathedral to restore order. He quieted the crowd, and suddenly the voice of a child rang out in the silence: "Let Ambrose be bishop!" Soon the entire crowd took up the chant - they all wanted their popular young governor to lead the church. Ambrose protested that he was totally unqualified. Not only wasn't he a priest, but he hadn't even been baptized! He even tried to run and hide, but the crowd would have none of it. He finally submitted to the wishes of the crowd, believing it to be the will of God. He was baptized, ordained to the priesthood, and consecrated as the bishop of Milan - all in the space of a week!

Ambrose immediately gave away his wealth and settled down to the task of making up for lost time. He studied the Bible and the writings of earlier church fathers, determined to do his best at the job to which God had called him. He turned out to be a capable leader indeed. He defended the orthodox Trinitarian position staunchly, much to the disappointment of the Arians who had helped to elect him. He encouraged high morals and simple living among the clergy and laymen alike, and introduced congregational singing into the Western Church. In fact, he wrote many hymns himself, some of which are still in use in the church today. As a preacher, he influenced the lives of many, particularly a young man by the name of Augustine who settled in Milan in a state of total religious confusion, but left to become the greatest theologian of the Ancient Church.

Ambrose's greatest contribution to the church, however, was in his relationship to the emperors who ruled during his time in Milan. At that time, Milan was the site of an imperial residence, so Ambrose had direct contact with a number of emperors. His dealings with them set precedents that influenced the church for years beyond his death.

The first of these incidents involved the Senate in Rome. Despite the rapid growth of Christianity in the empire, the old Roman aristocracy, from which the Senate was drawn, was largely pagan. The Senate chamber had in it a statue of the Goddess of Victory, which had been there since before the conversion of Constantine. The emperor Gratian finally removed the statue in 383, but was killed in battle soon after. When the Senate petitioned the new emperor to have the statue restored, it was Ambrose who wrote an impassioned plea to the new emperor, implying that anyone who allowed idolatry to continue unchecked would find no place in the church. The threat worked, and the statue was never replaced.

Two years later, Ambrose was challenged by the Empress Justina, who was ruling as regent for her young son Valentinian II. She was an Arian, and wanted the privileges previously enjoyed by the Arians in Milan to be restored. Her imperial guards were mostly Arian Goths, and she requested from Ambrose that one of the larger churches in Milan be turned over to these men for Arian worship. The threat of military force backed up her request. Ambrose, undaunted, refused to permit Arian worship in any way, shape, or form, and to counter the military threat, staged a two day sit-in by his congregation in the church she had wanted for her soldiers. The soldiers didn't dare attack these unarmed Christians, and Justina finally gave in. During the sit-in, Ambrose taught his people some of the hymns he had written, and they sang them together to keep their spirits up. This represents the first use of congregational singing in the Western Church.

In 388, a group of monks rioted in Callinicum and destroyed a Gnostic church and a Jewish synagogue. The emperor Theodosius ordered the local bishop to pay for the damages out of church funds, but Ambrose again resisted anything that smacked of support for false teaching. When Theodosius was in his congregation one Sunday, Ambrose preached on the parable Nathan told to David after the murder of Uriah, and implied that Theodosius was about to commit a similar sin. Theodosius offered a compromise, but Ambrose replied that he could not give Communion to anyone who fostered idolatry. Theodosius gave in, and the monks were never punished.

His final conflict with imperial power came in the year 390. Theodosius, a devout Christian who had made Christianity the official religion of the empire almost ten years earlier, had consolidated his power over the entire empire. He may have been a Christian, but he was also a hot-tempered soldier, and his temper sometimes got the better of him. In 390, a popular chariot-racer had been arrested in Thessalonica, and in the ensuing riot (violence at sporting events is not unique to the twenty-first century!), a Roman officer was killed. Theodosius ordered his troops to stage a circus in the hippodrome, but when the crowd had all arrived, the soldiers locked the gates and slaughtered everyone inside. Over seven thousand people died in the incident. When Ambrose heard about it, he sent Theodosius a letter telling him that he needed to repent. Theodosius failed to respond, and when he showed up at church the next Sunday, Ambrose refused to admit him. Theodosius attempted to turn the tables on the bishop by saying that David was admitted to worship even after his great sin, but Ambrose pointed out that David had repented, which Theodosius had not done. The emperor stalked out of the church, and for eight months stayed at home. Finally, he did public penance for his sin and was received back into the fellowship of the church.

The success of Ambrose in these encounters set a precedent in the West just as much as the failure of Chrysostom did in the East. They helped set the stage for the conflict between church and state that would dominate the history of the Middle Ages. Ambrose had put into practice the principle that, while the emperor was above the state, he was within the church, and thus subject to its authority.

B. JEROME (c.345-420)

Not all saints are saintly. Jerome,

probably the greatest scholar in the Western Church of his day, was a man devoted to God, but was not at all easy for his fellow-Christians to get along with. He left in his wake a trail of great writings and broken relationships.

Jerome was born in northeastern Italy, near present-day Slovenia, of Christian parents. Because his family was wealthy, he had the best education available in his day. He, like Chrysostom, studied rhetoric, and his ability to use words effectively was every bit as great as that of his Eastern contemporary, though his words flowed more smoothly through his pen than by means of his tongue. In his early twenties he joined a community of ascetics near his home town, but when the local bishop objected that Jerome expected too much austerity of others, Jerome responded by calling the bishop ignorant and well-suited to his misguided flock.

In 374, he headed east and settled down in a monastery in the desert outside Antioch, where he stayed for five years. While in the desert, his strict ascetic practices made him ill, and two of his companions died. One night, he dreamed that he had died and been taken before the judgment seat. There God accused him of being a Ciceronian rather than a Christian because of the pleasure he found in secular literature. God then ordered him to be flogged, despite the pleas of the angels for mercy. He finally vowed never to read a secular book again, though this was a vow that he did not always keep. This dream is a classic in the history of monasticism, and has influenced many generations of monks in the direction of ignorance of worldly things. Ironically enough, Jerome is one of the best examples of the futility of such imposed ignorance, since it is his knowledge of secular literature and the writing skills he gained by studying it that made him such an effective communicator of Christian truth.

His desert experience turned out to be one long struggle with temptation. He had gone into seclusion to avoid the desires of the flesh, but he found that they pursued him to his desert hideaway. While his dreams sometimes brought him visions of the Judgment Seat of Christ, they also gave him pictures of seductive dancing girls. Finally, in order to keep his mind away from such things, he took up the study of Hebrew with a converted Jew, which he found did the trick rather nicely.

In 379 he left the monastery and went to Antioch, where he was ordained to the priesthood, although he never served a congregation. He then traveled to Rome, where in 382 he became the secretary to Damasus, bishop of Rome. While in Rome, he became a popular preacher, and was especially effective in encouraging others to take up asceticism. Most of his success was among women, however, and his critics wondered why, unjustly accusing him of using the denial of the flesh as a cover for its indulgence. When one of the women who was fasting under his direction died in the effort and some of the pagans threatened to throw him into the Tiber, Jerome turned his back on Rome for the last time and headed East again, this time settling in Bethlehem, where he spent the last thirty-five years of his life in a cave that he believed to be the birthplace of Jesus, and supervised a monastic community, mostly made up of people who had accompanied him from Rome.

It was during the years in Bethlehem that Jerome did most of the writing for which he is famous. His greatest work was the translation of the Bible into Latin, the famous Latin Vulgate. Damasus was the one who started him on the project, encouraging him while in Rome to prepare a new translation of the New Testament and Psalms. Jerome was reluctant, knowing that people would object to changes in their favorite verses, whether the new translations were more accurate or not. He finally agreed to undertake the work when he realized how bad most of the available Latin translations were. In Bethlehem, he finished, not just the New Testament and Psalms, but the entire Bible, using the original Hebrew to translate the Old Testament, with the help of some Jewish rabbis he hired for the purpose, but who had to come at night so their congregations wouldn't know what they were doing. The Vulgate was a brilliant piece of work that soon gained acceptance from the whole Western Church, and eventually became the official Bible of Roman Catholicism. Like any one-man translation, it has its flaws and theological bias (one of the most notable is the persistent tendency to translate "repent" as "do penance"), but it brought the church of his day closer to the original manuscripts of Scripture than it had been in many years. Two ironies stem from Jerome's work on the Vulgate. One is that Jerome was motivated by a desire to get the Bible into the language of the people, but his work was used for years by the Catholic Church to prevent just that. In the Middle Ages, they opposed translation of any kind, and until the twentieth century, the Catholic Church required that any translation that was done had to be done from the Vulgate rather than from the originals. The other irony is that Jerome questioned the inclusion of the Apocrypha in the Bible, and never translated most of it because it was not found in the original Hebrew, yet the Roman Catholic Church included it in the official Bible based on Jerome's work.

In the years in Bethlehem, Jerome also carried on extensive correspondence with many of the church leaders of his day. Jerome was not kind to his critics, and his intense pride took offense easily and did not often either forgive or forget. His training in the classics gave him a sharp satiric wit that he used freely against any who opposed him. He even chided the mild-mannered Augustine, accusing the North African of criticizing him behind his back and implying that his own scholarship was far superior to that of the bishop of Hippo.

C. AUGUSTINE OF HIPPO (354-430)

"Thou madest us for Thyself, and our heart is restless until it repose in Thee." These words are found in the opening paragraph of the *Confessions*, the spiritual autobiography of Augustine of Hippo. Augustine was the greatest of the church fathers, leaving a legacy that touches deeply Catholic and Protestant churches alike.

Augustine did not begin like a saint of the church, however. Born in Tagaste (in present-day Algeria) to a pagan father and a Christian mother, he seemed determined to follow his father in frustrating his mother's prayers. His father, Patricius, was a local government official who shared the loose morals typical of the day. Augustine's mother Monica put up with her husband's infidelity, but prayed daily for his salvation, and that of her son. Augustine revealed his powerful mind at a young age, and his parents were determined to get him the best education available, despite their limited means. He began his education in nearby Madaura, where he acquired a life-long distaste for Greek, and became what teachers today refer to as an underachiever, not applying himself to anywhere near the extent of his ability. When he went away to school in Carthage, the provincial capital, at the age of eighteen, he quickly fell in with a rowdy crowd, and before long had acquired a mistress and fathered a son out of wedlock. To his credit, he remained faithful to this girl for the next thirteen years, though he never married her, and did his best to raise his son.

Spiritual and philosophical confusion accompanied his moral turmoil. Despite the pleas of his mother, he rejected the Bible as grotesque in its stories and poorly written, and turned to the popular Manichaean cult. Like many young people who are drawn into involvement with cults, he did so not so much because he believed the Manichaean doctrine as because he was dissatisfied with his life and had no answers. He remained a Manichaean for nine years, during which time he served as a teacher of rhetoric, first in Carthage and then in Rome. He didn't find any satisfaction, either in teaching or in Manichaeism. As a teacher, he was a brilliant lecturer, but had trouble controlling his classes. His students were often disruptive, and rarely paid their bills. When he expressed a desire to go to Rome, Monica objected, but Augustine sneaked aboard a ship while she was in a chapel near the dock praying that God would prevent his departure!

In 383, he arrived in Rome, ready for bigger and better things, but terribly confused. He wanted to know the truth and to do what was right, but he had no idea where to turn, and lacked the self-control to live morally. He gave up Manichaeism and tried Neoplatonism, but that didn't seem to help very much. After a year in Rome, he was offered a teaching post in rhetoric in Milan, where his mother Monica joined him and continued her praying and pleading. Monica finally convinced her son to settle down and get married, at which point he callously sent his mistress of thirteen years away. He then found out that the girl to whom his mother had engaged him was only ten years old, and that he would have to wait at least two years before marrying her. Crying out, "God, give me chastity, but not yet!", Augustine broke off the engagement and took another mistress.

By now he was at the end of his rope. While in Milan, his mother had asked him to go listen to Ambrose preach, and he had agreed, largely because of his interest in the bishop's rhetorical skills. The more he listened, however, the more the message began to penetrate, and the lessons Monica had been pounding into his head for thirty-two years finally began to take hold. One day in 386, while walking in a garden, he heard the voice of a child singing "Take and read." He picked up a Bible and read the first thing he saw - "Let us behave decently, as in the daytime, not in orgies and drunkenness, not in sexual immorality and debauchery, not in dissension and jealousy. Rather, clothe yourselves with the Lord Jesus Christ, and do not think about how to gratify the desires of the sinful nature" (Romans 13:13-14, NIV). These words were exactly what he needed. Right on the spot, he gave himself to Christ. The next Easter, he and his son were baptized by Ambrose, and his mother finally saw her prayers answered.

Augustine then left for North Africa, intending to live a life of seclusion. His mother died on the way home, and his son died two years later. He settled in his home town of Tagaste, but soon he was ordained to the priesthood in the nearby city of Hippo, and in 395 became the bishop of that city. Here he remained for the rest of his life, and died while the barbarian Vandals were besieging the city.

The great writing and teaching of Augustine grew largely from his struggles with the doctrinal controversies of his day. Since we will be looking at these in the next chapter, it is not my intention to say much about them here. But I should at least mention that his doctrine of the church was developed in opposition to the Donatists, his doctrine of man and salvation in opposition to the Pelagians, and his view of history developed in the light of the crumbling power of Rome and the barbarian invasions.

No teacher in the Ancient Church approached the influence of Augustine, both in his own day and in the years that followed. His formulations were critical in solving the Donatist and Pelagian controversies and in finalizing the orthodox doctrine of the Trinity. His spiritual pilgrimage from Neoplatonist philosopher to Christian theologian was a gradual one, and many of his early writings contain quite a bit of pagan thought. As a result, in many of the doctrinal disputes throughout the Middle Ages, Augustine was quoted as an authority by those on both sides! His view of the church, and of church-state relations, was adopted by Roman Catholicism, and his explanation of the Pauline doctrine of grace was the major inspiration for the work of Reformers like Luther, Zwingli, and Calvin. Thus Augustine can truly be called a father, by Catholics and Protestants alike.

MAKING DRY BONES LIVE

Has our look at men of iron with feet of clay been encouraging or discouraging? Does it bother you that the same men who fight for the doctrine of the Trinity tell people to avoid marriage, or that those who will not let the state dominate the church try to use church power to dominate the state, or that the same men who preach salvation by grace alone emphasize the grace of the sacraments and encourage people to pray to Mary? Does it bother you that some of the greatest men of the church were mean and vengeful in their dealings with other people? Do you sometimes wonder if anyone ever really had their doctrine completely straight?

The weaknesses, flaws, and sins of great men in the history of the church should affect us in the same way as the sins of Abraham, Moses, David, and Peter recorded in Scripture. They prove that God uses weak vessels to do His work, and that a person who is committed to Christ can be used by God in marvelous ways despite his imperfections. At the same time, as we look at the tremendous damage done to the church and to the reputation of God in the world by the sins of church leaders, we should recognize that while the good God does through His people goes far, so does the evil they do when they disobey Him.

Men of Iron with Feet of Clay

FOR REVIEW AND FURTHER THOUGHT

1. What is meant by the term "post-Nicene Fathers"?

2. What made Eusebius ideally suited for the position of imperial advisor?

3. Which of the men in this chapter were involved in some way with the Arian Controversy? What position did each of them hold in the dispute?

4. For what book is Eusebius best known? Why is it important?

5. Why did Athanasius believe that the deity of Christ was necessary for a proper understanding of salvation?

6. Why did Athanasius often think that it was "Athanasius against the world"?

7. Why is it foolish to trust the view of the majority on doctrinal questions?

8. Why was John Chrysostom a success in Antioch but a failure in Constantinople?

9. What characteristics of Chrysostom's preaching make it a model for preachers today?

10. What were the consequences for relationships between church and state of the careers of Chrysostom and Ambrose?

11. How is it possible to explain the success of Ambrose as a bishop when he was appointed to the job before he was even baptized?

12. Evaluate the four encounters between Ambrose and the emperors of his day. In which ones was Ambrose right, and in which ones was he wrong, and why?

13. Why is the Latin Vulgate important in the history of the church? In what ways has it been used that Jerome never would have favored?

14. Why did Augustine consider himself a living example of the grace of God? How does the quotation from the first paragraph of the *Confessions* fit his own life?

15. How is it possible for Augustine to provide the foundation for both Roman Catholic and Protestant doctrine?

16. Behind several of the great men of God in this chapter were great women of God, mothers who prayed and guided their sons into lives of service. What do these tell us about the importance of women in the advance of the Kingdom of God?

17. Identify the following in one sentence each: Pamphilus, Arius, Alexander, Anthony of Thebes, Libanius, Anthusa, Theodore of Mopsuestia, Flavian, Eudoxia, Arcadius, Theophilus, Gratian, Justina, Theodosius, Damasus, Monica.

7

THE WORD, THE LORD, AND THE WORK

We saw at the end of chapter three that heresy often forced the church to think through what it really believed in order to clarify the difference between truth and error. The church in the first five centuries was faced with challenges on many of the basic doctrines of the Christian faith, and the work done during this time laid the foundation for our understanding of what God's Word is, who Jesus Christ is, what the church is, and what the Bible teaches about man and salvation. Some of the conclusions arrived at by the early church, such as the doctrine of the Trinity and the full deity and humanity of Christ, have stood the test of time and have been recognized as truth by all Christians. Other conclusions have continued to be matters of debate, including the question of the makeup of the Bible, the respective roles of God and man in salvation, and the authority of the church.

The order in which the church faced these basic doctrinal questions was no coincidence. The content and authority of Scripture had to be tackled first because the Bible is the only basis for deciding how other doctrinal questions ought to be resolved. Once the composition of the Bible was determined, Christians turned to the question of the nature of the God who gave us the Bible - the doctrine of the Trinity. Though the major dispute here centered around the deity of Christ, the place of the Holy Spirit in the Godhead also came under discussion. After the church decided that Christ was truly God, it still had to deal with the matter of His humanity, and how the same person could be both God and man. With Christ as the bridge between God and man, the church next had to decide how that bridge could be crossed. Did a man come to God by the work of God alone, or was some cooperative effort on the part of the individual required? What part did the church play in all of this? If the church was part of the salvation process, how was the true church to be defined?

Though there are connections among these issues, the discussion of these matters in the early church may be divided into five distinct doctrinal controversies. As we examine these controversies, we will see how the decisions of the early church affected the beliefs and practices of the church for many centuries thereafter, in many cases right up to the present day.

THE CONTENTS OF THE BIBLE

When God sent His Son to earth to live, die, and rise again, He did something new. This new work required new revelation from God to explain it. Thus, while the church continued to accept the Scriptures of the Jews, which came to be known as the Old Testament, they also recognized that new Scriptures would need to take their place alongside them. The writings of the New Testament indicate as much, both by the authority with which the apostles write and through references such as II Peter 3:15-16, where Peter equates the writings of Paul with the Old Testament Scriptures. It took the church several centuries to finalize this collection of new Scriptures, however.

In the early part of the second century, no one even attempted to make a list of the books of the New Testament, at least as far as we know. The Apostolic Fathers quoted freely from the Gospels and the letters of Paul, showing that those books had already gained recognition as Scripture by the churches, but left no lists and said nothing about an official canon.

The heresies of the latter part of the second century, however, forced the church's hand. Gnosticism, especially the form taught by Marcion, forced the church to define the canon, while Montanism forced the church to close it. We already saw in chapter three that Marcion had completely rejected the Old Testament along with any first-century books that to him smacked of Judaism. He wound up with an edited version of Luke and ten of Paul's letters. When he began proclaiming that only these books were valid for the church, a response was necessary, and the churches began compiling lists. The earliest such list that has survived to the present is a part of a manuscript called the Muratorian Canon, which was probably compiled around the year 180. Irenaeus and Tertullian, among other leading churchmen of the day, also compiled lists. Though the various lists differed in some particulars, the following general conclusions may be drawn. The four Gospels, Acts, thirteen letters of Paul, I Peter, and I John were universally recognized as Scripture. II and III John, Jude, and Revelation were recognized by most, while many had serious questions about Hebrews, James, and II Peter. The main question in the minds of most of the church leaders of the day involved the authorship of these books. If it could be demonstrated that a book had been written by an apostle or the close associate of an apostle (such as Mark or Luke), it was accepted as Scripture. The churches questioned some of the books only because they were unsure about who had written them. At the time there were dozens of books circulating in the Roman world that bore the names of apostles, and most of them were forgeries. Some suspected Hebrews, James, and II Peter of being among them (ironically, Hebrews was ultimately accepted when the church became convinced that it was written by Paul, though many today would question that conclusion). There were also some in the church who recognized as Scripture books that are not part of our New Testament, such as *The Teaching of the Twelve Apostles*, *The Shepherd*, *The Epistle of Barnabas*, *The Apocalypse of Peter*, or even *I Clement*. Some of these were included in lists of the books of the Bible as late as the fourth century. They were eventually rejected, however, because of lack of apostolic authorship, or because they proved to be forgeries.

Montanism posed a different sort of challenge to the New Testament Scriptures. While Montanists didn't try to curtail the New Testament in the way the Gnostics did, they tried to expand it with their belief in continuing revelation. Montanists believed that the Age of the Father had produced the Old Testament while the Age of the Son had produced the (as yet undefined) New Testament. The Montanist prophets predicted that the Age of the Spirit was about to dawn, and that this age would be accompanied by still more new revelation from God. Thus they put the revelations of Montanus, Priscilla, and Maximilla on the same level as the writings of Peter and Paul. This explains another reason why the church insisted on apostolic authorship for the books they recognized as Scripture. When the apostles died, divine revelation ended, and the church had a basis for rejecting the novel teachings of the Montanists. Not surprisingly, some in the church used the general reaction against Montanism as a basis for questioning the place of the book of Revelation. When one reads the book literally, it paints a picture very much like that of the earthly Millennial Kingdom anticipated by the Montanists, and in their anxiety to reject the extremes of Montanism, some turned against the whole idea of an earthly kingdom, which had been very popular in the church up to that point. Some even went so far as to suggest that the book of Revelation had not been written by the apostle John at all, but by the first-century Gnostic teacher Cerinthus, who put the book in John's name in order to discredit his long-time opponent!

There is a bit of irony here as well, of course. We saw in chapter five that the development of the church hierarchy depended heavily on the teaching that the bishops and priests were the successors of the apostles. This in turn led to the position of the Catholic Church

THE DEVELOPMENT OF THE NEW TESTAMENT CANON

PERIOD	CHARACTER-ISTICS	APPROXIMATE DATES	SIGNIFICANT SOURCES	BOOKS RECEIVED	BOOKS QUESTIONED
APOSTOLIC FATHERS	No serious debate, no official pronouncements.	100-140	quotations in Apostolic Fathers	Four Gospels Pauline Epistles (unspecified corpus)	None
GNOSTIC OPPOSITION	Reaction against Gnostic truncation of canon (esp. writings of Marcion).	140-220	quotations in Church Fathers Muratorian Canon (c. 180) *Gospel of Truth* (Gnostic)	Four Gospels, Acts 13 Pauline Epistles I Peter I John Jude Revelation	Hebrews, James II Peter II-III John *Shepherd, Didache* *Apocalypse of Peter*
FINAL SOLIDIFICATION	General agreement by end of fourth century.	220-400	Origen	Four Gospels, Acts 13 Pauline Epistles I Peter I John Revelation	Hebrews, James II Peter II-III John Jude *Shepherd, Didache*
			Eusebius	Four Gospels, Acts 14 Pauline Epistles I Peter I John	James II Peter II-III John Jude, Revelation *Shepherd, Didache*
			Athanasius (Paschal letter of 367 - final acceptance in the East)	Present Canon	
			Synod of Rome (382 - final acceptance in the West)	Present Canon	
			Synod of Carthage (397 - acceptance by entire church)	Present Canon	

that the traditions of the church, including pronouncements of popes and councils, carry the same authority as the Word of God. Thus we find that the apostolicity of the New Testament documents was first used to deny the authority of extra-biblical teachings (i.e., the Montanists), and later became the basis, in combination with the doctrine of Apostolic Succession, for the authority of church tradition.

By the end of the second century, the church was in essential agreement on the content of the New Testament. Disputes over a few books continued up into the fourth century, but we can see that the church was for the most part unified on the question because, in an age when church councils were being called to deal with every doctrinal question imaginable, no church council was ever asked to determine the content of the New Testament. The first list that actually corresponds completely to our present New Testament was published by Athanasius in an Easter letter to his congregation in 367. Shortly thereafter, synods meeting in Rome (382) and Carthage (397) confirmed the same list, apparently without significant discussion or dissent.

One closing comment should be made concerning the books known as the Apocrypha, which were written during the Intertestamental Period, and are included in Roman Catholic Bibles, but not in those used by most Protestants. These books were never recognized as Scripture by the Jews of Palestine, and there is no evidence that they were used by Jesus and His disciples. The Jews in Alexandria used them, however, and included them in their translation of the Old Testament into Greek, called the Septuagint. When Jerome translated the Bible into Latin, he did not include the Apocrypha, since those books were not in the original Hebrew Old Testament. Augustine argued that they should be included, since the apostles quoted from the Septuagint, and the Septuagint contained the Apocrypha. The Catholic Church eventually adopted Augustine's position in the sixteenth century at the Council of Trent, while Protestants rejected the Apocrypha as not having divine authority.

THE DOCTRINE OF THE TRINITY

When Constantine professed conversion to Christianity, one of his greatest concerns was to unify the empire by means of the Christian religion. He quickly realized that it was impossible to use the church as a unifying force in the empire if the church itself was divided. One of the first major threats to that unity was the dispute over the doctrine of the Trinity that arose in Alexandria in the early part of the fourth century.

Disputes over the doctrine of the Trinity had been going on for quite a while before the conversion of Constantine. Christians had long before realized the difficulty of reconciling the belief in one God with the teaching of the New Testament that Jesus Christ was God in the flesh. In the second and third centuries, a teaching arose in the church known as Monarchianism, which sought to emphasize the oneness of God and guard against the polytheism so prevalent in Roman pagan religions. There were two major forms of Monarchianism, Dynamic Monarchianism (also known as Adoptionism) and Modalistic Monarchianism (also called Patripassionism or Sabellianism, after Sabellius, one of its major advocates). The Adoptionists espoused a belief somewhat similar to the Jewish-Christian Ebionites, maintaining that Jesus was a normal man, born of the Virgin Mary, but that God adopted him, either when the Holy Spirit came upon him at his baptism, or when he was raised from the dead. Modalists taught that there was one God who revealed Himself successively in three ways, first as the Father, then as the Son, and finally as the Holy Spirit. They stated quite bluntly that God the Father had suffered and died on the cross (the source of the name Patripassionism). Most Christians recognized that these explanations of the Godhead were inadequate; Adoptionism denied the full deity of Christ, while Modalism made the self-revelation of God a lie, and implied that God as He truly is is unknowable. It was in response to these Monarchian heresies that Tertullian formulated his teaching on the Trinity, maintaining that Christians worship one God in three Persons.

MAJOR ANCIENT CHURCH DOCTRINAL CONTROVERSIES

CONTROVERSY	MAJOR HERETICAL LEADERS	MAJOR ORTHODOX LEADERS	RELEVANT COUNCILS	ACCEPTED CONCLUSIONS
TRINITARIAN CONTROVERSY	Arius Eusebius of Nicomedia	Athanasius Hosius Basil the Great Gregory of Nyssa Gregory of Nazianzus Augustine of Hippo	Nicea (325) Constantinople (381)	Christ is "of the same substance with the Father." Father, Son, and Spirit are "co-eternal, consubstantial, and coequal."
CHRISTOLOGICAL CONTROVERSY	Apollinarius Nestorius Eutyches	Cyril of Alexandria Theodoret Leo I	Constantinople (381) Ephesus (431) Ephesus ("Robber Synod") (449) Chalcedon (451)	Christ is "one person in two natures, unmixed, unchanged, undivided, inseparable." Mary is "the Mother of God."
DONATIST CONTROVERSY	Donatus	Caecilian Augustine of Hippo	Arles (314)	"Outside the church there is no salvation."
PELAGIAN CONTROVERSY	Pelagius Coelestius John Cassian Caesarius of Arles	Augustine of Hippo Jerome	Ephesus (431) Orange (529)	Semi-Augustinianism; sacramental grace enables people to overcome their innate sinfulness.

While Tertullian's work for all practical purposes settled the issue in the West, the Eastern Church was not satisfied, and proceeded to dig into the issue further. The conflict in the East in the fourth century started with a popular preacher in Alexandria by the name of Arius, and the accusations that began to fly back and forth as a result of Arius' teaching soon brought Constantine into the picture. Arius feared that the doctrine of the Trinity was too close to Modalism for comfort, and felt that a stronger distinction between the Father and the Son was necessary. Consequently, he taught that the Son, while rightly called God, was a created being who had been made by God the Father before the beginning of time, and thus was subordinate to the Father. Alexander, the bishop of Alexandria, strongly objected to this teaching and tried to silence Arius, but Arius marshalled popular support by writing little songs about his teaching that were subsequently sung by the dockworkers at the city's busy port. When Alexander tried to excommunicate Arius, the latter wrote for support to some of his friends throughout the empire, and the conflict soon escalated. At this point, Constantine stepped in, rebuking both sides for this dispute "of a truly insignificant character and quite unworthy of fierce contention ... merely an intellectual exercise" (So much for his theological discernment!). He summoned the first church-wide council, to be held at Nicea in Asia Minor in 325, to settle the matter. Several hundred bishops were in attendance, mostly from the East, and Constantine himself presided over the deliberations. Arius and Alexander both had the opportunity to explain their positions, and each gained the support of a minority of the bishops present. The majority wanted some compromise between the two. When Arius presented his teaching, he clearly was outside the realm of Christian orthodoxy, and was quickly and almost unanimously condemned. Alexander, with the help of his deacon Athanasius, presented the Trinitarian position, staunchly defending the full deity of Christ, but the council was still uncertain. At that point, Eusebius of Caesarea suggested as a compromise a doctrinal statement used by his church in Caesarea. The council accepted it after modifying it to include the statement that Christ was "of the same substance" with the Father, and adding several declarations condemning Arius. This document became the Nicene Creed, though the form of the Creed that is in common use today was not written until over a century later. The Trinitarians thus emerged victorious from the Council of Nicea, and Arius and those who followed him were banished from their churches. Constantine also ordered their books to be burned. The issue was by no means settled, however.

The man who was to become the greatest defender of the doctrine of the Trinity, Athanasius, became bishop of Alexandria when Alexander died in 328. But the Arians were gradually working their way back into the favor of the emperor. Eusebius of Nicomedia, who was to become the torchbearer for Arianism after the death of Arius himself, had already been brought back from exile and restored to his church, at the same time becoming an advisor to the emperor. He did all in his power to obtain the rehabilitation of Arius and the removal of Athanasius. When Arius submitted a doctrinal statement to Constantine that sounded orthodox but avoided the issue in question, Constantine accepted it and ordered Athanasius to lift Arius' excommunication. Athanasius refused, and Constantine sent him into exile in Gaul after a trial on trumped-up charges before a council in Tyre in 335. When Constantine died two years later, Athanasius was permitted to return to his church. In the succeeding years, he was exiled four more times - to Rome from 339 to 346 by Constantius, the son of Constantine and an Arian, at the instigation of Eusebius of Nicomedia, who by then had become bishop of Constantinople; by Constantius again from 356 to 361, during which time Athanasius continued to run the church in Alexandria from a hideout in the Egyptian desert; by the pagan emperor Julian the Apostate in 361, after the emperor allowed him to come back, hoping that the dispute would destroy the church, but quickly found that Athanasius was too strong an enemy of paganism; and lastly by the Arian emperor Valens in 367, when Athanasius remained in the city of Alexandria, hiding for some months in his father's tomb!

Despite the political opposition, however, the Trinitarian position slowly but surely gained dominance in the church, championed by Athanasius and the Three Cappadocians, Basil the Great, Gregory of Nyssa, and Gregory of Nazianzus. Athanasius rightly insisted that the full deity of Christ was essential to the salvation of man. If Christ is not both fully man and fully God, he said, He is incapable of bringing man to God. Arianism was rejected, along with the Semi-Arian compromise that tried to assert that Christ was "of similar substance" with the Father. Finally, in 381, the Council of Constantinople settled the matter once and for all, adopting the Trinitarian position as the official doctrine of the church. The statement we now know as the Nicene Creed was formally adopted by the Council of Chalcedon in 451, and was a revision from the early part of the fifth century of the creed originally produced at Nicea.

THE GOD-MAN

Now that the church acknowledged that Christ was fully God and fully man, they faced the question of how this could be true. How can one Person be both God and man at the same time? How do the humanity and deity of Christ relate to one another? This dispute, like the one on the Trinity, had its roots in Greek philosophy, particularly the teachings of Plato. Those who had been influenced by Platonism found the doctrine of the Trinity hard to accept because Plato defined the concept of unity in such a way that it did not allow for any internal distinctions. Plato had also taught about the *Logos*, the fundamental rational principle of the universe;

since John uses the same term in his Gospel to describe Jesus ("In the beginning was the Word ..."), many Christians tried to harmonize Plato's philosophy with the Bible's teaching about Jesus, picturing Jesus as a man possessing the divine Reason or Wisdom. It should not surprise us in the least to find that the earliest efforts in this area came from the church in Alexandria. A Jewish philosopher named Philo who lived in the first century had made use of the *Logos* doctrine to produce a sort of Jewish Gnosticism. The idea was later applied to Christ by Clement of Alexandria and his famous pupil, Origen. In the latter part of the fourth century, Apollinarius of Laodicea, influenced by the teachings of the great Alexandrians, tried to use the *Logos* concept to solve the problem of the relationship between the humanity and deity of Christ. He taught that Christ was a man whose human spirit had been replaced by the *Logos*, whom Apollinarius identified as the Second Person of the Trinity. This early effort shared a fundamental problem with all attempts to solve the dilemma that followed - all wound up undermining either the humanity or deity of Christ, in this case the former. Asserting with Athanasius that a Christ who is not fully God and fully man cannot fully save, the Council of Constantinople in 381 condemned Apollinarianism as a heresy.

At this point, the dispute really gets messy. As in the Trinitarian Controversy, politics reared its ugly head, and Christian doctrine began to be disputed in a manner that was not Christian in the least. The major source of conflict was the rivalry that existed between the cities of Antioch and Alexandria, the two great cities of the Eastern Church prior to the rise of Constantinople. The church in Alexandria had historically concerned itself with the spiritual sense of Scripture, using allegorical interpretation to bring out the higher meaning of the text. It should come as no surprise that Alexandria tended to stress the deity of Christ, often at the expense of His full humanity. Antioch, on the other hand, was the center of literal interpretation, and focused on the grammatical and historical context as the basis for biblical interpretation, led by men such as Theodore of Mopsuestia and John Chrysostom. Antioch thus tended to emphasize the true humanity of Jesus as a man in history, sometimes at the cost of insufficient attention to the fact that He was also God. The Antioch-Alexandria rivalry produced one of the most disreputable conflicts in the history of the ancient church.

The conflict began when Cyril, the bishop of Alexandria, asserted in opposition to Apollinarianism that in Christ, the *Logos* had taken upon Himself the general characteristics of human nature, as opposed to a specific man's body and soul. In order to emphasize the deity of Christ, Cyril began to refer to Mary as the Mother of God, intending by that to affirm that Jesus was God even in the womb of His mother. Nestorius, the bishop of Constantinople who had been trained in Antioch, rejected this approach, insisting that Mary should be called only the Mother of Christ, since she could only legitimately be called the mother of His human nature. Cyril was furious, and began to write letters to other bishops throughout the empire, accusing Nestorius of teaching that Christ was two separate beings, God and man, inhabiting one body at the same time, but having no real connection with one another. An ecumenical (church-wide) council was called in 431 at the city of Ephesus to deal with the dispute. Here the politics really got nasty. Cyril and his supporters arrived early, and without waiting for the delegation from Antioch, quickly met and condemned Nestorius of heresy. They also stirred up the local population, who began to riot and threatened violence against the Nestorians. When the bishop of Antioch arrived, he and his people held their own council, at which they not surprisingly condemned Cyril and upheld Nestorius. When the representatives from Rome arrived, the council reconvened and voted to excommunicate the Antioch faction (Cyril's party was about five times as large as those supporting Nestorius). The emperor upheld the decision, and exiled Nestorius to a monastery for the rest of his life. He died a bitter man, to his last day disputing that he ever taught the things for which he had been condemned. His followers left the empire and headed East, where they formed Nestorian churches that at one time stretched from Persia all the way into the heart of China. Meanwhile, Cyril and John, the bishop of Antioch, made peace by agreeing on a document that each could interpret in his own way.

After John and Cyril died, the dispute flared up again, worse than ever. Cyril was replaced by Dioscurus, who was more ambitious than his predecessor, if such a thing is possible. Flavian, who had sympathy with the Antiochan school, became bishop of Constantinople at about the same time. Controversy was sparked by Eutyches, the elderly head of a monastery in Constantinople. He denounced the document upon which Cyril and John had agreed, and stated that, while there had been two natures, one human and one divine, prior to the Incarnation, that afterward there was only one divine nature, into which the human nature had been completely absorbed. Flavian recognized that this view undermined the full manhood of Christ, and excommunicated Eutyches. He sought an opinion from Leo I, the influential bishop of Rome, who agreed and sent a copy of a work called the *Tome*, which explained the position of the Western Church. This position had been expounded by Tertullian over two centuries before, and maintained that Christ was both fully God and fully man, two natures in one Person, but did not attempt to resolve the paradox implied by that statement.

Dioscurus quickly recognized that the position taken by Eutyches was similar in some ways to that of Cyril, and came to the defense of the elderly monk. The emperor called a council to resolve the issue, which was to meet at Ephesus in 449. Dioscurus dominated the discussion, would not even allow Leo's *Tome* to be read, reinstated Eutyches, and deposed Flavian and Leo, replacing both with Alexandrians. Leo refused to accept the decisions of this "Robber Synod," and appealed to the emperor, who called for another council to meet in 451 at Chalcedon, across the Bosporus from Constantinople. Over six hundred bishops came to the meeting, and the outcome was quite different from the farce at Ephesus. Leo's *Tome* was read and accepted, Eutyches was denounced as a heretic, and Dioscurus was excommunicated.

The Council of Chalcedon established the orthodox view of the human and divine in Christ that is accepted by most Catholic, Orthodox, and Protestant Christians today. It concluded that Christ was fully man and fully God, one Person with two natures, and that the natures were "unconfused, unchanged, undivided, and inseparable," thus stating what the Word of God teaches, but not attempting to resolve the paradox of the God-man. Though this became the orthodox position, not all agreed. Some in the East continued to insist that the distinction between nature and person was impossible, and that Christ had only one nature, a composite of human and divine. These came to be called Monophysites ("one nature"). They survive today in the Coptic (Egypt), Ethiopic, Jacobite (Syria), and Armenian Orthodox Churches. A further refinement of this occurred in Monothelitism ("one will"), which maintained an ethical unity of the Person of Christ, claiming that He had no human will, only the divine will. Monothelitism was condemned at the Third Ecumenical Council of Constantinople in 681.

THE TRUE CHURCH

The dispute over the nature of the church is usually called the Donatist Controversy, but it really consisted of a whole series of schisms in the church, of which Donatism was the largest. All of these schisms stemmed from the severe persecutions of the late third and early fourth centuries.

As we saw in chapter four, the first severe empire-wide persecution of the church occurred during the reign of Decius in the year 250. This persecution not only produced many martyrs, but also caused many to deny their faith out of fear, either by offering incense in order to obtain a *libellus* or bribing an official to say that they had. When the persecution ended with the death of Decius in 251, many of these, filled with guilt, repented and asked to be restored to the fellowship of the church. Among those who had remained faithful, opinion was sharply divided. Some believed that apostasy was the unpardonable sin, and one who had denied the faith could never return to the church, though

THE ECUMENICAL COUNCILS OF THE EARLY CHURCH

LOCATION	DATE	EMPEROR	KEY PARTICIPANTS	MAJOR OUTCOMES
Nicea	325	Constantine	Arius Alexander Eusebius of Nicomedia Eusebius of Caesarea Hosius Athanasius	Declared Son *homoousios* (coequal, consubstantial, and coeternal) with Father. Condemned Arius. Drafted original form of Nicene Creed.
Constantinople	381	Theodosius	Meletius Gregory of Nazianzus Gregory of Nyssa	Confirmed results of Council of Nicea. Produced revised Nicene Creed. Ended Trinitarian Controversy. Affirmed deity of Holy Spirit. Condemned Apollinarianism.
Ephesus	431	Theodosius II	Cyril Nestorius	Declared Nestorianism heretical. Accepted by implication Alexandrian Christology. Condemned Pelagius.
Chalcedon	451	Marcian	Leo I Dioscurus Eutyches	Declared Christ's two natures "unmixed, unchanged, undivided, inseparable." Condemned Eutychianism.
Constantinople	553	Justinian	Eutychius	Condemned "Three Chapters" to gain support of Monophysites. Affirmed Cyrillian interpretation of Chalcedon.
Constantinople	680-681	Constantine IV		Rejected Monothelitism. Condemned Pope Honorius (d.638) as heretical.
Nicea	787	Constantine VI		Declared veneration of icons and statues legitimate.

God may see fit to forgive him. Others said that God could forgive the worst of sins, and that apostasy was no exception, so that those who repented and demonstrated their sorrow with sufficient sincerity and consistency should be readmitted to fellowship. Too often, the two groups refused to recognize one another. We will now look briefly at a few of the more important schisms that resulted from this important issue of church discipline.

The first occurred in North Africa, in the city of Carthage. During the persecution, Cyprian, the bishop of Carthage, had hidden in the mountains in order to provide continued leadership for his flock. Many who suffered accused him of cowardice, especially when he returned to take a hard-line position against those who had denied the faith. Several things complicated Cyprian's problem. The first was the attitude of the "confessors," those who had been tortured and imprisoned for their faith without giving in. These people were thought to be the recipients of a special grace from God, and some believed that their special grace was sufficient to cover the sins of those who had denied the faith. Thus the lapsed members of the congregation were seeking out the confessors, confessing their sins, and asking for forgiveness, which the confessors were quick to grant. Cyprian felt control of the church slipping away from him, and was appalled by the easy forgiveness being granted to those who had given in during the persecution. To make matters worse, the confessors had the backing of Novatus, a priest who had opposed Cyprian's election as bishop and was ready to use this, or anything else, against him. Cyprian declared that only those who had given in under torture could be restored, and further maintained that any who broke fellowship with him were breaking away from Christ. The dissenting party soon disappeared, and Cyprian was martyred in 258.

Meanwhile, the church in Rome was facing a similar problem. The bishop of Rome had died during the Decian persecution. The new bishop, Cornelius, quickly restored many who had lapsed during the persecution, claiming that the church was like Noah's ark, and contained both clean and unclean animals. Novatian, a scholarly priest of unquestioned orthodoxy, was shocked, and led a schism that soon set up its own churches in opposition to those who recognized Cornelius. The Novatian churches not only refused to restore the lapsed, but also refused to recognize the priests or sacraments of the other churches. When someone joined a Novatian church, he had to be rebaptized. When the two factions sought support from other churches, it put Cyprian in a real bind. He sympathized with the principles of the Novatian church, but his zeal for unity was such that he wound up siding with the churches that followed Cornelius. The Novatian churches continued to exist alongside orthodox churches for two hundred years, though they eventually passed from the scene.

The persecution under Diocletian, more severe even than the one under Decius, produced more serious schisms as well. One of these was the Melitian schism in Egypt, where the strict party was led by a bishop named Meletius. But by far the most serious division to come from the persecutions was the Donatist Schism. The Donatist movement again had its start in North Africa. Though the issues here were the same as in the earlier schisms, a further matter made things worse, and that was the racial conflicts that existed between the North Africans of Latin heritage, the Punics of Phoenician ancestry, and the native Berbers. The latter two groups had a long-standing hatred of anything Roman, and when this schism gave them the opportunity to oppose the church at Rome, they seized it gladly. The conflict began when the lenient Caecilian became bishop of Carthage. His strict opponents were ready to take advantage of anything they could find to discredit him, and they found a convenient tool in the person of Felix of Aptunga. Felix was one of the bishops who participated in the ordination of Caecilian, and the strict party had heard a rumor that Felix had willingly turned over a copy of the Scriptures to be burned during the persecution. Felix denied it, but his opponents used the rumor as an excuse to reject Caecilian. They elected Majorinus as bishop, and when he died, replaced him with Donatus, after whom the schism is named. The schism spread as churches throughout the empire took sides, with each one refusing to recognize the ordinations and baptisms of the other. The Donatists, convinced they were right, appealed to Constantine, who referred the matter to the bishop of Rome. The Roman bishop supported Caecilian, as did the ensuing Council of Arles in 314, as did Constantine himself, who, as we have already noted, wanted nothing more than the unity of his empire and church. The Donatists refused to submit, however, and continued to start churches and spread their teaching throughout the empire. Within a hundred years, there were more Donatists in North Africa than there were Catholics.

At this point, Augustine entered the picture. The great North African theologian tried to win the Donatists back by persuasion, arguing, as had Cyprian, that there could be no salvation outside the church, and that the church was defined by the apostolic authority of the bishops. Such a line of argument did no good, since the Donatists were convinced that their bishops were in the apostolic line, and that the Catholic bishops were not. They maintained that sacraments were only vehicles of grace if administered by a godly priest, and that the sacraments of the Catholic Church were therefore invalid. Augustine responded by saying that sacraments belong to Christ, not the church, and therefore they carry divine grace irrespective of the moral or spiritual condition of the priest. The Donatists would not budge, and a council in Carthage condemned their teaching in 411. Augustine had to this point argued against the use of force, but in the face of Donatist stubbornness, he finally recommended overt persecution, reasoning that those brought back to the truth would thank those who had brought them back no matter how it had been done. This teaching was to have unfortunate consequences in succeeding years, especially as applied by the torturers of the Inquisition. In spite of everything, the Donatists refused to submit, and like the Montanists before them gladly sought persecution. The Donatist churches survived until the seventh century, when, with the Catholic churches, they were wiped out by the Muslim Conquest.

GOD, MAN, AND SALVATION

Another controversy in which Augustine played a leading role was the Pelagian controversy. While the Trinitarian and Christological controversies had largely affected the Eastern Church, the Pelagian controversy, like that of the Donatists, influenced mostly the West. In fact, the Eastern churches never seriously considered the issues raised by the Pelagian controversy, and to this day have retained the Athanasian view of salvation that sees Christ raising man to the level of the divine.

The Pelagian controversy is named after a British (perhaps Irish) monk named Pelagius who came to Rome early in the fifth century. He was a sincere man and a charismatic speaker who drew many by the force of his personality. The basis of his teaching was the idea that evil in the world came from following bad examples. Man was not born sinful, but learned to sin because he was surrounded by sinners. Man was fully able to overcome these bad examples if he chose to do so, and Christ had come to provide what man needed to help him - a good example. When he read the *Confessions* of Augustine, he was shocked by what he found there. When Augustine said that man was powerless to do good apart from the grace of God, Pelagius was convinced that he was providing thousands of people with excuses for loose living. Pelagius firmly believed that man could do good, and that therefore he should do so. Anyone who suggested that man could not do good would be providing him with an excuse for doing evil.

In Rome, Pelagius gathered a group of followers, one of whom was a young man named Coelestius. When Alaric sacked Rome in 410, Coelestius fled with many others to North Africa. When he arrived in Carthage, he began to spread the teachings of Pelagius. When Coelestius requested ordination, word of what was happening reached Augustine, and he began to write in opposition to the teachings of Pelagius. Pelagius, meanwhile, headed east, and in Palestine had the misfortune to run into Jerome. While Augustine criticized Pelagius' teachings with sincere respect for the godliness of the British monk, Jerome practically tore his head off verbally, and demanded that a council be called to excommunicate the heretic. The irony of this is that Jerome's own theology was probably closer to that of Pelagius than to Augustine's view of sovereign grace. In the years that followed, a number of local synods condemned Pelagianism, leading to the final condemnation of the teaching at the Council of Ephesus in 431.

The writings of Augustine on the subject provided the foundation for the church's views of man, sin, and the saving grace of God. Augustine taught that, as a result of the sin of Adam, all men were born in sin, and their wills were corrupted to the extent that they could not do good or even desire to choose good. Salvation was therefore a matter of God's grace from beginning to end. God had chosen before time began who would be saved, and it is to them alone that He gives His grace, which enables them to repent and believe. While Augustine believed that the grace of God was communicated through the sacraments of the church, he did not identify the Body of Christ with the visible church. He maintained that only the elect would persevere in their faith, and that one could not be sure of such perseverance until death. Therefore, no one could know whether or not he was elect, and none would have any reason to presume on the grace of God.

While the church clearly rejected Pelagianism, many were not at all comfortable with the teaching of Augustine. Shortly after the end of the Pelagian Controversy, a group of monks in Gaul led by John Cassian formulated a theology that came to be known as Semi-Pelagianism. While accepting the sinfulness of man from birth, the Semi-Pelagians saw this sin as a weakness rather than a disqualifying flaw. They taught that man needed the grace of God to be saved, but that man needed to cooperate with that grace. Man was thus able to choose to accept the grace of God, and also able to refuse it. Though it was recognized very early that any system that makes the will of man decisive in salvation is at its heart Pelagian, this Semi-Pelagian view has been remarkably persistent in the church, both among Catholics and Protestants.

Semi-Pelagianism was rejected by the church at the Council of Orange in 529, but the bishops still refused to endorse a full-fledged Augustinian doctrine of salvation. Instead, what emerged has been called Semi-Augustinianism. This theology, while maintaining the necessity of the grace of God in order for man to choose good, denies the Augustinian doctrine of predestination, insisting that such grace is accessible to all through the sacraments, and that God elects those who He knew would respond to His grace. This weak Augustinianism became the theology of the medieval church, but was rightly branded Pelagian by those occasional lonely souls who followed Augustine himself. When the time came for the Protestant Reformation, it was the doctrine of grace taught by Augustine that more than anything else provided the basis for the work of Luther, Zwingli, and especially Calvin.

MAKING DRY BONES LIVE

Having examined all of these doctrinal disputes, many of them decided on the basis of impure and selfish motives that had little to do with biblical truth and less to do with Christian love, we must ask ourselves a fundamental question: How do we know they were right? How far can we trust the results of these councils, the conclusions of these godly but flawed theologians?

The Roman Catholic Church solves this dilemma by insisting that God works through His church. They teach that, despite the flaws and sins of the men who lead the church, God brings them to the truth, and that what they proclaim to be the truth should be accepted as from God Himself. Protestants are decidedly uncomfortable with such teaching, and assert instead that the Word of God is the only basis for discerning the truth, and that all the pronouncements of popes, declarations of councils, and writings of the Fathers must correspond to the teaching of Scripture if they are to be accepted.

But what of the canon of Scripture itself? How can we be sure that the leaders of the ancient church gave us the right books to begin with? Two answers may be given, though both are in some ways less than satisfying. The first is that God is the Author of the whole Bible, not just the individual books that make it up. He supervised its compilation in the same way that He supervised its composition - through His Spirit. While this may sound suspiciously similar to the Catholic teaching cited above, note that we are not asserting any general validity to the decisions of the church, but are merely maintaining that God has preserved for us His revelation by which to discern the difference between truth and error.

The second reason is that the decision on the canon has resulted in complete unity in the church (the matter of the Apocrypha is really a different issue). People have continued to argue over the years about the deity of Christ, the nature of the church, and the doctrines of sin and salvation, but the church has accepted with no further major dispute the canon acknowledged by the early church. God not only gave us His Word, but also preserved it intact, and gave to the church assurance of its makeup through the work of His Spirit. That Word is the only basis upon which the doctrinal questions that have faced the church for two thousand years and continue to appear today may be rightly decided.

FOR REVIEW AND FURTHER THOUGHT

1. What was the major doctrinal issue with which each of the five controversies considered in this chapter dealt?

2. Why did the Apostolic Fathers not attempt to make a list of the books of the New Testament?

3. How did the Gnostics and Montanists force the church to define the canon of the New Testament?

4. What books were considered for inclusion in the New Testament that were eventually rejected? Why were they rejected?

5. What books now in our New Testament were questioned by some in the church? Why were they questioned?

6. When did the first list of books corresponding to our New Testament appear, and who wrote it?

7. When and why did the Catholic Church include the Apocrypha in its Bible?

8. What is Monarchianism? What is the difference between the dynamic and modalistic forms of the heresy?

9. The teaching of Arius was very similar to that of modern Jehovah's Witnesses. What did Arius teach about Jesus Christ?

10. Name three leading advocates of the doctrine of the Trinity in addition to Athanasius.

11. What major councils helped settle the Trinitarian controversy? What role did each play?

12. How did both the Trinitarian and Christological controversies relate to Greek philosophy?

13. Define the following heresies: Apollinarianism, Nestorianism, Eutychianism, Monophysitism, and Monothelitism.

14. What roles were played in the Christological controversy by Cyril of Alexandria, John of Antioch, Leo I, Flavian, and Dioscurus?

15. Why did the severe persecutions of the third and fourth centuries lead to splits in the church? What were the views of the two sides in these splits?

16. What roles were played by Cyprian, Novatus, Novatian, Cornelius, Felix of Aptunga, Caecilian, Majorinus, Donatus, Constantine, and Augustine in the Donatist controversy and other similar schisms?

17. Why did Augustine teach that outside the church there is no salvation?

18. Describe the following theological positions: Pelagianism, Augustinianism, Semi-Pelagianism, and Semi-Augustinianism.

19. What role did Jerome, Coelestius, and John Cassian play in the Pelagian controversy?

20. How were the following councils involved with the controversies discussed in the chapter: the Council of Arles (314), the Council of Nicea (325), the Council of Constantinople (381), the Council of Carthage (411), the Council of Ephesus (431), the Council of Ephesus ["Robber Synod"](449), the Council of Chalcedon (451), the Council of Orange (529), and the Council of Constantinople (681).

21. When church councils and theologians decide a particular doctrinal question, how can we know whether or not they are right? If different teachers disagree, how can we tell who is teaching the truth?

22. Many of the doctrinal issues discussed in this chapter were settled through state intervention in church affairs. Was this good or bad? Why do you think so?

8

OUT OF THIS WORLD

The great Cappadocian monk and theologian Gregory of Nazianzus tells the story in his eulogy on Cyprian of a beautiful young virgin named Justina who wanted to remain unmarried in order to serve Christ, but was being pressured into marriage by a smooth-talking lawyer who was not a Christian. Justina prayed to the Virgin Mary to help her keep her virginity, and finally managed to discourage her ardent suitor by disfiguring her face through fasting and self-torture. Her lawyer-friend eventually became a Christian - it was Cyprian himself!

Monks, self-torture, prayers to Mary - how did all of these become part of the church's understanding of holiness? In this chapter, we will look at how ascetic practices captured the imagination of the church, and how those practices were eventually incorporated into a special life of dedication to God, that of the monks and nuns. We will also see how the great respect given to martyrs, and their successors, the ascetics, led to the veneration of relics and saints, and chiefly to the honor given to Mary in the Catholic Church.

ASCETICISM IN THE CHURCH

Asceticism - the denial of the flesh in order to enhance the life of the spirit - is not unique to Christianity. It is common among the Oriental religions, most notably Hinduism and Buddhism, where it grows out of a denial of the reality or permanence of the body. Though Judaism teaches that the body is created by God, and is thus good, and underscores the value of the body by the doctrine of the resurrection, there have also been isolated examples of ascetics among the Jews. Men like Elijah and John the Baptist lived in the wilderness. The Nazirites in the Old Testament abstained from wine, refused to cut their hair, and avoided contact with the dead. The Essenes, who produced the Dead Sea Scrolls, lived in monastic communities, sharing all property in common; many of them avoided marriage, increasing their number by adopting orphans.

But the New Testament church recognized that there was something unhealthy and unbalanced about a life that denied the flesh. Paul, though he said that remaining unmarried allowed him more freedom to carry out his apostolic ministry, made it clear that most of the apostles had wives, and condemned those who would forbid others to marry or require abstinence from certain foods. While Jesus said that there were some who would make themselves eunuchs for the sake of the kingdom of heaven, He Himself lived the life of the world to such an extent that His enemies accused Him of being a glutton and a drunkard! How, then, did ascetic practices come to be recognized as a mark of holiness in the church?

There were two major theoretical impulses that stimulated the growth of asceticism, one heretical and one quite legitimate, though it was often misinterpreted and taken to extremes. Gnosticism and Neoplatonism had brought the church in contact with the Greek notion that the spirit was good while the body was evil. Many of the Gnostics were fierce ascetics, teaching that sex and marriage were the tools of Satan to produce more bodies in which to imprison the souls of men. While the church repudiated this sort of thinking, its prevalence in the Roman world influenced the church more than some would like to admit (Jerome, for instance, one of the prime motivators of monasticism in the West, said that the only reason marriage existed was to provide more virgins for the service of Christ!).

The legitimate theological basis for asceticism came from the biblical teaching concerning the conflict between the flesh and the spirit. While the term "flesh" as used by Paul refers more to the sinful nature than it does to the physical body, there can be no question that the temptations we face come through our senses. When Jesus talks about cutting off right hands and plucking out right eyes, and Paul speaks of beating his body to keep it under submission, we know that the body is a problem with which any serious Christian must learn to cope. The ascetics, however, soon developed an unhealthy imbalance in their lives that almost denied the reality of the body in order to minimize its sinful potential.

There were practical reasons for asceticism as well. One of the strongest was the rampant immorality that characterized Roman society. Like the world in which we live, imperial Rome was filled with temptations on every side, and the serious Christian could not help being offended at the corruption all around him.

Another practical motive involved the demands of Christian service. As Paul rightly pointed out, the single life was suited much better to full-time Christian ministry, especially when that ministry involved a lot of traveling, than was marriage. The persecutions made the same point even more strongly. One who might any day find it necessary to give his life for his faith did not want to take on the responsibility of a wife and family, only to leave them helpless upon his death.

The earliest ascetics voluntarily renounced marriage and property in order to devote themselves fully to prayer, contemplation, and deeds of service. It was not long, however, before the church began to see the ascetic life as more than an alternative open to those who desired it. It soon came to be viewed as the higher life, the road to perfection, and thus the ascetics became a class of super-Christians, devoting themselves to a form of obedience that was beyond the reach of the normal man or woman. Asceticism, and the monastic movement that grew from it, thus accomplished what the Gnostic and Montanist heresies had failed to do - it divided the church into two groups, representing higher and lower levels of spirituality. Those who were serious about their faith renounced the world and embraced the life of poverty and chastity, while those who lived in the world had little motive for self-control, since they had not received the "gift."

The church also eventually came to require of its priests and monks exactly those things that the Bible said should not be demanded of Christians. When Jesus told the rich young ruler to sell all he had and give it to the poor, the church taught that poverty was essential for all who desired the spiritual life. When Paul recommended celibacy "in the present distress," the church taught that men who were the representatives of Christ on earth could be married only to the church, while women who desired to serve Christ could be married only to Him. When recommendations to specific people in specific situations in Scripture become general principles for the church at large, the church is setting itself up for a great deal of trouble.

The matter of celibacy is especially curious because the Bible is so clear about the marriages of the apostles, and because Paul tells Timothy that elders and deacons are to be "the husband of one wife." In fact, it was this reference in I Timothy that began the push toward celibacy by encouraging many to ban second marriages, not only among the clergy, but among Christians at large. Despite the fact that Paul encouraged young widows to remarry, the church soon spoke against it, further creating the impression that celibacy was a higher state of purity and spirituality than marriage. In such an environment, it is no wonder that many ministers had unhappy marriages, and that most quickly found that unmarried ministers were more highly respected by their congregations than were married ones.

The next step after the prohibition of second marriages was the prohibition of marriage after ordination. Those who married before becoming priests were allowed to remain married, but priests who were single had to remain that way. Later, any married man who wished to become a priest was required to leave his wife (they were sent to convents and supported by their husbands). Celibacy became a source of spiritual pride for some, even to the extent that priests would live with virgins, sometimes sharing the same bed, in order to demonstrate and strengthen their victory over the lust of the flesh. That such arrangements were often fronts for immorality was obvious to all, and church leaders and councils alike strongly condemned the practice. Finally, total celibacy became the rule, though the Eastern Church requires it only of bishops, not of priests (thus most Eastern bishops are drawn from the monasteries rather than the priesthood), while the rule was not consistently enforced in the West until the eleventh century, through the efforts of Pope Gregory VII.

THE GROWTH OF MONASTICISM

As long as the church was a persecuted minority clearly separated from the Roman world at large, the ascetics lived within the Christian community. They may have been a church within the church, representing a higher order of spirituality, but they *were* within the church. The Edict of Milan changed all that, however. With the sudden popularity of Christianity, all sorts of pagans were flooding the church with their minimal understanding of the Gospel and their low pagan morality. Anyone who took his Christianity seriously could not help but feel disgust. Thus the ascetics found it not only necessary to flee the world, but also to flee the worldliness of the church.

During the persecutions, the greatest examples of men and women who denied themselves for the sake of the Gospel were the martyrs, and to a lesser extent the confessors, who had suffered great physical tortures and deprivations while bearing witness for Christ. The church had seen, time and time again, the special grace that God had given to those who suffered for the sake of His Son. Once the persecutions stopped, that grace was no longer in evidence, and the spirituality of the church plummeted. Many believed that the only salvation for the church was to regain the grace that had characterized the lives of the martyrs and confessors. Mistakenly believing that physical suffering was the basis upon which that grace had been given, the ascetics now sought a sort of synthetic martyrdom, a self-induced suffering that would, they hoped, bring them a taste of the same grace that had sustained the martyrs in their hour of trial. These self-appointed martyrs, desiring special grace and disgusted with the worldliness of the church, fled to the wilderness, hoping to save themselves while the church collectively went down the drain.

A. MONASTICISM IN THE EAST

The first monks arose in Egypt about fifty years before the Edict of Milan. After the persecutions of Decius and Valerian, there was a long period of time in which the state left Christians alone, and the church flourished, experiencing some of the watering down that would become a flood after the conversion of Constantine. Those repulsed by the decline of spirituality in the church found that the climate of Egypt was ideal for the solitary life. The fertile strip of land around the Nile quickly gives way to rugged mountains and desert, and the ascetics found they could live alone in caves, yet be close enough to civilization so that they could either grow their own food or have friends from nearby villages bring it to them. The climate was warm enough so that their food and clothing needs were minimal. Two types of monastic life developed in Egypt. One was the solitary life, in which a man would live by himself and shun all contact with society. These men were called hermits or anchorites, and the term *monk*, which means "solitary," properly refers to them alone, though it also came to be used of the second category of ascetics. The second group were communal monks, or coenobites, who lived in self-sustaining communities under the discipline of an abbot.

1. ANCHORITES

The first of the influential hermits was Anthony of Thebes (c.251-c.356). He was an Egyptian peasant who was orphaned in his teens and left with the family farm and a younger sister. At the age of eighteen, he heard a sermon on the rich young ruler, and determined to follow Christ's command to sell all that he had and give it to the poor. He thus sold his farm and distributed the money, leaving only enough to sustain his sister. Later, hearing that Christ had said, "Take no thought for the morrow," he gave away even that small reserve, and entrusted his sister to the care of a group of virgins in the church. He headed for the wilderness, living first in a nearby tomb, later moving to an abandoned fortress, and finally settling down in a cave on a mountaintop three days' journey from the Nile. In his successively more remote retreats, he lived alone with virtually no human contact, eating no more than one meal of bread, salt, and water each day, and frequently fasting for days at a time. He spent much of his time doing battle with Satan, who came to him in many forms, including wild beasts and seductive women. He emerged from seclusion only rarely. Once during the persecution of Diocletian, he went to Alexandria, hoping for martyrdom. Such was the respect he inspired that no one laid a hand on him, though he was able to comfort and encourage many of those who were in prison. Later, he made another appearance to oppose the Arian heresy. Though he was an uneducated man and read no Greek, he became a close friend of Athanasius, whom he met during one of the many exiles endured by the latter. Athanasius was later to write Anthony's biography, which is the source of most of our information about him. Though Anthony tried to avoid all human contact as much as possible, his fame spread to the point where he was unable to keep away the steady stream of pilgrims who arrived at the entrance to his cave. He finally somewhat reluctantly agreed to allow other hermits to live in caves in the vicinity, and instructed them periodically. This arrangement, whereby hermits live solitary lives in the same region and meet informally for instruction and worship, is called a *laura*.

Though the hermits tried by isolating themselves from the world to stamp out the temptations of the flesh, they often fell victim to the greatest temptation of all - spiritual pride. Individual monks would compete with one another to see who could undergo the greatest austerities, and this produced what can best be called the lunatic fringe of monasticism. Many hermits engaged in behavior that can only be described as bizarre. The most famous extremists were the pillar monks, led by Simeon the Stylite (c.390-459). He began by living in a cave in northern Syria, abstaining from food for long intervals, especially during Lent. One year he asked friends to wall him into his cave during Lent with only a little bread and water to sustain him. When they breached the wall at the end of the forty days, they found the bread and water in the cave untouched. Later, to escape the pollution of the world, Simeon built a six-foot pillar on which to live. Soon he found that six feet was not high enough, and he continued to build larger and larger pillars until he was living sixty feet in the air on a three-foot platform with only a railing to protect him. Friends climbed a ladder to bring up food and remove wastes. To keep himself from falling, he tied himself to the railing by a rope. The rope chafed his skin, and the resulting infection soon crawled with worms and insects. This didn't seem to bother Simeon, who would gently replace any worm that fell from his sores with the admonition, "Eat what God has given you." Simeon lived on his pillar for thirty-six years, drawing large crowds to whom he preached, evangelizing many, and allegedly healing many as well. His influence was such that he was consulted before the councils of Ephesus and Chalcedon were scheduled, and many imitators took up his peculiar form of austerity.

Some extremists ate only grass, grazing like animals, while others found virtue in avoiding soap and water. One monk refused to wear clothing, and became so hairy from exposure to the elements that a shepherd mistook him for a wolf and almost killed him. Another wandered naked in a swamp for six months, exposing himself to all sorts of insect bites in penance for killing a mosquito, until he looked like he had leprosy and could only be recognized by the sound of his voice. Some tied heavy chains to their waists, or lived in cells so small that they could neither stand, sit, nor lie down. Ascetic pride often fostered competitions, with some monks trying to outdo any austerity they heard had been accomplished by others. They would compete over who could go sleepless the longest, who could fast the longest, and even who had gone the longest time without seeing a woman!

2. COENOBITES

Many recognized that the extremes of the hermits did little good for the church's reputation. Regulation was necessary. There had to be some way to impose discipline on those who chose the ascetic life so that Christ would be praised rather than ridiculed. That way was devised by another Egyptian named Pachomius (c.290-c.346). He was a soldier in the Roman army who received such kind treatment from Christians that he became a Christian himself. After studying for several years with an old hermit, he became convinced that the solitary life contained too many temptations to foster real holiness. In 325, he established a community on the island of Tabennisi in the middle of the Nile in Upper Egypt. By the time of his death, he had established eight more monasteries, and was supervising seven thousand monks. His communities balanced devotion and work, and avoided the extremes of the hermits. The communal system also made it possible for women to participate in monastic life for the first time. In fact, the first convent was founded by Pachomius' sister, Mary.

Though Pachomius is looked upon as the founder of the communal system in the East, the man who was most influential in the development of Eastern monasticism was Basil the Great (c.329-379), the Cappadocian who was such a staunch supporter of Trinitarian doctrine. Being both a monk and a bishop, he was concerned that monastic discipline be within the context of the church. Not only did he require that monasteries be under the authority of the local bishop, but the instructions he included in his many writings on the subject became the basis for the monastic rule still in use by the Eastern Church today.

B. MONASTICISM IN THE WEST

Anchoritic monasticism never succeeded in the West, largely because of the cold climate. It did not take long for the West to pick up the enthusiasm for monastic life that had so captured the attention of the East, however. The man most responsible for bringing monasticism to the West was Athanasius, the great defender of the doctrine of the Trinity. In his several periods of exile in the West, he had plenty of opportunities to tell Western churchmen about his personal knowledge of the monks in Egypt, including the great Anthony. His encouragement spurred much monastic activity, and his biography of Anthony influenced Ambrose and Augustine, among others.

Though men like Ambrose, Augustine, and especially Jerome did much to stimulate monasticism in the West, the first to bring widespread popularity to the practice was Martin of Tours (c.335-c.400). Martin was the son of pagan parents, and entered the Roman army as a teenager. One winter day as he was traveling along the road in northern Gaul, he was approached by a naked beggar who was nearly frozen to death. Taking pity on the man, Martin took his heavy soldier's cloak, tore it in half, and gave half to the beggar. That night, he had a dream in which he saw Christ wearing half of his cloak. Shortly thereafter, he left the army, was baptized as a Christian, and went home to try to win his parents to Christ. His mother believed, but his father was too bitter at the loss of his son's promising career. Martin then returned to Gaul and lived the ascetic life of a hermit. Soon, however, the bishop of Tours died, and Martin was almost physically dragged from his cave to fill the post. He refused to live in the bishop's residence, but lived instead in a hut beside the church. Others soon gathered around him to share his lifestyle, and he established the first monastery in the West there in Tours. In addition to the kind of work done by the monks under Pachomius, who worked both to develop discipline and to support themselves so that they could remain apart from the world, Martin used his monks as missionaries to the largely unevangelized inhabitants of Gaul, where many soon came to Christ. Martin of Tours became the first non-martyr to be recognized as a saint by the Catholic Church.

In the same way that Basil established the rule that became the model for Eastern monasticism, the rule that was to dominate the West came from the pen of Benedict of Nursia (c.480-c.543). He was born shortly after the fall of Rome to the barbarians, and thus lived in a world where chaos was the order of the day. At the age of fifteen he became disgusted by the immorality of his friends and left school to become a hermit. He went through the usual temptations of the solitary life, at one point almost giving up to pursue marriage with a former girlfriend, but prevented such a rash action by rolling naked on a bed of thorns until the impulse left him. In order to encourage others to follow his example, he founded a group of twelve monasteries, which failed because the monks rebelled at his strict discipline, and at one point almost succeeded in poisoning him. Finally, in 529, he founded a monastery at Monte Cassino, Italy, which was to become the model for Western monasticism. It was for this monastery that he wrote his famous Benedictine Rule, which was later popularized by Pope Gregory the Great. Within a period of four to five hundred years, almost all of the monasteries in the West were following the Benedictine Rule. The Rule established a tightly scheduled daily routine of seven periods of prayer, interspersed with manual labor, reading, sleep, and two meals. Another major monastic task was introduced later by Cassiodorus (c.477-c.570), who after his retirement from a government post established monasteries for the purpose of instructing laymen and copying the Scriptures, the writings of the Fathers, and the classics of Greek and Roman literature.

Another style of monastic life developed among the Celts in Ireland. Though strong tradition traces the beginnings of these monasteries back to the work of Patrick (c.389-c.461), there is no direct evidence that the great missionary to the Irish ever founded a monastery, though he was certainly an ascetic. In following the example of Patrick, however, the Irish monks became the greatest missionary force of the early Middle Ages. Unlike the Eastern monks and the Benedictines, they were not restricted to their monasteries, and so traveled all over Europe preaching the Gospel.

C. EVALUATION OF MONASTICISM

From a Protestant standpoint, it is very easy to focus on the abuses of monasticism and condemn the movement as a perversion of Christian teaching. Both Roman and Eastern Catholics, on the other hand, find it easy to overlook the faults as minor aberrations. We can afford to do neither. We must recognize that, while the movement has made enormous contributions to the history of the church, it also incorporates some serious flaws.

1. CONTRIBUTIONS OF MONASTICISM

The greatest contribution of monasticism was its work in purifying the church. It arose at a time when the spirituality of the church was declining rapidly, and for almost a thousand years continued to stimulate the most dedicated Christian men and women to a life of service to God. The monks became models of spirituality to whom even the priests looked up, and many of the greatest leaders of the Middle Ages received their training in the monasteries.

The second great contribution of the monks is their work in preaching the Gospel.

Most of the barbarian tribes that overran the Roman Empire in the West could trace their conversion to Christianity to the labors of monks, particularly those from Ireland. Not only did the monks bring many to Christ through their preaching, but they also trained many young people in the faith through the schools that were established by many monasteries - the only schools to be found in the West through much of the Middle Ages.

The third great accomplishment of the monasteries was the preservation of the Scriptures. Their laborious efforts in the monastery *scriptoria* produced thousands of copies of the Bible, preserving the text until the invention of printing in the fifteenth century. They also copied the writings of the church Fathers and the great works of secular philosophers, giving the modern world access to these works as well. For all these things the monks deserve praise, and the gratitude of the entire church, both Catholic and Protestant. But the movement also had its problems, which cannot be easily ignored.

2. HARMFUL EFFECTS OF MONASTICISM

The most serious damage done by monasticism was in creating, or at least fostering, a two-tier view of Christianity. By teaching that holiness was only possible within the walls of a monastery, the monks left the vast majority of Christians with the belief that holiness was unattainable, and therefore should not even be pursued. Prayer and study were for monks. All normal Christians had to do was go to Mass regularly and obey their priests.

Monasticism also had a negative impact on the family. Although many would say that the monastic emphasis on purity was far better than the immorality that was rampant in Roman society, the fact remains that if virginity is better than marriage, it follows that sex is somehow dirty, and that those who choose to marry are giving in to the Devil. The best men and women in the church were turning aside from family life, which God Himself had created for the good of man. The result was that there were few good models of the Christian family for people to follow, and the most capable people in the church were not raising children to assume future church leadership roles. In addition, the ascetic ideal reduced women to the level of necessary evils for the propagation of the race and the production of more virgins, and pictured them as the chief instruments of Satan for the destruction of mankind.

The monks also had a negative impact on the church itself. Monasticism is only one of many super-spirituality movements to arise in the history of the church, and all flourish in the soil of corruption among the clergy. It is questionable, however, to what extent monasticism was a reaction against weak clergy, or whether it in fact contributed to the decline of the clergy.

Most monks were laymen. Some of the early hermits even scorned the sacraments because they were of the body. The prestige of these holy men grew to the point where the common people often respected the monks, with their other-worldly holiness, more than the priests and bishops, who were deeply involved in the politics and society of the day. The monks themselves often scorned bishops, and only reluctantly allowed themselves to be drawn into ecclesiastical affairs. The result of this is that not only did the people lose respect for their bishops and priests, but also the most dedicated men tended to become monks rather than priests or bishops. The monastic monopoly on education also meant that, while most monks could read and knew the Scriptures from long hours of copying, many priests were illiterate, and knew nothing of the Bible aside from the Lord's Prayer and a few psalms. Monasticism thus was not only a reaction against the decline in the clergy, but also contributed to that decline.

In summation, monasticism brought into the church what had been rejected as heresy by earlier generations. While the teaching of the Gnostics that the body was evil and the spirit was good had been condemned, the monks deprived the flesh in order to strengthen the soul. While the church had rejected the super-spirituality of the Montanists, it embraced the super-spirituality of the monks. The church that denounced the Manichaeans for their rejection of marriage now encouraged men and women to abstain from marriage as if it were something worldly. And the same church that condemned the British monk Pelagius when he taught that men could attain perfection in this life praised the men and women who sought spiritual perfection through purging from their bodies the lust of the flesh.

SAINTS AND RELICS

An indirect result of the monastic movement was the veneration of saints and relics. The New Testament, of course, uses the term *saint* to refer to all Christians, but during the later years of persecution it came to be reserved for those who had received a special measure of God's grace.

A. THE MARTYR CULTS

As far back as the second century, it was common practice for churches to remember the martyrs who had died in their midst with special celebrations. These "birthday" celebrations usually occurred on the anniversary of the martyr's death, and would involve a visit to the martyr's tomb and the reading of something written by the departed saint. This simple remembrance soon turned into something approaching worship, however.

Possessions, articles of clothing, or even bones of the martyrs were preserved in great honor by the churches where they had died. Like the bronze serpent made by Moses in the wilderness, these soon became snares, tempting the people to idolatry. By the fourth century, reputable people like Ambrose and Augustine were ascribing all sorts of miracles to these "relics." Like the bones of Elisha that raised a dead man and the handkerchiefs touched by Paul in Ephesus that healed the sick, the relics of the saints were thought to possess miraculous powers. Though the church opposed it, the market in relics eventually became big business, and forgeries abounded. One wag commented that at one point in the Middle Ages there were enough pieces of the True Cross in Europe to rebuild Noah's Ark!

People soon came to venerate the saints themselves as well as their relics. They reasoned that, if a man of God can pray for a person when he is on earth, how much more would he be able to pray when he is in the presence of God in heaven? Jerome argued that, since Christ is omnipresent, and the saints are said to be in His presence, that they, too, must be everywhere at once. Thus it became common practice to ask the saints to intercede when special needs arose, especially in matters thought to be the concern of that particular saint. The result was that certain saints came to be recognized as patrons who concerned themselves specifically with certain places, occupations, or certain types of problems.

B. THE VENERATION OF MARY

The most popular of the saints, of course, was and continues to be the Virgin Mary. At first, only martyrs were recognized as saints, but when martyrs were no longer common, synthetic martyrs - the ascetics - also gained recognition as having been given a special measure of grace from God. While the fourth-century incident mentioned at the beginning of the chapter is the first clear instance of the veneration of Mary, most of the pieces that now make up Catholic teaching on the subject were in place by that time.

The earliest contributions came from the writings of heretics and frauds. The apocryphal gospels of the second and third centuries contained all sorts of fanciful tales about Jesus and His family, and were the first to mention the idea that Mary had remained a virgin throughout her life. The brothers of Jesus were explained away as children of Joseph by an earlier marriage, and Joseph was described as a very old man whom Mary had married simply for the sake of her public reputation. In time, with the increasing emphasis being placed on celibacy, this view came to be accepted by most of the leaders of the church. Jerome, not surprisingly, went even further and suggested that Joseph also was a virgin, and that the "brothers" of Jesus were really cousins. Others took the idea of Mary's virginity to the extent of arguing that Christ must have passed through the entrance to her womb like He passed through the door of the Upper Room when He appeared to the disciples after His resurrection, thus leaving it unopened; still others said that she was impregnated by the words spoken by the angel Gabriel, and that the Holy Spirit entered her body through her ear!

When Augustine was arguing against Pelagius, he was willing to admit one possible exception to his argument. He agreed that Mary could possibly have lived a sinless life, though he insisted that she had been born with original sin that had later been removed when the Holy Spirit came upon her. Later theologians, rejecting Augustine's view of original sin, did not hesitate to say that Mary was born sinless, thus laying the groundwork for what was to become the Catholic doctrine of the Immaculate Conception. Even the Assumption of Mary, which did not become Catholic dogma until 1950, appeared in this era. It came from the teaching that since Mary, like her Son, was free from sin, she also was spared the pain of death, and went directly to heaven in her body.

When the Council of Ephesus in 431 asserted that Mary was the Mother of God, it was in opposition to what it saw as an attempt to separate the humanity and deity of Christ (Nestorianism). But a title that was intended to say something about Christ, the God-Man, came to be used to give honor to His mother. Other titles, such as Queen of Heaven, were borrowed from pagan cults when the pagans were converted, and the veneration of Mary quickly took its place in Catholic belief and practice. The humble maiden of Nazareth had become the all-powerful Co-Redemptrix, the object of devotion to millions, and the model of Catholic womanhood.

MAKING DRY BONES LIVE

No one can criticize the monks for seeking the highest level of spirituality possible, though, as we have already noted, there are many good reasons to criticize the way they went about it. But we need to consider a more fundamental question: Are there any such things as higher and lower levels of spirituality? Are there two ways to God?

The reason that the Protestant Reformers rejected monasticism is because they answered that question in the negative. Prayer, devotion, and study of the Word are for all Christians, not just the elite few. The monks and priests of the Middle Ages were able to manipulate the Christians under their care because the typical believer knew nothing of the Word of God except what he was told. Even today, many are amazed to find that the Scriptures say nothing about many doctrines they have been taught to believe from childhood.

The cult of super-spirituality carries with it two major dangers of which Christians today should be aware. The first is spiritual pride among the super-Christians. In the same way that many monks succumbed to pride because of what they thought was their spiritual vigor, so similar leaders today look down on the common Christian and indulge in the pride fostered by their own "holiness." This pride also causes the super-spiritual to defy authority, even as the monks often thought themselves superior to the priests and bishops who were the ordained heads of the church.

Super-spirituality also produces ignorance and docility among the "lower class," while at the same time providing an excuse for immorality. If those who are not among the elite need not study the Word for themselves, they become susceptible to manipulation, accepting what they are told rather than evaluating it on the basis of Scripture. These "lower" ones also have no motive to live holy lives, since such exalted behavior is beyond the reach of common people. Instead, all of God's people should be like the Bereans, who checked every word spoken by Paul against the Scriptures, and like the Thessalonicans, who followed Paul's example of holy living to the extent that they became models for all the believers in Macedonia and Achaia.

FOR REVIEW AND FURTHER THOUGHT

1. What is asceticism? Give examples of asceticism from other religions.

2. Were there any ascetics in the Bible? Give examples.

3. What key teaching from Greek philosophy influenced the growth of asceticism?

4. What were the two major things that ascetics thought it important to renounce?

5. From what verses in the Bible did the ascetics support their beliefs?

6. Were the ascetics using Scripture correctly when they taught that any who wish to serve Christ must give up all family and possessions? What other passages of Scripture contradict this teaching?

7. Why did ascetics remain with the churches during the period of persecution?

8. Why did the monastic movement appear suddenly when the persecutions ended?

9. What is the difference between anchorites and coenobites? What is a laura?

10. Who are the two Egyptians who are considered the founders of anchoritic and coenobitic monasticism?

11. Who are the two men who wrote the rules that dominated monasticism in the Eastern and Western Churches?

12. Why did some of the hermit monks engage in bizarre behavior?

13. Why did hermit monks never flourish in the West?

14. What role did Athanasius play in the spread of monasticism?

15. Did monks and priests generally get along well with each other? Why or why not?

16. What were the three great accomplishments of monasticism?

17. In what ways did monasticism help to shape the character of the Catholic Church?

18. What role did heresies play in the development of monasticism?

19. How did the veneration of saints and relics originate?

20. Why do Roman Catholics believe so many things about Mary that are not taught in the Bible?

21. Why are there no Protestant monasteries?

22. Why is the idea that there are two levels of Christianity dangerous to the church?

23. What role did the following play in the growth of monasticism: Simeon the Stylite, Martin of Tours, Cassiodorus, Patrick.

24. Identify the following: Justina, Essenes, celibacy, Tabennisi, Monte Cassino, *scriptoria*, relic, Immaculate Conception.

Part Two

THE MEDIEVAL CHURCH
(476-1517)

9

THE CLASH WITH THE INFIDEL

In the first century of its existence, the Christian church gained many of its converts from Judaism. Its persuasive claims to be the completion of what Judaism had begun fit in well with the Jewish expectation of a coming Messiah. Christianity began in Palestine, the very heart of Judaism, and then spread throughout the Roman world despite massive persecution, eventually coming to dominate that world. No other religion was able to stand against it. Temporary competitors such as Mithraism from outside and heresies like Gnosticism and Arianism within simply did not seize the public imagination like the Gospel of Jesus Christ.

In the seventh century, however, another religion arose. It claimed to be the completion of Christianity in the same way that Christianity had claimed to be the completion of Judaism. It was led by a prophet who said he was the Paraclete, and brought with him the final revelation of God to the world. But this new religion grew, not from the heart of Christendom, but out of the wild deserts of Arabia. The prophet was Muhammad, and his new religion was called Islam.

THE LIFE OF MUHAMMAD

The prophet Muhammad (c.570-632) grew up in the arid wastes of the Arabian desert. He was born into a primitive world that acknowledged many gods, including the *jinn*, the fire-demons of the desert. Among these gods they also worshipped Allah, the Creator of all things (the word is the rough equivalent of the Hebrew *Elohim*). Muhammad was born in the city of Mecca, and was a member of the clan that had the responsibility to care for the Ka'aba, the holiest shrine in Arabia. The Ka'aba, or Cube, was a tent containing 360 idols, one for each day of the lunar calendar used by the Arabs, and the Black Stone, a meteorite said to have fallen from heaven when man was created, but that turned black when Adam sinned. The Arabs believed that the tent itself had been made in heaven by the angels; that Adam had worshiped there after the Fall; and that Abraham and his son Ishmael had rebuilt it following the Flood.

Muhammad was the son of Abdallah, an Arab trader, and his wife Amina. His father died before he was born, and his mother died when he was six years old. He was then taken in and raised by his grandfather and later his uncle. From the age of four he was plagued with epileptic seizures, which he originally thought and his enemies always maintained were signs of demon possession. He later took these seizures as marks of divine inspiration. As a teenager, he had the opportunity to travel with his uncle on long camel caravans, visiting not only other cities in Arabia, but also journeying up through Palestine and into Syria. In the course of these trips, he came into contact with Jews and Eastern Christians, whose ideas were to contribute significantly to his later thinking.

In his early twenties, he entered the employ of a widow named Khadija to run the caravan business left behind by her dead husband. He managed the business with great success, and at the age of twenty-five married Khadija, who was forty at the time. Despite the age difference, their marriage was a happy one; she became his first and most ardent convert, and he idolized her as the perfect wife, much to the irritation of his later wives. She gave him six children, five of whom died in infancy. The only survivor was a daughter named Fatima.

In the year 610, Muhammad received his first revelation from Allah. This occurred as he was meditating in a cave on Mount Hira, about an hour from Mecca. He fell into a trance and heard voices, which he was sure were the voices of demons. He returned home and told Khadija, who assured him that he was not demon-possessed, but a prophet. He waited for more visions, but none came, and he returned to Mount Hira with the intention of committing suicide. It was then that the angel Gabriel appeared to him and told him that he was to be God's prophet. He continued to receive revelations until the time of his death. At times, Gabriel would appear to him in human form and speak. On other occasions, Muhammad said he heard the sound of a bell, and when the sound stopped, he was aware of new instructions that had been given to him. These revelations were later written down in the Qur'an. Muhammad himself was illiterate, but he told his visions to his wives and followers, who wrote them down on pieces of camel bone and palm leaves. These were collected and written down in one book after his death.

When Muhammad first began to spread his new religion, he had very little success. After three years of work, he had obtained fewer than fifty converts, mostly members of his own family. Furthermore, he was facing increasing amounts of persecution in Mecca. In proclaiming that there was only one God, Allah, he invited the wrath of his own clan, the guardians of the Ka'aba, as well as the merchants who reaped enormous profits from the pilgrims who came to visit the sacred shrine. He was at first mocked, then later physically abused. His followers were beaten, imprisoned, and showered with camel dung while at their prayers. But some of those pilgrims whom he was accused of chasing away had taken his message with them. In the city of Medina, two hundred and fifty miles north of Mecca, a sizable group had banded together, enthusiastic about the new religion. They sent a delegation to Mecca, inviting Muhammad to come to Medina and be their leader. When his own clansmen heard of this, they were determined to kill him. Muhammad sent his followers on ahead, and barely escaped from Mecca with his life. Upon arriving in Medina, he found a group of enthusiastic followers, and soon became the recognized head of a growing community. This flight from Mecca to Medina in 622, known as the *Hegira*, marks the beginning of the Muslim calendar.

From this point on, Muhammad knew nothing but success. His followers quickly conquered the other tribes in the Medina area, though he was disappointed when the Jews did not recognize him as a prophet sent from God (later, when they mocked him for his contradictions and inadequate understanding of the Old Testament, he had large numbers of Jewish men slaughtered, and their wives and children sold into slavery). The men of Mecca sent armies against him on several occasions, but he defeated them repeatedly, and finally in 630 entered Mecca itself with almost no opposition. His former enemies received his mercy, not his wrath, and they soon joined the religion of Islam. Upon arriving in Mecca, Muhammad cleansed the Ka'aba of its idols, but retained the Black Stone, which today remains the focal point of Islamic worship. It sits inside a large black tent, rebuilt in the seventeenth century, at the center of the Great Mosque in Mecca. Muhammad then returned to Medina, where he died in 632, the master of all Arabia.

Muhammad was a man of strong character who proved himself a capable leader when given the opportunity in Medina. He was also a great poet. The poetry of the Qur'an is considered the greatest in the Arabic language, and its beauty is such that Muslims have strongly resisted any efforts to translate it into other languages. Muhammad also possessed a disarming humility. He often helped his wives with chores around the tent, refused to live in the spacious quarters that his wealth and prestige might have afforded, and was accessible to the most humble of his followers. But, like many leaders who exercise absolute authority, he gave free reign to his sensual desires, especially later in life. Though the Qur'an permits only four wives, the Prophet made a special exception in his own case. For all practical purposes, he had access to any woman he wanted, and he took advantage of it, with over a dozen wives and numerous concubines. This preoccupation with sensuality also found its way into his religion.

THE ISLAMIC RELIGION

In his travels, Muhammad had had considerable contact with Christians and Jews. From them he learned the concept of one almighty God, the sovereign Creator, Allah. The Christians he met, however, were largely heretics who had been expelled by the Eastern Roman Empire, such as Nestorians and Monophysites, and thus the conception of Christianity that he gained was seriously distorted.

His understanding of monotheism - the oneness of God - had three important components that dominate the religion of Islam. The first is his understanding of the unity of God, which ruled out any possibility of Allah having a Son. Christ was viewed as a prophet, but not as God. In fact, Muhammad thought that the Christian Trinity consisted of God the Father, Mary the Mother, and Jesus the Son (perhaps he had heard Mary referred to as the "Mother of God," using the formula from the Council of Ephesus). He also emphasized the transcendence of God - the fact that He was completely different and apart from man and His other creatures. While Christians believe that the gap between a transcendent God and His human creatures was bridged by the God-man Jesus Christ, Muhammad taught that the gap was so wide it could never be bridged. Even prayer was largely a ritual to gain merit. The third key aspect of Muhammad's monotheism was the sovereignty of God. Allah is the cause of all that comes to pass, whether good or evil. This notion that everything that happens is the will of Allah has made Islam the most fatalistic religion known to man. The word *Islam* means "submission," and no religion is more aptly named.

The teachings of Islam come from three major sources, the first being the Qur'an. This book, which is slightly shorter than our New Testament, was compiled by Muhammad's followers after his death. The material is arranged neither chronologically nor topically. The 114 *suras*, or chapters, are arranged in descending order of length, with the exception of the first chapter, which contains the prayer repeated by Muslims five times daily. The contents are highly repetitious and even contradictory, but Muslims explain that the later revelations take precedence over the former. Other teachings come from the Hadith, which records the sayings and habits of Muhammad. These have become the standard of behavior for orthodox Muslims, down to such details as the proper way to eat a grapefruit. The third source is the Ijma, which contains the basics of Islamic law. These latter two perform a function much like that of the Talmud in Judaism. They flesh out and interpret the religion taught in the Qur'an much like the Talmud interprets the Torah, which we know as the Old Testament.

If the heart of Islamic doctrine is monotheism and its connected teachings, the heart of Islamic practice is the so-called Five Pillars. These include the recitation of the Creed ("There is no God but Allah, and Muhammad is His Prophet"), ritual prayer five times daily facing Mecca, almsgiving, fasting during the month of Ramadan, and a pilgrimage to Mecca at least once during a person's lifetime. Muhammad taught that prayer leads halfway to heaven, fasting brings a person up to the gate, but almsgiving opens the door. Muslims are required to give two and a half percent annually to the poor. While Jews and Christians are supposed to tithe their income, this ten percent is used both for the needy and for the support of the religious institutions. Muslims give two and a half percent of their possessions, and all goes to the poor. While this should theoretically encourage the redistribution of wealth, it has in fact spawned a class of professional beggars in Islamic countries.

The fast of Ramadan occurs in the ninth lunar month, which falls at various times in the solar calendar. During that month, Muslims must abstain from food, drink, and sexual activity during the daylight hours. This is supposed to be a time of repentance, but it has evolved into a time of feasting, as many Muslims make up after dark for what they've missed during the daytime.

The pilgrimage to Mecca shows the continuing prominence of the Ka'aba in the religion founded by Muhammad. The relatively small (about eight inches wide and six inches thick) meteorite it contains is smooth and shiny from the kisses of the faithful over the centuries. Only Muslims are permitted within fifteen miles of the holy city of Mecca, though a few infidels have risked death to get a glimpse of the Muslim shrine.

Islam is a male-dominated religion in a male-dominated society. The Qur'an not only permits men to have four wives and an unlimited number of concubines, it also instructs men to beat their wives if they are disobedient. Men have the right to divorce their wives for any reason, but women are not permitted to divorce their husbands. Women must be veiled in public, and must walk behind their husbands. Even the afterlife is strictly for the benefit of men. Paradise is a place of sensual gratification, and women, if they are there at all, are there only to give pleasure to men.

THE EXPANSION OF ISLAM

The story of the Muslim Conquest is one of the most amazing examples of empire-building in the history of man. Within a century after the death of Muhammad, the Caliphs of Islam ruled an empire larger than anything ever ruled by Rome. How was such a large empire built in such a short time? The simplest answer is the Jihad - the Holy War.

Muhammad, in his early revelations, taught that his new religion was not to be spread by force, but that soon changed. He initiated a policy whereby infidels were to be given the choice of Islam or the sword. Faced with such a choice, many quickly joined the swelling ranks of the Prophet. Jews and Christians, the People of the Book, were accorded a special privilege - they were permitted to keep their religion if they would submit to three conditions. The first was the payment of heavy tribute; this supposedly was to make up for their inability to participate in the Holy Wars. The second was an absolute prohibition of evangelism. Christians were free to evangelize Jews or other types of Christians, but any who tried to convert a Muslim faced death, along with their converts. The third condition was obscurity. Christians were prohibited from holding public processions or festivals, and were not even allowed to ring church bells. Many churches were converted into mosques, and permits to build new churches were often denied. Under these conditions, many nominal Christians became Muslims, preferring to go along with the prevailing power rather than suffer the disabilities associated with Christianity under Muslim rule.

There were several factors that contributed to the ease with which the Muslim armies were able to conquer Christian territory. The first was the political weakness of the Eastern Empire. In the early years of the seventh century, the Eastern emperors had fought a series of devastating wars against the Persians. These resulted in no significant territorial gains or losses, but severely weakened both sides militarily. Both Persians and Eastern Christians found the fanatical warriors of Islam impossible to stop. Another factor contributing to the defeat of the Christians was the weakness of the Christianity in the conquered regions. Christianity in the East had become a political tool, dominated by the Byzantine emperors. Continual fights with heretics had emptied the empire of its most zealous believers, and convinced the heretics that living under Islamic rule might be preferable to serving the emperors in Constantinople. In North Africa, the Donatist Controversy had so weakened the church that many turned to Islam, and those who did not fled to Italy or Gaul.

Whatever the reasons, the armies of Islam cut through Christian territory like a knife through butter. The fanatical desert warriors had been promised immediate entrance into Paradise if they died in a Jihad, and they fought with reckless abandon. Warfare aside, very few infidels were actually put to the sword. Most pagans converted to Islam, while Christians, Jews, and later Zoroastrians submitted to the conditions imposed upon them, and saw their communities gradually decline as later generations turned to the dominant Islamic religion.

By the time Muhammad died, his religion dominated Arabia. The first Caliph was the Prophet's father-in-law Abu Bakr, father of Ayesha, Muhammad's favorite wife after the death of Khadija. He and his successors conquered Syria by 636, Palestine in 638, Egypt in 642, and all of Persia by 650. At the same time, the warriors of Islam were advancing into Asia Minor and across North Africa. By 668 the Arabs were in a position to threaten Constantinople, but they were beaten back by the newly-invented "Greek fire," which proved too much for the invaders both then and again in 717. These defeats virtually ended the Muslim advance in the East until the sack of Constantinople in 1453, though they did conquer northern India in the ninth century. In the West, the Muslim armies continued to sweep across North Africa. Carthage fell in 697, and by 707 all of North Africa was in Muslim hands. In 711 the Muslim armies crossed the Straits of Gibraltar (named for al Tarik, the Muslim commander who led the invasion) into Spain, and soon conquered the Visigoths who controlled the region. They began to send raiding parties across the Pyrenees into Gaul, but their advance was finally halted in 732 at the Battle of Tours by a Frankish army under the leadership of Charles Martel, "The Hammer," and the grandfather of the great Charlemagne.

THE IMPACT OF ISLAM ON THE CHURCH

Though the Christians of the early Middle Ages often considered Islam a Christian heresy, it was far more than that. It was a new religion, and the greatest external threat the Christian church had ever faced. Muslims and Christians had an attitude of mutual hostility unlike anything the church had experienced up to that point. While Christian commentators were calling Muhammad the Antichrist, Muslims were asserting their superiority as followers of Allah's ultimate and final revelation to man.

The Muslim Conquest had a variety of effects on the church of the Middle Ages. First of all, Islam effectively destroyed the Christian church in the regions it conquered. Christians were allowed to practice their religion to a limited extent, but the inability to evangelize and the constant flow of nominal Christians into the ranks of Islam effectively killed the churches. Though many of those churches still exist today, they are small, insulated, and mired in traditionalism and empty ritual that is virtually devoid of spiritual life.

The second result of the Conquest was, quite obviously, the loss of territory. Very little of this ground has ever been reclaimed, the major exception being Spain, where the Muslims were driven out by Ferdinand and Isabella in 1492. The Eastern Church suffered the most from the loss of territory. The patriarchates of Jerusalem, Antioch, and Alexandria had fallen into Muslim hands, and Constantinople was under almost constant pressure. This secured the position of the Patriarch of Constantinople as the head of the Eastern Church, but also drove the Eastern Church into a shell from which it has never really emerged. While the Western Church was evangelizing the barbarians and expanding to the north and west, the Eastern Church was concentrating on survival, and having absolutely no success in evangelizing the followers of Islam. Even the Iconoclastic Controversy, the only major doctrinal dispute faced by the Eastern Church in the early Middle Ages, was at least partially stimulated by Muslim criticism of the idolatrous practice of using icons in worship.

In the West, the success of Charles Martel in turning back the Muslim invasion contributed to the eventual alliance between the popes and the Frankish kings that would mature into the Holy Roman Empire two generations later. The Conquest also enhanced papal authority by weakening the Eastern Church, which had never accepted the assertion of supremacy made two centuries before by Pope Leo I. But the greatest effects of the Muslim Conquest on the Western Church were not to appear for several centuries yet. It was the Muslim Conquest that motivated the Crusades, which from 1095 to 1291 sought to wrest the Holy Land from its infidel conquerors. These holy wars, along with a constant interchange between Christian Europe and Muslim Spain, brought to the West a renewed interest in the classical learning of Greece, which had been preserved by the Muslims, and an increase in knowledge in the areas of mathematics, astronomy, and medicine, in which the Muslims excelled. This ancient philosophy stimulated

Scholasticism in the Roman Catholic Church, while the new learning laid the groundwork for the Renaissance, which in turn paved the way for the Protestant Reformation.

MAKING DRY BONES LIVE

The final command that Jesus gave His disciples was to go into the world and make disciples among all nations. The extent to which they were successful in doing so is an irrefutable demonstration of the power of God. The Muslims spread their religion to many nations as well, but required force to do so. Those who are converted by the sword know nothing of the Spirit, whether they are being converted to Islam or to a formal, lifeless Christianity. Those Christians throughout the centuries who have thought to spread the truth by force could find no justification in the Word of God, and produced only nominal Christians whose path to hell was smoothed by their own presumptions of salvation.

But if Christianity cannot be like Islam and spread its teachings by force, it also cannot be like Judaism and view the work of evangelism as an option. It is no accident that the churches that submitted to the conditions imposed by the Muslim conquerors of their lands shriveled and died so that there was no spiritual life remaining. Christianity cannot be reduced to a moral or legal system; it is a relationship with the Living God through His Son Jesus Christ, and an integral part of that relationship is the obligation to communicate the truth to others. Any church that is not growing is dying, whether it be in Muslim North Africa or in an American suburb. A necessary part of loving God and loving one's neighbor is to spread the Good News to those to whom it is unknown.

The Clash With the Infidel

FOR REVIEW AND FURTHER THOUGHT

1. In what sense does Islam relate to Christianity in the same way Christianity relates to Judaism?

2. What was the religion of Arabia like before the time of Muhammad?

3. In what ways did Muhammad's background contribute to the religion he founded?

4. What is the Qur'an? How was it written?

5. What sort of reception did Muhammad get when he began to talk about his visions?

6. What conclusions did Muhammad draw from his conviction that there was only one God?

7. What are the Five Pillars of Islam?

8. What are the three major written sources of Islamic teaching?

9. What role do women play in the Islamic religion?

10. What factors within Islam itself contributed to its rapid spread in the Mediterranean world?

11. What factors weakened the Eastern and Western Churches so that they were unable to roll back the Islamic Conquest?

12. In what ways did the Muslim Conquest strengthen the leaders of the Eastern and Western Churches?

13. How did the Muslim conquest contribute to the Crusades? Scholasticism? the Renaissance?

14. Why is it impossible for true Christianity to be spread by force?

15. Why is it impossible for the Christian church to survive if Christians stop trying to evangelize others?

16. Identify the following in one sentence each: Black Stone, *Hegira*, *jinn*, Ka'aba, Mecca, Medina, Mount Hira, Ramadan, and *sura*.

17. What role did the following people play in the development and spread of Islam: Abu Bakr, al Tarik, Amina, Ayesha, Charles Martel, Fatima, and Khadija?

THE FALL AND RISE OF THE ROMAN EMPIRE

When T.S. Eliot concluded his poem *The Hollow Men* with the words, "This is the way the world ends, not with a bang but a whimper," he could just as easily have been talking about the Roman Empire in the West. Since the defeat of the emperor Valens by the Visigoths at Adrianople in 378, the barbarian tribes had been making steady encroachments into the territory controlled by Rome. Alaric and the Visigoths had sacked Rome in 410; Attila and the Huns were a constant threat throughout the middle of the fifth century; and the Vandals sacked Rome a second time in 455. All during this time, various barbarian tribes had been settling within the borders of the empire, and their warriors served as mercenaries in the Roman army. Thus when this same largely barbarian army replaced the weak emperor Romulus Augustulus with the barbarian chief Odovacar in 476, no one batted an eye, and few noticed that an era had ended.

The barbarian tribes that conquered the western Roman Empire had tremendous respect for the civilization they overcame. They recognized that Roman culture was in many ways superior to their own, and thus sought to preserve what remained of the Roman way of life. Aside from adopting the lifestyles of those they had conquered, however, they had no clear notion as to how this ought to be done. The barbarian conquests thus produced a vacuum in Western society - a vacuum that was filled by the church. In these days of chaos, the church brought stability to an uncertain and rapidly changing world. While the Muslim Conquest discussed in the previous chapter seriously weakened the Eastern Church, the church in the West gained greater prominence when the barbarians conquered Rome. The Western Church, with the pope at its head, faced two major tasks after Rome fell - preserving society and converting the barbarians.

PRESERVING SOCIETY

The barbarians who took over Rome were a primitive and superstitious people. They knew how to fight, but they had little experience in ruling an empire. Thus when the Ostrogoth leader Odovacar declared himself emperor, he gathered around him many prominent Roman aristocrats as advisors. Because of the prominence of the church in the empire of that day, many of these aristocrats were also Christians. A successor of Odovacar, the Ostrogoth king Theodoric, had in his court both Cassiodorus and Boethius. Cassiodorus would later retire and make his impact felt in the realm of monasticism, especially as he encouraged monks to copy manuscripts of Greek and Latin classics as well as the Scriptures. Boethius never had the opportunity to retire. His enemies accused him of treason against Theodoric, and he was imprisoned and eventually executed. While in prison, however, he wrote *The Consolation of Philosophy*, in which he became one of the first to try to formulate Christian truth on the basis of the categories popularized by Greek philosophy. He thus became a forerunner of Scholasticism, of which we will see more in chapter fifteen.

Of all the Christians who played key roles as advisors to the barbarian kings, however, none was held in higher esteem than the pope. Though the popes in the century and a half between Leo I and Gregory I were for the most part weak men, they were revered by the superstitious barbarians. They became in many ways the focal point of a society that was otherwise in constant flux. In the waning years of the Roman Empire in the West, the church had taken over many of the social services of the empire, such as hospitals and orphanages. The continuation of these institutions gave structure to early medieval society, and provided a base from which the church could branch out and augment its power. Another source of growing power within the church was the acquisition of land. Churches and monasteries came to control almost a third of the land in Italy by the early part of the sixth century. This came about because superstitious men believed that, if they willed their land to the church in exchange for masses to be said in their behalf, that their time in purgatory could be reduced. Land was wealth, and control of large amounts of land made the church powerful.

CONVERTING THE BARBARIANS

Very few of the barbarians who conquered the Roman Empire in the West were orthodox Christians, though not all were rank pagans. Several of the tribes had centuries before, during the Trinitarian Controversy, been converted to Arianism. The Arian view of Christ fit very well with the desire of the barbarians for a warrior-king, while the Trinitarian theology was too complex for their tastes. The church thus faced the task of converting these primitive tribesmen to catholic Christianity, whether from paganism or from Arianism. In carrying out this task, the church was remarkably successful.

There were two major sources of missionaries during the early Middle Ages. The first was the Irish monasteries. Founded by Patrick and his successors, these monasteries sent out a steady stream of traveling preachers who boldly confronted the barbarians and started monasteries all over Europe. Among these the most notable were Columba (c.521-597), who worked among the Picts and Celts in Scotland and founded the famous monastery on the island of Iona, from which many other missionaries later went out; Columbanus (c.543-615), who preached among the Franks and eventually found his way to Italy; and Willibrord (658-739), a missionary to the Frisians in what is now the Netherlands.

The second great source of missionary activity in the early Middle Ages was the papacy. Not all popes were equally zealous for the conversion of the barbarians, but those who were accomplished quite a bit. The two most noted papal emissaries were Augustine of Canterbury and Boniface, also known as Wynfrith. Augustine (d.c. 604), not to be confused with the illustrious bishop of Hippo, was a Benedictine monk sent out by Pope Gregory I at the head of a contingent of forty monks to evangelize England. Irish monks had earlier evangelized the peoples of the island, but Gregory wanted to see both the Anglo-Saxons converted and the churches and monasteries brought under papal authority. Augustine did succeed in converting Ethelbert, King of Kent, to Christianity with the help of his queen, Bertha, who was already a Christian. Like many of the barbarian tribes of the day, most of Ethelbert's tribesmen joined him in his new religious commitment. The kingdom of Kent then became a beachhead from which Christianity began to spread among the other tribes in Britain. Sixty years after Augustine died, the Celtic churches submitted to Rome and came under papal jurisdiction at the Synod of Whitby (664), though King Oswy of Northumbria favored the Romans over the Celts largely because he had been told that the Pope was the representative of Peter, and that Peter was the gatekeeper of heaven. Deciding that he wanted to be on the good side of the man who would decide whether he entered heaven or not, Oswy declared in favor of Rome, and the Celtic churches and monasteries were forced to conform their practices to those of the Catholic Church.

Boniface (680-755), an Englishman who was sent out by Pope Gregory II, has come to be known as the Apostle to the Germans. Boniface originally intended to assist Willibrord in his work among the Frisians, but was discouraged by the resistance he met there. He returned briefly to England, then went to Rome, where he received a papal commission to evangelize the

Goths. The barbarian Goths were a tribal people who had little unity even among themselves. Many had been converted to Arianism centuries before through the work of Ulfilas (c.311-c.381), but many remained pagan. For a period of thirty years, Boniface worked among the Goths, converting the pagans and bringing the Arians into the orthodox faith and under obedience to the pope. He was a man of great boldness, as the most famous incident of his missionary labors illustrates. In entering a new tribal area, he found that the barbarians worshipped Thor, the thunder god, and that his shrine was an ancient oak tree in the middle of a clearing. Boniface told them that Thor was no god, and proceeded to emphasize his point by taking an axe to the sacred oak. The Goths stood dumbfounded, waiting for lightning to fall from the sky and strike down this desecrator of the holy shrine. As Boniface chopped, a storm blew up. Instead of seeing the preacher struck by lightning, however, the Goths looked on in horror as the violent winds of the storm toppled the sacred tree. The storm passed, and Boniface stood unharmed, the tree dead at his feet. Convinced that the God whom Boniface represented had blown over their tree, the tribe became Christians, and built a chapel in honor of St. Peter out of the wood from the fallen oak. Boniface also played a key role in shaping the alliance between the papacy and the Franks, as we will see later in the chapter. At the end of his life, he returned to Frisia, and was martyred there, killed by an angry mob while preaching the Gospel.

BYZANTINES AND LOMBARDS

The Ostrogoths controlled Rome for less than sixty years. After years of confusion, the Eastern (Byzantine) Empire was taken over by the great Justinian in 527. He, like the Eastern emperors before and after him, was an advocate of caesaropapism - the notion that the emperor is also the head of the church. Though few Byzantine emperors would have stated it quite so bluntly, in practice they expected the leaders of the church to submit to their decisions in both political and theological matters. Justinian wanted to return to the glory that the Roman Empire had known in years past, and took several steps to bring this about. One was the preparation of a legal code that reduced to written form much of the legal tradition of ancient Rome, and included regulations for the church and the clergy. Another was the reconquest of the lands lost to the barbarians. Justinian entrusted his general Belisarius with the task of reuniting the Roman Empire and, given the small size of his army, he was incredibly successful in doing so. He reconquered North Africa from the Vandals, and in 535 managed to take most of Italy away from the Ostrogoths. Italy thus became a province of the Byzantine Empire, with its capital at Ravenna. Though the exarch in Ravenna was supposedly the imperial governor of Italy, the pope soon came to be recognized as the ruler of Rome, both because Justinian liked to combine civil and religious authority, and because the pope controlled more land around Rome than anyone else. When Justinian died in 565, however, Byzantine domination of Italy evaporated under the pressure applied by a new tribe of invaders, the pagan Lombards.

With the Byzantine Empire having authority over Italy in name only, it was left to the popes to protect the land from the Lombards. This they did, by negotiation, attempts at conversion, and even by warfare. By far the most successful at dealing with the Lombard menace was Gregory the Great (c.540-604), who was certainly the most influential religious leader in the early Middle Ages.

GREGORY THE GREAT

Numerous people throughout history have come to be known as "the Great," but few with better cause than this dedicated man who desired only to be called "a servant of the servants of God." Gregory was born into an aristocratic family in Rome and studied law in preparation for government service. His family had been dedicated Christians for generations. He had a pope in his family tree, and two of his aunts and his mother later joined him among the ranks of the saints. In the year 574, he was appointed prefect of Rome under the Byzantines. Gregory found public life very depressing, however, so he resigned as prefect to embark on a life of monastic seclusion. He used his family wealth to build six monasteries, then gave the rest to the poor and turned his family's palace into a seventh, where he himself took up residence. He was not permitted to enjoy his isolation for long, however. In 579, Pope Pelagius II appointed him as ambassador to the Byzantine court at Constantinople, where he served for six years. He then returned to Rome, where he became the abbot of the monastery he had left earlier, but continued to serve the pope in various public matters. When Pelagius died of the bubonic plague, Gregory was chosen to succeed him, thus becoming the first monk to ascend the papal throne (In those days, popes were chosen by the leading churchmen in Rome, but often under pressure from the political leaders and the population at large. It was not uncommon for riots to break out, or for popes to be placed in office by the faction with the most weapons. In this case, however, there could be no question. Gregory was the unanimous choice, though he himself hid in the forest to try to avoid the job).

Gregory accomplished an incredible amount in his fourteen years as pope, especially considering that he was a sickly man who spent much of his time confined to bed. His greatest strength was as an administrator. He not only administered the vast papal estates profitably, but used the produce of the land to feed the poor. He remedied many of the common abuses among the clergy and monks, setting an example himself of simplicity and purity in living. He also managed to keep the Lombards at bay through shrewd diplomacy.

In the church, Gregory became in fact what Leo I had claimed to be 150 years earlier. He exercised authority over almost all the churches of the West, and did not hesitate to speak out in response to conflicts in the East, as well. When the Patriarch of Constantinople assumed the title "universal bishop," Gregory objected in the strongest possible terms, saying that anyone who would claim to be a universal bishop was well on the way to being the Antichrist (later popes would have done well to heed this assertion). Somewhat ironically, however, Gregory, while refusing to use the disputed title, affirmed that he alone had the authority that the title implied.

Gregory was a man who was truly concerned for the spread of the Gospel. During his years as a monk, while walking through the marketplace in Rome, he had seen a group of fair-haired boys who were being sold as slaves. He asked who they were, and was told they were Angles. He responded that they were not Angles, but angels, and asked Pope Pelagius for permission to go to their land as a missionary. Pelagius needed him too badly in Rome, and refused to grant the permission. When Gregory became pope, however, he sent such a mission under the leadership of Augustine of Canterbury, the results of which we noted above. Gregory also, near the end of his life, was instrumental in turning a group of the Lombards from Arianism to Catholic Christianity, though this did not put a stop to their harassment of the countryside.

Gregory also made contributions to the theology and worship of the church that, while not original, came to be typical of medieval Catholicism. As a theologian, Gregory did little more than restate the teachings of the earlier Fathers, but the clarity with which he did so made him a popular author throughout the Middle Ages. He was generally semi-Augustinian in his theology, following the guidelines established by the Council of Orange in 529. As a commentator, he made generous use of allegorical interpretation in his writings (for instance, he taught that the passage in Leviticus 21 forbidding men with blemishes from serving as priests described spiritual requirements for the Christian priesthood; the blind are those who cannot see the light of Christ, the lame those who cannot walk perfectly in the truth, those whose noses are too small are those who lack wisdom, since the nose is used to distinguish good meat from bad, those who are hunchbacked are men who are overly burdened by the cares of this world, etc.). He piously followed the popular superstitions of the day, and did much to spread the belief in purgatory and the veneration of saints and relics. His stories of the lives of the saints established what was to become one of the most popular literary genres of the Middle Ages. He popularized the Benedictine Rule, and made it the standard for monasteries throughout the Western Church. Gregory also revised the liturgy, incorporating a style of music that bears his name (Gregorian chant), though the form in which it eventually became popular was established long after the time of Gregory himself. When he died in 604, his epitaph consisted of two words - "God's Consul," which was a highly appropriate summation of the career of a man who had so successfully blended the religious and political aspects of life into one harmonious whole.

THE FRANKISH ALLIANCE

The hundred years after the death of Gregory were years of chaos and confusion in Rome. While the city was nominally under Byzantine control, the Lombards continued to make trouble. Relations between Rome and Constantinople were becoming increasingly strained, and the popes soon realized that they were going to have to seek political protection for the church, not from the Eastern emperors, but from among the newly converted barbarian tribes. The tribe that soon proved a fruitful source of stability was the first of the barbarians to turn to Catholic Christianity, the Franks.

The Franks inhabited the region of Gaul, to which they later gave their name. They turned to Christianity in 496 during the reign of Clovis, the founder of the Merovingian dynasty. Clovis, like many of the barbarians of his day, sought friendly relations with the church in the realm he had conquered. His queen, Clothilde, was a Christian from Burgundy, and helped influence him in the direction of Christianity. In a scene reminiscent of the conversion of Constantine, Clovis pledged to become a Christian if the God of the Christians would help him defeat the Alemanni, another tribe of barbarians who had been rapidly eating up his territory. He won a resounding victory, and was shortly thereafter baptized, along with several thousand of his soldiers.

From that time on, the Merovingian kings supported the church, encouraging the founding of monasteries and supporting missionaries sent out from Rome. The line gradually declined over the next two hundred years, however. It got to the point where the kings held the title of office, but the real power in the kingdom lay in the hands of an administrator called the Mayor of the Palace, which had become an hereditary office in the seventh century. The first of these mayors of interest to us is Charles Martel, the famous Hammer who drove the Muslims out of France and back across the Pyrenees into Spain. It was during his tenure that the need of the popes for political support became especially acute. The Eastern Church was in the midst of the Iconoclastic Controversy (see chapter eleven), and relations between East and West were near the breaking point. In fact, the pope had just excommunicated the Byzantine emperor for destroying images used for worship, and the emperor had responded by removing most of Italy from the jurisdiction of the pope and placing it under the authority of the patriarch of Constantinople. The Lombards were threatening Rome again, and the pope had nowhere to turn. He asked Charles Martel, the deliverer of Christendom from the infidel, for help in removing the Lombard threat. Charles, who supported the church whenever it enhanced his own power but had no qualms about confiscating church lands whenever he needed money, refused on the grounds that the Lombards had been his allies in the fight against the Muslims.

Charles Martel was succeeded by his son Pepin the Short (c.714-768), who was much more positively disposed toward the church than his father had been, and also had greater ambitions. He had the power of the kingship, but he also wanted the title. He knew that he could not gain respect by simply overthrowing the decadent Merovingians. He was therefore open to making a deal with the pope. The deal was a simple one. In exchange for recognition as the rightful King of the Franks, Pepin would drive the Lombards out of Italy. The missionary Boniface, acting as the pope's representative, crowned Pepin King of the Franks in 752, thus initiating the Carolingian dynasty. Later Pope Stephen III visited Pepin personally and repeated the ceremony, after which Pepin accompanied the pope to Rome and defeated the Lombards, though not for long. Soon they attacked again, and the pope wrote to Pepin, asking for help and promising the new king one of the most beautiful mansions in heaven if he came quickly. Pepin came, again defeated the Lombards, and gave the conquered territory to the pope despite the fact that it at least theoretically was part of the Byzantine Empire. This "Donation of Pepin" in 755 provided the basis for the Papal States, a political entity ruled by the pope until the unification of Italy in 1870. It also further strained the already tenuous relationship between the eastern and western churches.

The historical foundation for the Donation of Pepin was provided by a document known as the Donation of Constantine. Though written in the middle of the eighth century, this document was supposed to be a will left by Constantine, the first Christian emperor. In this will, he left to Pope Sylvester and his successors political control of the whole western half of the Roman Empire, and also asserted the supremacy of the pope over the entire church. This forgery was blatantly used by popes throughout the Middle Ages to assert their power over church and state alike, and was never seriously challenged until proved to be a forgery by Lorenzo Valla in 1440. Some have tried to excuse this use of power politics by the popes on the ground that it was acceptable in past ages to give credibility to new ideas by putting them into the mouths of reputable men from the past. Historian Roland Bainton argued that

"... in antiquity men sought to gain authority for their convictions by attaching them to a great name, rather than prestige for themselves by avowing their authorship. Thus the Jews attributed their laws to Moses and their psalms to David, and the earlier Christians sometimes ascribed to the apostles books that modern scholarship considers of uncertain authorship."

One cannot excuse deceit, however, by blackening the Bible with the same brush. It is because the Word of God is absolutely truthful that deceptive means must be condemned, no matter how beneficial the motive behind them (and in this case, the motives are highly debatable). If the Donation of Constantine had been widely recognized as an expression of modern ideas in ancient garb, some excuse might be made for common practice. On the contrary, though, it is the very historicity of the document that was the basis for papal claims. No pope could have used the Donation to claim political power in Europe unless the ones against whom the club was being wielded really believed that Constantine had willed Western Europe to Sylvester and his successors.

Pepin was succeeded by his son Charlemagne (Charles the Great - c.742-814). This Frankish king dominates the politics of the early Middle Ages in the same way that Gregory the Great dominates the theology of the period. He was a great conqueror and administrator who had a sincere love for the church and a desire to revive learning in Western Europe. In the political realm, he built an empire that covered what today would be called France, Germany, Hungary, most of Italy, and much of Spain. He built the empire ruthlessly, at one point forcibly converting the Saxons to Christianity after beheading 4500 men in a single day. He encouraged education, and brought the greatest scholars of his day to teach in his court at Aix-la-Chapelle (Aachen). Among these was Alcuin of York, who headed the palace school and also undertook a revision of the Latin Vulgate, all while supervising the monastery at Tours. Though Charlemagne himself could not write and hated to read, he loved to be read to, his favorite book being Augustine's *City of God*.

In the religious realm, Charlemagne exerted control over the churches in his kingdom that rivaled the caesaropapism of Byzantium. He demanded that he have approval over all men appointed as bishops in his domain, and often just appointed them himself for the sake of simplicity. He supported the iconoclasts of the Eastern Church despite the fact that the popes favored the use of images in worship, produced a set of decrees that condemned the worship of images so strongly that Catholics at the beginning of the Reformation claimed they were a Protestant forgery, and refused to recognize the Seventh Ecumenical Council at Nicea (787), which had rejected iconoclasm. The popes themselves continually turned to Charlemagne for support. He put an end to the Lombard threat once and for all, but the factions in Rome continued to pose problems for the popes who were dependent on their good will. In 799, Pope Leo III was attacked by an angry mob and nearly killed. He fled to Charlemagne, who accompanied him back to Rome and supported him when he publicly denied all charges against him. The next year, Charlemagne again visited Rome, and went to the cathedral to celebrate Mass on Christmas Day. As he was kneeling at the altar, Leo placed a crown on his head and declared him to be Emperor of the Romans. Thus on December 25, 800, the Holy Roman Empire began. Though it never approached the glory of ancient Rome, it was to play a pivotal role in European politics for over a thousand years. When the pope crowned Charlemagne, he performed an action that was to become the source of a bitter dispute. Future popes would claim on this basis the right to make and unmake kings, and assert that no one could rule legitimately without papal approval. Charlemagne himself, and the kings who would follow him, would respond that the pope was thereby recognizing the king as sovereign in the political realm just as the popes were sovereign in the religious realm. What was intended to be a unification of the leadership of Christian Europe became instead the root of a great power struggle in which the church and state would battle one another for control of Christendom.

After the death of Charlemagne, Europe quickly descended again into chaos. According to the Frankish custom, Charlemagne's empire eventually was divided among his three grandsons, with the three parts corresponding roughly to France, Germany, and Italy. The resulting decentralization, accompanied and augmented by the invasions of a new group of barbarians, the Vikings, sent Europe reeling into what has quite rightly been called the Dark Ages, which would last for about two centuries.

MAKING DRY BONES LIVE

If there is ever a period of time when the bones of church history seem dry, even to a church historian, it is the early Middle Ages. What possible relevance can such a period have for a Christian in the twenty-first century?

Before we leave Charlemagne and his Holy Roman Empire, we ought to give some thought to the concept of Christendom - the idea of a Christian society ruled by a Christian prince in cooperation with the head of the church, the Vicar of Christ on earth. Looking at the issue from a practical standpoint, it is easy to assert that the concept has never worked. As we will see, the attempt to unify church and state has only produced constant conflict between church and state for the domination of society. Is this the necessary outcome? Is there some flaw in the whole idea of a Christian society that we ought to recognize?

When Jesus told the parable of the Wheat and the Tares in Matthew 13:24-30 and 36-43, He was making the point that the world would always be a mixture of Christians and unbelievers until the day of judgment, and to try to make it otherwise would accomplish nothing except to harm the wheat - the church. As the history of the church after the time of Charlemagne will abundantly illustrate, it is impossible to construct a Christian society. Those who try to do so by force, as Charlemagne did with the Saxons, will bring into the church those whose lack of true Christianity will corrupt it from within. Those who expect a Christian society to remain that way from one generation to the next are presuming on the grace of God. Each generation must be evangelized anew. As has often been pointed out, God has no grandchildren. Christendom was a myth from the beginning. In our own day, we should recognize that we are no more capable of building a Christian society by legislation than Charlemagne was of doing it by political power.

FOR REVIEW AND FURTHER THOUGHT

1. Why did the fall of Rome in 476 not produce a major change in the lives of the people of Western Europe?

2. Why did the collapse of the Roman Empire in the West increase the power of the pope?

3. Why did the barbarian kings often have Christians as their chief advisors?

4. How did the church become rich in the Middle Ages?

5. What roles did the following barbarian tribes play in the period of history considered in this chapter: Visigoths, Ostrogoths, Picts, Vandals, Lombards, Franks, Angles, Saxons, and Frisians?

6. Why did many of the barbarian tribes find Arianism attractive?

7. Describe briefly the work of the following missionaries: Columba, Columbanus, Willibrord, Augustine, Ulfilas, and Boniface.

8. Identify the following barbarian monarchs and their roles in the history of the early medieval church: Odovacar, Theodoric, Ethelbert, and Clovis.

9. Define caesaropapism. Why is Justinian a good example of this philosophy?

10. Summarize briefly the contributions to the church made by Gregory the Great.

11. Name two Christian queens who were instrumental in converting their husbands, and describe the circumstances under which these conversions occurred.

12. Why did Charles Martel refuse to help the pope against the Lombards? Why did Pepin give help under the same circumstances?

13. What was the Donation of Pepin? What is its historical significance?

14. What was the Donation of Constantine? How was it used in the Middle Ages?

15. Why did the formation of the Holy Roman Empire start a power struggle between the popes and the emperors?

16. Is it possible to create a Christian society? Why or why not?

11

EARLY MEDIEVAL THEOLOGY

An oxymoron is a word or phrase that contains an internal contradiction, such as when Juliet bid Romeo adieu by sighing, "Parting is such sweet sorrow." There are some who would suggest that the title of this chapter is also an oxymoron. After all, it was not for nothing that the centuries that ended the first millennium of the Christian era are called the Dark Ages. It is certainly true that this period of time produced no lasting theological works and few notable theologians. In fact, the theologians who are remembered from the period, such as Isidore of Seville and John of Damascus, are known more as compilers of the thought of others than as original thinkers (the one original thinker of the period was John Scotus Erigena, and he was so original that few people understood him; those who did recognized that his teachings were heretical). The theological disputes of the age were so entangled with power politics that they were argued on a level roughly comparable to that of children flinging mudpies at one another - whoever has the most mud wins. The three significant theological controversies with which we will concern ourselves in this chapter are the Iconoclastic Controversy, which centered in the East but had repercussions in the West as well, and the Predestination and Eucharistic Controversies, which involved only the Western Church.

THE ICONOCLASTIC CONTROVERSY

We saw in chapter nine the destruction that the warriors of Islam wreaked upon the Eastern Church during the years of the Muslim Conquest. There were a few areas, however, where interaction with Islam was beneficial to the church. One of these was the dispute in the Eastern Church over the veneration of icons.

With the growth of the veneration of saints and martyrs in the church, along with the paganizing influences brought in by mass conversions, the churches in both the East and West began to remember the saints by the use of visible representations, either statues or pictures. It was argued that such statues and pictures were not being worshipped in themselves, but that they served as visual aids to represent those to whom worship was rightly being directed. Besides, they helped to communicate the Christian religion to a pitifully illiterate population. In this superstitious age, however, it was not long before the statues and pictures themselves were being worshipped as sources of great spiritual and material blessing. They were carried in ceremonial procession in annual festivals, people knelt before them in prayer, and miracles of healing were ascribed to the images themselves. The Eastern Church confined itself largely to pictures of Christ and the saints known as icons, while the Western Church used statues as well. In the East, these icons were actually believed to embody something of the spiritual power of the departed saint. When the Muslims arrived on the scene, with their strict monotheism and strong opposition to any physical representation of deity, they rightfully mocked the Christians as idolaters and image-worshippers. Some Christians realized that the Muslims were right, and set out to do something about this crass idolatry that had wormed its way into the worship of the church.

One such man was the Byzantine Emperor Leo III, also known as Leo the Isaurian, who was emperor from 716 to 741. Born into a simple peasant family, he rose through the ranks of the army to become emperor. His legitimate concern with the idolatry around him was coupled with a despotic streak that inclined him to deal with the problem by force, and the caesaropapism of the East allowed him to step in and ride roughshod over the leaders of the Eastern Church. In his years in the army on the Eastern frontier, he had had much contact with the rampaging Muslims. As emperor, he successfully turned back an attack against Constantinople itself. He saw the worship of icons as the central evil behind the Muslim Conquest. Leo believed that Islam had conquered much Christian territory because pure monotheistic Islam was actually a religion superior to the debased Christianity practiced in the East, and that Christianity could never regain the lost land and people unless it returned to the purity of its youth. Muslims and Jews would never be converted to a religion that worshipped idols.

In 726, the tenth year of his rule, he issued a decree forbidding the worship of images, and ordered them moved beyond the reach of the people so they could no longer kiss or touch them. In 730, he ordered them destroyed completely throughout the realm. Pictures painted on walls were to be covered with whitewash, while hanging pictures were to be removed entirely. Even the magnificent picture of Christ over the gateway of the palace was to be taken down and replaced with a simple empty cross. Leo even had to depose the patriarch of Constantinople and replace him with an iconoclast. It was this order for the destruction of images that gave the iconoclasts their name ("iconoclast" means "image-breaker").

Leo's decrees drew strong opposition. Most of the clergy and the vast majority of the people rose up because Leo was taking away the only religion they knew. The monks, despite the fact that they were supposed to be separate from the world of the senses, also opposed iconoclasm because the monasteries derived significant income from the manufacture of icons. The most reasoned opposition to iconoclasm, however, came from a person who was far removed from the center of the controversy. John of Damascus (c.675-749), who served for many years as the chief advisor to the Muslim Caliph of Damascus, then retired to a monastery in Palestine in about 730, wrote three letters in opposition to iconoclasm, presenting arguments that are used by Catholics and Eastern Orthodox to the present day. In addition to the notion that icons are not worshipped, but merely represent what is being worshipped, John also argued that images were used in the worship of the Old Testament (such as the bronze serpent and the cherubim over the mercy seat on the ark of the covenant), and that the destruction of images would deny the incarnation, since it would imply that Christ had not had a physical body capable of being pictorially represented. He even argued that ascribing healing powers to icons was not unscriptural, since the book of Acts speaks of people being healed by Peter's shadow and Paul's handkerchief. Inanimate things may thus be instruments for the transmission of the power of those they represent.

Leo and his son Constantine V (reigned 741-775) imposed iconoclasm by force, though their edicts were widely ignored beyond the areas of their personal control. Christians in Muslim lands generally ignored the decrees, while the popes, though under nominal Byzantine authority, bluntly condemned them as so foolish as to be rejected by children. Pope Gregory III went so far as to excommunicate the iconoclasts, which led Leo III to remove most of Italy from papal jurisdiction and place it under the authority of the patriarch of Constantinople (as we saw in chapter ten, this helped push the popes into the arms of the Franks). Constantine V called a council in 754 in Constantinople that he intended to be the seventh ecumenical council. No prominent church leader was present, however, since the patriarchate of Constantinople was at the time vacant, the patriarchs of Alexandria, Antioch, and Jerusalem were under Muslim control and thus could not attend, and the Pope didn't even respond to the invitation. The council soundly condemned the worship of icons, though it also forbade the destruction of such images, and affirmed the duty of prayer to Mary and the saints. The council was never recognized by the church at large, and was later denounced as a council of heretics when the iconoclasts were overthrown.

Constantine V was succeeded by his son Leo IV, who reigned only for five years. When he died, his son was an infant, so his widow Irene ruled as regent on her son's behalf. Irene was both a shrewd and capable politician and a worshipper of icons. When she assumed power, she granted toleration to both sides in the dispute, but soon began filling the highest offices in the church and the empire with icon-worshippers. She was responsible for convening the Seventh Ecumenical Council of Nicea in 787, though it was technically under the auspices of her young son Constantine VI. This time the Pope sent representatives, though the patriarchs in Muslim territory were still unavailable. The council overturned the decrees of the Council of Constantinople of 754, asserting that icons could be used in worship with certain restrictions. Worshippers could kiss them, bow before them, light candles in front of them, and say prayers before them, as long as it was understood that these actions were in honor, not of the icons themselves, but of what the icons represented. While the results of the council were praised throughout the church and its decisions became the official position of both Roman Catholic and Eastern Orthodox, those decisions met opposition from an unexpected direction. Though the pope strongly supported the council, the Frankish king Charlemagne did not. In 790, Charlemagne, with the help of Alcuin of York, published the *Caroline Books*. These, which were confirmed by the Synod of Frankfurt in 794, spoke out against the use of images in worship, though they did permit the use of images for decorative purposes.

After the death of Irene, iconoclasm experienced a resurgence for almost forty years, though it was supported only by the emperors and the army. When the last and most brutal of the iconoclasts, Theophilus, died in 842, his widow Theodora took the throne as regent, promptly deposed the iconoclastic Patriarch of Constantinople, and replaced him with the monk Methodius, whose godliness was respected by all, and who favored the worship of icons. Images were restored to the churches, and the first Sunday of Lent has been celebrated in the Eastern Church as the Feast of Orthodoxy ever since.

Church historian Philip Schaff has pointed out that, though the iconoclasts were rejecting the worship of images for much the same reasons as those used by the Protestant Reformers eight centuries later, they failed because they were taking from the people the only Christianity they knew and offering nothing in its place. While the Reformers brought the Word of God as the point of contact between God and man, the iconoclasts left nothing but blank church walls.

THE PREDESTINATION CONTROVERSY

The biblical teaching on predestination had first become an issue in the church through the teaching of Augustine in opposition to Pelagius. We have already seen that, while the church rejected the views of Pelagius, few were willing to go as far as the great bishop of Hippo had gone in affirming the sovereignty of God and the gracious nature of salvation. Instead, the church of the Middle Ages espoused a watered-down "semi-Augustinianism," proclaimed by the Council of Orange in 529 and disseminated by men such as Gregory the Great. The issue is one that the church has never really settled to the satisfaction of everyone, however. It became a major source of conflict during the Reformation, when Luther and Calvin emphasized the grace of God in salvation as opposed to the works orientation of Roman Catholicism. Later, it divided Protestants themselves, as Calvin and Arminius, Whitefield and Wesley, and many more argued about the roles of God and man in salvation.

In the early Middle Ages, the Semi-Augustinianism of the Catholic Church was challenged by one lonely voice that was quickly silenced. That voice belonged to a reluctant monk named Gottschalk (c.805-868). He was the son of a Saxon aristocrat whose parents sent him to the monastery at Fulda, founded less than a century before by the missionary Boniface, as a young child. His parents intended him to be a gift to God as the child Samuel had been in the Old Testament. He never got used to monastery life, however, and when he reached adulthood, he applied for release from his monastic vows on the ground that they had been taken for him by others, and the Synod of Mainz agreed in 829. His abbot, Rabanus Maurus, argued against him, however, and succeeded in getting the emperor to overturn the decision of the synod. From that point on, Rabanus Maurus became the implacable enemy of Gottschalk.

Though Gottschalk was denied permission to renounce his vows, he was allowed to transfer to a different monastery. There he began to study the writings of Augustine, and soon realized that the teachings of the church were seriously lacking on the question of salvation. He began instructing the monks in his monastery for hours on end, emphasizing the matter of predestination in particular. He also began traveling around Italy preaching his newfound doctrine. Rabanus Maurus, who had by this time become Archbishop of Mainz, soon heard of this, and wrote a long letter condemning the views of Gottschalk, though much of what he condemned was a misunderstanding of what Gottschalk was teaching (like so many over the years, he falsely concluded that the doctrine of predestination made God the author of evil, that it made God unfair, and that it encouraged loose living). Gottschalk was called before a synod in Mainz in 848, where he was condemned for teaching, among other things, that God predestined both the elect to salvation and all others to damnation ("double predestination") and that Christ had died only for the elect ("limited atonement"); he was also condemned for having had the effrontery to preach such doctrines to the general public throughout Italy rather than confining them to monastery discussions where they belonged.

Gottschalk was then turned over to Hincmar, Archbishop of Rheims, for punishment. If Rabanus Maurus hated Gottschalk because he wanted to leave the monastery, Hincmar hated him because he had been ordained by a mere country bishop rather than an archbishop like himself. He had Gottschalk flogged within an inch of his life and confined to a monastery prison. There he wrote several defenses of the doctrine of predestination, along with some religious poetry. He even offered to test his doctrine in a trial by ordeal (one of the grosser medieval superstitions - the proponents of two opposing views would step into cauldrons of boiling water, oil, fat, and pitch, then walk through a blazing fire; presumably, whoever survived was right), but none of his opponents took him up on it. He remained in prison for the rest of his life. Shortly before his death, he asked to take communion, but Hincmar refused unless he would recant his views. He would not do so, and died soon after. He was buried in unconsecrated soil. A number of noble men came to Gottschalk's defense, but not for theological reasons. Instead, they rightly objected to the brutal treatment he had received at the hands of jealous men who showed no indication of Christian virtues.

The Predestination Controversy contributed nothing to the church's theological understanding of an issue that had been argued better by Augustine himself and would later be discussed in much more thorough and biblical fashion by the Reformers. It is valuable to us mainly as it provides insight into the low level of theological understanding and Christian morality that characterized the early Middle Ages.

THE EUCHARISTIC CONTROVERSY

We have seen that ever since the closing centuries of the Ancient Church period, the church had been moving in the direction of an understanding of the Lord's Supper that emphasized Christ's physical presence in the sacrament, and saw the Mass as a repetition of the sacrifice of Christ on the cross. Though transubstantiation did not become the official position of the Catholic Church until 1215 when sanctioned by Pope Innocent III, it was during the early Middle Ages that the dispute was really settled in the minds of most.

In this controversy, both sides agreed that Christ was actually present in the Eucharist. What was disputed was the manner of His presence. Some, who took the biblical description of the Last Supper and Jesus' words in John 6 literally, taught that the bread and wine were really the body and blood of Christ. Others understood the words of Jesus in a figurative sense, and affirmed that He was present spiritually in the sacrament, but not physically. The theologians of the Ancient Church had used both types of language almost interchangeably (Augustine, not surprisingly, was claimed by both sides), but the growing superstition of the early Middle Ages had pushed the church in the direction of the literal interpretation. As with the Predestination Controversy, the Eucharistic Controversy was carried on at an appallingly low level, both intellectually and spiritually. As occurred again at the time of the Reformation, professing Christians fought, condemned, and tortured one another while arguing about what is supposed to be the most sublime example of God's unifying love.

The chief supporter of transubstantiation was Paschasius Radbertus (c.785-c.865), abbot of the monastery at Corbie in France. Though the term "transubstantiation" was not introduced until several centuries later, what Radbertus taught was essentially what the Catholic Church later affirmed. He asserted that the bread and wine of the mass become the body and blood of Christ when the priest utters the words of consecration, even though they continue to look, smell, and taste like bread and wine. This is the identical body that was born to the Virgin Mary and the identical blood that was shed on the cross. All those who take the sacrament receive the body and blood of Christ, but only those who eat in faith benefit; others receive only condemnation. Radbertus supported his position by the aforementioned Scripture references, quotations from the Fathers, and descriptions of various miracles (in one such miracle, the bread on the altar took on the shape of a lamb; an angel then descended from heaven with a knife, killed the lamb, and its blood spilled into the chalice).

One of Radbertus' fellow monks at Corbie was a man named Ratramnus, who became the leading opponent of the transubstantiation doctrine. He argued that the elements of the Mass remain bread and wine throughout, but that Christ is spiritually present, and is received by faith through the sacrament. He used an analogy with baptism, arguing that the water of baptism did not become the Holy Spirit, but that the one who was baptized received the Holy Spirit through the symbol of water. The Protestant Reformers later adopted many aspects of Ratramnus' arguments, though the Catholic Church rejected them.

Though no final settlement occurred at this time, the writings of Radbertus on the subject became increasingly influential, and opinion in the Catholic Church gradually swung in favor of transubstantiation. The superstition of the age brought the dispute to a disgustingly low level of argument. In the tenth century, for instance, the supporters of transubstantiation were defining the literal view of Christ's presence by describing in such detail the chewing and swallowing of Christ that occurred in the Mass as to make it sound positively cannibalistic. Opponents responded by saying that if the body of Christ had been chewed and swallowed, it would also be eliminated with the waste products of the human body - a prospect that no one found particularly attractive. The proponents of the literal view finally decided that the body and blood of Christ never became part of the bodily wastes, but instead were supernaturally retained by the body, making up the eternal resurrection body in which the believer would live forever. After a final round of argument between Berengar (spiritual) and Lanfranc (literal) in the twelfth century, transubstantiation won out in a decree issued by Innocent III in 1215, only to be challenged again by the Protestant Reformers of the sixteenth century.

Though the views of Ratramnus and Berengar sound in some ways like those later espoused by the Reformers, it is important to realize that both were thoroughly Catholic in their theology. The key is that both believed that the presence of Christ in the sacrament was tied to the words of the priest. Such teaching put an unbridgeable gap between the priesthood and the laity, and was the foundation of the power of the clergy in the Catholic Church. As long as Christ's presence could be brought about by the priest, he had the power of eternal life and death over his congregation. It was only the Protestant teaching of the priesthood of all believers that freed the church from its bondage at the hands of the clergy.

One final consideration in this chapter should be the role played in the Predestination and Eucharistic Controversies by the most subtle theological thinker of the early Medieval Church, John Scotus Erigena (c.810-c.877). Scotus Erigena was born in Ireland and, after training in a monastic school, became a fixture in the court of Charles the Bald, the grandson of Charlemagne who ruled France. The quiet scholar was believed by the ignorant men of his age to know everything there was to know, and was consulted about both of the theological controversies of the ninth century. Fortunately for him, few people understood his answers. He was a Neoplatonist with definite mystical tendencies. In response to the Predestination Controversy, he argued that there could be no predestination to sin and damnation, since evil does not have any real existence, but is simply the absence of good. Free will is part of the nature of God, and thus is absolute in man and cannot be lost. Like liberal theologians over a thousand years later, he argued that God's election extended to the entire human race, and thus all would ultimately be saved. Such an argument was too much even for the opponents of predestination; some accused him of heresy, and others merely thought him insane.

In the Eucharistic Controversy, Scotus Erigena predictably opposed the transubstantiation doctrine of Radbertus. As a Neoplatonist, he believed that there existed an eternal world of ideas, of which the material world provided only particular representations. Thus reality existed in the idea rather than in matter. Coming from such a philosophical perspective, he naturally concluded that the bread and wine were only an outward symbol of a spiritual reality. He argued that the body of Christ was omnipresent, and only in that sense was to be found in the bread of the Eucharist. Such teaching came perilously close to pantheism (the idea that God is everything and everything is God), a position that grows naturally from Neoplatonism and of which John Scotus Erigena has often been accused in the centuries following his death.

MAKING DRY BONES LIVE

The theological disputes of the early Middle Ages give us a good picture of one of the greatest dangers surrounding all theological disputes, and that is that Christians tend to discuss Christian truth in a very unchristian way. If they are not torturing and imprisoning one another, we find them issuing anathemas and consigning one another to the fires of hell. How can such things be?

Such ugly disputes occur because of the undeniable fact that doctrine is important. Contrary to the easy relativism prominent in our own day, what a person believes does matter. If Christianity is true, it makes a difference what people believe and how they live. It is those who take doctrine seriously who face the greatest temptation to use it as a club to bash in the heads of those who disagree with them. On the other hand, the desire to display Christian love in our attitude toward others should not lead us to the point of saying that anyone is free to believe whatever he chooses because it ultimately doesn't matter. The Christian must walk the very fine line of affirming that everyone is free to believe as he chooses, but it makes a great deal of difference what one chooses to believe.

In disputes among Christians themselves, great bitterness is often generated over "minor" issues. In one sense, it does seem absurd to argue about whether people are predestined to go to heaven or hell when all agree that the saved go to one while the unsaved go to the other, and to fuss about how Christ is present in the Lord's Supper when everyone agrees that He is indeed present. We must recognize, however, that it is dishonest and unrealistic to brush such issues aside as fundamentally inconsequential. The doctrine of predestination has great consequences for a person's understanding of salvation and his approach to evangelism, while we have already seen that the doctrine of transubstantiation has had a significant role in enhancing the power of the priesthood in the Catholic Church. Thus while disputes among Christians cannot and should not be shoved into a corner to be disputed by theologians and ignored by everyone else, it is important for Christians to discuss areas of difference with other Christians on the basis of a common love of Christ and a common salvation through His work on the cross. Paul told the Ephesians to speak the truth in love. When either truth or love is ignored, the church suffers.

FOR REVIEW AND FURTHER THOUGHT

1. Why was the early Middle Ages not a period of great theological development?

2. What is an icon? What is iconoclasm?

3. How did the Muslim Conquest help to start the Iconoclastic Controversy?

4. What were some of the arguments used against the worship of icons?

5. What were some of the arguments used in favor of the worship of icons?

6. Where did the Western Church stand in the Iconoclastic Controversy, which was largely an Eastern Church dispute?

7. How did the Iconoclastic Controversy damage relationships between the Eastern and Western Churches?

8. What role did the following people play in the Iconoclastic Controversy: Leo III, John of Damascus, Gregory III, Constantine V, Irene, Charlemagne, Theodora, and Methodius?

9. What is the doctrine of predestination?

10. What role did the following people play in the Predestination Controversy: Gottschalk, Rabanus Maurus, Hincmar, Augustine, and John Scotus Erigena?

11. What is transubstantiation?

12. How did the Eucharistic Controversy contribute to the power of the clergy in the Catholic Church?

13. What role did the following people play in the Eucharistic Controversy: Paschasius Radbertus, Ratramnus, Berengar, Lanfranc, Innocent III, Augustine, and John Scotus Erigena?

14. To what extent was the spiritual view in the Eucharistic Controversy adopted by the Protestant Reformers? To what extent was it distinctively Catholic?

15. Why is it so hard for Christians to display love while engaged in doctrinal controversies? Why is it important that they do so no matter how hard it may be?

12

FROM THE DEPTHS TO THE HEIGHTS

The year 897 witnessed a most unusual trial in the Church of St. Peter in Rome. Pope Stephen VII presided over the trial. The defendant was Pope Formosus, who had by that time been dead for nine months. Stephen, in fact, was so anxious to bring his predecessor to justice for the crimes he had committed that he had ordered the body of Formosus exhumed. So there he sat, bones and rotting flesh covered in papal robes, amidst the splendor of St. Peter's. Though a defense attorney stood by the side of the putrid corpse, no witnesses spoke out in his behalf. It was not surprising, then, that Formosus was convicted of treason and various other crimes. Stephen decreed that the three fingers of Formosus' hand, those used to confer the pontifical blessing, should be severed, and that the corpse should be stripped of its regalia and thrown out the window to the waiting crowd in the courtyard outside. The crowd, stirred to a frenzy by the supporters of Stephen, seized the corpse, dragged it through the city, and threw it in the Tiber River.

It was not easy being a pope in the Dark Ages. The same Pope Stephen who conducted the trial described above was later strangled in a prison cell. Yet the church survived such degradation to become the most potent force in all of Europe by the beginning of the thirteenth century. The history recounted in this chapter, which will focus largely on the ebb and flow of relationships between the church and the state from the ninth to the thirteenth centuries, provides the backdrop for the topics to be covered in succeeding chapters. It is in the context of the political maneuverings described here that the Great Schism occurs, the Crusades are fought, the philosophical approach to Christianity known as Scholasticism develops, and the monastic reforms change the face of the church. While much of what this chapter recounts may seem overly complex and appear to have little to do with true Christianity, an understanding of these events is necessary if we are to grasp the changes that occurred in the Catholic Church that ultimately set the stage for the Protestant Reformation.

THE ERA OF CHAOS (814-962)

Charlemagne, like Alexander the Great, had built a mighty empire that was totally dependent for its strength on the powerful personality of its founder. The Roman Empire had in its heyday emphasized unity, and succession controversies were fought out until one claimant to the throne survived to rule the empire as a whole. Among the Franks, however, the laws of inheritance required that a father's estate be divided among his heirs. For the Holy Roman Empire of Charlemagne, this meant fragmentation. The empire remained intact during the reign of Charlemagne's son, Louis the Pious (814-840), but upon his death was divided among his three sons. Charles the Bald was given territory roughly corresponding to modern France, Louis the German was given Germany, and Lothair inherited a narrow strip of land running from the North Sea to northern Italy, which served as a buffer between the other two. All three grandsons of Charlemagne wanted the whole thing, of course. After a few years of inconsequential fighting, they finally agreed to a truce and signed the Treaty of Verdun in 843, establishing the boundaries that laid the groundwork for the eventual emergence of the French and German nations. Lothair's descendants were eventually restricted to northern Italy, leaving the French and Germans to fight over eternally disputed territories such as

Alsace and Lorraine. Though these fragments of the Carolingian Empire survived for almost 150 years after the Treaty of Verdun, most of the rulers were so weak that Europe quickly became fragmented into semi-independent local entities ruled by feudal lords. The development of feudalism was largely a response to the weakness of the kings, and was necessitated by the frequent invasions of Europe by a new group of barbarians - the Vikings. These brutal Norsemen terrorized Europe, and farmers and townsmen in their path were quite willing to trade land for protection. Thus the system of economic decentralization known as feudalism developed.

These were not easy years for the church. It, too, became decentralized. As one of the major landholders of Europe, it became an integral part of the feudal system. This almost total identification of church and society was the basis for the conflicts between the competing powers of a centralized church and centralized states that were to emerge later in the Middle Ages.

In the ninth and tenth centuries, however, there was only one pope who came close to the exercise of universal authority. That pope was Nicholas I (858-867). Like the other great popes of the Middle Ages, Gregory VII and Innocent III, Nicholas was a pious and humble man in his personal life, but an unflinching foe to those who in his eyes threatened the authority of Christ and His church. Nicholas was invited to mediate a dispute in the Eastern Church when the emperor deposed Ignatius, the patriarch of Constantinople, and replaced him with the scholar Photius, a layman who was quickly ordained to the priesthood and elevated to one of the highest offices in the church within a period of less than a week. Nicholas believed he had the right to do more than mediate, however. After investigating, he deposed Photius and reinstated Ignatius, despite the fact that his own legates had been bribed to send back a report favoring Photius. Nicholas' attitude infuriated the Eastern Church, and contributed another block to the growing wall that eventually separated Constantinople from Rome.

In the West, Nicholas was a terror to king and bishop alike. He forced Lothair II, king of Lorraine, to take back his wife after he had divorced her to marry his mistress. Though Teutberga, the wife, was less than excited about returning to a situation that she called more of an imprisonment than a marriage, Nicholas proved that the threat of excommunication could force even kings to submit to the moral dictates of the church.

Nicholas also made good on his claim to be the head of all bishops in the church. Many of these feudal lords of the church were unwilling to yield to anyone within their jurisdictions, and they often treated their lower clergy with contempt. We have already had an opportunity to sample the cruelty of Archbishop Hincmar of Rheims in the sad case of Gottschalk and the Predestination Controversy. But Gottschalk was not the only underling to suffer at the hands of the arrogant Hincmar. Once Hincmar deposed and imprisoned Rothad, one of his oldest bishops, for no apparent good reason. Nicholas heard about the case and intervened, but Hincmar insisted that Nicholas had no jurisdiction in the case. Nicholas summoned Rothad to Rome and restored him to his office, while Hincmar stood by helplessly and fumed. Such an exercise of authority over the church was bolstered by a document known today as the Pseudo-Isidorean Decretals, which Nicholas was the first to use. These forgeries, which included the Donation of Constantine (see chapter ten), attempted to demonstrate that the popes had been given authority over the entire church from the very beginning, and had exercised that authority from the second century onward. While the forgery became one of the cornerstones of papal authority in the Middle Ages, it was originally devised by a group of monks or lower clergy in France, not for the purpose of making the pope an absolute monarch in the church, but to protect the monks and lower clergy from abuse by such despots as Hincmar by giving the popes a weapon to use against them.

After the death of Nicholas I, the papacy declined into utter chaos. The collapse of political power in Europe meant that the popes had no powerful protectors against those who would abuse the office for their own ends. The result was that, for the next hundred years, the

From the Depths to the Heights

papacy became a private political football, used for the amusement of a few powerful Italian families. During this time, the men who filled the office of pope were almost all unworthy and openly immoral. One example of this degradation of the highest office in the church is the one with which this chapter began. Two others will suffice to convey the character of this dismal era in the history of the church.

One example that illustrates the sorry state of the church in the ninth and tenth centuries is the curious legend of Pope Joan. Though most historians have since rejected the story as unreliable, the fact that it was widely believed in the Middle Ages shows the depths to which the reputation of the papacy had sunk. According to one version of the legend, a young English girl disguised her sex and entered a monastery. Monastery life was such that she was able to conceal her femininity successfully, and meanwhile her native intelligence and ability allowed her to rise through the ranks until finally, around the year 850, she ascended to the papal chair under the name of John. After serving for a little more than two years, her secret was discovered when she gave birth during a papal procession, and died shortly thereafter. The story was so commonly believed that her bust was included with that of other popes at Siena in the fifteenth century. Many scholars today believe that the legend was a veiled reference to the domineering Marozia (see below). Interestingly, some feminists have argued for the historicity of the legend as a means of advocating female participation in church office.

A second example may be taken from the period from 904 to 964, when the papacy was under the thumb of the Roman senatorial house of Theophylact. The situation would have been bad enough if the ruling family had only appointed their favorites and retainers to the papal chair, but it was made far worse by the fact that the family was dominated by two powerful women - Theodora, the wife of Theophylact, and her daughter Marozia. Their tendency to secure the papal throne for their lovers and illegitimate children has earned for this period in papal history the term "Pornocracy." The Pornocracy began when Marozia became the lover of Pope Sergius III in 904. The next dominant pope of the period, John X (914-928), was rumored to have been the lover of Theodora, who was many years his senior. Later John XI, the illegitimate son of Sergius and Marozia, ruled as pope from 931 to 935. Finally, Marozia's grandson Octavian brought infamy to the church as Pope John XII (955-964). John XII was the first pope to change his name upon entering office. His behavior was so outrageous that, when he was deposed, the charges against him included not only adultery and murder, but rape, incest, drinking to the health of Satan, and calling on Jupiter and Venus for help when he gambled with the church's money! He cared so little for the dignity of the papal office that he didn't even bother to show up for his trial, but went hunting instead.

THE ERA OF RECOVERY (962-1059)

The papacy was delivered at least temporarily from this morass by the German king Otto I. This "deliverance" turned out to be a mixed blessing, for while Otto and his descendants were conscientious enough to appoint men of some character to the papacy, the fact remained that the highest office of the church was still under political control. After Otto rescued the notorious John XII from political domination at the hands of Berengar II, the pope crowned him Holy Roman Emperor and pledged loyalty to him as the ruler of Rome. No sooner did Otto leave, however, than John began scheming against him. When Otto got word of the pope's deceit, he returned to Rome and deposed John at the trial mentioned in the preceding paragraph. Though John tried to regain his post, he eventually was murdered while in bed with a woman who was not his wife.

Otto I and his son and grandson, Otto II and Otto III, sought to place decent men in the papacy, but were forced to fight constant battles with the family of Crescentius and the Counts of Tusculum, two warring Roman families both of whom had links to the notorious Theophylacts. Even when the German emperors were able to put good men in office, they struggled against rival popes set up by the Roman aristocrats. It was during this period that the first non-Italians held the papacy. Bruno, the twenty-four year old cousin of Otto III, became the first German pope as Gregory V (996-999). He was followed by Gerbert, a French scholar and the greatest mind of his era, who served as Pope Sylvester II (999-1003). The reign of Sylvester II was one of both great hope and great confusion. The pope chose the name Sylvester after the name of the pope who had baptized Constantine, thus expressing his hope that the ancient empire was about to rise anew under his powerful patron Otto. The people, meanwhile, were fully convinced that the return of Christ was about to occur. Many years earlier, when Augustine had identified the present age with the Millennium, he had assumed that the thousand years mentioned in Revelation 20 were to be understood literally. Thus as the year 1000 approached, Europe went into a frenzy. Confessions were made, wrongs were righted, property was sold, and pilgrims flocked to the Holy Land to be there for the big event. But when the year came to a close without the return of Christ, Europe breathed a collective sigh of relief - now life could once again get back to normal.

"Normal," of course, meant chaos for the papacy. When Otto III died while still in his twenties, the Roman aristocrats again dominated the papal office. From 1012 to 1048, the papal chair was again in the hands of the Tusculans, descendants of the Theophylacts. Benedict VIII (1012-1024) and John XIX (1024-1032), two brothers, were succeeded by their twelve-year-old nephew, who ruled as Benedict IX (1032-1048), and rivaled John XII for the distinction as the worst of the clan. His record of debauchery was so bad that he was eventually driven from the city in 1044 and replaced by Sylvester III. He returned shortly afterward to retake the throne, but soon tired of the old game and sold the office to a layman named John Gratian who assumed the name of Gregory VI. Gregory was a sincerely spiritual man who had bought the papacy because of a desire to reform it. To him belongs the credit for bringing to Rome a monk named Hildebrand, the man largely responsible for restoring to the papacy a large measure of dignity. Shortly thereafter, however, Benedict again returned to Rome, meaning that there were now three men in the city who claimed to be pope. This disgraceful situation could not long endure, and again the German emperor was the one to step in and settle the matter.

Henry III, the Holy Roman Emperor, was a truly godly man who wanted to see the church restored to its historical position of dignity. He convened a council at Sutri near Rome that deposed Benedict IX and Sylvester III. The devout Gregory VI then resigned, saying that he was unworthy to hold the office of pope because he had purchased it for money, no matter that his motives had been noble. After appointing two men who died after only a few months, Henry arranged for a bishop with a deep desire to reform the church to take office as Leo IX in 1049. He urged Hildebrand to remain as his advisor, and the young monk soon became the power behind the papal throne. Despite the zeal of these reformers, however, the papacy remained a political tool of the emperor. All this was changed by Pope Nicholas II in 1059. At the urging of Hildebrand, the new pope made changes that removed both the emperor and the population of the city of Rome from the papal selection process. From this time forward, popes were to be chosen by the College of Cardinals. Cardinals were originally "cardinal bishops of Rome" - the bishops of the leading churches in and around the imperial city. Later, leading churchmen throughout Christendom were chosen, though technically they were still considered pastors of Roman churches in which they rarely appeared (a technicality still observed today, by the way). These churchmen became papal advisors, and by the decree of Nicholas II, papal electors. The emperors were removed from the selection process by placing it in the hands of the churchmen, who theoretically were less susceptible to political and monetary inducements. The Roman population was removed by a provision that allowed the election to take place outside the city of Rome in times of political turmoil. While Nicholas specifically stated that the emperor was to be informed of the decision as a matter of courtesy, and the people of Rome retained the right to approve the choice by acclamation (but not to reject it), the fact of the matter is that the new decree went a long way toward removing the papacy from political control by laymen. The end of control by the state, however, ushered in a period of bitter conflict with the state, initiated by Hildebrand himself and the young emperor Henry IV.

THE ERA OF DOMINANCE (1059-1216)

Medieval society was a two-headed monster. Christendom had two leaders, one secular - the emperor - and one sacred - the pope. Theoretically, the two should have been able to work together to provide leadership for a Christian society. In practice, it never happened. The popes believed that they were Christ's representatives on earth, and that even the emperors should submit to their spiritual fathers. The emperors, on the other hand, believed that God had independently established the authority of the state, and that churchmen should submit to them as their feudal lords and protectors. Something had to give somewhere, and in Henry IV and Hildebrand, who ascended the papal throne in 1073 as Gregory VII, the irresistible force met the immovable object.

The reformers led by Hildebrand wanted to clean up the church. Freedom from political domination was only a means to an end. The ultimate goal was to produce a church that was both pure and powerful. The two major evils targeted for change by the reformers were the practices of simony and Nicolaitanism. Nicolaitanism was a name taken from the heresy described in Revelation 2-3, which was applied with no biblical warrant in the Middle Ages to sexual immorality among the clergy. Of course, to the reformers, sexual immorality did not just include adultery and fornication, it also included lawful marriage. Hildebrand and his cohorts insisted on clerical celibacy. One reason for this was the traditional one, that married men were in no position to devote their entire attention to the cause of Christ. Another aspect of the problem, however, was the fact that many church offices had become hereditary, being passed down from father to son through several generations. The reformers wanted all church officers to be directly under the authority of the pope. In their minds, this demanded that absolute celibacy become a requirement. Attempts to enforce celibacy were incredibly unpopular. Many argued that forbidding marriage for the clergy would simply increase the amount of immorality being practiced. Numerous priests left the priesthood rather than desert their families, while others simply ignored the papal dictum under the protection of their political sovereigns.

Simony, named after the sorcerer in Acts 8 who tried to buy the gift of the Holy Spirit, was the practice of buying and selling church offices. In the feudal system, church lands were held as fiefs under secular rulers, and these rulers would often raise money by selling them to the highest bidder. Because such rulers would also often give church lands and the accompanying offices to sons of nobles they wished to reward, the practice of lay investiture, which involved a church officer receiving his authority from a laymen, was also labeled as simony by the reformers. Stamping out simony was not going to be easy, however. When the Synod of Rome in 1049 declared excommunication as the penalty for simony, the outcry was so great that the reformers quickly reduced the penalty to a forty-day suspension when they realized that strict enforcement would soon leave the church without leaders. They didn't give up, though, as the clash between Hildebrand and Henry IV demonstrated.

When Hildebrand became Pope Gregory VII in 1073, the power behind the throne for twenty-five years now occupied that position for which he had been pulling the strings from behind the scenes. He believed that as pope he held in his hands all power, both spiritual and secular. He described the pope as the sun and the emperor as the moon, which was lesser in brilliance and derived its light from the sun. It was not long before he had the opportunity to put his theory into practice. In 1075, he called a synod that strictly forbade any layman from selling or giving a church office to anyone, forbade priests and bishops from receiving the insignia of their office from laymen, and prohibited anyone from receiving the sacraments from a priest or bishop who had received office through lay investiture. The same synod also excommunicated five of the counselors of the young emperor Henry IV for engaging in simony (the term used by Gregory for lay investiture). Henry realized that if he had no right to demand feudal loyalty from the bishops in his empire, almost half of his own land would be removed from his control, since the church controlled a significant portion of the land in Europe. Henry responded by restoring his counselors and continuing to practice simony openly. When Gregory threatened him with excommunication, Henry had the pope kidnapped and locked in a tower, from which the people of Rome soon released him. Henry then called a council that deposed the pope on the basis of all sorts of false and scandalous charges (Gregory may have been many things, but scandalous he most certainly was not). Henry then wrote to the College of Cardinals and invited them to elect a new pope. When the letter arrived, Gregory promptly excommunicated Henry, declared that he was no longer emperor, and absolved his subjects from their oaths of loyalty to him.

These were not empty words. The men of the Middle Ages took their religion seriously, and they were not about to follow an emperor who had just been consigned to the fires of hell by the head of the church. Furthermore, there were plenty of German nobles around who were more than ready to take Henry's place at the head of the Holy Roman Empire. Henry soon found that he had bitten off more than he could chew. His subjects were ready to overthrow him, and he realized that the only solution, unpalatable as it must have been, was to beg Gregory for forgiveness.

Henry knew he had to move quickly. Gregory was on his way to Augsburg to meet with some of the rebellious nobles. Henry took his wife and infant son and attempted a winter crossing of the Alps in the hope that he could reach Gregory before he got to Augsburg. The emperor caught up with the pope at the castle of Canossa in the Italian Alps. Gregory knew what was going on and realized that he had an obligation to forgive anyone who repented, but he was not about to give in easily. He forced Henry to stand in the courtyard of the castle for three days, barefoot in the snow, before admitting him, receiving his submission, and restoring him to the church and to his empire.

Despite the apparently total defeat experienced by Henry in this humiliation before the pope, he was not ready to quit just yet. He returned home to put down the rising rebellion, only to find that Gregory had awarded the empire to his chief rival, Rudolf. He then called a council in the town of Brixen to depose the pope and appoint a new one, Archbishop Wibert of Ravenna, who had earlier been excommunicated by Gregory on charges of simony. Now both Henry and Gregory had ambitious rivals with whom to contend. Henry was nearly defeated by Rudolf, but the latter was killed after victory in a decisive battle. Henry then took his army and headed for Rome, intent on removing Gregory and putting Wibert in his place. Gregory called on the Norman chieftain Robert Guiscard for help, but he did more harm than good. After entering the city, he and his men looted, burned, and raped, and Gregory was forced to flee into exile, where he died in 1085. His last recorded words were, "I have loved righteousness and hated iniquity, therefore I die in exile."

The death of Gregory did not mean victory for Henry, however. He wound up being driven from his throne by his own sons, and he too died in exile. The conflict over lay investiture was finally resolved by compromise with the Concordat of Worms in 1122. By this agreement, bishops were to receive their ecclesiastical authority from the pope and their feudal authority from the emperor. Similar agreements were made at about the same time in France and England.

Compromise did not mean peace, however. In the years that followed, church and state continued to struggle for the supremacy of Europe. In the century following the epic battle waged by Gregory and Henry, other notable conflicts developed. In England, archbishops of Canterbury such as Lanfranc and Anselm sought to impose the reform on the Norman conquerors, and Thomas à Becket quarrelled with Henry II over the right of the church to try clergy who broke the civil law. In the Holy Roman Empire, Pope Adrian IV, the only Englishman ever to hold the office, humbled Emperor Frederick Barbarossa by forcing him to kiss his foot, hold the stirrup of his horse, and lead him through St. Peter's Square on foot, while Frederick retaliated by convincing the jurists of the famous law school in Bologna to declare that the emperor's power was independently granted by God, and was not in any way dependent on the good graces of the pope.

These squabbles were mere preliminaries, however, to the reign of the most powerful pope in history. That honor belongs to Lothario, who as Innocent III (1198-1216) was more successful at putting into practice the papal claims of supremacy over secular rulers than anyone before or since. Lothario excelled in his studies of theology and canon law, and was named a cardinal at the age of twenty-nine. Despite being the youngest of the cardinals, he was given immediate responsibility, and was often asked to try the most complicated cases brought before the curia. He soon found that other cardinals sat in on his cases simply to hear him expound obscure points of law, and even those who lost their cases applauded his skill and brilliance. Everyone knew he was destined for greatness, and when Celestine III died in 1198, Lothario was quickly named to take his place, and ascended the papal throne as Innocent III.

Like Gregory VII before him a humble and devout man, Innocent made no bones about his view of papal authority. He not only borrowed Gregory's image about the sun and the moon, he expanded it. Previous popes had called themselves Vicars of St. Peter; Innocent called himself the Vicar of Christ. Believing he possessed the authority of Christ Himself, he was not reluctant to put it to what he saw as good use.

Shortly before Innocent became pope, the Holy Roman Emperor died at the age of thirty-two, leaving behind him a two-year-old son and heir. Innocent quickly moved into the confusion, played rivals off against one another, convinced the widow to submit to his authority, and upon her death a year later, took the child Frederick in as his personal ward. Thus Innocent for all practical purposes became the emperor until the child grew old enough to rule on his own. Clever as this appeared to be at the time, the move ultimately failed to ensure papal dominance. Frederick II grew up to be his own man, making Innocent's last years difficult ones and making life miserable for a succession of popes thereafter.

Innocent felt free to interfere in any political situation where the cause of Christ was at stake - and to Innocent, that meant any political situation at all. He once overturned the results of a German election because, though one candidate had garnered a majority of the votes, Innocent decreed that the loser had gotten the "saner" votes. Amazingly enough, Innocent's decision carried the day. His most famous conflict, however, was with the disreputable King John of England. John had usurped the throne while his brother Richard the Lion-Hearted was in the Holy Land on a crusade, and had immediately proceeded to make himself grossly unpopular with his subjects. Being unpopular with his subjects was nothing compared to getting on the wrong side of the pope, however, as he found out when he tried to appoint a new archbishop of Canterbury without Innocent's approval. Innocent nullified John's selection and instead installed Stephen Langton, a capable and scholarly English cardinal. John responded by confiscating the Canterbury monastery and accusing the monks of treason. Innocent's answer was to place England under interdict. What this meant was that no sacraments could be performed throughout the entire country with the exception of baptism and last rites. Men could not be ordained, married, or buried with the church's blessing. Mass could not be said, nor could confessions be heard. In a church where men were taught that the saving grace of God was communicated through the sacraments, this was a grave situation indeed. Yet John continued to be stubborn. A year later, Innocent excommunicated John, but he still held his ground. Finally, four years later in 1212, Innocent played his last card. He deposed John, and not only declared the throne of England vacant, but also invited Philip Augustus of

France to cross the English Channel and take it for himself. Philip gladly agreed, and began to prepare his army for the crossing. The combination of the threat of invasion, four years of popular unrest that was by now on the verge of panic, and a king who was unpopular and incompetent to begin with finally had the desired effect on the English barons. They forced John to give in to the pope or else abdicate his throne. In 1213, John humbled himself before Innocent's representative, offering England to the pope and receiving it back again as a fief, while agreeing to pay an annual rent of a thousand marks (the combination of the humiliation and the rent helped gain popular support for Henry VIII's break with Rome over three hundred years later).

One interesting sidelight of this whole conflict was that the English barons, now conscious of the power they held over the king, forced him two years later to sign the Magna Carta. Innocent strenuously objected to this document, claiming that the king had signed it under duress (as if the submission of 1213 had not been!). In fact, Innocent was much more comfortable with a corrupt king who wielded absolute power within his domain than with nobles who were getting their first whiff of constitutional democracy.

Innocent was also responsible for convening the Fourth Lateran Council in 1215, which ended the Eucharistic Controversy by ruling in favor of and defining transubstantiation, established the Inquisition as a tool to be used against the Waldensians and Albigensians, and granted a papal charter to the Franciscan monastic order. When Innocent died a year later, he was the most powerful man in Europe. No pope would ever reach such heights again. Many tried, but political conditions were changing. Soon threats of interdict and excommunication would no longer motivate nobles to revolt against their kings, and popes would again become the puppets of powerful monarchs.

MAKING DRY BONES LIVE

The events of the ninth through the thirteenth centuries seem like they must have happened in another world to most modern citizens of a secular society. It is difficult for us to conceive of a society where everyone believes that God is real, and that He rules over the affairs of this world. We are so used to that kind of thinking being a minority opinion that we can't imagine what it would be like for everyone to think that way. If the events of the Middle Ages are any indication, it was certainly no paradise. The universal belief in the rule of God became the basis for bitter power struggles among His representatives on earth. Things were done in the name of God that were anything but godly, and His church was turned almost entirely away from the spiritual realm to a concern with the affairs of this world (though as we will see in later chapters, this was mercifully not the case for all).

There are at least two lessons to be learned from this. The first is that such a world has passed from the scene forever. We will never live in a world where all men acknowledge God until Christ Himself returns and all men bow before Him. The example of the Middle Ages shows us that there is little reason to mourn its passing. When all claim to be Christians, it is difficult to recognize the enemy. At least Christians today can understand what Jesus meant when He said that His kingdom was not of this world, and that the way to life is a narrow one found only by a relative few. The cause of Christ is not served by those who would seek to dominate the world in His name.

The second lesson is that Christians today often do not have a sufficient grasp of the direct involvement of God in the affairs of this world. God is not a God of the past and the future, who did great things once upon a time and will one day come to earth and fulfill amazing prophecies, but who is now on vacation. God is indeed in charge, as the men of the Middle Ages sincerely believed Him to be. The fact that all men no longer believe this does not mean that Christians should not act as if it were true. It is too easy for us to forget that Christ is the King, even though the pope is not, and even though secular rulers no longer tremble at the threat of judgment.

From the Depths to the Heights

FOR REVIEW AND FURTHER THOUGHT

1. How did the Frankish laws of inheritance contribute to the collapse of Charlemagne's empire?

2. What was the relationship between the Viking raids and the growth of feudalism?

3. How did the Treaty of Verdun contribute to the eventual establishment of national boundaries in Western Europe?

4. How did the church get to be part of the feudal system?

5. How did Nicholas I attempt to exert his authority over the Eastern Church? over kings in the West? over his own bishops and archbishops?

6. Why were the forgeries known as the Pseudo-Isidorean Decretals written? For what purpose were they used?

7. What was the Pornocracy, and why was it given that name?

8. In what way was Otto I's interference in papal affairs beneficial to the church? In what way was it harmful?

9. Why did many people in Europe believe that Christ was coming back in the year 1000 A.D.?

10. What role did Sylvester III play in the reform of the church?

11. What change was made in 1059 in an attempt to remove the papacy from the control of politicians and the Roman mob?

12. What is a cardinal?

13. Why were the church and state unable to work together in harmony in leading the society of medieval Europe?

14. What were simony and Nicolaitanism? Why did the popes oppose them and the emperors favor them?

15. What is lay investiture? What compromise was eventually reached on the practice in the Holy Roman Empire?

16. Evaluate the behavior of Henry IV and Gregory VII in their conflict over lay investiture.

17. What is an interdict? Why was it such a powerful weapon in the hands of the popes?

18. How did Innocent III force the submission of King John of England? Why did he oppose the Magna Carta?

13

RENDING THE SEAMLESS ROBE

The four great marks traditionally associated with the true church, and which the Roman Catholic Church continues to claim to the present day, are unity, holiness, catholicity, and apostolicity. These marks were used to distinguish the church from various heretical groups in the early years (for instance, the apostolicity of the church was a potent defense against Gnosticism, while the unity of the church was argued against the Donatists). In the year 1054, however, the visible unity of the church was irremediably destroyed when Cardinal Humbert, the legate of Pope Leo IX, ceremoniously placed a bull of excommunication on the altar of the Church of Holy Wisdom (Hagia Sophia) in Constantinople, excluding from the church the patriarch of Constantinople and all who followed him. Shortly thereafter, the patriarch, Michael Cerularius, excommunicated the members of the papal delegation and anathematized the pope himself, not realizing that Leo had died months earlier. With these mutual excommunications, the seamless robe of Christ to which the church liked to compare itself was forever rent asunder.

THE CAUSES OF THE SCHISM

When the mutual excommunications occurred in 1054, few people noticed. The reason for this is that the churches of the East and West had been growing apart for centuries, and each had already developed an attitude of thorough contempt for the other. Furthermore, the death of Leo IX had left the binding nature of the action taken by his legates in question. As a result, only those who look back over centuries of history see the events of 1054 as constituting a major turning point in the history of the church. For the people of that day, it was business as usual. What, then, were some of the causes of the separation between the churches that had grown so serious by the eleventh century that such a serious matter as mutual excommunication could pass with little notice?

A. POLITICAL RIVALRY

Aside from the Muslims, who posed a constant threat, the main rivals for power in the Mediterranean world of the Middle Ages were the Byzantine emperor in the East and the Holy Roman Emperor (first Frankish, then German) in the West. While the Eastern Church was almost completely dominated by the caesaropapism of Byzantium, the popes in the West both helped and were helped by the Holy Roman Emperors, at least until they became rivals for power in their own right. In the early Middle Ages, the popes were technically agents of the Byzantine Empire in Italy. Thus when the popes turned to the Franks for support after Byzantine Emperor Leo III removed much of Italy from papal jurisdiction and placed it under the patriarch of Constantinople, they were actually committing treason against their emperor. Until the fall of the Byzantine Empire in 1453, the two emperors continued to uphold competing claims for the crown of ancient Rome, a dream after which the medieval mind never stopped groping. Thus the churches of East and West were divided by competing political loyalties.

B. DIFFERENCES IN LANGUAGE AND CULTURE

The same linguistic and cultural barrier that had begun to separate the churches of the East and West as early as the fourth century continued to grow as the years passed. The culturally rich oriental potentates of the East viewed the Westerners as barbarians. Even a man such as Charlemagne, who gave his name to a rebirth of learning in the West, was viewed as an uncultured boor by the Byzantines because of his illiteracy. And if Charlemagne was thought to be uncultured, what about the popes of the Dark Ages? By the eleventh century, the East had written off the West as being totally devoid of learning.

The other side of the coin was that the West considered themselves practical in contrast to the perpetual theological wrangling of the Greeks in Byzantium. They rightly pointed out that the Greeks were great at starting arguments, but rarely were able to settle them, while the popes in Rome, for all their shortcomings, at least could settle disputes. If the East viewed the West as ignorant, the West looked upon the East as being stagnant and impotent.

C. DIFFERENCES IN THEOLOGY

The theological differences that separated the Eastern and Western churches began as far back as the time of Augustine. While the two main branches of Christendom agreed on the conclusions of the ecumenical councils concerning the Trinity and the relationship of the humanity and deity of Christ, the two parted ways over the doctrine of salvation. From the time of Augustine on, the West's view of salvation centered on the work of redemption, though the Roman Catholic Church was never completely comfortable with Augustine's emphasis on the sovereign grace of God in salvation. The East, on the other hand, continued to view salvation in terms of what was taught by men such as John Chrysostom - an incarnational emphasis that said essentially that God became man in order that man might become like God.

For all practical purposes, then, the Eastern Church never went beyond Chalcedon in its theological understanding. While the Roman Catholic Church grappled with the questions raised by the Protestant Reformation and, at least from a Protestant point of view, came up with all the wrong answers, the Eastern Church never even asked the questions. While the Eastern Church considered the ecumenical councils of the Ancient Church to have achieved such a state of theological perfection that any further development could represent nothing but decline, the West continued to struggle with its understanding of Christ and His Church, and in the process grew farther and farther away from the Eastern Orthodox.

In addition to the general theological trends in the two churches, there were also specific disputes that drove a wedge between them. We have already looked at the Iconoclastic Controversy in chapter eleven. Though this was almost totally a dispute within the Eastern Church, the continual sniping and criticism of the popes in the West did nothing to improve relationships between the two branches of the church. Things only got worse when the illiterate Charlemagne responded to the Ecumenical Council of Nicea of 787, which found in favor of the use of icons in worship, by rejecting its conclusions out of hand and presuming to instruct the learned doctors of the East through the mouths of his untutored bishops.

The other major theological dispute that separated the two branches of the church is known as the Filioque Controversy. The argument centered around whether the Holy Spirit proceeded from the Father alone (the position of the Eastern Church), or whether He proceeded from the Father and the Son (the position of the Western Church). The controversy got its name from the Latin word *filioque* ("and the Son"), which was added to the Nicene Creed's description of the Holy Spirit in the West. The argument seems absurd enough on its face, but further explanation only makes it more so. Both churches agreed that the Holy

THE PRIMARY CAUSES OF THE EAST-WEST SCHISM OF 1054

CAUSE	EASTERN CHURCH	WESTERN CHURCH
POLITICAL RIVALRY	Byzantine Empire	Holy Roman Empire
CLAIMS OF PAPACY	Patriarch of Constantinople was considered second in primacy to Bishop of Rome.	Bishop of Rome claimed supremacy over the entire church.
THEOLOGICAL DEVELOPMENT	Stagnated after Council of Chalcedon.	Continued to change and grow through controversies and expansion.
FILIOQUE CONTROVERSY	Declared that the Holy Spirit proceeds from the Father.	Declared that the Holy Spirit proceeds from the Father and the Son.
ICONOCLASTIC CONTROVERSY	Engaged in 120-year dispute over the use of icons in worship; finally concluded they could be used (statues prohibited).	Made constant attempts to interfere in what was purely an Eastern dispute (statues permitted).
DIFFERENCES IN LANGUAGE AND CULTURE	Greek/Oriental	Latin/Occidental
CLERICAL CELIBACY	Lower clergy were permitted to marry.	All clergy were required to be celibate.
OUTSIDE PRESSURES	Muslims constricted and put continual pressure on Eastern church.	Western barbarians were Christianized and assimilated by Western church.
MUTUAL EXCOMMUNICATIONS OF 1054	Michael Cerularius anathematized Pope Leo IX after having been excommunicated by him.	Leo IX excommunicated Patriarch Michael Cerularius of Constantinople.

Spirit was co-equal and co-eternal with the Father and the Son; furthermore, both churches agreed that the Holy Spirit had been sent into the world by both the Father and the Son. What, then, was the point of disagreement? The two churches differed over their understanding of the relationships among the members of the Trinity in eternity. Though the Spirit was eternal in the same way as the Father and the Son, who was to be thought of as the eternal source of the eternal Spirit? The Eastern Church maintained that it was the Father alone, or else the Trinity would be divided by having two sources; for the Western Church, the Spirit must proceed from both the Father and the Son or else it would seem to imply that the Son was in some sense subordinate to the Father.

This hardly seems like the stuff of which church splits are made. Cooler heads on both sides frequently acknowledged that it makes little difference in the long run whether the Holy Spirit is said to proceed from the Father, from the Son, or from the Father through the Son. Yet the dispute persisted, growing more bitter as the years passed, and as usual, there were political conflicts at the root of the problem.

The insertion of the disputed word in the Nicene Creed was first made at the Synod of Toledo in Spain in 589. The change at the time applied only to the churches in Spain, and was done largely in response to the continued presence of the Adoptionist heresy, which denied the full deity of Christ, in that country. Charlemagne later favored the insertion, though when he appealed to the pope to include it in the creed, the pope refused, though he agreed with the concept, because he considered the creed to be inviolate.

The dispute between Pope Nicholas I and Photius changed the picture drastically, however. In the previous chapter we saw that Nicholas I had been invited to mediate a dispute between Ignatius, the deposed patriarch of Constantinople, and Photius, the scholar who had been appointed in his place. Nicholas had rather high-handedly deposed Photius and restored Ignatius to his office. Photius did not take this lying down, however. In response to the pope's action, he charged the Western church, and the pope along with it, with heresy because of their acceptance of what was now called "the double procession" - in other words, the *filioque* in the Nicene Creed. The West was now forced to defend its position, and in the years following Nicholas, the insertion was accepted by churches all over the West, and finally approved for inclusion in the creed by the pope himself, probably during the reign of Benedict VIII (1014-1015). Thus the stage was set for the division of Christendom over a single Latin word. The battle lines were hardened to the extent that, to the present day, they remain an insuperable barrier to union. The East refuses to retract their charges of heresy unless the West removes its insertion into the greatest of the ecumenical creeds, and meanwhile views the double procession as the root of all theological error. The West, on the other hand, sees the question as one of papal authority over the church as a whole, and cannot retract the filioque without admitting that the popes were in error on a theological issue. Thus the division remains.

D. DIFFERENCES IN PRACTICE

If the theological disputes that divided the churches seem trivial, the practical issues are even more so. Yet any difference becomes for those who are convinced of the complete rightness of their own cause a basis for condemnation of any who disagree in the slightest particular. Perhaps the most serious of the practical differences between East and West lay in the matter of priestly celibacy. The East permitted lower clergy to marry, while insisting that bishops remain celibate (thus insuring that the vast majority of their higher clergy would be drawn from the ranks of the monasteries). In the West, total celibacy of all priests was a rule that was honored more in the breach than in the observance, especially during the scandalous days of the Dark Ages. Ironically, the Hildebrandine reform, with its emphasis on enforcing the church's standard of celibacy, drove a deeper wedge between the churches of East and West, since the insistence on celibacy in the West was viewed as unbiblical by the East, while the West viewed the East as sanctioning Nicolaitanism.

Other differences included variation in clerical vestments (robes worn by priests), minor disagreements about the liturgy (for instance, the West did not sing the Hallelujah during Lent), and the fact that the Western churches fasted on Saturday during Lent while the churches of the East did not. The Eastern churches also accused the West of violating the provisions of Acts 15 by eating animals that had been strangled, and claimed that they were reverting to Jewish practice by using unleavened bread during the mass. The West, in turn, accused the East of delaying baptism until the eighth day to conform with the Jewish practice of circumcision, and having the temerity to rebaptize those from the West who joined churches in the East. All these differences, needless to say, became important only because of the amount of animosity already existing between the churches.

E. RESPONSE TO OUTSIDE PRESSURES

Outside pressures also served to drive the churches of the East and West apart. In the West, the pressures came largely from barbarian tribes, from the Goths and Huns of the fourth century to the Viking invaders of the ninth and tenth centuries. The Western church was immensely successful in Christianizing these barbarians, though the depth and reality of the conversions that occurred remains at best an open question. At the same time that the conversion of the barbarians was expanding the territory, power, and influence of the Western church, it was changing that church and moving it farther and farther from the traditions and culture of the East.

Meanwhile, the Eastern church was facing terrible pressure from the Muslim invasions. While the West was converting barbarians, the East was seeing an appalling number of its adherents converting to Islam. While the territory of the Western church was continually expanding, the Eastern church saw its own sphere of influence continually shrinking under the persistent assaults of the Muslims. The failure to deal effectively with the Muslim threat both forced the Byzantines into a defensive shell and placed them in a position where they almost had to beg for help from the vigorous rulers of the West. Such humiliation could do little but increase their hatred of the Western barbarians.

F. THE CLAIMS OF THE PAPACY

All of the reasons discussed so far are nothing more than blowing smoke compared to the one insuperable barrier that separated the churches. As long as the pope claimed to be the supreme head of the church on earth, the churches of the East could never give him complete allegiance. While the Eastern church was willing to recognize the pope as first among equals in terms of primacy, they were not ready to acknowledge that the primacy of the Bishop of Rome carried with it supreme authority over the other patriarchs. Thus every attempt by a pope to interfere in the affairs of the Eastern church was viewed as just another exercise of papal arrogance. The claims of the pope to infallibility and supremacy continue today to divide the churches. Agreement might be possible in all other areas (for instance, certain Eastern rite congregations associated with the Roman church are permitted to retain married clergy), but even the conciliatory spirit of Vatican II is not enough to break down the barrier that the Roman Catholic view of the papacy has erected between the churches of East and West.

THE SCHISM OF 1054

When the reform movement in the Roman church gained control with the election of Leo IX in 1049, the energetic new patriarch immediately tried to bring as much of the church as possible within the scope of his reforms. One of his first targets was southern Italy - the same region that had been removed from papal jurisdiction by Leo III during the Iconoclastic Controversy. The territory was now under the control of the Normans, but despite the fact that these descendants of the Vikings had been converted to Christianity, they were systematically brutalizing priests, monks, nuns, and Christians in general in their domain. Michael Cerularius, a man no less ambitious and capable than Leo, had become patriarch of Constantinople in 1043, and wanted southern Italy under his control as much as Leo did. Complicating matters further was the fact that the region contained churches that observed the doctrines and forms of worship characteristic of both major rivals.

Leo immediately attempted to impose celibacy on the married clergy of the region. Meanwhile, Leo of Ochrida, the Metropolitan of Bulgaria who was an associate of Michael Cerularius, wrote a letter to the churches of southern Italy warning them against the terrible heresies being perpetuated by the pope and the Western Christians. When Pope Leo visited the region himself to try to win support, he was captured and imprisoned by the Normans. While a captive, he wrote a letter to the patriarch of Constantinople demanding his submission, and sent the letter by the hand of three legates, chief of whom was the ardent reformer Cardinal Humbert.

The result of this visit was the mutual excommunication described at the beginning of the chapter. When Michael Cerularius refused to submit, Humbert issued the papal bull of excommunication, unaware that the pope who had empowered him to serve it had died three months earlier. Cerularius in turn excommunicated the legates, and the breach was complete.

ATTEMPTS TO REPAIR THE SCHISM

Despite the mutual animosity that characterized the two churches, both wanted the schism to be repaired. The West, because of its belief in the unity of the church and the ambition of the popes, wanted Christendom united. The patriarchs and emperors of the East, though they considered themselves to be Orthodox in contrast to the heretics of the West, knew that the Byzantine Empire could not survive the continued onslaught of the Muslims without help from the West. Several attempts were thus made to heal the breach, though they ultimately proved to be fruitless, and often made matters worse instead.

The Crusades were the first of these efforts at reconciliation. The popes were convinced that if the Muslims could be driven out of the Holy Land, the Eastern Orthodox churches would submit to papal authority and the church would again be one. As we will see in the next chapter, however, the mistrust between representatives of the two churches was simply too great. Cooperation became impossible in the light of the bitterness that characterized many of the participants. The final indignity came when the Crusaders actually sacked Constantinople in 1204 and established a Roman patriarch in competition with the Eastern Orthodox patriarch of Constantinople. On top of everything else, the Crusades ultimately failed to remove the Muslim threat, but so weakened the Byzantine Empire as to accelerate its fall.

It became increasingly evident, however, that the Byzantine Empire required Western help in order to survive. As the emperors of the East became more and more desperate, they became increasingly willing to submit to the Roman point of view on theological matters in the hope that the armies of the West could deliver them from what appeared to be certain destruction. Emperors such as Michael Palaeologus at the Council of Lyons in 1274, Manuel Palaeologus on his visit to Paris and London around 1400, and John VII at the Council of Ferrara in 1438 offered total capitulation to the Western position in return for military salvation. Though spirits were high and many were optimistic, nothing ever came of these agreements. In the West, the popes were unwilling to encourage military adventures in the Eastern Mediterranean. Unlike the era of the Crusades, the late Middle Ages was a time of increasingly aggressive and powerful secular monarchs, and the last thing the pope wanted was a Holy Roman Emperor or French king who controlled both ends of the Mediterranean. In the East, the clergy rejected as capitulations the compromises worked out by the emperors. The agreements became worthless pieces of paper, and Constantinople fell to the Turks in 1453, bringing the Byzantine Empire to an end.

RESULTS OF THE SCHISM

In the West, the schism unquestionably increased the power of the popes. Though they still faced numerous struggles with the secular powers of kings and emperors, they had no serious rivals on the religious front, though the domain over which they exercised power had become smaller through the exodus of the Eastern Orthodox churches. Their unquestioned authority was to be short-lived, however, as the councils of the fifteenth century and the Reformation of the sixteenth century would amply demonstrate.

The schism and the fall of the Byzantine Empire that followed drove the Orthodox churches of the East further into isolation. They have never gone beyond Chalcedon in the realm of theology, and have never known either Renaissance or Reformation. The conversion of Vladimir of Russia in 988 meant that the Orthodox Church had a place to go after the fall of Constantinople, but the rise of Moscow as the Third Rome has done little to change the character of Orthodoxy. The caesaropapism of the Eastern Church has simply been passed on from the Byzantine emperors to the Russian czars to the Soviet dictators. The Eastern Orthodox Church is as much a tool of the state today as it was a thousand years ago.

Interestingly enough, the entrance of the Russian Orthodox Church into the World Council of Churches in 1961 produced a nice bit of irony. The state-dominated church only sent those representatives abroad who adhered to the party line, of course, so the Russian Orthodox were voices of leftist political radicalism in an organization known for its radical politics. On the other hand, the theological tradition of the Russian Orthodox Church has made it one of the most theologically conservative bodies in the WCC, although that is not really saying much.

Today, the claims of the papacy remain the major barrier dividing the Roman Catholic and Eastern Orthodox Churches. Despite the fact that the mutual excommunications of Leo IX and Michael Cerularius in 1054 were lifted by Pope Paul VI and Patriarch Athenagoras of Constantinople in 1965, the churches remain far apart, though their actual differences are of a relatively trivial nature.

MAKING DRY BONES LIVE

The sad saga of the schism contains many lessons that could be of value for us in the church today. Perhaps one of the most useful may be learned from the development, or lack thereof, experienced by the Eastern Church throughout the Middle Ages and beyond. Though we readily affirm that the Christian faith is an unchanging faith based upon the unchanging revelation of an unchanging God, the fact remains that a church that does not grow soon dies. The Eastern Orthodox Church believed that it had come to a complete and perfect understanding of doctrine, and thus in effect stopped thinking and criticizing itself. As a result, the church today is little more than a relic of ancient tradition. We must understand that, though God is perfect, our understanding and application of His Word is not. This one fact requires us to fight stagnation, to reevaluate ourselves and our churches on a constant basis, in order to grow more and more like Christ Himself. What the Apostle Paul said about himself as an individual may appropriately be applied to churches as well: "Not that I have already obtained all this, or have already been made perfect, but I press on to take hold of that for which Christ Jesus took hold of me. Brothers, I do not consider myself yet to have taken hold of it. But one thing I do: Forgetting what is behind and straining toward what is ahead, I press on toward the goal to win the prize for which God has called me heavenward in Christ Jesus" (Philippians 3:12-14, NIV).

FOR REVIEW AND FURTHER THOUGHT

1. Why was the agreement by which Charlemagne was crowned as Holy Roman Emperor by the pope really an act of treason on the part of the latter?

2. Why did the Byzantine Emperor Leo III remove southern Italy from the control of the pope?

3. Why did the leaders of the Eastern Church view the Westerners as ignorant?

4. How did the teachings of Augustine produce theological differences between the Eastern and Western churches?

5. Why did the Eastern Church oppose any form of theological development?

6. What does the Latin word *filioque* mean?

7. What was the theological issue over which the churches disagreed in the Filioque Controversy? What beliefs concerning the Holy Spirit did they have in common?

8. Why was the term *filioque* originally added to the Nicene Creed in Spain?

9. How did the conflict between Nicholas I and Photius affect the Filioque Controversy?

10. How does the Filioque Controversy relate to the issue of papal infallibility?

11. List some of the differences in practice that divided the Eastern and Western churches.

12. How did the reform of the Western church under Hildebrand widen the gap between East and West?

13. In what areas did each church accuse the other of holding to Jewish practices?

14. How did the invasions of Vikings and Muslims serve to increase the distance between the churches of East and West?

15. What is the most important barrier dividing the Roman Catholic and Eastern Orthodox Churches, and why?

16. Why were both sides motivated to repair the schism after it occurred in 1054? Why did all attempts to do so fail?

17. Identify the following in one sentence each: Athenagoras, Benedict VIII, Humbert, Leo of Ochrida, Michael Cerularius, Michael Palaeologus, Vladimir.

14

GOD WILLS IT

It was perhaps the most powerful piece of motivational preaching in history. Pope Urban II, worthy successor of the great reformer Gregory VII, stood before the Council of Clermont in southern France in November in the year 1095. Gathered around him was an enormous throng of bishops, priests, monks, nobles, and peasants. After appealing to their pride as Frenchmen, he aroused their anger with graphic descriptions of the torture and rape of Christian pilgrims to Jerusalem by the infidel Turks. He then implored them to take action:

"On whom therefore is the labor of avenging these wrongs and recovering this territory incumbent, if not upon you? You, upon whom above all other nations God has conferred remarkable glory in arms, great courage, bodily activity, and strength to humble the heads of those who resist you.... Let the Holy Sepulchre of our Lord and Savior, which is possessed by the unclean nations, especially incite you, and the holy places which are now treated with ignominy and irreverently polluted with the filth of the unclean. O, most valiant soldiers and descendants of invincible ancestors, be not degenerate, but recall the valor of your progenitors....

"Let therefore hatred depart from among you, let your quarrels end, let wars cease, and let all dissensions and controversies slumber. Enter upon the road to the Holy Sepulchre; wrest that land from the wicked race, and subject it to yourselves. That land which as the Scripture says `floweth with milk and honey,' was given by God into the power of the children of Israel. Jerusalem is the center of the earth; the land is fruitful above all others, like another paradise of delights. This the Redeemer of mankind has made illustrious by His advent, has beautified by His residence, has consecrated by His passion, has redeemed by His death, has glorified by His burial.

"This royal city, however, situated at the center of the earth, is now held captive by the enemies of Christ, and is subjected to those who do not know God, to the worship of the heathens. She seeks therefore and desires to be liberated and does not cease to implore you to come to her aid. From you especially she asks succor, because, as we have already said, God has conferred upon you above all other nations great glory in arms. Accordingly undertake this journey for the remission of your sins, with the assurance of the imperishable glory of the kingdom of heaven."

The response to this impassioned piece of oratory startled even Urban himself. The crowd began to shout with one voice, "God wills it!" Nobles came forward to kneel at the feet of the pope and dedicate themselves to the liberation of Jerusalem. The peasants were ready to leave for Palestine immediately. The Crusades had begun.

THE REASONS FOR THE CRUSADES

The desire expressed so eloquently by Urban was not a new idea with him. Several popes had earlier advocated the liberation of Jerusalem, the most recent being Gregory VII himself, though his involvement in the lay investiture controversy with Henry IV prevented him from doing anything about it. A number of conditions in the eleventh century made the idea of a Crusade to the Holy Land attractive to Europeans.

The first and most obvious was the invasion of Palestine by a new breed of Muslim. The Arabs who had held the land for the previous four centuries had permitted free access to the holy places of Christianity for the payment of a nominal fee. In fact, they profited greatly by the tourist trade and had every reason to encourage it. When the Seljuk Turks stormed into the region from central Asia and wrested control of it from the Arabs, their fanatical devotion to Islam was such that they no longer looked kindly on Christian visitors. As a result, European pilgrims who sought to visit the holy places of Palestine often encountered harassment, imprisonment, or worse, though no doubt the atrocity stories were considerably inflated by the time they reached the European population.

Molesting pilgrims was serious business. The system of penance in the Catholic Church required that those who confessed their sins do something to make restitution, and often the required payment included a trip to some holy shrine. Thus the pilgrims to Palestine were more than tourists; they were looking to gain forgiveness of sins by means of their journey. The Turks who stopped them from visiting the holy places were consequently interfering with their reception of God's grace of forgiveness. As a result the Crusades became fighting pilgrimages. The Crusaders were looking to gain forgiveness of their own sins while at the same time making Palestine safe for other Christian pilgrims. Their romanticized view of the Holy Land did not hold up to the harsh reality - their "land of milk and honey" turned out to be mostly barren desert - but the superstitions that drove them to believe that God's grace could be found more readily in Jerusalem than anywhere else were perpetuated throughout the crusading era. The pilgrimages were also tied in with the superstitious belief in the power of relics. It was to be expected that physical remains of the saints would be more plentiful in the Holy Land than in Europe, and the popular belief that such relics contained great power to do miracles and forgive sins motivated many to make the dangerous journey to the East.

The Seljuk Turks also posed a threat to the Byzantine Empire. The Greeks and Arabs had been living peacefully side by side for many generations, but the Turks turned out to be more aggressive than the Arabs had been. They invaded the Byzantine holdings in Asia, nearly wiped out the Greek army at the Battle of Manzikert in 1071, and as a result reduced the land of the Byzantine Empire by almost half. It was the Byzantine Emperor Alexius Comnenus who sent an urgent letter to Pope Urban pleading for help against the Turks. He got more than he bargained for, but we will see more of that later.

The popes still had a strong desire to reunite all Christians under their leadership and end the great schism between East and West, and the Crusades became a tool for fulfilling that goal. Different popes looked at it in different ways. Some really believed that if they were to deliver the Byzantines from the Turks, the Greeks would be so grateful that they would submit to papal authority for the sake of Christian unity. Others somewhat more cynically treated the Crusaders as a bargaining chip, offering to send soldiers in return for the submission of the Eastern Church. Some kings and emperors went so far as to suggest that the best way to reunite Christendom was by the outright conquest of the Byzantine Empire - an idea that was repudiated as wicked even by such a politically-minded pope as the great Innocent III.

In addition to the religious motives, there were also political and economic ones, of course. While the French, and to a lesser extent the Germans, threw themselves into the Crusades because of their religious zeal, the Italians sat back and tallied up the potential profits of such ventures. The Italians, having seen the inner workings of the church firsthand for hundreds of years, were cynical about the church in general and popes in particular. They refused to be taken in by all the talk of recovering the land of the Savior from the hand of the infidel Turk, but were more than willing to make a handsome profit by lending money, selling supplies at inflated prices, providing ships, and taking the lion's share of the lucrative spice trade that resulted from the Crusades.

There was also the problem of overpopulation in Europe. While the population was only a fraction of what it is today, the feudal economy was having trouble supporting the growing number of people. In addition, feudal lords were occupying much of their time in fighting one another, reducing the peasant population in the process, and younger sons of the nobility were becoming increasingly unruly because the feudal system left them out in the cold. The Crusades turned out to be a useful outlet for all of this excess energy - the young men turned to killing Turks instead of each other, though they were not always quite as discriminating in their carnage as the leaders of the Crusades might have wished. The wars in the East also occupied the leading monarchs of Europe and kept them from interfering with papal political ambitions, at least through much of the twelfth century.

The Crusades also involved a new understanding of the nature of war. The Christian concept of the just war had been defined centuries before by Augustine, who had taught that wars may legitimately be fought by the state, which had the God-given responsibility to defend its people and mete out justice to aggressors. A just war, then, was one that was fought in defense of one's own land and people, and Christians could in good conscience participate in such a war. Just wars were to be fought between opposing armies, with mercy shown to prisoners and the wounded, while non-combatants were to be left alone. The church had tried to put further restrictions on war during the Middle Ages by introducing the Truce of God and the Peace of God, whereby fighting was forbidden on weekends and holidays (which, by the time saints' days were included, didn't leave much time for warfare), and monks and their monasteries and farmers and their fields were declared off-limits for the quarrelsome knights. But when it came to the Turks, all rules were cancelled. The Crusades differed little in this respect from the Holy Wars of Islam, though many historians suspect that the Muslims were more merciful to those they conquered than the Crusaders were to their victims. The atrocities perpetrated by the Crusaders were justified on the grounds of the instructions given to Joshua for the total extermination of the Canaanites, though they surely outdid Joshua, not only in their lust for blood, but also in their unrestrained torture, rape, and plunder.

The preachers of the Crusades did much to stir up this fanaticism. The popes maintained that the church had legal right to Palestine by virtue of the preaching of the apostles and the conquest of the land by the Roman Empire. Bernard of Clairvaux argued that it was no sin to kill an infidel because Christ would be glorified by the death of His enemy. He maintained that the Crusader should rejoice in the death of the pagan, and even more so glory in his own death in the holy cause. The popes augmented this attitude by granting all sorts of privileges, both temporal and spiritual, to the Crusaders. Urban II declared the Crusades to be pilgrimages, thus substituting for other forms of penance. By the time of the Second Crusade, eternal life was being promised, not only to the Crusaders, but also to parents who sent their sons to Palestine. Later Crusaders were excused from all debts, taxes, and interest payments (which excited the Jewish moneylenders beyond bounds). Innocent III ultimately extended the offer of plenary indulgence (the forgiveness of all sins and the promise of eternal life) to any who helped in a Crusade in any way - by fighting, building ships, or even contributing money.

THE FIRST CRUSADE (1096-1099)

The enthusiastic response of Urban's audience at Clermont caught him totally by surprise. While he thought a Crusade would be a great idea, he had made no preparations to set one in motion. The three most powerful kings in Europe were at that time excommunicated because of the lay investiture controversy, and the only leadership Urban could provide was an elderly papal legate. As a result, leadership of the crusade fell to the lesser French nobility. Some of these men were noble and motivated by genuine piety, but others were much more interested in carving out fiefs for themselves in Palestine than in delivering Jerusalem from the Turks. The fall of 1096 was set as the date for the crusade to begin.

The peasants couldn't wait that long, however. Galvanized into action by wild-eyed monks with names like Peter the Hermit and Walter the Penniless, they swarmed across Europe with little or no advance preparation. Peter had himself taken a pilgrimage to Jerusalem, and it was his stories of Turkish atrocities that had helped to convince Urban of the need for a crusade. Urban encouraged Peter to spread the word, and he had done so very effectively. As he traveled from town to town exhorting the populace, his reputation for holiness grew to the point that people were plucking hairs from the tail of his donkey and treating them like holy relics. Peasants followed him by the thousands. The bands led by Peter, Walter, and others like them were totally unprepared for the journey to the East. They brought little food and less water, and when their provisions ran out, they began to plunder the Christian towns through which they were passing. They also took out some of their lust for blood on the Jewish ghettoes in settlements along the Rhine. Many were killed on their way through Hungary and Bulgaria. When those who remained reached Constantinople, the emperor quickly hustled them across the Bosporus, where they were ambushed and slaughtered by the Turks outside of Nicea. In all, the Peasants' Crusade took the frightening toll of 300,000 lives - about one tenth of all those who were to die in the two-hundred-year history of the Crusades died before they even officially started.

The main armies gathered in the fall of 1096 and set off for Palestine. They, too, lived off the land on their way, though they were better prepared than the peasants had been. When they arrived at Constantinople, Alexius was glad to see them, but feared that they had more interest in conquering Byzantine territory than in fighting Turks. He therefore made them swear fealty to him as their feudal lord before agreeing to transport them across the Bosporus. The warriors of the First Crusade met with success largely because the Turks were divided and fighting among themselves. They conquered Nicea in 1097 and Antioch in 1098, though they were then besieged inside the city by a Turkish army. The Crusaders were heartened by a vision that told them that the holy lance with which Christ's side had been pierced was buried in the city. They dug under the Church of St. Peter and discovered a rusty lance, which they took with them into battle as a sacred relic, and under its inspiration routed the Turks.

The Crusader army arrived outside Jerusalem in 1099 with only 12,000 knights remaining out of the original 300,000 with which they had left Europe. The Turks refused to take the Crusaders seriously, and had left only a small garrison to defend the Holy City. The Crusaders, convinced that they were carrying out the will of God, marched barefoot around Jerusalem, expecting its walls to collapse before them as the walls of Jericho had fallen in the time of Joshua. The Muslim defenders found this quite amusing, to say the least, and the walls did not cooperate. When the Crusaders did storm the city, however, they overwhelmed the Muslims, and released all of their pent-up frustrations in an unrestrained slaughter of the population of the city. Men, women, and children were beheaded, tortured, and burned. Babies were torn from their mothers and thrown over the walls of the city. One observer of the carnage described the scene on the Temple Mount by using the apocalyptic image of blood flowing up to the horses' bridles. The Jews, having been accused of helping the infidels, were herded into the synagogue and burned alive. Finally the bloodshed was over, and the Crusaders gathered at the Church of the Holy Sepulchre and knelt in prayer, praising God for His mercy.

The First Crusade was the only one that gained any measure of success. It resulted in the establishment of four Crusader kingdoms, led by the Latin Kingdom of Jerusalem. These remained more or less intact for the next two hundred years. The Crusader kingdoms were an interesting mix of East and West. They imposed the feudal system of Europe on an alien culture, and installed patriarchs loyal to Rome in Jerusalem and Antioch, where Eastern patriarchs were already functioning. But in clothing and manner of life, they quickly adopted the customs of the orientals. They wore burnooses, ate Turkish delicacies, and often acquired harems. It quickly became apparent that it was only the newcomers to Palestine who had any real zeal for fighting. The veterans of life in the Crusader kingdoms found co-existence with the Turks to be more comfortable and more profitable than war.

THE SECOND CRUSADE (1147-1148)

To speak of the Crusades by numbers is somewhat misleading. It gives the impression of widely-spaced organized expeditions with long periods of time in between. This was hardly the case. It would be more accurate to speak instead of a Crusading Era. While there were a number of major expeditions that have been given numbers by historians (though different historians number them in different ways), the fact is that there were numerous smaller organized ventures between the major ones, and the entire period was characterized by a steady flow of adventurers, merchants, and reinforcements from Europe to the East.

The First Crusade appeared to have attained the chief goal of the movement with the capture of Jerusalem, but those who populated the Crusader kingdoms knew how tentative their hold on the land really was. As the Muslims settled their own internal squabbles, they again turned their attention to the cities controlled by the Crusaders. In 1144, the city of Edessa fell to the Turks. Knowing that the infidels would not stop there, the Crusaders sent a message to Rome begging for reinforcements. Pope Eugene III called on the great monk Bernard of Clairvaux to preach a second Crusade. Bernard somewhat reluctantly left his cloister and embarked on his task. He enlisted the French king Louis VII and the Holy Roman Emperor Konrad III to lead the crusading armies. Louis undertook the journey as a penance for burning a church with over a thousand people inside, while Konrad was convinced by the moving eloquence of Bernard. The two armies traveled separately because of the rivalry of their leaders and the mutual hatred of their knights. They obtained some Greek guides in Constantinople, but the guides hated the Western barbarians and the Crusaders mistrusted the subtle Byzantines. After numerous wild goose chases through the mountains of Cappadocia and several ambushes by the Turks, less than one tenth of the armies remained by the time they reached Palestine. They decided to attack Damascus rather than Edessa, and were virtually wiped out by the Turkish army.

The dismal failure of the Second Crusade came as a great shock to the Europeans. How could an expedition that was the will of God fail? It was necessary to blame someone, and blame was eventually directed in one of three places. Some blamed the Greeks. It was the deceitful Byzantine guides who led the Crusaders astray and caused the failure of the expedition, they maintained. Such bitter feelings did not bode well for the future of the crusading ventures, and eventually bore bitter fruit in the Fourth Crusade.

Others blamed the sins of the Crusaders. They pointed to the loose living of the European inhabitants of Palestine and argued that such immoral men did not deserve the deliverance of God. The crusading armies were not blameless, either. The most notorious example was provided by the young, beautiful, and vivacious queen of France, Eleanor of Aquitaine. She accompanied her husband on the Crusade, but wound up engaging in a well-publicized affair with her young uncle, the ruler of Antioch. Louis VII wound up requesting and getting a divorce from the pope, and Eleanor went on to marry Henry II of England and become the mother of Richard the Lion-Hearted and the villain King John.

Some thought more deeply, however, and began to question the whole crusading enterprise. They began to question whether or not the pope was really speaking for Christ on earth. Such doubts ultimately contributed to the undermining of papal authority in Europe.

THE THIRD CRUSADE (1189-1192)

All doubts were swept aside near the end of the twelfth century by the rise of a new leader in Islam. Saladin, who along with Richard the Lion-Hearted and Louis IX of France remains one of the few noble figures of the period, succeeded in uniting the warring factions among the Turks. He would have been satisfied with maintaining the current situation had not a minor noble named Reginald of Chatillon invaded

Arabia with the intention of destroying the tomb of Muhammad in Medina and smashing the Ka'aba in Mecca to powder. Though his army was easily intercepted and destroyed, Saladin was enraged by such a violation of the truce between the Turks and the Crusader kingdoms. He stepped up his efforts against the Crusaders, but wound up agreeing to another truce. Reginald again violated it, however, by capturing a richly-laden camel caravan. Unfortunately for him, Saladin's sister was one of the passengers. Saladin immediately declared a holy war. He defeated the main Crusader army and killed Reginald with his own hands. He then moved on to Jerusalem in 1187, where the sparsely-defended city surrendered after a brief siege. Quite in contrast to the behavior of the Crusaders who took Jerusalem in 1099, Saladin freed all the captives upon payment of a ransom, and even allowed them to take their holy relics with them. He also agreed to allow pilgrims continued access to the city as long as they bore no arms. He made the prisoners promise never to bear arms against him again, but once they were safe in Antioch, they prepared for another assault, reasoning that a promise given to an infidel is not binding.

The fall of Jerusalem to Saladin in 1187 motivated what has been called the Crusade of the Kings. Holy Roman Emperor Frederick Barbarossa, Philip Augustus of France, and Richard I of England promised to set aside their differences to unite in the holy cause. Such promises turned out to be empty indeed. The entire venture was beset by constant quarrels among the participants, along with the now commonplace Byzantine treachery. When the Crusaders reached Constantinople, the emperor Isaac Angelus threw some of Frederick's commissioners in prison, and meanwhile made a secret treaty with the Turks. Frederick later drowned while swimming in a river in Cilicia. Meanwhile, Richard and Philip argued constantly. When Richard conquered Cyprus, he celebrated the occasion by marrying, in the process breaking his engagement to Philip's sister, who he claimed had slept with his father, Henry II, while visiting in the English court. Richard continued his military success with the recapture of the port city of Acre. Like Saladin, he offered to release the prisoners upon payment of a ransom, but when the ransom was not paid quickly enough to suit him, he had 2700 prisoners beheaded in full view of the Muslim troops outside the city. Meanwhile, Philip stormed back to France in a fit of jealousy.

Richard was now the only leader who remained. He was a brave and capable general, and a fit rival for Saladin. The two came to respect one another highly, though their battles were never conclusive. Once when Richard had lost his horse in battle, Saladin sent him one of his own, saying that such a noble warrior did not deserve to fight on foot. When Richard fell ill, Saladin sent his personal physician to minister to him and nurse him back to health. Richard later offered to end the fighting by giving his sister to Saladin's brother in marriage, and suggested that they should be given Jerusalem as a wedding present. Saladin approved of the idea, but the pope did not, and the agreement fell through. Eventually, all that was accomplished by the Crusade was a treaty giving pilgrims access to the city of Jerusalem - which Saladin would have been willing to grant before all the fighting began. In 1192, Richard returned to England to deal with the usurper John who had stolen his throne. He vowed to return and continue the war, but he was captured in Austria by the jealous successor of Frederick, and never made it back to Palestine.

THE FOURTH CRUSADE (1200-1204)

When Innocent III became pope in 1198, one of his great desires was to revive the crusading spirit. He realized by now that the Byzantines were not to be trusted, so he proposed that the Crusaders travel eastward by sea, departing from Venice and landing in Egypt. He reasoned that if Egypt could be captured, the soldiers of the cross could then have a base of operations closer to Palestine from which to regain the Holy Land. First, however, the

THE CRUSADES

CRUSADE	DATE	CHIEF MOTIVATORS	NOTABLE PARTICIPANTS	GOAL	RESULTS
FIRST CRUSADE	1096-1099	Urban II Peter the Hermit	Walter the Penniless Peter the Hermit Raymund of Toulouse Godfrey Tancred Robert of Normandy	Liberate Jerusalem from the Turks.	Crusaders captured Nicea, Antioch, Edessa, Jerusalem; established feudal Crusader kingdoms.
SECOND CRUSADE	1147-1148	Bernard of Clairvaux Eugene III	Konrad III Louis VII	Retake Edessa from Turks.	Mistrust between Western Crusaders and Eastern guides led to decimation of Crusader army; attempt to take Damascus failed.
THIRD CRUSADE	1189-1192	Alexander III	Frederick Barbarossa Philip Augustus Richard I	Retake Jerusalem from Saladin and the Saracens.	Frederick drowned; Philip returned home; Richard captured Acre and Joppa, made treaty with Saladin, and was captured and imprisoned in Austria on the way home.
FOURTH CRUSADE	1200-1204	Innocent II	Thibaut of Champagne Louis of Blois Baldwin of Flanders Simon de Montfort Enrico Dandolo	Undermine Saracen power by invading Egypt.	Christian city of Zara was sacked to repay Venice for transportation; for this the Crusaders were excommunicated; they then sacked Constantinople.
CHILDREN'S CRUSADES	1212	Nicholas of Cologne Stephen of Cloyes		Supernatural conquest of Holy Land by "the pure in heart."	Most of the children were drowned at sea, sold into slavery, or slaughtered.
FIFTH CRUSADE	1219-1221	Honorius II	William of Holland John of Brienne	Undermine Saracen power by invading Egypt.	Crusaders succeeded in taking Damietta in Egypt, but soon lost it again.
SIXTH CRUSADE	1229		Frederick II	Regain Jerusalem.	Crusaders made treaty with Sultan, giving Frederick control of Jerusalem; Frederick was excommunicated for this.
SEVENTH CRUSADE	1248		Louis IX	Relief of Holy Land through invasion of Egypt.	Crusaders were defeated in Egypt.

Crusaders had to convince the Venetians to help them. They readily agreed - for a price. The old blind Doge of Venice, Enrico Dandolo, promised to provide ships and provisions in return for the payment of the equivalent of several million dollars up front and a promise of half the profits of the venture later. The Crusaders, having no alternative, agreed, and many sold their families' estates to raise the money. By the time they were ready to leave, however, only about two-thirds of the money had been raised. Dandolo was the cooperative sort, and suggested that he would be willing to forget about the rest if the Crusaders would destroy the town of Zara on the Adriatic Coast - Venice's chief trading rival, and a Christian city under the control of the king of Hungary. Meanwhile, Dandolo secretly made a non-aggression pact with the Sultan of Egypt.

Innocent III warned the Crusaders that he would excommunicate the whole lot of them if they sacked Zara, but the temptation of riches was too great, and they burned the city to the ground. Meanwhile, Emperor Isaac Angelus of Byzantium had been overthrown, blinded, and imprisoned by his brother. Isaac's son Alexius came to the Crusaders and begged for help. The old Doge drove a hard bargain, but the young prince agreed to his heavy price. Hoping to get Innocent off his back, the Doge also got Alexius to agree to the submission of the Eastern Church to the pope. Innocent was not fooled, however, and warned the Crusaders that he would not be a party to any expedition against Constantinople.

The Crusaders were by now beyond caring what Innocent thought, however. They captured Constantinople and threw out the usurper, restoring old Isaac to the throne. Though the Greeks were pleased to have order restored, they blanched when they heard the price. They would never agree to such a heavy payment, and would die before submitting to the pope. When the Greeks refused to complete the bargain made by young Alexius, the Crusaders took it out on the city. They slaughtered thousands, raped nuns, burned buildings, robbed churches (the stolen treasures even today grace some of the finest museums and churches in Venice), destroyed priceless works of art and literature, and carried off an amazing number of "holy relics," including the stone Jacob used as a pillow, Moses' rod, John the Baptist's head, the finger that Thomas thrust into Jesus' side, the crown of thorns, teardrops and blood from Christ Himself, and innumerable fragments of the True Cross. When they were done, they set up the Latin Kingdom of Constantinople, which endured from 1204 to 1261. As much as Innocent deplored their actions, he was not reluctant to take advantage of the situation. He quickly sent a new patriarch to Constantinople, and, at least on the surface, reunited Christendom.

THE CHILDREN'S CRUSADES (1212)

In an era filled with one sordid account after another, perhaps none is so tragic as that of the Children's Crusades. The unspeakable wickedness of the Fourth Crusade started some people thinking even more seriously about the sins of the Crusaders being at the root of their failure. In 1212, a twelve-year-old French shepherd boy named Stephen of Cloyes claimed that Christ had appeared to him and told him to lead a crusade to the Holy Land. He was told that earlier efforts had failed because of the wickedness and selfishness of the participants, but that an army of children would succeed where adults had failed because they were pure of heart. They would not even need weapons, he said, because God would be on their side. All they needed to do was march to the Holy Land - even the waters of the sea would part before them. When he appeared before Philip Augustus, the king told him to go back to his sheep, but the lad, convinced he was a prophet, continued to gather supporters. Soon he had an "army" of 20,000 children, and together they headed for Marseilles. When they arrived, the seas remained undivided, but they found a pair of helpful local merchants named Hugo the Iron and William the Pig who promised to transport them to the Holy Land for nothing. Seven ships soon set sail bearing the children, and most of them were never heard from again. It was later discovered that two of the ships had sunk near Sardinia, drowning all aboard. The other five

THE MUSLIM CONQUEST AND THE CRUSADES - A COMPARISON

AREA OF COMPARISON	MUSLIM CONQUEST	CRUSADES
DATES	633-732	1095-1291
INITIATION	Death of Muhammad	Council of Clermont
TERMINATION	Battle of Tours	Fall of Acre
MOTIVATION	They desired to spread the true faith among the infidels by means of Jihad, or Holy War.	They sought to defend pilgrims and the glory of God and to recapture the holy places of Christendom from the infidel Turks.
INDUCEMENTS OFFERED	Immediate entrance to Paradise promised to those who die in Jihad.	Plenary indulgence offered - forgiveness of sins past, present, and future; for those who died, immediate entrance into heaven; for all others, forgiveness of debts and freedom from taxation.
TREATMENT OF ENEMIES	Pagans were required to convert or die; Jews and Christians were allowed to keep their religions but were required to pay tribute and refrain from proselytizing or public religious display.	Conquered Muslims were indiscriminately put to the sword; inhabitants of Jewish ghettoes were slaughtered.
RESULTS	Palestine, Syria, Asia Minor, Egypt, North Africa, Spain were subjugated; Greek learning was preserved through the "Dark Ages."	No permanent territorial gains were made; classical Greek and Roman culture was rediscovered; there was increased enmity between Eastern and Western churches and among Christians, Jews, and Muslims.

were auctioned by the "helpful merchants" to Muslim pirates, who took the children to North Africa and sold them into slavery. The few educated youngsters among them were purchased by the Sultan of Egypt. It was one of these, a nameless priest, who returned to Europe eighteen years later and told the tale of the tragic fate of the children.

Meanwhile, in Germany, ten-year-old Nicholas of Cologne was stirring up enthusiasm for the same sort of venture. Despite opposition by priests and other adults of all kinds, he gathered up a motley aggregation of about 30,000 and headed across the Alps for Italy. Many died on the way, and when they reached Genoa, they found that, not only did the seas not part, but no one was willing to transport them to Palestine. When Innocent III got wind of their idea, he gently advised them to go back to their homes. Some did, but many remained in Genoa, eventually merging into the population there.

THE DECLINE OF THE CRUSADING MOVEMENT

When Innocent III died in 1216, the Crusades died with him - it just took a while for rigor mortis to set in. The Fifth Crusade was launched by the Fourth Lateran Council in 1215, and succeeded in taking the key Egyptian port of Damietta in 1219. The Sultan of Egypt offered to *give* Jerusalem to the Crusaders in exchange for Damietta, but they refused, reasoning that they could take it for themselves once they had conquered Egypt. Two years later, Damietta again fell to the Turks.

The Sixth Crusade was led by the excommunicated Holy Roman Emperor Frederick II, who hoped by his efforts to get back into the good graces of the church. He quickly found that he got along much better with the Turks than he did with other Europeans, however, and he wound up regaining Jerusalem by treaty in 1229. The church was unwilling to countenance any dealings with the Muslims, however, and not only refused to ratify the treaty, but put the city of Jerusalem under interdict! In 1244, Jerusalem fell to the Turks for the last time, and remained in Muslim control until the British captured the city in 1917, near the end of World War I.

The crusading era was brought to a close under the leadership of the pious king of France, Louis IX (the same St. Louis after whom the city in Missouri is named). He led the Seventh Crusade in 1248, which succeeded in recapturing Damietta. An unexpected (to them) flooding of the Nile led to the defeat of the crusading army, and Louis himself was captured by the Turks at Mansura. He gained release by the payment of a ransom, and tried again in 1270, but died of the plague in Tunis in what is called by some the Eighth Crusade. When the port city of Acre fell to the Turks in 1291, the last of the Crusader kingdoms came to an end, and the crusading era with it.

THE RESULTS OF THE CRUSADES

The Crusades produced none of the intended results, but contributed to a great many changes in the church and in Europe. While no territory in the Holy Land was permanently regained, the two hundred years of interaction between East and West sparked a cultural exchange that led to the Renaissance in Europe. While trade with the Turks opened up interest in things Eastern, the fifty-year Latin control of Constantinople reacquainted Europeans with the art and philosophy of ancient Greece and Rome. European knowledge of mathematics and medicine was also greatly enhanced through contact with the Muslim world.

While the Crusades were intended to bring unity between the Eastern and Western Churches and between the warring feudal states of Europe, they only produced greater disunity. The duplicity of the Byzantine monarchs and the sack of Constantinople by the Crusaders ended any possibility of bringing the churches of the East and West back together. Meanwhile, the destruction wrought by the Crusaders had so weakened the city that it was easy pickings for the Muslims, who took some time to recover from the Crusades themselves, when they assaulted it in 1453.

Other kinds of disunity also stemmed from the Crusades. The treatment accorded to Muslims by Christians has never been forgotten, and is to this day a major stumblingblock in the path of evangelism in the Muslim world. Jews, too, have not forgotten the ghettoes that were destroyed or the synagogues that were burned by the Crusaders. In Europe, the idea of a united Christendom was laid to rest once and for all. People far and wide had come to think of themselves as Frenchmen, Germans, or Italians. Europe was well on its way toward the solidification of nations by the time the Crusades were over.

Perhaps the greatest result of the Crusades was its effect on the papacy itself. The popes had taken the lead in sparking the Crusades. When they succeeded, the popes shared the credit, but when they failed, the popes shared the blame. Exposure to other cultures naturally produced questioning - especially when those cultures appeared to prove themselves superior by success on the battlefield. The heavy taxes levied by the popes to support the Crusades embittered many monarchs along with their people, and the increased abuse of indulgences for fund-raising purposes upset enough people that it eventually produced the Protestant Reformation. The end of the Crusades also signalled the end of papal supremacy in Europe.

When we return to European politics in chapter seventeen, we will find the popes virtually powerless before the aggressive new national monarchs.

MAKING DRY BONES LIVE

"My kingdom is not of this world. If it were, my servants would fight." Thus Jesus spoke before Pilate when on trial for His life. When those who claimed to be the servants of Jesus forgot those words, the result was deep disgrace to the name of Christ that has not been erased from the minds of Muslims and Jews for almost a millennium. Worse yet, the pattern of violence for the cause of the church was perpetuated in Europe through "crusades" against excommunicated kings and emperors, heretical groups like the Albigensians and Hussites, and through the notorious Inquisition.

There is, of course, a better way. Francis of Assisi accompanied the warriors of the Fifth Crusade in 1219 with the intention of winning the Sultan of Egypt to Christ. He received a polite hearing, and the Sultan was much impressed with the gentleness and sincerity of the young monk. A century later, the Spaniard Raymond Lull took the time to learn Arabic from a Muslim slave before embarking on a mission to North Africa. His words serve as a fitting conclusion to our study of the Crusades:

"The conquest of the Holy Land should be attempted in no other way than as Christ and the Apostles undertook to accomplish it - by prayers, tears, and the offering up of our own lives. Many are the princes and knights that have gone to the Promised Land with a view to conquer it, but if this mode had been pleasing to the Lord, they would assuredly have wrested it from the Saracens before this. Thus it is manifest to pious monks that Thou art daily waiting for them to do for love to Thee what Thou hast done for love to them."

FOR REVIEW AND FURTHER THOUGHT

1. What were the main goals that the Crusades were trying to accomplish?

2. What conditions in the church, in Europe, and in Palestine made the Crusades an attractive idea at the end of the eleventh century?

3. Why were pilgrimages so important to the Roman Catholics of the Middle Ages?

4. What were some of the ways in which the Byzantines betrayed the Crusaders who were trying to help them?

5. What were some of the ways the Crusaders harmed the Orthodox Christians they were supposed to be helping?

6. What economic benefit did Europe gain from the Crusades?

7. What approach to war had been defined by Augustine in the fifth century, and how did the Crusaders violate this standard?

8. What were the Truce of God and the Peace of God?

9. How did the Crusaders justify the wholesale murder of Muslim women and children?

10. What promises were made by the popes to encourage people to go on the Crusades?

11. Who were Peter the Hermit and Walter the Penniless, and what role did they play in the First Crusade?

12. What role did relics play in the conduct of the Crusades?

13. In what way was the culture of the Crusader kingdoms European? In what way was it Oriental?

14. What event in Palestine motivated the Second Crusade?

15. What effect did the failure of the Second Crusade have on Europe?

16. What role did Reginald of Chatillon have in causing the Third Crusade?

17. How would you explain the undeniable fact that the pagan king Saladin conducted himself more like a Christian than many of the Christians associated with the Crusades?

18. What new idea did Innocent III introduce into the conduct of the Crusades?

19. How did Enrico Dandolo, the Doge of Venice, use the Fourth Crusade for his own profit?

20. Why did Innocent III excommunicate the Crusaders of the Fourth Crusade?

21. Why did the Crusaders sack Constantinople in 1204?

22. How did the sack of Constantinople wind up helping Europe? How did it harm the Byzantine Empire?

23. Why did the children who organized the Children's Crusades believe they would succeed where trained warriors had failed?

24. What were the outcomes of the Children's Crusades?

25. What role was played by Louis IX in the closing years of the Crusades?

26. In what ways did the Crusades contribute to the development of the Renaissance and Reformation in Europe?

27. How did the Crusades help accelerate the development of modern science?

28. In what way do the Crusades continue to have an influence on modern missionary efforts in the Middle East?

29. How did the Crusades contribute to the decline of papal power in Europe?

30. Why do you think so few Europeans in the Middle Ages thought about evangelizing the Muslims instead of slaughtering them?

15

CATHEDRALS OF THE MIND

Peppermint Patty was in trouble, as usual. She sat there with the test in front of her, and didn't know what to do. The question on the test said, "How many angels can stand on the head of a pin?" After puzzling over the question for a while, she finally answered, "Eight if they're skinny, and four if they're fat!" Though there is no evidence that the theologians of the High Middle Ages, known as Schoolmen or Scholastics, actually asked the question that stumped Peppermint Patty, they did ask many other questions that seem to us to be equally irrelevant. They asked these questions, not out of idle intellectual curiosity, but out of a desire for completeness. They believed that all questions could be answered through the proper application of the principles of logic, and were naive enough to believe that all knowledge could be brought together in a single comprehensive textbook. These textbooks were called *Summae*, or summaries.

Scholasticism dominated the thought of the Middle Ages during the twelfth and thirteenth centuries, the period of papal supremacy, as well as the period during which the great Gothic cathedrals were constructed. The popes were trying to build a Christian society with themselves at the head; the cathedral builders were searching for a visible expression of communion between man and God, with spires stretching toward the heavens and brilliant stained-glass windows admitting the light of God to the congregation below. The Scholastic notion that all knowledge could be brought together into a single unified whole was an intellectual expression of these same ideas. In the same way that Christendom was to be united under the pope, all knowledge could be united under the auspices of theology; in the same way that God and man met in the Gothic cathedral, faith and reason met in the logical arguments for Christian dogma presented by the Schoolmen.

The twelfth and thirteenth centuries were also the period of the Crusades, of course. The religious wars against Islam contributed to the development of Scholasticism because they raised new questions in men's minds. As Europeans were exposed to societies in the East that were very different from their own, they began to question their concepts of unity. The real bombshell, however, came near the beginning of the thirteenth century with the reintroduction into Europe of the writings of Aristotle. These had for many centuries been lost with the exception of a few Latin translations made in the early Middle Ages by men like Boethius. The increased contact with the Muslims in Spain, along with the plunder of the cultural and material wealth of Constantinople in 1204, brought to Western Europe both Greek and Arabic translations of Aristotle's works that had the newly-formed universities abuzz. The philosophy of Aristotle, especially as that philosophy had been interpreted by the Muslim scholar Averroës, was luring many young thinkers away from the basic doctrines of Christianity.

The Schoolmen (so named because most of them were university professors) took upon themselves the task of showing that Aristotle and philosophers like him were not really a challenge to the Christian faith. They believed that faith and reason were fully compatible because all knowledge, whether it came through the Bible, the mind, or through observation of the physical world, had its ultimate source in God, and thus could not be contradictory. They thus attempted to use the forms of logical argument devised by Aristotle to prove the truths established by the doctrine of the church. Though they finally failed in their efforts to unify all knowledge, their attempts produced the most amazing intellectual achievement of the Middle Ages.

Scholasticism did not involve a search for new knowledge. The Schoolmen believed that the teachings of the Bible and the church were right; they simply wanted to demonstrate that they were also reasonable. They thus attempted to prove what they already knew to be true, both to strengthen the faith of those who already believed and to meet the challenges of the young radicals in the universities who were abandoning the faith in a headlong rush after the faddishly popular teachings of Averröes.

It would be false to assume that Scholasticism was a single unified whole, however. The Schoolmen differed among themselves, often violently, on certain philosophical issues that they believed to be at the heart of their endeavors. The most important of these was the issue of the existence of universals. Since this is a rather obscure subject, an example might be useful. In the world, there are many cows. These cows come in different shapes, sizes, and colors, yet all are identifiably cows. If the essence of what made them cows instead of horses, the fundamental "cowness," could be isolated, that would be a universal. Centuries before the time of Christ, the Greek philosopher Plato had affirmed that universals (he called them ideas) really existed. In fact, he said that the particular objects of our experience are only shadows of these universals, which are the true reality. In other words, individual cows are simply shadows of the ideal cow. Aristotle disagreed, maintaining instead that the particulars (individual cows) were indeed real, while universal concepts like "cowness" were only mental categories that helped us to classify things according to their characteristics.

The Schoolmen divided themselves into four major approaches to the question of universals, with probably a dozen shades of difference in between. Those who followed Plato in believing in the existence of universals were called Realists. While they did not assert that somewhere in the universe was an ideal cow, they did believe that the concept of "cowness"

existed in ideal form in the mind of God before the creation of cows on earth. The Realists were particularly fond of pointing out how helpful their philosophy was for understanding the doctrine of the Trinity. After all, if God the Father, God the Son, and God the Holy Spirit all partake of the universal of "deity," Realism allows one to conclude that the universal really exists. Consequently, the three Persons of the Trinity may also be said to be one universal God. Realism also helped the popes in their concept of the universal church. The church is not a mere abstraction, but a very real entity that both incorporates and supersedes its individual members. The weakness of Realism only appears when one gets away from theology and ventures into the realm of philosophy. Is it not true that all creatures share the common characteristic of Being? There then must be a real universal Being of which they all partake. Carrying this sort of thinking out consistently led to pantheism - the idea that man, and indeed the entire universe, partakes of the divine.

Those who denied the real existence of universals were called Nominalists. They taught that universals were mere words, categories devised by our human minds to help us make sense of the world around us. The Nominalists of the Scholastic period often found themselves being charged with heresy. The reason can be seen easily if we turn again to the question of the Trinity. If "God" is no more than a name that we use to denote what God the Father, God the Son, and God the Holy Spirit have in common, then God is not really a single being. Instead we must conclude that there are really three separate Gods whom we perceive to have something in common. Those who denied the unity of God did not tend to fare well before the Inquisition.

There were some who, realizing the weaknesses of the two extreme positions, tried to compromise, and in so doing arrived at a position very close to that of Aristotle. They were called Moderate Realists or Conceptualists, and they maintained that universals were real, but lacked independent existence. In other words, while there may be some actual essence of "cowness" that allows us to distinguish cows from horses, a person would search the universe in vain for the ideal cow. The universals then are real, but exist only in the particulars of our experience. This proved to be both the most satisfactory and most productive approach, and dominated Scholasticism in its heyday.

There were some, of course, who thought all of this to be total nonsense. They thought that the attempt to prove the truths of Christianity by reason was destructive because it caused men to fall in love with their own minds rather than devoting their attention to God. They believed that the only true knowledge of God came through the mystical experience of the Beatific Vision. Through meditation, these Mystics taught that one could come to know God as He is in Himself. This, they said, is the only knowledge that is in any way worthwhile.

We turn now to a survey of the period through the lives of six of the most prominent Scholastic theologians: Anselm, Peter Abelard, Bernard of Clairvaux, Thomas Aquinas, Duns Scotus, and William of Ockham.

ANSELM OF CANTERBURY (1033-1109)

Scholasticism finds its beginnings in the work of Anselm, Archbishop of Canterbury from 1093 to 1109. In his own day, he took part in the Hildebrandine reform of the Catholic Church and the lay investiture controversy, but his greatest contribution to the church came through his writings. Though the work of earlier scholars like Boethius in the sixth century and John Scotus Erigena in the tenth had set the stage for such an approach, Anselm started a trend when he consciously tried to strengthen the faith of the people of his day with what he considered an airtight philosophical proof for God's existence. This proof is known today as the Ontological Argument. Simply put, Anselm defined God as the greatest imaginable being. He then went on to say that two alternatives were available to us - either this greatest imaginable being existed, or he did not. Of the two alternatives, the first is clearly the greater; after all, even a living dog is better than a dead lion. Since, therefore, God has already been defined as the greatest imaginable being, and such a being that exists is clearly greater than one who does not, God must exist. Such an argument clearly put Anselm in the Realist camp (the universal in which all perfections find their basis is God Himself, who exists in reality, independent of the particulars who derive their existence from Him), based as it was upon Augustine, who himself was strongly influenced by Plato. While the Ontological Argument has some rather serious weaknesses (some have asserted, for instance, that it could equally well be used to prove the existence of pink elephants), we must remember that it was addressed to those who already believed. It was not Anselm's intention to convince unbelievers, but to strengthen the faith of Christians.

Anselm also contributed greatly to our understanding of the meaning of the death of Christ. In his book *Cur Deus Homo* ("Why God Became Man"), he tried to prove that the Incarnation and death of Christ were logically necessary. The church had always struggled with the question of why Christ had to die. After all, if God was God, couldn't He simply decree that the sins of men were forgiven, without having to put Christ through the humiliation of becoming man and the pain of dying on the cross? Unless a satisfactory answer could be given, there was a tendency to view God as a bit of a sadist. The popular answer to the question in Anselm's day was what some have called the Devil Ransom theory. They said that man, by his sin, had come under bondage to Satan. In order to deliver man, God had to pay Satan off. The price was the death of His Son. God got the better end of the deal, however, because He not only delivered men from Satan, but also regained His Son through the Resurrection. Satan was left only with the pitiful souls of those destined for Hell.

Anselm's explanation, though again derived from a Realist (i.e., Platonic) philosophy, was much more biblical. He argued that the real tragedy of the Fall was not that it enslaved men to Satan, but that man's sin offended a holy God. The death of Christ was therefore not a payment to Satan, but the satisfaction of God's honor and justice. No other alternative was possible. Since human nature, concentrated as it was in Adam at the time of the Fall (here is where the Realism comes in; Anselm viewed human nature as an independently-existing universal), had been alienated from God, no man could satisfy God's justice. Since the offense was infinitely great, only an infinite payment would do. The only way to pay for man's sin and satisfy God's honor was for one who was both God and man to make the payment. While further refinements needed to be made, Anselm's view of the death of Christ as satisfying the justice of God was a major advance on the Devil Ransom theory.

PETER ABELARD (1079-1142)

Abelard is a man whose life speaks so loudly, even today, that it is difficult to concentrate on what he said. He was an undeniably brilliant man whose popularity with his students, arrogance with his superiors and colleagues, and notorious affair with the beautiful Heloïse caused those around him to view his ideas in the worst possible light. We must treat his ideas, then, in the context of the events of his life.

Abelard was born in Brittany, the oldest son of a noble family. He could have inherited the family estate, but he declined the family wealth in favor of the life of the mind. He traveled all over France seeking out the most famous teachers, but almost always got himself into trouble by challenging his teachers, saying uncomplimentary things about their scholarship, and claiming that his understanding was far advanced beyond theirs. Though he was probably right, it didn't win him any popularity contests, except with his fellow students, who loved to see the professors taken down a peg. During these years, he studied under Roscelin, the first of the Nominalists, who was condemned for his views on the Trinity, and William of Champeaux, an extreme Realist, who eventually changed his views under the intense questioning of Abelard.

When Abelard got frustrated and set up his own school, students flocked from all over Europe to study under him. He was a friendly, outgoing man, an entertaining lecturer, and a ferocious debater. His students loved him, but those who were the targets of his attacks detested his arrogance. What really got him into trouble, however, was the student who loved him too much. While teaching in Paris, Abelard met Heloïse, the teenage niece and ward of Fulbert, a canon of the cathedral. She was by all accounts a remarkable girl - beautiful, intelligent, and far more interested in the world of ideas than most women of her era. Abelard, who up to that time had remained celibate (though according to his testimony he could have seduced almost any woman he desired), was determined to get to know Heloïse better. He convinced Fulbert to allow him to become a boarder in his home in return for payment of rent and free tutoring for Heloïse. Fulbert, whom Abelard describes as a greedy fool, immediately agreed, and thus exposed his lamb to the attentions of the wolf. Fulbert, unwilling to disturb their studies, left Abelard alone with his niece for long hours of every day and night, and soon they were devoting precious little of their time to intellectual discourse. The two fell head over heels in love with one another, and soon all Paris knew what was going on - all, that is, except for the blissfully ignorant Fulbert. Abelard found he could no longer pay attention to his teaching. He devoted his time to writing love songs, while his students, caring little about the poor education they were getting, reveled in the scandal. Fulbert may have continued in his ignorance indefinitely had not Heloïse become pregnant. Abelard quickly spirited her away to his sister's home in Brittany, where she bore a son named Astrolabe (an astrolabe was an instrument for reading the positions of the stars; this was roughly equivalent to naming your child Telescope). Abelard tried to pacify the enraged Fulbert by offering to marry the girl, but Heloïse opposed the idea, knowing that marriage would put an end to any chance Abelard had for academic advancement (it was necessary for high-ranking academics to be priests, and priests, of course, were supposed to be unmarried). She said she preferred to remain his mistress. Instead, Abelard went through with the marriage, but then sent Heloïse away to a convent. Fulbert, disgusted with this shabby treatment of his niece, arranged for some thugs to break into Abelard's apartment and make sure he would never pose a threat to any young lady again. Thus rendered incapable of fulfilling his marital responsibilities and ineligible for the priesthood at the same time, Abelard entered a monastery. The remainder of his life was a sad cycle of moving from place to place, having students swarm to hear him, then being forced to move on by the authorities. He was finally excommunicated for heresy, and died on his way to seek reconciliation from the pope.

With such a life, it is easy for a man's ideas to get lost in the shuffle, yet Abelard was a man whose ideas had a great impact on his age. That impact is most easily seen in his most important book, *Sic et Non* ("Yes and No"). In this book, Abelard compiled a series of quotations from the Bible, the writings of the church fathers, the decisions of popes and councils, and even secular philosophers, under 158 topics. Each topic was introduced by a question, and then quotations dealing with the topic were arranged in two columns, one of which answered the question affirmatively, while the other set of quotations indicated a negative response. Since Abelard believed, as did most Schoolmen, that all truth is one and that the Bible, the church fathers, and the popes and councils spoke the truth, as did the best insights of the secular philosophers, he concluded that these apparently contradictory quotations really didn't contradict one another at all. He left to his students the task of harmonizing the contradictions.

Such an approach to education had several effects. First of all, it got Abelard in trouble. The idea that people learn by questioning established beliefs was not an acceptable one to the authoritarian church of the twelfth century. Even though Abelard insisted that he believed what the church taught, who could tell what conclusions other people would reach once they started asking questions? The fact of the matter is, of course, that the church fathers, popes, and councils *did* contradict one another and the Scriptures in many places. Abelard was merely encouraging people to allegorize the Scriptures even more than had already been done. In the long run, the impossibility of reconciling opposite ideas destroyed Scholasticism and sent people searching in other directions. In the short run, however, *Sic et Non* established a pattern that became standard practice among the Schoolmen. The great *Summae* developed to a fine art the practice of demonstrating the truth of something by disproving those ideas that contradicted it. Questioning once again became a constructive force, as it has been in education ever since.

In philosophy, Abelard was the first of the Conceptualists. He sought a middle way between Realism and Nominalism, and came amazingly close to the views of Aristotle before most of the writings of the great Greek philosopher were even available in medieval Europe. While he was very skilled at puncturing the balloons of others, his own theology was somewhat suspect in many areas. As his most persistent foe, Bernard of Clairvaux, said, "He savors of Arius when he speaks of the Trinity, of Pelagius when he speaks of grace, and of Nestorius when he speaks of the person of Christ." His moral philosophy was suspect as well. In a book called *Know Thyself*, he argued that it was only intentions that were sinful, not actions in themselves. Even murder (or adultery?) would not be sinful if done out of pure motives. This sort of thinking anticipates the relativism of modern ethics, and leads one to suspect that in many ways Abelard was a man ahead of his time. Despite the fact that he was twice condemned by church councils, once at Soissons in 1121 for his views on the Trinity and later at Sens in 1141 for a variety of other teachings, it was his attitude rather than his teachings that aroused the intense opposition against which he struggled throughout his life. Bernard said it best:

"Peter Abelard is trying to make void the merit of the Christian faith when he deems himself able by human reason to comprehend God altogether ... Not content to see things through a glass darkly, he must behold all things face to face ... The faith of the righteous believes, it does not dispute. But this man has no mind to believe what his reason has not previously argued."

BERNARD OF CLAIRVAUX (c.1090-1153)

Bernard of Clairvaux was the most dominant figure of the twelfth century. In the last chapter, we noted his involvement in stimulating the Second Crusade. In the next chapter, we will talk about the leadership he provided for monastic reform among the Cistercians. In addition to his preaching and reforming work, however, Bernard was also a capable theologian, and the finest example of mysticism during the Scholastic period.

As we have already seen, the mystics believed that knowledge of God was not to be obtained through reason or argument, but through contemplation. Bernard taught that God was to be known through prayer and holy living, and that the greatest good that a man could pursue was to learn to love God. His works raised the church, not to a new level of knowledge, but to a new level of praise. Among other extant works are a series of eighty-six sermons on the Song of Solomon, in which he soars to great heights in praise of the love of God. He treats the entire book as an allegory, insisting that the literal meaning is unworthy of Christian consideration. Instead, he sees it as speaking of the love between Christ and His church (though he also sees in the Shulamite the figure of the Virgin Mary at times). Bernard's legacy in the Catholic Church includes an emphasis on devotion to Mary, while he left to the church at large a number of great hymns, including *Jesus the Very Thought of Thee* and *Jesus Thou Joy of Loving Hearts*. He is also given credit for a long poetic meditation on the Crucifix from which the words to the hymn *O Sacred Head Now Wounded* are taken.

THOMAS AQUINAS (c.1225-1274)

Thomas Aquinas was to the Middle Ages what Augustine was to the Ancient Church and Calvin was to the Protestant Reformation - the theological genius who brought together the best of all that captured the attention of the church in his age. Thomas was born into a wealthy family in Aquino, Italy. As a young boy he entered the Benedictine monastery at Monte Cassino, where his education was supervised by his uncle, the abbot. When he decided to become a Dominican monk at the age of nineteen, his family violently opposed the move, and had him kidnapped and confined on the family estate. He finally convinced them, however, and went on to become one of the greatest theologians of all time. A gentle bear of a man, tall, heavy, and soft-spoken, Thomas' shyness hid his skills from many observers. The astute, however, saw in the quiet student an intensity and power of concentration that would make him the most thorough scholar of his age.

Though he wrote brilliantly on many practical as well as theological issues, Thomas tended to be a bit absent-minded in his personal life. Though he loved to eat, he would sometimes become so absorbed in thought that his plate would be removed and the table cleared without him realizing it. Once, while eating dinner at the palace of Louis IX, the pious king of France who led the last of the Crusades, he became lost in thought. Suddenly he started, pounded the table with his sizeable fist, and announced, "That is the decisive argument against the Manichaeans!" The other guests were a bit taken aback, but Louis calmly ordered writing implements to be brought so Thomas could write down his new insight.

Despite the fact that he died at the relatively young age of 48, Aquinas left behind an enormous body of work. The most notable of his achievements are *Summa Theologica* ("A Summary of Theology") and *Summa Contra Gentiles* (a book of arguments intended to refute the teachings of Islam on the basis of reason). Like Abelard, Aquinas was a Moderate Realist, but unlike his predecessor, Thomas was a man of unimpeachable purity in life and orthodoxy in theology.

Unlike Anselm, Aquinas did not believe that all truth was susceptible to explanation by human reason. He taught instead that reason and revelation were like two great circles that overlapped but did not coincide. Some things could be known only by reason, while other things could be known only as God revealed them in His Word or through His Church. There were some truths, however, that had been revealed by God but could also be demonstrated by reason. Thomas believed that God had revealed these things to man because it was very difficult for reason to perceive them. They made up what he called Natural Theology, and form the key to his greatest work, the *Summa Theologica*. The most basic of these truths is the existence of God. Aquinas taught that the existence of God could be proved in five ways. While he rejected the Ontological Argument of Anselm, he maintained that God's existence could be proved from motion (all motion is caused by prior motion, and God is the first or Prime Mover), causality (every effect has a cause, and God is the First Cause), the derivative nature of being (every being derived its existence from another being, and God is the original and self-existent being), relative imperfection (we judge things to have degrees of perfection, but there must be a standard of perfection to which such things are compared, which is God), and design (the order found in the universe requires an intelligent Designer, who is God).

Aquinas relied heavily on Aristotle, not so much for content as for method. He refuted some of Aristotle's conclusions as contrary to church teaching, but used his logic in an effort to demonstrate the truth of Catholic doctrine. Such an approach could have gotten him into considerable trouble had he not been so good at it. Few could fault his careful logic, and his conclusions supported the teachings of the church in almost every particular. Needless to say, the fact that he demonstrated the logic of such matters as papal supremacy and infallibility did his cause no harm. In fact, the only issue on which he differed from the accepted teaching of the Catholic Church was his opposition to the Immaculate Conception of Mary - the idea that Mary was preserved from original sin at the time of her conception - which became official church dogma in 1854. As Thomas reaffirmed church doctrine, the Catholic Church has also affirmed its approval of his explanation of that doctrine. In 1879, Pope Leo XIII declared Thomism eternally valid, and that position was reiterated in 1923. To this day, the man who wishes to understand the doctrine of the Roman Catholic Church must read Thomas Aquinas.

JOHN DUNS SCOTUS (c.1266-1308)

If Thomas Aquinas marks the height of Scholasticism, Duns Scotus signals the beginning of its decline. "The Subtle Doctor" revealed the inherent weaknesses in the system without providing anything constructive to take its place. He stands at the forefront of the theology of the Franciscans as Thomas does for the Dominicans. As he opposed the writings of Aquinas, so the Thomists and Scotists fought, sometimes bitterly, in the years that followed. Little is known of his personal history. He was born somewhere in the British Isles (several locations vie for the honor), and taught in universities at Oxford, Paris, and Cologne, where he died at an early age.

The only theological contribution for which Duns Scotus is remembered is the doctrine of the Immaculate Conception of Mary. It is his one lasting legacy to the church. Otherwise, his ideas were primarily negative. He denied that the doctrines of the faith could be proved by reason (thus brushing aside Aquinas with a single sentence), but insisted that they must therefore be accepted on the authority of the church. This led to his famous conclusion that a thing may at the same time be true in philosophy and false in theology. His followers drew finer and finer distinctions between the realms of faith and reason, and such nit-picking sophistry eventually caused the leaders of the Reformation to label any hair-splitting fool a Dunce.

WILLIAM OF OCKHAM (c.1280-1349)

The complexity of Duns Scotus' writings may have kept his ideas out of the hands of the general population, but the division between faith and reason that he initiated was completed by the work of the Nominalist William of Ockham. Like Duns Scotus, Ockham was British, and like him became part of the Franciscan order. It was his involvement with the Spiritual Franciscans, who espoused the doctrine of absolute poverty (which was hardly what the very rich and very corrupt church hierarchy of the fourteenth century wanted to hear), rather than his Nominalism, that led to his condemnation by Pope John XXII in 1324, and eventual excommunication. He escaped from prison with the help of Louis of Bavaria, and spent the remainder of his career in the service of that prince writing dissertations on the independent authority of the state as established by God.

Ockham's teachings contributed in a variety of ways to both the Renaissance and the Reformation. His understanding of Nominalism led him to an absolute separation of revelation and reason. He argued that, since our experience, by which he meant both senses and reason, brings us knowledge of individual things, it is not necessary to bring universals into the picture at all (the principle that an argument based upon few assumptions is superior to one that requires many assumptions has come down through history as Ockham's Razor). Because of the limitations of our experience, such knowledge can never be more than probable. Absolute knowledge comes only from divine revelation.

The men of the Renaissance focused only on Ockham's view of human experience. To them, man should be free to explore his world and learn its secrets without being fettered by church dogma. Eventually, in later centuries, this view was extended to a complete denial of divine revelation, and an affirmation that all knowledge comes through human experience, relative and limited though it may be.

To Luther and some of the other Reformers, however, Ockham's philosophy was a valuable weapon against church authority. While the Church exists in the mind of God, the visible church on earth does not necessarily correspond to it. Therefore if final truth were only discernable through divine revelation, the church could not claim to corner the market. Fathers, councils, and popes could err; only the Scriptures were infallible. While William of Ockham would never have used these ideas in the same way Luther used them, he began to pry loose a few of the stones in the foundation of the edifice of church authority that the German Reformer eventually brought tumbling to the ground.

THE LEGACY OF SCHOLASTICISM

The most obvious legacy of the Schoolmen was the formulation of Roman Catholic doctrine in the manner in which it continues to a large extent to be expounded today. The theology of Thomas Aquinas is the theology of the Roman Catholic Church. But as historian Will Durant has indicated, Scholasticism contained the seeds of its own destruction:

"Scholasticism was a Greek tragedy, whose nemesis lurked in its essence. The attempt to establish the faith by reason implicitly acknowledged the authority of reason; the admission, by Duns Scotus and others, that the faith could not be established by reason shattered Scholasticism, and so weakened the faith that in the fourteenth century revolt broke out all along the doctrinal and ecclesiastical line. Aristotle's philosophy was a Greek gift to Latin Christendom, a Trojan horse concealing a thousand hostile elements. These seeds of the Renaissance and Enlightenment were not only `the revenge of paganism' over Christianity, they were also the unwitting revenge of Islam; invaded in Palestine, and driven from nearly all of Spain, the Moslems transmitted their science and philosophy to Western Europe, and it proved to be a disintegrating force; it was Avicenna and Averroës, as well as Aristotle, who infected Christianity with the germs of rationalism."

Scholasticism had begun in the late eleventh century with Anselm, convinced that revelation and reason could be represented by two coinciding circles, both containing identical truth. With the Moderate Realism of Aquinas, the circles became overlapping - revelation and reason, each with its own sphere, but sharing a point of contact in natural theology. With the coming of William of Ockham and Nominalism, however, the circles ceased to overlap. The separation of revelation and reason forced men to choose. Some rejected revelation and chose reason - "the revenge of paganism" of which

Durant spoke. Others affirmed that revelation is the only true source of truth, and thus rejected human reason, fleeing into mysticism to seek revelation in an immediate form; for still others, the primacy of revelation over reason meant that all truth obtained by the senses and the mind (or affirmed by the Church) needed to be subjected to the authority of Scripture before it could be acknowledged as truth indeed. But for the vast majority, the dichotomy between revelation and reason meant nothing so dramatic as a choice. For them, as for so many today, it meant hanging on to both for dear life despite the fact that there was no connection between the two. Men's lives came to be divided into the secular and sacred realms, with neither one having any bearing on the other.

What, then, is the legacy of Scholasticism? Roman Catholic orthodoxy? Renaissance humanism? Mysticism? The Reformation emphasis on Scripture? The schizophrenic separation of secular and sacred? Our conclusion must be that the answer is, "All of the above."

MAKING DRY BONES LIVE

To those of the twentieth century, there are few sets of bones that seem drier than the skeleton of medieval Scholasticism. Yet the development and decline of Scholasticism contains an important lesson for us. When the writings of Aristotle first became readily available in the West near the beginning of the thirteenth century, they were banned by the church. Scholars read them anyway, of course, and the ban probably even increased the popularity of Aristotle's works among university students. By the middle of the century, however, respected churchmen like Thomas Aquinas were arguing that Aristotle could be an asset to the Christian faith, and developing complex systems of doctrine to harmonize the two. Once Thomism came to be accepted by the Roman Catholic Church at large, it became important to defend the philosophy of Aristotle, since in their view the rational basis of Christian doctrine depended on his reliability. Thus by the early part of the seventeenth century, men like Galileo were being charged with heresy and threatened with the stake for challenging, not the Bible or even church councils or popes, but Aristotle. Within the space of four centuries, Aristotle had gone from *persona non grata* to foundation of orthodoxy!

It is with precisely this kind of subtlety that Satan infiltrates the church with the wisdom of this world. What is prohibited today will be permitted tomorrow and required the next day, not only in the realm of worldly philosophy, but also in the area of ethics. Often in their desire to respond to the attacks of the world, Christians use and then accept the methods of the world. If there is one thing that we can learn from the sad story of Scholasticism, it is that God's work must be done in God's way. The Word of God must be the foundation, not only for what we believe, but for the way we defend and live out that belief.

FOR REVIEW AND FURTHER THOUGHT

1. What is Scholasticism?

2. What is the relationship between Scholasticism and Gothic cathedrals?

3. How did the Crusades contribute to the development of Scholasticism?

4. What made the Schoolmen so sure that faith and reason were compatible?

5. What did the Schoolmen hope to accomplish by proving what they already knew to be true?

6. What was the key difference between Realism and Nominalism?

7. What was Conceptualism? How did it relate to Realism and Nominalism?

8. What is the connection between Realism, Nominalism, Conceptualism, and the philosophies of Plato and Aristotle?

9. In what way did Realism tend to support and Nominalism tend to undermine the doctrine of the Trinity?

10. How did the mystics view the relationship of faith and reason?

11. Summarize in your own words the Ontological Argument for the existence of God.

12. How was the Ontological Argument an outgrowth of Realism?

13. Summarize Anselm's satisfaction theory of the Atonement. How was this an improvement on the view that prevailed at the time?

14. In what way is Peter Abelard an illustration of the adage, "Your life speaks so loudly, I can't hear what you say"?

15. What role did Roscelin, William of Champeaux, Fulbert, Astrolabe, and Bernard of Clairvaux play in the life of Abelard?

16. What was the method of education followed by Abelard in *Sic et Non*?

17. How did this approach undermine Scholasticism in the long run? How did it encourage misinterpretation of Scripture?

18. What ideas of Abelard later became a standard part of Scholasticism?

19. In what sense did Abelard advocate relativism in ethics?

20. How did Bernard of Clairvaux believe that God could best be known?

Cathedrals of the Mind

21. Why is Thomas Aquinas considered the greatest of the Schoolmen?

22. What is the realm of knowledge covered by natural theology?

23. Explain in your own words one of Aquinas' proofs for the existence of God.

24. What is the single doctrine about which the Catholic Church today differs from the teaching of Thomas Aquinas? Who was the man largely responsible for defending this doctrine?

25. How could Duns Scotus assert that something could be true and false at the same time?

26. What did the Spiritual Franciscans believe? Why were they persecuted?

27. How did William of Ockham contribute to the Renaissance? the Reformation?

28. What is Ockham's Razor?

29. Why did Will Durant call Scholasticism a Greek tragedy?

30. How did the church's view of the relationship between faith and reason change from the time of Anselm to the time of William of Ockham?

31. How did humanists, mystics, and Protestant Reformers deal with the dichotomy between revelation and reason with which the Scholastic period ended?

32. How many angels can stand on the head of a pin?

16

THE POOR IN SPIRIT

The chief characteristic of life in Western Europe in the High Middle Ages was dissatisfaction. People simply were not satisfied with their lives. Nobles dissatisfied with petty wars with their neighbors sought new adventures in the Holy Land. Scholars dissatisfied with the barren thought of the Dark Ages banded together in universities to learn new ideas. Even peasants became dissatisfied with their lot in the feudal system and migrated in droves to the towns, where they might improve their position in society. But the deepest dissatisfaction of all that marked the latter part of the Middle Ages was the widespread conviction that something was seriously wrong with the church. As we saw in chapter twelve, there was good reason for this. The church was in bad shape at the end of its first millennium, and something needed to be done about it. The push for change in society at large was in the forward direction - new places, new ideas, new economic structures - and those who sought to reform the church for the most part also sought to move ahead. The reforming popes from Gregory VII to Innocent III, for instance, were looking to make the kingdom of God on earth a reality by building a theocracy in which all of Europe was ruled by Christ's earthly representative, the pope, while at the same time extending Christ's dominion into the lands of the eastern Mediterranean.

Not all agreed that the right direction to look was forward, however. The monastic reformers saw the ideal in the distant past, and sought to recover the purity and simplicity of an earlier age by cleansing the church of all its worldly accretions. Whether they went back to the early monks or to the apostolic age is a matter of indifference; what they all had in common was the conviction that the cure for the corruption in the church was to turn the clock backward. In the eleventh through the fourteenth centuries, the church repeatedly channeled these "back-to-basics" movements into monasteries, thus minimizing their impact on society. Those that could not be channeled into monasteries were either used by the hierarchy to further their own purposes or stigmatized as heretics and violently suppressed. As long as the church ruled Europe, popular religious movements had little chance of producing permanent change. As the power of the papacy declined in the face of the rising nation-states of Europe, however, the drive for reform finally found an outlet that could neither be channeled nor suppressed - the Protestant Reformation.

The High Middle Ages was the greatest period of monastic activity in the history of the church. The corruption in the church produced reform after reform, so much so that the Fourth Lateran Council in 1215 finally proclaimed that no more new monastic orders were to be permitted - a decision that was violated almost immediately with the formation of the Franciscans and Dominicans. The monks represent both the best and the worst examples of medieval Christianity, ranging from the simple piety of Francis of Assisi to the vicious repression of the Inquisition. But monasticism contained within itself the seeds of its own downfall. The sure path to success for a monastic movement was austerity, but success brought recognition, gifts from nobles and peasants alike, and papal favors, all of which soon removed both the means and the motivation for the austerity that had brought success to the movement to begin with. Thus a new reform was required, and the cycle went on and on.

REFORMERS IN THE MONASTERIES

The order founded by Benedict of Nursia in the sixth century had gradually come to dominate Western monasticism. As the early Middle Ages passed into the Dark Ages, the Benedictine monks preserved what there was of the Christian faith, but they also gradually slipped away from the strict observance of the Rule given them by their founder. In the same way that the petty feudal barons of the ninth and tenth centuries dominated and perverted the papacy, so similar men corrupted the monasteries, appointing as abbots men who looked only for a comfortable living, and allowed the monks to live in open violation of their vows.

A.   THE CLUNIACS

The first stirrings of reform came from the Benedictine monastery at Cluny, France. The monastery was founded by William of Aquitaine in 910, and his concern for the purity of monastic life led him to stipulate that the monks were to be free to elect their own leaders and govern their own affairs without interference from the local barons. Over the next two or three centuries, the monastery at Cluny was led by a succession of pious and capable abbots who enforced the Benedictine Rule in their own house while at the same time extending their influence to hundreds of other monasteries all over Europe. The Cluniac movement thus became a major force in returning the monasteries to their original purpose of solitary labor and contemplation.

The major impact of Cluny, however, was not its effect on monasticism, though that effect was significant. More than any other single source, the Cluniacs produced the men who powered the Hildebrandine reform of the clergy and papal hierarchy. Hildebrand himself spent some time at Cluny, as did Urban II and two other men who served as popes. In addition, many bishops and abbots who supported the reform were in sympathy with the Cluniac movement.

Like the Benedictine movement they sought to reform, the Cluniacs soon became rich and powerful, and their influence drew them away from their own stated purposes. By the twelfth century, other, newer houses were criticizing the Cluniacs for their laxness in discipline and ostentatious shows of wealth. The reformers themselves were in need of reformation.

B.   THE CISTERCIANS

When Robert of Molesme left his Benedictine monastery in Burgundy to start a new house at Citeaux in 1098, he had in mind another back-to-basics movement, much like that begun at Cluny almost two centuries earlier. He also incorporated some new ideas, however, that he was convinced would enable the monastery to fulfill its purpose more faithfully. More than anything else, the Cistercians, as they came to be called, suspected that the fundamental cause of Cluny's decline was the wealth it had accumulated. While this wealth had come largely because of the success of the Cluniacs, which brought gifts and endowments, it had ultimately undermined the whole monastic purpose by making the monasteries places of comfort and even luxury rather than retreats from the world. The Cistercians sought to avoid this by extending the vow of poverty from the individual monks to the order as a whole. While the monks of Cluny owned little themselves, the monasteries accumulated enormous wealth. The Cistercians were determined that this would not happen to them. They consequently decided to shun the elaborate buildings and expensive vestments and instruments of worship favored by the Cluniacs in favor of simple structures of wood and vestments of common cloth.

In order to encourage austerity, the Cistercians located their monasteries far from civilization. Instead of building monasteries near towns and cities, the Cistercians found isolated valleys and mountain peaks where their monks could live apart from the corrupting influences of the world. They also sought to ensure dedication among the monks by refusing to accept oblates - children sent to monasteries at an early age by their parents as a sort of sacrifice to God, after the model of Samuel in the Old Testament. Instead, they insisted that applicants must be of age, and come of their own free will.

The Cistercians also adopted an organizational structure designed to maintain discipline. While the Cluniacs had been ruled by a single abbot, who was physically incapable of supervising the hundreds of monasteries under his care, the Cistercians established a system whereby each monastery would have its own abbot. The abbots of the first five Cistercian monasteries would each supervise a district, and would visit the monasteries in their district on a regular basis. They would also be accountable to one another, submitting to each other's inspections. The abbots would all then meet at Citeaux annually to discuss matters of concern to the order.

Many were drawn to the movement because of its severe discipline, but many more were drawn because of its greatest single representative, the saintly Bernard of Clairvaux. Bernard had been raised by devout parents near the monastery at Citeaux, and entered that monastery in 1112, at the age of 22. He convinced all but one of his brothers to accompany him, along with several dozen other friends. These thirty men brought to Citeaux such a zeal for holiness that they turned the monastery upside down. Bernard himself was so dedicated to the monastic life that he later felt it necessary to repent of the ways in which he had abused his body. The number of residents at Citeaux grew so rapidly that soon another house was needed, and the young Bernard was chosen to lead a group of twelve monks in the formation of a new settlement. Bernard chose an isolated valley that he named Clairvaux, and there founded the second monastery of the Cistercian order. He remained as the abbot of the monastery at Clairvaux for the rest of his life, though he rarely had the opportunity to enjoy the peace and quiet for which he so desperately longed.

Bernard was a man of such sterling qualities that the world could not leave him alone for very long. He became the outstanding religious leader of his generation. He inspired thousands to enter monastic life, so that it was said that mothers hid their sons and young women their lovers whenever they heard he was coming to town, lest they be convinced to devote their lives to the monastery. He also dominated the popes and kings of his day by the sheer force of his personality. When preaching the Second Crusade, he convinced both the King of France and the Holy Roman Emperor to participate. When two rival popes were elected at the same time and the monarchs of Europe were divided in their support of them, Bernard threw his weight behind the one he considered most morally fit and convinced the rulers to fall into line with his choice. When one of his own monks became Pope Eugene III, Bernard did not hesitate to write to him and encourage him to live like Jesus instead of like an oriental potentate. He used his influence to bring about the condemnation of Peter Abelard and his rabble-rousing pupil Arnold of Brescia. Meanwhile, his own purity of life and evident love for God continued to inspire respect among people both high and low.

As with the Cluniacs, the success of the Cistercians led directly to their decline. The movement grew rapidly, but the wealth and papal favor that came with popularity soon undermined the discipline that had made the Cistercians so attractive to so many in the first place.

C. THE RULE OF SAINT AUGUSTINE

From the sixth century through the eleventh, the Benedictine Rule dominated Western monasticism. When the Hildebrandine reformers came to power in the eleventh century, however, one of their major goals was to enforce discipline among the clergy. In addition to the monks and priests, other minor church functionaries were also expected to abstain from marriage. Among these were a class of clerics known as canons regular, who attended to many administrative duties on the local level. The reformers were convinced that such men could more easily be held to the ideal of a celibate life if they, too, had a Rule to follow. The Rule chosen by many was the Rule of Saint Augustine. While Augustine of Hippo ran his diocese in

North Africa, he himself had lived a semimonastic life with a group of men in his city. They remained celibate, lived simply, and followed strict discipline. Though this "Rule" was not formally stated, but only contained in a letter from Augustine to one of his friends, it became the basis for the Augustinian Canons. The generality and flexibility of the Rule made it immediately popular, and it quickly spread throughout large areas of Europe.

One notably successful group that adopted the Rule of Saint Augustine was the Premonstrants, founded in 1119 at Premontre, France by a German named Norbert, who was dissatisfied with the laxity he found among the Benedictines. Norbert modeled the discipline among the Premonstrants after that of the Cistercians, but he allowed the canons to travel about preaching to the populace, though strangely enough he also forbade the reading of books.

Though the Premonstrants never became a large order, their practice of preaching influenced the later mendicants. This was particularly true of the Dominicans. Dominic himself was an Augustinian canon, and his order initially adopted the Rule of Saint Augustine. Later, a group of monks in Italy in the thirteenth century formed the Augustinian Friars (or Austin Friars), a mendicant movement that came to be closely associated with the Dominicans, and that produced as its most famous member a young German named Martin Luther.

D. THE EXTREMES OF ASCETICISM

Like the monks of the early church, some were never satisfied with the level of austerity achieved by others. They were convinced that holiness was only to be found in total separation from the world and complete denial of the flesh. Most notable among these were the Carthusians. The order was originated by Bruno of Cologne, who founded a house at Chartreuse in the French Alps. The standards of asceticism practiced by Bruno and his followers included strict vegetarianism, regular self-flagellation, and the complete exclusion of women from the premises. Because of their strictness, the Carthusians had much more success than most of the other orders in shutting out the temptations of the world, and thus maintained their discipline and devotion to the principles of their founder for many centuries.

Another group that sought after strict asceticism was the Order of Our Lady of Mount Carmel, generally known as Carmelites. The order was founded on Mount Carmel in Palestine by a crusading knight named Berthold in 1156, though the members of the order insist that it dates instead from the time of Elijah. Allegedly the sons of the prophets formed a monastic community on Mount Carmel that still existed in Jesus' day. At that time, the monks were converted to Christianity, and perpetuated a Christian monastery in that location until the time of the Crusades. No evidence of such an order has ever been found, however, so most historians date the Carmelites to the time of Berthold. In fact, the issue of the origin of the Carmelite order became a bone of contention between the Carmelites and the Jesuits in the seventeenth century. When the Jesuits insisted that Berthold had founded the order rather than Elijah, the Carmelites objected. The dispute caused such great bitterness that it was finally brought before the pope, who ordered them both to remain silent on the issue until he rendered a decision. He never did, and the dispute soon faded into insignificance.

The Carmelites originally followed the same type of austere regimen as the Carthusians, but eventually became mendicants. The mystic Theresa of Avila made an effort to bring the order back to its original discipline in the sixteenth century, but she eventually formed a separate order known as the Barefoot Carmelites. The Carmelites are distinguished by the veneration and use of the scapulary, a sort of vest that they claim was received from the Virgin Mary by a thirteenth-century general of the order. According to the story, Mary promised to visit Purgatory every Saturday and deliver from there anyone who had worn the vest. Pope John XXII accepted the account in 1322 when he proclaimed that all members of the order would indeed be delivered from Purgatory on the first

Saturday after they died, and Pope Benedict XIV included it in the official teaching of the Catholic Church in the eighteenth century.

E. THE DEFENDERS OF THE FAITHFUL

If the Crusades could be glorified as fighting pilgrimages, there is no reason to expect that the Crusaders themselves could not be pictured as fighting monks. Thus it should come as no surprise that the crusading era produced a number of military orders that attempted to combine the asceticism of the monk with the Crusader's zeal for the faith. The three most prominent of the military orders were all founded in the twelfth century in connection with the Crusader kingdoms - the Knights of St. John, also known as Hospitallers (1113), the Knights Templar (1119), and the Teutonic Knights (1190). All three originally devoted themselves to caring for and protecting pilgrims, but they later turned to fighting, and often put formidable armies into the field against the Turks. While Saladin respected Richard the Lion-Hearted, he despised and mistrusted the military orders, and showed them no mercy.

The Hospitallers, a French order, were originally dedicated to caring for wounded Crusaders. After the fall of Acre and the end of the Crusades, they established their headquarters on Cyprus, later moved to Rhodes, and were finally given the island of Malta. They became very rich through donations and powerful as a result of receiving papal privileges, and did much to defend Europe from Turkish invasion in the late Middle Ages.

The Templars, so called because their first headquarters was located near the Temple mount in Jerusalem, were explicitly military in their purpose from the very beginning. They, too, became rich and powerful, but their power and wealth made them lax and made their critics jealous. The order was eventually suppressed in 1312 on the basis of serious charges of immorality, including rumors of occult practices, though the confessions were obtained by torture under the supervision of Philip the Fair of France, who coveted the wealth of the Templars and mistrusted their power.

The Teutonic Knights were a German order who also ran hospitals for the wounded during the Crusades. After the Crusades they continued to establish hospitals in Germany, and used their military might to tame the wild lands near the German-Polish border. They eventually became the lords of Prussia and controlled a significant portion of the land in Germany. In 1523, Luther convinced the grand master of the order to renounce celibacy and turn to the Reformation. The Teutonic Knights ultimately went on to found the great noble families upon which the kingdom of Prussia was established.

THE FRIARS - IN THE WORLD, BUT NOT OF IT

The greatest change introduced into monasticism in the Middle Ages was the idea that monks were not to isolate themselves from the world, but be instruments of God to bring Christ to the world, while themselves remaining apart from its temptations. This was the ideal of the Mendicants, or Begging Friars, the most important of which were the Franciscans and Dominicans.

A. THE FRANCISCANS

Historically, the ranks of the monasteries had been filled by members of the aristocracy. The rich had both the leisure and education to allow them to focus their minds on spiritual things; furthermore, their experience of the world taught them that the things of the world were empty, and whetted their appetites for spiritual things. On a more practical level, monasteries and convents were often convenient places for noblemen to dump extra sons and daughters, and became for those sons and daughters their best chance to gain an education and make a way for themselves in the world.

The breakup of feudalism brought a new awakening to the peasants who migrated to the towns, however. Now they, too, saw things that stimulated them to seek a deeper level of spiritual experience. In addition, the growing middle class of merchants and artisans sought an outlet for their religious desires. For most of these people, the traditional monastic orders simply were not a practical alternative. They had families and businesses that depended upon them, and they could not afford to leave them and enter a monastery. Yet they wanted to serve Christ in some way.

From such desires sprang a whole series of lay religious movements in the late Middle Ages. Most chose a simple lifestyle, and many observed voluntary celibacy. While a few, such as the Waldensians, eventually deviated from Catholic orthodoxy, most remained well within the confines of church teaching. Such groups as the Beghards, Beguines, and Humiliati sought nothing more than to live the life of Christ where they were, though they were periodically accused of heresy or immorality by a church hierarchy suspicious of anyone who was not directly under papal supervision. By far the most notable of these lay religious movements among the poor and middle class was the Franciscans, founded by Francis of Assisi in the early part of the thirteenth century.

Francis is probably the most attractive personality of the Middle Ages, but his life did not begin like the life of a saint. He was the son of Pietro Bernardone, a rich merchant in the town of Assisi in northern Italy, and took advantage of his father's wealth to live a life of pleasure. In 1204, at the age of 22, he took part in a minor Italian war and was taken prisoner. He then became ill, and the time of enforced idleness gave him a chance to reflect on his life. He did not like what he saw. He began to spend more and more time in the chapels in and around Assisi, while his father grew increasingly puzzled by the change in his son's behavior. Finally, when young Francis sold some of his father's property and gave the money to the poor, Pietro had had enough. He hauled his son before the local bishop and demanded that his goods be returned. Francis promptly stripped himself naked and handed his clothes and all they contained to his astonished father, and vowed from that moment on to be the son only of his Father in heaven.

Francis then began a career of preaching and service to the poor. He was especially concerned for lepers, and often would minister to them and dress their sores and wounds. He was ashamed whenever he met anyone poorer than himself, and his followers complained of always having to find him new clothes after he gave his away to some naked beggar. Francis' love of nature was proverbial. He loved all creatures, not in the sense that a pantheist sees God in nature, but in the sense that he believed God reveals Himself through what He has made, and wanted all God's creatures to praise Him. Thus he preached to birds, supposedly calmed a wolf who was about to attack him and rebuked him for harming God's creatures, and wrote the famous Canticle of the Sun, a hymn of praise to God for His wonderful creation.

Francis' preaching was ethical rather than doctrinal. He encouraged his hearers to live simply and love all creatures. As followers gathered to his side, he gave them no other rule than the instructions of Jesus found in Matthew 16:24-26; 19:21; and Luke 9:1-6. When he was told that he needed the permission of the pope to preach, he went to Rome in 1210 and met with Innocent III. Innocent was impressed with Francis' obvious sincerity and piety, but doubted that many would be able to observe the life of absolute poverty that Francis himself had chosen. He gave Francis permission to preach, but only with the consent of the local bishop. Francis agreed, and soon gained fame far and wide. Wherever he went, crowds would gather to see, hear, and touch him. Followers multiplied. The Order of Friars Minor (the official name of the Franciscans) soon added a branch for women. Because it was initiated by a young girl from Assisi named Clara, they came to be called the Poor Clares. Francis then began to send his followers out on missionary journeys to spread the Good News. His own desire was to preach to the Muslims and win them to Christ. In 1219, he accompanied the soldiers of the Fifth Crusade to Egypt, where he spoke at length with the Sultan, though he was unable to convert him to Christianity. He returned a year later to Italy, disillusioned with the barbarity of the entire crusading enterprise, and determined that his followers should seek after peace with all of God's creatures.

When he arrived home, he found that his order had moved far from his original purpose.

While he had sought simplicity and freedom to preach, he found a rule of discipline similar to other monastic orders. While he opposed learning as a distraction from ministry to the poor, he found Franciscans actively seeking entrance into the university faculties. Worst of all, the man who advocated and himself set a standard of absolute poverty found his followers compromising by allowing the pope to hold property for the use of the order. Most of these changes had been instituted by Cardinal Ugolino, a close friend of Francis who later became Pope Gregory IX, who firmly believed that the order should be transformed into an instrument of the church. This saddened Francis, who turned the order over to an associate who was more administratively inclined and went into virtual seclusion. In the years that followed, his health declined, possibly because of diseases contracted in Egypt, and he died in 1226 at the age of 44. He is said to have received the *stigmata* (the marks of the wounds of Christ in his hands, feet, and side) two years prior to his death, though the evidence for this is somewhat debatable.

The Franciscans thus departed from the principles of their founder very early in their history. They went on to produce numerous contributors to the medieval church, including scholars like John Bonaventure, Duns Scotus, Roger Bacon, and William of Ockham, and many missionaries. In the succeeding centuries some in the order sought to return to the absolute poverty and simplicity of Francis. They came to be called the Observants, Spirituals, or *Fraticelli*, and were often persecuted by the church, with some of the more radical being excommunicated for heresy and burned at the stake by the Inquisition. Thus it was that some of his followers were tortured and executed for the same teachings and practices for which Saint Francis was canonized two years after his death.

B. THE DOMINICANS

If the Franciscans were organized for the purpose of converting the Muslims, the Dominicans were intended to evangelize the heretical Albigensians of southern France. When Dominic Guzman, a young Spanish Augustinian canon, accompanied his bishop to a conference in France, he was appalled by the heresy that dominated the region. He wondered why the church had been unable to put a stop to these false teachings, but when he met three papal representatives who had been sent to the region, he understood. The papal legates wore rich clothing and were accompanied by all the trappings of power. As far as the Albigensians, who valued simplicity and poverty and who thought the Catholic Church to be the false church of the Antichrist, were concerned, the haughty emissaries of the pope only confirmed their judgment. Dominic insisted that the Albigensians would never be won to the true faith except by those who lived lives of simplicity and holiness, and he determined to do just that. Though he had some small measure of success, Innocent III had already decided that the heretics needed to be stamped out by violence if necessary.

When Dominic went to Rome to appear before the Fourth Lateran Council in 1215 and seek approval for a new monastic order, Innocent encouraged his work, but refused to authorize a new order. Instead, he told Dominic to choose a Rule that was already in use. Having been an Augustinian, he adopted the Rule of Saint Augustine. After Innocent's death, Honorius III established the Order of Preaching Friars, better known as the Dominicans. Dominic met Francis on several occasions, and in 1220 committed his order to mendicancy on the same basis as the Franciscans, though the standard of absolute poverty was never strictly observed and was soon dropped.

After Dominic's death in 1221, his order spread rapidly throughout Europe. While Francis of Assisi had sought to reach the heart, Dominic targeted the mind. He had thus encouraged learning, and the Dominicans produced some of the most notable of medieval scholars, including Albertus Magnus and Thomas Aquinas. Like the Franciscans, they also produced many missionaries, including the famous missionary to the Americas, Bartolomeo de Las Casas. The work for which they are best known, albeit somewhat unfairly, is the conduct of the Inquisition. Such Dominicans as Bernardo Gui and Tomas de Torquemada head the list of the administrators of that brutal institution.

THE DISSENTERS

Periods in history that are characterized by great bursts of creative energy are usually also characterized by heresy in the church. There can be no heresy where there is no independent thought, but where there is independent thought, some minds will wander off in the wrong direction. Thus it should not surprise us that there was little in the way of heresy in the Dark Ages. With the stimulating events of the eleventh century, however, came intellectual and spiritual ferment, not all of which moved people in a direction approved by the church. The two most notable heretical groups, the Cathars and the Waldensians, were vastly different from one another in almost every way, yet they elicited the same response from the church - the Inquisition.

A. THE CATHARS

There can be little doubt that the Cathars were genuine heretics. They appear to have gotten their teachings through contact with the Paulicians and Bogomils, who were heretical groups in Eastern Europe. The Cathars were also known as Patarenes (from a district in Milan where they were prominent) and Albigensians (from the city of Albi in southern France that was one of their strongholds). The only disadvantage we face in evaluating them is that the only surviving sources of information were written by their enemies, whose objectivity is at best questionable. From all available accounts, it appears that the Cathars (from the Greek word for "pure") were dualists who perpetuated the heresy of the Manichaeans from the Ancient Church era, who taught that there were two gods, one good, who had created Spirit, and one evil, who had created matter. They were strict ascetics who shunned marriage, meat, and manual labor. They were divided into two groups: the perfect, who devoted themselves to complete commitment to the practices of the group, and the believers, who supported the perfect and honored them to an extent that was little short of worship. They rejected the sacraments of the church because they partook of the evil of matter, and rejected transubstantiation for the same reason. Satan had been cast from heaven when he had tempted the other angels with women, and Adam had fallen through sexual intercourse with Eve. They taught that the Jehovah of the Old Testament was the evil god who created matter, while Jesus was a life-giving Spirit who came to bring light to the earth. Because He did not have a body, He never suffered or died, however. Salvation was obtained by receiving the *consolamentum*, the only sacrament practiced by the group. It involved a sort of spiritual baptism, in which a copy of the Gospel of John was placed on the breast of the initiate, and one of the perfect laid hands on him. The recipient of the *consolamentum* then became one of the perfect. Most believers declined to receive the *consolamentum* until death was imminent, because they feared lapsing again into sin and losing their salvation. In fact, some accounts survive of newly-perfected Cathars who were smothered at their own request when they unexpectedly recovered from what was thought to be a fatal illness, or who starved themselves to death to avoid lapsing. Cathars denied the existence of hell or purgatory, however, believing that a loving God would never cause one of the souls He had made to suffer - even if it required several incarnations to reach the state of perfection.

The Cathars of southern France were the objects of a series of brutal crusades in the first half of the thirteenth century. Innocent III, frustrated that the scourge of Catharism had not been eradicated by the local nobles and bishops and angry that his papal legate, Peter of Castelnau, had been murdered by an unknown assassin, called for a Crusade against them in 1208, reasoning that if the faithful could take up arms against the Turk, how much more should force be used to put an end to those who were destroying the Church of Christ from within. The nobles of northern France, eager to take advantage of the promised indulgences and have a chance to gobble up the fertile land of the south, responded enthusiastically under the leadership of Simon de Montfort. The resulting wars were vicious. Perhaps the worst example of the atrocities that were committed in the name of orthodoxy was the fall of Beziers. After the city had been conquered, the crusading soldiers began to slaughter the inhabitants. Realizing that there were many Catholics in the city, they asked the papal legate how they could tell the difference between Catholics and Cathars. The legate responded, "Kill them all. The Lord knows His own." On that day, twenty thousand men, women, and children were massacred, seven thousand of whom had taken sanctuary, unarmed, inside the city's largest church. By the time the Crusades and the Inquisition had finished their bloody work in 1244, the Cathars were no more, and most of the beautiful countryside of southern France had been reduced to rubble.

B. THE WALDENSIANS

The Waldensians are usually lumped with the Cathars because they flourished in the same general area at the same time as the Cathars, and shared the same persecution at the hands of the Catholic Church. The Waldensians, however, have far more in common with the Franciscans than they do with the Cathars. In fact, had the Franciscans preceded the Waldensians instead of the other way around, the latter may never have had a reason to exist at all.

The Waldensians, or Poor Men of Lyons, were founded by a rich merchant of Lyons named Peter Waldo in about 1170. He heard a minstrel sing a ballad about a young man who had abandoned his new wife to go on a Crusade, then returned home years later to beg unrecognized on the doorstep of his former home. The ballad challenged Waldo to place spiritual things above the things of this world, and he gave sufficient property to his wife to sustain her, placed his two young daughters in a convent, and gave away the rest of his money and possessions to the poor. He then found a priest who was willing to translate portions of the Bible into the language of the people. He took these, memorized them, and went around preaching and counseling others to follow his example. When the archbishop of Lyons told him to stop preaching, he went to Rome to appeal to the pope, and appeared at the Third Lateran Council in 1179. In order to be sure of his orthodoxy, the pope required him to be examined by Walter Map, a subtle English aristocrat. Map wanted nothing to do with the ignorant merchant, and ridiculed him for his lack of theological knowledge. The pope approved of Waldo's ministry, but told him that he and his followers could only preach with the permission of the local bishop. This, of course, was exactly the same response Francis of Assisi received over thirty years later. But Francis was a saint, a man of such remarkable character that most bishops gladly gave him permission to preach. Waldo had no such advantage, and quickly found that no one was willing to grant the permission he sought. He soon decided that God had called him to preach, and he ought to obey God rather than men. He continued his preaching, and sent his followers out two by two to spread the Gospel. As a result, they were excommunicated in 1184, and in the process lumped with the Cathars by the church.

When the church rejected the Waldensians, they in turn rejected the church. They maintained that the only authority by which men should live was the Scriptures; popes and councils could err, but the Bible could not. They then proceeded to reject those teachings of the church that were not found in the Scriptures, such as transubstantiation, purgatory, and especially the mediatorial role of the clergy. The Waldensians, in fact, insisted that there were only two sacraments, baptism and the Lord's Supper; that these only had power when received in faith; and that any godly man or woman could preach or forgive sins. While many of these teachings sound like they came right out of the Protestant Reformation, the Waldensians were not Protestants. Missing was the key teaching that defined the Reformation - justification by faith. The Waldensians were still looking for salvation through the holiness of their lives. Though this was certainly superior to salvation through the sacraments, it was a far cry from the emphasis on the grace of God in salvation that the Reformation brought to the church.

The Waldensians were persecuted by the same Crusades and Inquisition that destroyed Catharism. Many died, but large numbers fled into the mountains of northern Italy, where they survived until the sixteenth century as an identifiable community. They had much in common with the Lollards and Hussites, whom we will discuss in chapter 18, and like those groups threw in their lot with the Protestant Reformation in the sixteenth century. The Waldensians still exist today in Italy as the oldest Protestant body native to that country.

C. THE INQUISITION

When people think of the Inquisition, the first thing that usually comes to mind is some bloody account of torture like Edgar Allen Poe's *The Pit and the Pendulum*. While the Inquisition was undoubtedly bloody, it must be understood in the context of its times.

For centuries, the church and state in the Middle Ages had been struggling for power, and one of the bones of contention had been the right to try offenders. The church had insisted that religious offenders should be tried in church courts, while the state should restrict itself to civil matters. This sounds good in theory, but in an era where the realms of church and state were not easily distinguishable, it was very hard to put into practice. As far as heresy was concerned, it was widely recognized that, since the church was the glue that held society together, false teaching threatened the state as well as the church. Thus those convicted of false teaching by the church would be subject also to civil penalties by the state. At this point, things tended to get a bit hypocritical. The church was not permitted to shed blood (thus bishops who fought in the Crusades used maces - heavy clubs - rather than swords, for instance), so it could do no more than excommunicate the heretic. The next step was up to the state. Of course, the church then proceeded to threaten excommunication for any monarch who refused to punish heretics.

The Inquisition was based on a procedure in Roman law whereby officials would "inquire" into the charges brought against someone. In such inquiries, the accused would have to prove his innocence, and would not have the opportunity to face his accusers, or even to know who they were. The church adopted these procedures in its own courts. When the Cathar heresy first appeared in France, the bishops were encouraged to examine their parishioners on a regular basis to root out heresy. The bishops, however, usually had little taste for this sort of thing, and Catharism grew by leaps and bounds. In 1229, at the Council of Toulouse, the Inquisition was turned over to the Dominicans, who fulfilled their charge with cold efficiency. They soon came to be called "The Lord's Watchdogs" - a pun on their Latin name (*Dominicanes = domini canis*). The pope added a final weapon to their arsenal in 1252, when he authorized the use of torture to extract confessions. When the Inquisitor arrived in a town, he announced his intention to hold court, and offered a one-week grace period in which heretics could confess and be forgiven, with the assignment of certain penances. He also encouraged the people to report any suspected heretics. Those who were brought before the Inquisition could be condemned on the basis of the testimony of two witnesses; wives and children of the accused could testify against them, but not for them; the accused was not represented by an attorney (he had that right, but since anyone who defended a heretic could be accused of heresy himself, few volunteered for the task). Those who confessed were sentenced to life in prison, while those who refused to do so were usually burned at the stake.

After the destruction of the Cathars, the Inquisition increasingly became a political weapon in the hands of the rulers of Europe. Ferdinand and Isabella used it to gain control of Spain, and the Spanish later turned it against Protestants in the Netherlands. For many, it became a convenient way to dispose of political enemies. In later years, it became a tool to stamp out witchcraft, which again was so loosely defined that many were tempted to turn the Inquisition to their own profit.

MAKING DRY BONES LIVE

The monastic movements of the eleventh through the thirteenth centuries came about because of a hunger that those movements could never satisfy. The power politics and rationalistic theology of the popes and Schoolmen left a dry taste in people's mouths. They hungered for the Word of God and the life of Christ in the church. Monasticism could provide neither. Instead, the people were told that the only way to find the Christlike life was to leave family and society and deny the world, even while living as a part of it. The Word of God became an abstraction for scholars to debate; when men like the Waldensians dared to bring it to the common people in their own language, they were excluded from the church. In fact, the Council of Toulouse in 1229 put the Bible on the Index of Forbidden Books, and condemned all who would translate it into the common language.

When the church becomes divorced from the Word of God and fails to demonstrate the life of Christ, it ceases to be the church. When those who professed to represent Christ on earth lived like the devil and persecuted those who spread the Word, the church was setting itself up for judgment. When the Protestant Reformation came in the sixteenth century, nothing the church did could stop those who preached the Word of God and manifested the life of His Son.

FOR REVIEW AND FURTHER THOUGHT

1. Why was there such general dissatisfaction with the church at the beginning of the eleventh century?

2. In what sense were the monastic reforms of the Middle Ages an attempt to return to the past?

3. Why did the monastic reform movements almost always decline as a result of their success?

4. How did the Cluniacs attempt to reform the Benedictine monasteries?

5. What was the relationship between the Cluniacs and the Hildebrandine reform of the clergy?

6. What new ideas did Robert of Molesme introduce into the Cistercian order? How were these intended to prevent corruption?

7. Why did the Rule of Saint Augustine become popular among minor clerics in the church?

8. In what sense did the Premonstrants prefigure the work of the mendicants?

9. Why did the Carthusians avoid corruption more effectively than the other monastic orders of their day?

10. How did the Carmelites explain the origin of their order?

11. What is a scapulary, and what is its special relationship to the Carmelites?

12. What were the three most prominent military orders, and what were the distinctives of each?

13. What are mendicants? How did they differ from other monastic orders?

14. Why were many early monastic orders populated largely by the aristocracy?

15. How did Francis of Assisi's love of nature differ from pantheism?

16. In what ways did the Franciscans deviate from the principles laid down by their founder?

17. What were the original missionary enterprises pursued by the Franciscans and Dominicans?

18. Why was there no significant heresy in the Dark Ages?

19. What were the major teachings of the Cathars?

20. What was the *consolamentum*? Why did most Cathar believers postpone it until the time of death?

21. In what ways were the Waldensians similar to the Franciscans?

22. What were the distinctive teachings of the Waldensians?

The Poor in Spirit

23. Why is it inaccurate to classify the Waldensians as Protestants before the Reformation?

24. What aspects of the Inquisition were derived from Roman law?

25. How did church and state cooperate in the Inquisition?

26. Why were the Dominicans called "The Lord's Watchdogs"?

27. What happened to those who confessed to heresy before the Inquisition? to those who were convicted on the testimony of others?

28. Why could monasticism not meet the needs for Christlike living and the Word of God that had stimulated the monastic reforms in the first place?

17

FINANCIERS AND HUMANISTS

In 1302, Pope Boniface VIII issued the bull known as *Unam sanctam*, perhaps the most arrogant piece of papal self-aggrandizement in history. In speaking of the church, Boniface said,

"That in her and within her power are two swords, we are taught in the Gospels, namely, the spiritual sword and the temporal sword. For when the Apostles said, `Lo, here' - that is, in the Church - `are two swords,' the Lord did not reply to the Apostles, `It is too much,' but, `It is enough.' It is certain that whoever denies that the temporal sword is in the power of Peter, hearkens ill to the words of the Lord which He spake, `Put up thy sword into its sheath.' Therefore, both are in the power of the Church, namely, the spiritual sword and the temporal sword; the latter is to be used for the Church, the former by the Church; the former by the hand of the priest, the latter by the hand of princes and kings, but at the nod and suffrance of the priest. The one sword must of necessity be subject to the other, and the temporal authority to the spiritual."

Boniface seems to have forgotten that Jesus also said that he who lived by the sword would die by the sword. From the time of Gregory VII to the height of papal power under Innocent III, and on beyond to the time of Boniface, the popes insisted on seizing for themselves the sword of political power. In the last two centuries of the Middle Ages, that same sword brought the papacy down to depths unknown outside of the tenth-century Pornocracy, and by the time the Reformation was ready to dawn, the popes were in few ways distinguishable from the petty Italian princes who occupied their time promoting the arts, enriching themselves, and fighting with their neighbors.

When Boniface VIII became pope in 1294, it was his intention to maintain the same absolute power that had been claimed by every pope since the middle of the eleventh century. The things he said about the papacy were not new; he made no claims that had not been made many times before, although it might well be argued that he made those claims more obnoxiously than any of his predecessors. But the world in which he lived was not the world of Innocent III. The Crusades, which had been a great source of papal moral influence, were over, though the ideal would live on for two more centuries. The wars against the Muslims had sparked the growth of nationalism in Europe, and the fact that people had begun to think of themselves as Englishmen, Frenchmen, or Germans spelled the beginning of the end for the effectiveness of papal threats of excommunication and interdict. Gregory VII and Innocent III had been able to foment revolts against monarchs by threatening their countries with interdict, but Boniface found that the new, more secular nobility now supported their kings against what they saw as "foreign interference." Another change was in the economic system of Europe. Feudalism was declining fast in the wake of the rapid growth of towns. The economy of Europe was becoming more and more based on money and less and less tied to the possession of land. The church by this time had plenty of land; it found that it was going to need money to keep itself going. The struggle for increasingly greater revenues dominated the thinking of the late medieval popes, and brought them into repeated conflict with the monarchs of Europe.

Most of Boniface's troubles were with Philip IV (the Fair), the energetic young king of France. The French kings had greatly expanded their territory through the defeat of the Albigensians and the seizure of the lands of the house of Toulouse in southern France. Only a few small tracts of land on the coast remained outside their power, and those belonged to the king of England. In fact, France and England were at war at the time over a dispute concerning those same lands. In order to support the war effort, both Philip and Edward I of England were demanding taxes of the clergy in their domains. The bishops and abbots felt that this was an unreasonable invasion of their immunity, and appealed to Boniface. In 1294, Boniface issued the bull *Clericis laicos*, which stated that no king could tax the clergy without papal permission, and that any king who levied such a tax, and any priest who paid it, would be subject to excommunication. The kings, however, were not about to give in so easily. Edward threatened to haul every priest in England into court and try them as traitors if they didn't pay, while Philip promptly put an embargo on the export of gold, thus preventing Boniface from collecting any revenues in France. Boniface was forced to back off, and issued another bull stating that kings could collect money from the clergy in times of emergency. Since the kings were left free to define what constituted an emergency, this calmed the waters considerably.

The situation appeared to improve significantly when Boniface declared 1300 to be a Jubilee Year. In connection with this, he offered a plenary indulgence - forgiveness of all sins - to anyone who visited Rome during the year. This, of course, had the effect of bringing vast sums of money into the city, so much so that one historian of the day reports that two priests were kept busy all day every day doing nothing but gathering with rakes the money that was cast before the altar in St. Peter's.

Problems with Philip cropped up again the following year, however, when the French monarch began to seize church lands and use church tithes to finance his war against England. Boniface sent a legate to demand that Philip return the land and the money, and Philip arrested the legate and charged him with treason. After an exchange of less than friendly correspondence, the pope issued the famous bull *Unam sanctam* quoted above. The document closed by stating, "Furthermore, that every human creature is subject to the Roman pontiff - this we declare, say, define, and pronounce to be altogether necessary to salvation." Boniface prepared to excommunicate Philip, and invited the Holy Roman Emperor to occupy the throne of France. The emperor declined, but Philip responded by calling a council of French clergy that accused Boniface of all sorts of crimes, including the murder of his predecessor. Finally, in 1303, as the day arrived for the formal excommunication of Philip, a French knight by the name of William of Nogaret traveled toward the pope's home in Anagni with a band of men. They burst in upon the pope, who was now in his eighties, and humiliated him shamefully. His Italian supporters finally rescued him, but the shock was too much, and he died within a month. Contemporary historians summed up his career by saying that he "came in like a fox, reigned like a lion, and died like a dog." Thus in the span of a few brief years, the prestige of the papacy, which had reached such great heights, came tumbling to the ground.

THE BABYLONIAN CAPTIVITY

Boniface was succeeded by Benedict XI, who was determined to make peace with Philip, and in so doing retracted everything Boniface had decreed. He only lived for eight months, and was allegedly dispatched by his enemies by means of a bowl of poisoned figs. Benedict was succeeded by the French archbishop of Bordeaux, who took the name Clement V. He was in France at the time of his election, and never did make it back to Rome. He had been advised that Italy was not a safe place for a French pope, and so he located his capital in the city of Avignon, in the territory of the king of Naples, just across the Rhone River from the land of Philip the Fair. Thus began the Avignon papacy, which lasted from 1309 to 1377.

Because of its duration of almost seventy years, it has come to be called the Babylonian Captivity of the papacy.

It was not really a captivity, of course. Though the seven Avignon popes were all French, they were not so much under the thumb of the French kings as is commonly thought. They maintained some measure of independence, and in fact, during the Avignon years, the papal court had greater revenues than those of any European monarch, and Avignon became the center of European cultural life. The strength of the French influence can be seen, however, in the fact that of the 134 cardinals appointed during the 68 years of the Avignon papacy, 113 were French.

If the Avignon popes were controlled by anything, though, it was not the French monarchy - it was the monstrous financial network that they themselves had helped to create. It could well be said that the sign under which the Avignon papacy lived was not the sign of the cross, but the sign of the dollar (or in this case, the franc). The financial genius among the Avignon popes was John XXII (1316-1334). He belongs on any list of history's most creative fund-raisers. During his reign, everything within the power of the popes had a price. Not only were church offices openly sold to the highest bidder, but papal dispensations for divorces, second marriages, legitimizing illegitimate offspring, and almost anything else imaginable had their designated fee. The wheels of the papal bureaucracy also had to be greased with appropriate gratuities, of course. As the bureaucracy gobbled up more and more cash, more creative means of squeezing money from those seeking favors were required. The popes began demanding annates, which meant that anyone appointed to a church office had to remit his first year's income to the papal treasury. They soon discovered that if they filled vacancies by transferring people from one office to another rather than just appointing someone new, a large amount of fresh revenue could be generated. Furthermore, the popes claimed the right to reservations, which meant that the income from any vacant office went directly into the papal treasury; on many occasions, they found it prudent to wait a while before filling church vacancies, thus collecting revenues while waiting for the highest possible bid for the office. The selling of offices to the highest bidder produced the dual abuses of pluralism and absenteeism. Often a wealthy nobleman (or a papal relative) would purchase or be given several offices at the same time. It was not unheard of for the same man to hold three or four bishoprics, several abbacies, and a dukedom or two simultaneously. Of course, under these circumstances, there could be no thought of actually fulfilling the duties of the office in question. The actual officeholder might never even visit the church or monastery over which he was supposed to preside; instead, he would hire someone to do the actual work for a small fraction of the income he derived from the office. The worst fund-raising abuse of all, however, was the sale of indulgences. Urban II had initiated these at the end of the eleventh century to encourage people to go on the First Crusade. They had gradually been applied, not only to later crusades, but to wars against heretics and recalcitrant princes in Christendom. By the fourteenth century, they were being offered for almost any provocation. After all, anyone who opposed the pope was by definition a heretic, and anyone who contributed to stamping out heresy deserved a spiritual reward.

The result of these abuses was that the papal court became the jewel and ornament of European society, but the papacy itself lost the respect of anyone in Christendom who cared for spiritual things. Scholars in the universities began speaking up against what the church had become, and mystics like Catherine of Siena and Brigitta of Sweden urged the popes to remove themselves from the worldliness and corruption of Avignon and return to Rome. Rome, however, was itself in dismal condition. The city had been deprived of its greatest source of revenue with the departure of the papal court, and during the fourteenth century had sunk to a deplorable condition. The population had dropped to less than twenty thousand, the buildings were in ruins, goats grazed in the broken-down churches, and brigands controlled the city. When later Avignon popes visited the city, they were horrified, and quickly scurried for their lives back across the Alps. The chaos that threatened to overwhelm the city also was on the verge of costing the papacy control over the Papal States. The last of the Avignon popes, Gregory XI, visited Italy in 1377 to try to reestablish his authority over the threatened territory. While he was in the city of Rome preparing for his return to Avignon, he died, thus bringing to an end the Babylonian Captivity. This, of course, did not by any stretch of the imagination solve the problems that were making life increasingly difficult for the occupants of the papacy. In fact, things quickly got worse.

THE GREAT PAPAL SCHISM

The cardinals who met in Rome to elect a successor to Gregory XI soon found the Vatican surrounded by a Roman mob that threatened to kill all the French cardinals unless they elected a Roman pope, or at least an Italian. At one point during the deliberations, the mob stormed through the doors and demanded to know who was being favored for election. The cardinals panicked and quickly pushed forward an elderly Roman cardinal who hadn't even been in the running. Satisfied, the mob left, and the cardinals proceeded to elect an archbishop from Naples who took office as Urban VI. The cardinals then fled for their lives.

Urban turned out to be a poor choice indeed. Despite urgings to return the papal court to the safety of Avignon, he insisted on remaining in Rome. He also rather tactlessly began to attack the privileges that the cardinals had come to expect as part of their office. He vowed to put an end to corruption, and make the papacy once again a universal office rather than the personal property of the French. The cardinals quickly decided that they had made a mistake. They met again, declared Urban to be an apostate, claimed his election had occurred under duress, deposed him, and elected a new pope, a French prince who took the name of Clement VII. Urban quickly appointed twenty-nine Italian cardinals, but it was too late. The cardinals who had elected Clement returned with him to Avignon, and the papacy was in a state of schism.

Antipopes, of course, were nothing new. There had been so many rival claimants to the papacy during the Middle Ages that in the three and a half centuries prior to the schism, the papal throne had been occupied by a single claimant less than half the time. What made this schism far more serious than those that had preceded it, however, was that both of the rival popes had been appointed by the same college of cardinals (earlier antipopes were usually set up by kings or emperors, along with a few cardinals who were loyal to them). Furthermore, the nations of Europe quickly lined up and took sides. France, of course, supported Clement, while Italy stood by Urban. England was at war with France, so naturally supported Urban, while Scotland, always willing to oppose England in any quarrel, backed Clement. The Holy Roman Empire mistrusted the French and wanted no more of its revenues flowing into Avignon, and thus supported Urban, though there were major pockets of support for Clement throughout Germany. Spain vacillated, but finally chose Clement, which meant quite naturally that Portugal backed Urban. Thus Europe was almost evenly divided. The result was chaos. The two popes excommunicated not only each other, but also the supporters of their opponent. No one could be quite sure whether baptisms, marriages, ordinations, or even last rites were valid - matters of eternal destiny were thrown into utter confusion. Along with this, the financial situation became intolerable. Each pope made war on the supporters of the other, and levied taxes to support these wars. Some districts received two tax bills, one from each pope! It was clear to everyone in Europe that something had to be done, and fast, in order for the church to survive.

The schism was perpetuated because whenever one of the popes died, his cardinals would immediately elect a successor so the other pope would not win the struggle by default. Everyone claimed to hate the schism, but no one was willing to step aside in order to end it. Every pope elected during this time promised to work to end the schism,

THE GREAT SCHISM OF THE PAPACY (1378-1417)

DATE	ROMAN POPES	AVIGNON POPES	CONCILIAR POPES
1375		GREGORY XI (1370-1378) Died in 1378, setting stage for Schism.	
1378			
1381	URBAN VI (1378-1389) Ended "Babylonian Captivity" but caused Schism by alienating French cardinals.	CLEMENT VII (1378-1394) After three years of warfare with supporters of Urban VI, moved to Avignon in 1381.	
1384			
1387			
1390	BONIFACE IX (1389-1404)		
1393			
1396		BENEDICT XIII (1394-1417) Deposed by Council of Pisa in 1409, but refused to step down; deposed by Council of Constance in 1417; returned to Spain, convinced to his dying day that he was the true pope.	
1399			
1402			
1405	INNOCENT VII (1404-1406)		
1408	GREGORY XII (1406-1415) Deposed by Council of Pisa in 1409, but refused to step down; deposed by Council of Constance in 1415.		
1411			ALEXANDER V (1409-10) Appointed at Pisa.
			JOHN XXIII (1410-15) Deposed by Council of Constance in 1415.
1414			
1417			MARTIN V (1417-1431) Named by Council of Constance to end Schism.
1420			
1423			

even if he had to resign to do it, but not one of them followed through on the promise. The closest the popes ever came to ending the schism themselves was in 1406, during the reigns of the Roman pope Gregory XII and the Avignon pope Benedict XIII. Gregory actually offered to resign if Benedict would do the same. Benedict offered an alternative, suggesting instead that the two sets of cardinals meet to discuss the matter, with the popes agreeing to abide by their verdict. Both popes were maneuvering for their own advantage, however, and could not agree on a place for the cardinals to meet, since each wanted the meeting to occur in territory controlled by his own supporters.

The scholars at the University of Paris, meanwhile, came up with several ideas for ending the schism. They thought the best suggestion would be for both popes to abdicate, but that clearly wasn't going to happen. The next best idea was to submit the dispute to an impartial arbitrator, but the popes, who still considered themselves the highest power on earth, were unwilling to submit to the authority of anyone else. The final suggestion for healing the schism was to call a general council of the church. The scholars argued that, in the same way ecumenical councils resolved disputes in the ancient church, so this dispute could be handled by a gathering of the best and brightest in Christendom. The popes continued to insist that no council could meet unless a pope summoned it, however, and there was no way they were going to call a council that was likely to depose them. Finally, however, the situation became intolerable, and the cardinals decided to take matters into their own hands.

THE CONCILIAR MOVEMENT

As early as the beginning of the fourteenth century, men like Marsilius of Padua and William of Ockham had been disputing the absolute authority of the papacy. Both insisted that the authority of Christ lay in His church as a whole, not in one man. One man could err, but the gates of hell could not overcome the church as a body. Thus the ultimate authority in the church lay in a council of its leaders, not in a single man, who could surely be mistaken. It was this attempt to make the papacy a constitutional monarchy rather than a dictatorship that was at the heart of the Conciliar Movement, which began at the Council of Pisa in 1409 and ended when the Council of Basel collapsed in 1449. The chief theorists of the Conciliar Movement were John Gerson, Peter D'Ailly, and Nicholas of Cusa, all of whom were active at the University of Paris.

A. THE COUNCIL OF PISA (1409)

The Council of Pisa, which was not called by a pope, is not recognized as an ecumenical council by the Catholic Church. It was an abject failure, not because of lack of papal support, but because it failed to overcome political rivalries that had contributed to the schism in the first place.

Cardinals from both Rome and Avignon met in Pisa and summoned a general council in 1409. Attendance was large, as everyone in Christendom wanted to see the schism ended. Peter D'Ailly argued that the first church council was neither called nor led by Peter, but was headed by James. John Gerson, though not present at the council, made his presence felt through a tract that argued that a council had the authority to remove a pope from office who was not serving the welfare of the church. The council proceeded to depose both popes, and elected a Cretan who took the name of Alexander V. Satisfied with themselves, they then went home without ever addressing the deeper needs for reform within the church.

The actions of the Council of Pisa only made matters worse, however. The two deposed popes refused to step down, branding the council as illegal. One of their more ingenious arguments was that, if they were not popes, then the cardinals whom they had appointed were not cardinals, and had no authority to depose them or elect another pope! The crux of the problem, though, was that the Council of Pisa lacked the political support to make its actions stick. Though most of Europe backed Alexander, the other two popes still had large pockets of

Financiers and Humanists

support. Instead of two popes, the Christian world now had three.

B. THE COUNCIL OF CONSTANCE (1414-1418)

Alexander died after only a year in office. The Pisan cardinals regathered and elected a Neapolitan nobleman who took the name of John XXIII. This shrewd lawyer disgraced what up to that point had been the most popular papal name so badly that it was not chosen again until the middle of the twentieth century, when a gentle old man who later summoned the Second Vatican Council took the name John XXIII. The Pisan Pope John spent his entire time in office engaged in political maneuverings, most of which involved making contradictory promises to two different rulers at the same time. When one of these rulers got wise to John's tricks, he drove him out of Rome. The pope took refuge with the soon-to-be Holy Roman Emperor Sigismund, who pressured him into agreeing to another council. The council met in the city of Constance in 1414, and was the largest gathering of church leaders in history to that point.

John, knowing that he was not the most popular man in Europe at the time, quickly appointed a large group of Italian cardinals and other church officials whom he could count upon to support him at the council. The council foiled his plans, however, by instituting a rule that had never been used before and has not been used since; they determined that the voting of the council would be by nations rather than on an individual basis. Thus the eighty Italians, most of them sworn to support John, had no more clout than the dozen men who came from the British Isles. This unusual procedure not only recognized the political realities of growing nationalism, but also virtually guaranteed widespread political support for the council's decisions.

The Council began by declaring its own legitimacy as an ecumenical council, declared that councils had authority over popes, then turned to the matter of ending the schism. John XXIII, being present at the council, was the first target. A list of charges was drawn up against him. John was unquestionably a rascal, but the charges drawn up by his enemies were so severe that the council rejected a third of them as being outrageous beyond belief. The others were easily enough to bring about his ouster, however. When John saw which way the wind was blowing, he tried another one of his patented tricks. He openly submitted to the council, agreeing to resign and humbly kneeling before the entire assembly to remove his papal robes. He then fled from Constance disguised as a groom, and traveled about Europe condemning the council and attempting to drum up support for himself. He was finally captured, arrested, and imprisoned, but was later released upon payment of a huge bribe, and appointed a cardinal, though he died six months later. The Roman pope Gregory XII agreed to abdicate on condition that the council would permit him to reopen the council under his authority as pope and then submit his resignation. They agreed, and Gregory resigned, was appointed a cardinal, and died as a well-respected member of the curia two years later. The Avignon pope proved a bit more difficult to convince, however. Benedict XIII, despite a personal plea from Sigismund, refused to step down, despite the fact that almost all of his supporters had gone over to the council. He finally was deposed as a schismatic, and he retired to a mountaintop in Spain with four of his cardinals, believing to his dying day that he was the true pope. In fact, two of his cardinals succeeded him, the last one dying in prison in 1433.

The Council of Constance thus succeeded in ending the schism. It appointed Martin V as the new pope, and he was quickly recognized by all of Europe. They then turned to the matter of reform. In an attempt to deal with the heresies that were then plaguing the church, they condemned the teachings of the Lollards and burned John Huss at the stake after the emperor had given him safe conduct to the council. We will see more of these things in the next chapter. The council also decreed that the College of Cardinals should be limited to 24 members, proportionally divided among the different parts of the church; that no relatives of popes or cardinals should be given cardinal's hats; and that councils should be held on a regular basis to deal with problems in the church. Martin also concluded treaties known as concordats with the major nations of Europe to regulate church business in those countries.

The Council of Constance accomplished its immediate purpose, but in the long run it was a failure. The popes simply were not willing to give up their absolute authority, and they therefore did everything in their power to undermine the Conciliar Movement. In fact, the major contribution of the Council of Constance, aside from ending the schism, may have been in its failure. The demand for reform had been frustrated once again, and that demand became increasingly louder as the fifteenth century wore on. The Council of Constance had declared that popes were fallible; it had also taken on the rather uncomfortable chore of proving that councils were fallible, since it had to set aside the pope chosen by the Council of Pisa. Its conclusion was that the decisions of councils were infallible unless set aside by other councils. This clearly unsatisfactory line of reasoning was not taken to its logical conclusion until Luther argued that it is not the church, whether represented by pope or council, that is infallible at all, but the Scriptures as illuminated by the Holy Spirit of God.

C. THE COUNCIL OF BASEL (1431-1449)

If it was the popes who killed the Conciliar Movement, the Council of Basel played right into their hands. Called by Martin V in the year of his death, the Council of Basel met determined to carry forward the reforming zeal of Constance. Martin's successor, Eugene IV, at first tried to disband the council, but eventually agreed reluctantly to support it, and even issued a bull acknowledging his own error in trying to suppress the council and submitting himself to its decisions. But he was not about to cave in quite that easily. He sent letters to rulers all over Europe exaggerating the danger of the reforms the council was pursuing. He also inflamed national jealousies, convincing each monarch that the council was giving advantages to his rivals. All of these behind-the-scenes maneuverings might have accomplished nothing, however, if the Turks had not bailed him out.

In 1434, representatives from Constantinople arrived in Europe to beg for help against the Turks, who by this time were threatening to overrun the city. Everyone agreed that this was a vital matter of concern, and Eugene slyly arranged for the council to be moved from Basel to Ferrara in order to meet with the Greeks. This move completely ended any possibility that the council would institute any meaningful reforms. Many of the most influential participants in the council packed up and headed for Ferrara, and later to Florence, where lengthy but ultimately meaningless discussions went on interminably (the Greeks agreed to reunion with Rome, but were nearly run out of town when they returned to Constantinople; when Constantinople fell to the Turks in 1453, the whole matter became moot in any case). Meanwhile, a minority contingent remained at Basel, and issued more and more radical decrees. These alienated most of the responsible participants in the council, who left for Italy. Those who were left eventually wound up deposing Eugene in 1439 and appointing an antipope, Felix V, who was the last antipope in the history of Catholicism up to the present day. As their numbers and support dwindled, they finally realized that the reform effort was dead. In 1449, Felix resigned, and the Council of Basel declared itself ended, resulting in a total victory for the papacy. Ever since, popes have been very reluctant to call councils. In fact, even the threat of the Protestant Reformation did not bring forth a council until twenty years too late; the pope wanted to be sure the council would be under his control, and could not guarantee that until the Jesuits emerged as a major force in the sixteenth-century church.

MEDIEVAL ECUMENICAL COUNCILS

COUNCIL	DATE	KEY PARTICIPANTS	RESULTS
LATERAN I	1123	Callistus II	Confirmed Concordat of Worms. Forbade marriage of priests. Granted indulgences to Crusaders.
LATERAN II	1139	Innocent II	Anathematized followers of antipope Anacletus II. Condemned schismatic groups. Confirmed decisions of Lateran I.
LATERAN III	1179	Alexander III	Condemned Cathari. Required two-thirds vote of cardinals for papal elections.
LATERAN IV	1215	Innocent III	Established Inquisition. Confirmed election of Emperor Frederick II. Denounced *Magna Carta*. Defined doctrine of transubstantiation. Confirmed Franciscans. Condemned Cathari and Waldensians. Prepared for Fifth Crusade.
LYONS I	1245	Innocent IV	Deposed Emperor Frederick II. Mourned loss of Jerusalem to Saracens.
LYONS II	1274	Gregory X	Reaffirmed *filioque* clause. Prohibited new monastic orders, Attempted to reunite Eastern and Western churches. Decided that cardinals were to receive no salary during papal elections.
VIENNE	1311-1312	Clement V	Suppressed Knights Templar. Attempted to encourage new crusade, but failed. Condemned Beguines and Beghards.
PISA	1409	Peter D'Ailly Peter Philargi Guy de Maillesec	Asserted conciliar authority over papacy. Deposed Gregory XII (Rome) and Benedict XIII (Avignon) and elected Alexander V. Lacked power to enforce its decisions, left church with three rival popes. Not considered an official ecumenical council.
CONSTANCE	1414-1418	John XXIII Sigismund Peter D'Ailly John Gerson	Ended papal schism by deposing all three claimants and appointing Martin V. Tried and executed John Huss. Affirmed authority of councils over church and insisted they be called as often as necessary.
BASEL	1431-1449	Martin V Eugene IV Julian Cesarini Nicholas of Cusa	Affirmed authority of council after pope tried to disband it. Pope used disunity of council to reassert his authority. Reached compromise settlement with Hussites. Moved to Ferrara after arrival of Eastern delegation.

THE RENAISSANCE PAPACY

The failure of the Conciliar Movement opened the doors for a level of blatant corruption in the church the likes of which had not been seen since the tenth century. If during the Babylonian Captivity the popes were pawns of the French kings, during the Renaissance they became the bishops on the chessboard of Italian politics. This dismal period in the history of the papacy virtually guaranteed that reform would come. The only question was what form the reform would take. A few examples will suffice to show why the need for reform was so universally recognized by the beginning of the sixteenth century.

Nicholas V (1447-1455), the first of the Renaissance popes, was a patron of the arts who helped establish the great Vatican library. When Constantinople fell in 1453, he called a Crusade to deliver it from the Turks, but nobody came. One of his secretaries, the noted humanist Lorenzo Valla, had been the critic who had demonstrated that the Donation of Constantine was a forgery; Nicholas hired him anyway.

Pius II (1458-1464), a humanist who had been one of the leading participants in the Council of Basel and a supporter of Felix V, issued a bull *Execrabilis* that stated that papal decrees were final and could never be appealed to councils.

Sixtus IV (1471-1484), who had been the general of the austere Franciscans, proved very generous with the church's money, lavishing it on his relatives and on artists who beautified the churches of Rome. He built the Sistine Chapel, which bears his name. He also extended indulgences beyond the realm of the living, maintaining that they also had power to free souls from Purgatory. Sixtus was also the pope responsible for sanctioning the Spanish Inquisition.

The most notorious of all the Renaissance popes, and perhaps the most wicked pope in the history of the church, was Roderigo Borgia, who reigned as Alexander VI (1492-1503). Alexander devoted most of his attention to advancing his large number of illegitimate children, including the unspeakably vicious Cesare Borgia, for whom he had earlier arranged an appointment to the College of Cardinals, and his beautiful sister Lucrezia. No desecration of his office was too great for the benefit of his dear children. They were married with great honors in the Vatican, and the papal palace was also available for the orgies that Cesare enjoyed so much. Alexander devoted all the resources of the papal treasury to win power and influence for his son - the same son who was used as the model of the utterly unscrupulous but successful ruler by Machiavelli in *The Prince*. Alexander was also the pope responsible for the death of the Florentine preacher Savonarola, whom we will meet in the next chapter.

Julius II (1503-1513) was another great patron of the arts who hired Michelangelo and Raphael, among others, to decorate the Vatican and other churches in Rome. He also was a warrior, leading his armies against the noble families of Italy, and on one occasion personally scaling the walls of Bologna in full armor. It was during the papacy of Julius that Luther visited Rome for the first and only time, and was appalled by the blatant corruption he found there. At about the same time, a young priest named Ulrich Zwingli came to Rome as a chaplain for a group of Swiss mercenary soldiers. He, too, had his eyes opened to a degree of immorality he had never suspected.

The last of the Renaissance popes was Leo X (1513-1521), of the famous Medici family. He saw the papal office as no more than a source of personal pleasure, and never really understood what all the fuss was about when he had to excommunicate some bothersome priest from Germany by the name of Martin Luther.

The Renaissance papacy was an open sewer that smelled to high heaven. Monk and humanist alike were revolted by the nepotism and public immorality of popes who would not only keep mistresses and father illegitimate children openly, but would then turn around and make those same children cardinals in the church. The church was like Amos' basket of overripe fruit - the time for judgment had arrived.

MAKING DRY BONES LIVE

The great tragedy of the Renaissance popes was that it never occurred to them that they should be significantly different from other Italian nobles. Some of these men were personally religious, even devout, but it seemed to have little effect on their conduct of church business. At the height of the Middle Ages, there was no distinction between the sacred and the secular. The popes sought to bring everything in submission to Christ by putting all men under their own authority. By the time of the Renaissance, however, the influence of paganism had opened a crack in the solid wall constructed by men like Innocent III. Men were now being told that certain aspects of life are outside the realm of the church. In a sense that is true; no one wants to return to the theocratic dictatorship of the High Middle Ages. Yet the separation of church and state need not mean the separation of God from certain realms of life. To force God into a corner is bad for society. How much more is it devastating to the professing Christian to restrict God to a corner of his life? The hypocrisy of the Renaissance popes, who honored God with their lips while breaking every law He had ever given, is painfully obvious to us. But how often do Christians today go along unquestioningly with the secular world that tells us that religion is best left at home and in church? Might not our hypocrisy be every bit as visible, and just as painful, to future generations?

FOR REVIEW AND FURTHER THOUGHT

1. What was the significance of each of the following papal bulls: *Unam sanctam*, *Clericis laicos*, and *Execrabilis*?

2. What changes in the political and economic environment of Europe made it impossible for Boniface VIII to exercise the same power that had been wielded by Innocent III a century earlier?

3. How had the crusades against the Cathars in southern France augmented the power of the French kings?

4. How did Edward I and Philip IV prevent Boniface from enforcing *Clericis laicos*?

5. How did the proclamation of a Year of Jubilee enrich the papal treasury?

6. What factors caused the shift of the papal headquarters to Avignon?

7. Why is the Avignon papacy known as the Babylonian Captivity?

8. What were annates, reservations, pluralism, absenteeism, and indulgences, and how did they bring enormous amounts of money into the papal coffers at Avignon?

9. Who were Catherine of Siena and Brigitta of Sweden, and what role did they play in ending the Avignon papacy?

10. Why did the city of Rome fall into ruin during the Babylonian Captivity?

11. What factors contributed to the Great Schism of the Papacy?

12. What made this schism more serious than all the papal schisms that had preceded it?

13. How and why did the nations of Europe divide themselves in support of the two competing popes?

14. Why were the popes opposed to allowing a council to settle the schism?

15. What were the three ideas proposed by the University of Paris for resolving the papal schism?

16. How did Marsilius of Padua and William of Ockham lay the groundwork for the Conciliar Movement?

17. Why is the Council of Pisa not recognized by the Catholic Church as a legitimate ecumenical council?

18. Why did the Council of Pisa fail to end the schism?

19. What key role did Sigismund play in the Council of Constance?

20. How did the Council of Constance foil John XXIII's efforts to pack the council with his supporters?

Financiers and Humanists

21. How did the Council of Constance succeed in ending the papal schism?

22. Why did the popes who reigned after the schism do all they could to squelch to Conciliar Movement?

23. In what ways did the Council of Constance help lay the groundwork for the Reformation?

24. What tactics did Eugene IV use to undermine the reform efforts of the Council of Basel?

25. Why did the efforts at reunification of the Greek and Roman churches fail?

26. What is the significance of Felix V?

27. Identify the contributions of the following popes in one sentence each: Alexander V, Alexander VI, Benedict XIII, Boniface VIII, Clement V, Clement VII, Eugene IV, John XXII, John XXIII.

28. Identify the contributions of the following popes in one sentence each: Gregory XI, Gregory XII, Julius II, Leo X, Martin V, Nicholas V, Pius II, Sixtus IV, Urban VI.

29. Identify the following in one sentence each: Peter D'Ailly, Anagni, antipope, Cesare Borgia, Ferrara, John Gerson, Machiavelli, Nicholas of Cusa, Lorenzo Valla.

30. What factors contributed to the separation of life into the realms of the sacred and secular that occurred in the late Middle Ages, and which is still with us today?

Part Three

THE PROTESTANT REFORMATION
(1517-1648)

18

REFORM EFFORTS THAT FAILED

The condition of the Roman Catholic Church in the latter part of the Middle Ages was such that almost everyone, with the possible exception of the popes, recognized the need for reform. The cries for change came from outsiders like the Cathars and Waldensians in the thirteenth century, and from within the hierarchy itself in the fifteenth-century Conciliar Movement. Many others during these years were seeking reform in various ways. Most took as their starting point the obvious corruption of the church during the Avignon papacy, the schism, and the Renaissance, and worked to bring the church's practice back into line with her profession. Such were the leaders of the reforming councils, and though they failed, they earned the respect of the church with their efforts. A few also criticized the church's theological foundations. Men like Thomas Bradwardine (c.1290-1349), the Archbishop of Canterbury who died in the Black Plague, and Gregory of Rimini (d.1358), the head of the Austin Friars, accused the church of being Pelagian because of its emphasis on human effort in gaining salvation. Though these men did not go so far as the Protestant Reformers did in teaching justification by faith alone, their emphasis on the grace of God in salvation would be one that the Reformers would echo. These men, too, earned the respect of their church.

Some who fought for change earned hatred rather than respect, however. What brought down the wrath of the system upon their heads was not the fact that they challenged the doctrine or practice of the church, which many did to one extent or another, but the fact that they challenged the authority of the church. The popes could afford to stand by and do nothing when they were accused of simony, immorality, or even heresy, but they could not permit anyone to undermine their authority. Like the Sanhedrin of Jesus' day, when someone dared to threaten their power, they moved in for the kill. It is somewhat ironic that few today have heard of doctrinal reformers like Bradwardine or Gregory of Rimini, or great conciliarists like Gerson, D'Ailly, and Nicholas of Cusa, but that almost everyone knows of Wycliffe, Huss, and Savonarola - men whose undying fame was assured by their persecution and/or martyrdom at the hands of the Roman Catholic Church.

JOHN WYCLIFFE AND THE LOLLARDS

The first to stir the waters of reform was an Oxford don named John Wycliffe (c.1329-1384). Wycliffe was a man who wrote a great deal about his ideas and very little about himself, so we know next to nothing about his early life. He attended Oxford University and later became a professor there, and was undoubtedly influenced by the teachings of Bradwardine, who taught there in the 1340's, though he ultimately rejected Bradwardine's full Augustinianism in favor of an espousal of the freedom of the human will. He rose quietly through the ranks until he came to be recognized as the leading Scholastic theologian in England. Though the prevailing philosophy of the day was the Nominalism espoused by William of Ockham and others, Wycliffe was an unabashed Realist. He first gained public attention in 1366 when he argued against papal interference in the affairs of the English church. This was the time of the Avignon papacy; it was also the era of the Hundred Years' War between England and France. The English were not at all happy to see their tithes leaving the country and going to Avignon, where they were being sent "on loan" to the French king to help in his war effort against England. When the pope demanded the tribute that Innocent III had extracted from King John, which had not been paid for many years, Parliament refused. Wycliffe appears to have been one of the leaders in this struggle, because a document critical of Parliament's decision addresses Wycliffe by name.

In the years that followed, Wycliffe developed a philosophy to support his politics. One of the hot issues in academic circles in the fourteenth century was the question of "lordship" or "dominion." Who really owned the land? the pope? the king? Wycliffe argued that dominion belonged to God alone, and that men had been given the privilege to use God's property. This privilege, however, was retained by men only as long as they lived righteously. Of course, nothing could have been clearer in those years of open corruption than that the church did not qualify as worthy to use God's property. Wycliffe thus argued that the state had the right to confiscate property that was being misused by the church, and give it to those who would make good use of it. Needless to say, such a theory delighted the English nobility, especially the king's son John of Gaunt, the duke of Lancaster, who was the power behind the throne. Wycliffe thus gained powerful protectors against the opposition that was soon to come. The bishop of London tried to silence Wycliffe, but John of Gaunt defended him. Then the last of the Avignon popes, Gregory XI, entered the fray, condemning certain of Wycliffe's writings as dangerous and issuing five bulls against him in an attempt to have him silenced by the English authorities. Shortly thereafter, Gregory died, and the bulls were promptly ignored.

When Gregory died in 1378, the papal schism began, and so did Wycliffe's career as an outspoken critic of the church. To this point, his opposition had been largely of a political nature. Now the sight of two rival popes, excommunicating and anathematizing one another while taxing Christendom to support their wars against each other's supporters, turned Wycliffe into a radical. He began to argue that the pope was not the head of the church, that priests had no control over the sacraments, and that the bread and wine of the Mass had to remain bread and wine, though he did acknowledge that Christ was present in the elements. Whether he saw Christ's presence as physical or spiritual is still a matter of debate, and both Lutheran and Reformed claim him as a forerunner of their views of the Lord's Supper. Whatever his actual teaching, his denial of transubstantiation led to his condemnation in 1382 by the Earthquake Synod, so called because of the tremors that occurred while it met. The archbishop of Canterbury led the proceedings, and Wycliffe was condemned as a heretic and deprived of his teaching position at Oxford. He thereupon retired to his church at Lutterworth, and died peacefully two years later. Though he died in peace, Wycliffe was not allowed to rest in peace. His teachings were condemned as heresy by the Council of Constance, and in 1428 his body was exhumed and burned, and the ashes were cast into the River Swift.

Wycliffe made two lasting contributions to the history of the church. The first was his translation of the Bible into English, in which he was assisted by Nicholas Hereford and John Purvey. Wycliffe knew neither Greek nor Hebrew, and thus made his translation from the Latin Vulgate. Though the accuracy of such a second-level translation was not good, some of his wordings survived in later English translations such as that done by Tyndale over a century later.

Wycliffe's Bible translation was at the heart of the ministry of a group of poor preachers who were inspired by Wycliffe's teachings. These men, called Lollards by their enemies, traveled all over England preaching the Word of God and spreading Wycliffe's ideas, following much the same pattern as that adopted by the Waldensians a century earlier. Though Wycliffe had gone to his grave in peace, the Lollards who followed him suffered severe persecutions. Many of the early Lollards recanted under torture, while some were burned for their faith. The greatest of the Lollard martyrs was Sir John Oldcastle, who was involved in a revolt against the worst persecutor of the Lollards, Henry V, and perished in the flames in 1418. Ironically, Sir John Oldcastle was the name Shakespeare originally used for the clown in the historical plays dealing with the reigns of Henry IV and Henry V. When the descendants of the Lollard martyr objected, Shakespeare changed his name to Sir John Falstaff. After the death of Oldcastle, the Lollard movement went underground for over a century, and was composed largely of peasants. It remained a quiet undercurrent in English society until the arrival of the Reformation, in which the Lollards enthusiastically enlisted.

JOHN HUSS AND THE BOHEMIAN BRETHREN

In 1382, Anne of Bohemia, the godly sister of the Bohemian king Wenceslaus IV, married Richard II of England. Soon large numbers of Bohemian students were traveling to England to study at Oxford University. Many of these students absorbed the teachings of Wycliffe, which were still highly controversial, and took them back to Bohemia. There they were adopted by a young Czech priest by the name of John Huss (c.1373-1415), who spearheaded a popular movement that went far beyond that spawned in England by Wycliffe. Though Huss was not as radical in his doctrine as was Wycliffe, he captured the attention of the people to a much greater extent than had his scholarly predecessor.

Huss was born into a poor peasant family in what is now the Czech Republic, and worked his way through the University of Prague. After being ordained to the priesthood, he became a professor at the university and rose to a position of influence on the faculty. He also became the preacher in Bethlehem Chapel, where he preached to large throngs in the Czech language. He soon gained a reputation as a supporter of two things - Wycliffe's theology and Czech nationalism. Bohemia had come under the domination of the Holy Roman Empire, and the Czechs resented the Germans. At the University of Prague, the Germans held most of the prominent positions, and when the Czech faculty managed to shift the balance of power in their favor in 1409, most of the Germans left and formed the University of Leipzig. Ironically, Huss now came to be viewed as the villain of the piece - the hero who had won the day for the Czechs was now held responsible for reducing the University of Prague to a second-rate, backwater institution. As had been the case with Wycliffe, the loss of university support proved a turning point in his career. While up to this point the issues raised by Wycliffe had been considered a matter for open debate, the archbishop of Prague now ordered a public burning of Wycliffe's books, and attempted to stop Huss from preaching. He threatened Huss with excommunication if he continued to spread Wycliffe's ideas. Huss refused to keep quiet, and soon riots broke out in the streets between the supporters and opponents of Wycliffism. Huss was then excommunicated by order of Cardinal Colonna, who was later to be made Pope Martin V by the Council of Constance. Huss protested his innocence of the charge of heresy, and wrote to the conciliar pope John XXIII to insist that he had been accused of teachings that he did not hold (indeed, Wycliffe's view of the Lord's Supper, called *remanence*, had never been taught by Huss, who affirmed transubstantiation).

In 1411, the controversy was renewed when John XXIII began selling indulgences in Bohemia to finance his war against the king of Naples, who supported Gregory XII, his rival claimant to the papal chair in Rome. Huss openly denounced what he considered to be an abuse of indulgences. He considered it a travesty that a pope should sell heavenly benefits to raise money for wreaking death and destruction upon a rival Christian monarch. He argued that the pope had no right to use the sword, and that forgiveness came only from God, and could not be granted by the church. In these arguments he relied heavily on Wycliffe's view of the church as the congregation of the elect, and roundly denounced the pope as the Antichrist. These denunciations gained him great popular support, but cost him many of his followers among the clergy of Prague. The archbishop placed the city under interdict and ordered Huss arrested and Bethlehem Chapel razed to the ground, but Huss' support among the people still kept him safe. He finally agreed to leave Prague in 1412 so that the interdict could be lifted. During his exile he continued to preach and attract large crowds. His preaching was no more moderate than before, and he also took the time to reduce his ideas to writing in a work called *De ecclesia*, which borrowed heavily from the works of Wycliffe.

When Sigismund, the soon-to-be Holy Roman Emperor, organized the Council of Constance in 1414, one of his goals was to clear the church in Bohemia of charges of heresy. His naivete in believing that Huss and his followers were orthodox was exceeded only by that of Huss himself, who was convinced that he could prove his orthodoxy if given the opportunity to defend himself before the council. Sigismund therefore offered Huss a safe-conduct to appear before the council, and Huss accepted it. Huss, however, as Luther did a century later in his early dealings with Leo X, imputed to the hierarchy of the church a level of godliness that simply did not exist. Sigismund's safe-conduct turned out not to be worth the parchment it was written on. After less than a month in Constance, Huss was arrested and imprisoned on a trumped-up charge. His cell was next to the latrines, and he soon became weak and sick. When John XXIII fled Constance after his resignation, many feared Huss would follow suit, and his imprisonment was made yet more severe. Ironically, when John XXIII was finally captured and returned to Constance, he was imprisoned in the same fortress in which Huss was being held. In the end, the council released the scoundrel to the honor of a cardinal's hat, while releasing the godly preacher to the flames.

It was not the scoundrels of Constance who hounded Huss to the stake, however, but the guiding lights of the Conciliar Movement like Gerson and D'Ailly. The latter was appointed to head the heresy commission charged with examining Huss. D'Ailly was no fool, and quickly realized that Huss' view of the church undermined the authority of councils every bit as much as it denied the infallibility of popes. He also was a Nominalist, and hated the Realism that Huss shared with Wycliffe. Huss had hoped to clear himself of the charge of heresy before the council as a whole, but he was never really given a chance to do so. In 1415, the council declared the views of Wycliffe to be heresy. Huss had already espoused many of those views. He argued that they must be tested against the standard of Scripture, but the council declared that the authority of the church was final. By the time Huss was permitted to appear before the council, the issue had already been decided. Every time he tried to explain his views, he was shouted down, and told that he was only to answer "yes" or "no" to the charges against him. In the end, he was caught on the horns of a dilemma. Of the charges against him, some were true and some were false. He could not affirm the charges without confessing to heresies he had never taught, but his conscience would not permit him to deny those teachings that he firmly believed had their source in the Word of God. He was ultimately condemned on the testimony of others, stripped of his priestly robes, and turned over to the secular authorities. Sigismund, who was said to have blushed at his own faithlessness, sent Huss to the stake, where he died singing praises to God. Huss' ashes, along with the ground in which the stake had been planted, were cast into the river so that no one could preserve his remains as relics.

Meanwhile, Huss' followers back in Bohemia were not about to forget Sigismund's treachery. When Wenceslaus died, Sigismund inherited Bohemia, but the people rebelled against him. John Zizka, a one-eyed general who was one of the shrewdest military leaders in Europe, led the revolt. Martin V, the pope who had been appointed by Constance, called for a crusade against the rebellious Hussites, and the Germans quickly took up arms. The Hussites beat back five successive attacks, and eventually even succeeded in invading Saxony. When the Council of Basel convened in 1431, one of their major goals was to deal with the Hussite problem. One of the radical ideas that eventually discredited the council was their notion that it was possible to compromise with heretics. They met with representatives of the Hussites (the safe-conduct was honored this time), and agreed to allow the Bohemian churches to administer the wine as well as the bread to laymen during the Mass (so-called "communion in both kinds" had recently been denied to laymen to keep careless peasants from spilling the "blood of God" onto the cathedral floor), and to restrict the sale of indulgences in Bohemia. The Hussites in turn agreed to recognize papal authority.

The agreement brought peace to Bohemia, but it caused a split among the Hussites themselves. Those who approved of the settlement called themselves Utraquists (from the word for "both," because of their insistence on communion in both kinds), while the more radical Taborites rejected papal authority. The latter were eventually exterminated. In the middle of the fifteenth century, a group known as the *Unitas Fratrum* ("Unity of the Brethren") emerged from the remnants of the Taborites under the influence of a group of Waldensians in Austria. These so-called Bohemian Brethren persisted until the Reformation, and like the Waldensians and Lollards, accepted Protestantism in the sixteenth century. After going through terrible persecution at the hands of the Jesuits, they became the nucleus of the Moravian Church under the leadership of Count von Zinzendorf in the eighteenth century.

GIROLAMO SAVONAROLA AND THE FLORENTINE REPUBLIC

The third reformer to whom we now turn our attention is very different from the first two. While Wycliffe and Huss attacked the corruption of the church from a doctrinal basis drawn from the Scriptures, Savonarola adhered to every particular of Catholic dogma. He attacked only the corruption of the church, but did so in such a spectacular way as to draw attention to the abuses of Rome in a manner unlike any who preceded him. Luther admired him greatly, and considered him a forerunner of the reforming effort in which he himself was engaged.

Girolamo Savonarola (1452-1498) was born into a family whose father and grandfather were physicians, and he quite naturally pursued the same career. He quickly became restless, however, and decided to enter the Dominican order against the wishes of his parents. While in the convent, he studied the Bible diligently and committed large portions of it to memory. When he was called to St. Mark's in Florence in 1481, he began to preach, but found he had few listeners. They found his preaching dry and dull, and he was quickly reassigned to train other monks. Eventually he was sent to preach in other cities in Italy, and it was during this time that he changed his style of preaching. No longer the dull pedant, he began to denounce the immorality of the church hierarchy in the words of the prophets, and used the imagery of the Book of Revelation to predict the doom of the unrepentant. He quickly attracted attention, and in 1489 was invited back to Florence.

The Italian Renaissance was then in full bloom, and nowhere was this more evident than in Florence, which was ruled by the great patron of the arts, Lorenzo de Medici. There was probably nowhere on earth where Savonarola's message of judgment was less welcome, or more needed. The humanism of the Florentine Renaissance verged on paganism, and Savonarola lost no time in denouncing the rulers of the city for their immoral and worldly lifestyles. The result was that Savonarola earned the animosity of those in power and the love and devotion of the population at large. His preaching also had a remarkable impact on scholars such as Pico della Mirandola and artists like Botticelli and Michelangelo. Lorenzo de Medici respected Savonarola's hold over the people, and sought to win him over rather than opposing him openly. The austere friar could not be moved by presents or offers of advancement, however, and even refused to give the last rites to Lorenzo on his deathbed because the worldly aristocrat refused to repent of his sins.

Savonarola had in him something of the mystic, and ultimately became convinced that he was a prophet sent from God. He believed he had received divine revelations and angelic visits, and predicted the future with the assurance of an Old Testament prophet. He boldly announced to the Florentines that the city would fall to the king of France after the death of Lorenzo, but that it would be restored eventually to an even greater glory, in which it would become the ruler of all Italy. Then would come the advent of a Golden Age over which Florence would preside, in which the Muslims would be converted to Christianity and all the world would be ruled by

Christ Himself. When Charles VIII of France invaded Italy and drove the Medici from Florence, Savonarola's stock went up immeasurably. Because of his support of Charles, Florence was allowed to keep its liberty, and Savonarola set about to change the city into a theocracy. He established a republic with God as its head. The democratic (at least for the fifteenth century) form of government he instituted was accompanied by a radical change in the morals of the city. One of the most notable examples of this was the change that occurred during carnival season. Every year prior to Lent, the young men of the city used to run through the streets, looting and destroying as they went. Savonarola recruited many of these adolescents, and instead of running through the streets spreading terror, they would sing hymns, knock at the doors of the homes they passed, and ask for any worldly things such as gambling devices, immodest clothing, or immoral books or works of art. These were then taken to the public square, piled up into a huge heap, and burned to the ringing of bells and singing of hymns. This "bonfire of the vanities" occurred in two successive years. While they show the extent of Savonarola's influence over the city, these demonstrations also contained the seeds of his downfall. The aristocrats of Florence simply were not ready to abandon the Renaissance. Resentment against Savonarola grew, abetted by the Franciscans, who had no desire to see a Dominican exercise so much power, and the Medici family, who were waiting in the wings for the new republic to fall.

The pope at this time was the openly wicked Roderigo Borgia, Alexander VI. It really didn't bother him that Savonarola was condemning his immorality - everyone was doing that. What bothered him was that Savonarola was using his influence to keep Florence in the camp of the French king, against whom Alexander was engaged in fighting a war. He determined that the bothersome friar had to be stopped. He first tried to buy Savonarola off by offering to make him a cardinal. When the friar refused, propaganda against Savonarola began to circulate in Florence, and teams of assassins were sent out to silence him. Savonarola responded by intensifying his condemnation of the pope and all who supported him. While Savonarola was attacking only a particular pope rather than the institution of the papacy, as Wycliffe and Huss had done, this particular pope was not about to put up with it. In 1497 he excommunicated Savonarola and ordered him to stop preaching. The friar agreed, but soon returned to the pulpit, as outspoken as ever. He had worn out his welcome, however. His enemies were becoming more numerous by the day, and even his supporters were staying away from his preaching out of respect for the pope's decree of excommunication. The pope ordered Savonarola to come to Rome, and threatened Florence with interdict if they harbored him. At this point, a Franciscan friar accused Savonarola of heresy and challenged him to an ordeal by fire. This was a medieval practice in which the two contestants would walk through flames, and whichever one survived was assumed to be right (if they both died, as usually occurred, both were assumed to be in error; this didn't solve the argument, but it eliminated the troublemakers). Savonarola was opposed to the ordeal, but one of his followers accepted the challenge. The Franciscan who had suggested the idea in the first place then withdrew, and was replaced by another monk who was less than enthusiastic about the whole business. When the appointed day arrived, the fire was prepared, and an enormous crowd gathered in the public square. The Franciscans repeatedly delayed the proceedings, insisting that the Dominican could not wear his red robe, nor carry a cross or the consecrated host, nor have any contact with Savonarola, lest he be able to survive the fire by the use of witchcraft. They then started a theological debate about whether or not the body of Christ would be consumed if the host were burned in the fire. By the time the disputes had ended, the sun had set, and the ordeal had to be called off - much to the relief of the Franciscan who had been drafted. The failed ordeal destroyed Savonarola's popular support. Many argued that he should have braved the flames himself rather than permitting a substitute, and the people, denied their long-awaited spectacle, accused him of cowardice. They assumed that, because he had not passed the trial by ordeal, he must be guilty.

Shortly thereafter, Savonarola and two of his followers were arrested. The pope, glad that he did not have to deal with this messy business himself, sent representatives to the trial with orders to make sure that Savonarola died, "even if he were John the Baptist." As was customary, Savonarola was put to the torture, and eventually succumbed and confessed to all the charges against him. That he later came to his senses and denied the charges mattered little to anyone. On May 23, 1498, Savonarola and his two companions were hanged in the public square, then their bodies were burned. Like Huss, their ashes were thrown in the river to leave no potential relics behind.

THE CHRISTIAN HUMANISTS

Before we conclude this chapter, a word needs to be said concerning the so-called Christian humanists. Though the Renaissance was the enemy of reformers like Savonarola, it, too, helped pave the way for the Protestant Reformation. The humanists valued the individual, and asserted the right of the individual to decide for himself the questions of truth and authority. This humanist perspective undermined the absolute claims of the Roman hierarchy and sent men searching the Scriptures for themselves. The Renaissance was also the enemy of the Reformation, of course, in that it advanced secularism and caused men to believe that there was no higher authority outside themselves. That sort of thinking remains the enemy of the church to the present day. Before we conclude the chapter, however, we need to look at two examples of humanists who advanced the cause of the Reformation - the Brethren of the Common Life and the great Dutch thinker Desiderius Erasmus.

The Brethren of the Common Life was a lay monastic movement begun by a mystic named Gerhard Groote (1340-1384) in the Netherlands. They emphasized simple and chaste living in communal homes, and eventually founded schools all over Germany and the Netherlands, one of which was attended by the young Martin Luther. From these schools came many of the leaders in the movement for church reform. Thomas à Kempis, the German mystic who was a champion of reform from within the heart of the individual and wrote the devotional classic *The Imitation of Christ*, spent most of his adult years in a Brethren of the Common Life household. The conciliar leader Nicholas of Cusa also received his training from the Brethren of the Common Life.

More in the line of the Reformers was John Wessel or Wessel Gansfort (1420-1489). A noted scholar who learned both Greek and Hebrew, he sought a simple life in the confines of the houses of the Brethren of the Common Life. Once when he visited Rome, Pope Sixtus IV asked him what gift he wished to receive. The pope was used to constant streams of visitors asking for church offices, and he laughed aloud when Wessel asked him for nothing but a Greek manuscript of the Bible from the Vatican library. His teachings anticipated those of the Reformers in many ways, including his repudiation of many of the traditions of Catholicism. His writings were not widely known prior to the Reformation, but when Luther became acquainted with his work, he said, "Had I read his works sooner, my enemies might have thought I had derived everything from Wessel, so much are we of one mind." Luther later published an edition of Wessel's works, for which he wrote the preface.

A man who is often confused with Wessel Gansfort also contributed to the coming Reformation, though he had no connection with the Brethren of the Common Life. John of Wesel (d.1481) taught at the University of Erfurt, where Luther later studied his writings. His repudiation of papal authority, transubstantiation, indulgences, priestly celibacy, and the mediatorial role of the church caused him to be brought before the Inquisition, where he recanted his views, afterward spending the rest of his life in prison. His emphasis on Scripture as the only authority for the Christian and on the grace of God in salvation makes him a true forerunner of Luther, despite his forced recantation.

The most famous of the Christian humanists, and a man who also had ties to the Brethren of the Common Life, was the Dutch scholar Desiderius Erasmus (c.1466-1536). He opened the door of the Reformation for many, but never entered in himself. On the negative side, he launched a series of scathing attacks against the hypocrisy of the Catholic Church, including his satirical *In Praise of Folly*. Though he clearly saw the failings of the Catholic Church, he thought the cure proposed by Luther worse than the disease itself. He never left the Catholic Church, though the church repaid him by putting most of his books on the Index. On the positive side, he helped pave the way for the Reformation by editing a Greek text of the New Testament that opened the Bible in its original language to many who previously had not had access to it. That Greek text was not only the basis for Luther's translation of the New Testament into German, but also contributed to the *Textus Receptus*, which was the manuscript foundation for the King James Version of the Bible in English.

Though the Brethren of the Common Life did much to bring the people back to simple piety and provided many voices calling for reform, they, like Erasmus, remained within the Roman Catholic Church, electing not to follow groups like the Waldensians, Lollards, and Hussites into the Reformation. Because they were primarily concerned with moral living rather than theology, they were satisfied when the Catholic Church cleaned up its act at the Council of Trent, and saw no reason to leave.

MAKING DRY BONES LIVE

The attempts at reform in the fourteenth and fifteenth centuries demonstrated that the salvation of the church was not to be found in replacing bad works by good works. The view of Wycliffe and Huss that saw the church as the elect, and identified the elect as those who lived godly lives, was an improvement on the sacramental salvation and identification of the Body of Christ with the visible church advocated by the Scholastics, but it was still far from the teaching of salvation by grace through faith that would become the rallying cry of the Reformation. The negative criticism of prophets like Savonarola and humanists like Erasmus was even farther from the truth; like the man of Jesus' parable, they chased out one demon, only to find seven more ready to come in. The austerity of Savonarola failed, but was succeeded by the austerity of the Jesuits, who did more to oppose the Protestant Reformation than any other single organization. The humanism that was the basis for Erasmus' critique of the church became, in Protestant Europe, the impetus for a secularism that to the present day has increasingly undermined Christianity.

In the life of the individual, as in the life of the church, change is not enough. One does not become a Christian by working to rid his life of vices, nor by trying to live a good life. In the same way that the church could not be truly reformed until it recognized that salvation was by the grace of God alone, so no man can hope for salvation as long as he depends upon his own efforts. The church that taught the grace of God gained God's blessing; the man who trusts in the grace of God gains salvation through His Son.

Reform Efforts That Failed

FOR REVIEW AND FURTHER THOUGHT

1. What factor distinguished the protests of those who were rejected by the church from the objections of those who remained respected members of it?

2. How did the Realism of Wycliffe influence his theology?

3. What political circumstances motivated the English revolt against the financing of the Avignon papacy?

4. How did Wycliffe use the question of dominion to attack the corruption of the Catholic Church?

5. What role did the papal schism play in turning Wycliffe into a reformer?

6. How did Wycliffe lose the support of the English nobility? of the Oxford faculty?

7. Why was Wycliffe's translation of the Bible into English important?

8. In what way was the Wycliffe Bible a poor translation?

9. Who were the Lollards, and how did they keep Wycliffe's teaching alive?

10. How did Huss come in contact with the teachings of Wycliffe?

11. In what ways did the teachings of Huss and Wycliffe differ?

12. How did Huss lose the support of the Prague authorities?

13. How did indulgences lead to the downfall of Huss?

14. What false assumptions led Huss to travel to the Council of Constance?

15. Why did the leaders of the Conciliar Movement at the Council of Constance fight for Huss' destruction?

16. How did the Council of Basel solve the Hussite conflict?

17. Who were the Utraquists and Taborites, and how did they differ?

18. Who were the Bohemian Brethren?

19. Why did Savonarola believe himself to be a prophet? How did he exercise his prophetic gifts?

20. What do you think was behind the prophecies of Savonarola? Explain your answer.

21. Why did Savonarola oppose the Renaissance?

22. What caused Savonarola to lose the popular support of the people of Florence?

23. What was an ordeal by fire? How did it contribute to Savonarola's downfall?

24. How did the Renaissance help pave the way for the Reformation?

25. In what ways was the Renaissance the enemy of the Reformation?

26. How did the Brethren of the Common Life help pave the way for the Reformation?

27. Why did the Brethren of the Common Life refuse to join the Protestant Reformation?

28. In what ways did Erasmus further the cause of the Reformation?

29. In what way did Wycliffe and Huss fall short of Protestant doctrine?

30. How does the history of the fifteenth century illustrate the statement of Tertullian that "the blood of the martyrs is seed"?

19

A WILD BOAR IN THE VINEYARD

In June of 1520, the Medici pope Leo X published a bull known as *Exsurge domini*, which began as follows:

"Arise, O Lord, and judge thy cause. Be mindful of the daily slander against thee by the foolish, incline thine ear to our supplication. Foxes have arisen which want to devastate thy vineyard, where thou hast worked the winepress. At thy ascension into heaven thou hast commanded the care, rule and administration of this vineyard to Peter as head and to thy representatives, his successors, as the Church triumphant. A roaring boar of the woods has undertaken to destroy this vineyard, a wild beast wants to devour it."

This "roaring boar" was an Augustinian monk from Wittenberg named Martin Luther, the father of the Protestant Reformation. In previous chapters, we have seen many other men who "protested" against the evils in the Roman Catholic Church. What was there about Luther and the revolt that he led that set them apart from previous reform efforts?

There can be no question that the time was right. From a religious standpoint, the corruption of the Catholic hierarchy was an open, festering sore. Everyone knew that change was needed. From an intellectual standpoint, the Renaissance had taught people to think for themselves rather than submitting to authority. In the political realm, growing nationalism was breeding deep feelings of resentment against "foreign" (i.e., papal) interference in national affairs. Economically speaking, the financial burdens imposed by Rome were becoming increasingly unbearable, and rulers, peasants, and especially the members of the growing middle class, were unwilling to underwrite the pope's artistic and military ventures. To view the Reformation primarily in terms of such factors, however, is like explaining the spread of the Gospel in the first century in terms of the *Pax Romana* and the sterility of pagan religion. While all of these factors contributed to the Reformation, they must be seen, not so much as causes, but as providential preparation by God for the work He was about to do. To characterize the Reformation as anything other than a religious movement is to miss the point.

The key question of the Reformation was the question the Philippian jailer asked the Apostle Paul: "What must I do to be saved?" The fact that Luther gave Paul's answer caused the Reformation to be a radical departure from medieval Catholicism. The Catholic Church had over the years interposed a succession of mediators between God and man. When men sought God, they prayed to Mary or the saints; when God gave His grace to men, it was distributed by the priest, through the sacraments of the church. A veil much thicker than that which kept men out of the Holy of Holies in the Jewish Temple had been lowered between man and God.

Luther tore that veil. Like the pre-reformers, he taught that God spoke through the Bible, which every individual was to read and understand for himself. No longer were people dependent upon the priest to tell them what the Bible said and meant. Like a few of his predecessors, Luther emphasized the grace of God in salvation. He returned to the Augustinian (and Pauline) teaching that men are incapable of saving themselves, and can only be saved by a free and sovereign act of God's mercy. Like some who had gone before, he taught the priesthood of all believers. He said that all men could come to God without the need of a human mediator. While all of these teachings represented departures from medieval Catholicism, they were not in themselves new. Various reformers in the centuries before Luther had said each of these things, though no single man had said them all. What made Luther the father of the Reformation was his teaching of justification by faith alone. What was it that brought the simple German monk to the understanding of salvation that would shake the church to its very foundations?

LUTHER'S EARLY YEARS

By all accounts, there was nothing remarkable about Luther's childhood. He was born on November 10, 1483, the oldest son of Hans and Margaret Luther of Eisleben. His parents were good Catholics, and named him after Martin of Tours, the fifth-century saint on whose day he was baptized. The Luthers were strict disciplinarians, but the whippings he described from his youth were nothing out of the ordinary for a child of his or any other day. His father was a miner, a hard-working peasant who managed to amass considerable wealth for himself by the time young Martin was ready to go to school. Luther studied at a school run by the Brethren of the Common Life, then went off to the University of Erfurt, then the best and largest university in Germany. His father wanted him to study law. Luther was a good student, and finished second in his class, then went on to study for his Master's degree.

In the summer of 1505, he was returning to school after a visit home when a sudden thunderstorm arose. Lightning was flashing all around him, and Luther was terrified. In his fear, he called out to St. Anne, the patron saint of miners, and promised that if he survived the storm he would become a monk. Much to the displeasure of his father, he kept his vow, and two weeks later entered the Augustinian monastery in Erfurt.

Luther turned out to be a good monk in everyone's eyes but his own. He took the rigors and responsibilities of monastic life very seriously, and often went far beyond what was required in terms of fasts and deprivations, to the point where he nearly ruined his health. The harder he struggled to make himself acceptable to God, however, the more unworthy he felt. He would go to confession for hours on end, then worry that he had forgotten something, and that the omission would cost him his salvation. He became increasingly conscious of his own sins, and realized that he could never possibly confess to God, or even remember, all the evil thoughts that went through his mind in even a single day. At times he despaired of his own salvation, and in his frustration admitted that he hated God. Johann von Staupitz, the head of the order, encouraged young Martin to read the Scriptures and the writings of the German mystics, and the young monk found these a source of some comfort.

Luther became a priest in 1507, then in 1508 was sent to teach at the newly formed University of Wittenberg, which Frederick the Wise, Elector of Saxony, had established in 1502. After teaching there for one semester, Luther was called away to deal with some business for the Augustinian order. Part of this business involved a trip to Rome in 1510. What an incredible eye-opener that trip turned out to be for Luther! The following are some of Luther's later reflections on his trip:

"In Rome I was a frantic saint. I ran through all the churches and catacombs and believed everything, their lies and falsehood. I celebrated several masses in Rome, and almost regretted that my father and mother were still living, for I would have liked to redeem them from purgatory with my masses and other good works and prayers. There is a saying in Rome: `Blessed is the mother whose son celebrates a mass in the Church of St. John on Saturday.' I surely would have liked to make my mother blessed! But there was a great commotion and I could not get close. I ate a salted herring instead.

"I did not stay long in Rome, but found occasion to celebrate and hear many a mass. I still shudder when I think of it now. I heard people laughingly boast in the inn that some celebrated mass, saying to the bread and wine, `Bread thou art and bread wilt thou remain.'

A Wild Boar in the Vineyard

Then they elevated it. I was a young and pious monk who was hurt by such words.... If pope, cardinals, and the courtiers celebrated mass that way, I had been deceived, since I had heard many masses by them. I was especially annoyed over the speed with which they said the mass. By the time I reached the gospel the priest next to me had already finished mass and shouted, `Come on, finish, hurry up.'"

Luther saw for the first time some of the abuses that had led so many others to criticize the church, and what he saw shocked him. He still somewhat naively believed that the pope was above it all, however. Even after the Reformation had begun, he continued to believe that change could be made if only the pope were informed of the abuses going on around him.

Luther returned to Wittenberg in 1511 to teach Bible and theology while studying for his doctorate. It was during these years that his understanding of justification by faith developed. As he lectured on the books of Romans and Galatians, he came to understand that justification was an immediate and judicial act of God. In other words, salvation was not so much God making a person righteous through doing good works and taking the sacraments as it was God declaring a person to be righteous because of the saving work of Christ on the cross. Good works were thus not the cause of salvation, but the result of it. Once Luther realized that his continued sin did not separate him from God, but that God accepted him because he trusted in the death of Christ on the cross, it was like a great burden had been lifted from his shoulders. From that point on, justification by faith became, not only the keynote of Luther's preaching, but the rallying cry of the Reformation.

THE SPARK IS IGNITED

The pope needed money. That in itself was nothing new, especially for Leo X. Leo was such a generous patron of the arts that it was said that he spent the funds of three popes; he quickly emptied the full treasury left behind by his thrifty predecessor Julius II, spent every penny that came in during his papacy, and left behind him an enormous debt that his successor had to spend his entire reign making up. At the moment, the project in question was the restoration of the Basilica of St. Peter. In order to finish this marvelous piece of architecture with artwork of a suitably grand nature, Leo turned to that old tried-and-true technique, selling indulgences. Most of the monarchs of Europe had caught on to the scam by now, and demanded some kind of kickback for allowing indulgence peddlers to operate in their jurisdictions. In Germany, the demand came from Albrecht, Archbishop of Mainz, who had just finished paying the pope an enormous bribe in order to gain that valuable office (he was only in his twenties, and he already had two bishoprics, so the bribe had been well over a million dollars). Albrecht had borrowed the money from the banking house of Fugger in Augsburg, and the interest rates were atrocious. The Fuggers wanted their money back, so they demanded that the pope pay to Albrecht half of the indulgence receipts collected in his district; they then sent a representative along with the indulgence peddlers to make sure they didn't get cheated.

The indulgence seller hired by Albrecht and the Fuggers was a Dominican named Johann Tetzel. He had been in the indulgence racket for a long time, and he was good at it. His tear-jerking sermons were calculated to wring hard-earned money from the pockets of the ignorant and superstitious. He would preach, for instance,

"Don't you hear the voices of your wailing dead parents and others who say, `Have mercy upon me, have mercy upon me, because we are in severe punishment and pain. From this you could redeem us with a small alms and yet you do not want to do so.' Open your ears as the father says to the son and the mother to the daughter, `We have created you, fed you, cared for you, and left you our temporal goods. Why then are you so cruel and harsh that you do not want to save us, though it only takes a little?'"

Though the official teaching of the Catholic Church was that indulgences could take the place of earthly penances (such as prayers and pilgrimages), but only God could forgive sin, the two soon became muddled in the preaching of the indulgence peddlers. With regard to purgatory, the church taught that an indulgence would pay for the pope's intercession on behalf of the one for whom the indulgence was bought, but that didn't stop Tetzel from proclaiming that "as soon as the coin in the coffer rings, the soul from purgatory springs."

Frederick the Wise had refused to allow Tetzel to operate in Saxony, but when he arrived just across the boundary line from Wittenberg, Luther found out what was going on. The blatant commercialism of Tetzel's sales pitch shocked him, and he decided to issue a challenge. On October 31, 1517, he posted a list of ninety-five debate topics having to do with indulgences on the door of the castle church in Wittenberg. This was common practice. Academic debates were frequent in university towns, and the church door served as a sort of community bulletin board. Though no one stepped forward to accept the challenge, friends of Luther took the Ninety-five Theses to a printer and had copies made, which within two weeks were all over Germany. Soon a copy even found its way to the pope in Italy. Before long, all Europe was in an uproar. The Reformation had begun.

Why should these debate topics cause so much trouble? After all, Luther was only criticizing the abuse of indulgences, he wasn't challenging the doctrine or even the authority of the church - yet. One reason for this, of course, is money. The mercenary officials of the church hierarchy could take almost any kind of criticism except the kind that hurt their pocketbooks. When sales of indulgences dropped off, something had to be done to silence Luther. From the other side, the theses sparked a major response because they articulated and gave focus to a protest that had been growing under the surface for a long time. The resentment that so many had been feeling toward the abuses of the church hierarchy now could come out into the open through support of this new-found champion.

THE FIRE SPREADS (1517-1525)

Luther had no idea what all the commotion was about. He had no more desire to start a religious movement than he had to join a circus. He remained certain that if the pope could only be convinced of the abuses indulgence sellers were perpetrating in his name, he would quickly put a stop to them. Fortunately, Luther's supporters were not quite so naive. When Leo summoned Luther to Rome in 1518, Frederick the Wise arranged to have the summons canceled. The pope then sent Cardinal Cajetan to examine Luther. The conference was cordial, and Luther became convinced more than ever that the pope did not approve of Tetzel's actions.

Tetzel became the scapegoat for the whole business. Cajetan criticized him severely, and he became the butt of jokes all over Germany. One favorite story told about a man who came to Tetzel and asked if he could buy an indulgence for a sin not yet committed. Tetzel readily agreed, as long as he paid in advance. The man quickly purchased the indulgence, and later Tetzel left for the next town. During his journey, a robber jumped him, beat him up and stole all his money. The robber was none other than the man who had bought the indulgence earlier. He thereupon informed poor Tetzel that this sin was the one he had in mind when he purchased the indulgence! Things got so bad that even Luther later wrote a letter to Tetzel to encourage him and tell him that it was his superiors who were really at fault.

The next year, in 1519, another papal representative named Karl von Miltitz visited Luther and arranged a truce of sorts. Luther agreed to keep quiet about indulgences if his opponents would do the same. He even wrote a very submissive letter to the pope. The truce didn't last long, however. Later that year, someone finally accepted Luther's challenge to debate. Johann Eck, a noted humanist and professor at the University of Ingolstadt, agreed to debate Luther, but wanted the topic to be broader than simply indulgences (as it turned out, indulgences were hardly mentioned). The reason for this was that he wanted to trap Luther into some declaration of heresy that could be used against him. The debate was held at Leipzig, and though both sides claimed victory, Eck achieved his purpose. During the debate, he maneuvered Luther into an open criticism of the Council of Constance, along with an affirmation of the truth of some of John Huss' teachings. This was heresy indeed, and the pope now had a handle by which he could grasp the troublesome Wittenberg monk. The coin had two sides, however. Luther was not far from Bohemia, and his defense of Huss gained him a large number of new supporters. He was becoming more popular by the day, and Eck soon found it difficult to walk the streets in safety.

The press had been the chief weapon of the Reformation, and it became even more so in 1520. In that year, Luther published a series of pamphlets in German that were soon circulated all over the country. These included *Address to the German Nobility*, in which he encouraged the secular rulers to undertake a reform of the church and society, since the hierarchy refused to do so. He based this on the concept of the priesthood of all believers. The princes were to cleanse the church of unbiblical practices, but do so without violence. In *The Babylonian Captivity of the Church*, he attacked the sacramental system, maintaining that Scripture only sanctions two sacraments rather than seven. He also criticized the doctrine of transubstantiation as an innovation in the church. In *The Freedom of the Christian Man*, he tried to do two things. On the positive side, he asserted that each man was free to read and interpret the Scriptures for himself, and need submit to the hierarchy only insofar as it was in accord with the Bible. On the negative side, he emphasized that freedom means nothing apart from faith and love, thus attempting to silence the critics who had insisted that his teachings would lead to anarchy, where each man would do what was right in his own eyes.

Meanwhile, the pope was writing as well. While Luther was writing pamphlets, Leo was drafting a bull of excommunication - *Exsurge domini*, the document quoted at the beginning of the chapter. By this time, however, it was clear to Luther that the only solution was to break away from the corruption of the hierarchy. Calling Leo the Antichrist, he posted another announcement in Wittenberg, calling all to a public burning of the papal bull.

By this time, Luther had become a national hero. Leo simply could not deal with a man who had such enormous popular support. He turned instead to the newly crowned Holy Roman Emperor, Charles V, the grandson of Ferdinand and Isabella of Spain. While Charles was a devout Catholic, he had good reason to mistrust the pope. Leo had actively worked for the election of his rival Francis I of France as Holy Roman Emperor, and had shown little enthusiasm for the religious reforms introduced into Spain through the Inquisition. He badly wanted to put a stop to the turmoil in Germany, however, so he agreed to summon Luther to a meeting of the German parliament, or Diet.

In 1521 the Diet was to meet in the city of Worms. Luther's friends begged him not to go, and reminded him of what had happened to John Huss when he had depended on an emperor's safe-conduct. The fact that Frederick the Wise also offered a safe-conduct convinced Luther that he was on his home turf, however, and he agreed to go. Like Huss, Luther hoped to have the opportunity to explain his teachings before the assembled nobility of Germany, but also like Huss, that opportunity was denied. The Diet only permitted Luther to answer two questions: "Did you write these books?" and "Are you willing to recant their contents?" He readily affirmed that the books were indeed his, but asked for a day to consider the matter of recantation. This request was not because of any uncertainty on Luther's part - that night he wrote to one of his supporters that he did not intend to recant a single word. He simply wanted to make sure that what he was affirming was according to Scripture and not simply the product of his own imagination. The next day, he returned to the Diet and asserted that he simply could not recant what he had written, for to do so would be to deny the truth revealed by God in his Word. While he agreed to give up any views that could be shown to be wrong from Scripture, he refused to submit to the edicts of popes or councils.

Charles V condemned Luther as an outlaw, but insisted on honoring the safe-conduct (though on his deathbed he said that his failure to do away with Luther was the greatest regret of his life). On the way back from Worms to Wittenberg, a group of men surrounded Luther's carriage, seized him and carried him off. They had been sent by Frederick the Wise, and they took Luther to the Wartburg Castle, where he remained in hiding for almost a year. Not even his friends knew where he was, and some of them thought he had been killed by agents of the pope or emperor. Why Frederick protected Luther continues to be somewhat of a mystery. The two men never met. Frederick certainly valued Luther as the most famous professor in the university he had founded, and heartily approved of the monk's denunciation of papal practices in Germany. Yet he never clearly understood the theological basis for Luther's activity; to the end of his days, he maintained one of the largest relic collections in Europe (it consisted of over 5,000 relics; a pilgrim viewing them all could earn almost two *million* years off his time in purgatory).

Luther lived in the Wartburg disguised as a nobleman named Junker George. While he was there, he went on occasional hunting trips, wrote letters to his friends to let them know he was safe (though he didn't tell them where he was), but spent most of his time translating the New Testament into German. This translation, based on the Greek text of Erasmus, became as important in shaping the German language as the King James Version was later to be for English. He later added the Old Testament, so that the entire Bible was available in German by 1534.

While Luther was in hiding, the Reformation almost collapsed before it even had a chance to get started. Luther's followers tried to provide leadership while he was gone, but they lacked his sense of judgment, and soon Wittenberg was in chaos. The two most prominent among Luther's followers were Philip Melanchthon and Andreas von Carlstadt. Melanchthon was a great scholar, and wrote the first Protestant work of systematic theology, *Loci Communes* ("Theological Commonplaces"), but was not a leader of men. Carlstadt, on the other hand, was full of fire, but had absolutely no common sense. He immediately established himself as the leader of the church in Wittenberg. He encouraged the magistrates to remove every remnant of Catholicism from the worship of the church. The people began to destroy works of art and drive monks from their monasteries. Meanwhile, Carlstadt began referring to himself as Brother Andreas. Things only got worse when a group of "prophets" arrived from the nearby town of Zwickau. Thomas Münzer, Nicholas Storch, and Marcus Stübner claimed that they had received revelations directly from God, and that the existing order was soon to be overthrown. They taught community of property, rejected infant baptism, and advocated the violent overthrow of everything Catholic.

When Luther heard about this, he knew he could not remain in hiding any longer. Despite the sentence of death that hung over him (and remained there for the rest of his life), he would not allow the Reformation that he had begun to disintegrate into fanaticism. He returned to Wittenberg and soon brought things under control. Carlstadt accused Luther of compromising his principles, and eventually went into exile. He never seemed satisfied wherever he went, despite being openly received in Switzerland. He died a bitter man, but his ideas did have somewhat of an influence on the Anabaptists. Luther, by stepping in and restoring order, assured that the Reformation would focus on theology rather than practice. He was determined to reject only those things that were directly against Scripture, and to this day the Lutheran Church retains many of the Catholic practices that Luther considered to be compatible with Scripture, though not contained in it.

Meanwhile, Charles V was trying another tactic to gain control of the situation in Germany. When Leo died in 1521, Charles used his influence to get his Dutch tutor elected to the papacy as Adrian VI. Adrian was fully committed to the Spanish reforms, but was wholly incapable of carrying them out. To begin with, his notion that church leaders should live simple and pious lives did not sit well with the members of the curia. Furthermore, Adrian was an outsider - he didn't even know how to speak Italian. As a result, any attempt he made to change things in Rome was quickly sidetracked by the cardinals behind his back; when he died in 1523, many suspected that he had been poisoned. The experience with Adrian was one that the cardinals had no desire to repeat; he was the last non-Italian pope elected by the College of Cardinals until the election of the Polish cardinal Karol Wojtyla as Pope John Paul II in 1978.

Luther, meanwhile, was in the process of losing the support of many who had followed him for reasons that had little to do with his theology. The humanists had stood to one side and cheered while Luther skewered the pope and his cardinals, but when he led an open schism, they were unwilling to follow. Besides, they were uncomfortable with his theology. Humanists valued the freedom of the individual man above everything. When Luther wrote about freedom, they were behind him one hundred percent. However, it soon became clear that Luther had adopted the Augustinian doctrine of predestination. Like Augustine, he taught that man was incapable of doing anything to please God, and that therefore salvation was entirely a work of God's grace, to which man could contribute nothing, not even his assent. To the humanists, this sounded like a denial of free will. Luther, however, was not denying man's volitional freedom - his ability to make responsible choices, he was denying man's moral freedom - his capacity to choose God apart from God's grace. Erasmus voiced this humanistic discontent when he penned *The Freedom of the Will* in 1524. Luther responded by writing *The Bondage of the Will*, which clarified his theological position, but alienated many of his humanistic supporters.

At about the same time, he lost the support of the German peasants, also because they misunderstood his teachings about freedom. They saw in Luther's teachings about the priesthood of all believers an affirmation of the fundamental equality of all men before God. For them, this meant they now had a theological justification for throwing off the oppression under which the German nobility had kept them for centuries. A Peasants' Revolt broke out in 1525, led by Thomas Münzer. Luther at first sympathized with the peasants, and advised them to proceed slowly. When they began burning and looting across the countryside, however, he wrote a pamphlet condemning their rebellion against authority established by God (*Against the Thieving and Murdering Hordes of Peasants*), and encouraged the authorities to put down the revolt by force. The nobles needed little encouragement in that area, and over a hundred thousand peasants were slaughtered. As a result, Luther lost the support of the peasantry of southern Germany, who viewed him as a traitor; many returned to Catholicism, and some joined the new Reformed movement that had recently begun in Switzerland.

The year 1525 also marked an important transition in Luther's life. That year he married a former nun named Katherine von Bora. He had always resisted marriage because of the threat of death hanging over his head, but he finally succumbed, both to set a good example for others, and because Katherine made it clear to him that she was more than willing to take the step. She provided firm support for him for the rest of his life, managed the funds of the household (he time and again refused to take any money for the publication of his books, and was so generous that he would have given everything away to the needy had not "Katie" kept an eye on things), and bore him six children. Their family conversations at mealtime became the basis for *Table Talk*, a record of Luther's often-rambling dinner discourses as transcribed by his students.

THE STRUGGLE FOR SURVIVAL (1525-1555)

Though Luther remained an influential figure in Germany until his death in 1546, control of the movement passed from his hands after 1525, and into the hands of the Lutheran princes like Philip of Hesse and the theologians like Melanchthon. Charles V still wanted to bring the German situation under control, but he was preoccupied with war in France and conflicts with the new pope, to say nothing of the conquest of the New World. Thus when the German Diet met at Speier in 1526, they simply agreed to maintain the status quo, thus in effect giving the Lutheran princes the authority to continue making changes in their domains. By the time a second Diet met at Speier in 1529, however, Charles had made peace with the pope and the French, and was ready to deal with the Lutherans. He took a hard-line position, insisting that Lutheranism spread no farther. He outlawed Lutheranism in Catholic lands, and demanded that the Lutheran princes tolerate Catholicism in their domains. The Lutheran princes protested against this unfair treatment, and thus earned for themselves the name of Protestants, which later came to be applied to the entire movement. The Lutheran princes earned the right to present their case before another Diet at Augsburg in 1530. They commissioned the scholarly and tactful Melanchthon to prepare a statement of Lutheran belief; the result was the Augsburg Confession. The Lutheran position was weakened because they were unable to come to terms with the newer branch of Protestantism that had sprung up in Switzerland and spread into southern Germany. The Swiss reformers, led by Ulrich Zwingli, were far more radical than the Germans, and insisted that worship in the church should contain only those elements commanded in Scripture. They thus rejected every aspect of Catholic worship on which the Bible was silent. The Lutheran prince Philip of Hesse realized that if the Protestant house were divided, it would soon fall, and invited Luther, Zwingli, and some of their supporters to his castle in Marburg to resolve their differences. This Marburg Colloquy (1529) proved to be a failure. Though the Germans and Swiss could agree on fourteen of fifteen articles, they could not come to terms on the Lord's Supper. Luther insisted that Christ's body was truly present in the sacrament along with the bread (sometimes called "consubstantiation"), while Zwingli believed that the Supper was a memorial service to celebrate Christ's death, and that the bread and wine merely symbolized Christ's body and blood. The disagreement was so bitter that soon the two sides were using the same kind of language to describe one another that they had earlier reserved for Catholics.

By the time they arrived at the Diet of Augsburg, they were totally incapable of presenting a united front against the Catholic opposition. While the Lutherans submitted the Augsburg Confession, the Reformed submitted two other confessions to explain their beliefs. Charles, who was now determined to enforce conformity at any cost, rejected all of them. The Lutheran princes formed the League of Smalcald to defend themselves against the attack they felt sure would come. Charles soon became embroiled in other wars, however, and was unable to devote any attention to Germany until the year of Luther's death.

Luther lived out the rest of his days in Wittenberg, suffering from poor health and becoming increasingly crotchety and violent in his verbal outbursts against his enemies. He exercised notably bad judgment in the incident involving the marriage of Philip of Hesse in 1540. Philip had contracted an arranged marriage at age nineteen, and his wife had been both faithful and fruitful, while Philip had engaged in constant extramarital flings, like most of the aristocrats of his day. His immorality genuinely bothered his conscience, but he felt unable to control himself. He therefore asked Luther's blessing to marry a seventeen-year-old girl with whom he had become infatuated, having already gotten permission from both his wife and the girl's parents. Luther reluctantly agreed, arguing that polygamy was better than divorce (he had given the same advice to Henry VIII fifteen years earlier). Since plural marriage was against the law, however, Luther told Philip to keep the marriage a secret. Word soon got out, though, and the scandal did much to damage Luther's credibility and reputation (despite the fact that some Catholic theologians had given the same advice).

Meanwhile, the pope had finally gotten around to calling a general council of the church at Trent in 1545. Protestants had been asking for a council for years to discuss their grievances, but the Conciliar Movement of the fifteenth century had taught the popes to be cautious. Thus the Council of Trent was called only after the pope had assured himself of complete control of the outcome (largely through the instrumentality of the Jesuits, founded a decade earlier). When the delegates got word of Luther's death in 1546, some said that it was a pity that they didn't have the pleasure of burning him at the stake. Obviously the Protestants could hope for little from such a council.

In 1546, Charles V finally got around to using military force against the Smalcald League. Because of treachery on the part of some of the Lutheran princes, Charles was able to defeat the League and imprison Philip of Hesse. War soon broke out again, however, and a compromise settlement was reached at the Peace of Augsburg in 1555. The treaty established the principle of *cuius regio, eius religio*, meaning that the prince had the right to determine the religion of his people. The treaty guaranteed that those whose religion differed from that of their prince would be free to sell their property and move. The result was that Germany became a religious checkerboard. This not only set the stage for the Thirty Years' War, but also prevented the unification of Germany until late in the nineteenth century. The Peace of Augsburg only recognized Catholicism and Lutheranism as legal; the Reformed Church was still not granted toleration in Germany. Charles, meanwhile, abdicated his throne and in frustration retired to a monastery.

Thus the Peace of Augsburg institutionalized state control of the Lutheran Church. Luther himself had wanted congregational control as an expression of his belief in the priesthood of all believers, but also realized that an uneducated peasantry simply was in no position to run a church. Since the bishops for the most part remained loyal to Catholicism, the only option left was the nobility. Thus what Luther considered a practical expedient passed into the structure of the Lutheran Church.

THEOLOGICAL AND POLITICAL WARFARE (1555-1648)

The interval between the Peace of Augsburg and the Thirty Years' War was one of theological conflict among German Lutherans. After Luther's death, the mantle of leadership fell to Melanchthon, but he was insufficient for the task. He had such a strong desire for peace and reconciliation that he seemed incapable of taking a strong stand on anything, and appeared to many to be willing to give away the essentials of the faith in order to purchase peace. As a result, he lost the respect of many of his fellow Lutherans. In many ways, they were right. Though he held to the basic tenets of Lutheranism, he compromised in some key areas. In an attempt to make peace with the Reformed, he supported the teaching of the spiritual presence of Christ in the Lord's Supper, causing Lutherans to accuse him of being a crypto-Calvinist. To make peace with Catholics, he declared himself willing to accept certain Catholic practices that Luther had rejected, and his frequent use of pagan philosophers made many suspicious. He moved closer to the humanists by allowing room for the human will to cooperate with God in salvation, thus vacillating on perhaps the most basic doctrine of the Reformation.

Melanchthon's major opponent in these disputes was Matthias Flacius, a Wittenberg professor of Hebrew who was as prickly as Melanchthon was peaceful. He himself got into trouble, and was eventually forced into exile, for teaching that the image of God was lost by man at the time of the Fall. The German Lutherans finally decided to settle some of these matters, and produced in 1577 the Formula of Concord, under the leadership of Martin Chemnitz, who forged numerous compromises between the strict Lutherans and the followers of Melanchthon. While these disputes were raging, the Reformed branch of Protestantism was making steady gains in southern Germany under the leadership of Martin Bucer, Zacharius Ursinus, and Caspar Olevianus.

In 1618 the Thirty Years' War broke out, and the Protestants stopped fighting one another theologically long enough to join against the Catholics on the battlefield. The war started with the infamous Defenestration of Prague, when Bohemian Protestants, unhappy with their treatment by the emperor's Catholic counselors, threw several of them from a window into a moat eighty feet below. Though no one was seriously hurt, the insult was enough to start one of the most devastating wars in the history of Europe. By the time it was over, as much as half the population of central Europe had perished, and the countryside had been so badly devastated that Georgia after General Sherman got done with it would have looked relatively unscathed. The war originally pitted Protestants against Catholics, but soon political considerations overwhelmed the religious issues. At first, things went badly for the Protestants, and the Jesuits nearly succeeded in eradicating Protestantism in Austria, Hungary, and Bavaria. Then Cardinal Richelieu, the power behind the French throne, brought France in on the Protestant side to prevent the German emperor from gaining too much power and territory. Later, the tide was turned by the entrance into the war of the Lutheran King Gustavus Adolphus of Sweden, whose military genius won battle after battle for the Protestants. The war finally ended in 1648 with the Peace of Westphalia, which redrew the map of Europe along the same basic lines it retains today, and gave legal recognition to the Reformed Church alongside Lutherans and Roman Catholics. Thus the fiction of a united Europe was dead, and the fiction of a united organizational church along with it. Protestantism became a political reality that the Catholic Church could not deny, no matter how strongly it continued to refuse to grant it recognition.

MAKING DRY BONES LIVE

There are many important lessons to be learned from church history, but perhaps now is the time to pause for a moment to consider what we should *not* learn from our study of the subject. A good illustration of my point is found in the following statement by John Eck (not the same Eck of the Leipzig debate), addressed to Luther at the Diet of Worms in 1521:

"Your plea to be heard from Scripture is the one always made by heretics. You do nothing but renew the errors of Wycliffe and Huss. How will the Jews, how will the Turks, exult to hear Christians discussing whether they have been wrong all these years! Martin, how can you assume that you are the only one to understand the sense of Scripture? Would you put your judgment above that of so many famous men and claim that you know more than they all? You have no right to call into question the most holy orthodox faith, instituted by Christ the perfect lawgiver, proclaimed throughout the world by the apostles, sealed by the red blood of the martyrs, confirmed by the sacred councils, defined by the Church in which all our fathers believed until death and gave to us as an inheritance, and which now we are forbidden by the pope and the emperor to discuss lest there be no end of debate."

Eck, in short, used the history of the church to attempt to prove that Luther was wrong, not because he contradicted the Bible, but because he contradicted the great Christians of the past. History is valuable, and can be a great aid in ascertaining truth. It is not, however, infallible. Only God is infallible, along with the Word He has revealed to us. That Word is the only standard by which we may judge truth.

It is this principle that is both the glory and the Achilles' heel of Protestantism. Because the Word is infallible, all human judgments must be tested against it. But because man is a fallible interpreter, there will always be debates about what the Word means. History cannot settle those debates, though it can shed light on them. As Christianity enters its twenty-first century, it must do so with firm adherence to what the Bible says - not to what someone in the history of the church said it meant. The study of the history of the church should not make us followers of men, but convince us that the only way for the church to prosper is as its people become followers of Christ.

FOR REVIEW AND FURTHER THOUGHT

1. What teachings did Luther share with the pre-reformers?

2. What teaching of Luther set him apart from those who had preceded him?

3. Why did Luther find monastery life unsatisfactory?

4. Why was Luther's visit to Rome a significant turning point in his life?

5. How did Luther's understanding of justification differ from that of the Catholic Church?

6. When Johann Tetzel sold indulgences in Germany, for what was he trying to raise money?

7. According to Catholic teaching, what could an indulgence accomplish?

8. In what ways was Tetzel deviating from Catholic teaching on indulgences?

9. What were the Ninety-five Theses?

10. In what ways did Frederick the Wise protect Luther between 1517 and 1525?

11. Why did the Ninety-five Theses stir up such a fuss?

12. In what way did Eck trap Luther during the Leipzig debate of 1519?

13. What were the main topics addressed by Luther in the pamphlets he wrote in 1520?

14. Which of Luther's three pamphlets do you think the Catholic Church found most objectionable, and why?

15. Why was Charles V unsuccessful in putting a stop to the spread of Lutheranism?

16. In what sense was the Diet of Worms a triumph for Luther, and in what sense was it a disappointment?

17. Why did Frederick the Wise kidnap Luther after the Diet of Worms?

18. How did Luther's followers almost destroy the Reformation while he was in hiding?

19. Why was Luther's translation of the Bible into German important?

20. What were the major contributions of Melanchthon to the development of Lutheranism?

21. Who were the Zwickau Prophets, and what did they teach?

22. How did the Lutheran and Reformed Protestants differ on their views of worship?

23. Why did Adrian VI fail in his efforts to reform the abuses in the Roman curia?

24. Why did Luther lose the support of many European humanists?

25. Why did Luther oppose the Peasants' Revolt despite sympathizing with the desire of the peasants to rid themselves of their yoke of oppression?

26. What was accomplished at the two Diets of Speier and the Diet of Augsburg?

27. How did the followers of Luther come to be called Protestants?

28. What was the Marburg Colloquy?

29. How did the Lutheran and Reformed Protestants differ in their views of the Lord's Supper?

30. What was the League of Smalcald?

31. Why did Luther agree to the polygamous marriage of Philip of Hesse?

32. What is the meaning of *cuius regio, eius religio*?

33. Why did Luther favor state control of the church?

34. Why did Melanchthon turn out to be an ineffective leader after the death of Luther?

35. What was the Defenestration of Prague?

36. In what senses were the opponents in the Thirty Years' War not strictly divided along religious lines?

37. Why can church history never be used as an infallible guide to the truth?

20

THE SCHOOLS OF CHRIST

On Ash Wednesday in the spring of 1522, a group of men gathered in the home of Christoph Froschauer, a printer in the city of Zurich. Froschauer's maid fried two sausages, which the men then cut into small pieces and solemnly shared. This was no simple breakfast, but instead a symbolic protest. The Catholic Church of the sixteenth century prohibited the eating of meat during Lent, which of course extends from Ash Wednesday to Easter. The Swiss men who violated this prohibition did so because they were convinced that the Church could not legitimately require anything of its people that the Bible did not also require. The protesters soon found themselves called before the town council to give account of their actions. Ulrich Zwingli, the people's priest of the largest church in Zurich, came to their defense. Though Zwingli himself had not taken part in the symbolic breakfast, he defended the men who had done so on the ground that the Bible specifically affirmed that eating and fasting were matters about which no one could legitimately bind the conscience of another person. Such a novel idea was hard for the members of the council to swallow, and they called for a public debate between Zwingli and the representatives of the local bishop. The debate was no contest, and the council declared within a year that all preachers were to preach only what could be proved from the Bible, and avoid teaching based on "human inventions."

Zwingli's breakfast-table coup and its aftermath speak volumes about the differences between the manifestations of the Reformation in Switzerland and Germany. First of all, while the spread of the Lutheran Reformation lay largely in the power of monarchs, that of the Swiss Reformation was subject to the rule of magistrates. The religion that developed in the semi-democratic republics of Switzerland differed markedly from that of the Holy Roman Empire. Though both Lutheran and Reformed (the term used to describe the churches that trace their roots to the Swiss Reformation or to its cousins in France, Scotland, the Netherlands, and Hungary) churches maintained close ties to the state, the Lutherans were much more submissive to governmental authority, as befits the mindset of men used to living in a monarchy, while the Reformed were much more inclined to see church and state as working together in a partnership within a Christian society. In fact, as we will see, the Swiss Reformers were determined to produce not only Christian churches, but Christian societies. When the young John Knox fled to Geneva to avoid persecution in his native Scotland, he found there what he referred to as "the most perfect school of Christ that ever was in the earth since the days of the Apostles." This was precisely what the Swiss Reformers had in mind. All of society was to be a school in which men were taught to be Christians. In order for this to happen, it was essential for state and church to work together.

The second major difference between the German and Swiss Reformations that can be seen through the Zurich protest was the attitude of the Reformers toward the traditions of the Catholic Church, and thus toward the Bible itself. As we saw in the last chapter, Luther averted the radicalism of some of his followers by insisting that only those practices that were clearly contrary to Scripture should be removed from the church. The Swiss went at the matter quite differently. They maintained that any human doctrine, even if not explicitly condemned in Scripture, constituted adding to the Word of

God, and should therefore be rejected. The Swiss Reformation was consequently much more radical in principle than that in Germany. Required fasting was not allowed to stand, even though there may not have been anything in Scripture against it. The fact that the Bible was silent on the matter was enough to convince the Swiss Reformers that it should be removed from the practice of the church. The result was a way of practicing religion that differed from Catholicism in a much more significant way than the Lutheranism of Germany.

Switzerland is a country that has long cherished its independence from the powerful political influences surrounding it. The Swiss Confederation began as a loose association of independent republics in the Middle Ages, and by the time of the Reformation consisted of thirteen cantons and associated territories. Each canton functioned independently of the others with regard to its internal affairs, and dealt with matters of mutual concern through a Diet, a representative body in which each canton had the same number of members. The equal representation given to each canton worked to the advantage of the older members of the confederation, the so-called "Forest Cantons," who though smaller in population than the cantons containing the larger towns of Zurich, Bern, and Basel, could always outvote them in the Diet. We will see later the significant effect of this situation on the development of the Reformation in Switzerland.

Another characteristic of Switzerland that played an important part in the Swiss Reformation is the division of the country on the basis of language. Switzerland has no language of its own, but speaks variations of the languages of the countries surrounding it on all sides. Northern Switzerland is largely German-speaking, the southwestern part of the country speaks French, and those in the southeast speak Italian. It should come as no surprise, then, that the Reformation in Switzerland can be fairly neatly divided according to language and geography. We will devote our attention in this chapter to the manifestations of the Reformation in German and French Switzerland (the impact of the Reformation in Italian Switzerland was restricted largely to the descendants of the Waldensians who became Protestants).

THE REFORMATION IN GERMAN SWITZERLAND

Ulrich Zwingli (1484-1531), the key figure in the Reformation in German Switzerland, was, like Martin Luther, born into a peasant family. This fact is about all the two men have in common, however. Zwingli was born in a small cottage in the village of Wildhaus in what is now the canton of St. Gall. He was the third son in a family of ten children, his father was the village magistrate, and two of his uncles were priests. One of his uncles was influential in furthering his education, and he successively passed through a Latin school in Basel, a college in Bern, and the University of Vienna, where he encountered the teachings of the Renaissance humanists, which impressed him favorably. He was especially fond of the writings of Erasmus. Later he returned to Basel and received his Master of Arts degree while teaching in a school in the city.

In 1506 Zwingli was ordained to the Catholic priesthood. Though he was a good Catholic, he viewed the priesthood as little more than a respectable career for a younger son of a public official, and never went through the agonies of soul that plagued Luther during his years in the monastery. He was given a church in Glarus, where he remained for ten years, meanwhile teaching himself Greek - like any good Renaissance scholar, he was not satisfied until he had studied an important document (in this case, the New Testament) in its original language. While at Glarus, he made several trips to Italy as the chaplain for a group of Swiss soldiers who had been hired by foreign governments as mercenaries (the Swiss had not yet developed their present reputation for peace-loving neutrality). What he saw while traveling with the mercenaries made his Swiss blood boil. These young men were giving their lives for the benefit of foreign rulers (including the pope, who believed that Swiss fighting men were the best in the world, and always tried to hire them for his wars against other Italian cities), meanwhile enriching the Swiss businessmen who acted as brokers and got rich from the blood of others. Worse yet, the mercenaries were at the same time engaging in the grossest kinds of immorality to which they were tempted in foreign lands, and which they would then bring back to Switzerland with them when and if they returned. Zwingli fumed at the foreign rulers who bought wealth for themselves at the cost of Swiss lives, while at the same time sending an endless stream of corruption into Swiss society. Equally to blame were the fat brokers who lined their pockets through this shameless trade in human flesh. He began to speak out, and wrote eloquent tracts against the mercenary trade, using to good effect the training he had received from the humanists.

He soon gained a reputation as a powerful and convincing speaker, and in 1516 obtained the pastorate of the church in Einsiedeln. The pulpit here was much more influential, since Einsiedeln was the site of the most popular shrine in Switzerland, the Shrine of the Black Madonna, possessor of an image of Mary that had supposedly fallen from heaven. Here, Zwingli began to speak out against the same abuse in the Catholic Church that had first drawn Luther into the public eye - the sale of indulgences. While Zwingli experienced no radical conversion, it was at Einsiedeln that the Word of God began to play an increasingly greater part in his ministry. His Renaissance passion for original sources drove him to deeper and deeper study of the text, and his preaching reflected his passion.

In 1518, an opening occurred in the Grossmünster in Zurich. Zwingli badly wanted the post, and wrote to several of his friends in the city to encourage them to speak out in his behalf. He was offered the post of people's priest with some reservations. Many had heard of his powerful preaching, but they had also heard rumors about immorality. One critic even charged that Zwingli had seduced the virgin daughter of one of Einsiedeln's town fathers. Zwingli denied the charge, though he was candid enough to admit that he struggled mightily with the whole issue of sexual purity. In his own defense, however, he maintained that he had never defiled a virgin, a nun, or a married woman. That seemingly was enough for the men of Zurich, and Zwingli got the job. One of the first things he did in Zurich was to petition the bishop for an end to clerical celibacy, which he saw as the cause of great temptation. He eventually married, though he kept the marriage secret for two years before solemnizing it publicly in 1524.

He began work on January 1, 1519, and immediately departed from tradition when he started preaching straight through the Gospel of Matthew rather than following the assigned texts for each Sunday from the Catholic liturgy. Such expository preaching quickly gained the attention of the city, especially when Zwingli included many direct practical applications of the texts he was expounding. His first challenge in Zurich came from a monk named Bernard Samson who came into the canton to sell indulgences for the pope. Zwingli immediately preached against the practice, and the town council followed his advice and sent Samson packing. The pope apparently had learned his lesson from the Tetzel fiasco in Germany, and, realizing that the Swiss had been far more deeply infected by the independent thinking of the Renaissance than had the Germans, made no effort to foist any more indulgence peddlers on the Zurichers. Later that same year, the plague hit Zurich, killing almost one third of the city's population of about eight thousand. Zwingli himself became ill and almost died as a result of his efforts to minister to the sick.

The real beginning of the Reformation in Zurich did not occur until the protest against the Lenten fast mentioned at the beginning of the chapter. The public debate sponsored by the council led Zwingli to present Sixty-Seven Conclusions, debate topics similar to yet far more wide-ranging than Luther's Ninety-Five Theses. When the council backed Zwingli in 1523, ordering that preachers should confine themselves to the Bible only, the door was opened for departure from Rome. When the town council abolished the Mass the following year, the break was complete. By 1525, the churches of Zurich had been completely cleansed of the remnants of Catholicism - images were crushed or burned, candles and organs were removed, and relics were given a Christian burial. One should not imagine that the removal of idolatry was accompanied by the sort of wild iconoclasm that characterized the German radicals whose behavior had brought Luther rushing from the Wartburg to Wittenberg in 1522. What occurred in Zurich was an orderly process supervised by the magistrates and applauded by the vast majority of the people. In some cases, those who had paid to have images erected participated in their removal. Zwingli also opened a theological school called the Carolinum for training young men to be pastors.

Like Luther, Zwingli had his problems with followers who thought he hadn't gone far enough in his departure from the Catholic Church. In Zurich, these men were called Anabaptists, and Zwingli persecuted them with all the zeal of a man convinced he is right. Since we will take up their story in the next chapter, however, we will not deal with it here. Meanwhile, Zwingli's teachings were spreading throughout German-speaking Switzerland. By 1529, Bern and Basel had joined Zurich in the Protestant camp. Whenever the Swiss Diet took up the question of reform, however, the rural Forest Cantons voted together to slam the door in the faces of the Protestants. The Renaissance had not made the same inroads in the Forest Cantons as it had in the larger towns - the rural villagers clung firmly to their superstitions. In addition, the sturdy farmers were being well paid to serve as mercenaries, and saw Zwingli's attacks against the trade as assaults at both their pope and their income. Even when the Diet called for a debate, the deck was stacked so badly against the Protestants that many of them declined to waste their time by participating, and Zurich wouldn't even let Zwingli attend because they feared for his life at the hands of the Catholics.

The growing animosity between Catholic and Protestant cantons set the stage for civil war. Zwingli, like most of the men of his day, had no conception of the separation of church and state, and often found it difficult to draw much of a definable boundary between the two. His role as pastor overlapped his role as prominent Swiss citizen, and his Christianity was often intermixed with patriotism. Though the Swiss Diet had agreed that each canton was free to pursue its own religious agenda, it soon became obvious that no one's religious agenda included toleration of opposing views. Protestant cantons banned Catholic practices, and Catholic cantons burned Protestant preachers. The Catholic and Protestant cantons formed into opposing alliances, and when the Catholics sought the help of the Duke of Austria, Switzerland's closest enemy and a threat to their independence, war became almost inevitable. When the Catholic canton of Schwyz burned a Protestant preacher named Jacob Kaiser at the stake, Zwingli advised war as the only way to hold the Confederation together. He feared the growing influence of Austria in Swiss affairs, and felt justified for both patriotic and religious reasons in attacking the Forest Cantons before it was too late. The two armies met near Kappel on the border between Zurich and the Canton Zug. Before battle could begin, however, some of those in the Protestant alliance begged for negotiation rather than bloodshed. Over Zwingli's objections, they won the day, and a treaty was concluded that ended the Catholic alliance with Austria in return for mutual toleration of Catholics and Protestants in one another's districts. Thus the "First Kappel War" of 1529 ended without a drop of blood being shed.

Zwingli knew the peace would never last. He believed that as long as Switzerland was divided, the great powers of Europe would always be waiting like hungry vultures at her borders, waiting to gobble her up. He believed that the only solution was a great Protestant alliance, including the German Lutherans and the French Huguenots, that would be powerful enough to challenge even the great Catholic house of Hapsburg - the Holy Roman Empire itself. Philip of Hesse shared his vision, and invited Zwingli to his castle at Marburg to meet with Luther and iron out their differences. As we saw in the last chapter, the Marburg Colloquy failed over the issue of the Lord's Supper, leaving the Lutheran and Reformed Protestants as isolated from each other as they were from the Catholic Church.

Emotions were too strong for the cantons of Switzerland to tolerate one another's beliefs. Persecution broke out anew, accompanied by charges of treason based on the renewed overtures made by the Catholics to Austria at the same time Zwingli was courting the support of both the German Protestants and the French king Francis I. When Spanish troops invaded Switzerland from the Italian side, the Diet couldn't even agree on whether or not to repulse the invasion. Zwingli saw that prolonged division would destroy the confederacy, and again advocated war. The other Protestant cantons, however, were still reluctant to fight, and instead advised a blockade of the Forest Cantons. Zwingli, his ideas rejected, saw nothing but doom and disaster ahead. When Halley's Comet appeared overhead, Zwingli saw it as a sign of his own coming death and the defeat of the Protestant cause. Deprived of food and commerce, the Forest Cantons gathered an army and attacked Zurich in the "Second Kappel War" of 1531. The Zurichers were badly outnumbered, and received little help from the other Protestants. Zwingli accompanied his flock into battle unarmed, and fell during what quickly became a slaughter. When Catholic soldiers discovered his body on the field of battle, they quartered it, burned it, mixed the ashes with those of a pig, and scattered them in the wind. He was succeeded as chief pastor of Zurich by his friend and associate Heinrich Bullinger, who possessed a much greater spirit of diplomacy, and was instrumental in eventually bringing the Reformed churches of German and French Switzerland together when he helped to author the Second Helvetic Confession in 1566. In his day, Zurich became a refuge for many persecuted Protestants, as happened on a much greater scale with Geneva, the great city of the Reformation in French Switzerland.

THE REFORMATION IN FRENCH SWITZERLAND

The French cantons were relative newcomers to the Swiss Confederation. Geneva was until 1526 under the rule of the Duke of Savoy. By the time they affiliated themselves with the Swiss, the Reformation was already under way. The men of Geneva retained close ties with France, however. Some of the greatest leaders of the Swiss Reformation came from France, while Geneva became a haven for persecuted Protestants who later returned to France and provided leadership for the struggling Huguenots there.

A. GUILLAUME FAREL (1489-1565)

The man who first brought Geneva into the Protestant camp was a fiery red-headed French preacher who fit every stereotype that often goes with that particular shade of hair. Though never formally ordained, Guillaume Farel was a powerful preacher and evangelist, and a man who seemed to be followed by conflict wherever he went. He was a man of strong words in an age of strong ideas. He cursed idolaters and sought the eradication of any who taught or practiced error. Moderation was not a part of his vocabulary or his life.

Farel learned to treasure the Word of God while studying in Paris under the tutelage of Jacques Lefevre d'Etaples, an early champion of biblical truth who translated the Bible into French. He quickly realized that much of Catholic teaching was foreign to the Bible, and began preaching against the doctrines and practices of Catholicism, insisting that salvation could be obtained through Christ alone, apart from any human mediators. Such views were not tolerated in France, and Farel was forced to flee for his life. For a number of years he traveled around Switzerland, meeting with many of the leaders of the Swiss Reformation, including Zwingli in Zurich, John Oecolampadius in Basel, and Martin Bucer in Strasbourg, Germany. He finally found himself in Geneva, where his preaching stirred up considerable opposition, so much so that the local priests ran him out of town with stones and clubs. He eventually returned with the support of some of Geneva's leading citizens, and in public disputations much like those carried out by Zwingli in Zurich convinced the town council that the doctrines of the Reformation were true to the Word of God. As a result, Geneva accepted the Reformation in 1535, abolishing the Mass and instituting biblical preaching and worship. The city was still notorious for its immorality, however. Much work remained to be done, and in the summer of 1536, the man arrived who was to undertake that monstrous task - a young Frenchman by the name of John Calvin.

B. CALVIN'S EARLY CAREER

Calvin was born in Noyon, France, in 1509. He was one of seven children, two of whom died in infancy. His mother died when he was young, and his father remarried. His father was the secretary of the local bishop, and as such had powerful friends. He used his influence to get young John a benefice at the age of twelve, which supported him throughout his education. The elder Calvin was apparently a man with a firm mind about many things, and his inflexibility eventually got him into trouble with the local bishop, leading to his excommunication prior to his death in 1531.

From his youth young John was headed for a career in the church. His family saw this calling in much the same way as we already saw with Zwingli - a respectable vocation for a younger son. Calvin was sent away to study in Paris at the age of fourteen, where he immediately showed himself to be a careful and dedicated student. He avoided the temptations that surrounded him in the big city, and his life was such a rebuke to his fellow students that they sometimes jokingly referred to him as The Accusative Case. At about the same time that his father was having his problems with the Catholic clergy in Noyon, he ordered his son to change directions in his studies. Rather than becoming a priest, he now wanted John to be a lawyer. Whether he saw in legal studies a surer path to fortune and security or simply recognized that his troubles at home ended the possibility of his son getting a coveted clerical post, the fact remains that the son obeyed the father with little evident reluctance. He undertook studies at the universities of Orleans, Bourges, and Paris. He was as good a law student as he had been a divinity student, and there is no question that God used this period of training as preparation for the task that Calvin was later to perform in Geneva. After his father's death, he gave up his legal studies in favor of the classics, and finally returned to theology again.

It was probably at some time during the year of 1532 that Calvin was converted. He says very little about this in his writings, but does mention at one point that only the power of God could have broken his obstinate adherence to superstition, and that he was suddenly converted during this period in his life. By this time he had already developed a reputation as a fine scholar, and even while he was continuing his studies he was treated by his professors more like a colleague than a student, often substituting for them in their classes and giving lectures at the university. In 1533, when one of his close friends, Nicholas Cop, was elected rector of the university, Calvin helped him to prepare his inaugural address. That address plainly presented the ideas of the Protestant Reformation, which had been for several years the talk of people all over France. Talk among students and professors was one thing, but a formal address was quite another. Such a public presentation of ideas challenging the authority of the church was not something the French authorities were ready to tolerate. Cop was forced to flee the country, and Calvin wisely followed suit. By the time the authorities arrived to search Calvin's rooms at the university, he was already gone.

For the next three years, Calvin wandered throughout Switzerland, France, and Italy, spending time with other Reformers such as Lefevre d'Etaples, Bucer, and Bullinger, all of whom helped to mold his thinking. He also had brief contact with a brash Spanish heretic named Michael Servetus, who challenged him to a debate on the doctrine of the Trinity, then failed to show up. What Calvin wanted more than anything else during this time was to find a place where he could settle down and lead the life of a scholar. He had already proven himself to be a capable writer, and he wanted to use his gifted pen to advance the cause of the Gospel. During his wanderings, he worked on a brief exposition of Christian truth called *Institutes of the Christian Religion*. The main purpose of the work was to demonstrate that Protestants weren't heretics, but accepted all the foundational truths of Christianity. In a prologue addressed to Francis

I of France, he pleaded for toleration for persecuted Protestants in France. The first edition of this short work of six chapters was published in Basel in 1535, and created an immediate sensation. Others had explained Protestant teaching before, but never so clearly and powerfully as this young Frenchman. Revised and expanded many times under the encouragement of his friends, the *Institutes* eventually became, in the final revision of 1559, a magnificent systematic theology of over a thousand pages in length.

C. CALVIN IN GENEVA

After the publication of the first edition of the *Institutes*, Calvin decided that he wanted to settle down in Strasbourg. Because of a war going on at the time, he had to take a detour through Geneva. He only intended to stay one night, but when Farel heard that the author of the *Institutes* was in his city, he knew that the man who was capable of undertaking the reformation of this wild and notorious town had arrived. He went to Calvin's room and asked him to stay and help bring Geneva under the rule of God's Word. Calvin refused, insisting that he was a scholar, not a reformer, and that he could serve the Lord best by means of his pen. Farel, however, would not take no for an answer, and loudly told Calvin that the curse of God would be upon both him and his studies if he left Geneva in its time of need in order to pursue his own preferences. Such an argument was hard to resist, and Calvin reluctantly agreed to stay in Geneva. He began to give theological lectures almost immediately, and was soon ordained and appointed pastor of one of Geneva's churches.

Calvin believed that instruction and discipline were the two keys to reforming the society of Geneva. The instruction took place through daily preaching and teaching in the churches, and through the preparation of a catechism through which the basic doctrines of the faith could be mastered by the citizens. Discipline involved exclusion from the Lord's Supper of anyone who either refused to assent to the Confession of Faith prepared by Calvin, or who lived in unrepentant disobedience to God's Word. The magistrates who governed Geneva were happy to see the instruction instituted, but were not quite as thrilled about Calvin's proposals for discipline. They felt that church discipline was a matter of law enforcement, and thus should rest in the hands of the magistrates themselves. When they refused to give to the church the power of excommunication, Calvin and Farel resisted, convinced that discipline by the church was a biblical mandate. The council then voted to expel Calvin and Farel, giving them three days to get out of town.

Thus the reforming of Geneva had lasted only two years, and appeared to end in failure. Farel left for Neuchatel, where he ministered for the rest of his life. Calvin, with a sigh of relief, headed for Strasbourg, where he had intended to go originally. Here he spent perhaps the happiest three years of his life (1538-1541). Martin Bucer, the chief pastor of Strasbourg, asked Calvin to take over the care of a congregation of French refugees. Calvin agreed, meanwhile pursuing his writing, both revising the *Institutes* and beginning work on his Bible commentaries, which by the time of his death covered 49 of the 66 books of Scripture. He also got married during this time, to Idelette de Bure, the widow of an Anabaptist. Their union seems to have been happy, though their only child, a son, died in infancy, and Idelette herself died in 1549, after only nine years of marriage.

Meanwhile, back in Geneva, the city was under attack. Calvin's critics were not doing a very good job of running things, and the new pastors who had replaced Calvin and Farel had lost the respect of everyone. Seeing an opportunity to win the city back to the Catholic faith, Cardinal Jacopo Sadoleto, a learned man and one of the smoothest writers of the period, addressed a friendly letter to the town council, arguing that it was time for them to return to their ancient faith. No one in Geneva was capable of giving any sort of intelligent response to Sadoleto's letter, and more and more people began to talk seriously about returning to Catholicism. When Calvin heard about Sadoleto's letter, he drafted a response, covering each of Sadoleto's arguments point by point. The result was devastating. Not only did the people of Geneva now have a sound basis upon which to resist the siren call of the Roman Church, but the friends of Calvin could now point to his support of their city in a time of crisis. Many of the citizens came to realize that the critics of Calvin had failed in their attempt to provide positive leadership for the city, and public opinion soon shifted in favor of inviting him back again to assume his old post as chief pastor.

When the invitation from Geneva arrived, Calvin did not want to go. He liked life in Strasbourg, and knew that in Geneva he would face nothing but trouble. After many months of pleading by the officials of Geneva and encouragement from Protestants in other Swiss and German cities, Calvin agreed to go back, under the condition that the power of church discipline be returned to the church without the interference of the council. The magistrates agreed, and Calvin arrived in Geneva to an enthusiastic welcome.

Calvin never held any official post in the city of Geneva other than that of chief pastor, but his influence was enormous. He was so widely respected that almost any issue that arose brought people to his door to consult him and get his opinion. His ability to expound the Word of God with accuracy and power meant that few could stand against him. His reforms in the city were far-reaching. They included a new liturgy for the church, as well as a new form of church government. The church was organized under four types of officers - pastors, who preached and led the churches; teachers, who instructed the people in church, in their homes, and in the schools; elders, who were laymen who exercised oversight over the people, dealing with problems that arose in the lives of those assigned to their care; and deacons, who were responsible for helping the sick and needy. Pastors and teachers were chosen by the pastors, while elders and deacons were elected by the people at large. All church office holders were subject to the approval of the council. This form of government was very close to that used by Presbyterian churches today. Calvin also established a school system for the city of Geneva (which later developed into the University of Geneva), and even helped to rewrite the city's legal code.

Calvin firmly believed that the state and the church should work together in a Christian society. Because the pastors were citizens, they were subject to the same laws and penalties as other citizens (unlike the Catholic Church, where priests and monks could not be brought to trial before secular magistrates, but only before a church court). Because the magistrates were Christians (it may be difficult for us to imagine, but virtually everyone in Geneva was a professing Christian at this time), they were subject to church discipline when they acted against God's Word. It should not be surprising, then, that the lines of demarcation between church and governmental responsibilities sometimes were less than clear. The magistrates, enthusiastically following the biblical teaching of the pastors, did their best to make the Bible the law of the city. Thus they provided civil penalties for religious offenses such as missing church or being disrespectful toward the church's leaders. On the other hand, they didn't hesitate to stick their noses into the church's business when they thought it appropriate, and often went on record as advising a certain pastor to cut down on the length of his sermons.

Such attempts to enforce biblical morality naturally met with opposition among some segments of the population. Calvin's main opponents during his years in Geneva were a group known as the Libertines. They believed in a Christianity without moral strictures, and strongly resisted the efforts of the church's elders to enforce biblical living. Most of them came from the old families of Geneva and they used the fact that Calvin was a foreigner (he didn't even become a citizen of Geneva until 1559) to turn some against him, especially when refugees from other parts of Europe started streaming in, swelling the numbers of his supporters.

Geneva did indeed become a haven for persecuted Protestants from France, England, Scotland, and elsewhere. The refugees studied in Calvin's "school," and returned to their homes prepared to put his teachings into practice there. Many of those who returned to France perished within weeks of crossing the border, but Geneva provided a steady stream of pastors for the persecuted Huguenots. Calvin's influence extended into Hungary, the Netherlands, England, and Scotland as well. In each of these places, a church grew up following the Reformed model that the refugees in Geneva had observed. The result was that Calvin's influence extended far beyond that enjoyed by Luther. While the Lutheran church expanded throughout Germany and into Scandinavia, Reformed churches were planted everywhere; perhaps the ideas of Calvin found their most fertile ground when they spread across the ocean with the Puritans to America, where an effort was made to found a theocracy that followed the model established by Calvin in Geneva.

When Calvin died in 1564, his work was carried on by Theodore Beza, the first head of the Academy founded by Calvin in Geneva. Beza maintained the standards of Geneva until his death in 1605, and often served as an advisor to Reformed Protestants all over Europe, especially in France and England. When Calvin died, he left behind him an enormous legacy. Not only did he develop a theology that is the clearest statement of what Protestants believe and a form of church government that has become the standard for modern Presbyterians, but he also left behind a Christian view of society that influenced the development of such great ideas as democracy, capitalism, and modern science. While Luther had taught the priesthood of all believers, Calvin put it into practice in his policy of electing church leaders. It is no exaggeration to state that the election of church leaders helped teach people how to elect political leaders as well, and no one should be surprised to notice that the countries most strongly influenced by the Reformed churches are the countries where democracy has flourished. Both capitalism and modern science relate to Calvin's teachings for the same reason. Calvin emphasized the Cultural Mandate - the idea that man is to glorify God in all his works, whether "sacred" or "secular," and that there is no area of life outside the realm of God's plan and purpose. Thus people in the Reformed churches were encouraged to pursue "secular" work with vigor, and to learn all they could about the universe in which God has placed us - no longer were the best minds channeled exclusively into monasteries or the priesthood because these were the only suitable ways to serve God.

D. CALVIN'S THEOLOGY

Martin Luther was not a theologian; his ideas were largely systematized by his colleague and successor Philip Melanchthon. Ulrich Zwingli was a theologian, but few read his theological works today - he is known largely as a powerful preacher. Calvin, however, was a theologian *par excellence*. There has perhaps been no more competent theological mind in the history of the church. When most people think of Calvinism, they think of the doctrine of predestination. While predestination was certainly an important part of Calvin's teaching because of his emphasis on the sovereignty of God, it should be noted that the subject takes up only four chapters out of eighty in the final revision of the *Institutes*. More than anything else, Calvin was the premier expositor of the foundational truths of Scripture. Not only do the *Institutes* stand as one of the finest systematic discussions of Christian thought ever written, but Calvin's commentaries set the pattern for the modern exposition of Scripture. No longer did people wander through the Bible, losing themselves and others in endless allegorizing. Following Calvin, they learned to draw the meaning of a passage of Scripture from its context. For this principle alone, the modern evangelical church owes Calvin an enormous debt.

We must spend a little time, however, on those distinctive doctrines most readily associated with the name of Calvin. What about the notorious Five Points? The fact of the matter is that the famous TULIP formulation never came from Calvin himself. In fact, the Five Points were drawn up more than fifty years after Calvin's death in 1619 by the Synod of Dordt in response to five points of belief affirmed by the followers of James Arminius. Though some would dispute whether or not these five points are an accurate representation of Calvin's teachings, they provide perhaps the best way to summarize his understanding of Christian theology. The acronym TULIP can be used to summarize the Five Points of the Synod of Dordt in the following way:

    T - Total Depravity
    U - Unconditional Election
    L - Limited Atonement
    I - Irresistible Grace
    P - Perseverance of the Saints

Total depravity is simply an affirmation of the fact that man is a sinner in every aspect of his being and is thus incapable of doing anything to please God, let alone to save himself. This does not mean that people never do anything in any way good; it simply means that, in their unsaved state, they neither desire to please God nor are capable of pleasing Him.

Unconditional election follows logically from the first point. If man can do nothing to please God, then it must follow that God does not choose to save a person because of anything good in that person. In particular, God does not choose to save anyone because He foresees that that person will believe, since without the gift of God's grace, no one desires to believe, let alone being able to do so.

Limited atonement is the idea that there is continuity in God's plan of salvation from beginning to end. Those who are chosen by the Father are redeemed by the Son and regenerated by the Spirit. There are none chosen by the Father who are not redeemed by the Son, and there are none who are redeemed by the Son who are not regenerated by the Spirit. In simple terms, Christ's death accomplished salvation for Christians rather than making salvation possible for everyone but accomplishing it for none.

Irresistible grace conveys the idea that the work of the Holy Spirit in a person's life is as sovereign as God's choice of that person before time began. In other words, those whose hearts are changed by the Holy Spirit are saved; it does not require some cooperative effort on their part to complete the transaction.

Perseverance of the saints simply means that God will finish what He started. All who have been saved by the work of Christ will remain true to Him. This does not mean that anyone who professes faith in Christ is automatically and eternally saved. Many who claim to be Christians have no real relationship with God, and will ultimately be condemned to hell. On the other hand, no one who truly belongs to Christ can ever be lost, since his perseverance in the faith is as much a matter of the grace of God as his original salvation.

As you may at this point recognize, there is really nothing original about these teachings. We have seen them before in the work of Augustine in the Ancient Church period and Gottschalk, Thomas Bradwardine, and Gregory of Rimini in the Middle Ages, they were to a large extent shared by the other Reformers, and we will encounter them many times more in our study of the history of the church. Calvin's name is associated with these ideas, not because he invented them, but because he explained them more clearly than anyone had before his time. The basic truth that underlies all of Calvin's theology is the fact that salvation is all of Christ. Any attempt to insert human effort into the process of salvation is to be rejected as a matter of sinful pride.

MAKING DRY BONES LIVE

We cannot leave our account of the Swiss Reformation without commenting briefly on the sad case of Michael Servetus. It seems that the one man burned at the stake for heresy in Calvin's Geneva draws more attention and approbation than the thousands tortured and executed in the long history of the Inquisition. Why should that be the case?

Servetus was a Spaniard, a brilliant man in his own right, who refused to submit himself to the authority of any man. From his reading of the Word of God, he came to the conclusion that the doctrine of the Trinity was unbiblical. While Christ may have been the Son of God, He can never be viewed as equally eternal with the Father. His views combined several of the heresies rejected by the Ancient Church, and led to a sort of pantheism that saw God in all men because of the divinity of the human soul. In addition to his heresies, Servetus was an incredibly arrogant person. He openly scorned any who disagreed with his teachings, and it

THEOLOGICAL ISSUES - LUTHERAN VERSUS REFORMED

ISSUE	LUTHERAN POSITION	REFORMED POSITION
ORDO SALUTIS	Calling, illumination, conversion, regeneration, justification, sanctification, glorification.	Election, predestination, union with Christ, calling, regeneration, faith, repentance, justification, sanctification, glorification.
GRACE OF GOD	Grace received through baptism or preaching, enabling one to avoid resisting the regenerating grace of God.	Irresistible.
REPENTANCE	Leads to faith.	Flows from faith.
BAPTISM	Works regeneration, removing guilt and power of sin.	Incorporation into the Covenant of Grace.
LORD'S SUPPER	Christ present in the sacrament objectively.	Sign and seal of the Covenant of Grace to believers; Christ present by faith.
CHURCH AND STATE	State church to tutor in the faith the rulers who support Protestantism.	Holy Commonwealth, in which church and state are both Christian, yet perform their separate functions.
REGULATIVE PRINCIPLE	Whatever is not forbidden in Scripture is permissible.	Whatever is not commanded in Scripture is forbidden.

seemed to bother him very little that almost everyone did. After his writings against the Trinity were condemned as heresy by the Catholic Church, he went into hiding, used an assumed name, and hypocritically functioned as a practicing Catholic for years. In fact, he was commissioned by a Catholic bishop in France to prepare an edition of the Bible for publication - the bishop never realized that his scholar and the notorious Servetus were one and the same. All during this time, Servetus carried on an active correspondence with Calvin, asking a thousand questions to try to undermine what Calvin taught, while at the same time arrogantly rejecting without comment any response Calvin made to him. Calvin finally tired of these games, and sent Servetus a copy of the *Institutes*, saying that the book explained exactly what Calvin believed, and why. Servetus later returned the book, filled with all sorts of insulting marginal notes. During all the time that Servetus was expressing these heterodox convictions in his correspondence with Calvin, he continued to live as a practicing Catholic in France.

When a young French refugee in Geneva found out what Servetus was up to, he wrote to a friend of his in the city where Servetus was living. He had been trying to win his friend to the Protestant cause, and as an example of the weakness of Catholicism, he mentioned that the pastors in Geneva cared enough about people's lives to watch over them, while in his friend's own town, the bishop was employing a notorious heretic. When word of this reached the bishop, Servetus was called in for questioning. He delayed long enough to burn all the manuscripts in his house, then went before the court. Once he arrived he denied being Servetus, despite the fact that the incriminating letters were in his handwriting. He maintained that as a young man he had met the heretic Servetus, and that he had foolishly copied some of his writings for later study. Despite his blatant lies, the Catholic court condemned him to death. He was put into prison to await execution, but escaped by climbing over the roof when allowed to relieve himself in the prison garden.

It was at this point that Servetus betrayed his incredible arrogance even more than before. He could have gone anywhere and concealed himself under a false name as before. Instead, he chose to go to Geneva. Calvin had already determined that if he did so he would never leave the city alive. Servetus, however, must have believed that he could stir up enough trouble among Calvin's enemies to topple the great Reformer (this was at the height of Calvin's conflict with the Libertines). If Servetus believed that, though, he was sadly mistaken. After his arrival in Geneva, he had the effrontery to appear in Calvin's church; he was arrested shortly thereafter. He was put on trial for heresy, and showed himself to be totally unrepentant. He not only boldly asserted his teachings as if they were the only truth, but accused Calvin of heresy and demanded that the magistrates put him to death and give his goods to Servetus! Even while the trial was going on, many tried to go out of their way to be fair. Servetus was offered the opportunity to return to France if he chose. Since he was under sentence of death there, he decided that that might not be a wise move. The council in Geneva also insisted on getting opinion from other cities before passing judgment; the responses were almost unanimous in considering Servetus a dangerous heretic worthy of death. The extent of Servetus' misjudgment is shown in the fact that, despite the council being controlled by Calvin's opponents, Servetus was condemned to death. Calvin begged for mercy to the extent that he asked for decapitation rather than burning, but the council ignored his pleas. Servetus was condemned to burn at the stake. Upon hearing the sentence, he broke down completely, but at the end, he was completely immovable, despite the fact that Farel accompanied him all the way to the place of execution, pleading for him to repent. He died while crying out, "Jesus Christ, thou Son of the eternal God [rather than the eternal Son of God], have mercy on me."

In assessing this tragic event, we can certainly in no way condone the use of the death penalty to punish false teaching. We must note, however, where Calvin and the other Reformers were coming from when they advocated the death of heretics. In the Old Testament, God commanded that false prophets should be put to death. Israel was a theocracy, a nation under God, and therefore offenses against God were to be treated as offenses against the state. Calvin viewed Geneva the same way - as a biblical commonwealth where God's rule must be acknowledged and His Word obeyed and enforced. Sadly, he and Zwingli both forgot that Christ said, "He who lives by the sword will die by the sword."

The Schools of Christ

FOR REVIEW AND FURTHER THOUGHT

1. Why was the breakfast in Zurich on Ash Wednesday in 1522 such an important event?

2. How did the German and Swiss Reformers differ in their view of the relationship between church and state?

3. How did the German and Swiss Reformers differ in their treatment of church practices not mentioned in Scripture? If you were to go into a Lutheran church and a Presbyterian church and participate in the worship services, how would you expect them to differ?

4. Why did the older cantons, though smaller in population, dominate the Swiss Diet?

5. In what ways did the characters and experiences of Luther and Zwingli differ?

6. Why did Zwingli object to the Swiss practice of hiring themselves out as mercenary soldiers?

7. How did Zwingli's preaching differ from that of his predecessors in Zurich?

8. Why was Protestantism never accepted as the religion of all Switzerland, despite the fact that a majority of its people were Protestants?

9. Why did Zwingli argue for war against the Forest Cantons?

10. Why did Zwingli want to form a military alliance with Protestants in France and Germany?

11. What significance did Zwingli place on the appearance of Halley's Comet in 1531?

12. What role did Farel play in turning Geneva to the Reformation?

13. In what ways were the backgrounds of Zwingli and Calvin similar? How did their temperaments and characters differ?

14. How did Calvin's background and early years help prepare him for the work God had for him to do?

15. What incident forced Calvin to flee France for Switzerland?

16. How did Farel convince Calvin to remain in Geneva and help with the Reformation there?

17. Why was Calvin reluctant to remain in Geneva?

18. What were the two basic concepts that Calvin attempted to put into practice in reforming the city of Geneva?

19. Calvin was really the first of the Reformers to take the need for church discipline seriously. Why did he consider it so important?

20. Why were Calvin and Farel expelled from Geneva in 1538?

21. How did Cardinal Sadoleto attempt to win Geneva back to the Catholic Church?

22. What were the four types of church officers established in Geneva by Calvin, how were they chosen, and what were their duties?

23. How did Calvin view the relationship between church and state?

24. Why did the church and state in Geneva wind up competing with one another for power? How did the lines of authority between them become blurred?

25. Who were the Libertines? Why did they oppose Calvin?

26. How did Calvin help persecuted Protestants from other European countries? How did they enhance his own ministry, both in Geneva and elsewhere?

27. In what countries outside Switzerland was the influence of Calvin felt most strongly?

28. How did Calvin contribute to the growth of democracy, though Geneva would hardly have qualified as one?

29. What is the Cultural Mandate, and how did Calvin's view of it encourage the development of capitalism and the growth of modern science?

30. What are the Five Points of Calvinism, and what do they mean?

31. What other teachers in the history of the church taught doctrines similar to those of Calvin?

32. What did Servetus teach that made Protestants and Catholics alike consider him a heretic?

33. What was there about the character of Servetus that contributed to his harsh treatment at the hands of others?

34. Why did Calvin believe that it was right to execute Servetus? Do you agree with him, or not? Why?

21

REFORMING THE REFORMERS

In January of 1527, the authorities in the city of Zurich took young Felix Manz from his prison cell and led him out to the Limmat River, which runs through the center of the town. They then bound him hand and foot, while the executioner prepared to push him into the river. As he approached his watery grave, his mother and brother encouraged him to stand firm in his faith. His last words before drowning in the river were, "Lord, into thy hands I commend my spirit."

About a year later, a former professor at the University of Ingolstadt named Balthasar Hubmaier was arrested in Austria. After being taken to Vienna for trial, he was condemned to death. The authorities ordered that he be tortured with hot irons, then burned at the stake. Three days later, his saintly wife was drowned in the Danube.

The Reformation period was one of bitter warfare and persecution, but few experienced greater persecution than the small group to which Manz and Hubmaier belonged. Who were these men and women who were persecuted by Catholics and Protestants alike? Why were they considered so dangerous that Protestant Zurich and Catholic Vienna could agree on their eradication?

Manz and Hubmaier were representatives of a group of people who have come to be known to history as Anabaptists. This was not a name that they themselves chose. In fact, since the name means "rebaptizers," they emphatically rejected it. Zwingli may have been closer to the point when he called them *Catabaptists*, which means "against baptism." These men and women did not oppose baptism as such; what they really opposed was infant baptism. They maintained that baptism was an affirmation of faith, and that it therefore could not legitimately be performed upon those who were too young to exercise faith. They refused to be called rebaptizers because they insisted that infant baptism was no baptism at all.

Anyone who tries to understand the Anabaptists largely in terms of their teaching and practice concerning baptism misses the point, however. To them, the practice of believer's baptism flowed naturally from their convictions about the nature of the church. In the last chapter we saw that Zwingli and Calvin, believing that the Reformation in Germany had stopped short of total biblical Christianity, determined to reject anything that was not commanded in Scripture. Thus Roman Catholic worship was almost wholly rejected and refurbished, leaving the Swiss Reformers with a simple, unadorned service celebrated in a simple, unadorned building. There were some, however, who took the principles enunciated by the Swiss Reformers and extended them even further. They noticed that the New Testament said nothing about things like candles and church organs, but they also noticed that the church of the New Testament was a church made up only of committed believers. The church in Rome was not governed by the Emperor, nor was the church in Corinth subject to the dictates of the town council. The Anabaptists thus concluded that, in order to be faithful to God's Word, the church must not only change the particulars of worship, but also must radically alter its relationship to society. It was this conviction that set the Anabaptists apart from the other Reformers, and put them on the opposite side of an issue that was one of the few upon which Catholics and Lutheran and Reformed Protestants could agree.

Because of this marked departure from the way in which church and society had worked together for over a thousand years, Anabaptism is often referred to as the Radical Reformation. Perhaps this term is really more to the point; baptism was not the real issue, but a radical departure from the status quo was. Those who agreed in the need for this radical departure agreed on little else, however. Consequently, anyone who undertakes the task of describing and classifying the different movements that make up the Radical Reformation faces the discouraging prospect of bringing together groups of people who share little more than a common rejection of the church-state relationship assumed by almost everyone else in the sixteenth century. Some of these were largely orthodox in their doctrine, while others were rank heretics. Some were mystics, while others were simple people of the land. Some had political goals, while others sought nothing more than a total divorce from anything of a political nature. Furthermore, the Radical Reformation had no organization, no creed, and no universally-recognized leader. In an attempt to bring some order out of this hodge-podge of men and movements, we will examine two major areas in this chapter. In the first place, we will discuss the major teachings and practices that a significant number of the Radical Reformers drew from their understanding of the nature of the church. Secondly, we will look at some of the more notable examples of the radical fringe of the Protestant Reformation.

THE TEACHINGS OF THE RADICAL REFORMERS

In 1527, a group of Swiss Anabaptists met at Schleitheim, near the Swiss-German border, and drew up a brief document called the Schleitheim Confession of Faith. The main author of the work was a former Benedictine monk named Michael Sattler, who within four months of the Schleitheim meeting suffered martyrdom in Austria. The Confession is not in any sense a formal doctrinal statement, but emphasizes the distinctives that the Anabaptists drew from their understanding of the Scriptures and the nature of the church. It consists of seven articles, and serves as a good basis from which to launch into a discussion of Anabaptist beliefs and practices.

The first article dealt with baptism, and noted that, "Baptism shall be given to all those who have learned repentance and amendment of life, and who truly believe that their sins are taken away by Christ." The Anabaptists believed that baptism was a sign of a grace that had already been received, not the means by which that grace was received. As a result, they would administer it only to those who had demonstrated their reception of God's grace by a clear profession of faith accompanied by a changed life. Such a policy not only ruled out infant baptism, but put the Anabaptists at odds with all of Christendom. Catholics, of course, saw baptism as conveying saving grace, and were horrified that anyone who called himself a Christian would deliberately deny to infants the grace of Christ in baptism. After all, a baptized infant who died was assured of a place in heaven, but an unbaptized infant could expect no more than eternity in limbo. Calvin, using the analogy of circumcision, insisted that baptism was a sign and seal of the covenant, and initiated an infant into the covenant community to which he belonged by virtue of being born into a Christian family. Zwingli, like the Anabaptists, saw baptism as a sign only, and perhaps struggled more with this issue than any other Reformer. Early in his career in Zurich, he actually had expressed serious doubts about infant baptism, but had eventually rejected the concept of believer's baptism when the practical implications of the doctrine became clear to him, and he saw that such a practice would completely undermine the concept of a Christian society. Luther was more sacramentally-oriented than the Swiss Reformers, and maintained that the sacraments actually conveyed the grace of God in some sense. In fact, he agreed with the Anabaptists in seeing baptism as a sign of faith in God. This led him, however, to assert that infants who are baptized actually exercise faith, which is given to them by the grace of God, even though it is not visible until much later. Against all of this, however, the Anabaptists insisted that the Bible nowhere taught the baptism of infants, and that to do so was to practice "the highest and chief abomination of the pope."

The second article of the Schleitheim Confession deals with the issue that was to prove the most divisive among Anabaptists themselves - the matter of church discipline. Among the major Reformers, only Calvin really took church discipline seriously. The Anabaptists, however, recognized that it was only through the exercise of church discipline that the church could possibly remain what they believed it to be - an association of committed believers. They found the basis for their practice in Christ's words in Matthew 18. All agreed with the need for discipline to keep the church pure. Where they differed, however, was in the lengths to which that discipline should be carried, particularly excommunication, or the ban. The extent to which a disciplined brother or sister should be "shunned" by the community caused many a division in Anabaptist circles, some of which persist to the present day.

The Confession next spoke of the Lord's Supper, which for Anabaptists was a memorial celebration of the death of Christ. It was open only to baptized believers, and church discipline was specifically for the purpose of keeping the Lord's Table free of those who were not living orderly lives before God and their fellow Christians.

While the modern descendants of the Anabaptists may no longer be distinguished by their baptismal practices, they are certainly distinguished by the next issue tackled by the Confession - the matter of separation from the world. Since the children of light can have no communion with the children of darkness, it is incumbent upon God's people to separate themselves from the world of sin. For many Anabaptists, this meant living apart in their own communities, having little contact with the outside world. Their concept of separation included avoidance of "all popish and antipopish (e.g., Protestant) works and church services, meetings and church attendance, drinking houses, civic affairs, the commitments made in unbelief and other things of that kind, which are highly regarded by the world and yet are carried on in flat contradiction to the command of God, in accordance with all the unrighteousness which is in the world." Anabaptists today practice separation to varying extents, from the Mennonites who have to a large degree accommodated themselves to modern society, to the Amish and Hutterites who live in virtual isolation from the outside world.

The fifth article dealt with pastors, and provided that they should be chosen and supported by the members of the congregation rather than being chosen by a bishop or king and supported by the state. The Confession also, in a provision that reflects the experience of the Anabaptists at the time, insists that replacements should be chosen immediately for pastors who are martyred, "so that God's little flock and people may not be destroyed."

The Confession next moves on to the matter of the sword. Most, though not all, of the Anabaptists were pacifists, believing that force was never to be used, either to propagate the faith, or to defend the faithful against aggression. While they recognized that, according to Romans 13, God had given magistrates the power of the sword, they concluded from this, not that the use of the sword was legitimate, but that Christians could not therefore be magistrates. Many Anabaptists took this further and argued that Christians could in no way support the violence of the state, either by participating in government in any way, or even by paying taxes that were used to support military activity.

The final issue with which the Confession deals is the matter of taking oaths. Using Jesus' teaching in the Sermon on the Mount, Anabaptists refused to take oaths, maintaining that their answers should consist of nothing more than "yes" or "no."

Although the Schleitheim Confession is by no means a doctrinal statement, we must note in passing that it is perhaps the closest that we can come to a statement of Anabaptist belief. The reason for this is that Anabaptists, unlike Catholics, Lutherans, and the various groups of Reformed Protestants, did not write doctrinal statements. This was not a matter of ignorance or carelessness, but by design. Anabaptists wished to live and worship by the simple precepts of Scripture, which they believed all men were able to interpret for themselves. It was an abomination for anyone to try to force his beliefs on someone else. When they looked at the history of the church, they discovered that the confessions of faith by which the church had been living for over a thousand years had been drawn up under imperial sponsorship and enforced by the arm of the state. They refused, therefore, to be bound by such universally received documents as the Nicene and Athanasian Creeds.

The rejection of the foundational doctrinal statements of the church did not make the Anabaptists heretics, but heresies sprang up rather freely in the soil of Anabaptism. Whenever anyone asserts the right to interpret the Scriptures for himself under the guidance of the Spirit of God, he is being biblical. But when he divorces himself from the entire history of the church, thus cutting himself off from the wisdom of godly men through the ages, he is being foolish. Too many Anabaptists wound up justifying the charges of heresy being leveled against them by "throwing out the baby with the bath water" - not only rejecting the state church, but disposing of doctrines such as the Trinity and the full humanity and deity of Christ at the same time because these doctrines had been first enunciated under the sponsorship of the state. Even those who were personally orthodox were accused of heresy because they refused to affirm creeds for reasons other than their content.

Why, then, were these people persecuted? Why, in a period of about fifty years in the middle of the sixteenth century, did thousands of these gentle people go to their deaths by the sword, at the stake, or by drowning - the ironic "one-way baptism" thought by many to be poetic justice? While we may understand, but not condone, the execution of heretics practiced by Catholics and Protestants alike, and see why Catholics in particular would object to those who denied the grace of baptism to infants, it is nonetheless difficult for people in the late twentieth century to understand exactly what there was about the Anabaptists that produced such hatred in their fellow-countrymen, Protestant and Catholic alike.

The simple fact of the matter is that the vast majority of people in the Europe of the Reformation period saw the Anabaptists as a threat to the very fabric of society. Catholics and Protestants both believed that society ought to be Christian. To this end, both saw the necessity of a partnership between the church and the state, notwithstanding the fact that such a partnership had proven over the centuries to be notoriously troublesome to work out in practice. Theories as to how the church and the state should function together varied widely, and were as different from one another as Rome was from Geneva. No one, however, was ready to entertain the idea that the state should be abandoned to the devil. That way lay anarchy and chaos. While the Anabaptists saw a church of outcasts, separate from the sinful world, as a duplication of the New Testament picture, most others saw it as a major step backward, a rejection of all the progress God had given to His people over many centuries. It was therefore as subversives and revolutionaries - destroyers of society - that the Anabaptists were martyred and hounded from place to place throughout Europe. Neither was such a harsh opinion of the tendencies of Anabaptism totally without foundation. For decades, the horrible episode at Münster, which we will consider at a later point in the chapter, provided confirmation for everything the enemies of the Anabaptists feared about the ultimate consequences of their beliefs and practices.

RADICAL REFORM MOVEMENTS IN EUROPE

We now turn to the Anabaptists themselves. As already noted, the Anabaptists resist classification: by doctrine and practice, because of the considerable variety that existed in their ranks; and by geography, because many of the most important Anabaptists were itinerant, either by choice or because of persecution, and exerted influence in many different regions.

While many have asserted that Anabaptism was no more than a continuation of the radical movements of the Middle Ages, such as the Waldensians, Albigensians, and Catholic mystics, and while they certainly both had many ideas in common with the medieval dissenters and had points of contact with them, the fact of the matter is that there is something peculiarly

Protestant about Anabaptism. Therefore the logical place to begin any survey of prominent Anabaptists of the sixteenth century is in Zurich.

Luther may have talked about Scripture as the only source of authority for the Christian and emphasized the priesthood of all believers, but his application of these principles was really very conservative. He saw no problem with retaining many Catholic practices that had no biblical basis, nor did he give the common people much of a role in the church. In Zurich, however, Zwingli worked out these principles in a far more extensive way, undoubtedly aided by the democratic spirit of the Swiss cantons. Some of his enthusiastic young followers simply could not wait for the relatively stodgy town council to enact the reforms that Zwingli was preaching, however. Such men as Conrad Grebel and Felix Manz not only wanted reform immediately, but didn't understand what the town council had to do with the whole matter in the first place. The church should obey God, not men. They even received encouragement from Zwingli himself, who questioned whether or not infant baptism was really biblical. But once Zwingli understood exactly how far these men wished to go in their departure from the Catholic Church, he backed off. To him, these men and their doctrines were dangerous. As was the usual practice in Zurich, the result of the dispute was a public debate. Grebel, a well-educated man, held his own against the eloquent Zwingli, and was later assisted by the scholar and former professor Balthasar Hubmaier. The town council, however, decided that Zwingli had won the debate, and therefore ordered that all inhabitants of Zurich should baptize their children shortly after birth. Those who refused were to be imprisoned or exiled. When Grebel's wife got pregnant, the situation became critical. Grebel, Manz, and several of their friends gathered to decide what course of action to follow. One of their number, Georg Blaurock, asked Grebel to baptize him upon profession of faith, and he then baptized the others. By this open act of rebellion, they took their stand against the will of the council. They marched through the streets crying out woe against the city (including some rather uncomplimentary references to Zwingli), and were quickly arrested. They escaped, and soon spread their ideas in surrounding towns and cantons, where they found many willing listeners. Grebel soon died of the plague, but the others were arrested again upon returning to Zurich. Manz, as a citizen of Zurich, was drowned in the Limmat, while Blaurock and Hubmaier were beaten, sent out of the city, and threatened with drowning if they ever returned.

Blaurock and Hubmaier both soon met death as martyrs, but not before Hubmaier had traveled to Moravia, where he established numerous Anabaptist communities in the somewhat more hospitable feudal atmosphere that had a century earlier produced the Hussite movement. The communities founded by Hubmaier were then led by Jacob Hutter, who gave to those communities his own characteristic stamp. Hutter believed that the early chapters of Acts provided the model for the ideal Christian community. He therefore advocated community of property. The commitment and diligence of the Moravian Anabaptists made them prosperous in a tolerant environment, and they were soon valued by the surrounding Catholics for their skilled craftsmanship and their contributions to the economy of the region. When the Catholic Counterreformation began, however, they again experienced persecution, and suffered severe losses during the Thirty Years' War. The Hutterites eventually wound up in the Dakotas and Manitoba, Canada, after years of wandering around Europe to avoid persecution. They remain today as largely isolated communities, strict in their ways, separated from the outside world, and continuing to prosper in their diligence.

It was neither the biblically-oriented Swiss Anabaptists nor the solid-citizen Hutterites who fueled the fears of Catholics and Protestants alike, however. There were extremists among the Anabaptists. In the same way that the Zwickau prophets had appeared in Wittenberg, predicting the end of the world and advocating the violent overthrow of the infidel in order to make way for the Kingdom of God, so some in the Anabaptist movement fulfilled every fear that their enemies had ever entertained about them. Perhaps the most notorious example of this is the tragic incident at Münster, in Westphalia near the Dutch border.

In 1526, a Dutch leatherworker by the name of Melchior Hoffmann announced that the Kingdom of God was to be established in 1533. Hoffmann had been influenced by Lutheran ideas early in his career, and had later had contact with some Anabaptists, and had adopted their views. After periods of exile in Sweden and Denmark, he had returned to Holland in 1530, and soon the whole region was in an uproar, anticipating the imminent coming of the Kingdom. Hoffmann announced that the city of Strasbourg would be the site of the New Jerusalem, but that he himself would be imprisoned for the cause of the Gospel. He predicted, however, that the prophet Enoch would come, and lead in establishing the Kingdom. Hoffmann accordingly went to Strasbourg in 1533 and gave himself up to the authorities. They obliged by putting him in prison, where he died ten years later, all the while moving back, year by year, the date when the Kingdom was to come to earth.

Hoffmann's prophecies had not gone unnoticed, however. A young Haarlem baker by the name of Jan Matthys, caught up in the spirit of the end times, announced shortly after the imprisonment of Hoffmann that he was the prophesied Enoch. He began to preach the Kingdom, proclaiming to all who would listen that the true Israel would soon come into the promised land, but that this would only happen after the destruction of the Canaanites - in other words, he openly advocated the slaughter of all who opposed him. Unlike most Anabaptists, Matthys was no pacifist! Meanwhile, the city of Münster had been undergoing a Reformation of sorts under the leadership of a young preacher named Bernard Rothmann. His experience was similar to that of Zwingli, in that he found that simply preaching the Bible brought him great attention and enormous crowds in his church. Despite opposition from the Catholic bishop of Münster, he continued to preach, and finally his followers won control of the town council, and soon established the Reformation in the city.

When Rothmann, who was now recognized as the religious leader of Münster, came out in favor of believer's baptism, Anabaptists from all over flocked to Münster, convinced that here they had found a place of their own. In their number were several followers of the prophet Enoch, Jan Matthys. These followers, who included the fanatical Jan of Leyden, announced that Enoch had arrived to bring in the Kingdom, and that from now on all property was to be shared in common, and the saints were to live under God's law without the need for civil magistrates. Within a week, hundreds were baptized, while hundreds more left the city. Soon Matthys himself arrived, and announced that Münster, rather than Strasbourg, was to be the New Jerusalem. The reign of the saints had begun!

The bishop of Münster was not prepared to relinquish his city quite so easily, however. He gathered an army and prepared to besiege the city. Matthys and his followers took up arms, prepared to destroy the Canaanites in the strength of the Lord. After one particularly encouraging vision, Enoch gathered a group of about twenty men and marched through the city gates, convinced that the Lord would deliver the enemy's thousands into his hands. Instead, Matthys was quickly captured and summarily executed, and the soldiers entertained themselves during the siege by throwing various parts of his body around among themselves.

Jan of Leyden now assumed leadership of the Münster Anabaptists. He called himself King David, and began to travel throughout the city in royal robes - or at least the closest things to them he could find. He put the city under virtual martial law, with severe and immediate penalties for any who disobeyed. Numerous executions followed, with all suspected of disloyalty being put to the sword. Jan also proclaimed the reinstitution of the practice of polygamy, using the Old Testament patriarchs as his precedent (the city contained about three or four times as many women as men). He soon accumulated sixteen wives, including the beautiful widow of Jan Matthys.

The siege soon began to take its toll, especially when the besieging army received reinforcements from several surrounding regions. The reinforcements arrived shortly after word got out that the Münster Anabaptists were encouraging peasants in other towns to revolt against their masters. In Amsterdam, for instance, a group of men and women had run naked through the streets in imitation of the prophet Isaiah, announcing that the Kingdom was at hand. As the men and women of Münster were reduced to eating dogs and cats, meanwhile looking on as King David "preserved his own health for the good of the people," a spirit of discontent spread among them. In 1535, an Anabaptist captured by the besieging army told them where the walls of the city could be breached, and Münster was soon taken. The men were herded together and slaughtered and the women suffered various other forms of abuse, but the conquerors reserved their worst for the leaders of the revolt. Jan of Leyden and two others were tied to stakes in the public square while flesh was torn from every part of their bodies with hot pincers. When they could no longer feel pain, the executioner drove knives through their hearts. Their bodies were put into cages and hung from the steeple of the largest church in Münster. Thus ended the Münster rebellion.

The debacle at Münster also almost ended the brief history of Anabaptism. Now the enemies of the Anabaptists had something concrete to support their fears. "They may look and talk like law-abiding citizens now, but what do you think will happen when they get what they want?" Clearly the only appropriate response to such fanatics was total annihilation. Indeed, the persecutions drove the Anabaptists out of Switzerland, Germany, Austria, and Moravia. Many traveled farther east, going as far as Russia, while some eventually migrated to the tolerant shores of America, settling in Pennsylvania or some other place where they were permitted to live in peace.

That Anabaptism survived in the Netherlands, however, can be credited largely to the influence of one man. Menno Simons, a former Catholic priest, distanced himself completely from the Münster fanatics. While maintaining the Anabaptist distinctives, he preached a Gospel of peace, emphasizing the non-resistance that clearly had not been the hallmark of the Anabaptists of Münster. He pictured himself as a descendant of the Waldensians, and gradually brought respectability to a movement on the verge of annihilation. His followers are by far the most numerous of the Anabaptist groups today. They call themselves Mennonites, and have made pacifism one of their major distinctives. They have often disagreed among themselves over the years about the issues of separation from the world and the administration of church discipline, and the result is a wide variety of Mennonite sects, ranging from the evangelical General Conference Mennonites to the strict Old Order Amish.

We could cite other examples of Anabaptism as well, from the mysticism of Hans Denck and Caspar Schwenkfeld to the antitrinitarian extremism of Michael Servetus, about whom we spoke in the last chapter, and Laelius and Faustus Socinus, the forerunners of Unitarianism. Though the Anabaptists have had their share of mystics, such as Jacob Boehm, and have often harbored those of questionable orthodoxy (Menno Simons himself taught that Christ's human flesh did not come from Mary, but was a direct creation of God, thus denying Christ's full humanity), these are hardly representative of the movement.

MAKING DRY BONES LIVE

What, then, are we to learn from these radicals of the Reformation? The lessons for us come both from what the Anabaptists have become and from what we have become because of them. To begin with, the Anabaptists themselves have developed in a way that illustrates two of the weaknesses in their teachings. When any group of Christians emphasizes total separation from the world, they repeat all over again the error of the monks. A church that is cut off from the world ceases to have an impact on that world. What, after all, distinguishes the self-contained Amish communities from the monasteries of the Middle Ages, except that the Amish "monasteries" contain families as well as individuals? Christians cannot be salt and light by isolating themselves from the sinful world in which God has placed them.

Secondly, while church discipline is biblical, it must be administered on biblical grounds. When pride is defined as wearing buttons, and wearing buttons thus becomes an offense worthy of discipline, legalism has taken over the church. While it might be easy to criticize some Anabaptist groups for legalism, the fact of the matter is that any church that takes discipline seriously runs the same risk. As we saw in the last chapter, Calvin's Geneva also had its problems in this area.

On the other side of the coin, there can be no question that the Anabaptists have left in their wake an enormous legacy from which all of us have benefitted, especially those who live in the United States of America. Their radical notion of separation of church and state may have sounded dangerous to Protestants and Catholics alike in the sixteenth century, but it has become the only way for religious people to worship according to their consciences in today's pluralistic society. While some would argue that the notion of religious toleration and separation of church and state were inevitable consequences of the political settlements following the great religious wars of the sixteenth and seventeenth centuries, the fact of the matter is that the Anabaptists were pioneers, preaching toleration when everyone else was preaching intolerance, and for this we owe them a great debt.

It is somewhat ironic, of course, that today's Anabaptists are far more threatened by that very freedom they were the first to advocate than they are by the persecution they once feared. It is not intolerance that worries today's Amish and Hutterites. Instead, it is the prospect of losing their children, and thus their long heritage, to the secular world that surrounds them on all sides.

FOR REVIEW AND FURTHER THOUGHT

1. Why were the subjects of this chapter called *Anabaptists* or *Catabaptists* by their enemies? To what extent were these titles appropriate?

2. In what way was the Anabaptist view of baptism an outgrowth of their doctrine of the church?

3. In what sense did the Anabaptists go beyond even the Swiss Reformers in challenging the doctrines and practices of the Catholic Church?

4. How did the Anabaptist view of baptism differ from those of the Catholics, Lutherans, and Reformed Protestants?

5. How did the Anabaptist view of church discipline differ from that of Calvin?

6. In what way did the Anabaptists themselves differ over the issue of church discipline?

7. According to the Anabaptists, what does the Bible mean when it tells Christians to come out and be separate?

8. In what sense does the Anabaptist procedure for selection and support of pastors demonstrate their conviction that the church should be separate from the state?

9. Why did the Anabaptists believe that Christians should not hold positions in government?

10. What caused some Anabaptists to question such doctrinal statements of the early church as those defining the doctrine of the Trinity and the relationship of the two natures of Christ?

11. Why did Protestants and Catholics alike in the sixteenth century consider Anabaptists to be worthy of death?

12. Why was it more likely that Anabaptists would find encouragement in Zurich rather than Wittenberg?

13. What were the distinctives of the Anabaptist communities in Moravia influenced by the leadership of Jacob Hutter?

14. Why were the Hutterites for a time tolerated more than other Anabaptist groups elsewhere?

15. What roles did Melchior Hoffmann, Bernard Rothmann, Jan Matthys, and Jan of Leyden play in the Münster debacle?

16. Why did the Münster incident almost destroy the Anabaptist movement?

17. In what ways was the incident in Münster *not* typical of the Anabaptist movement as a whole?

18. In what ways have modern descendants of the Anabaptists emphasized the distinctives of those who arose in the sixteenth century?

19. What weakness was manifested by the Anabaptists that also posed a problem in Calvin's Geneva?

20. What is the major contribution made by the Anabaptists to the American religious landscape?

22

GENEVA'S CHILDREN

In 1536, the city of Geneva won its independence from the Duke of Savoy, largely because of the aid supplied by the Swiss cantons of Bern and Freiburg. The German-speaking Swiss referred to the patriots of Geneva who were struggling against the oppression of Savoy as *Eidgenossen* ("confederates"). That this term for patriotic Genevans eventually evolved into *Huguenots*, the word used to describe French Protestants, is a small measure of the enormous influence exerted by Calvin's Geneva on the Reformation in his native France. Because Geneva served for many years as a haven for persecuted Protestants from all over Europe, it also had the opportunity to export Calvin's understanding of Christian faith and life to many places beyond its borders. In this chapter, we will look briefly at three countries to which the Reformation of Geneva was exported - France, Scotland, and the Netherlands.

All three of these countries were ripe for revolt against Rome in the sixteenth century. The French had long chafed against papal interference from Rome. In the fourteenth century, Philip the Fair had taken matters into his own hands and actually moved the papacy to Avignon (the infamous "Babylonian Captivity"). Even after the papacy returned to Rome, the French church affirmed certain "liberties" in the Pragmatic Sanction of Bourges in 1438. In Scotland, many had viewed ties to Rome as little more than a source of foreign overlords since the days of the old Celtic church. Spain ruled the Netherlands in the sixteenth century, and the sturdy Dutch were just as freedom-loving as the Scots.

It would not have required a great deal for all three of these countries to move into the Protestant camp. The bombs were ready to explode. All that was needed was someone to light the fuse. That someone turned out to be John Calvin. As A.G. Dickens has noted, "Geneva supplied the current and the wires which led to the plentiful local stores of dynamite." Calvin's *Institutes of the Christian Religion* supplied the theological framework for those aching for reform. Geneva became the model for church government and Christian society, and the Academy in Geneva provided trained pastors for persecuted Protestants all over Europe. Furthermore, Calvin gave the rebels an excuse to revolt against their oppressors. Luther was a convinced monarchist, and would neither countenance revolt among his followers or approve it in others, as became clear when he condemned both the Peasants' Revolt of 1525 and the Kappel Wars in Switzerland a few years later. Calvin, while strongly asserting the responsibility of Christians to submit to their governments, did open a loophole large enough for freedom-loving French, Scots, and Dutch to plunge through. Calvin taught that lawful officials could justifiably revolt against tyrannical rulers when their duties as protectors of the people required it. This was all that French "Princes of the Blood" and Scottish barons needed to hear. As long as they could justify their revolts as being in line with their duties as public officials, they could enter into battle against kings and emperors with clear consciences. Though Calvin by no means approved of the bloodshed that resulted from putting his theory into practice, there can be no question that his justification of revolution was a significant contributing factor to the spread of the Reformation in Europe. As we will see in a future chapter, it also played a role in drawing staunch Puritans into the American Revolution two hundred years later.

THE REFORMATION IN FRANCE

The Reformation in France began before the time of Calvin, of course. Calvin himself was influenced by the Christian humanists at the University of Paris, led by the biblical scholar Jacques Lefevre d'Etaples. During Calvin's early years in France, the French king was Francis I, the same sort of pleasure-loving, politically-oriented monarch as his English counterpart Henry VIII. Francis never could quite make up his mind about the Protestants in his realm. He alternately persecuted and tolerated them, depending upon whether he was seeking an alliance at the time with Catholic Spain or with the Protestant German states. He fancied himself a patron of the new learning, and encouraged the humanism under which Protestantism blossomed. At the same time, he was not above burning or beheading any who stirred up public commotion, which Protestants also tended to do. Ironically, it was the actions taken against Protestants by Francis that did the most to promote the Protestant cause. When he ordered the massacre of the inhabitants of several Waldensian villages in 1545, Protestant protests poured in from Germany and Switzerland, while many Catholics expressed their dismay somewhat less vocally. Furthermore, it was the sporadic persecutions of Francis that provided the occasion for Calvin to write the first edition of the *Institutes*, which he addressed to the French monarch.

When Francis I died in 1547, he was succeeded by his son Henry II. Henry continued the persecutions initiated by his father, though his opposition did not prevent the Protestants from organizing themselves formally in 1559. In that year, representatives from about fifty Protestant churches met in Paris and adopted the Gallican Confession (based on the one written by Calvin in Geneva), along with a form of church government modeled on that of Geneva, though somewhat more democratic in nature, and allowing for provincial and national synods in addition to the local consistories. Anne du Bourg, a scholarly and respected representative in Parliament, gave speech after eloquent speech in defense of the Protestants, for which he was eventually arrested and executed. His death brought much sympathy for the Protestant cause, and by the time Henry II died in 1559, there were thousands of Protestants scattered throughout France.

Henry's death initiated a thirty-five-year period of almost continual civil war between the Protestants and Catholics of France. During these years, France was ruled by a succession of weak kings, and this weakness at the top encouraged jockeying for power among the French noble families. Three of these families played a major role in the progress of the French Reformation. On the Catholic side was the Guise family, represented by Henry, Duke of Guise, and his brother Charles of Lorraine, a cardinal in the Catholic Church. The fact that the Guise family was from Lorraine, near the German border, caused many to view them as foreign interlopers, thus driving many Frenchmen to the Protestant side for patriotic reasons. The champions of the Protestant cause were the Bourbon and Chatillon families. The Bourbons were Princes of the Blood, and ruled the kingdom of Navarre, near the Spanish border in the south. The Bourbons provided military leaders for the Huguenots, including Louis, Prince of Conde, and Henry of Navarre, who later became King Henry IV. Perhaps the most noble Bourbon of all was Henry's mother, Jeanne d'Albret, who fervently espoused the Protestant cause, and showed far more spiritual devotion than her son, or many of the other "political" Huguenots. From the Chatillon family came Odet, who openly supported Protestants despite being the Roman Catholic Cardinal of Chatillon, and Gaspard de Coligny and François d'Andelot, Huguenot military leaders. In the middle of this power struggle among the French nobility was the queen mother, the Italian Catherine de Medici. While three of her sons ruled France as Francis II, Charles IX, and Henry III between 1559 and 1589, she tried to maintain a precarious balance between Catholic and Protestant forces in order to keep her sons on the throne of France.

In the beginning, the major threat came from the ambitious Guises. Francis II was only fifteen when he became king, and he was in no position to control these powerful men. When a Protestant plot to arrest the Guises (the "Tumult of Amboise") failed in 1560, large numbers of Protestants were slaughtered, and the leading Huguenots were arrested and condemned to death despite the fact that they disavowed any involvement with the plot. Before the executions could be carried out, however, Francis died, leaving his ten-year-old brother Charles on the throne. Catherine de Medici promptly seized the regency and released the Huguenot leaders, hoping to use them to counterbalance the powerful Guises. She initiated a public debate among leading Catholics and Protestants called the Colloquy of Poissy, where Theodore Beza came from Geneva to defend the Protestant cause. Protestants gained a small measure of official toleration, but the peace did not last long. Open war broke out in 1562 when the Guises massacred a group of Huguenots gathered for worship in a barn (their excuse was that the Protestants had thrown stones at their horsemen), and continued with little break until 1593.

In a period filled with brutal episodes that reflect no credit on either side of the struggle, the worst incident was the St. Bartholomew's Day Massacre of 1572. Catherine's latest step in her balancing act was to propose a marital union between Henry of Navarre and her own daughter, Margaret of Valois. Young Henry was not a very good Protestant, and his mother Jeanne d'Albret strongly opposed the union, though she died before the wedding took place. Margaret was a good Catholic, and was even less enamored of the whole idea than her prospective mother-in-law was. She was willing to submit to her mother, however. The wedding was planned for August of 1572, and leading members of Catholic and Huguenot parties alike were invited to Paris for the festivities. Catherine had more in mind than a wedding, however. She was also busy plotting the assassination of the most powerful leader of the Huguenots, Admiral Gaspard de Coligny, who had begun to exert an alarming influence over the young Charles IX. Four days after the wedding, a hired assassin in the employ of the Guises attacked de Coligny, but only succeeded in wounding him. The king, who knew nothing about the plot, was horrified, but Catherine came to him and convinced him that the old Admiral had to be killed. She lied to Charles, telling him that de Coligny was involved in all sorts of plots against the throne. Charles finally agreed to the death of de Coligny, but childishly insisted that all the other Protestants would have to die, too, so he wouldn't have to worry about them taking revenge against him for the death of the Admiral.

Two days later, on August 24, 1572, the bells rang at daybreak to announce the Feast of St. Bartholomew. On this day, the bells were a prearranged signal. When they rang out from churches all over the city, Catholics began to search out and destroy Huguenots. Gaspard de Coligny was one of the first to die. Armed men entered his bedroom, thrust a sword into his body, and threw it out the window into the street below. Others cut off his head and held it aloft on a pike, while his headless body was dragged through the streets of Paris. By the time the blood lust had spent itself, ten thousand Huguenots lay dead in the streets of Paris, along with many Catholics who had been caught in the frenzy. The scene was reenacted in other towns around the country as news of the massacre spread, and within a week as many as twenty thousand Huguenots had been slaughtered in the towns and villages of France. The incident brought almost universal disgust, with two exceptions. Philip II wrote a congratulatory letter, and suggested that such means would not be necessary if the French would have the sense to make use of the Inquisition the way he did in Spain. The pope was also pleased. While Pius V had earlier encouraged Charles to exterminate every Huguenot in France, using the example of King Saul and the Amalekites, Gregory XIII, the pope at the time, received news of the massacre by calling for rejoicing in the streets of Rome and ordering a commemorative medal struck in honor of the occasion.

Henry of Navarre was spared in the slaughter, and went on to become the leader of the Huguenots. Catherine's weakling sons continued to die without leaving sons behind them, and finally Henry found himself heir to the throne of France. After thirty years of war, the Catholics, who still held a significant majority of the population, were not about to sit idly by and watch a Protestant assume the throne of France. Henry, realizing that he would never be secure if he tried to rule a Catholic kingdom as a Protestant, converted to Catholicism in 1593 and assumed the throne as Henry IV. He protected his former coreligionists, however, when he issued the Edict of Nantes in 1598, granting religious toleration to the Huguenots and allowing them significant political power in the cities and regions where they held a majority.

Henry IV was assassinated in 1610, and Huguenot freedoms quickly disintegrated. The power behind the throne in the following years, Cardinal Richelieu, saw the Huguenots as a political threat to the absolute power of the monarchy, and encouraged the king to break them. After the fall of the major Huguenot stronghold, La Rochelle, in 1628, Huguenot political power eroded, though they maintained their religious freedoms. Even these were gradually removed by Louis XIV. When he revoked the Edict of Nantes in 1685, it was because he foolishly believed that there were few Huguenots left. He soon learned otherwise when almost half a million fled France, decimating both the middle class and the economy of the country.

Long years of warfare and persecution broke the backs of the French Protestants, however. The "conversion" of Henry IV ensured that France would remain a Catholic country, and much of the Protestant population eventually wound up settling in other parts of Europe and the Americas. By the time the Huguenots regained toleration on the eve of the French Revolution, there was truly little left to tolerate.

THE REFORMATION IN SCOTLAND

As the Reformation era dawned, Scotland may have been ripe for change, but it is no surprise that change took a great deal of time. Scotland in the sixteenth century was a land little changed since the Middle Ages, a land of warring nobles and kings dependent on those nobles for their power. Shakespeare's MacBeth would have been right at home. In fact, the kings of Scotland often began their reigns as children because their fathers had died violent deaths at the hands of disgruntled nobles, or been killed in battle. A kingdom ruled by child kings is dominated by regents, and the real powers in Scotland were often the corrupt Catholic clergy. This, too, contributed to the openness of the Scottish people when reform finally arrived.

The first glimmer of reform came from a young Scottish nobleman named Patrick Hamilton. Hamilton had been educated abroad, spending time in Wittenberg and Marburg, and when he returned to Scotland, he brought with him the ideas of Luther and Melanchthon. James Beaton, the Archbishop of St. Andrews, quickly put a stop to Hamilton's preaching by burning the twenty-four-year-old preacher at the stake in 1528. Meanwhile, William Tyndale's translation of the New Testament into English began circulating into Scotland. The teachings of the Reformation spread rapidly, enhanced by a growing division between those who favored alliance with France and those who wanted to see closer ties with England. The Stuart kings of Scotland had already formed ties with France through the marriage of James V to Mary of Guise. Catholics heartily approved of the union, and viewed England, the traditional enemy of the Scots, as an even more dangerous foe since the apostasy of Henry VIII. Many others feared that Scotland would be swallowed up by the French, however, and saw England as the savior. As a result, as in France, Scottish Protestants were abetted by patriotic motives among those whose religious concerns were minimal. Any who feared the ambitions of the French in Scotland were of necessity driven toward Protestantism.

By this time, the chief power in Scotland lay in the hands of Cardinal David Beaton, the nephew of James Beaton. David Beaton hated Protestants with a vengeance, but often contributed to the growth of Protestantism by his openly scandalous lifestyle. A firebrand former priest by the name of George Wishart began preaching Reformed ideas in Scotland, and Beaton had him arrested and burned at the stake in 1546. As he was dying, Wishart called down the wrath of God upon the corrupt cardinal; many were impressed when Beaton was murdered in his bed a short time later.

When Wishart had been traveling around Scotland preaching the Gospel, his life was often threatened. At times, it was necessary for him to surround himself with armed bodyguards while he preached. Among these sword-wielding adventurers was a forty-year-old Catholic priest named John Knox. After the martyrdom of Wishart and the assassination of Beaton, Knox went to St. Andrews to minister to the men who had taken the castle there and murdered Cardinal Beaton. He served as their chaplain, and was hopeful that the death of the corrupt Beaton would lead to the reformation of Scotland. Before long, however, French troops landed in the harbor and soldiers surrounded the castle. Knox and the others were captured, and he served for the next year and a half as a galley slave on a French ship. After being released as part of a prisoner exchange, he went to England and began to prepare for his eventual work of reforming the Church of Scotland.

Knox arrived in England during the reign of Edward VI, the young son of Henry VIII whose advisors favored Protestantism. He gained enough respect while preaching in England to be offered the post of Bishop of Rochester, but he declined. When Edward died in 1553 and was replaced by his half-sister Mary Tudor ("Bloody Mary"), Knox fled to the continent along with many other Protestants. For the next six years, he traveled from place to place, serving English-speaking congregations in Frankfurt and Geneva, and spending much time taking in all he could learn in Calvin's "School of Christ." Despite Calvin's admonitions to move cautiously, Knox published a pamphlet in 1558 called *The First Blast of the Trumpet Against the Monstrous Regiment of Women*, in which he attacked female rule as against Scripture and nature. While his primary targets were such Catholic stalwarts as Mary Tudor of England, Mary Stuart (later to be come Queen of Scots, then just married to the Dauphin of France, who was later to become Francis II), and Mary of Guise (who was regent in Scotland in the place of her daughter Mary Stuart), the pamphlet was a classic of bad timing. Shortly after its publication, Mary Tudor died and was succeeded by her sister Elizabeth, who was determined to rule England as a Protestant. Despite the fact that Knox and Elizabeth should have been on the same side, the broadside alienated them so completely that he was never able to regain her trust.

Meanwhile, Protestantism had been growing rapidly in Scotland. People increasingly feared a French takeover of the country, between Mary of Guise serving as regent and a young queen who was married to the Dauphin of France. In 1557, a small group of Scottish noblemen met in Edinburgh and signed a covenant in which they agreed to defend the Reformed faith with their lives. These men soon came to be known as the Lords of the Congregation, and it was they who spearheaded the drive to reform the Church of Scotland. By the time Knox was invited to return to Scotland in 1559 by the Lords of the Congregation, Mary of Guise was getting desperate. The Reformed movement was growing at an increasing rate, and the situation in France, where King Henry II had just died after getting a lance through the eye during a tournament, was too chaotic for her to expect much help from that quarter. When Elizabeth of England sent troops to support the Protestant lords, the battle was over. France sent some soldiers, but they were too little and too late, and when Mary of Guise died suddenly, they turned around and sailed home, leaving Scotland firmly in Protestant hands.

Knox was in his glory then. He proceeded to do in the country of Scotland what Calvin had done in the city of Geneva. Parliament passed law after law intended to establish the Reformed faith, and, somewhat surprisingly, the majority of the people followed this course enthusiastically. The Scottish Kirk (Church) became the first national presbyterian church, and adopted a confession of faith modeled on that of Geneva. While Knox, like Calvin, held no public office, he was so widely respected in Scotland that his influence was every bit as great among his own people until his death in 1572 as that of the Genevan Reformer. By 1560, Parliament had passed the major elements of the Scottish Reformation, and within a year these reforms had spread throughout the country.

Not everyone in Scotland loved Knox, however. While his strict sense of discipline made him unpopular among the loose livers of Scotland in the same way the Libertines of Geneva hated Calvin, his greatest challenge came in the political arena. One year after Francis II became King of France, he died, leaving a beautiful eighteen-year-old widow - Mary, Queen of Scots. Mary had been raised in the Catholic court of France since she was five years old, and had really known nothing other than Catholicism. When she arrived in Scotland after her husband's death, she found herself in the awkward position of being a Catholic monarch in an overwhelmingly Protestant country, and where Protestantism had swept into authority to a large extent as a reaction against the Catholicism in which Mary had been raised. When Mary innocently called for a priest to celebrate Mass in her chambers, Knox exploded, insisting that one Mass was more dangerous to the health of the realm than if thousands of French troops were to land on the shores of Scotland. Knox had several interviews with the young queen in the years that followed, but she did not budge an inch under the pressure of the great reformer. Though she made no outwardly aggressive moves against Protestantism, she worked subtly behind the scenes to return Scotland to the Catholic faith. She eventually brought about her own downfall through foolish marriages. She first married the dashing but empty-headed Catholic nobleman Lord Darnley, but found out too late that there were no brains behind those good looks. She began to rely more and more on an Italian advisor in her court named David Rizzio. Darnley, jealous of Rizzio and afraid he was losing his influence with the queen, arranged to have Rizzio murdered in Mary's presence. This only alienated her more, and she soon became enamored of another nobleman, Lord Bothwell. In 1567, Lord Darnley was murdered, and Mary married Lord Bothwell shortly thereafter. When Lord Bothwell was implicated in the murder, the scandal brought the wrath of the people down upon Mary's head. She was forced to abdicate, and turned the throne over to her one-year-old son James VI, who later became James I of England when he succeeded Elizabeth in 1603.

Mary left the country and sought refuge in England. Elizabeth received her, but it soon became apparent that the arrangement could never work. The Catholic powers, especially France and Spain, had a great desire to topple Elizabeth from power. They were determined to use Mary Stuart as a pawn, claiming that she was the rightful Queen of England by virtue of her descent from Henry VII of England, and that Elizabeth, the daughter of Henry VIII and Anne Boleyn, was the issue of a marriage that had never been recognized by the pope, and therefore had no legal standing. When Elizabeth found out that Mary herself was being drawn into some of these plots, she had no choice but to have her cousin beheaded in 1587, after twenty years in custody.

Meanwhile, the Protestant Earl of Murray was serving as regent for the young James I. The Earl was a Protestant and an early supporter of the reforms, but he was no presbyterian. In fact, he worked overtime to impress upon his young charge the theory of the Divine Right of Kings, which states that the king is not only appointed by God, but also is God's representative on earth, and thus wields absolute power. Such ideas put James in conflict with the Scottish Presbyterians, who had to fight hard under the leadership of Andrew Melville to maintain the form of church government they favored over against the episcopal system that, according to James, was the only one suited to a monarchy. What was merely a struggle in the sixteenth century was to break out into open warfare several times in the seventeenth century, after the Stuarts had become rulers of England as well as Scotland.

THE REFORMATION IN THE NETHERLANDS

While the countries we are considering in this chapter have much in common, there are also significant differences. While France and Scotland were independent countries, the Netherlands was at this time under the rule of Spain. While Scotland was relatively poor and backward, the Netherlands was in some senses the most advanced region in Northern Europe.

In the late Middle Ages, the Brethren of the Common Life began in the Netherlands. The region had been the center of the Northern Renaissance and the birthplace of Erasmus. It was an area of flourishing commerce and free thought. It was also inevitable that the teachings of Martin Luther and John Calvin would have an impact in an area such as this, where people were already accustomed to thinking for themselves. In fact, it was in the Netherlands that the earliest Lutheran martyrs died in the early 1520's.

The Reformation did not come easily to the Netherlands, however. The Holy Roman Emperor Charles V had been raised in the region and had a special love for it. As a result, he was determined that the troubles that were tearing Germany apart would not harm his beloved Low Countries. His solution to the problem was the Inquisition. Despite the execution of many, the Reformation spread throughout the region, not only in its Lutheran form, but also the Anabaptist variety, as we saw in the last chapter. Ultimately, though, it was the Reformed branch of Protestantism that came to predominate. Reformed churches were started by pastors sent from Geneva, and augmented by refugees from England during the reign of Bloody Mary. When Charles V abdicated in 1555 in favor of his son Philip II, the young king, a rabid Catholic, decided that it was time for a crackdown. He initially appointed his half-sister as regent over the Netherlands, but she proved ineffective in stemming the tide of Protestantism. Finally he sent the Duke of Alva in 1567, complete with the troops necessary to enforce his will, to do something about the Protestant menace. The Duke approached his job with great enthusiasm, and between 1567 and 1573, thousands of Protestants were tortured and executed, and thousands more were driven from their homes and had their towns destroyed.

Such repressive measures may have had a negative impact in the short run, but in the long run they simply made the people more determined to resist Spanish tyranny. Again, Protestantism came to be identified with patriotism. Under the leadership of William the Silent, the Dutch waged a long and bloody war of independence, culminating in a truce in 1609 that in effect recognized the autonomy of the six northern provinces (now the Netherlands), leaving the southern provinces (present-day Belgium) under Spanish control. Though the independence of the Netherlands was not officially recognized until the Peace of Westphalia in 1648, the issue was really settled in the late sixteenth century by three factors. The first was the Dutch domination of the sea. Merchant ships that called themselves Sea Beggars constantly harassed Spanish shipping, making it difficult to wage any kind of consistent war. In one remarkable battle, the city of Leyden was under siege, and nearby villagers broke holes in the dams surrounding the city so that the Sea Beggars could sail in across the fields and break the siege. The second incident, which dealt a death blow to Spanish sea power, was the sinking of the Invincible Armada when Philip II tried to invade England in 1588. The reason he was trying to invade England was because Elizabeth had been sending aid to the Protestant defenders of the Netherlands, which had kept them afloat during the darkest days of the war. The third factor was the determination of the Dutch themselves. Despite the assassination of William the Silent in 1584, they continued the fight until the Spanish finally agreed to a truce.

During the fighting, Dutch Protestants had set up the Dutch Reformed Church in 1574, based on the Belgic Confession, which had been drawn up by Guido de Bres in 1561, and the Heidelberg Catechism of 1563. Though efforts were made after independence was secured to establish the Reformed Church, internal conflicts prevented any united front among Dutch Christians. The result is that the Netherlands became one of the earliest havens of religious freedom in Europe, and a place in which those being persecuted elsewhere could find freedom to worship as they pleased. Among these persecuted believers seeking sanctuary were many English Separatists, some of whom later settled in Plymouth, Massachusetts.

THE SPREAD OF CALVIN'S THEOLOGY

Many a great man in the history of Christianity has had good cause to pray, "O Lord, deliver me from my disciples." John Calvin was certainly such a man. In the years following his death, an incredible amount of bickering grew up around the tenets of his theology, much of which has continued down to the present day. Though the system of theology presented by Calvin has come to be called by his name, "Calvinism" was not a radical innovation in the history of the church. Calvin taught little that was different from such men as Augustine, Gottschalk, and Thomas Bradwardine on the issue of salvation, and agreed with the other major Reformers in his doctrine of the church. After his death, however, Theodore Beza further expounded his teachings, laying special emphasis on the subject of predestination, which Calvin had taught without stressing. Beza's treatment of predestination became a matter of conflict in both France and the Netherlands. Beza emphasized what has been called "double predestination" - the idea that God predestined the elect for salvation and also predestined the reprobate (those who are not among the elect) for eternal damnation before time began. Not even those who believe this teaching find it a particularly pleasant one, but those who are committed to it affirm it because they believe it to be biblical (see Romans 9). Things got even messier when those who believed in double predestination began to argue about *how* this had occurred. Some maintained that God had chosen who was to be saved and who was to be lost in eternity past, and then had planned the fall of man and salvation through Christ in order to bring it about (these people were called supralapsarians). Their opponents taught that God had decreed the fall of man, and then determined to save some men from their sinful condition through the sacrifice of Christ, leaving others to their just damnation (infralapsarians). In other words, the two groups were arguing about the order in which God had made certain decisions before the beginning of time! In an environment of such extreme thinking, it is natural that some would seek compromising or mediating positions.

In the Netherlands, such a person appeared in the form of James Arminius, former student of Beza at Geneva and professor at the University of Leyden. Arminius had early been an advocate of the form of Calvinism taught by Beza, but began to question it when he was asked to defend it against a vocal critic of Calvin's system. After several years as a pastor, he came to the University of Leyden, where Dutch Calvinists strongly opposed his appointment. Though he often claimed he had no argument with the Belgic Confession, he continued to dispute tenets of Reformed theology, especially the matter of irresistible grace (see chapter 20 for a summary of Calvinism). The dispute took on political overtones when those in favor of a centralized government for the Netherlands lined up behind the strict Calvinists, while those favoring a looser confederation of the Dutch provinces stood behind the free-thinking Arminius. Though Arminius did publish his views in his *Declaration of Sentiments* in 1608, he died the following year, before the conflict really came to a full boil.

After the truce of 1609, the Dutch were able to catch their collective breaths sufficiently to turn their attention to theological disputes. The champion of the Calvinist position was a professor at Leyden named Francis Gomarus. The Arminian view was upheld by several of his followers, led by his successor Simon Episcopius. Episcopius and the other Arminians drew up a document presenting their views called the *Remonstrance*, after which they came to be called Remonstrants. For several years following, the two sides argued over how the dispute should be conducted. The Calvinists favored a national synod, while, the Remonstrants wanted each province to deal with the matter on its own. The Calvinists won the procedural dispute, and the Synod of Dordt met from late 1618 to early 1619. This meeting was more representative than any other council of the Reformation period in the sense that it included Protestant theologians from the Netherlands, Switzerland, England, and several of the German Protestant states. It was not, however,

THEOLOGICAL ISSUES - CALVINIST VERSUS ARMINIAN

ISSUE	CALVINIST POSITION	ARMINIAN POSITION
ORIGINAL SIN	Total depravity and guilt inherited from Adam.	Weakness inherited from Adam.
HUMAN WILL	In bondage to sin.	Free to do spiritual good.
GRACE OF GOD	Common grace given to all; saving grace given to elect.	Enabling grace given to all; saving grace given to those who believe; persevering grace given to those who obey.
PREDESTINATION	Rooted in God's decrees.	Rooted in God's foreknowledge.
REGENERATION	Monergistic.	Synergistic.
ATONEMENT	Christ's death a substitutionary penal sacrifice.	Christ's death a sacrifice that God benevolently accepted in place of a penalty.
EXTENT OF ATONEMENT	Intended only for the elect.	Intended for all.
APPLICATION OF ATONEMENT	By power of the Holy Spirit according to the will of God.	By power of the Holy Spirit in response to the will of the sinner.
ORDO SALUTIS	Election, predestination, union with Christ, calling, regeneration, faith, repentance, justification, sanctification, glorification.	Calling, faith, repentance, regeneration, justification, perseverance, glorification.
PERSEVERANCE	Perseverance of all the elect by the grace of God.	Perseverance dependent on obedience.

an open debate. The Arminians appeared only as defendants, and to no one's surprise the *Remonstrance* was condemned. The articles drawn up by the Synod of Dordt in response to the *Remonstrance* set forth for the first time what have come to be known as the Five Points of Calvinism, discussed in chapter 20 (to get an idea of what the Remonstrants taught, imagine the opposite of each of the points summarized there). Though many Arminian pastors and professors were forced to leave the country, by 1625 the restrictions against Arminians were no longer being enforced, and by 1630 Arminian churches were being openly established in the Netherlands. In fact, it was the Dutch Arminians who wound up having a significant impact on the Church of England, which espoused (though never officially) many Arminian tenets in the seventeenth century and beyond.

The dispute over Calvinist theology also affected France in the seventeenth century. The focus of attention here was the University of Saumur. A series of theological professors at the university, beginning with the Scotsman John Cameron, and including Placaeus and Moses Amyraut, challenged certain facets of the Calvinist system. While Arminius had begun to question Calvinism when he entertained doubts about irresistible grace, Amyraut simply could not accept the notion that Christ did *not* die for everyone (limited atonement). His approach, rather than rejecting the entire Calvinist system as Arminius had done, was an attempt to compromise between Calvinism and Arminianism (some have referred to Amyraldianism as two- or three-point Calvinism, though this is really a misnomer). Amyraut taught that, while Christ died for everyone (at least hypothetically), it is only those who believe who actually benefit from His death. These are the chosen of God, and the only ones to whom He gives saving grace (this differs from Arminius' position in that the Dutchman affirmed that God chose those whom He knew would believe; Amyraut said that no one would believe on his own, so God graciously saved some). Thus Amyraldianism lacks the consistency of either the Calvinist or Arminian positions, yet it has continued to be enormously influential, especially among American evangelicals, where many affirm some combination of Calvinist and Arminian tenets that approximates the teachings of Amyraut. The French-speaking Reformed churches viewed Amyraldianism as dangerous, however, and rejected it at the Helvetic Consensus in 1675.

MAKING DRY BONES LIVE

Before we conclude our consideration of the Reformation movements in France, Scotland, and the Netherlands, we need to return to Henry of Navarre, the Huguenot who converted to Catholicism in order to become King Henry IV of France. Despite the obvious political advantages, was he right to do what he did? He certainly could not have granted toleration to the Huguenots through the Edict of Nantes had he never become king. On the other hand, could not God have brought the Huguenots victory despite their smaller numbers, and thus made France a Protestant country? We will, of course, never know what the practical consequences would have been had Henry stuck to his convictions and remained Protestant. On the other hand, there is a very real question as to whether Henry had any convictions to begin with. When he reputedly said "Paris is worth a Mass" prior to converting to Catholicism, he was expressing what was apparently his philosophy of life. This was, after all, the eighth time he had changed religions. It seems that he chose religions in the same way he chose clothes - use whatever is appropriate for the occasion.

As we will see in chapter 25, the Roman Catholic Jesuits were often criticized for teaching and acting upon the precept that the end justifies the means. Henry IV demonstrates that they had no corner on that particular philosophical market. Many of the military heroes of the Protestant Reformation did what they did, not because they were motivated by sincere piety, but for the purposes of political or economic gain. Religion was to them no more than a tool for their own advancement.

It is no less important today than it was in the sixteenth century for people to examine why they claim to believe what they believe. Too often people profess one religious faith or another for reasons that have nothing to do with any real relationship to God. A Christian should never be one for whom the ends justify the means. For a Christian, both the ends and the means must be dictated by the Word of God, and that alone.

Geneva's Children

FOR REVIEW AND FURTHER THOUGHT

1. How did the work of Calvin in the city of Geneva come to influence the development of Protestantism in France, Scotland, and the Netherlands?

2. Why were these three countries ripe for reform even before the Reformation began?

3. What political factors aided the progress of Protestantism in the three countries covered in this chapter?

4. Do you think it was helpful that Protestantism and patriotism were often identified with one another in the sixteenth century? Why or why not?

5. How did Calvin's view of the responsibility of civil governments help to justify the religious wars carried on in France, Scotland, and the Netherlands?

6. How did the persecution of Protestants by Francis I of France actually contribute to the growth of Protestantism?

7. What role did each of the following play in the French Reformation: Anne du Bourg, Jacques Lefevre d'Etaples, Jeanne d'Albret, Gaspard de Coligny, and Henry of Navarre?

8. How did Catherine de Medici try to balance the powerful families of Guise and Bourbon to try to maintain her position of authority, along with that of her sons?

9. Identify the following: Gallican Confession, Tumult of Amboise, Colloquy of Poissy, St. Bartholomew's Day Massacre, Edict of Nantes.

10. What excuse did Charles IX use for approving the St. Bartholomew's Day Massacre?

11. What role did each of the following play in the Scottish Reformation: Patrick Hamilton, George Wishart, David Beaton, Mary Stuart, Andrew Melville?

12. Why did regents play such an important role in the Scottish Reformation?

13. How did John Knox alienate Elizabeth of England?

14. How did Mary, Queen of Scots bring about her own downfall, exile, and eventual execution?

15. What factors contributed to the reputation of the Netherlands as a hotbed of free-thinkers?

16. What role did each of the following play in the Dutch Reformation: Philip II, the Duke of Alva, William the Silent, Guido de Bres, Elizabeth of England?

17. Who were the Sea Beggars, and how did they help the Protestant cause?

18. What emphasis did Theodore Beza give to Calvinism as a theological system that Calvin himself had never stressed?

19. What was the point of dispute between supralapsarians and infralapsarians?

20. How did Arminius come to question Calvin's view of salvation? What were his basic objections?

21. Who were the Remonstrants? What did the Synod of Dordt conclude about their teachings?

22. In what way did the professors at the University of Saumur in France try to compromise between the teachings of Calvin and Arminius? Were they successful? If so, in what way?

23. Do you believe that Henry of Navarre should have converted to Catholicism in order to secure his position as King of France? Why or why not? Does the end ever justify the means?

23

THE MIDDLE WAY

When Elizabeth I ascended the throne of England in 1558, one of the tasks she faced was that of appointing a number of bishops and archbishops to provide leadership for the Church of England, since the Catholic bishops from the reign of her sister Mary had either died or resigned. She did discover one elderly bishop, however, who had held office through all the religious changes in the country since the reign of Elizabeth's father Henry VIII. Elizabeth asked him how he had managed to survive all the turmoil, and his response was, "I smacked of the willow more than of the oak." In a century in which Henry VIII's religious policy was such that "those who were against the Pope were burned, and those who were for him were hanged," where "Bloody Mary" earned her infamy by burning almost three hundred Protestants at the stake, and where Elizabeth executed numerous Catholics for plotting against her throne and her life, most of the oaks were indeed cut down. It is little wonder, then, that the Reformation in the Church of England produced a compromise between Protestantism and Catholicism known as "The Middle Way" - a compromise born out of decades of bloody persecution.

While each manifestation of the Reformation had its political overtones, none was dominated by political considerations more than the Reformation in England. In Germany, the religion of each principality was determined by its prince, resulting in a sort of religious checkerboard. The same was true of England as a whole in the sixteenth century. Unfortunately for most of those committed to either the Protestant or Catholic cause, the rulers of England alternated - if Germany was like a checkerboard, England was more like a yoyo. For this reason, the simplest way to study the English Reformation is to divide the sixteenth century among the members of the Tudor family who ruled England during those years.

HENRY VIII (1509-1547)

England was prepared for the Reformation for many of the same reasons we have already seen in our study of Protestantism in continental Europe. The church was openly corrupt to the point of being a public disgrace. When Chaucer wrote his *Canterbury Tales* in the late Middle Ages, few of his clergymen come off as sympathetic characters. Instead, they are almost uniformly worldly, wealthy, pleasure-seeking, and corrupt. During the reign of Henry VIII, the most visible example of the corruption of the church was the Lord Chancellor of England, Cardinal Wolsey. Besides being Lord Chancellor (chief advisor to the king) and a cardinal, he held numerous church offices, including the archbishopric of York, and was also the papal legate (official representative) in England. He possessed enormous power and wealth second only to the king himself, and showed little or no concern for spiritual matters. Following the example set by several of the Renaissance popes, he not only fathered illegitimate children, but elevated them to high church office.

The desire for reform had its roots in several sources. The work of Wycliffe over a century before had spawned a movement known as the Lollards - poor persecuted lay preachers who were dedicated to spreading the Word of God among the people in the towns and villages of England. The Lollards survived into the sixteenth century, and the hunger for God's Word that they helped to stimulate certainly prepared some for the Reformation. The new learning of the Renaissance also led many to question the church's authority. The Dutch humanist Erasmus had visited England a number of times, and his writings were given wide circulation. The universities were full of talk of reform, stimulated not only by Erasmus, but also by Luther. At Cambridge University, the White Horse Inn became the meeting place for reform-minded students. They spent so much time discussing Luther's teachings that students called the place "Little Germany." Among these were the men who were to lead the English Reformation - Thomas Bilney, Robert Barnes, William Tyndale, John Frith, Thomas Cranmer, Hugh Latimer, Nicholas Ridley, and Miles Coverdale, among others. Yet their talk of reform might never have advanced beyond the point of talk had it not been for the great political crisis of Henry's reign - his obsession with the need for a male heir.

It is all too easy for people in our day to think of Henry VIII as a womanizing buffoon, complete with his six wives and numerous mistresses. Nothing could be further from the truth. Henry was one of the shrewdest rulers of his age, and one of the best examples of the ideal prince pictured by Machiavelli in his famous work on power politics. If it is foolish to picture Henry as a buffoon, however, it is equally wrong-headed to view him as a Reformer. Despite the fact that he initiated the break between the Church of England and Rome, he remained throughout his life more a Catholic than a Protestant, and more a humanist than a Catholic.

England had just passed through an age of terrible turmoil - the civil wars known as the Wars of the Roses that had torn England apart in the fifteenth century. These wars had ended only when the Lancastrian prince Henry Tudor had married the Yorkist princess Margaret and ascended the throne as Henry VII. In order to assure the stability of his realm, Henry had arranged to marry his son and heir, Arthur, to Catherine of Aragon, the young daughter of Ferdinand and Isabella of Spain. Unfortunately, Arthur spoiled his plans by dying less than six months after the marriage. Henry had no intention of losing his alliance with Spain, or of allowing Catherine to return home with the enormous dowry she had brought with her, so he offered to marry his second son, Henry, to Catherine, despite the fact that he was considerably younger than the Spanish princess. Such an arrangement posed a problem because the Catholic Church had taught for centuries that marrying one's brother's widow amounted to incest, based on Leviticus 20:21 (they seem to have missed the point that the marriage is forbidden because the brother is still alive; Deuteronomy 25:5 clearly states that a brother not only could, but *should* marry his deceased brother's widow in order to carry on the family inheritance). Such problems were minor, however, because the popes were always ready to grant dispensations allowing such marriages, if the price was right. Thus the young Henry was permitted to marry Catherine, and the marriage was consummated when Henry ascended the throne as Henry VIII upon the death of his father in 1509.

The marriage appears to have been relatively happy, though Henry did have several mistresses, but Catherine failed to produce a male heir. All her sons died in infancy, and the only surviving child was a daughter, Mary. By 1525, Henry was beginning to wonder if God was punishing him for marrying his brother's wife (Leviticus 20:21 does mention childlessness as the penalty). Catherine by this time was pushing forty, and the chances of getting a male heir from her looked slim indeed. Without a male heir, England might be plunged into renewed civil war when Henry died, so Henry decided that, for the security of realm, he needed a new wife. It didn't hurt in the least that an attractive young lady in court, Anne Boleyn, had come to Henry's attention as a possible replacement. He thus told his Chancellor, Cardinal Wolsey, to arrange with the pope to have the marriage with Catherine annulled (divorce was unthinkable to a Catholic such as Henry; the marriage could not be ended - it must be declared to have never existed in the first place).

Such a procedure did pose certain problems, however, as Wolsey soon discovered. Though such things had been done before, the pope could not easily cancel the special dispensation given by his predecessor - such a move would undermine the authority of the papacy, which would be hard-pressed to maintain a claim to infallibility when one pope directly contradicted the man who had reigned before him. Secondly, the pope found himself caught in a political dilemma from which there seemed to be no escape. In 1527, the Holy Roman Emperor Charles V had sacked Rome and taken the pope prisoner. Charles just happened to be the grandson of Ferdinand and Isabella, and the nephew of Catherine of Aragon. The pope was thus in no position to do anything that might upset Charles. On the other hand, he could ill afford to let Henry VIII follow through with his threat to cut the Church of England off from the authority of Rome. Consequently, the pope took the only course open to him - he stalled. He sent his representative, Cardinal Campeggio, to England with explicit orders to do nothing, and to take as much time as possible doing it.

The pope's stall tactics only served to antagonize Henry further. Poor Wolsey became the scapegoat for his wrath. Because of his inability to obtain the desired annulment, he lost his offices and most of his property, and was on the way to the Tower of London to await execution when he died, contemplating the insecurity of life as a royal favorite. Few mourned him, however. Henry next elevated the great Renaissance scholar Thomas More to the post of Chancellor, but found that More was too much a man of conscience to give the king what he wanted. Like many other Englishmen of this era, his principles cost him his head. Henry finally found a man after his own heart, however, in a young Cambridge scholar named Thomas Cranmer. Cranmer first came to the king's attention when he suggested that the matter of the annulment would be more profitably submitted to the theological faculties of the great universities, rather than waiting around for a papal dispensation. Henry saw this as his way to get around the pope, and immediately sent Cranmer off to Europe to gather opinions. The opinion poll produced mixed results, and some of the opinions, particularly from the English universities, were given under considerable duress, but there were enough positive opinions that Henry felt warranted in proceeding with his plans. When the Archbishop of Canterbury, the highest church official in England, died in 1532, Henry knew exactly whom he wanted as his new archbishop. Cranmer, however, did not want the job. He wanted nothing more than to return to Cambridge and spend his life in teaching, writing, and quiet study. Henry, however, was a hard man to refuse, and Cranmer became the Archbishop of Canterbury in 1533. Shortly after, he not only annulled Henry's marriage to Catherine of Aragon, but also pronounced the secret marriage between Henry and Anne Boleyn (contracted in January of that year because Anne was already pregnant with the child who was to become Elizabeth I) legitimate. Within a year, Catherine and her daughter Mary were virtually imprisoned in separate remote castles, Elizabeth had been born, and Parliament had declared Henry "the only supreme head on earth of the Church of England" - quite a step for one who had been declared "Defender of the Faith" by the pope in 1521 for his pamphlet attacking Luther's view of the sacraments. The pope quickly excommunicated Henry and declared the throne of England vacant, but the time had long passed when such steps posed a serious threat to European monarchs.

Henry VIII initiated the break with Rome because he wanted power, not because he wanted reform. In fact, the only reforms he permitted during his reign were those that enhanced his own power. The most notable of these was his order to disband the monasteries. His excuse for doing this was his contention that the monks had given allegiance to a foreign power - the pope - which was a violation of the medieval law of *Praemunire*. Any opposition to his action was quickly silenced. The monks themselves were for the most part sent into retirement with generous pensions, while the monastic lands were sold off to the nobility at good prices, which pleased both the nobles and the king, whose treasury benefitted from the transaction. The most powerful men in the land now had a vested interest in maintaining Henry in power and in keeping the pope's nose out of English affairs.

As far as the doctrine and practice of the Church of England were concerned, Henry never intended to deviate significantly from traditional

Roman Catholicism. Three factors contributed to the growth of reform during his reign despite his intentions, however. The first of these was Henry's own participation in European politics. In his dealings with the Catholic powers of France and Spain, he often found it useful to maintain a balance by negotiating with the Protestants of Germany. Such negotiations necessitated certain concessions to English Protestants, and provided several opportunities for change in the English church. Those changes were stimulated by several of Henry's closest advisors, notably Thomas Cromwell, a pragmatic politician to whom Henry had entrusted the task of dissolving the monasteries, and Thomas Cranmer, the Archbishop of Canterbury. Cromwell favored reform for reasons of political expediency. In fact, he tried to construct a formal alliance with the German Protestants by arranging a marriage between Henry and the German Anne of Cleves (wife number four, if anyone is counting). Henry detested Anne at first sight, however, and Cromwell was executed for treason shortly thereafter. Cranmer, meanwhile, had slowly been developing Protestant convictions as a result of his own study. He was also convinced that the Christian owed absolute obedience to his God-ordained sovereign, however, so he rarely opposed anything that Henry wanted to do (he personally dissolved three of Henry's marriages, for instance, and often assented to the execution of stubborn religious extremists). In doctrinal matters, Cranmer was not afraid to express his views to Henry, and objected strongly to the explicitly Catholic *Six Articles*, for instance, but willingly submitted to his king after a decision had been rendered. In fact, since the *Six Articles* forbid clerical marriage, among other things, Cranmer sent his wife to Germany when they were passed (the inconvenience she suffered in this and other times, when she was required to travel while concealed in a chest, caused historian Roland Bainton somewhat facetiously to refer to her as "one of the minor martyrs of the Reformation"). Cranmer's loyalty and discretion allowed him to survive under Henry's protection at a time when many more outspoken men became victims of the block and the stake.

The third factor that contributed to reform during the reign of Henry VIII was the dissemination of the English Bible. We have already seen that the Catholic Church generally opposed the translation of the Bible into the common languages of the people on the ground that it would stimulate heresy among the ignorant. By the beginning of the sixteenth century, the only translation of the Bible into English was the one done by Wycliffe, which was of rather poor quality because it was translated from the Latin Vulgate rather than from the Hebrew and Greek originals. The man who saw the need for a good English translation of the Bible and was determined to fill that need was William Tyndale. Tyndale became convinced of the need for an English Bible while studying at Cambridge. When he presented his idea to some of the leading churchmen of England, they showed no interest, realizing that the king would never approve the work. Tyndale decided to do the work in the friendlier confines of Protestant Europe, and ship the results back to England. He found a friendly publisher at Worms in Germany, but when his work began to circulate, the Catholic authorities moved to put a stop to it. The result was that Tyndale was constantly on the move, traveling from place to place, concealing his manuscripts, and smuggling his Bibles into England in bales of merchandise. These Bibles (Tyndale eventually finished the entire New Testament and several portions of the Old Testament, but died before the entire Bible could be completed) caused a major sensation in England, and Henry ordered his men to put a stop to the smuggling. One bishop came up with a particularly brilliant idea. He decided to buy the copies as soon as they landed in port, and then burn them in the public square before anyone could read them. He contacted a merchant who was familiar with the cross-channel trade, and the merchant agreed to make the necessary arrangements. The merchant went straight to Tyndale, however, and told him that he had found a buyer for his Bibles. Tyndale objected that the bishop was buying the Bibles only to burn them, but the merchant convinced Tyndale that the money could finance a much larger second printing, while the burning of the

The Middle Way

Bibles would produce all sorts of publicity that would encourage the people to obtain Bibles, while making the king and his bishop look like villains. Tyndale finally agreed, and so for several years the English church actually financed Tyndale's underground press! The authorities finally did catch up with Tyndale, and he was arrested, strangled, and burned at the stake in 1536 in present-day Belgium, but his work became the foundation for most of the English translations made in the century following his death. His work was used extensively by his associate Miles Coverdale, who worked on the Great Bible and the Geneva Bible, among others, and also contributed much of the language that was later incorporated into the King James Bible of 1611.

By the time Henry died in 1547, he left behind one wife (Catherine Parr - wife #6), three children, all of whom were to rule England (Mary Tudor, daughter of Catherine of Aragon, Elizabeth, daughter of Anne Boleyn, and Edward, son of Jane Seymour - wife #3), and a church that was essentially Catholic in its doctrine and practice, yet was bursting at the seams with the drive for reform.

EDWARD VI (1547-1553)

That drive found expression during the brief reign of Henry's only surviving son, a sickly child of nine named Edward. Though his body was frail, however, his mind was sharp, and the precocious lad was unquestionably committed to the Protestant cause. Under the guidance of the regents who ruled as Protectors during his reign, first his uncle the Duke of Somerset, and later the Duke of Northumberland, Edward openly encouraged the process that made the Church of England truly Protestant. The leaders of the reform were three men from that group who had gathered to discuss the writings of Luther in that Cambridge tavern some twenty-five years earlier - Hugh Latimer, Nicholas Ridley, and Thomas Cranmer.

Latimer was a great and eloquent preacher whose outspokenness had led to some time in the Tower of London during the reign of Henry VIII. When Edward took the throne, Latimer was often invited to preach at court, and his sermons spread the Gospel of salvation by the grace of God throughout the land. Ridley, meanwhile, was the theological "brains" behind the English Reformation. This quiet scholar helped to formulate the Forty-Two Articles, the new doctrinal statement adopted for the Church of England during Edward's reign. Revised as the Thirty-Nine Articles during the reign of Elizabeth, this document continues today as the theological foundation of the English church. Cranmer, meanwhile, lent his hand to a revision of the liturgy, producing during the reign of Edward two editions of the *Book of Common Prayer*, the beauty of whose language continues today to grace the worship of the Church of England. These men were assisted by Protestant Reformers from the continent who were invited by Cranmer to teach in English universities - men such as Martin Bucer and John à Lasco, along with John Knox, who had recently been liberated from his imprisonment in a French galley.

If Edward had lived to assume the sole rule of England, the Church of England might have been much different than it is today. The direction in which these Reformers were moving was much like that of Calvin in Geneva. But Edward did not live to reign by himself or produce an heir - he died at the age of sixteen. The Protectors who ruled during his minority may have encouraged Protestantism, but they were politically corrupt, grasping for themselves and their friends whatever they could manage to accumulate. Not only that, but the Duke of Northumberland initiated a scheme to keep Edward's sister Mary from ascending the throne after Edward's death. He suggested that Mary should be declared an illegitimate daughter of Henry VIII (this would require an alteration in Henry's will), and that a cousin, sixteen-year-old Jane Grey (who wanted nothing to do with the whole mess), should be declared the rightful heir. Northumberland convinced Edward to approve the scheme because Jane was devoutly Protestant while Mary was just as obviously Catholic, but meanwhile Northumberland arranged for Lady Jane to marry his son. When Edward died, many nobles agreed to recognize Jane as the rightful queen, but the majority of the people saw through Northumberland's power play, and, sick of the corruption under the Protectors, rushed to support Mary. The conspirators, including poor Lady Jane, were quickly arrested and executed, and Mary Tudor ascended the throne.

MARY (1553-1558)

When Mary Tudor became queen, she was a thirty-seven year old who had aged well beyond her years. For most of her life, she had been abused by members of her own family: disowned by her father Henry, separated from her mother Catherine, made subservient to her sister Elizabeth, and disgraced as the illegitimate offspring of a non-existent marriage by much of the general population. The harsh treatment she had received produced in her two characteristics that were to dominate her brief reign: a deep bitterness against her father and all he had accomplished, which was transferred to the English Protestants in general, and a personal insecurity that led to her pathetic, unrequited love for her dashing young husband, Philip II of Spain.

When Mary came to the throne, everyone knew she was Catholic, but few realized the extent to which Catholicism dominated her thinking. Many in England rejoiced when she threw out the corrupt regency that had controlled England during the reign of Edward. Protestantism had successfully penetrated the upper levels of British society, but the vast majority of peasants were every bit as Catholic as they had always been, and neither knew nor understood very much about the disputes going on among the leaders of church and state. They took occasional changes in the prayer book in stride, and continued to believe what they had always believed. Most of the nobles anticipated that Mary would return to the independent form of Catholicism established by her father. Many had no firm ties to Protestantism (Northumberland, for instance, openly returned to the Catholic Church before his execution; as with many others, for him religion was a matter of political convenience), and would not mourn in the least at the departure of the Calvinists who had been pushing so hard for change in the church.

Had Mary indeed followed in the footsteps of her father, her reign would be remembered much differently today. The people praised her for clearing the corrupt nobles out of the government, and many cheered her restoration of Catholicism when she removed the Forty-Two Articles and *Book of Common Prayer* produced during the reign of Edward. Two moves by Mary began to turn the people against her, however. A year after she took the throne, Cardinal Reginald Pole, an Englishman who had been in exile since Henry VIII declared himself Supreme Head of the Church of England, returned as papal legate. He immediately made it clear that his purpose was to return England and its church to the Catholic fold, not only in belief and practice, but also in submission to the pope. Parliament indeed did agree to this, and Pole granted absolution to the English church for their rebellion, but many of the nobles started to get nervous. What if Mary tried to reestablish the monasteries? There was hardly a noble family in England that did not by that time possess land that had formerly belonged to the church. The nobles may have wanted a Catholic Church of England, but they had no intention of giving their land back to the pope or his representatives. After several abortive attempts to reestablish monasteries in England, Mary recognized that what she was attempting here was politically suicidal, and gave up the effort. But the nobles never forgot that their queen was a woman whose religion caused her to put principle above politics - an attitude for which they had little liking.

Her second error was her marriage to Philip of Spain. Charles V, the Holy Roman Emperor and Mary's cousin, had long coveted greater influence in England. He gave some thought to the possibility of marrying Mary himself, but realized that his reign was almost over and that such a union would have limited political benefit. Instead, he arranged for Mary to marry his son Philip, to whom he was planning to abdicate his domains in the near future. Mary, who had known little affection in her sad life, fell pitifully in love with Philip, who was eleven years younger than she, but he saw the marriage as a political expediency and no more. After the marriage was contracted, Philip remained in England for a year to try to produce an heir (without success), then returned home to become King Philip II of Spain, and rarely saw his wife thereafter. The marriage to Philip had far more serious consequences than Mary's unrequited love, however - it was enormously unpopular with the English people. To them, Spain was a greedy, grasping neighbor, and the last thing they wanted to see was their sickly queen married to a vigorous young Spanish king. With little difficulty, people began visualizing what England would look like as a Spanish province.

It was only after her popularity began to wane that Mary initiated the terror that was to earn her the nickname "Bloody Mary." The leading Protestants had been in prison since the beginning of her reign, some for having lent their support to the plot to put Lady Jane Grey on the throne, others for their refusal to submit to the Catholic Church. Among these were bishops Latimer, Ridley, and Hooper, and Archbishop Cranmer. In 1555, the executions began. Latimer and Ridley were burned at the stake on the same day, with Latimer encouraging Ridley by telling him that they would, in their deaths, light a candle in England that would never be put out. Cranmer received special attention. Because he was an archbishop, and a papal appointee (he had become Archbishop of Canterbury shortly before the break with Rome), he could not be executed without papal consent. Mary made good use of the waiting period, pressuring Cranmer to recant his Protestant faith and return to the Catholic fold. After months of mental and physical duress he did indeed recant, affirming that he had been mistaken in his repudiation of Catholicism. This did not satisfy Mary, however. She could never forget that Cranmer had been responsible for annulling her mother's marriage to her father and forever branding her as illegitimate in the eyes of many Englishmen. Recantation or not, Cranmer had to die. Before being taken to the stake, he was forced to read his recantation in public from the front of the church. To everyone's surprise, he announced instead that his recantation had been false, that he had made it under pressure, and that he wished to reaffirm his faith in all he had taught in his years of service to the church. He was dragged from the platform and hurried to the stake, where he deliberately thrust his right hand into the fire first, so that the part of his body that had given offense by signing the recantation could first be consumed.

In all, somewhat less than three hundred people were sent to their deaths during the final three years of Mary's reign. There have been many rulers who shed more blood than Bloody Mary, but few whose executions have made a greater impact. As was true in the early years of the Roman persecutions, the blood of the martyrs proved to be seed. Men and women were cheered by crowds who gathered as they were led to the stake, and when Mary died in 1558, it was with the almost universal loathing of her countrymen. Her infamy was assured with the publication of accounts of the deaths of many of the Marian martyrs by the Protestant John Foxe, whose *Book of Martyrs* concentrates much of its attention on those who died during the reign of Mary Tudor.

ELIZABETH I (1558-1603)

One of the great ironies of the Tudor dynasty is that the son Henry VIII schemed so much to produce, that "chip off the old block," ultimately turned out to be a daughter - the baby born to Anne Boleyn shortly after their marriage. Elizabeth ascended the throne at the age of twenty-five, and reigned for almost half a century. The "Virgin Queen" was with little question the shrewdest and most capable politician of the sixteenth century.

It was during the reign of Elizabeth that the Middle Way of Anglicanism began to take on many of its characteristic features. While Elizabeth herself had no religious convictions that anyone has ever been able to discern (if she had any, she worked very hard to keep them to herself), she knew that her handling of the religious issue was the key to her success and survival as queen. For her, Protestantism was the only serious alternative. The pope had never recognized the annulment of Henry and Catherine's marriage, and thus considered Elizabeth to be illegitimate. Besides, two Catholic claimants to the throne waited in the wings to dispute her legal title at the first opportunity. Mary Queen of Scots was the granddaughter of Henry VII, and thus Elizabeth's cousin. Since Edward and Mary had died childless, she would be next in line if Elizabeth were disqualified. Philip II of Spain also had his claim to the throne, having been the husband of the recently-deceased Mary. Elizabeth knew she would get no support from the pope; she had to seek it among the Protestants. She had no taste, however, for the strict, narrow, and divisive approach to Christianity spreading out of Geneva. Her path was one of inclusion through compromise.

Elizabeth recognized that England contained a wide variety of religious viewpoints. Her hope was that if religious practice could be unified, people would be willing to keep their beliefs to themselves, and eventually would come to believe what they were reciting in church each Sunday. She thus sought to place pragmatic moderates in all major church offices, and watered down the wording of the prayer book and creed to the extent that almost everyone in England could use them, even if doing so required reading into them their own favored interpretations. Elizabeth didn't really care whether or not everyone thought the same way, as long as they acted uniformly and submitted themselves to her rule. In this she was remarkably successful. As long as people went to church, read the prayer book, and affirmed the Thirty-Nine Articles (her revision condensed the old creed a bit), she persecuted no one. As it turned out, only two types of people succeeded in earning her wrath - Catholics and Puritans.

The new liturgy was such that many Catholics could use it in good conscience, but not all were willing to do so. Some were determined to bring the Church of England back to full submission to the pope, and plotted to do so. An Englishman named William Allen, with the help of the Jesuits, established an English seminary at Douai in Belgium (later relocated to Rheims). This seminary was the source of the Catholic translation of the Bible into English - the Douai Version - which served for many years as the Catholic equivalent to the King James Version. The teachers at the seminary also trained priests who would then return to England and agitate for the restoration of Catholicism. Some of these zealots hatched plots that included the overthrow or assassination of Elizabeth in favor of Mary Queen of Scots. When these plots were uncovered, Jesuits and students from the Douai seminary were banned from England, and numerous Catholics were executed. After one particular plot to which Mary herself had been a party was foiled, Elizabeth was forced somewhat reluctantly to have Mary, who had been in custody in England since being forced from the throne of Scotland by Knox and the Scottish Protestants, executed for treason. After Mary's death, Philip II decided that the time was ripe for the invasion of England. As long as Mary lived, overthrowing Elizabeth would only help the cause of France, where Mary had been raised and where she had married her first husband. With Mary safely out of the way, Philip now was prepared to advance his own interests. In 1588, he gathered the Invincible Armada and sent it into the English Channel. The defeat of the Armada by the smaller, faster English ships not only ended the commercial dominance of Spain and opened the way for England to expand her empire, but also sounded the death knell for state Catholicism in England.

In much the same way that Elizabeth disliked and feared the Catholic zealots who would not conform and submit to her rule, so she hated the extreme Protestants who refused to be satisfied with the religious compromise of the Elizabethan Settlement. The men who had gone into exile during the reign of Mary Tudor had studied at the schools of Christ in Geneva, Zurich, and elsewhere, and came back to England full of zeal to turn the Anglican Church into something resembling the Reformed Churches of continental Europe. This was the last thing Elizabeth wanted. She allowed these men, who came to be called Puritans because of their desire to purify the church according to the Word of God, to talk as much as they wanted - as long as they used the prayer book and affirmed the creed. She also made sure they did not have access to high church office, and that those in power kept their eyes on any efforts made by the Puritans to bring about change in the church. Thus she suppressed Puritan meetings known as *prophesyings*, which were basically preaching services held in homes and public buildings, insisting that any preaching that was to be done must be done in church buildings at the appointed times, with the permission of the local bishop. She wanted no rabble-rousers in her kingdom.

The Puritans responded to her strictures in different ways. Some conformed and waited for the day when change from within would be possible. Others sought reform within the church through outspoken preaching and teaching; many of these suffered imprisonment or exile because of their insistence on publicizing their views. Still others left the church altogether, deciding like the European Anabaptists that the true church could only be found in a voluntary society of committed believers. These last came to be known as Separatists or Independents. As Elizabeth's reign progressed, the Puritans won more and more Englishmen to their way of thinking. Their beliefs, and the conflicts among the different varieties of Puritans, became the dominant issue during the Stuart monarchy - the subject of our next chapter.

MAKING DRY BONES LIVE

While there are many lessons to be learned from the history of the Reformation in Tudor England, I want to concentrate our attention on one of the most ambiguous men in an age of ambiguity - Thomas Cranmer, the scholar who earned Henry VIII's favor by his willingness to dissolve the royal marriage, later proceeded to help Henry shed two more unwanted wives, survived much criticism as Henry's Archbishop of Canterbury, became a leader of the Reformation during the reign of Edward VI, then suffered imprisonment, torture, recantation, and death during the reign of Mary Tudor.

What was Thomas Cranmer? Was he a sincere Christian who wanted nothing more than to return to his college to study and teach, one who shunned the public eye but found it unavoidable, one whose own religious convictions deepened during his years of public service through his own study, and finally one who overcame a momentary weakness to die bravely as a hero of the faith? Or was he a pragmatic politician to the core, one who was willing to change his convictions freely to please his sovereign, who earned the favor of Henry through abject sycophancy, manipulated the young and impressionable Edward, and finally took his stand only after recantation had failed to save his life in the face of Mary's vengeance?

To view Cranmer in either of these ways is to miss the point. Thomas Cranmer was the type of Christian and scholar who was sincere enough about his beliefs, and committed strongly enough to the truth, to recognize that he did not have a monopoly on that very important commodity. Men who go through true agony of soul are those who are humble enough to believe that they just might be wrong about certain things. Ironically, one of Cranmer's few certainties was the one that ultimately got him into trouble. In addition to the basics of the Christian faith, there was one thing Cranmer was sure of, and that was that Scripture commanded Christians to submit to the sovereign under whose authority God had placed them. As long as he was convinced that his sovereign was not demanding anything contrary to God's Word, Cranmer gave that sovereign his complete allegiance. This approach was successful during Henry's reign, when Cranmer's own convictions were still forming, and gave glorious freedom during the reign of Edward, when the Archbishop did so much to shape the doctrine and practice of the English Church. When Mary came to the throne, however, Cranmer faced a dilemma. Who, in fact, was England's true sovereign? A case could be made for Lady Jane Grey, certainly. But what about Mary? Cranmer himself had annulled her parents' marriage, yet now she had been proclaimed monarch of the realm. Cranmer entertained just enough uncertainty in his mind about his former judgments that the long period of imprisonment and deprivation caused him to recant. Long months in isolation, repeated arguments presented by his opponents, and even seeing the executions of his long-time friends all worked on his mind, so that he finally gave in under the pressure. He regained a measure of assurance and conviction only after the pressure was removed and he faced certain death.

Which, then, is better - to be sure and unbending in the face of all opposition, or to be humble and open to the arguments of others? The first way leads to a sure and confident witness - or to bigotry and division. The second may produce harmony, or it may lead to tortuous hours of doubt and vacillation. The key here is to recognize the difference between those certainties about which there can be no doubt, and those issues over which there will always be differences. The former are worth dying for; the latter require compromise for the peace of the church and the testimony of Christ in the world. A man of conscience knows that he must never waver on the essentials of the faith, but humbly acknowledges his uncertainty on the multitude of issues that divide Christians. Thomas Cranmer was a man of conscience who was humble enough to doubt his own opinions, but who ultimately stood firm for the truth in the face of death. His doubts and uncertainties should not be held against him.

FOR REVIEW AND FURTHER THOUGHT

1. Why is the Church of England often spoken of as the *Middle Way*?

2. What developments in England prior to the sixteenth century paved the way for the acceptance of the Reformation?

3. What was "Little Germany," and what role did it play in the English Reformation?

4. In what senses may Henry VIII be viewed as a participant in the Protestant Reformation? In what senses would such a view be ridiculous?

5. What events led to the marriage between Henry VIII and Catherine of Aragon?

6. Why did some consider Henry and Catherine's marriage unlawful?

7. What is the difference between a divorce and an annulment? Why did Henry want the latter rather than the former?

8. Why did the pope find it impossible to nullify Henry's marriage to Catherine?

9. How did Thomas Cranmer first come to the attention of Henry VIII?

10. What reforms did Henry introduce into the English church, and why did he want them?

11. What was the medieval law of *Praemunire*, and how did Henry use it to strengthen his power in England?

12. How did Henry's political maneuvers contribute to the growth of the Reformation?

13. In what way did the church authorities in England actually contribute to the circulation of Tyndale's translation of the New Testament?

14. What were the major contributions made to the growth of Protestantism in England during the reign of Edward VI by Latimer, Ridley, and Cranmer?

15. In what ways did Calvin's work in Geneva influence the development of the English Reformation?

16. Why were the people of England glad to see Mary come to the throne after the death of Edward?

17. What were the political and religious reasons for the attempt by the Duke of Northumberland to place Lady Jane Grey on the throne of England after the death of Edward VI?

18. What aspects of Mary Tudor's upbringing made her bitter against the English Protestants?

19. Why did most Englishmen oppose the marriage of Mary to Philip II of Spain?

20. Why was Mary so determined that Thomas Cranmer should be put to death, even after he recanted his Protestant faith?

21. What book was largely responsible for the fact that Mary Tudor came to be known as Bloody Mary?

22. What made Elizabeth realize early in her reign that she would have to come out in favor of Protestantism?

23. What did Elizabeth do to enable as many people as possible to support her policies and her church?

24. What led Elizabeth to persecute English Catholics?

25. What were the most notable accomplishments of the English seminary at Douai, Belgium?

26. Who were the Puritans, and where did they get their name?

27. Why did Elizabeth dislike the Puritans?

28. What were *prophesyings*, and why did Elizabeth forbid them?

29. How did the Puritans respond to Elizabeth's repression?

30. How would you evaluate the character of Thomas Cranmer? Do you think he was a hero of the faith or a cowardly compromiser? Why?

24

THE HOLY COMMONWEALTH

If someone today refers to another person as a "Puritan," it is not likely to be a compliment. We tend to think of the Puritans as a bunch of sour-pussed stick-in-the-muds whose greatest mission in life was to keep people from having any fun. While the Puritans, both in England and America, did oppose certain kinds of amusements they considered immoral, especially those practiced on the Sabbath, most people don't realize that they were considered radicals in their own time. In the face of an English church determined to follow the path of compromise, they clamored for radical change - change that would "purify" the church and society and bring both in line with God's Word. In this chapter, we will examine the success and failure of the Puritan enterprise in England in the seventeenth century, while reserving the American Puritans for consideration in chapter thirty-five.

THE EARLY STUARTS - THE DIVINE RIGHT OF KINGS

When the great compromiser Elizabeth died in 1603, James VI of Scotland, son of Mary Queen of Scots and Lord Darnley, came to the English throne as James I of England. Since James had been raised under the tutelage of Scottish Presbyterians, the Puritans saw an opportunity to institute the change Elizabeth had been unwilling to pursue. A group of Puritans met James on his way to London and presented him with a petition bearing over a thousand signatures. Called the Millenary Petition (from the Latin word for "thousand"), the document outlined various practices that the Puritans considered unbiblical (mostly carryovers from the Catholic Church), and requested that James remove these from the practice of the Church of England. The new king agreed to a conference, which was to be held the following year at Hampton Court.

What the Puritans did not realize is that James' experience with the Scottish Presbyterians had made him resentful rather than making him presbyterian. He had had his fill of commoners telling him how he should live and how he should run his kingdom. Besides, several representatives of the High Church party had already visited James in Scotland, and their fawning and flattery had made an enormous impression on this most egotistical of monarchs. James quickly decided that it would be far better to deal with a few bishops, who not only were aristocrats like himself but also clearly recognized his absolute God-ordained authority, than with these pestilential Puritans.

When the Hampton Court Conference began in 1604, the Puritans found that the deck was hopelessly stacked against them. Only a handful of Puritans were permitted to attend the conference, and it soon became clear that James had already made up his mind. The king fancied himself to be a great scholar, and personally responded to the arguments set forth by the Puritans. It mattered little that his arguments were weak - the only person those arguments needed to convince was James himself. James treated the Puritans very rudely at the conference, and flatly rejected all of their proposals except one. Recognizing that a church organization in which all elders were equal could easily give people the idea that all were equal in the political realm as well, he insisted that monarchy and the presbyterian system agreed as well as God and the devil, and that a church with no bishop would soon produce a state with no king. James told the Puritans that they would either conform to his wishes, or he would harry them from the kingdom. The tragedy is that his stubbornness, and that of his son, directly contributed to the fulfillment of his apprehensions.

The one Puritan proposal that James did accept involved a new English translation of the Bible. While the churches of England had had authorized English Bibles since the time of Henry VIII, the most popular version among the people was the Geneva Bible, translated by English exiles in Geneva during the reign of Mary Tudor. The first Bible to divide the text into verses, it was remarkably easy to use, and included Calvinistic marginal notes that the people found helpful (somewhat like a modern reference Bible). James considered these marginal notes politically explosive, however - after all, they were presbyterian - and was glad for the opportunity to put a Bible into the churches and into the hands of the people that would not steer their thinking along dangerous lines. He thus commissioned fifty-four scholars of varying theological positions to prepare a new translation. The translators relied heavily on the earlier work of Tyndale and others, and consulted the best manuscripts of the Hebrew and Greek testaments available to them at the time. The result was the Authorised Version, or King James Version of 1611, which was to become the most widely-used English Bible in history, remaining the most popular English translation for some 350 years.

The Puritans made great gains during the reign of James I, largely because James succeeded in identifying himself with the forces of tyranny, thus driving most of those who favored greater political liberties into the arms of the Puritans. Three policies contributed to this movement of many toward Puritanism for political reasons. The first was James' open-minded attitude toward Catholicism. His mother had been Catholic, of course, but he had never really known her well, and had been raised by Protestants. He and his royal successors, however, could never seem to resist the fascination of the Roman Church with its absolute authority emanating from the top. James had married a Catholic (Anne of Denmark), and spent most of his reign trying to form an alliance with Spain. When that effort failed, he managed to marry his son Charles to the French princess Henrietta Maria, a devout Catholic. Parliament did not favor these alliances with Catholic powers, and was particularly upset when James refused to help the Protestant side when the Thirty Years' War broke out in Germany.

James probably would have developed even stronger Catholic sympathies had it not been for one of the most notorious conspiracies in English history, the famous Gunpowder Plot of 1605. A group of Catholic noblemen, aided and abetted by the Jesuits, planned to overthrow the English government and return the country to Catholicism. In order to accomplish this, they arranged for a fanatic named Guy Fawkes to blow up the Parliament building when the king and his son Charles were in it. Word of the conspiracy leaked out, however, and Fawkes was caught with thirty-six barrels of gunpowder in a cellar of Parliament. James may have formed alliances with foreign Catholics, but this attempt on his life guaranteed that he would never trust English ones.

The second aspect of James' policy that alienated many was his attempt to force an episcopal form of church government on his Scottish subjects. He was determined that the Scottish church would be ruled by bishops, and in 1610 appointed several of them. As long as these bishops did not tell the Scottish churches what to believe or how to worship, they caused little trouble, but the seeds were sown for conflict during the reign of Charles I.

Probably the greatest contribution James made to Puritan popularity was his effort to provide greater funding for the support of the Anglican clergy. His first Archbishop of Canterbury, Richard Bancroft, determined that the clergy in each parish should receive a full tenth of the goods produced in that parish. He worked hard to remove many of the exceptions from paying tithes the nobles had been granted during the previous century. The nobles, of course, resented the threat to their pocketbooks greatly indeed, and began screaming about the liberties of Englishmen from the tyranny of church and king. They and the Puritans quickly became strange, though somewhat predictable, bedfellows.

The Holy Commonwealth

Meanwhile, James was keeping his word, energetically harrying the Puritans at every opportunity. He revived the Star Chamber, a court introduced by Henry VII over a century before in which normal civil liberties did not apply, to deprive Puritans of their liberty. Those who refused to conform to the state church were often physically mutilated; their ears were cropped, their noses slit, and they were branded on cheeks or forehead. To rub salt into their already smarting wounds, James introduced the Book of Sports in 1618. This was allegedly a physical fitness program, but was calculated to upset the Puritans. The Book of Sports encouraged everyone to engage in physical activities, supposedly so that England would be able to put a physically fit army into the field in the event of war (this was the same year the Thirty Years' War started on the continent). The problem was that the recommended time for engaging in such sports was Sunday afternoon - a blasphemous thought to the Puritans, for whom Sabbath observance was very important indeed. James even required all ministers to announce the Book of Sports from the pulpit on Sunday mornings. Some Puritans bluntly refused, while others dutifully read it, then followed it with a rather pointed reading of the Fourth Commandment ("this is what man says, but God says this...").

James' policies toward the Puritans not only won them sympathy and supporters, but succeeded in driving many both from the kingdom and from the church. While most Puritans remained steadfast in their desire to purify the church from within, some gave up hope of ever accomplishing that and became Independents. Among these Independent congregations were the one from Scrooby, led by John Robinson, which first fled to Holland and later crossed the ocean to America - the Pilgrims. Another Independent congregation was led by John Smyth and Thomas Helwys. They too settled in Holland, where they became convinced of the truth of believer's baptism. Smyth baptized himself and then the rest of the congregation, thus making them the first English Baptists. Smyth eventually joined the Mennonites, while Helwys returned to England to form the first Baptist church on English soil.

The churches that grew from this small beginning came to be known as General Baptists, because they followed the Arminian theology the founders had acquired in the Netherlands. Another type of Baptist soon arose in England known as Particular, or Calvinistic Baptists. The Particular Baptists originated in an Independent congregation in Southwark, near London, which had been founded by the Puritan Henry Jacob. In 1633, several within the congregation became convinced of believer's baptism, and asked permission to form a new church that would conform to their beliefs. Several others joined them five years later, and by the end of the seventeenth century there were a significant number of Baptist churches scattered throughout England.

When James I died in 1625, he was succeeded by his son Charles I. Charles was every bit the absolutist his father had been, but though he had a much higher level of personal morality, he was so cold and aloof that he generated even less popularity among the people of England than his father had been able to muster. He was so convinced of the need for absolute monarchy that he was determined to rule without Parliament if at all possible, so from 1629 until 1640, he did exactly that. The English people felt they had no redress for their grievances, and grievances there were aplenty.

The source of most of these grievances was a narrow-minded little pedant named William Laud, who had risen through the church hierarchy during the latter years of James I and became Archbishop of Canterbury in 1633. Laud believed in the absolute supremacy of bishops over the church every bit as much as he believed in the divine right of kings. His vision of the church was one in which what he called the Beauty of Holiness would be returned to Christian worship. This meant a return to many of the rituals of Catholicism, to altars and vestments, and the Puritans would have none of it. Laud was determined that all within the church should conform down to the last detail, or suffer the consequences. During his administration, the Star Chamber became a sort of Protestant Inquisition, producing public outrage and driving thousands of Puritans to the continent and the New World (the population of

Massachusetts Bay colony grew to over 20,000 within the first ten years of its existence).

It was Charles' determination to continue his father's policy toward Scotland, however, that brought England to the point of civil war. Incited by Laud, Charles in 1637 imposed on the Scottish Church a prayer book very much like the *Book of Common Prayer*, and incorporating many elements carried over from Catholicism. Doing this in England was one thing, but in Presbyterian Scotland, which had thoroughly purged all remnants of Catholicism over a half-century before, the king's decree constituted fighting words. When a bishop, decked out in full ecclesiastical regalia, began to lead a service in Edinburgh using the new prayer book, a vegetable peddler named Jenny Geddes became so enraged that someone would dare to "say Mass" at her that she picked up the stool on which she was sitting and flung it at the bishop's head. The bishop was able to duck the projectile, but a riot ensued, and soon all Scotland was in an uproar. Thousands of Scots signed the National Covenant, in which they swore to uphold presbyterianism at the cost of their lives if necessary.

When Scotland took up arms, Charles realized that he had no money with which to raise an army to put down the rebellion. He would have to call a session of Parliament to try to raise the needed funds. This was the biggest mistake of his life. When Parliament came together in 1640, it was for the first time in eleven years. People had been without a voice for so long they were bursting to be heard on numerous subjects, most having little to do with the problem the king had caused in Scotland. Member after member stood up to call for reform in the government and the church, completely ignoring the king's pleas to deal with the problem of raising an army. Finally the king got fed up and disbanded the Parliament after only three weeks. This "Short Parliament" did not give the king his money, but it should have given him some idea how deep the resentment was against him and his policies.

When Scottish troops crossed over the border into England, Charles realized he had no alternative and called Parliament back into session. This "Long Parliament," which sat in one form or another for the next twenty years, was completely dominated by Puritans, whether they identified themselves as such for political or religious reasons. Parliament refused to talk to Charles about money until he listened to their demands for reform in the church. They passed the Grand Remonstrance in 1641, which called for a council for the purpose of reforming the Church of England. Even then, the army, which was largely made up of Puritans and Independents of various stripes, made it clear that they had no intention of fighting the Scottish Presbyterians. The Scots then went home, convinced that the king would never be able to force the unwanted prayer book on them. By 1642, Charles had fled London, and the Royalists in Parliament had left to join the king. The Puritans were now free to do what they had been longing for years to do - reshape the English church and society along the lines laid out in Scripture. In 1643, Parliament accepted the Solemn League and Covenant, in which they agreed to work with the Scottish Presbyterians to unify the churches of England, Scotland, and Ireland along biblical lines, and with a presbyterian form of church government. In order to accomplish this purpose, the leading Puritan theologians were summoned to meet at Westminster Abbey. The Westminster Assembly, which met from 1643 to 1648, drew up the Westminster Standards - the Confession of Faith and Larger and Shorter Catechisms, which are considered the classic statement of Reformed theology and presbyterian polity. While these continue in use today in Presbyterian churches, the documents have also had a major influence on Independents and Baptists, since the Savoy Confession of 1658 (Independent) and the London Confession of 1689 (Particular Baptist) are to a large extent modeled on the work of the Westminster theologians. While the Westminster Standards were accepted immediately by the Church of Scotland, they never were fully adopted in England. Though they were passed by Parliament, they were only used in a few places in England because of the civil war then in progress. Later conflicts led the English church to discard them altogether.

The Holy Commonwealth

While the Westminster divines were deliberating, civil war broke out between the forces of the king (Cavaliers) and the Parliamentary army (Roundheads). The army was led by a brilliant and devout general named Oliver Cromwell, who knew the strength of men dedicated to a cause. His Puritan forces were accompanied by chaplains who held church services for them every Sunday, organized prayer meetings before going to battle, and marched to war singing hymns. They never lost a battle. The king's forces were more interested in plunder than anything else, and were quickly demoralized by Cromwell's New Model Army.

Two factors arose during the civil war, however, that were ultimately to spell doom for the Puritan dream. The first was the disunity among the Puritans themselves. Not only did the Puritans have a wide variety of motives for opposing the king, but they also had many different ideas about what the ideal biblical church and society should look like. The Westminster Assembly, for instance, was dominated by Presbyterians, though some Independents and Anglicans presented a minority voice. The army, however, was made up largely of Baptists and Independents, including Cromwell himself. The latter feared that the Presbyterians were merely trying to impose a different form of church tyranny on them; as John Milton put it, "Presbyter is priest writ large." These fears and disputes among the Puritans themselves not only led to the ultimate rejection of the Westminster Standards, but finally to the failure of Parliament to govern the country after the civil war ended.

The Puritans also gradually lost popular support. Some became disenchanted when they realized that the Puritans wanted some of the same strictness of discipline that had characterized Calvin's Geneva (Sabbath-keeping was now required by law, and public blasphemy was a punishable offense). Perhaps more than anything else, though, the thing that turned the country against the Puritans was what had generated so much support for them in earlier years - they created some very visible martyrs. The first of these was Archbishop Laud. Shortly after it convened, the Long Parliament arrested him for treason. This stirred up little opposition - Laud was not a popular man. However, when his case came to trial in 1645, he was acquitted because of the lack of concrete evidence against him. Parliament then made the terrible mistake of passing a Bill of Attainder (which allowed them to condemn a man to death for the safety of the realm), and executing him anyway. The public response was not at all favorable. This was nothing, however, compared to the response when Charles himself was executed by Parliament in 1649. The king had been caught trying to convince the Scots to invade England and fight for him against Parliament; he had promised to support presbyterianism in England if they would do so. After the king was captured and imprisoned, evidence was produced to prove that he had no intention of keeping his word to the Scots. Even then, few were willing to put him to death. Cromwell eventually purged all Presbyterians from the Parliament until only Independents remained, and this Rump Parliament condemned the king to death. The execution of a reigning monarch brought cries of horror from all over Europe - Catholic and Protestant countries alike. When a booklet began to circulate around England showing the king, on the night before his death, on his knees in prayer with an open Bible before him, his crown on the floor, a crown of thorns in his hand, and his gaze fixed on the crown of glory he was soon to inherit, his image as a martyr was assured. The Puritans had gone from heroes to villains with one blow of the headsman's axe.

COMMONWEALTH AND PROTECTORATE - THE PURITAN EXPERIMENT

The die was now cast against the Puritans, but Cromwell made a noble effort to institute a Commonwealth in England. Contrary to the somewhat dubious reputation he often enjoys in modern circles, Oliver Cromwell was a tolerant man, given the spirit of his age. In place of a state church that required one form of worship and outlawed all others, he instituted a system within which Presbyterians, Independents, and Baptists were all openly tolerated. The bishops were supplanted by a Board of Triers, made up of representatives of all three legal church groups, who would examine candidates for the ministry in order to determine their moral and doctrinal fitness. Congregations were free to call ministers according to their own persuasion. Only Catholic and Anglican worship were forbidden, and these more for political than religious reasons (Catholics were considered a threat to the nation because of their sympathy for foreign powers and their history of involvement in plots of all kinds, while Anglicans were considered a threat to the Commonwealth because of their allegiance to the Stuart monarchy). Even these were left alone as long as they kept their worship to themselves and disturbed no one. Another notable example of Cromwell's attitude toward toleration is that, during his regime, Jews were permitted to worship openly in synagogues in England for the first time since the Middle Ages.

Cromwell faced numerous political and military problems during his years in power. Rebellions arose in Scotland and Ireland, both of which he put down with brutal efficiency. Parliament turned out to be increasingly ineffective, and Cromwell finally disbanded it in 1653, and until his death in 1658 the Lord Protector ruled England as a virtual military dictatorship.

The Cromwell years also demonstrate clearly how religious toleration breeds religious dissent. During the Commonwealth and Protectorate, all sorts of fringe groups appeared, most of whom made little lasting impact. These groups included the Levellers, who insisted on the complete equality of all men ("any he is as good as any other he in England") and wanted to tear down all social distinctions; the Diggers, who believed that private property was the root of all evil, and got their name by digging up a plot of land on a Surrey hillside belonging to a local nobleman, planting a garden, and giving the vegetables to the poor; the Muggletonians, followers of a London tailor who thought he and his cousin were the two witnesses of Revelation 11, taught that only preachers with short hair were worthy of attention, and that reason was of the devil; and the Quintomonarchists or Fifth Monarchy Men, who believed that the fifth kingdom of Daniel 2, the Kingdom of God, was about to come to earth, and that it would do so as soon as the Antichrist (Cromwell) was overthrown.

The one group that came to prominence during the Cromwell years that did leave a significant mark on history was the Quakers, or Society of Friends. Founded by an uneducated shoemaker named George Fox, the Quakers picked up many of the tenets already espoused by the Anabaptists of Europe, such as pacifism and simplicity of lifestyle. They also followed the medieval mystics in seeking God through an Inner Light rather than by means of a visible church or an external revelation such as the Bible. The Quakers faced a great deal of persecution in their early years, largely because of the frequent disruptions of worship in which Fox engaged and the fact that Quakers refused to take oaths when called into court. Fox mellowed with age, however, and the movement mellowed with him, gradually gaining acceptance in England and making a major impact in America through the colony founded by the Quaker William Penn. Cromwell himself had a great deal of personal respect for George Fox.

There were many in England who wanted Oliver Cromwell to accept the crown and begin a new royal dynasty. Cromwell repeatedly refused, knowing that to do so while the rightful heir to the throne, Charles I's son, lived in France would be to invite renewed civil war. When Cromwell died in 1658, he was succeeded by his son Richard as Lord Protector, but Richard had none of his father's abilities, and soon submitted his resignation to Parliament. With overwhelming popular approval, Parliament invited young Charles II to return from France and restore the Stuart monarchy to the throne of England in 1660.

THE LATTER STUARTS - THE GROWTH OF CONSTITUTIONAL MONARCHY

After the Cromwell years, it would no longer have been possible to return to the absolutism of James I and Charles I. People had had a taste of liberty, and were unwilling to relinquish it. The same was true of religious toleration. Before Charles II was permitted to return to England, he was required to sign the Declaration of Breda, in which he acknowledged the authority of Parliament, and agreed to permit "liberty to tender consciences" in religion as long as it did not threaten the peace of the realm. While the years of Puritan rule had left a legacy in many areas that people wanted to retain, it also generated a major reaction in the area of public morality. Many in England were sick and tired of enforced Sabbath observance, prohibitions against public swearing, the closing of the theaters, and many other irritations from the Cromwell years. The result was a political reaction that swept into power a Parliament dominated by Anglicans. This Parliament was so anxious to wipe England clean of the remnants of Puritan rule that Charles found it impossible to keep his promises of toleration. The Anglican bishops were quickly restored to authority, and those Puritans who had had places of influence during the Protectorate, such as the Puritan poet John Milton and the Independent theologian John Owen, were forced into retirement. Parliament soon passed act after act designed to suppress the Puritans. Collectively known as the Clarendon Code, these acts included the Act of Uniformity (1662), which required the use of the Anglican prayer book in all churches; the Conventicle Act, which forbade attendance at all religious meetings not authorized by the bishop and permitted preaching only at stated services of the church; and the Five Mile Act, which required dissenting ministers to stay more than five miles from any parish in which they had previously ministered, or from any incorporated town that was large enough to send a representative to Parliament - in effect, this prevented dissenting ministers from earning a living by preaching. One of the many Puritan ministers who felt the wrath of the anti-Puritan reaction was a Baptist preacher in Bedford named John Bunyan. He spent over ten years in the Bedford jail because he would not conform to Anglican worship. It was while he was in jail that he wrote the most famous allegory in the English language, *Pilgrim's Progress*.

Morally, the Restoration era was a disgrace. Charles himself led the way by openly resorting to numerous mistresses and producing many illegitimate children (although he produced no legitimate heir to the throne). It was as if all the evil in men's hearts had been forced behind closed doors during the era of Puritan rule, but could be contained no more, and came out in one explosive orgy of immorality during the reign of Charles II. The theaters reopened, of course, and the stages were filled with bawdy comedies the likes of which are not considered fit to include in most English textbooks, even in our own permissive era. Charles was also a spendthrift, and had practically bankrupted the English treasury by the time of his death (he wound up giving William Penn the grant for Pennsylvania, for instance, because he owed a large debt to Penn's father that he was simply unable to repay).

Politically, Charles fell into the same foolish errors that had resulted in the execution of his father. His desperate need for money led him to make a secret agreement with Louis XIV of France. Charles agreed to become a Roman Catholic (he did convert to Catholicism on his deathbed) and bring England back into the Catholic fold in return for much-needed financial relief from the French king. The agreement did not become known until after Charles' death, but it was a significant factor in his brother's fall from power. He also fomented open rebellion in Scotland by trying again to force episcopacy on the Scottish church (see chapter twenty-seven). The nation never did return to Catholicism, however, because Parliament refused to cooperate with Charles' plan. In fact, in 1673, it passed the Test Act, which required all candidates for public office or for university degrees to take Anglican communion, affirm allegiance to the king as head of church and state by taking the Supremacy Oath, and repudiate transubstantiation. This act kept Catholics from public office, as well as excluding them from England's universities, until it was repealed in 1829.

Nevertheless, when Charles II died in 1685 without leaving an heir to the throne, he was replaced by his brother James II, who was an avowed Roman Catholic. He was determined to return the English Church to the arms of Rome, but he quickly found that it was not possible for a Catholic monarch to rule a Protestant nation and church successfully. When Parliament officially invited James' Protestant daughter Mary and her Dutch husband William of Orange to come to England (with an army if necessary) and assume the throne, James saw the handwriting on the wall and retired quietly to France. Accomplished without any bloodshed, the ascent of William and Mary to the throne in 1688 came to be known as the Glorious Revolution. By 1689, acts had been passed assuring that all future monarchs of England would be Protestant, and granting freedom of religion to the dissenting groups outside of the Church of England. Over a century and a half of religious conflict had finally come to a close.

MAKING DRY BONES LIVE

Many people today decry the evils of denominationalism. Why, they say, must there be so many different churches? Why can't God's people be one, the way Jesus wanted them to be? Certainly the existence of hundreds of denominations in Christendom is hard to reconcile with the biblical teaching concerning the unity of the church. But which is better - an organizationally divided church where each denomination recognizes the legitimacy of the others while maintaining its own distinctives (this is idealistic in itself, of course - many churches refuse to acknowledge the legitimacy of any outside their own circle), or a unified church that must rely on coercion or persecution to maintain outward unity?

In the end, we must recognize that denominations are the fruit of sinners living in a sinful world. Our understanding of God's Word will only be perfect when we reach heaven, so as long as we are in this world, Christians will disagree about what it means to follow Jesus Christ. Truth is important, and Christians should always be willing to stand up for what they believe. But when that certainty of truth translates into oppression of those who differ, we cease to follow our Lord. Which is better, a "unity" in which Catholics persecute Protestants, Anglicans suppress Puritans, or Puritans outlaw Catholicism, or a "disunity" that recognizes that all should be free to worship God according to the dictates of their consciences?

The Holy Commonwealth 273

FOR REVIEW AND FURTHER THOUGHT

1. Why were the Puritans considered radicals in their own day?

2. Why did the Puritans believe that James I would be sympathetic to their desire for change in the church?

3. What was the Millenary Petition, and what resulted from it?

4. What was the Hampton Court Conference? Why did James treat the Puritans so rudely?

5. What was the only positive result of the Hampton Court Conference?

6. What factors contributed to the growth of the Puritan movement during the reign of James I?

7. What was the Gunpowder Plot, and how did it influence the reign of James I?

8. How did James I and Charles I use the Star Chamber and Book of Sports to harass Puritans?

9. How did the policies of James I and Charles I contribute to the settlement of the American colonies?

10. Identify the following people in one sentence each: Guy Fawkes, Richard Bancroft, John Robinson, John Smyth, Thomas Helwys, Henry Jacob, Jenny Geddes.

11. What was the difference between the General Baptists and the Particular Baptists?

12. Why did the Puritans grow to hate Archbishop of Canterbury William Laud?

13. How did Charles I's determination to impose episcopacy on Scotland lead to his death?

14. What was the National Covenant? the Solemn League and Covenant?

15. What Protestant churches were influenced by the work of the Westminster Assembly?

16. Why did the Church of England ultimately reject the Westminster Standards?

17. What aspects of the executions of Laud and Charles I contributed to the loss of popular support sustained by the Puritans?

18. In what senses was Oliver Cromwell a tolerant ruler?

19. What was the Board of Triers, and how did it function during the Commonwealth era?

20. What dissenting groups appeared during the Cromwell regime, and what were some of their peculiarities?

21. What were some of the sources from which the Quakers acquired their teachings and practices?

22. What was the Declaration of Breda? Why was it necessary for Charles II to rule as a constitutional monarch?

23. Why was Charles II unable to keep his promises of religious toleration?

24. Why was the Restoration period characterized by such flagrant immorality?

25. What was the Clarendon Code, and how was it used to harass Puritans?

26. Identify the following in one sentence each: George Fox, John Bunyan, William Penn, Louis XIV, William and Mary.

27. What was the Test Act, and how did it foil the plans of Charles II?

28. What was the Glorious Revolution, and how did it succeed in ending religious strife in England?

29. Do you think the existence of denominations is good or bad for the church, and for the testimony of Christ in the world? Support your answer.

25

REFORM, REACTION, AND RENEWAL

The cannonball had shattered his leg. The young Spanish soldier lay on the ground at Pamplona in excruciating pain. Enemy troops soon came to collect the wounded, and they gently provided treatment for his broken limb. The military doctor set the bone badly, however, and it soon became clear that the young soldier would never again walk without a limp. After being allowed to return home, he had the bone broken and reset two more times, but his leg was never the same. Now incapable of serving his king, and having read the life stories of various saints during his period of recuperation, the young man was determined to continue his life as a soldier, not of Spain, but of Christ. He gave to Christ and His Church the same unswerving loyalty with which he had served his king. In the same way that a soldier should never question the command of an officer, he believed that the true soldier of Christ "ought always to be ready to believe that what seems to us white is black if the hierarchical Church so defines it." The young Spaniard, whose name was Ignatius Loyola, instilled this same commitment to absolute obedience into the members of the organization he later founded - the Society of Jesus, otherwise known as the Jesuits.

It is more than a little ironic that Ignatius Loyola went through many of the same doubts and fears that Luther experienced prior to his conversion. While Luther found peace in the concept of justification by faith, trusting the grace of God alone, and was willing to stand up against the entire church hierarchy on the authority of the Scriptures, Ignatius silenced his personal demons through complete surrender to Christ as personified in His Church. The difference between the two men is a perfect illustration of the difference between the Protestant reformers who left the Church of Rome and the Catholic reformers who remained within it. For the former, the authority upon which they rested was the Word of God - *sola scriptura* - even if it meant challenging the established church. For the latter, it was the Church through which the authority of Christ was administered, and they dedicated their lives to purifying that Church.

The reform movement within the Catholic Church is often erroneously referred to as the Counterreformation. The name implies that what occurred in the Church of Rome was largely a reaction against Protestantism. While the Catholic reform movement did in many ways eventually take on the character of an anti-Protestant reaction, it was initially a positive movement, a continuation of the work of the reforming councils of the fifteenth century. In fact, one of the key elements of the Catholic Reformation was in place long before Luther posted the Ninety-five Theses, while a second developed initially with little or no reference to the growth of Protestantism.

In this chapter, we will focus our attention on the three key elements of the Catholic Reformation - the Inquisition, the Jesuits, and the Council of Trent. We will also take this opportunity to summarize developments in the Roman Catholic Church from the Reformation to the present, as we summarized the history of the Eastern Church in chapter thirteen. The remainder of the book will be devoted to the growth and development of the various churches in one way or another identified as Protestant.

REFORM BEFORE THE REFORMATION

Any effort to understand the Catholic Reformation must begin in Spain. The failure of the fifteenth-century conciliar movement guaranteed that reform would not come to the church through general councils, and the blatant corruption of the Renaissance popes gave little hope that impetus for change would come from the top of the church hierarchy. If change were to occur, it must come from the increasingly independent monarchs of Europe. For many of these monarchs, the church was a tool for furthering their political ambitions. We have already seen that Henry VIII of England broke away from Rome because of his overriding concern for the stability of the Tudor dynasty. In Spain, however, the major concern was not stability, but unity, and the Spanish monarchs saw a strengthened church as the essential tool for obtaining that unity.

Prior to the fifteenth century, Spain had not been a recognizable political entity. The Iberian peninsula was broken up into numerous petty kingdoms, including Aragon, Castile, Navarre, and Portugal. The marriage of Ferdinand of Aragon and Isabella of Castile in 1469 united the two largest of these kingdoms, and the new rulers then set out to secure a united and powerful Spain. They wanted to dominate the church as much as Henry VIII did half a century later, but they found no need to look beyond the church as it then existed for the key that would unify Spain. The unity of thought they required could be produced by means of a tool already in existence - the Inquisition.

The Inquisition had first been formally used in France in the thirteenth century in opposition to the Albigensians and Waldensians. Since the virtual destruction of those groups (the Albigensians had disappeared, but the Waldensians remained in hiding in the mountains of Italy), the Inquisition had fallen into disuse. Ferdinand and Isabella brought it back, in a form far more vicious than anything experienced by the medieval heretics. The original targets of the Spanish Inquisition were converted Muslims and Jews. The consolidation of Christian power in Spain was often accompanied by violence against Muslims and Jews. Since both groups were automatically suspect in terms of their loyalty, they were often given the choice of exile or conversion. Not surprisingly, many professed conversion because of an unwillingness to leave their homes and businesses. Such "conversions" were merely on the surface, however, and most such "converts" continued to practice their original religions in secret. Ferdinand and Isabella saw these false converts as a threat to Spanish unity, and were determined to remove them from Spanish society.

The task was carried out with brutal efficiency by Tomas de Torquemada, who was appointed Grand Inquisitor in 1483. Thousands died and many more thousands suffered loss of property, torture, and imprisonment during his fifteen-year reign of terror. The inquisitors frightened the population into conformity by secrecy and ceremony. The courts of the Inquisition were closed to the public. People would simply disappear from the streets, and not even their families would know where they were. Often the accused were not even informed of the charges against them, and were tricked by shrewd prosecutors into incriminating themselves. Confessions were obtained by torture, not only of the accused, but also of potential witnesses. Once one had been accused before the Inquisition, the burden of proof rested upon his shoulders - he was presumed guilty unless he could prove himself to be innocent. Those who confessed their guilt were often sentenced to imprisonment for life, while the condemned faced the dreaded *auto-da-fé* ("act of faith") - burning at the stake. These very public burnings served to augment the terror produced by the Inquisitors, and the surrounding ceremony became a circus in much the same way as persecution of Christians over a thousand years before and the beheadings of the French Revolution three centuries later.

No one can doubt that the Spanish Inquisition accomplished its intended purpose. Not only did it quell dissent in Spain, but it also had some other side-effects. In some areas, the Inquisition became a tool for the suppression of Protestantism. This occurred most notably in the Spanish domain in the Netherlands, under the brutal Duke of Alva, and in Italy, where the Inquisition was used to stamp out the Protestant threat. Needless to say, Protestantism never really had a chance to get started in Spain itself. But the conformity desired by Ferdinand and Isabella also had its negative side. Many believe that the Inquisition so stifled the creative drive of the Spanish people that Spain lost its position as the dominant power in Europe by the end of the sixteenth century.

While the Inquisition was certainly the major tool used by Ferdinand and Isabella to dominate the church and bring political unity to Spain, it is only fair to note that they also had a genuine concern for reforming the church. The reform effort was entrusted to Francisco Ximenes (or Jimenes), confessor of Queen Isabella and later the Archbishop of Toledo (the Spanish equivalent of the English Archbishop of Canterbury). Ximenes gave special attention to cleaning up moral abuses in the church, as well as to providing for the education of the clergy. As somewhat of a Renaissance scholar, he not only helped to found the University of Alcala, but also supervised preparation of the Complutensian Polyglot, an edition of the Bible in three languages (Hebrew, Greek, and Latin), along with marginal notes, so that scholars could study the Bible in its original languages. Typical of the attitude of the Catholic Church, however, he did not include Spanish as one of the languages in which the Bible was published.

THE SHOCK TROOPS OF THE CATHOLIC REFORMATION

The reforming zeal of Ximenes was not unique. Throughout the church, men of good will and spiritual sensitivity ached inwardly at what the church had become, and longed to see her brought back to her true mission. One such group of men, the Oratory of Divine Love, met together in Rome from 1517 to 1527, encouraging devotional and pastoral activities and ministering to the poor. The Oratory, which numbered about fifty men, included many of those who would rise to positions of leadership in the Catholic reform movement, including Jacopo Sadoleto, who tried to bring Geneva back into the Catholic fold, and Giovanni Caraffa, who went on to become the reforming pope Paul IV.

The early part of the sixteenth century witnessed the birth of many monastic movements - more than the church had seen since the birth of the Franciscans and Dominicans three centuries earlier. Included in this group were orders such as the Carthusians and the Ursulines. Other orders, like the Carmelites and the Observant Franciscans, gained new life from the reform movement. By far the most influential of the new orders, however, was the Society of Jesus - the Jesuits.

While Ignatius Loyola was recovering from his war wound, he spent long hours meditating on the life and sufferings of Christ, the terrors of hell, and the glories of heaven. These times of meditation led him to the whole-souled commitment to Christ that finally gave him peace in place of the torment through which he had been going. He was convinced that what had been good for him would be good for others as well. In the years after his recovery, he worked hard to get a good education for himself. He returned to grammar school despite being twice the age of most of his classmates. He then went on to university studies, everywhere seeking to initiate others into the spiritual meditations that he had found so beneficial in his own life (these meditations are recorded in his *Spiritual Exercises*, which is used not only by the Jesuits, but by other Catholics as well who are in search of deeper spirituality). On several occasions he ran afoul of the Inquisition, and was imprisoned twice for teaching without church approval. Finally he moved on to the University of Paris. Here the forty-year-old Ignatius studied in the same college at the same time as the brilliant young Frenchman John Calvin, who was then in his early twenties, though there is no evidence that they ever met one another. While Calvin, the scholar, was soon to become a leader of the revolt against Rome, the plodding Ignatius, who always found his schoolwork exceptionally difficult, went on to found the organization that did more than any other to limit the spread of Protestantism in Europe. While in Paris, Ignatius gathered around himself a group of young men who were willing to commit themselves as fully to Christian devotion as he had. They banded themselves together into the Society of Jesus, taking the traditional vows of poverty, chastity, and obedience. They originally intended to go to the Holy Land and evangelize the Muslims, but political conditions in Europe at the time made such a trip impossible. They served the poor in Rome for a number of years, and finally gained official papal sanction in 1540. Included in this small group of men were several who were to become key figures in the Catholic Church of the sixteenth century - James Laynez and Alfonso Salmeron, who played major roles in the Council of Trent, and Francis Xavier, perhaps the greatest Catholic missionary of the modern era.

What made the Jesuits such a potent force in the hands of the reforming popes? Their vow of obedience was nothing new, certainly. Yet the care given by the Jesuits to the preparation of their members produced a single-mindedness completely foreign to many of the orders that preceded them. The Jesuits believed that a thorough and comprehensive education was essential for one who was to serve Christ effectively in the world. Their schools were among the best in Europe, and the preachers they trained, unlike most Catholic priests, were able to hold their own in competition with Protestant preachers. The Jesuit schools did not, therefore, produce mindless automatons. They early on recognized a truth that has been brought out thoroughly by modern psychologists - the importance of a child's early training. They boasted that, if they were given a child for his first seven years, that child would surely remain a Catholic for life. The Jesuits thus took thoroughly indoctrinated, convinced pupils, and carefully placed them in positions that made the most effective use of their individual talents. These were men of strong will and great ability who were nonetheless convinced that God spoke through the pope and through their superiors in the order, and consequently were convinced that their own wills had to give way when their opinions and desires conflicted with the orders they were given.

Such unquestioning submission to authority produced a potent army in behalf of Catholicism, but it also opened the door to some disgraceful moral abuses. Three teachings of the Jesuits, in particular, generated a situation where the order was almost universally hated and feared by Protestants and Catholics alike, was ejected from most of the countries of Europe, and was finally banned by the pope himself in 1773, only to be reinstituted in 1814.

The first of these teachings is the notion of probabilism. As early as the first century, the church struggled with gray areas in morality, issues on which Christians disagreed. Paul included discussions of these matters in his letters to Corinth and Rome (I Corinthians 8, Romans 14). Probabilism began as an approach to dealing with these gray areas. It was argued that, in the absence of concrete teaching by the Bible or the church, many probable solutions existed for a given moral problem. Though one solution might be more probable than another (because it enjoys greater support among respected teachers, for instance), each solution, if espoused by a reputable person, has at least some degree of probability. As a result, the Jesuits argued that it could not be a sin to choose an action even though the probability of its rightness may be somewhat less than that of another approach. In practice, what this meant is that the Jesuits justified themselves in doing anything for which they could find even minimal support among the church fathers - even if the vast majority of teachers in the church concluded that the action was wrong. A good example would be the assassination of tyrants; though most Christian teachers throughout the centuries argued against the legitimacy of such an act, the fact that a few favored it made it at least somewhat probable, and therefore justifiable. The fact that the Jesuits seemed very willing to label any ruler who did not energetically further their vision of the church as a tyrant, of course, made their use of probabilism that much more objectionable.

A second practice that brought the Jesuits into disrepute was their advocacy of mental reservation. This meant that a person could legitimately withhold information to which he believed his listener was not entitled. For instance, if a Jesuit had been implicated in a plot against the king, and the king asked him where he had been on a certain day at a certain time, the Jesuit would feel justified in responding, "I was in my room praying [this morning]," with the final phrase being confined to his mind and not spoken to the king. Obviously, such an approach could easily be used to justify the most blatant of lies. One Jesuit in India even took on the garb and lifestyle of a Brahmin, and later forged a Veda (an ancient Hindu holy book) that taught Catholic doctrine for the purpose of convincing the Hindus of India that the early teachers of their religion had supported what the Jesuit missionaries were proclaiming. It is not at all surprising that the adjective "Jesuit" soon came to be used as a synonym for deceitful double-dealing.

The practices of probabilism and mental reservation, however, were only specific examples of the broad principle for which the Jesuits were most often condemned - the idea that the end justifies the means. Though the Jesuits steadfastly denied teaching such a doctrine, even the pope condemned them for practicing it. For instance, the Jesuits were noted for running the softest confessionals in Catholicism. They regularly gave mild penances and absolved those who came to them of the most heinous sins. Consequently, they became the confessors of choice for the rich and powerful, and often used the confessional as a means to gain inside information, which was then used to further the ambitions of the order. The willingness of individual Jesuits to submit their own judgments to the orders of their superiors made them ready tools for unscrupulous power-grabbers, and caused them to be feared and hated, not only in Europe, but in the Americas and the Far East as well.

Though it is easy to focus on the negative aspects of Jesuit history, we also must acknowledge their positive accomplishments, at least from the perspective of Catholicism. The Jesuits stand out in at least two areas. The first is the leadership they provided in the intellectual combat against Protestantism. Protestants gained many adherents among the well-educated because their careful exegetical preaching stood out in contrast to the widespread ignorance of many of the Catholic clergy. The Jesuits proved themselves to be worthy opponents, able to argue theology with the Protestants on their own terms. Jesuits such as Peter Canisius and Caesar Baronius prepared histories of the church designed to refute the Protestant *Magdeburg Centuries*, which had argued that the Catholic traditions were innovations of which the primitive church had known nothing. The Catholic historians responded by trying to show that the beliefs and practices of Catholicism had their roots in the apostolic church. History thus became a weapon in a propaganda war between Catholics and Protestants. Like statistics, history clearly can be made to serve widely differing purposes.

The second major contribution of the Jesuits to the life of the Catholic Church was their leadership in the field of foreign missions. While other orders were active in the lands discovered and colonized by the conquistadors, it was the Jesuits who took the lead. Francis Xavier, one of the original members of the Society of Jesus, traveled to India, Southeast Asia and Japan, baptizing hundreds of thousands of converts in the process, and died while attempting to enter China. While the depth of many of the conversions he produced is open to question, most credit his work for the continued existence of a Catholic Church in Japan during the era when it was completely closed to Westerners.

THE LONG-AWAITED COUNCIL

The popes of the Catholic Church had defeated the conciliar movement of the fifteenth century, which had attempted to place the authority of a general council over that of the pope. The conciliar ideal was by no means dead, however. The open corruption of the Catholic Church again generated an outcry for a reforming council to deal with and eliminate abuses. With the rise of Protestantism, the need became even greater. Luther himself had called for a council, believing that a serious treatment of doctrinal differences could still produce a united church.

The cries for a council, whether emanating from theologians, reformers, or kings, fell on deaf ears when they reached the papacy.

Incredibly enough, the popes during the early years of the Reformation saw no need for a council largely because they simply did not take the Reformation seriously, contemptuously shrugging it off as a "monks' quarrel." They were so absorbed in European politics, and so concerned about increasing their own power and wealth, that they failed to notice the major threat to the church being mounted by the Protestants. Thus Leo X (1513-1521) excommunicated Luther, but soon turned his attention to more important matters of politics and the arts. Adrian VI (1522-1523), the Dutch tutor of Charles V, wanted to bring the Spanish reforms to Rome, but was so distrusted by the Italian-dominated curia that he was able to accomplish nothing of any significance. He was followed by Clement VII (1523-1534), a sincere man who was completely paralyzed by his desire to please competing rulers like Charles V, Henry VIII of England, and Francis I of France.

Finally, with the accession of Paul III to the papal throne in 1534, the reformers within the Catholic Church began to make some headway. Paul appointed several of the more influential members of the Oratory of Divine Love to the College of Cardinals, along with Gasparo Contarini and the Englishman Reginald Pole, who was later to supervise Mary Tudor's efforts to turn England back to Catholicism. A group of these reformers were commissioned to prepare a report on the status of the church, and to make recommendations for reforming the church. When the report came back, it included a long list of abuses, and lay responsibility for those abuses squarely at the feet of the popes. The cardinals recommended that celibacy be enforced, that indulgence selling be drastically curtailed, that clergy be required to live and preach in their parishes, and that no church official should be permitted to hold more than one office at a time. Their recommendations did not address doctrinal issues at all, however.

While Paul favored the recommended reforms, he still had no desire to convene a general council. Charles V was loudly demanding that a council meet in Germany to deal with the Protestant problem. The Protestants, while agreeing that a council was needed, insisted that such a council must be "free" (i.e., not under papal control) - a demand to which Paul could not possibly accede. The pope had no intention of yielding his authority to a council or an emperor. Furthermore, Francis I of France made it clear that he would not support a council, particularly one on German soil. While clothing his rejection in pious language, the fact of the matter is that he was glad to see Charles V tied up in conflict with the German Protestants - the last thing he wanted was peace and unity in Germany.

One effort to mend the break in the church was made when Catholic and Protestant representatives met in 1541 at Ratisbon for a conference. Both sides sent moderates rather than extremists. The Catholic cause was represented by Contarini, who had considerable sympathy with the Protestant teaching of justification by faith, while the Protestants sent Melanchthon and Bucer, the most able compromisers in a group where compromise did not frequently occur. The conferees were able to agree rather quickly on the basic doctrines of Christianity represented in the ancient creeds, and to everyone's amazement actually came up with a definition of justification with which all were comfortable. The conference foundered on the issue of the sacraments, however. Contarini could no more give in on the matter of transubstantiation than Melanchthon and Bucer could accept it. They thus adjourned without reaching complete accord, and went home to find that their own people rejected their efforts. Luther scoffed at the declaration on justification as a bunch of ambiguous nonsense, while Contarini was promptly confronted with charges of heresy and being a "crypto-Lutheran."

Finally, a general council was convened at Trent near the Italian border in 1545. While Charles V and the Catholic reformers were looking for the council to clean up the church, Paul wanted doctrinal matters to take priority. For him, the best way to deal with the Protestant problem was to eliminate the Protestants, and the best way to do that was by using the Inquisition. To apply the Inquisition, however, he needed definitive doctrinal statements on the issues the Protestants were raising. Finally, a

THEOLOGICAL ISSUES - PROTESTANT VERSUS CATHOLIC

AREA	ISSUE	PROTESTANT POSITION	CATHOLIC POSITION
SCRIPTURE	SUFFICIENCY	*Sola Scriptura.*	Tradition of equal authority with Scripture.
	APOCRYPHA	Rejected.	Accepted.
ANTHROPOLOGY	ORIGINAL SIN	Total depravity and guilt inherited from Adam.	Corruption and predisposition to evil inherited from Adam.
	HUMAN WILL	In bondage to sin.	Free to do spiritual good.
SOTERIOLOGY	PREDESTINATION	Rooted in God's decrees.	Rooted in God's foreknowledge.
	ATONEMENT	Christ's death a substitutionary penal sacrifice.	Christ's death the merit for blessings of salvation - blessings passed on to sinners through sacraments.
	GRACE OF GOD	Common grace given to all; saving grace given to elect.	Prevenient grace, given at baptism, enabling one to believe; efficacious grace cooperating with the will enabling one to obey.
	GOOD WORKS	Produced by the grace of God, unworthy of merit of any kind.	Meritorious.
	REGENERATION	Work of the Holy Spirit in the elect.	Grace infused at baptism.
	JUSTIFICATION	Objective, final, judicial act of God.	Forgiveness of sins received at baptism, may be lost by committing mortal sin, regained by penance.
ECCLESIOLOGY	CHURCH AND SALVATION	Distinction between visible and invisible church.	Outside the (visible) church there is no salvation.
	SACRAMENTS	Means of grace only as received by faith.	Conveying justifying and sanctifying grace *ex opere operato*
	PRIESTHOOD	All believers are priests.	Mediators between God and man.
	TRANSUBSTANTIATION	Rejected.	Affirmed.
ESCHATOLOGY	PURGATORY	Denied.	Affirmed.

compromise was reached, and the council set out to deal with matters of doctrine and reform together.

The Council of Trent met in three distinct periods - 1545-7, 1551-2, and 1562-3. Though Protestants were invited to participate, they largely realized that such an effort would be futile in a council clearly stacked against them from the beginning. A few Protestants did come to the second session of the council, but when their demand that doctrinal matters be decided on the basis of Scripture alone without reference to papal authority or tradition was rejected, they went home, realizing that their position would not be given a hearing. In doctrinal matters, the council went systematically through every major issue raised by the Protestant Reformation, and in each case came down firmly on the side of medieval Catholic tradition. They affirmed transubstantiation and the seven sacraments, gave tradition equal authority with Scripture, included the Apocrypha officially in the canon, declared the Latin Vulgate to be the accepted version of the Bible, rejected the doctrine of justification by faith alone, and expanded the Index of Prohibited Books to include vernacular translations of the Bible, along with the works of Protestant authors and many Catholic humanists like Erasmus - in fact, by the time the Council of Trent was done its work, the Index included almost seventy-five percent of all the works currently coming off the printing presses of Europe.

In the area of reform, the council did its work well. The administration of the church was tightened up and discipline was strengthened, largely through the efforts of the Jesuits James Laynez and Alfonso Salmeron. The reforms were instituted in such a way that papal authority, far from being challenged, was actually strengthened. By the time the Council of Trent adjourned in 1563, the church was more firmly in the grip of the pope than ever. The council concluded its efforts by submitting its work to the pope for his approval. Disciplinary authority rested firmly in his hands, as did the loopholes that allowed him to make exceptions when he chose to do so. Thus the presence of the Jesuits succeeded in preventing what the pope feared most - conciliar decisions that would allow others to challenge his authority.

The Council of Trent was the most influential council since the ecumenical councils of the Ancient Church, largely because it defined the character of Roman Catholicism for the next four centuries. The doctrinal affirmations of Trent represented a defeat, not only for Protestants, but also for the humanists among the Catholics; Trent saw to it that the medieval Scholasticism of Thomas Aquinas became the official theology of Catholicism. In the process, the conferees at Trent also rejected the pleas of those Catholics who favored an Augustinian understanding of salvation, an emphasis on grace without human works that had much in common with the teachings of Luther and Calvin. Though Augustinians continued to appear periodically in Roman Catholicism (the most notable being the French Jansenists in the seventeenth century), Trent firmly established Catholic teaching upon the position that meritorious works contributed to a person's salvation. Meanwhile, all hope of reunion with Protestants was lost, and the authority of the pope over the church would never again be effectively challenged to the present day.

FROM TRENT TO VATICAN II

While the Council of Trent fixed the basic character of Catholicism, there were nonetheless several significant developments in the church in the centuries that followed. The years after Trent witnessed a great expansion of Roman Catholicism. The church expanded through missionary efforts abroad, largely in the colonies of Catholic powers like Spain, Portugal, and France, but also in Europe, as the gains made by Protestants during the Reformation period were systematically rolled back through the efforts of the Jesuits. Austria, Belgium, Poland, and large parts of Germany were regained for Catholicism. Though political dealings contributed to the Catholic successes, educational efforts and church reform also played a major role. The fact of the matter is that many had turned to Protestantism more than anything

Reform, Reaction, and Renewal

else out of disgust for the corruption in the Catholic Church. When the Council of Trent acted to eliminate some of the more blatant forms of corruption, many who had left the church returned, glad to see the church of their fathers cleaning up its act.

The Catholic Church also prospered because it succeeded in weathering the challenge of the Enlightenment far better than most Protestant churches. While Protestants had always emphasized the importance of studying and interpreting the Bible for oneself, the Catholic Church had emphasized the authority of the church as the only trustworthy interpreter of the Scriptures. Thus, when the Age of Reason came to dominate Europe, many Protestant churches fell under the sway of rationalism, as we will see in succeeding chapters. The Catholic Church, however, because it did not encourage people to think for themselves, but rather to submit to authority, experienced far less upheaval than did the Protestants during the heyday of Reason in Western Europe.

While the popes were maintaining their spiritual authority, however, their political authority was being progressively undermined. The Age of Revolution in the eighteenth and nineteenth centuries generated increasingly greater resentment toward the absolutist claims of the papacy in the political realm. Finally, the political power of the popes was stripped away almost entirely when Garibaldi reunified Italy in 1870. Since then, Vatican City, where the pope continues to be the recognized political sovereign, is all that remains of the Papal States and papal claims to political jurisdiction.

The loss of political authority was counteracted by an explicit claim to spiritual authority, however. With Garibaldi's army bearing down on the city of Rome, the First Vatican Council met in 1870, and proclaimed the dogma of papal infallibility to be official church doctrine. They declared that the pope was the representative of Christ on earth, and that when he spoke from the papal chair (*ex cathedra*) on matters of faith and morals, he was to be considered infallible. Thus what popes had been claiming for over a millennium finally became official Catholic doctrine. While secular rulers no longer paid heed to papal proclamations, the Catholic faithful were bound to adhere to the words of the Supreme Pontiff at peril of their souls.

As the Catholic Church entered the twentieth century, it remained largely conservative in nature. Papal proclamations vocally denounced innovations like democracy, labor unions, communism, and existentialism. The church also hardened its position against other Christians and other religions. Jews continued to be condemned as bearing direct responsibility for the death of Christ, while Protestants were "enemies of the cross of Christ." In a rapidly changing world, the Roman Catholic Church stood against the tide. The church soon found, however, that it did not possess enough fingers to seal the dike against the encroaching waves of change.

MODERN ROMAN CATHOLICISM

In the same way that a small leak in a dike soon gives way to a rushing torrent, so change in the Catholic Church came suddenly, and in a way that few expected. When the stern Pius XII died in 1958 after a reign of almost twenty years, there was conflict in the College of Cardinals over his successor. Finally a compromise was reached, and the elderly Angelo Roncalli became Pope John XXIII. Many considered this gentle man to be a caretaker, a do-nothing pope who would reign quietly and soon die, clearing the way for a stronger candidate who would have by then gained sufficient support to be elected. John fooled them all, however, by following up his election with a call for an ecumenical council, the first in almost a century. Vatican II, which met from 1962-1965, turned out to be as radical in many ways as the Council of Trent had been conservative.

Vatican II brought enormous changes in the practices and attitudes of the Roman Catholic Church. As far as church practices are concerned, the Second Vatican Council permitted Bible translation into common languages from the original Hebrew and Greek,

MODERN ROMAN CATHOLIC ECUMENICAL COUNCILS

	COUNCIL OF TRENT	FIRST VATICAN COUNCIL	SECOND VATICAN COUNCIL
DATES	1545-1563	1869-1870	1962-1965
CALLED BY	Paul III	Pius IX	John XXIII
PAPAL BULL	*Laetare Hierusalem*	*Aeterni Patris*	*Humanae Salutis*
NUMBER AND DATES OF SESSIONS	3 sessions - 1545-47, 1551-52, 1562-63	1 session - 12/8/69-7/18/70	4 sessions -10/11-12/8/62; 9/29-12/4/63; 9/14-11/21/64; 9/14-12/8/65
KEY FIGURES	Paul III Julius III Pius IV James Laynez Giovanni Morone	Pius IX Henry Manning Karl J. Hefele Felix Dupanloup	John XXIII Paul VI Karl Rahner Hans Küng
CENTRAL FOCUS	Reform the church. Halt Protestant Reformation	Papal infallibility.	*Aggiornamento* - updating the church.
MAJOR DECISIONS	Tradition bears same authority as Scripture. Apocrypha was included in canon of Scripture. Vulgate was declared official Bible of the church. Protestant teachings on original sin and justification by faith alone were rejected. Number of sacraments were fixed at seven, giving grace *ex opere operato*. Transubstantiation was affirmed. Moral standards for clergy were reaffirmed. Index was greatly expanded by the addition of Protestant writings.	Promulgated dogma of papal infallibility when speaking *ex cathedra* on matters of faith and morals.	Protestants were referred to as "separated brethren." Dialogue with other faiths was encouraged. Translation and reading of Bible was encouraged. Mass was required to be in vernacular, with laity participating. Religious freedom for all was upheld. Excommunications of Great Schism of 1054 were revoked. Index was eliminated. Papal infallibility, tradition, Catholic Church as only way of salvation were reaffirmed. Veneration of Mary was encouraged. Laity were recognized as spiritual priests. Collegiality of pope and bishops was recognized.

rather than requiring the use of the Vulgate, it authorized the saying of Mass in the vernacular rather than in Latin, and encouraged greater involvement by the laity in the life and worship of the church. Old attitudes were challenged as well. Protestants were now "separated brethren" rather than enemies; dialogue between Catholics and people of other religions was encouraged; even the excommunications of the Great Schism of 1054, when the Eastern Orthodox and Roman Catholic Churches formally separated, were officially revoked.

While changes in practice and attitudes were encouraged by Vatican II, however, the council made no more progress in resolving doctrinal differences than had the Council of Trent. In a sense, therefore, the changes brought about by Vatican II were cosmetic rather than changes in the fundamental nature of Catholicism. As long as the authority of the pope and tradition remain, the gap between Protestant and Catholic will be unbridgeable. The greater openness engendered by Vatican II has had beneficial effects, however. Catholics are reading their Bibles and going to Bible studies in greater numbers than ever before, and many are being drawn away from the traditions of the church as their eyes are being opened to the teaching of God's Word.

Another agent of change in twentieth-century Catholicism has been the growth of the Catholic Charismatic Renewal. Beginning in the 1960's, the breeze that had been blowing through Protestantism for several years moved in the direction of the Catholic Church. While Catholic charismatics have exhibited some of the same excesses found among their Protestant counterparts, they have also shown much of the same desire for spiritual growth, commitment to meaningful worship, and hunger for the Word of God that characterize Protestant charismatics. Ironically, the Catholic charismatic movement has done much to pave the way for Protestant missionary efforts in Latin America, where charismatics have proved to be more open to the preaching of God's Word than traditional Catholics.

MAKING DRY BONES LIVE

In looking at the Catholic response to the Protestant Reformation and the developments of the church in the years that followed, it is very easy for us to focus on the negatives - the Inquisition, the Jesuits, papal infallibility. We need to recognize, however, that cruelty in the name of religion, questionable moral teachings, and convenient doctrinal proclamations are by no means the exclusive province of the Roman Catholic Church. As we concentrate our attention on the Protestant churches in the remainder of our study, we will see many examples of teachings and practices that are every bit as self-seeking and sinful as those recounted in portions of this chapter.

We need to remember above all else that such things do not find their root in institutions or organizations, but in the human heart. The same innate sinfulness that allowed the Jesuits to succumb to the temptation to use sinful means to accomplish what they considered to be worthy goals tempts us to excuse our own choices when those choices lead to a "good" result. The next time you are tempted to cheat on a test, lie to a parent or teacher, or steal a small item from a convenience store, ask yourself if the end, whatever it may be, really does justify the means. Then recognize that you are not really that different from Jesuits of the sixteenth and seventeenth centuries, and pray that God would help you to make decisions based on biblical principle rather than what you foresee as the consequences of those decisions.

FOR REVIEW AND FURTHER THOUGHT

1. What was the key difference between how the Protestant reformers sought Christ and how the Catholic reformers went about the same task?

2. Why is the term "Counterreformation" somewhat misleading?

3. How did the use of the church for political purposes by Ferdinand and Isabella differ from that of Henry VIII?

4. How did Ferdinand and Isabella use the Inquisition to unify Spain?

5. Why had many Muslims and Jews in Spain converted to Christianity?

6. Why was the loyalty of converted Muslims and Jews in Spain considered questionable?

7. How did the Spanish Inquisition generate the fear needed to keep the population in line?

8. What roles did the following Spaniards play in the Catholic Reformation: Tomas de Torquemada, Francisco Ximenes, Ignatius Loyola, Francis Xavier, and James Laynez?

9. What was an *auto-da-fé*? Why was this ceremony called an "act of faith"?

10. What was the Complutensian Polyglot, and why was it a landmark publication in Catholic history?

11. How did the Oratory of Divine Love embody the spirit of the Catholic Reformation?

12. What made the Jesuits different from other monastic orders?

13. Why were the Jesuits able to undo the work of the Protestant Reformation where others had failed to stem the tide?

14. In what way was the Jesuit principle of absolute obedience to authority an invitation to abuse?

15. What is probabilism? Give an example of a modern situation where this philosophy could lead to moral abuse.

16. What is the doctrine of mental reservation? Compare this teaching to what Abraham did in Genesis 12:10-20.

17. Do you think there is any difference between the practice of mental reservation and lying? Why or why not?

18. How did the Jesuits use the confessional as a means of increasing their power?

19. How did Catholics and Protestants alike use history as a propaganda tool?

20. In the chapter you have just read, point out specific passages that indicate the point of view of the author regarding the Catholic Reformation.

Reform, Reaction, and Renewal 287

21. Why did the popes fear general councils? Why did the king of France oppose the idea?

22. Why did Charles V want the pope to call a council? Why did the Protestant Reformers want one?

23. Why do you think the pope was willing to reform the practice of the Catholic Church, but was unwilling to consider doctrinal change?

24. Why was the Ratisbon conference able to achieve wide-ranging agreements on some very sensitive issues that separated Catholics and Protestants? On what issue could the conferees not reach agreement?

25. Why did the Ratisbon conference ultimately fail to heal the breach between Catholics and Protestants?

26. Why was Paul III eager to have the Council of Trent consider the doctrinal questions raised by Protestants?

27. Why did most Protestants consider the invitation to participate in the Council of Trent an empty one?

28. What segments of Catholicism experienced defeat as a result of the Council of Trent?

29. In what important ways did the Council of Trent shape the character of Roman Catholicism?

30. How did the reforms instituted by the Council of Trent contribute to the regaining of territory in Europe by the Catholic Church?

31. What enabled the Catholic Church to deal more effectively with the challenge posed by the Enlightenment than did the Protestant churches?

32. What was the main accomplishment of the First Vatican Council?

33. Under what circumstances is the pope considered to be infallible?

34. What made the Catholic Church of the early twentieth century basically conservative in nature?

35. In what ways was Vatican II different from the Council of Trent? In what ways were the conclusions of the two councils similar?

36. What good results have come from the change introduced into the Catholic Church by Vatican II?

37. What impact has the charismatic movement had on the Catholic Church in recent years?

38. What are some situations in which you are tempted to act as if the end justified the means?

Part Four

EUROPE AFTER THE REFORMATION
(from 1648)

26

GOD, MAN, AND MONKEYS

According to Psalm 93:1 (NIV), "The Lord reigns, he is robed in majesty; the Lord is robed in majesty and is armed with strength. The world is firmly established; it cannot be moved." Galileo, however, believed that the world did indeed move, and tried to prove it. The Inquisition was not impressed. The authorities forced him to recant, and suppressed his writings. Why should the church get so upset about what seems to us today to be an obvious truth about the world of nature? The heliocentric theory contradicted the Catholic understanding of Scripture, but the Catholic Church of the sixteenth and seventeenth centuries was hardly known as a bastion of sound biblical interpretation. No, Galileo's crime was far more serious than going against the church's interpretation of a few relatively obscure passages of Scripture. What he said challenged an entire way of looking at and thinking about the natural world. Such a revolution brought stiff resistance, as revolutions usually do.

In fact, much of the history of the relationship of Christianity and science has been one of conflict. In this chapter, we will attempt to take an overview of the history of modern science, particularly focusing on its relationship to Christianity, from the debate over the heliocentric theory to the modern disputes over creation versus evolution and the age of the earth. Is it necessary that science and Christianity be opponents, or is it possible for them to complement one another?

THE MEDIEVAL CONSENSUS

There are two common misunderstandings people frequently have about the science of the Middle Ages. The first is that there was none. Most scientific knowledge was lost during the so-called Dark Ages, but many classical texts were reintroduced to Western Europe as a result of the Crusades. While it is true that Europeans in the Middle Ages had little interest in experimentation, they did spend quite a bit of time thinking about the world around them. That thinking, however, was guided by two basic principles - authority and deduction. The philosophers of the ancient world, particularly Plato and Aristotle, had provided a way of thinking about the created universe. Few men in the Middle Ages thought to challenge that way of thinking. When they did make observations of the natural world, those observations were always interpreted in the light of the basic framework provided by the philosophers of the classical era, whose authority was unquestioned.

With the rise of Scholasticism, the logic of Aristotle gained special prominence in Western Europe. Thomas Aquinas had used Aristotle's principles of logic to expound in great detail a system of Christian theology, and the church's acceptance of Aquinas' work meant also an acceptance of the logic of Aristotle. Aristotle's logic was primarily deductive, reasoning from accepted premises by logical steps to arrive at conclusions that should then be considered to be as valid as the premises from which they had been derived. Such an approach to understanding nature simply does not require experimentation. After all, if the basic premises are correct and the logic is airtight, why should the conclusions need testing?

Such an approach works nicely, of course, except when the basic assumptions upon which the deductions are based are themselves flawed. Two examples of such faulty assumptions inherited from the ancient world are the belief that motion on earth is qualitatively different from motion in the heavens, and that the natural, fundamental form of motion is motion in a circle. Aristotle, and the Egyptian astronomer Ptolemy after him, had taught that the heavens are naturally in motion (circular, of course, revolving about the earth), while in the earthly realm, objects are naturally at rest. All motion on earth therefore had to be explained by the continuous exertion of forces of some kind, while the movements of planets in the heavens always had to be explained in terms of the constant motion of transparent spheres upon which the planets and stars were believed to be mounted. The more observations people made, the more complicated the explanations became, but no one thought to question the basic assumptions.

The second common misunderstanding about science in the Middle Ages is that there was very little disagreement among thinkers in the medieval era. We already have seen that this was hardly the case in theology; no more was it true in the realm of science. The disagreements, however, centered around competing explanations that were rooted in the same fundamental assumptions about the nature of reality. Medieval men differed in their understanding of science, but their differences were about conclusions, not presuppositions.

THE BEGINNINGS OF MODERN SCIENCE

The Italian Renaissance did not produce much of a change in the medieval pattern at first. The Renaissance was initially a conservative movement in the sense that it was an attempt to get back to the ancient texts and classical writings of the Greek and Roman era and reproduce and interpret them with greater fidelity. The great Polish astronomer Nicholas Copernicus (1473-1543) fits precisely this pattern. He really was not an innovator, though his work had revolutionary results. Copernicus accepted without question the astronomical observations made by Ptolemy, and added a few of his own to them. He applied to those observations the medieval philosophical doctrine of simplicity, namely, that a simple explanation of any event is naturally superior to a complicated one. By the time of Copernicus, the accepted explanation of planetary motion had become complicated indeed. In order to explain the motion of the planets, which from the perspective of the earth is quite irregular, on the basis of solid transparent spheres, astronomers had found it necessary to introduce dozens of extra spheres, some of which were mounted a bit off-center, and other smaller ones that rolled around the outside of larger spheres. Copernicus discovered that the calculations for these odd spheres all had something in common - they all depended in one way or another on the "motion" of the sun. This led him to suspect that an alternative explanation might be a lot simpler, and indeed he found that, if he placed the sun at the center of the planetary system, the need for all those extra spheres suddenly disappeared. While his system did have some bugs in it, it also had the virtue of simplicity. Though some within the Catholic Church apparently supported his work, Copernicus had the good sense to have his findings published posthumously. Not surprisingly, they eventually appeared on the Index, where they remained for many years. While Luther, who was a contemporary of Copernicus, thought the heliocentric theory to be so much hogwash, and in his inimitable way referred to the Polish scientist as "the fool who would overturn the whole science of astronomy," he never suggested that Copernicus be burned at the stake, or that his works be banned.

The Renaissance only became a threat to the Catholic Church and a stimulus to scientific development when scientists started challenging those cherished medieval assumptions about the nature of the universe. In the same way that the Renaissance had helped to stimulate the Reformation by encouraging people to think for themselves about the Bible, it contributed to the growth of science by opening up the world of nature to new ways of thinking. Not surprisingly, the Protestant countries of Europe tended to be open to this new kind of thinking about nature, while the Catholic countries opposed the new science almost as much as they opposed the new Christian churches of the Reformation. Galileo was persecuted in Italy, while Isaac Newton was knighted in England.

We noted in the last chapter that the authoritarian nature of the Catholic Church proved to be an effective shield against the liberalism that plagued Protestantism from the Age of Reason onward. That same authoritarianism, however, tended to stifle scientific development in Catholic countries. In Protestant countries, on the other hand, the belief that every man, under the guidance of the Holy Spirit, was free to interpret the Bible for himself carried over into the field of science, so that people were encouraged to think about the natural world in new ways. The rapid growth of science in the Protestant countries of Europe gave those countries an economic and technological advantage over their Catholic counterparts that remains to the present day.

Another aspect of Protestantism that tended to encourage scientific inquiry was the emphasis, especially among Calvinists, on the Cultural Mandate (Genesis 1:28). The Reformed churches taught that, in the same way that the church was to conform completely to the teachings of Scripture, the Christian was to bring every aspect of society under submission to the Kingdom of God. Thus no human endeavor could rightly be viewed as secular, since everything was to be done to the glory of God. Men thus turned their attention to gaining dominion over the natural world. Science was not a threat to the church, but a way of bringing the world under subjection to God.

Perhaps the greatest examples of the typical Protestant approach to science are Isaac Newton, who revolutionized physics and mathematics, and Robert Boyle, the Irish chemist. Both men were devout Christians (though Newton was by all accounts a rather disagreeable man personally), and spent much of their later lives writing devotional literature (Boyle) and Bible commentaries (Newton). They viewed their pursuit of science as an effort on their part to know God better through gaining a better understanding of the world He made. Newton's numerous contributions included the law of gravitation, the three laws of motion, discoveries in optics, and the invention of calculus, while Boyle is best known for Boyle's Law, which describes the behavior of a gas exposed to changes in pressure or volume.

In what ways, then, did the new scientific thinking challenge the medieval consensus? What was this new way of thinking that the Catholic Church considered to be such a threat? In order to see how people's thinking was reoriented by the Scientific Revolution, we need go no further than the four basic rules of reasoning outlined by Isaac Newton in his *Principia Mathematica*.

The first principle states that "we are to admit no more causes of natural things than such as are both true and sufficient to explain their appearance." This is no more than a restatement of the notion of simplicity that had stimulated the thinking of Copernicus, yet it has revolutionary implications. Specifically, the doctrine of simplicity states that if a natural explanation for a natural phenomenon exists, then a supernatural explanation is not required. Many of the events that had been explained supernaturally in the Middle Ages no longer required the intervention of God, angels, or demons. The supernatural seemed in danger of shrinking into a corner in the face of ever-expanding knowledge of the natural world. As we will see, this kind of thinking proved to be, not only a threat to the authority of the Catholic Church, but also a stimulus to the eventual exaltation of science itself to a position formerly occupied by God in the minds of many.

Newton's second principle was that, "to the same natural effects we must, as far as possible, assign the same natural causes." Newton succeeded in doing what Copernicus and Galileo had been unable to do. Copernicus proposed the heliocentric theory with no thought of questioning the medieval notion of the uniqueness of the earth in the universal scheme of things. Galileo suspected that earthly and heavenly motion could be explained in the same way, but was unable to formulate such an explanation mathematically. Newton's law of universal gravitation, however, tied together in mathematical form the motion of the planets in space and the behavior of an apple as it falls from a tree on earth. The medieval belief in the uniqueness of the earth was dead. [NOTE: Newton also successfully challenged the medieval notion that circular motion was "natural." His laws of motion stated that the fundamental natural motion was motion in a straight line at constant velocity.]

The third principle outlined by Newton states that, "the qualities ... which are found to belong to all bodies within the reach of our experiments, are to be esteemed the universal qualities of all bodies ...." In other words, observations may be extrapolated and applied to other phenomena outside the reach of experimentation. Behind this principle is the assumption that we live in an orderly universe, and that this universe is susceptible to explanation. The fact that this is God's world means that it *can* be understood, not that man is presumptuous to attempt to probe into divine mysteries.

Finally, Newton asserted that, "we are to look upon propositions collected by general induction from phenomena as accurately or very nearly true, notwithstanding any contrary hypotheses that may be imagined, till such time as other phenomena occur, by which they may be made more accurate, or liable to exceptions." Newton here alludes to the scientific method previously proposed by Francis Bacon, by which scientific hypotheses are formed through observation and experimentation. Newton goes on to argue that the only effective way to challenge a scientific theory is to provide evidence to the contrary. The experimental evidence, then, becomes the final arbiter of scientific truth. While Newton, as mentioned above, saw this principle as leading to a deeper understanding of God through the study of His world, later scientists used the same principle to rule out biblical authority altogether, arguing that the teachings of Scripture were to be given no weight whatsoever unless they could be supported by experimental evidence.

THE TRIUMPH OF SCIENTISM

While Newton saw science as opening the door wide for a deeper human understanding of God and His ways, later scientists used Newton's work to shove God out that same door and slam it in His face. Science became scientism when it arrogated to itself the role of final arbiter of truth. To understand how that came to pass, we need to look at the contributions to scientific thought made by the French mathematician René Descartes and the English Deists.

Descartes was educated in a Jesuit school, but was monumentally bored by his educational experience, and considered that his professors had been able to teach him little of value. The constant appeal to authority by his Jesuit teachers frustrated him no end. He finally decided that the only way to come to any certain knowledge was to tear down everything and start from the beginning. Descartes therefore resolved to doubt everything that could reasonably be doubted, and rebuild a rational system of belief from what was left. He quickly found that it is relatively easy to doubt almost anything if one puts one's mind to it. He could easily doubt the reality of his own perceptions, for instance. How could he be sure he was not at that very moment dreaming? One thing, he concluded, could never be doubted, however, and that was the existence of the person doing the doubting. One could not doubt if he did not exist. Descartes thus reduced his level of certainty to the famous *cogito ergo sum* - "I think, therefore I am!" Starting with his certain knowledge of his own existence, Descartes then proceeded to build upon that foundation. He used the Ontological Argument devised by Anselm to prove the existence of God (see chapter fifteen), and then used the existence of God to prove the general reliability of our sense perceptions. The result of this approach was that Descartes effectively divided human knowledge into two realms - the realm of experience, where the senses reign supreme, and the realm of faith, where God is our only source of knowledge. Unfortunately, there is no real correspondence between the two realms. Faith is every bit as unnecessary in the natural realm as the senses are in the realm of the supernatural. God is thus pushed out the door of the natural world like an elderly relative who no longer is able to contribute to the life of the family. While Descartes left the door open, leaving God to reign over that realm which is beyond human experience, many soon began to question the need for such a realm at all. Indeed, some of

Descartes' critics, such as the Jansenist Blaise Pascal, suspected that he had included God in his argument largely for the purpose of avoiding the attentions of the Inquisition.

It was the Deists, however, who built upon Newton's foundation an edifice he would have found appalling, and in so doing shut God out of the universe completely. The Deists had argued that Newton had proved the world to be a great machine, capable of being explained entirely in mathematical terms. The fact that scientists could not explain everything mathematically did not mean that everything was not capable of mathematical explanation; it simply meant that the proper formulas had not yet been devised. The Deists maintained that the Bible was no more than a republication of the Book of Nature. Those truths that Descartes relegated to the realm beyond experience were rejected entirely by the Deists as nothing more than the superstitions foisted upon the gullible population by priests seeking to enhance their own power over men. Even religion, they argued, could be derived from nature. Such religion told us that the world had been created by an orderly God, who had endowed man with the capacities to determine his own fate. He was to do this by learning about and controlling his world for the good of himself and others. True religion is thus an attitude of benevolence toward all mankind. Any talk of doctrine is divisive, and should be banned for the good of society. Thus the Deists dismissed, in one fell swoop, every major teaching of the Christian religion except for the doctrine of creation - miracles, providence, the Incarnation, the deity of Christ, the resurrection - and left man with a religion that consisted almost solely of ethical principles. Such thinking was supported by the voyages of discovery, which gave many Europeans a new awareness of non-Christian cultures and religions. They came to believe that all religions had a core of ethical behavior in common and, once stripped of all doctrinal peculiarities, would correspond to the universal religion of nature proposed by the Deists.

Science thus shifted, in the century following Newton, from being the handmaiden of theology to becoming the replacement for theology. Any knowledge that did not come by way of science was not worth having, nor was it worthy of the name of knowledge. Such an attitude, of course, has dominated the thinking of many down to our own day. In the same way that the theologians of the sixteenth century often scoffed at science as irrelevant nonsense, the scientists of the twentieth century frequently dismiss religion out of hand.

THE DARWINIAN REVOLUTION

The worst was still to come, of course. If Newton had undermined the medieval belief in the uniqueness of the earth by showing that the same natural laws were in operation throughout the universe, there remained, even in the eyes of the Deists, one thing that could not be denied, and that was the uniqueness of man. The Deists may have been ready to banish God from the contemporary world, but they continued to cling to God as Creator, both to explain the orderliness of the universe and to support their belief in the dignity of man as God's greatest creation. All of that changed, however, with the coming of Charles Darwin (1809-1882).

Somewhat ironically, Darwin had as a young man aimed toward a career in the church, but he was deflected from his purpose by his interest in the natural world. The turning point was an invitation to accompany a ship called the *Beagle* in a voyage around the tip of South America; on this voyage Darwin served as volunteer naturalist. A man with a keen eye for observation, Darwin kept voluminous records of bird, animal, and plant life, as well as fossil remains encountered by the company. He was most interested in the peculiar life forms found to exist in the Galapagos Islands in the Pacific Ocean off the coast of Ecuador. His observations became the basis for a theory of organic evolution expounded in his two major works, *The Origin of Species* and *The Descent of Man*. In these, he argued that complex organisms, including man, had developed from simpler life forms over millions of years by means of gradual adaptation and genetic variation. Those variants better suited to their environment had survived to reproduce and pass on their characteristics. By these means, the variety of living beings on the face of the earth had developed from primitive organisms in the planet's distant past.

Such a blatant denial of biblical teaching was quickly rejected by most churches in the nineteenth century, though some of the more liberal church bodies soon adapted their teaching to the new science. The world at large, however, embraced Darwin's theory enthusiastically. The nineteenth century was an era when belief in the inevitability of progress and the perfectibility of man dominated the popular mind. The popular revolutions in the middle of the century had brought a measure of liberty to many who had never known it before, and the world had been spared major wars of any consequence since the Napoleonic Wars of the early eighteen hundreds. The optimists now had scientific evidence to support their optimism. Man, the pinnacle of evolution, was himself destined to advance to ever greater heights.

Darwin's theory thus had a marked influence on areas of human thought only tangentially related to biology. A group of people called Social Darwinists justified European imperialism by citing Darwin's doctrine of the survival of the fittest. Adaptation to and domination of the environment had allowed European civilization to advance, and therefore it either had the right to dominate the clearly "backward" cultures of Asia, Africa, and the Americas, or had the duty to bring those peoples into the glorious light of Western civilization. Some even argued for social policies at home that would allow the unfit to die out through "benign" neglect. Aid for the poor would only allow them to survive and multiply. This is clearly against nature. For the good of the nation, social policy should be directed toward encouraging the fit, not the unfit. Similarly, Karl Marx argued that the evolution of society was determined by economic factors to follow a certain inevitable progression. Though progress would require conflict and even bloody revolution, the result would be a classless society where all were equal.

A few men in the nineteenth century realized, however, that Darwin's theory of evolution did not necessarily imply an optimistic view of human history in which everything inevitably progressed onward to a peaceful and prosperous future. German philosopher Friedrich Nietzsche understood the implications of Darwin's theory better than most men of his age. He realized that, if man is not a unique organism, but an animal like all other animals, then the entire Judeo-Christian ethical system was a fraud. If only the fittest survive, then the only fundamental determiner of right is power. Nietzsche spoke of Supermen who, like Napoleon, seized history by the scruff of its neck and directed it according to their own desires - a procedure later attempted by a German madman named Adolf Hitler, who saw human evolution as leading ultimately to a super race, and was determined to bring such an end to pass.

Though few have cared to follow the implications of evolutionary theory in the direction taken by Nietzsche, twentieth-century evolutionists have in general lost their optimism. The perfectibility of man is no longer taken seriously, nor do men believe in the inevitability of human progress. The horrible wars of the twentieth century have demonstrated that optimism is unwarranted, and many have even begun to question the kind of "progress" that destroys the natural environment for the sake of human consumption. Many evolutionists have become pessimists, seeing the entire process as at best pointless, having no meaning, and at worst a cruel joke perpetrated on the human race by a mindless, faceless Mother Nature.

THE CRUMBLING FOUNDATIONS

The optimism about man and society encouraged by Darwin's work in biology was being echoed by the physicists of the era. Ever since Newton had shown that natural phenomena could be reduced to universally applicable mathematical equations, physicists and chemists had been busy describing one discipline after another in mathematical terms, from astronomy to mechanics to light to electricity to magnetism. Their success had been such that some reluctantly concluded toward the end of the nineteenth century that the science of physics had almost completed its work. All the major discoveries had been made, all the fundamental questions had been answered, so that all that remained was technology - finding new ways to put this knowledge to use. Some even suggested that the mathematics of the universe might some day be fine-tuned to the extent that a man equipped with all the necessary data could predict infallibly the entire course of human history that lay ahead.

It was technology, however, that soon led to the overthrow of any such pretensions to completeness. Improved instruments allowed scientists to observe in greater detail than ever before the movements of the heavenly bodies and the elementary building blocks of matter. In both realms, the very small and the very large and distant, disturbing new observations appeared that brought into question the foundation of all physics - Newton's laws, the formulas that were believed to describe all motion, both celestial and terrestrial.

One man who realized that Newton's laws were applicable only within certain frames of reference, and who first devised a theory that accurately predicted the forms of behavior observed by scientists in contradiction to Newton's laws, was a German scientist named Albert Einstein. His theory of relativity destroyed the popular notion of a universe where space and time were constants. Later scientists who worked in the field of quantum mechanics demonstrated that all scientific measurements must involve a certain degree of uncertainty, since the very act of measurement alters the behavior that is being measured. Furthermore, scientists found that the most fundamental behavior of matter - the movement of electrons, for instance - could only be described in terms of probability. Some theorists today are suggesting that some things, such as weather patterns and earthquakes, by their very nature are incapable of prediction, and that we must recognize that chaos is at the very heart of certain natural phenomena. Thus the twentieth century, with its recognition of indeterminism and the limitations of science, has brought an end to the pride that characterized much of scientific inquiry in the years that preceded.

People who had learned to throw off the superstitions of religion for the certainties of science have responded to this development in a number of ways. Some have continued to cling to the outmoded notion that science has all the answers, and that only that which can be shown to have scientific validity may be regarded as true. Such an approach smacks of desperation. Having rejected all other alternatives, these people cling to science because it is all they have left.

Others have taken the short-sighted approach of ignoring ultimate issues in favor of concentrating on matters of application. For them, ultimate questions about the meaning of life and the role of man in the universe can be left for others to discuss. They instead occupy themselves with technology, immersing themselves in one narrow field of endeavor and refusing to think about the broader applications of the changes wrought by the crumbling of the foundations.

Many of those who have taken the time to think through the implications of modern science have gazed into the face of an empty universe and have been unable to live with the nothingness they have seen there. They thus leap into mysticism, a modern version of the dualism of Descartes, where the facts of this life are totally divorced from some reality beyond the realm of experience. The growth of oriental cults such as Hare Krishna, the widespread use of Transcendental Meditation, and the recent New Age movement in its various forms are all examples of the flight from reason when the rational foundations of science proved inadequate, and the unfilled void was too much to bear.

MAKING DRY BONES LIVE

Christians, of course, do not need to focus with tunnel vision on technology or throw themselves into some other-worldly mysticism. Christians realize that science can never provide a total understanding of the world, since it deals only with what is seen. If it is wrong to see science as the key to all knowledge, it is also wrong to divide knowledge into two realms, as Descartes attempted to do. The history of science clearly shows that, when science is left in control of the natural realm, God is soon pushed into an increasingly small portion of reality, and quickly becomes redundant.

Instead, the Christian is one who views all knowledge as one. All we know comes from God, whether that knowledge pertains to the natural world that He has both created and given us the senses and minds to perceive and understand, or whether that knowledge has been directly revealed to us through His Word. The Christian thus is able to benefit from science because he puts science in its proper place, as a God-given tool by which God's world may be better understood, but never as a source of ultimate knowledge.

How, then, is a Christian to deal with conflicts between the Bible and science? What about differing views of Creation, the Flood, or the age of the earth? First of all, we must recognize that, because the Bible and the natural world both have the same origin - God - they can never be in conflict with one another. The conflicts come in the interpretation of the Bible and nature. There is always, of course, a temptation to twist either the Bible or science to produce an unnatural harmony between the two. Someone who does that is not being intellectually honest. Others attempt to impose a popular understanding, whether scientific or biblical, and soon find themselves with egg on their faces when that popular interpretation changes. Those who wed themselves to popular interpretations run the risk of going the way of the Catholic Church in the time of Galileo, which went down in history as identifying geocentrism with Christian truth.

In conclusion, the Christian approach must be one of caution. While the Christian may without shame insist loudly on the total reliability of God's Word, he must cultivate humility in recognizing that his own sinful limitations allow for the possibility of misunderstanding the infallible Word. Christians who insist they have all the answers on the relationship of Scripture to the natural world all too often embarrass the cause of Christ. We must combine complete trust in God with a healthy skepticism about our own opinions.

God, Man and Monkeys

FOR REVIEW AND FURTHER THOUGHT

1. How did the science of the Middle Ages differ from science in the centuries following the Renaissance?

2. In what way was the way men thought about the natural world in the Middle Ages governed by the authority of the great Greek philosophers?

3. What is deductive thinking? Why does it remove the need for experimentation?

4. What were some of the faulty assumptions about the natural world passed down by the ancient philosophers?

5. In what sense is it accurate, and in what sense is it misleading, to speak of the medieval view of science as a "consensus"?

6. In what sense was the Renaissance a conservative rather than a revolutionary movement?

7. What was the medieval doctrine of simplicity, and how did Copernicus use it to arrive at the heliocentric theory?

8. Why did science tend to progress much faster in Protestant countries than in Catholic countries?

9. What is the Cultural Mandate, and how was it interpreted to encourage scientific work by Calvinists in particular?

10. What were the four basic principles of scientific reasoning outlined by Newton in his *Principia*, and how did each challenge the prevailing thought of his day?

11. How were some of Newton's principles later used to undermine the authority of Scripture and almost totally exclude God from the universe?

12. How did Descartes attempt to arrive at a theory of human knowledge?

13. How did Descartes divide human knowledge into two unrelated realms?

14. How did the Deists effectively shut God out of the universe?

15. How did the Deist teaching that God had created the world as a great machine and then left it on its own undermine most of the great doctrines of Christianity?

16. How did the voyages of discovery contribute to the popularity of "natural religion"?

17. How did the work of Darwin undermine the belief in the uniqueness of man?

18. What factors in popular nineteenth-century thinking paved the way for the widespread acceptance of Darwin's theory of evolution?

19. How did the theory of evolution fit in with the prevailing optimism of the nineteenth century?

20. What was Social Darwinism, and what conclusions about social policy did the Social Darwinists draw from the theory of evolution?

21. What role did the theory of evolution play in the development of Marxism?

22. Why did some conclude that the theory of evolution does not in fact support an optimistic view of human history?

23. What made nineteenth-century physicists optimistic about the future of science?

24. How did improving technology contribute to the overthrow of the mechanistic view of the universe?

25. In what ways has twentieth-century science come to recognize more clearly its limitations?

26. Why has a recognition of the limitations of science often led to either technology or mysticism?

27. How should Christians view the relationship between the Bible and science?

28. Why is it important for Christians to be cautious in their pronouncements about scientific theories?

29. What must the church today do to avoid the humiliation experienced by the Catholic Church at the time of Galileo?

30. How can a Christian be certain about God's Word and at the same time be humble about his own understanding of it? Give an example using a contemporary Bible-science dispute.

27

MEN OF THE COVENANT

During the winter of 1778, a captain of the Hessian mercenaries stationed in Philadelphia wrote these peculiar words about the American Revolution: "Call this war, my dearest friend, by whatsoever name you may, only call it not an American Rebellion, it is nothing less than an Irish-Scottish Presbyterian Rebellion." Such was the impact of a small band of Scottish rebels on American history that their determination to resist tyranny became the governing principle of the revolt of the American colonies. Who were these Scottish rebels? The goal of this chapter is to provide an answer to that question.

When Jenny Geddes threw her famous, though possibly apocryphal, stool in 1638 (see chapter twenty-four), the people of Scotland were roused to action in opposition to Charles I's efforts to impose an episcopal prayer book on the Scottish Presbyterian Church. They responded by drafting and signing a document called the National Covenant. The National Covenant affirmed the intention of the signers to uphold presbyterianism and keep the church free from royal interference. The concept of a covenant, which was taken from Scripture, involved a sacred oath sworn before God. By it the people of Scotland bound themselves perpetually to its terms. In the succeeding years, this covenant, along with the Solemn League and Covenant drafted by Alexander Henderson in 1643, became the rallying point for the Scottish battle against the tyranny of the Stuarts. Those who bound themselves by these documents and remained faithful to them in the face of great odds were known as Covenanters.

THE EARLY COVENANTERS

We have already seen in chapter twenty-four how the uprising in Scotland led to the downfall of Charles I. The Scottish revolt forced Charles to summon Parliament in order to finance the war against Scotland, but Parliament had no intention of paying for such a war, and the result was the English Civil War. The Civil War produced an alliance between the English Puritans and the Scottish Presbyterians that was summarized in the Solemn League and Covenant. When Oliver Cromwell came to power, however, the alliance was fractured. Cromwell favored independency over presbyterianism, and a republic over a monarchy. The Scots, as much as they hated tyranny, wanted a king, and would have nothing to do with the concept of an independent church. To them, Cromwell's notion of toleration was nothing less than base compromise. The Scots thus backed a move to restore Charles II to the throne in 1651. Cromwell sent troops across the border into Scotland, and the young king was forced to flee to the continent. Meanwhile, the English Parliament repudiated the Solemn League and Covenant, which infuriated the Scots even more.

The Scots also found that it was difficult for them to agree among themselves. Many argued that the toleration of presbyterianism under Cromwell should be viewed as a blessing, while the hard-liners maintained that anything less than the imposition of presbyterianism throughout the British Isles according to the terms of the Solemn League and Covenant would be a serious sin indeed, since the Bible clearly has some very dire things to say about covenant-breakers. The Covenanters, holding to the eternal validity of the National Covenant and Solemn League and Covenant, thus became a minority in their own land.

The strongest voice of the Covenanters in this period belonged to Samuel Rutherford (1600-1661). Rutherford was a godly pastor in the parish of Anwoth who was among the first to be silenced for opposing episcopacy. When rebellion broke out in 1638, he signed the National Covenant, later became Professor of Divinity at the University of St. Andrews, and served as one of Scotland's representatives at the Westminster Assembly. His greatest contribution to the Covenanter movement, however, was his book *Lex Rex* ("The Law and the Prince"). The book consisted of an argument for constitutional monarchy, and included a number of principles that were later to characterize the Covenanters.

Rutherford argued first of all that the king was subject to the law, in opposition to the Stuarts, proponents of divine right, who maintained that the king, because he had been given authority by God alone, was accountable to no man, and therefore was above the law. Rutherford based his conclusion on the idea that only God had absolute power, and that for a monarch to claim such power was nothing less than blasphemous.

Another key Covenanter concept enunciated by Rutherford was that a careful distinction must be made between a man and his office. The Covenanters could thus loudly uphold the principle of monarchy while at the same time rebelling against a king they considered to be a blasphemous tyrant. If the man were distinct from his office, of course, that did open the door to rebellion. The key question then became, "What sort of behavior disqualifies a man from office?" Rutherford argued that the king was bound to uphold the laws of God, and could legitimately be removed from office when he failed to do so. To the Covenanters, upholding the laws of God was equivalent to maintaining the Covenants, and when the Stuarts repudiated the Covenants, the Covenanters repudiated the Stuarts.

To Rutherford, the greatest sin a king could commit was to force on his people a false and idolatrous religion. If that were to happen, Rutherford taught that the people were to act as if they had no king, since the king had forfeited his right to rule. Such decisions were not to be made lightly, however. Rutherford cautioned against those who would be overly eager for martyrdom, as well as against those who would replace tyranny with anarchy. Neither extreme was pleasing to God, though the former was one the later Covenanters often seemed to approach.

Rutherford pursued this issue further when he argued that the king reigned by consent of the people, and that he could also be removed by their consent. Such thinking was considered radical and dangerous in the seventeenth century, but by the end of the eighteenth century, it was very popular indeed. In fact, it was this very concept of government by the consent of the governed that was to become the heart of American democracy. While many recognize the debt owed by Thomas Jefferson to men like Locke and Rousseau, fewer see that Locke drew on the Covenanter Rutherford for key elements of his political thought.

PERSECUTION UNDER CHARLES II AND JAMES II

Since the Scots had been ready to put Charles II on the throne as early as 1651, one would think that the Restoration in 1660 would have been even more popular in Scotland than in England. Such was not the case, however. When Charles promised at Breda to allow each man to worship according to his conscience as long as it did not threaten the peace of the realm, the English saw it as a breath of fresh air after what they considered to be the stifling strictness of the Puritans, but the Scots saw in Charles' profession of openness nothing less than the repudiation of the Covenants he had sworn to uphold at his coronation in 1651. Charles, who had no moral standards to speak of, thought nothing of breaking his word, and fully believed that oath-breaking was part of his kingly prerogative. When the Covenanters began to criticize him openly as a "treacherous and lecherous prince" (his bedroom escapades were beyond counting, and his illegitimate children numbered in the dozens), Charles understandably took offense, and began to view the staunch presbyterians as traitors to the realm.

Thus began a series of persecutions that would not come to an end until the overthrow of the Stuarts in the Glorious Revolution of 1688. Two of the most visible Covenanter leaders, the

Marquis of Argyle and a presbyterian pastor named James Guthrie, were executed almost immediately on trumped-up charges. Soon the Scottish Parliament began to make life increasingly difficult for any who would not acknowledge the king's sovereignty over the church. This "Drunken Parliament" (the nickname requires no elaboration) made every effort to outstrip the hardships forced on English dissenters by the notorious Clarendon Code. In 1662, episcopacy was restored and presbyterianism outlawed in the Church of Scotland. Anyone wishing to hold an office of any kind was required to repudiate the Covenants. All ministers were ordered to submit their credentials to the bishops for affirmation; those who refused to do so were removed from their churches. The originators of these acts suspected at the time that perhaps a few dozen pastors would refuse to submit to the episcopal bishops, and were amazed when fully one-third of the pastors in Scotland resisted the order. These men were duly excluded from their churches, but that left the bishops with two major problems - how to replace the ousted pastors, and how to keep them from continuing to minister to their former flocks. Finding new pastors for that many churches turned out to be a serious problem. Not only were those sent in as replacements woefully unqualified, but the congregations also refused to acknowledge them as legitimate pastors. Parliament then passed a law requiring everyone to attend the episcopal worship, and threatening fines to all who refused. Enforcement was left to the military - often Catholic soldiers imported from Ireland or the Scottish Highlands who had no love for presbyterians. Not only did these "enforcers" tend to line their own pockets with exorbitant fines, but they also abused the people frightfully, beating, raping, and pillaging any who resisted their demands.

As far as the pastors were concerned, Parliament devised the Conventicle Act and the Mile Act to drive them out of business. The Conventicle Act forbade any religious gathering of more than five persons that did not follow the episcopal prayer book. The Mile Act required the ousted ministers to remain more than twenty miles from their former parishes, as well as six miles from any cathedral town and three miles from any royal city. In effect, this law gave the dissenting ministers quite literally no ground on which to stand.

Harassment of presbyterians and their ministers was bad enough, but harassment quickly became persecution because Charles viewed any repudiation of episcopacy as a challenge to his royal authority. Thus one could not be a dissenter without also being a rebel and a traitor. In the years that followed, most of the leading Covenanter ministers were forced into exile or arrested and executed. Occasionally open warfare broke out, such as the Pentland Rising of 1666, when some thousand Covenanters took up arms in defense of their liberties, and were quickly cut down by the king's forces. In 1679, Archbishop Sharp, the former Covenanter who initiated many of the persecutions, was assassinated, and the following year Richard Cameron, after declaring that Charles had forfeited his right to be king by breaking his oath to uphold the Covenants, led a short-lived revolt that ended in his violent death (thereafter the more radical Covenanters were known as Cameronians).

Each of these risings brought a bloody response from the government. The worst bloodbath, called the Killing Time, followed the Test Act of 1683. The Test Act required an oath of loyalty to the king that included a repudiation of presbyterianism and the Covenants, along with a promise not to try to change anything in church or state. Like the anti-Covenanter acts of twenty years before, this was enforced by free-lancing soldiers who had orders to execute on the spot any who would not swear the oath. It is estimated that during the reigns of Charles II and James II, over eighteen thousand Covenanters were either exiled or executed. Many others gave up the fight and yielded to the king's offers of "indulgence" (which involved freedom for a pastor to return to his parish if he willingly acknowledged the king's authority over the church). Thus by the time of the Glorious Revolution, the covenanting movement, which had begun with over a quarter of a million Scots signing the National Covenant in 1638, had dwindled to about seven thousand bedraggled zealots

COVENANTERS AFTER THE GLORIOUS REVOLUTION

The Glorious Revolution, which brought to the thrones of England and Scotland William III and Mary, should have ended the struggles of the Covenanters, but did not do so. The tolerant William quickly restored presbyterianism to the Church of Scotland, but still the Covenanters were not satisfied. For one thing, William would not reaffirm the Covenants, which the Covenanters considered eternally binding on all of Britain. Furthermore, William made no effort to institute presbyterianism in England or Ireland, which to the Covenanters was an inexcusable compromise. Worse yet, the Covenanters viewed the whole notion of toleration as an affront to the sanctity of truth. They would be no part of a church that would tolerate error.

During the reign of Queen Anne, who ascended the throne after the death of William in 1702, the Covenanters were further offended, first by the union of England and Scotland in 1707, which united the Parliaments, and then by an act of Parliament in 1711 that reinstituted lay patronage. The practice of lay patronage involved the right of a local nobleman to nominate a man of his choice for a vacant pastoral position in his parish. Though the appointment had to receive the approval of the church, the mere fact that a pastor had been nominated by a layman often was enough to turn his parishioners against him.

Finally, the Covenanters followed the inevitable course and seceded from the Church of Scotland. Ebenezer Erskine, one of the severest critics of lay patronage, led the secession. He and his followers came to be known as Marrowmen, after a book published shortly before called *The Marrow of Modern Divinity*.

The secession of the Covenanters had two effects on the Scottish Church. First of all, it left the moderates firmly in charge of the church, and it was not long before the church in Scotland was moving along the same path toward Deism and Unitarianism that the Church of England followed, as we will see in the next chapter. Secondly, the Covenanters, as had been the case all during the years of persecution, were so determined to uphold the truth that they were unable to maintain any kind of unity among themselves. They soon split over a variety of issues, including the lawfulness of an oath requiring officeholders to support "the true religion presently professed within this realm" (the two parties were called Burghers and Antiburghers). Thus the love of peace became associated with doctrinal laxity, while the zeal for truth begat perpetual schism. Such has continued to be the case, not only among Presbyterians, but in much of the church over the last three centuries.

We should also note briefly the impact of the Covenanters in the American colonies. While the Covenanter movement had died out to the point where they made up only a very small minority in Scotland by the time of the Glorious Revolution, the persecutions of the Stuarts had driven many of them to seek refuge abroad. While many went to the Netherlands, a large number eventually found their way to America, settling mostly in the Middle Atlantic region. As we will see in a later chapter, the Presbyterians quickly gained a foothold in Pennsylvania and New Jersey, and contributed greatly to the Great Awakening. They also brought with them the same hatred of tyranny that had upheld them through years of persecution, and soon became leaders in the struggle of the colonies against England. Thus the quotation with which our present chapter began.

MAKING DRY BONES LIVE

The actions of the Covenanters raised serious questions that are still with us today about the responsibility of Christians to obey their governments. When, in fact, may a Christian disobey the government under which he lives? The answers given by the Covenanters may help us to examine our own thinking on the subject.

The question of civil disobedience may be answered in three basic ways. One may affirm that a government may be legitimately disobeyed, (1) when the government itself is illegitimate, (2) when the legitimate government does something sinful enough to disqualify itself as deserving of the obedience of Christians, or (3) when the government forces the Christian to sin, so that to obey the government would be to disobey Christ.

The Covenanters clearly repudiated the first answer. They steadfastly maintained that the powers that be had been ordained by God, and genuinely sought a godly monarchy for Scotland. They used the second principle, however, to argue that a king who broke his oath no longer deserved the loyal obedience of Christians, so that rebellion against Charles was not in fact defying God's ordained authority, but upholding it. The men of the Covenant also used the third answer when they argued that submitting to the authority of the king in the church would be sinning against Christ, who was the church's only rightful Head.

In America, the issue took on new dimensions because of the separation of church and state. Though many of the colonies had established churches and some were driven to rebellion by the fear that England would eventually impose the episcopal form of church government throughout the colonies, none could legitimately argue in America that to submit to the king in and of itself constituted sin. Thus those who justified civil disobedience on the ground of the second answer given above tended to support the American Revolution, while those who favored the third answer could find no legitimate reason for the colonies to rebel. As we will see in chapter thirty-seven, there were sincere Christians on both sides.

We should note that the same debate continues today in connection with such social issues as abortion. Is this a matter that permits, or even requires, civil disobedience? Some Christians argue that abortion is such a terrible crime that laws may be legitimately broken to draw attention to it and fight against it. Thus they block abortion clinics and stage sit-ins and illegal demonstrations. Extremists have even tried to destroy clinics in several places. Others say that, while the government may be allowing sin to go on unhampered, it is not requiring Christians to take any part in that sin, and therefore disobedience is not justified. While Christians should do all in their power to put an end to wholesale slaughter, they may not break laws in the process. The right of civil disobedience extends only to those statutes to which obedience would entail sin. There is no doubt about what answer the Covenanters would give, but what answer is right for Christians today?

FOR REVIEW AND FURTHER THOUGHT

1. What is a covenant?

2. What was the National Covenant?

3. Upon what basis did the Solemn League and Covenant seek to unite the churches of England and Scotland?

4. Why did the Covenanters dislike Oliver Cromwell?

5. What was the attitude of Charles II toward the Solemn League and Covenant?

6. What arguments did the author of *Lex Rex* use in favor of resistance against the Stuart monarchs?

7. How did the principles of *Lex Rex* influence the American Revolution?

8. Why did the Covenanters charge Charles II with being "treacherous and lecherous"?

9. Identify the following in one sentence each: Alexander Henderson, James Guthrie, Samuel Rutherford, Richard Cameron, Ebenezer Erskine.

10. How were the Conventicle Act and the Mile Act used against presbyterian ministers in Scotland?

11. Why did the Test Act lead to such great bloodshed?

12. Why were the Covenanters dissatisfied with the religious settlement made after the Glorious Revolution?

13. What was lay patronage, and why did the Covenanters oppose it?

14. What are the similarities and differences between the lay patronage controversy in eighteenth-century Scotland and the lay investiture controversy in medieval Europe?

15. Who were the Marrowmen, and why did they leave the Church of Scotland?

16. On what grounds did the Covenanters who had come to America favor the American Revolution?

17. Of the three views of civil disobedience outlined in the chapter, which one most nearly describes the view of the Covenanters?

18. Of the three positions on civil disobedience, which do you think is most biblical, and why?

28

BABEL REVISITED

When the entire human race gathered together on the plain of Shinar and began to build a tower, God came down to view their work. He concluded that, "If as one people speaking the same language they have begun to do this, then nothing they plan to do will be impossible for them" (Genesis 11:6, NIV). God spoke these words, not because He felt threatened by man's growing power, but because He could see into men's hearts. He knew that their growing pride and self-sufficiency made them believe that nothing on earth or in the heavens was beyond their grasp. When God confused the languages of mankind at Babel, He showed them how fragile their power really was. But the human race has demonstrated the need to be taught this lesson repeatedly. The pride of the men of Babel has been duplicated over and over again in the history of the human race, not least in the period of time commonly known as the Enlightenment.

The Enlightenment, also sometimes called the Age of Reason, encompasses the latter part of the seventeenth century and most of the eighteenth. It was an era of great contrasts for the church. The deification of human reason turned many away from Christianity and the Church, but God refused to let men brush Him aside so easily. Thus the same era known for its scoffing at God is also known as one of the greatest periods of revival in the history of the church. In the chapters to come, we will examine both the declines and the revivals of the Age of Reason in some of the major countries of Europe. In this chapter, however, we will be focusing our attention on the church in England.

THE DECLINE OF PURITANISM

After two decades of dominating the English political and religious landscape, the Puritans virtually dropped out of sight following the restoration of the monarchy in 1660. The decline of Puritan political influence is understandable, since Charles II would not be expected to place in positions of authority men who had been connected in any way with the execution of his father. In fact, the persecutions directed against the Puritans under the Clarendon Code surprised only those who had been foolish enough to trust the word of a king whose entire family had made it a matter of principle to place themselves above the law.

Puritan control of the church was a different matter. One would have expected that, during twenty years in power, the Puritans would have secured dominant positions in the governmental machinery of the church. This was far from the case, however. Because of the Puritan desire to reform the church along biblical lines, most of them had developed a strong aversion toward episcopacy. Many participated in the Westminster Assembly, which tried to turn the Church of England into a presbyterian church much like that in Scotland. Others favored independency, and openly associated themselves with Independent or Baptist churches during the Cromwell years. As a result, when the bishops regained power over the church at the time of the Restoration, most of the Puritans found themselves on the outside looking in. While the majority of Puritans were suffering discrimination and persecution as members of dissenting congregations, there remained little or no Puritan voice in the Church of England. Men like John Owen and John Bunyan continued to be influential, but their influence was exercised from retirement or from prison, not from the seats of authority in the church.

The churches where the Puritan presence continued soon found themselves caught up in the prevailing spirit of the age. The rationalism that dominated European thought affected Presbyterians, Independents, and Baptists as well as Anglicans. As we shall see, most of the dissenting churches quickly followed the Anglicans into Unitarianism. The one significant exception was the Particular Baptists, who remained firmly committed to their revision of the Westminster Confession (the London Baptist Confession of 1689). Rationalism also had an impact on the Particular Baptists, however. For them, it took the form of hypercalvinism - an overemphasis on the sovereignty of God that led many Particular Baptists to teach that Christian obedience to God's law was unnecessary (since salvation was entirely by grace, one who was saved would continue to be saved no matter how he lived), and that any attempt to win the lost to Christ would be a positive insult to the divine prerogative (since only God could save a person, and He saved only those whom He had chosen, why witness?). They also became very narrow in their refusal to involve themselves either with other Christians or with the unsaved. Clearly, such a church would have little impact on the society around it.

On the level of common society, few people mourned the passing of Puritanism. Most had chafed at the moral strictness of the Cromwell regime, and breathed a sigh of relief when the Restoration brought to the throne a man with whom the common people could identify - one whose irresponsibility and immorality had made him a legend in his own time. In general, people were sick to death of conflicts rooted in religious differences. The best religion, in their view, was one that caused the least disturbance. Not surprisingly, that is exactly the kind of religion that England soon manufactured for itself.

ARMINIANISM IN THE CHURCH OF ENGLAND

The Church of England had never really been comfortable with Calvinism. Though the early reformers of the English church like Cranmer, Latimer, and Ridley were in many ways similar to the great Genevan reformer in their theology, and though the Thirty-Nine Articles could be called broadly Calvinistic, the theology of Calvin never really gained a foothold among the English people. Elizabeth I had openly opposed the doctrines of Geneva because she thought them doleful and sour, to say nothing of narrow and divisive. James I disliked Puritans and Scottish Presbyterians, which generally eliminated Calvinism as far as he was concerned. During the reign of Charles I, the Church of England was dominated by Archbishop of Canterbury William Laud, who openly favored Arminian teaching. Many of those restored to positions of power in the church under Charles II had first come into the church during Laud's time, so it should not surprise anyone to find that the theology of the Church of England following the Restoration was largely Arminian.

Arminianism, you should recall, involved the belief that salvation was a cooperative effort between God and man. Denying the teaching, made popular by men such as Augustine, Luther, and Calvin, that man could do absolutely nothing to contribute to his own salvation, so much so that even faith was seen as a gift of God's grace, the Arminians taught instead that man's free will allowed him to respond in faith to the Gospel of salvation freely offered to all men. The Arminianism of the Church of England in the latter part of the seventeenth century, however, was not so much the result of doctrinal conviction as a result of doctrinal laxity. All the people knew was that they were tired of the somber Calvinism of the Puritans, and everyone was quite prepared to feel good about himself and mankind in general. They thus became Arminians by default rather than by decision. Arminianism, however, proved to be only a brief pause on the path to much more serious deviations from the faith of the Bible and the Reformation.

LATITUDINARIANS AND COMMON-SENSE RELIGION

After the fall of James II in the Glorious Revolution, the Church of England came under the control of a group of men known as Latitudinarians. Led by Archbishop of Canterbury John Tillotson, these men were weary of religious conflict, and quite prepared to give a liberal interpretation to the standards of the church in order to include as many people as possible. Toleration became the watchword of the day, and enthusiasm the only really serious sin ("enthusiasm" was a word similar in its meaning to what we would today label fanaticism). As has always been the case, those who preach toleration were able to be open-minded about almost anything except those who insisted that their way was the only right way. Thus when John Wesley and George Whitefield began preaching biblical faith and biblical morality, they received little but scoffing from the churchmen of their day.

Religious peace often comes at a terrible price. For the Church of England in the early eighteenth century, the price was lowest-common-denominator Christianity. If Christianity was to appeal to the educated man of the Enlightenment, it must be reasonable. To most people, reason was equated with common sense, and reasonable religion was religion that made few serious demands upon a person's life. Any reasonable person could see that God had made the world and that He expected people to live in harmony with one another, but any effort to go beyond these basics was rejected as irrelevant. As a result, worship became immersion in tradition, sermons became lectures on morality, and the Christian life soon came to be equated with the happy life of a good Englishman. As in the Middle Ages the bishop had been indistinguishable from the baron in his lifestyle, so in the England of the Enlightenment the rector's life was little different from that of the country squire - a life devoted to fox-hunting, parties, and taverns. It soon became apparent, however, that a church devoted to making people feel good about themselves is hardly necessary. People are quite capable of feeling good without the church, and in fact can usually find much more satisfactory ways of doing so. For many, religion became a frightful bore, no more necessary than an appendix. The toleration of the Latitudinarians bred peace, but also apathy.

THE IMPACT OF DEISM

We have already seen something of the teachings of Deism in chapter twenty-six. Deism was sparked, not only by the scientific discoveries of men like Isaac Newton, but also by the prevailing confidence in human reason that permeated European society in the eighteenth century. The transition in thought represented by Deism was subtle yet drastic. The early scientific thinkers like Francis Bacon and Newton were convinced that science was merely a means for gaining greater knowledge of God through learning about His creation. They had no doubt that the book of nature and the book of Scripture would harmonize perfectly. Those who followed, however, drew two conclusions that radically changed people's perceptions of Christianity. The first conclusion was that God had made nature so flawless that His intervention was not necessary; the second was that natural revelation was so complete that God's revelation of Himself in Scripture was an exercise in redundancy. To put it another way, natural revelation and Scriptural revelation were first thought to be complementary, then coincident, and finally contradictory.

In addition to the scientists already cited, a good representative of the first view is John Locke (1632-1704). Locke, whose political theories were later to influence the American Revolution, believed that the human mind was a blank slate upon which was written the perceptions that came to us through the senses. Locke naturally assumed that these perceptions would be in harmony with the teachings of the Scriptures, as he explained in his book, *The Reasonableness of Christianity*.

The great English Deists largely fit into the second category. Men such as Matthew Tindal (1655-1733) and John Toland (1670-1722) taught that the Bible was a republication of nature, so that what the Bible really taught was identical to the truths discoverable through reason and natural revelation. Because nature is perfect, the Bible can add nothing to it. Obviously, such an approach to Scripture involved ignoring much that the Bible taught. One of the earliest Deists, Lord Herbert of Cherbury (1583-1648), had maintained that true religion could be reduced to five basic propositions: God exists, we are obliged to worship Him, virtue is the purest form of worship, failure to live virtuously is to be repented of, and virtue will be rewarded and lack of virtue punished in this life and in the life to come. It does not require a great deal of strenuous mental activity to produce a substantial list of foundational Christian teachings omitted from Lord Cherbury's list. The Deists simply wrote off the remainder of Christian teaching as unnecessary priestly invention. Thus the intellectualizing of the Deists corresponded completely with the apathetic temperament of the English population at large. When it came to matters of doctrine, no one cared any more.

In the end, of course, the Deists could not continue to ignore doctrine while preoccupying themselves with the beauty and symmetry of nature. The plain fact of the matter is that what the Deists were teaching contradicted the Bible. If the Deists were to triumph, the teachings of the Bible would ultimately have to be attacked and undermined. Such an attack was mounted by a group of men who styled themselves Freethinkers. They openly admitted that the Bible did not correspond with modern thought, and set out to convince people that the Bible should therefore be rejected. Anthony Collins (1676-1729) argued that biblical prophecy, which has often been used to demonstrate the truthfulness of Scripture, is no more than a sham, and that the life of Jesus corresponded very little if at all to the Old Testament predictions about the Messiah. Thomas Woolston (1669-1733) set out to defend the Bible in his *Six Discourses on the Miracles of Our Saviour*, but proceeded to do so by insisting that the miracles of Jesus were symbolic, intended to underscore the truths He taught, and had never really happened. With such friends, enemies are redundant at best. One contemporary remarked that many had believed in the miracles of Christ until Woolston had set out to defend them!

The man who struck the final blow was the Scottish philosopher David Hume (1711-1776). Interestingly, his philosophy was as much an attack upon Deism as it was an attempt to undermine Christianity. Hume argued that, if the senses indeed are our source of knowledge, miracles must be ruled out by definition. Miracles, after all, are those things that are not part of normal human experience, and it is normal human experience that provides our basis for understanding the world. Miracles must therefore be viewed as at best highly improbable. It is much easier to believe that one who claims to have experienced a miracle was either deluded or a charlatan than it is to believe that the laws of nature and common experience have been violated. He also attacked Deism, however, by asserting that experience alone provides no basis for belief in cause and effect. We know that two events often succeed one another, but we can know nothing about their causes. He concluded that man is thus reduced to skepticism - he can have no certain knowledge of anything. Hume even questioned Descartes' maxim, denying that the mere act of thinking proves the existence of the human soul. By the time Hume was finished, Christianity may have been reduced to a pile of rubble in the minds of many, but so was Deism, and there was little on the horizon to take its place. Reason had failed to win the day.

RATIONAL ARGUMENTS FOR THE CHRISTIAN FAITH

Thankfully, there were Christians in the eighteenth century who did not take these attacks lying down. Unwilling to yield the high ground to the Deists, they fought fire with fire, successfully turning many of the Deists' arguments against them. The greatest of these apologists was Joseph Butler (1692-1752), an Anglican clergyman who eventually became the Bishop of Durham. The Deists won a significant following by contrasting the certainties of science and the natural world with the unverifiable beliefs of religion. Butler, in his *Analogy of Religion, Natural and Revealed, to the Constitution and Course of Nature*, argued that the certainties of science were not certain at all, but rather represented a high level of probability based upon accumulated experience. The Christian religion was also able to cite thousands of years of accumulated experience, which gives the truth of Christianity just as high a probability as the truths of science. Furthermore, the mysteries and dilemmas of religion are paralleled by many things in the world of nature that cannot be understood or explained. If science is not rejected because it cannot provide an explanation for the nature of light, why should Christianity be rejected if it cannot rationally explain the Trinity? Many in Butler's day considered his arguments decisive, and in fact the Deists never refuted them successfully. His *Analogy* was used for two centuries after its publication as a textbook in apologetics courses in colleges and seminaries, though his approach is powerless against the more radical attacks of skeptics like Hume and the critics of modern times.

Butler never attempted to provide a rational proof for God's existence, since that was one teaching the Deists did not deny. Another apologist of our era did, however - William Paley (1743-1805). Paley expanded and refined the argument from design earlier used by Thomas Aquinas to prove that God exists. He spoke of a man walking across a field and happening upon a watch lying on the ground. Even if he had never seen a watch before, and even if the watch were broken and inoperable, he would immediately recognize that the watch had been created by an intelligent mind for a specific purpose. Paley then argued that the world, like the watch, gave evidence of an intelligent Designer - even if the mechanism was "broken" by sin and the purpose only generally intelligible to human observers.

Another interesting apologetic was provided by William Warburton (1698-1779). While Butler and Paley had tried to use the Deists' own weapons against them by showing that the Christian religion was every bit as reasonable as science, Warburton argued for the reliability of Scripture because of its *lack* of reasonableness. He asserted that, had the Bible been written by men in the normal way, it certainly would have approached matters differently than it in fact does. For instance, people are clearly interested in and concerned about life after death. If the Bible were merely a human book, it would have a great deal to say about this subject. In fact, however, the Old Testament hardly mentions it at all. Warburton concluded that such an unreasonable lack of information on a subject of intense interest to man proves that the Bible is divine revelation rather than human speculation.

An even stronger reaction against the cult of reason is found in the work of William Law (1686-1761). While Law is primarily known as a devotional writer whose works profoundly influenced John Wesley, he also entered the debate against the Deists with his book *The Case of Reason*. In this work, he argued that no one should expect God or the truths revealed in His Word to correspond to human reason. If in fact God could be rationally explained, He would not be God, since a God able to be comprehended by the mind of man would have to be a very small God indeed. He thus attacked the very basis of Deism - the notion that only those things that conform to human reason are worthy of acceptance by man.

SOCINIANS AND UNITARIANS

An age that had begun by questioning the importance of many Christian teachings inevitably ended by denying the truth of those same teachings. The Latitudinarians had to a large extent believed the truths of orthodox Christianity, but had not considered most of them to be very important, and certainly not worth arguing about. Soon, though, those same truths began to be attacked, first because they were beyond the verification of experience, then because they contradicted reason. The final steps in the transition to a religion of man were provided by the Unitarians.

Unitarianism reduces Christianity to the simplest form imaginable. Unitarians affirm the belief in one God; aside from this, Unitarians are free to believe whatever they please. Such a creed, of course, involves the denial of such insignificant teachings as the doctrine of the Trinity, the Incarnation, the deity of Christ, the

Resurrection, etc. Unitarians generally affirm the basic goodness of man, and teach that man's basic duty is to live a good life.

Unitarianism in England grew from ground that had been well prepared by the scientific rationalism of the Deists, but it was also stimulated by an influence from abroad - Socinianism. Laelius and Faustus Socinus (uncle and nephew) were sixteenth-century Italians who had rebelled against the corruption in the Catholic Church by advocating a return to the church of the first century. For them, such a move backward involved not only the rejection of over a thousand years of tradition, but also a repudiation of the doctrinal decisions of the councils of the Ancient Church. Like other back-to-basics movements in the history of the church, they tended to throw the baby out with the bath water, and wound up with a rather creative set of teachings that would have made them feel right at home among some of our modern cults. Faustus Socinus eventually fled Italy and settled in Poland, where he and his followers established a thriving church. During the Counterreformation, the Socinians were driven from Poland, and some settled in England, where their doctrines began to spread, particularly through the universities.

The religious climate in England was right for the acceptance of the rational approach to Scripture advocated by the Socinians. Men had been conditioned by the Deists to set up their own minds as the final standard of truth, and the Latitudinarians had convinced the English people that there was room in the church for all kinds of teaching. As a result, one church after another fell under the influence of Unitarianism in the eighteenth century. In 1719, a Presbyterian minister in Exeter named James Pierce was accused of denying the doctrine of the Trinity. A group of ministers met to discuss the matter at the Salters' Hall in London, and by a slim margin of 57 to 53, agreed that ministers should not be held to any specific human interpretation of the doctrine of the Trinity - in other words, Presbyterian ministers were free to deny the deity of Christ without fear of censure by the church. The General Baptists soon moved in the same direction, to the extent that the majority of General Baptist churches became Unitarian.

The Church of England followed suit, though it took a bit longer. In 1772, a group of ministers led by Theophilus Lindsey petitioned Parliament to allow men to be ordained to the Anglican priesthood upon affirmation of the Scriptures rather than the Thirty-Nine Articles. Though such a request sounds very pious - after all, our loyalty is to the Word of God rather than to documents produced by mere men - the fact is that Lindsey and the others wanted to affirm the Bible rather than the creed because they denied what the creed said about the Bible's teachings. They wanted to be free to interpret the Bible in their own way. When Parliament refused, Lindsey left the Church of England and formed an independent Unitarian congregation in London. A few years later, Parliament dropped the doctrinal requirement, and the Church of England was soon firmly in the hands of Unitarians.

Another influential Unitarian was the chemist Joseph Priestley (1733-1804), who departed far from the Calvinism of his youth to lead a movement he called "Rational Dissent." He saw Jesus as no more than a noble man and good moral teacher whose example was worthy of emulation. His support of the French Revolution led to the destruction of his home and laboratory by an angry mob, after which he emigrated to the friendly confines of Pennsylvania, where he established the first Unitarian church in the state, and was honored by scientists and statesmen until his death in 1804.

Thus by the end of the eighteenth century, most of the English churches had fallen under the spell of the cult of Reason, and Unitarian "doctrine" (such as it is) dominated the religious scene. God will not be silenced so easily, however, and during this same era, a revolt against the deadness of the churches was being led by a pair of fiery preachers - John Wesley and George Whitefield. The revival that grew from their evangelistic work will be the subject of chapter thirty.

MAKING DRY BONES LIVE

After struggling through a century and a half of religious warfare in the years following the Protestant Reformation, Europe was sick of war, and convinced that wars were caused by focusing on religious dogma. The antidote to all the suffering during the religious wars was a new attitude of religious toleration, in which all who lived good lives and respected their fellow men were to be welcomed with open arms. While such an approach may sound good in theory, in practice it led to the rapid decline of the churches. If during the Reformation men made the mistake of thinking that the most minor point of doctrine was worth dying for, the Enlightenment proved that those who believe that no doctrine is worth dying for soon are succeeded by those who think that no doctrine is worth believing.

If such an attitude brought about the decline of the church, many would consider it a consummation devoutly to be wished. The spirit of the Age of Reason touched more than just the church, however. Men who relied on reason for all the answers to society's problems soon found that reason did not have those answers, and having discarded religion long before, discovered nothing but emptiness. If David Hume professed skepticism in theory, the French Revolution demonstrated in brutally practical terms that the worship of the Goddess of Reason was an empty religion.

The Enlightenment was not the only era in history in which man has practiced self-glorification, of course. Our own age, though one in which the churches of America are flourishing in many ways, is an age in which man looks to himself for ultimate answers and discards as foolish superstition anything that may not be verified scientifically. When C.S. Lewis sought an image by which to communicate his critique of modern man in his science fiction novel *That Hideous Strength*, it is no accident that he chose the Tower of Babel. Self-worship in our age expresses itself in many ways, from the narcissism of health and beauty fads to the conviction that technology can cure all ills. The lesson of the Enlightenment - that man is *not* the measure of all things - is one we need desperately to relearn today.

FOR REVIEW AND FURTHER THOUGHT

1. What similarities exist between the Enlightenment and the Tower of Babel in Genesis 11?

2. Why did the Restoration cause the Puritans to lose political power?

3. For what reasons did the Puritans cease to have a significant voice in the Church of England after the Restoration?

4. What is hypercalvinism? How did the Particular Baptists during the Enlightenment misuse the teachings of Calvin?

5. Why were the common people of England generally glad to see the Puritans fall from power?

6. Why had the Protestant monarchs of England disliked Calvinism?

7. What is the basic teaching of Arminianism? What factors influenced the English Church in the direction of Arminian theology?

8. Who were the Latitudinarians, and what did they believe?

9. What did eighteenth-century Englishmen mean when they spoke of "enthusiasm," and why did they dislike it?

10. Why are those who preach religious toleration often intolerant of those who believe in absolute truth?

11. Do you think it is possible to stand up for the truth and at the same time be tolerant of others? If so, how?

12. Why did the tolerant attitude of the Enlightenment lead to a "lowest common denominator" brand of Christianity?

13. Why is it true that a church whose main goal is to make people feel good soon works itself out of a job and ultimately out of existence?

14. How did the Deists succeed in undermining people's confidence in the Bible?

15. How did the Deism of John Locke differ from that of Matthew Tindal and John Toland?

16. When Lord Herbert of Cherbury summarized true religion, what important doctrines of Christianity did he leave out as unimportant?

17. Who were the Freethinkers, and why did they find it necessary to attack the Bible?

18. Why was the philosophy of David Hume as much of an attack against Deism as it was against Christianity?

19. Why did Hume argue that miracles are improbable?

20. How did Joseph Butler turn the arguments of the Deists against them?

21. Why would Butler's arguments be useless against Hume's skepticism?

22. In what sense did William Paley's argument for God's existence play into the hands of the Deists rather than refuting their views?

23. What novel approach was used by William Warburton to argue for the divine inspiration of the Bible?

24. In what sense did William Law strike at the roots of Deism rather than seeking to hack off the branches one by one as other apologists had done?

25. What, basically, do Unitarians believe about God? about Jesus? about man?

26. Why did Laelius and Faustus Socinus rebel against the Catholic Church, and what kind of church did they try to form?

27. Why did the Socinians reject the doctrine of the Trinity?

28. How did Deism and Latitudinarianism contribute to the spread of Unitarianism?

29. Why did Theophilus Lindsey want ordination in the Church of England to be based on the Bible rather than the Thirty-Nine Articles?

30. In what sense does a creed or doctrinal statement serve as a safeguard of orthodoxy in the church?

31. What dangers could possibly be associated with the use of a creed to define a church's doctrine?

32. Why did religious toleration lead to a decline in the churches in England?

33. What characteristics of the Enlightenment are shared by our own era?

29

THE DEEP LONGINGS OF THE HEART

Like many young aristocrats of his age, the nineteen-year-old Lutheran nobleman would not have considered himself adequately educated had he not been exposed to the great cultural centers of Europe. While traveling the continent, he had occasion to visit the art gallery in Dusseldorf. There he saw a painting by Domenico Feti entitled *Ecce Homo* that pictured Christ wearing the crown of thorns. Under the picture was the inscription, "All this I did for you. What are you doing for me?" The young count's conscience was smitten, and he determined from that day onward to devote his life to the service of Christ. His name was Nikolaus Ludwig von Zinzendorf, and the deep longing of his heart to know and serve God characterizes an entire movement in the history of the church that has come to be known as Pietism.

The teachings of Pietism were not unique to the eighteenth century, of course. Throughout all ages of the church there have been men and women whose hearts were drawn to God in pure devotion - simple believers, monks and mystics, Anabaptists and Puritans, Protestant, Catholic, and Orthodox alike. But never has the religion of the heart known such widespread influence in the church as may be seen in the eighteenth century. While the term "Pietism" is thus often reserved for the movement in eighteenth-century Germany that will be the subject of our consideration in this chapter, it may also be applied to similar movements at other times and other places, as we will see in succeeding chapters.

BACKGROUNDS OF GERMAN PIETISM

The Thirty Years' War was a tragedy for all of Europe, but nowhere more so than in the German states. The war had robbed Germany of many of its young men, denuded the land, impoverished the people, and brought with it a frightfully low standard of morality. German Protestantism had lost considerable territory as a result of the war, and the leading theologians had to a large extent buried themselves in a defensive cocoon in which they did little but argue the finer points of Lutheran orthodoxy and criticize any who differed from them to the slightest degree. Henry Melchior Muhlenberg, a German Pietist who became the father of American Lutheranism, caught the spirit of the age with unfortunate accuracy when he described one staunchly orthodox woman as holding to "the unaltered Augsburg Confession with an unaltered heart," and spoke of a Lutheran elder "who wanted to be saved by grace but expected to see God without sanctification." A religion of doctrinal precision and intolerance coupled with deadness of heart and little effort in the direction of Christian morality could not help but pain the hearts of those who truly loved God. There seemed at the time little hope for improvement, however, since the German princes who had since the time of Luther controlled the churches in their domains were becoming increasingly cynical in their efforts to manipulate the church for their own political and economic ends.

Some spoke out against this dead orthodoxy. George Calixtus (1586-1656), a professor of theology at Helmstadt, criticized the narrow dogmatism of most Lutheran theologians and advocated tolerance among Christians. In his teaching he focused, not on the doctrines that divided believers of different churches, but rather on those all shared in common. As is always the case with men of moderation, he soon found himself attacked on all sides.

The Lutheran pastor Johann Arndt (1551-1621) opposed the Protestant Scholasticism of his day on a more practical level. From his own pulpit, he preached sermons that focused on living a Christian life on a daily basis. These sermons were quite unlike the theological lectures dealing with obscure points of doctrine that emanated from most Lutheran pulpits of the day. His greatest influence came, however, through his book *True Christianity*, in which he encouraged Christians to live fruitful lives of devotion to God.

A third contributor in the developmental years of the Pietist movement was Paul Gerhardt (1606-1676), a scrupulously orthodox Lutheran pastor whose lasting contribution to the life of the church lies in his hymns. Many of these hymns were later translated into English by John and Charles Wesley, and have continued to inspire the hearts of worshipers in both German and English up to the present day.

SPENER, FRANCKE, AND THE UNIVERSITY OF HALLE

The man who was able to crystallize the growing desire for deeper, more meaningful religion was the Lutheran pastor Philip Jacob Spener (1635-1705). During his pastoral career, which spanned almost forty years, he served churches in Frankfurt, Dresden, and Berlin, and rose to great influence in the courts of the nobility. While in Frankfurt, he realized that the lives of the people in his pews were not being influenced by the doctrinal sermons typical of the day. He abandoned the prescribed texts and instead began to preach through extended passages of Scripture, giving his attention to explaining and applying to the lives of his congregation the basic truths found in his texts. The response, when it came, was miraculous. People who had been content year after year to do their duty to God by coming to church on Sunday, thinking that they thereby had earned the right to ignore Him the rest of the week, suddenly began to hunger for the Word. Members of Spener's congregation began to meet on Sunday afternoons to pray together and discuss the morning sermon. Realizing that they were in need of pastoral guidance, Spener assumed leadership of the group. Soon similar devotional groups, called *collegia pietatis*, sprang up all over the city. It is from these conventicles, or home Bible study groups, that Pietism is believed to have gotten its name.

It may be difficult to imagine how anyone could object to a movement that did nothing more than encourage people to study their Bibles, pray together, and live moral lives, but Spener soon found that the critical theologians of his day could object to almost anything. The orthodox Lutherans feared enthusiasm almost as much as did the rationalists in England. They claimed that the Pietist conventicles were little more than nests of heresy, that they undermined the authority of the church, and that the emphasis on living a holy life contradicted the foundational Lutheran doctrine of justification by faith. The theological faculty at the University of Wittenberg displayed Luther's contentious spirit without an ounce of Luther's heart for God when they compiled a list of two hundred eighty-three errors of which they believed Spener to be guilty.

In 1675, Spener published what was to become the manifesto of Pietism - a little book called *Pia desideria* ("Pious Desires"). In this work he criticized the cold, dead orthodoxy of German Lutheranism, and expressed six heartfelt desires for which he longed. These six provide a concise summary of Pietism. Spener's first and most urgent desire was for Christians to study the Bible for themselves. The conventicles were an outgrowth of this. Secondly, he wanted to reaffirm the Lutheran doctrine of the priesthood of all believers by giving laymen responsibility in the conventicles and in the churches. In Spener's day, as in many ages both before and since, the tendency of the people in the pews was to sit like sponges and soak up the sermon, but never use what they had heard to cleanse either their own lives or the lives of those around them. Thirdly, Spener saw the doctrinal emphasis of the Lutheran church producing crippled Christians whose growth was stunted, if indeed there was any growth at all, and desired for people to view Christianity as a way of life, not just a set of beliefs. His fourth desire was that, when it was necessary for Christians to disagree on matters of doctrine and practice, that such disagreement could be carried out in a spirit of mutual love and respect. Fifthly, Spener saw around him many knowledgeable men in the pulpits of Germany - men who knew every detail of Lutheran doctrine, but gave no evidence of knowing Jesus Christ. He believed that pastoral training should go far beyond biblical and theological studies to include devotional materials as well as practical experience in ministering to the needs of people. Such pastors, Spener was convinced, would then be able to fulfill his sixth and final desire - that the pulpit ministry in the churches would focus on expounding the Word of God and feeding the flock rather than emphasizing obscure theological disputes. Spener's six pious desires summarize the strengths of Pietism, but they also hint at some of the weaknesses that have followed Pietism wherever it has spread, and which will be the subject of the concluding section of this chapter.

If Spener was the man who enunciated the foundational principles of Pietism, August Hermann Francke (1663-1727) put those ideas into practice in a way that became a model for Pietist endeavor in Germany, England, America, and elsewhere. Francke came under the influence of Spener as a young man, and while teaching Hebrew at the University of Leipzig formed a Bible study group among the faculty called the *Collegium Philobiblicum*. The theological faculty at Leipzig objected both to the rather free-wheeling and subjective interpretation of Scripture encouraged by Francke in these Bible studies, and also to the not-so-subtle implication that those who had not found the deeper religious life earnestly sought by the Pietists were in fact not saved at all. When Francke had the unmitigated gall to suggest that members of the Lutheran church in good standing, and even certain pastors, were themselves in need of evangelizing, he was dismissed from his post at the university. He then moved on to Erfurt, where the same cycle of revival, opposition, and removal repeated itself. He then spent some time with Spener in Berlin, in a period of fellowship that encouraged both men. When the Elector of Brandenburg founded a new university at Halle, Spener convinced him to include Francke on the faculty. It was at the University of Halle that Francke was to do his greatest work, while the university itself became the center of Pietist activity in Germany.

At Halle, Francke for the first time had the opportunity to put into practice on a large scale what he believed to be the essence of Christian living. For him, a Christianity that was not given to practical service was no Christianity at all. Thus, in the thirty-five years he spent at Halle, he founded an orphanage, started schools for children of all ages, both rich and poor, helped organize a Bible society for the publication and dissemination of inexpensive copies of the Scriptures, and encouraged dozens of young men who passed through his schools to give their lives to foreign missionary service. The impact of his work was extended, not only by the travels and varied ministries of his students, but also by his voluminous correspondence with Christian leaders in many churches all over the world. By the time of his death, Halle had become the most influential university in Germany, and had trained thousands of men for Christian service.

ZINZENDORF AND THE MORAVIANS

The young man in the art gallery with whom we began the chapter was the Halle student who, perhaps even more than Francke, came to embody the Pietist ideal. Count Nikolaus Ludwig von Zinzendorf (1700-1760) never knew his father, a nobleman who died when Nikolaus was still an infant, and was raised by his godly grandmother, who was a friend of Spener. Young Zinzendorf studied at one of Francke's schools in Halle between the ages of ten and sixteen, and there developed a strong love for God and a deep desire to serve Him. While in school, he organized a group of students into what he called the Order of the Grain of Mustard Seed, dedicated to living godly lives and bringing the Gospel to all regardless of religious or national background. Though his real desire was to pursue a career in foreign missions, his family would not hear of such a risky and uncertain life, and convinced him to study law instead. He then entered the University of Wittenberg, where he prepared for government service. It was during a break in his studies that he recommitted his life to the service of Christ in the Dusseldorf museum. From this time on, Zinzendorf was determined to serve his Master first, no matter what profession he practiced.

After his graduation from Wittenberg in 1721, he began serving in the royal court in Dresden. At about the same time, he purchased from his grandmother the family estate at Berthelsdorf. A year later he married a young countess who shared his Pietist ideas, and together they entered into a life of service. Late in 1722, a carpenter by the name of Christian David visited Zinzendorf. He asked if he and several other families who were fleeing religious persecution might be allowed to settle on the Berthelsdorf estate. The count readily agreed to give them sanctuary. The refugees, under the leadership of David, built a settlement that they named Herrnhut ("The Lord's Watch"). Zinzendorf at first had no direct involvement with the group beyond providing a place for them to live, but he soon began to take a more active interest in their affairs.

Within a few years, David and the others were joined by a group of refugees who described themselves as members of the *Unitas Fratrum*, or Bohemian Brethren. These Brethren were descendants of the fifteenth-century Hussite movement in Bohemia who had maintained their identity for almost three centuries. The Brethren had for a time been dominant in Bohemia and Moravia, and had affiliated themselves with the Protestant cause when the Reformation appeared on the scene. They had suffered much persecution during the Counterreformation, however, and had been forced to flee from place to place under the leadership of the great educational theorist Jan Amos Comenius (1592-1670). The Brethren had been persecuted by all sides during the Thirty Years' War, during which their numbers had been reduced drastically. Many of their remaining families were now welcomed into Zinzendorf's fast-growing religious community.

With growing numbers came growing problems, however. Settlers from Lutheran and Reformed backgrounds had joined the Brethren at Herrnhut, and they quarreled to the point of schism over forms of worship and church practice. In 1727, Zinzendorf himself finally stepped in, spent much time counseling the individual families involved, encouraged them to pray together, and was overjoyed to see an outpouring of the Holy Spirit that to a large extent ended the strife. Zinzendorf then helped prepare a "Brotherly Agreement" that became the rule of community life. By it the settlers were divided into small "bands" for devotional purposes, in which people were grouped with those of like mind. With Zinzendorf now recognized as their leader, the Herrnhut community became one big Pietist conventicle, in which the lives of the people were strictly regulated, and all gave frequent attention to Bible study and prayer.

Zinzendorf, a good Lutheran, had no desire to leave the Lutheran Church, and in fact sought ordination as a Lutheran minister in order to avoid conflicts. He also was ordained by the lone surviving bishop of the *Unitas Fratrum*, and thus brought into the Herrnhut community the concept of apostolic succession. Conflict soon broke out with the local Lutheran leaders, however, over many of the same issues that had brought such fierce criticism to Spener and Francke. Ultimately, Zinzendorf was banished from Saxony (1736), with the result that his followers became a separate church, known formally as the Unity of the Brethren (after the older *Unitas Fratrum*), but more commonly referred to as the Moravian Church.

In the same way that the persecution of the Jerusalem Church mentioned in Acts 8:2 scattered the Christians and led ultimately to the spread of the Gospel throughout the Roman Empire, so the banishment of the Moravians contributed to the first great Protestant missionary outreach. Zinzendorf had always been interested in missions, and the Herrnhut community shared his vision. Beginning as early as 1732, missionaries were going out from Herrnhut, and for the first two centuries of Moravian history, the church sent an astounding one percent of its members (actually, one out of 92; a typical figure for most churches is one out of several thousand) into missionary work. Not surprisingly, the Moravian Church spread rapidly into other parts of Europe, North America, the Caribbean, India, and elsewhere.

Zinzendorf had a vision for Christian unity as well as foreign missions. He believed that doctrinal differences, while having some validity, could and should be overlooked so that Christians could join in common devotion to Christ. Thus, when he spent part of his exile from Saxony visiting the Moravian settlements in Pennsylvania, he attempted to join all the German settlers together into one church - a true Unity of the Brethren. His efforts failed, largely and somewhat surprisingly because of the efforts of Henry Melchior Muhlenberg, the Halle-trained Pietist who had assumed leadership of the American Lutherans.

One of Zinzendorf's greatest legacies is his devotional spirit, reflected in his writings, but even more so in his hymns. Despite the extremes to which some Moravians took their devotion to the blood and wounds of Christ (some of their literature dwells in gory detail upon Christ's suffering, and especially His wounded body), Zinzendorf has given to the church some of its most powerful devotional poetry, including the great hymn *Jesus, Thy Blood and Righteousness*.

PIETIST INFLUENCE OUTSIDE GERMANY

We have seen that the Pietists, both those from Halle and the Moravians, spearheaded the first organized Protestant missionary outreach. There are many reasons why Protestants had not engaged in significant missionary work prior to this, and these will be enumerated in chapter thirty-four. In any case, the Pietists were the ones who first saw the importance of such an effort.

In 1706, King Frederick IV of Denmark expressed a desire to send missionaries to the Danish colony on the coast of India. He was unable to find any volunteers in Denmark, so he sent word to Francke at Halle to see if any suitable men might be found. Francke leaped at the opportunity, and soon recommended to the king two young men, Bartholomew Ziegenbalg and Heinrich Plutschau. After commissioning in Denmark, they set sail for India. Once they arrived, they faced much opposition, mostly from the Danish traders and European Roman Catholics in the settlement. At first they couldn't even find a place to live or anyone willing to teach them the native language. God blessed their work greatly, however, and by the time Ziegenbalg died in 1719, he had seen over 400 Indians baptized, and had translated a major portion of the Bible into the Tamil language. The Danish-Halle mission continued to bear fruit through the efforts of men such as Christian Friedrich Schwartz (1726-1798). During his forty-eight years in India, Schwartz led many to Christ, and also gained such high respect for his personal integrity that he was entrusted with raising a Hindu ruler's son, and called upon more than once by a Muslim prince to negotiate treaties with European powers.

The Moravians soon joined their Pietist brethren in enthusiastic missionary activity. In 1732, Leonard Dober and David Nitschmann became the first missionaries sent out from Herrnhut when they sailed for the island of St. Thomas in the Caribbean, where they established a church after much suffering and hardship. Christian David eventually traveled to Greenland, while August Gottlieb Spangenberg (1703-1792) came as a missionary to the wilds of North America, ministering first in Georgia, then heading up the Moravian settlements in Pennsylvania (towns in eastern Pennsylvania with biblical names such as Bethlehem, which is still the American Moravian headquarters, and Nazareth were originally Moravian settlements). David Zeisberger (1721-1808) gave his life to ministry among the Indians of North America, sharing with them in the persecution they faced at the hands of white settlers and pagan Indians as well. As they were forced by persecution to migrate from place to place, Zeisberger accompanied them, finally settling in Canada shortly before his death.

The most far-reaching result of Pietism outside Germany may not have been in India, Greenland, the Caribbean, or Pennsylvania, however, though there can be no question that the missionary efforts of the Pietists established a pattern later followed by many. Instead, if we are to see the area of Pietism's greatest influence, we must look to England. There, in a church driven to the point of rationalistic skepticism and traditional apathy by the Enlightenment and Deism, God introduced one of the greatest revivals in the history of the church through the preaching of John Wesley and George Whitefield - a revival largely stimulated by the influences of Pietism in the lives of these men. This revival not only touched the British Isles, but overflowed into America as well, and made a lasting impression on the American religious character.

STRENGTHS AND WEAKNESSES OF PIETISM

Pietism provided a needed corrective to the dead orthodoxy of German Lutheranism and the cold rationalism of Enlightenment England. But any medicine, if taken too often or for too long, can ultimately do as much damage as the disease it was intended to cure. Thus Pietism's very strengths, which did so much to revive the church, contained the seeds of future trouble when they became the exclusive focus of the churches that sprang from the Pietist movement.

Because Pietism was a reaction against the preoccupation of the German Lutheran church with doctrinal trivia, the Pietists rightly emphasized the importance of living a Christian life. Believing the right things means nothing if that truth is not put into practice. While the emphasis on holy living was badly needed, it also produced problems in the long run. First of all, the Pietist effort to diminish the importance of doctrine tended to produce churches that were at best doctrinally ignorant and at worst tolerant of heresy. The early Pietists were strong Christians because they built their emphasis on holy living upon the foundation of orthodox doctrine, which they assumed but did not stress. The second generation, however, was raised in an environment in which Christianity was understood to be a certain style of life and form of devotion, but where doctrine simply was not taught. It should surprise us very little to find that the second generation of Pietists produced some who were quite willing to jettison the foundational doctrines of the faith and define Christianity as little more than moral living (see chapter thirty-one).

Another problem associated with downgrading doctrine is that the Pietist emphasis on the Christian life tended to spawn legalism. The American evangelicalism so typical of our own culture in the twentieth century revealed its Pietist heritage when it understood Christian living as being centered in the avoidance of certain "worldly" practices. Much like the Anabaptists earlier, an approach to Christianity that defines the faith in terms of external practices easily falls prey to a legalistic spirit.

A second important emphasis of Pietism was on the need for a personal devotional life, including private and corporate Bible study and prayer. The devotional life stressed by the Pietists was a major factor in reviving many of the churches with which they became involved. This aspect, too, brought with it its share of problems, however. The most obvious of these is the tendency toward spiritual pride. The Pietists in their conventicles found it very easy to look down upon the poor benighted souls in the churches, and occasionally developed a two-level view of Christianity almost as strong as that spawned by monasticism in the Catholic Church. Those in the churches may claim to be Christians, they might think, but anyone who *really* cared about spiritual things would surely join our devotional group. They thus came to think of Christians as divided into two categories, the "spiritual" and the "carnal" - i.e., Pietists and those who were not.

Similarly, the conventicles tended in the long run to undermine the authority of the church. As much as Zinzendorf and Wesley after him may have expressed their desire to reform the church from within, their use of laymen in places of authority in the conventicles made it inevitable that their Bible study groups would ultimately become separate churches. After all, what did it say about the local pastor's spirituality and authority if a Bible study group was started in his parish without his knowledge, and leaders were appointed without consulting him?

In addition, the separation of the conventicles from the church's authority structure, along with their encouragement of personal and group Bible study, tended to produce a high degree of subjectivism in biblical interpretation. The conventicles tended to ask the question, "What does this passage mean to me?" without first asking the question, "What does this passage mean?" Francke even went so far as to assert that the simple believer who approaches the Bible with a spirit of devotion will always benefit more from it than the man who studies the minutiae of grammar and doctrine. While the Pietist approach may serve well the cause of application, it does little for the cause of truth. The Pietist approach to Scripture ultimately undermined the authority of the Bible as well, since what the Bible means to me becomes the standard for my life, even if what it means to me may differ from what it means to you. In the long run, Pietism produced a situation where no one is in a position to say what the Bible *really* means.

Finally, the subjectivism of Pietist religion tended to drive a wedge between the Christian and the larger society. While the early Pietists showed a great desire to influence the world around them through orphanages and other social services, the emphasis on personal religion in the long run produced a group of people who were quite willing to attend to their devotions, content that they were on their way to heaven while the society around them was going to hell. It's not that Pietists were not concerned for men's souls - that was one of their greatest strengths. The problem was that the responsibility of the organized church to make an impact on the secular world was pushed aside in favor of a private religion that had little to do with the public life of the Christian or the church.

The third great emphasis of the Pietists was their conviction that Christians had the responsibility to spread the Gospel to the ends of the earth. They thus became the first great Protestant missionaries, laying the groundwork for the monumental missionary endeavors of the nineteenth and twentieth centuries. Nor did they ignore home missions. In fact, the Pietists often offended the people in their own churches by at least inferring that many in those churches needed to be born again, despite the fact that they had been born and baptized into the church. By stressing that not all those who say, "Lord, Lord" are going to enter into the Kingdom of Heaven, the Pietists brought revival to many churches, while at the same time drawing upon themselves the wrath of many "respectable" Christians.

MAKING DRY BONES LIVE

The history of the Christian church all too often resembles the pendulum of a grandfather clock. We have seen since the beginning of our studies that false teaching very often enters the church, not because of deliberate rejection of biblical truth, but rather because of an overemphasis on one particular area of truth to the exclusion of all others. When such extremes of teaching appear, they are usually recognized by the majority of Christians as being unbalanced representations of the message of God's Word. Unfortunately, the response of the church to false teaching has often been to stress the truth that is being ignored by the false teachers. The result, of course, is simply imbalance in the opposite direction. Thus the history of the church looks like a pendulum, with periods of emphasis on certain truths succeeded by times when the complementary truth receives the bulk of attention, with precious few examples of a genuine biblical balance in between.

The development of Pietism is a perfect example of this "Pendulum Effect." The German Lutheran church was undoubtedly guilty of focusing on doctrine to such an extent that the importance of practical daily application of the Christian faith was being ignored. The Pietists saw this gaping hole in the life of the church, and sought to correct the balance by stressing the need for personal holiness and devotion to Christ. Had the movement been able to retain the doctrinal roots upon which the founders of Pietism built their views of Christian living, all would have been well, but that did not turn out to be the case. Instead, Pietism swung to the other extreme, ignoring doctrine as if it counted for little, and defining Christianity so much in terms of outward behavior and inner devotion that soon people knew nothing of the doctrines that had shortly before been the objects of such intense debate. The pendulum thus swung from the purely objective study of doctrine to the opposite extreme, the purely subjective attention to personal Christianity. It should come as no surprise that the next step involved a swing back to objective rationalism, as we will see in chapter thirty-one, though this time the objective approach was almost tantamount to the denial of Christianity altogether.

Christians need to recognize that the only way to know the Bible truly is to know it fully. Those who stress some teachings to the exclusion of others will always wind up with an unbalanced Christianity that is in serious danger of becoming no Christianity at all. When Paul spoke to the Ephesian elders for the last time before traveling to Jerusalem, he said that he had not hesitated to preach to them "the whole counsel of God" (Acts 20:27, KJV). True Christianity is not a narrow focus on some favorite truth or religious hobby-horse. Only the complete teaching of the Word of God will keep the church from the errors and extremes of the Pendulum Effect.

FOR REVIEW AND FURTHER THOUGHT

1. What was the condition of the Lutheran church in Germany in the middle of the seventeenth century?

2. How did the Thirty Years' War contribute to the pitiful condition of the German church?

3. How did George Calixtus, Johann Arndt, and Paul Gerhardt help pave the way for the development of Pietism?

4. Why is Philip Jacob Spener known as the Father of German Pietism?

5. What were the *collegia pietatis*, and what role did they play in the development of Pietism?

6. Why did the Lutheran leaders of Spener's day object to the Pietist movement?

7. List the six "pious desires" expressed by Spener in his book, and explain how Pietism sought to put them into practice.

8. Why did some of the professors at Leipzig object to Francke's *Collegium Philobiblicum*?

9. What role was played by the University of Halle in the spread of Pietism?

10. What practical expressions of Christian service were initiated by Francke at Halle?

11. What was the Order of the Grain of Mustard Seed? Where did Zinzendorf get his name for the group?

12. Identify the following in one sentence each: Christian David, Jan Amos Comenius, Henry Melchior Muhlenberg, Frederick IV, Bartholomew Ziegenbalg, Heinrich Plutschau, Christian Friedrich Schwartz, August Gottlieb Spangenberg, David Zeisberger.

13. What was Herrnhut, and how did it get started?

14. Who were the *Unitas Fratrum*, where did they come from, and how are they related to the Moravian Church?

15. Do you think Zinzendorf's desire to unite all Christians into one organization was a good thing? Why or why not?

16. How did the king of Denmark and the Halle Pietists come to cooperate in missionary work? Where did the Danish-Halle mission operate?

17. Where in the American colonies did the Moravians concentrate their efforts? Why do you think they chose this particular colony?

18. What was the major impact of Pietism in England?

19. Name three strengths of Pietism, and tell why these strengths were badly needed by the German church.

20. Name three weaknesses of Pietism, and tell how these weaknesses developed from the strengths of the movement.

21. What is the Pendulum Effect? What causes it? Why is Pietism a good example of it?

THE WORLD FOR A PARISH

The Latitudinarians and Deists had done their jobs well. Eighteenth-century England was filled with people who were not inclined to take their religion very seriously. One aristocratic lady was even heard to suggest, with tongue firmly planted in cheek, that Parliament should consider a bill to remove the word "not" from the Ten Commandments and insert it in the creed. The empty moral platitudes emanating from the pulpits satisfied no one, least of all the spiritually starving people in the pews. When satirist William Hogarth drew a cartoon picturing the typical church service of his day, he showed the preacher reading his sermon to a sleeping congregation.

Such dead churches were in no position to meet the needs of a rapidly changing English society. The Industrial Revolution had created a whole new class of people, the urban working poor, who to a large extent were not being reached by the churches. These men and women had left the small towns where they had been raised to seek jobs in the cities, and found little welcome in the upscale churches of England's larger municipalities. Industry also brought with it enormous social problems, from the abuse of workers by their employers to female and child labor to crowded and filthy city slums to gin, the potent drug of choice in eighteenth-century England. With churches unable and Parliament unwilling to deal with these problems, unrest bubbled under the surface of English society not unlike that stirring the peasants across the Channel in France. In 1789, the unrest in France broke out in bloody revolution, in which thousands lost their lives on the guillotine. In 1789 England, however, almost every city and town had one or more groups of Christians meeting for prayer, praise, and Bible study, while Christians in positions of power were working to correct the injustices of English society.

What made the difference between England and France in 1789? While many factors were involved, one of the most important was the Methodist Revival, which changed the face of English society and left a significant mark on America as well. Not only did the revival save England from a bloody revolution, but it also was used by God to bring thousands of people to a saving knowledge of Christ.

THE EARLY LIFE OF THE WESLEYS

John (1703-1791) and Charles (1707-1788) were the fifteenth and eighteenth children, respectively, of Samuel Wesley, an Anglican rector in the town of Epworth, and his wife Susanna. The Wesleys were strict parents. While Samuel fancied himself to be a bit of an intellectual, Susanna devoted herself tirelessly to the task of raising her large family. She ran the house with a firm hand that would have elicited the envy of a drill sergeant. She administered the rod freely, and taught her children to cry softly by the time they had reached the age of one year. Time was allotted each week for private conversation with each child, during which Susanna looked after the spiritual welfare of her offspring. She also took upon herself the task of educating the children in their early years. Given such an environment, it should surprise us little to find that, of the eleven Wesley children who survived beyond infancy, three eventually became preachers. The oldest son, Samuel, followed in his father's footsteps, while John and Charles became leaders in the greatest revival in English history. John Wesley freely acknowledged his debt to his parents, particularly his mother. He clearly inherited her substantial organizational ability, and he sought and valued her advice until the day of her death.

Samuel Wesley's preaching was not always popular with his congregation in Epworth, particularly when he boldly pointed out the sins of the people in his pews. In 1709, some of the townspeople became so enraged that they set fire to the parsonage. The members of the Wesley family scrambled out of bed and got safely outside of the house, all except for young John, who was trapped in an upstairs bedroom. He was finally rescued by a neighbor who stood on the shoulders of another man and lifted the terrified boy out of a window. From that day onward, John thought of himself as "a brand plucked from the burning," and believed that God had spared him for some special task.

When the time came to obtain his university education, John enrolled at Christ Church, Oxford. After earning his degree, he was ordained to the Anglican ministry, and spent several years assisting his father in the vicinity of Epworth. He then returned to Oxford as a fellow of Lincoln College. By that time, Charles had arrived in Oxford, and had gathered around him a small group of students who met regularly for prayer and Bible study. John soon became the leader of this little group of undergraduates. They practiced regular fasting, took communion weekly, visited the sick and the inmates of the local prison, and encouraged one another in holy living. Most of the other students at Oxford thought they were crazy. They sneered at the devotional practices of the little band, derisively referring to them as the Holy Club, the Bible Moths, or, because of the strict disciplines they imposed upon themselves, Methodists. Though the group probably never exceeded twenty-five in number, the Holy Club produced several men who later went on to play prominent roles in the revival, including an innkeeper's son from Gloucester named George Whitefield.

In 1736, both John and Charles Wesley responded to an invitation from General James Oglethorpe, the founder of the American colony of Georgia, to come over to America as missionaries. John was to serve as chaplain, while Charles would be the governor's personal secretary. They soon set sail for the New World, full of enthusiasm for the work God had called them to do. John was particularly interested in bringing the Gospel to the American Indians, whom he envisioned as noble savages hungering for the Good News. The trip to Georgia was not an easy one. The seas were rough, and on several occasions the young men were convinced that they were about to meet their Maker. On board with them was a group of Moravians bound for the Moravian settlement in Georgia. John and Charles were amazed at the peace and confidence displayed by the Moravians during the storm. These Brethren did not appear to fear death at all, while the Wesleys were terrified. What kind of religion could give men, women, and even children such courage in the face of death? John and Charles began to wonder whether they knew Christ at all.

Upon arriving in Georgia, the idealism of the Wesleys was punctured like an over-inflated balloon. Charles found the climate disagreeable, and soon got sick and went back to England. John, meanwhile, was encountering resistance on all sides. The Indians were anything but noble savages. John found them to be drunkards, liars, and thieves who had absolutely no interest in the Gospel. The English colonists were not much better. Most had little desire to follow the strict disciplines and High Church practices John wanted to institute, and he quickly made many enemies. His refusal to marry or bury anyone who had not undergone Anglican baptism infuriated the Dissenters in the colony. Even those who were willing to join with him in spiritual disciplines became a source of trouble. One such young lady, Sophia Hopkey, caught John's eye as a potential wife. When he determined by casting lots that he should not propose marriage, however, she rather abruptly married someone else. When she then stopped attending John's religious meetings, he placed her under church discipline and refused to admit her to communion. Her new husband promptly took John to court, where the jury turned out to consist largely of his enemies. He decided it was time to return to England.

GERMAN PIETISM AND ENGLISH METHODISM - A COMPARISON

	PIETISM	METHODISM
FOUNDER	Philip Jacob Spener (1635-1705)	John Wesley (1703-1791)
RELIGIOUS SITUATION	Stagnant orthodoxy of post-Reformation scholastic Lutheranism	Rationalistic Deism of post-Puritan Anglicanism
FOUNDATIONAL BOOK	Spener, *Pia Desideria*	William Law, *A Serious Call to a Devout and Holy Life*
EDUCATIONAL CENTER	University of Halle	Oxford University
ORGANIZATION	Conventicles	Methodist societies
OTHER KEY FIGURES	Auguste H. Francke (1663-1727) J.A. Bengel (1687-1752) Nikolaus von Zinzendorf (1700-1760) Peter Boehler (1712-1775) Alexander Mack (1679-1735)	Charles Wesley (1707-1788) George Whitefield (1714-1770) Thomas Coke (1747-1814) Francis Asbury (1745-1816) Selina Hastings, Countess of Huntingdon (1707-1791)
RESULTING CHURCHES	Church of the Brethren Moravian Church	Methodist Church Calvinistic Methodists (Countess of Huntingdon's Connexion)
COMMON EMPHASES	Practical holiness Personal Bible study Need for conscious conversion Evangelistic preaching Devotional exercises Relief of poor and needy Experience more than doctrine	
PIETIST INFLUENCES ON METHODISM	Wesleys met Moravians on ship to Georgia, were impressed with their quiet confidence (1735) Moravian Spangenberg questioned John Wesley in Georgia. John Wesley sought out Moravians in London; Boehler was instrumental in his conversion (1738) John Wesley visited Zinzendorf at Herrnhut (1738) Methodist societies were established, based on model of Pietist conventicles (1738)	

While in Georgia, John Wesley had sought out the Moravian leader August Spangenberg to try to find out the secret behind the behavior he had observed among the Moravians on board the ship that brought him to America. The conversation with Spangenberg only produced more doubts, however. The Moravian leader had asked John a simple question: "Do you believe in Jesus Christ?" John had responded, "I believe that He is the Savior of the world," but Spangenberg had insisted that more than that was necessary. He told Wesley that he would never find peace until he could say with conviction that Christ had died for him personally.

By the time he returned to England, John Wesley was convinced that he was not a Christian at all. While he had gone to America to convert others, he had discovered that he himself needed to be converted. In London, he spent many hours conversing with the Moravian leader Peter Boehler, who encouraged him to wait upon the Holy Spirit. He tried everything he could think of, but still found no peace. Then, on the night of May 24, 1738, he somewhat reluctantly went to a small Bible study in Aldersgate Street in London. When he arrived, the leader was reading from the preface to Luther's commentary on the book of Romans. When the leader began to speak about justification by faith, Wesley writes in his journal that his "heart felt strangely warmed," and he at last knew that Christ had died for *his* sins. He had found the peace he had sought for so long. He quickly rushed off to tell his brother Charles, but when he arrived he found that Charles had had a similar experience three days earlier. The two now set out with renewed enthusiasm to serve God in whatever way He called them to do so.

GEORGE WHITEFIELD

At this point in our story, we turn to the man God used to show John Wesley the method that was to become the hallmark of his long preaching ministry. George Whitefield (1714-1770) came from a background very different from that of the Wesleys. He was the son of a Gloucester innkeeper. His father died when George was two years old, and he was raised by his mother and stepfather in the atmosphere of an English tavern. While Whitefield did show some concern for religious things as a young man, he also was involved in some of the vices that surrounded the life of an English public house.

He was able to save a little bit of money by tending bar, and proceeded to work his way through Oxford University by hiring himself out as a servant to other students. While at Oxford he was converted, and soon became a member of the Holy Club. After graduation, he was ordained to the Anglican priesthood. His first sermon apparently made quite an impression - the local bishop complained that his preaching had driven fifteen people mad! In a church that was deathly afraid of "enthusiasm," Whitefield soon found that few clergymen were willing to let him preach in their parishes.

He was not deterred by these refusals, however, and was determined to take the Gospel to those people whom the churches were not reaching. He thus went to the coal-mining region around Bristol, and began to preach to the miners as they entered and left the mines. The Good News preached by Whitefield melted the hearts of these men to such an extent that the tears flowing from their eyes made white rivers down their coal-blackened faces. Such "field preaching" was forbidden by the Church of England (under normal circumstances, a preacher had to get the permission of the local priest if he wanted to preach in the parish), but Whitefield felt that the need of these unreached miners justified violation of the church's policy. Whitefield saw such responsiveness among the miners that he wrote to John Wesley in London and invited him to come up to Bristol and help with the work. Wesley, a devout High Churchman, was very reluctant to go against church policy, but nonetheless responded to Whitefield's invitation. The joyful response of the miners to the preaching of the Gospel soon removed all doubt from Wesley's mind. From that point on, when he was rebuked for preaching in another man's domain, he responded that the world was his parish. The spiritual blindness of men and women everywhere compelled him to preach wherever the Good News was needed.

Field preaching thus became the primary method by which the Methodist Revival was spread. Whitefield and Wesley drew enormous, though often hostile, crowds wherever they went. Whitefield was one of the most eloquent preachers of his or any other era. His voice was a marvelous instrument, and he used it to move throngs of people to respond to Jesus Christ. Even those who had little interest in spiritual things marveled at the power of Whitefield's oratory. David Garrick, the greatest English actor of the eighteenth century, claimed that Whitefield could move audiences to ecstasy or tears by the way he intoned the word "Mesopotamia," and swore that he would gladly

JOHN WESLEY AND GEORGE WHITEFIELD - A CONTRAST

	WESLEY	WHITEFIELD
PARENTAGE	Son of an Anglican rector in Epworth	Son of a tavern-keeper in Gloucester
EARLY LIFE	Strict religious upbringing supervised by mother, Susanna	Raised surrounded by worldly influences by mother, Elizabeth, who was widowed when George was 2
CONVERSION	Aldersgate Street, London, at age 35	Oxford University, at age 21
ORDINATION	Church of England, 1728, at age 25	Church of England, 1736, at age 22
PREACHING STYLE	Intellectual, doctrinal	Dramatic, emotional
DOCTRINE	Arminian (though closer to Pietist semi-Augustinianism than to Dutch Arminianism)	Calvinistic
ORGANIZATIONAL ABILITY	Exceptional organizer; maintained personal control over total organization of Methodist societies	Not a good organizer, preferring to preach and leave organizing to others
MINISTRY OUTSIDE ENGLAND	Did early unsuccessful missionary work in Georgia; later preached in Scotland and Ireland; appointed bishops to supervise work in America.	Visited Scotland 14 times, participating in Cambuslang revival; visited America 7 times, becoming catalyst of First Great Awakening
LEGACY	Methodist Church	Calvinistic Methodists; influence on Evangelical Party in Church of England

"pay a hundred guineas to be able to say `Oh!' like Mr. Whitefield." Benjamin Franklin, an old skeptic if there ever was one, writes of going to hear Whitefield speak in Philadelphia:

"I perceived that he intended to finish with a collection, and I silently resolved that he should get nothing from me. I had in my pocket a handful of copper money, three or four silver dollars, and five pistoles in gold. As he proceeded, I began to soften, and concluded to give the copper. Another stroke of his oratory determined me to give the silver; and he finished so admirably that I emptied my pocket wholly into the collector's dish, gold and all."

During a preaching career spanning over thirty years, Whitefield traveled all over the British Isles, and crossed the ocean thirteen times while making seven trips to the American colonies, where he died in 1770. Wherever he went, revival followed. Whitefield was a man of toleration who could comfortably work with men of varying religious persuasions. His flexibility enabled him to work with and stimulate revivals in the American colonies, Wales, and Scotland as well as England. In America, his preaching tied together the various manifestations of the Great Awakening (see chapter thirty-six). In Wales, he helped stimulate the growth of the revival started by men such as Howell Harris and Daniel Rowland, while his preaching in Scotland gave new impetus to the Cambuslang revival begun by the ministry of William McCullough.

Whitefield was not much of an organizer, and left behind him no structure such as that created by John Wesley. His legacy included an orphanage in Georgia, a small group of Calvinistic Methodists in England and Wales under the patronage of Lady Selina Hastings, the Countess of Huntingdon, and thousands of souls won to Jesus Christ. Many of those converted under his preaching remained within the Church of England, and became the foundation for the Evangelical party within that church.

METHODIST ORGANIZATION

Whitefield may not have been a capable organizer, but John Wesley had order in his genes. He grew up in the tightly-organized household run by Susanna Wesley, and applied the same principles of discipline to the Holy Club at Oxford. His contacts with Spangenberg in Georgia and Boehler in London had given him a great deal of respect for the Moravians, and after his conversion he traveled to Saxony to visit Herrnhut. There he observed the orderly community life on Zinzendorf's estate, though he was distressed by the lurid mysticism of the Brethren, and felt that Zinzendorf himself was encouraging the growth of a personality cult. Wesley learned much from the Moravian model, however.

When people began to respond to Wesley's preaching, he encouraged them to meet in small groups for mutual edification. He never intended these small groups to be churches, and specified that they should never hold their meetings at times that conflicted with the worship services of the church. His desire was not to pull people out of the church or to split the church, but to revive the church from within - a goal he shared with the German Pietists.

Wesley modeled the organization of these Methodist societies on that of the Pietist conventicles. Each society was divided into small groups of about ten people, and each of these "classes" had a leader, who at first was responsible for collecting the penny per week that each member was to contribute, but later was charged with the spiritual oversight of the class. These class leaders were personally appointed by Wesley as his "assistants," and could be removed from their positions whenever he wished to do so. He kept a very close rein on his helpers, and many were removed from leadership positions for moral and spiritual offenses of various kinds. Originally, Wesley intended to visit each one of the Methodist societies personally on an annual basis, but as the number of societies increased, this became impossible. Wesley then established "circuits" that incorporated all the Methodist societies in a given geographical area, and appointed "superintendents" to oversee these circuits. All the leaders then met annually at a General Conference called by Wesley himself.

Several aspects of the organizational structure of the Methodist societies generated opposition from the Anglican Church of which Wesley was a member, and also contributed to the character of the Methodist Church when it eventually came into being. First of all, the Methodist societies, as discipleship groups for those converted under Wesley's preaching, had no doctrinal or church membership requirements, and emphasized holy living rather than doctrine (another characteristic Wesley shared with the German Pietists). Societies might consist of Anglicans, Baptists, Presbyterians, or even Quakers - doctrinal differences were not considered as long as a person was willing to commit himself to a life of dedication to Christ. It should be no surprise, then, that when the Methodist Church was formed, though it had its doctrinal distinctives (see the next section), doctrine was never a major consideration.

Secondly, the structure of the Methodist societies tended to undermine the authority of the local Anglican clergy. Most of Wesley's assistants were laymen, and they preached in their society meetings (and often in the open air as well) with no thought of gaining the approval of the local bishop. Members of the Methodist societies understandably soon came to believe that the true spiritual leaders in the community were the heads of the Methodist societies rather than the Anglican priests or Dissenting ministers. Not surprisingly, the extensive use of laymen in ministry became one of the notable characteristics of the Methodist Church when it came into being.

A third area of difficulty arose from the fact that Wesley, because he had no thought of forming a church, gave no attention to biblical teaching on church government when he formed the Methodist societies. His decisions were governed totally by practical considerations. The result of this was that, when the Methodists did break away from the Anglican Church, their organizational structure had little relationship to that described in the New Testament, and remains today largely pragmatic in orientation.

Though it was never Wesley's intention to form a separate church, certain actions he took toward the end of his life made the formation of a distinct Methodist Church inevitable. When Wesley appointed superintendents, he also ordained them as ministers. He argued that, since in the New Testament the terms "bishop" and "elder" are synonymous, any priest had the right to ordain ministers. Besides, when he asked Anglican bishops to ordain men for his societies, they refused to do so. While his exegesis was sound, his ordinations clearly contradicted the policy of the Anglican Church. By ordaining men without a bishop's participation, he laid the groundwork for schism.

In fact, the schism came in America even before Wesley's death. Francis Asbury and Thomas Coke, who had been sent to America by Wesley as superintendents of the Methodists there, soon began to refer to themselves as bishops (over Wesley's loud objections). Then, in 1784, at the Christmas Conference of the American Methodists in Baltimore, Maryland, the conferees voted to form the American Methodist Episcopal Church, and formally named Asbury and Coke as its first bishops.

In the same year, Wesley made plans for the continuation of English Methodism after his death by preparing a legal document called the Deed of Declaration. In this deed, Wesley named one hundred men who would legally make up the Methodist General Conference after his death, and would control the funds and property accumulated by the Methodist societies. It was this General Conference that eventually formed the Methodist Church in 1795, four years after Wesley's death.

THE THEOLOGY OF JOHN WESLEY

Like Luther, John Wesley was not a systematic theologian. Though he had some very definite opinions on theological issues, he was much more concerned about evangelism and practical Christian living, and many of the theological positions he took were based on what he saw as the practical implications of those teachings. Three particular areas of Wesley's thought are worth noting here - his teachings on Arminianism, antinomianism, and perfectionism.

The Church of England had been Arminian ever since the time of the Restoration. Wesley had grown up in that environment, and though he professed great admiration for Calvin, he hated and feared the doctrine of predestination. He firmly believed that the doctrine of predestination undermined the work of evangelism. After all, he argued, if only the elect could be saved and those elect were certain to be saved, why preach? Whether a person preaches the Gospel or not, the result will be the same. What Wesley failed to realize, of course, was that the motive for evangelism is first of all a desire to please God rather than being primarily oriented toward results. One who obeys God has the privilege of being part of His work of saving the lost, while one who ignores the commandment to preach the Gospel to every creature does not share that blessing.

Wesley thus considered himself to be an Arminian, though his Arminianism was nowhere near the extreme position taken by Arminius himself and his Remonstrant followers. In fact, when Wesley began publishing a periodical for his Methodist societies, he called it *The Arminian Magazine*. His theological stance wound up causing a serious rift with his friend and co-worker George Whitefield, however. Whitefield was a Calvinist, and when Wesley published a sermon entitled *Free Grace* in 1740, he and Whitefield parted company. Though they remained friends and had a great deal of respect for one another, their theological differences prevented them from working together. Unfortunately, the followers of Wesley and Whitefield were much less tolerant than their leaders. Calvinists like Augustus Toplady attacked Wesley with great enthusiasm, while Wesley's followers saved some of their sharpest barbs for the doctrine of predestination. The attitude of the great men themselves can best be seen in the famous reply made by Whitefield to one of his Calvinistic friends. When Whitefield was asked by this man whether or not he expected to see John Wesley in heaven, Whitefield replied, "I fear not. He will be so near the throne, and we shall be at such a distance, that we shall hardly get a sight of him."

One of the reasons why Wesley disliked Calvinism, besides the belief that it discouraged evangelism, was his great fear of antinomianism. As we saw in chapter twenty-eight, antinomianism is the belief that, since a Christian is saved by grace, he is then free to live in any way he chooses. Wesley, with his emphasis on holy living, greatly feared anything that would minimize Christian obedience, and he felt that Calvinism would do just that. Of course, any cursory study of Calvin's work in Geneva or the Puritan efforts in England and America would show that Calvinism produces an enormous concern for personal holiness. Antinomianism is an abuse of Calvinist theology, not its natural result. Interestingly enough, in the same way that his fear of antinomianism contributed to Wesley's rejection of Calvinism, it also led him to repudiate the mysticism of the Moravians. Some of the Moravians in London had developed a practice of "waiting on God" that approached that of the Quakers (and which was later repudiated by Zinzendorf). Wesley broke off relations with them because he was convinced that such an approach to religion undermined the importance of Christian service and took away the motivation to live a holy life.

As far as perfectionism was concerned, Wesley spent a large proportion of his life trying to make people understand exactly what he believed on this subject. Wesley did teach that perfection was attainable in this life, though he never claimed to have attained it himself. The perfection that he taught, however, was not sinless perfection, but "perfection in love" - a purity of motive that meant that a person did not deliberately violate the laws of God. Three consequences resulted from Wesley's perfectionist teaching. The first is that Methodism has from the beginning had a tendency to define sin only in terms of deliberate disobedience to the Word of God. Only such a narrow definition of sin can support a doctrine of perfectionism. In addition, since Wesley taught that such perfection could sometimes be attained through a single experience, there developed in some Wesleyan circles the doctrine of a second blessing, the teaching of entire sanctification that has passed from Methodism into much of modern Pentecostalism. Thirdly, since Wesley taught that the perfection attained by the Christian was not necessarily permanent, Methodists have traditionally believed that while it is possible for a Christian to have assurance of present salvation, it is not possible to have assurance of final salvation. One who ceases to obey could conceivably fall from a state of grace and lose his standing before God. Thus Wesley, though his theological concepts were primarily practical in their motivation and orientation, left a doctrinal legacy that has influenced the Methodist Church to the present day.

ANGLICAN EVANGELICALS

Though the most obvious product of the Methodist Revival was the Methodist Church, the impact of the efforts of Wesley and Whitefield extended far beyond that single organization. We have already noted the influence of Whitefield on revivals in Wales, Scotland, and America, and the Calvinistic Methodists that came from among his converts. Perhaps a greater legacy may be found among those Christians who did not join the Methodists, but remained within the established and dissenting churches. The Methodist Revival left behind not only a Methodist Church, but also a strong and active Evangelical party in the Church of England. Many preachers within the Anglican Church, encouraged by the revival, began proclaiming the Gospel in their churches, and in the process breathed new life into a nearly-dead body. Perhaps the best known of these evangelical preachers was John Newton, the former slave-trader who was miraculously converted and went on to become one of London's most influential pastors.

The Methodist Revival also spurred tremendous activity among Christians in an effort to address abuses in society. Robert Raikes, a newspaper publisher in Gloucester, was encouraged by Wesley to finance Sunday Schools. These schools were intended for the poor city children who often worked in factories six days a week, and thus had no time to go to school. Raikes wanted to teach them the Bible, but first had to teach them to read and write. Raikes was not the first to try this, but through his efforts the idea caught on and spread throughout England and America. These schools were the forerunners of free public education in England. John Howard also received encouragement from Wesley in his efforts at prison reform.

By far the greatest social achievement of the evangelicals, however, was the termination of slavery in the British Empire. Led by William Wilberforce, who made eradication of the slave trade his personal crusade during almost forty years in Parliament, the evangelicals succeeded, against overwhelming odds and wealthy and powerful opposition, to end first the slave trade (1807), and finally slavery itself (1833) in Britain and its colonial possessions. The Clapham Sect, a group of wealthy and powerful evangelicals who lived near one another in the London suburb of Clapham, worked not only for the abolition of slavery, but also tried to help those slaves who had gained their freedom establish themselves in their new lives. One of these wealthy men, Granville Sharp, was instrumental in founding the colony of Sierra Leone in West Africa, where freed slaves could go and make a new life for themselves if they were unable to find employment or housing in England. The members of the Clapham Sect also were active in providing relief for the urban poor and publishing Bibles and other Christian literature that could be distributed widely among the needy both in England and abroad.

The Methodists also spurred other Christians on in the area of missionary work. The Pietists had laid the groundwork, but the Methodists encouraged many to follow their path, so that both the Anglicans and the dissenting churches began to give attention to foreign missions. The pioneering work of William Carey (see chapter thirty-four) in a sense grew out of the environment created by the Methodist Revival.

One legacy of the Methodist Revival that is often overlooked is the great wealth of Christian hymns produced by the Methodists and those associated with them. Charles Wesley alone is said to have penned almost seven thousand hymns, including beloved standards like *And Can It Be That I Should Gain*, *Hark, the Herald Angels Sing*, *O, For a Thousand Tongues to Sing*, *Christ the Lord is Risen Today*, and *Love Divine*. John Newton (*Amazing Grace* and *Glorious Things of Thee Are Spoken*) and William Cowper (*God Moves in a Mysterious Way* and *There is a Fountain Filled with Blood*), in their Olney Hymns, and the Welsh Calvinistic Methodist William Williams (*Guide Me, O Thou Great Jehovah*) also contributed significantly to the outpouring of praise that accompanied the revival and has enriched the church ever since.

MAKING DRY BONES LIVE

There are many lessons to be learned from the Methodist Revival, but certainly it shows us that one man, when that man is totally committed to God, can make a difference in an indifferent world. England was changed by the efforts of John Wesley, George Whitefield, and others like them. Not only was England spared the trauma of a bloody revolution by the great movement for social reform stimulated by the Methodists, but the church was renewed by the influx of thousands of new believers and just as many reinvigorated professing Christians. We need to recognize, however, the time frame in which these changes occurred. Revival in the church, which results from the sometimes dramatic movement of the Spirit of God in the hearts of men and women, can turn things around in an incredibly brief time. Social change usually takes much longer. Wilberforce fought for forty years to end slavery, and only on his death bed in 1833 did he see his dream come to pass.

If Christians today want to see the world changed, they need to recognize three things. The first is that the man or woman who changes the world for Christ is the one who is totally committed to Christ. When George Whitefield's health declined as a result of his extensive travels and brutally demanding preaching schedule, his friends told him that he needed to ease up. He responded that he would much rather burn out than rust out. The world needs people who are willing to burn out in service to God. Secondly, Christians must realize that revival is not the result of human effort, but the work of the Spirit of God. Too often we tend to rely on using the right methods or saying the right things, when what we really need to do is pray for the powerful working of the Spirit of God in the hearts of those who hear the Word. Thirdly, Christians need to recognize that social change only comes through perseverance. Those today who are working and praying for an end to the practice of abortion need to take a lesson from Wilberforce. It is possible for Christians to make a difference, but such change only comes through persistent effort.

The World for a Parish

FOR REVIEW AND FURTHER THOUGHT

1. What social changes generated unrest in eighteenth-century England?

2. Why were the churches ill-equipped to deal with this unrest?

3. How did the family environment in which John Wesley was raised equip him for the ministry he was eventually to undertake?

4. What was the Holy Club, and how did it come into being?

5. What factors caused John Wesley to question his salvation during his time in Georgia?

6. What were the major reasons for the failure of the Wesleys' efforts in Georgia?

7. In what ways did the Moravians influence the development of Methodism?

8. What happened at the Aldersgate Street Bible study that changed John Wesley's life? Compare this with what we know of Luther's conversion.

9. What was field preaching? Why did the Church of England oppose it?

10. How did Whitefield and Wesley get started in the practice of field preaching?

11. What did John Wesley mean when he said, "The world is my parish"?

12. What roles did the following places play in the revival of the eighteenth century: Epworth, Gloucester, Aldersgate Street, Cambuslang, Bristol?

13. Identify the following in one sentence each: Howell Harris, Robert Raikes, Francis Asbury, John Newton, John Howard, William Wilberforce, William Cowper, Augustus Toplady, Peter Boehler, Selina Hastings.

14. In what ways were the goals and practices of the Methodist societies similar to those of the German Pietists?

15. What relationship did the organization of the Methodist societies have to the New Testament's teachings on church order?

16. Why did the Methodist societies have no doctrinal requirements for membership?

17. Why did the organizational structure of the Methodist societies cause conflicts with the Anglican establishment?

18. In what ways did the organizational structure of the Methodist societies influence that of the Methodist Church that developed from them?

19. Upon what basis did Wesley move to ordain ministers for his Methodist societies?

20. What was the Deed of Declaration, and how did it contribute to the eventual independence of the Methodist Church?

21. Why did Wesley oppose the doctrine of predestination?

22. How would a Calvinist respond to Wesley's charge that the doctrine of predestination undermined evangelistic zeal?

23. What is antinomianism, and why did Wesley consider it such a serious threat to the church?

24. Why did Wesley believe that Calvinism produced antinomianism? In what way is this a distortion of Calvin's teachings?

25. Why did Wesley eventually break off his relationship with the Moravians?

26. What was the difference between Wesley's teaching of perfectionism and the idea of sinless perfection?

27. What consequences have been produced among some branches of the Methodist Church as a result of Wesley's perfectionist views?

28. What impact did the Methodist Revival have on the Church of England?

29. What was the original purpose of Sunday Schools? How did they contribute to the development of education in England?

30. What was the Clapham Sect, and what were some of the causes to which they addressed their efforts?

31. Why was the colony of Sierra Leone founded?

32. What lessons can Christians who are working for social change today learn from the Methodists?

31

GOD'S ORPHANS

During the Enlightenment of the eighteenth century, the Deists in England and France had defined God largely as a "God of the gaps" who was needed only to explain the things that man could not explain on his own. As scientific progress continued throughout the century, the gaps got increasingly smaller until God was left with very little room indeed. In the nineteenth century, leadership in European thought shifted to Germany, and the liberal theologians, who based their conclusions on the views of philosophy and history propounded by the great German thinkers, succeeded in putting God out of His misery. Though the liberals gleefully undermined every aspect of orthodox Christianity, most of them ironically could not bring themselves to take the next logical step - the total rejection of Christianity in favor of a religion of Man. Like the adolescent who killed his parents and then begged the court for mercy on the ground that he was an orphan, the German liberals and those who followed them continued to define themselves in terms of what they had destroyed.

This chapter constitutes our last visit to Germany, and in it we will focus our attention on the development of German liberalism in the nineteenth and twentieth centuries. While it may not be completely fair to slap the label "liberal" on a collection of theologies that differ as much from one another as do the Tübingen School, the Social Gospel, Existentialism, and Neo-Orthodoxy, the fact of the matter is that, while they differ significantly from one another, what they have in common is far more important than their differences. The men upon whom we will be focusing our attention in this chapter categorically reject the teaching that the Bible is God's infallible revelation of propositional truth to mankind. Once the Bible has been rejected as the inerrant ground of Christian truth, man is left to define God and Christianity for himself. The result, not very surprisingly, is that such men remake God in their own image. Though their definitions of God may differ widely, those definitions have in common the fact that they are humanly devised, rooted in the philosophies of man. It is no less valid to group the German liberals together than it is to generalize about non-Christian religions. Though they have certain important differences, they are united by what they deny.

THE PHILOSOPHERS

Throughout the history of the church, there has been significant interaction between philosophy and theology. As we have seen with the impact of Platonism on the early church and the effect of Aristotle on the medieval Scholastics, attempts to harmonize Christian teaching with a philosophy that is not itself derived from Scripture have done great damage to the Christian cause. German liberalism, too, is rooted in philosophies inherently alien to Christianity. Before we are able to understand German liberalism, we must understand something of those philosophies.

A. IMMANUEL KANT (1724-1804)

By far the most influential philosopher in the period before us was Immanuel Kant. He spent most of his life in the German city of Königsberg, and was the stereotypical ivory-tower academic. Kant was a philosopher who, through reading the works of David Hume, recognized the weaknesses of the rationalism popular in France and the empiricism that dominated British thought. He was not ready to accept Hume's conclusion that skepticism was all that remained, however. He believed that the flaws of rationalism and empiricism could be overcome to produce a solid basis for human knowledge.

Kant agreed with the empiricists when they said that human beings gained knowledge through the use of their senses. He differed from them, however, when they said that the human mind was nothing more than a blank slate upon which our senses write the story of our experiences. Kant argued instead that the mind should not be pictured as a blank slate, but as a series of pigeonholes, rather like the mail boxes in a post office. When the senses conveyed information to the mind, the mind organized that information on the basis of the categories that were built into it. Thus, the senses provided the raw data that the mind then acted upon, resulting in what we call knowledge.

This synthesis of the rationalist emphasis on the mind and the empiricist focus on the senses seems on the surface quite adequate as a description of human knowledge, but it is vital that we realize the implications of Kant's description. To begin with, Kant's philosophy eliminates the possibility of knowing anything as it really is. Since the mind organizes and alters everything the senses put into it, what we "know" can never correspond to what is really "out there." The problem is very much like that of the physicist who realizes that what he is measuring is changed by the insertion of the measuring instrument into the environment. Kant's description of knowledge really involves giving up on the possibility of absolute knowledge. Everything we "know" is by definition relative simply because our minds have "arranged" everything they encounter.

Kant's philosophy of knowledge has devastating implications for theology. First of all, he clearly placed God in the realm of pure data. We cannot know Him as He really is, because any experience we have of the divine is filtered through the grid of our minds. Knowledge of God is therefore impossible. As for the Bible, it obviously belongs in the realm of human knowledge in the sense that it contains the record of men's experiences of God. Of course, these experiences have been filtered through the minds of the authors, and thus should not be imagined to contain objective truth about either God or man. Kant thus destroyed once and for all the concept of propositional revelation among those who followed his lead. Even those liberals who differed radically from his teaching agreed with him on this one key particular - that objective revelation from God to man was inconceivable.

Kant referred to his philosophy as a Copernican revolution. Copernicus reoriented man's thinking about the heavens so that it was no longer possible for anyone to take seriously the celestial spheres of the old Ptolemaic universe. In the same way, Kant redefined human knowledge to such an extent that belief in the Bible as God's objective word to man was viewed by many as no less an anachronism than the Flat Earth Society. From the time of Kant onward, intellectuals, including liberal professing Christians, have been unable to take seriously anyone who believes that the Bible is the Word of God in the traditional sense of that phrase.

Kant was not an atheist, however. Having slammed the front door in God's face by denying the very possibility of theology in his *Critique of Pure Reason*, he then turned around in his *Critique of Practical Reason* to sneak God in the back door by way of man's moral sensibilities. While Kant denied the possibility of absolute knowledge, he insisted on the existence of moral absolutes. He argued that all men could and should live on the basis of what he called the Categorical Imperative. What he meant by this was that any action could be deemed as right if the person about to perform the action could without contradiction will that such an action would become a universal law. In other words, if I am about to do something, what would happen if everyone else did the same? Clearly, on this basis, murder is wrong, since if everyone were to commit murder, it would soon be impossible to commit murder, since no one would be left to kill. Similarly, large-scale thievery would be self-contradictory, since such a practice would quickly undermine the concept of private property, and when nothing belongs to anyone, stealing becomes impossible. Kant then went on to argue that such a moral system requires the existence of God, for where else could such notions of morality have their source? Furthermore, he believed that God was necessary in order to provide rewards and punishments in the next life, since clearly virtue is not always rewarded nor vice always punished in this one. As we will see, the resulting emphasis on the moral aspect of religion was picked up and amplified by a number of theologians in the nineteenth and twentieth centuries.

B. G.W.F. HEGEL (1770-1831)

Hegel, for many years a professor at the University of Berlin, refused to accept Kant's conclusion that the human mind could never know what was outside of itself. Instead, he argued that "the rational is the real and the real is the rational." Hegel is called an Idealist because he believed that the human mind and human experience are simply outworkings of the Absolute Idea. This Absolute Idea, which some may call God, is not separate from man and the universe. Instead, man and the universe are part of the Absolute Idea, or Spirit. While this concept may sound like nothing more than garden-variety pantheism, Hegel gave it a new twist. He argued that the Absolute Idea was not static, but was in a constant state of flux. This change occurred through a dynamic process called a dialectic in which opposites were combined to form new ideas. The conditions at any particular time might be described as a thesis. This thesis would contain within itself a contradictory idea, or antithesis, which would then arise to oppose it. The struggle between thesis and antithesis would result in a new idea, a synthesis, which would contain elements of both competing concepts from which it arose. The synthesis would then become a new thesis, and the process would repeat itself again and again. Thus the only constant in the universe is change.

Clearly, though Hegel was adamantly opposed to Kant, he joined Kant in asserting the impossibility of objective divine revelation. Like Kant, however, he rejected atheism, and even asserted that Christianity was the highest form of religion - once it had been cleansed of all its superstitious accretions, of course. While Kant's greatest impact on liberal theology came through his views of knowledge and morality, Hegel, as we shall see, influenced generations of liberal theologians through his understanding of history.

C. LUDWIG FEUERBACH (1804-1872)

Ludwig Feuerbach was originally a follower of Hegel, but he eventually rejected Hegel's Idealism in favor of a philosophy centered in man himself. Feuerbach taught that the Absolute Idea was no more than the sum of human social consciousness. Man thus truly is the measure of all things. While he retained Hegel's dialectical view of history, he saw religion as no more than a projection of man's needs and desires. It corresponds to no outward reality. For Feuerbach, man created God in his own image.

The philosophy of Feuerbach had an enormous influence on Karl Marx, the founder of communism. Marx reduced Hegelianism even further to the point of materialism, and argued that economic and political forces would, through conflict and revolution, lead ultimately to the dictatorship of the proletariat in a stateless society. Religion was no more than a tool used by the bourgeoisie to oppress the masses, an opiate that kept the poor in their state of peaceful subservience as they awaited the fulfillment of their needs and desires in a future life that their religion assured them would come.

D. FRIEDRICH NIETZSCHE (1844-1900)

If Kant removed the possibility of knowing God, Hegel pictured man as an extension of an ever-changing God, and Feuerbach saw God as the wish-projection of man, Nietzsche cut through all the nonsense and arrived at the only honest conclusion that could be drawn from the work of those who preceded him - he declared that God was dead.

Nietzsche understood the implications of Darwin's theory of evolution far better than most of the men of his age. Though he rejected many elements of evolutionary theory, such as Darwin's totally illogical assertion that evolution must produce upward progress, he agreed that history should be viewed as a struggle for survival. Man is no more than an animal, and religion was suitable only for his more primitive stages of development. In such a climate, traditional concepts of morality are not only meaningless, but positively harmful. Nietzsche believed that Judeo-Christian ethics encouraged weakness and made men helpless in the face of their ruthless enemies. The only true ethic, he argued, was the Will to Power. Might makes right - only with such an ethic will man survive and prosper.

Nietzsche also believed that history existed for the sole purpose of producing those superior individuals he called Supermen. The vast majority of men contribute nothing to humanity, but the great men, the men of power such as Alexander the Great and Napoleon, are the true triumphs of human history. Such a view of history is perverted enough in itself, but when it becomes a tool of a madman like Adolf Hitler who is convinced it is his destiny to create a race of Supermen, tragedy is inevitable.

SCHLEIERMACHER AND ROMANTICISM

We are ready now to turn to the German theologians. It should not surprise us in the least to find that the theological teachings of the period derive much of their foundation from the philosophers of whom we have already spoken.

Without question, the most influential theologian of the nineteenth century was Friedrich Schleiermacher (1768-1834). Schleiermacher was raised in a strict Pietist family, received early schooling from the Moravians, and attended the University of Halle. He was the leading theologian of the Romanticist movement, which emphasized the importance of human emotion. He provides the classic example, not only of the orphan mentioned at the beginning of the chapter, but also of the dangers inherent in Pietism. Schleiermacher agreed with Kant that knowledge of God was unattainable, but was unwilling to see religion reduced to a mere rational system of ethics. He maintained instead that religion had little to do with the sort of cognitive knowledge expressed in the doctrinal formulations of the church. For Schleiermacher, true religion consisted of a feeling of absolute dependence on something outside of oneself. This feeling, whether it was generated by gazing at the starry heavens or contemplating the complexity of the human mind, is what it means to know God. While all religions seek this end, Christianity is the highest religion because it comes closest to achieving it.

For Schleiermacher, Christ was God only in the sense that He manifested absolute dependence upon God in every phase of His life. He thus becomes the example of the totally dependent man. The church has value because it is the community where dependence may be learned and practiced. The doctrinal statements of the church over the centuries have value as concrete expressions of what it means to depend upon God, but that value is only secondary. What really counts is a person's own experience.

In Schleiermacher, we thus find Pietism run amok. While the early Pietists like Spener and Francke considered doctrine divisive and emphasized Christian devotion and moral living, they nonetheless assumed the basic doctrinal foundation that Christians have shared since the time of Christ. Schleiermacher and those like him, however, were raised in Pietist homes where Christianity was defined in terms of devotion and holy living, but where doctrine was not really taught at all (others in this chapter who came from Pietist backgrounds include Kant, Hegel, Baur, and Ritschl). Thus it was very easy for Schleiermacher, when he encountered the writings of Kant, to reject the doctrine that to him was insignificant anyway. It didn't bother him in the least that Kant had undermined the objective knowledge of God. As far as he was concerned, true religion didn't need it. We thus wind up with a religion of feeling without any objective foundation for that feeling. As Hegel somewhat sarcastically remarked, if Schleiermacher's definition of religion is the true one, dogs would be the best Christians. After all, who shows more consistent feelings of dependence than a dog?

THE TÜBINGEN SCHOOL

While Schleiermacher had developed his theology in the wake of Kant's philosophical system, most of the nineteenth century's leading liberals took their point of departure from Hegel. This was certainly true of the Tübingen School, a group of liberals who studied and/or taught at the University of Tübingen, which in the nineteenth century became the hub of German criticism. When we refer to these men as critics, we mean not that they criticized the Bible (though they certainly did that often enough), but that they tried to interpret the Bible in the light of its historical and cultural backgrounds. While there is nothing wrong with this in itself, the liberal critics carried out their criticism on the basis of certain assumptions; these assumptions included not only the Hegelian view of history, but also the idea that the Bible was a human book, and nothing more.

The first of the shock waves produced by the Tübingen School came from the pen of David Friedrich Strauss (1808-1874), who studied at Tübingen University. In 1835 he published a *Life of Jesus* in which he denied the historicity of almost everything in the Gospel narratives. He argued that the supernatural elements in the Gospels reflected the imaginative mindset of the first century in which myths were objectified into historical narratives. He even left hanging the radical possibility that there never had been a man Jesus at all. Such destructive criticism was too much even for most of those who accepted Strauss' Hegelian presuppositions. Like so many liberals, they were unwilling to face up to the logical conclusions of their own teachings, and Strauss soon found that no German university was willing to have him on their faculty. Later in life, he rejected Christianity altogether, opting instead for a pantheistic Religion of Man based on Hegelian philosophy.

By far the most influential of the Tübingen liberals was Friedrich Christian Baur (1792-1860), who taught at Tübingen University for thirty-four years. Baur had been one of Strauss' professors, and though he was unwilling to go quite so far as his outspoken pupil had gone in rejecting the historicity of the Gospel narratives, he in reality provided the framework in which the type of radical criticism practiced by Strauss could prosper. Baur attempted to take the Hegelian view of history and apply it directly to the New Testament. He identified the early Jewish Christian church under the leadership of Peter and the other apostles as the thesis, which in turn produced the antithesis of the Gentile church under the leadership of Paul. Baur capitalized on the accounts of conflict between Jews and Gentiles found in Galatians and Romans in order to argue that the Jewish and Gentile Christians were fundamentally opposed to one another. In true Hegelian fashion, however, this conflict resolved itself into a synthesis, out of which came the old catholic church of the late second century. Having assumed this historical framework, Baur then proceeded to date the books of the New Testament on the basis of what they had to say about the Jewish-Gentile conflict. Those books that showed conflict, such as Romans, the Corinthian epistles, and Galatians, were clearly early, and most probably were written by Paul. Those books, however, which showed harmony and cooperation between Jews and Gentiles (i.e., the rest of the New Testament) must have been produced during the period of synthesis - the second century - and therefore could not possibly have been written by the authors with whom they are traditionally associated. For example, Baur believed that the accounts in the book of Acts that show Peter preaching to the Gentile Cornelius and the Jerusalem Council settling the Gentile question clearly prove that the book was a product of the synthesis, and therefore must have been written in the second century.

Although he was not directly associated with the University of Tübingen, another liberal whose approach to the Bible was very similar to that of the Tübingen School was the Old Testament critic Julius Wellhausen (1844-1918). Wellhausen was the greatest popularizer of the Documentary Hypothesis, in which he argued that Moses could not have written the first five books of the Old Testament. He theorized that the two most frequently used names of God in the Pentateuch, *Elohim* and *Jahweh* (or *Jehovah*), reflected two source documents out of which the

Books of Moses had been constructed. Like Baur, Wellhausen postulated a framework of historical development and dated the Pentateuchal material on the basis of that supposed history. He believed that the religion of Israel had evolved from a primitive polytheism to the noble monotheism of the prophets. The Elohim and Jahweh documents reflect the polytheism current in Israel during the Divided Monarchy, and therefore must have been written by some unknown scribe during that period. He further argued that the book of Deuteronomy had been written during the revival of monotheism under Josiah, and then conveniently "found" in the Temple in order to spread that revival among the people. The detailed laws found in the book of Leviticus and other places in the Pentateuch must have been written during a time when priests had the upper hand in Jewish society, so Wellhausen dated them after the Babylonian Captivity. Thus he arrived at four source documents, often labeled J (Jahweh), E (Elohim), D (Deuteronomy), and P (Priestly), out of which he believed some unknown redactor (editor) had woven the Books of Moses at some time during the Intertestamental Period. As with Baur, Wellhausen's historical framework was purely speculative, and is supported by not one shred of manuscript evidence.

Wellhausen's theory of the "evolution" of the Pentateuch has much in common with Darwin's theory of the evolution of the human race. As with Darwin's theory, scholars have long rejected the foundational arguments upon which Wellhausen's theory was based. For instance, Wellhausen argued that Moses must have been illiterate because only a few scholars in his day knew how to write. Massive archaeological discoveries since have demonstrated that writing was a widespread skill in Moses' day, and certainly would have been known by a man raised in Pharaoh's palace. In addition, many of the historical "errors" Wellhausen believed pointed to a late date for the composition of the Pentateuch have since been shown to be accurate. Wellhausen's blunders in his supporting arguments have not led scholars to reject his theory any more than Darwin's use of mutations as an evolutionary mechanism or his suggestion that embryonic development recapitulates the evolutionary history of a species have caused biologists to reject the theory of evolution. Liberal Old Testament scholars today continue to assume that the Books of Moses are in reality a late compilation of an anonymous editor based on anonymous documents from the period of Israel's monarchy. Why do they continue to cling to such a totally groundless position? The answer is a simple one. For liberal scholars, the alternative - divine revelation - is every bit as unthinkable as divine creation is for evolutionists.

RITSCHL AND THE SOCIAL GOSPEL

While Baur and the Tübingen School adopted the historical framework provided by Hegel for their criticism of the documents of Scripture, another school of German liberals who rejected Hegel's approach grew up around one of Baur's students, Albrecht Ritschl (1822-1889). Ritschl, taking his lead from Kant, rejected any possibility of knowing God in any metaphysical sense. As far as he was concerned, Hegel's Absolute Idea was too far removed from the common experience of mankind. For Ritschl, true religion had to do with moral value, and was only to be found in community. He pictured Christianity as an ellipse with two foci - a relationship with Christ as the Son of God and involvement with the community of believers in the Kingdom of God. When Ritschl spoke of Christ as Son of God, however, he meant merely that the man Jesus had lived a life of such supreme moral influence that others had come to express the value of his example in their lives by calling him God. Christians, similarly, are called to influence others to lead moral lives, and by so doing spread the Kingdom of God on earth.

Ritschl's "Theology of Moral Value" has been enormously influential on succeeding theologians. One of Ritschl's best-known followers was Adolf von Harnack (1851-1930), who dominated the German theological scene in the years preceding World War I. Harnack's greatest scholarly achievements were in his studies of the history of the ancient church, but his most popular book was a series of printed lectures entitled *What Is Christianity?* Harnack argued that Christianity could be reduced to three basic teachings - the Fatherhood of God, the Brotherhood of Man, and the infinite value of the human soul. Such teaching implied both that all men were saved and that the true mission of the church is to unite all mankind in brotherhood and peace. As we will see later, these ideas had a tremendous influence on the Social Gospel movement in America and the ecumenical efforts that would characterize twentieth-century liberal Protestantism.

Another liberal who by his teachings and personal life emphasized the ethical aspects of Christianity was Albert Schweitzer (1875-1965), the medical missionary who was awarded the Nobel Peace Prize for his work in West Africa. Schweitzer's most interesting theological contribution was his book on *The Quest of the Historical Jesus*. Schweitzer showed brilliant insight in his criticism of the old liberalism represented by men such as Baur and Strauss. He noted that most of the nineteenth-century liberals had brought to their study of Jesus certain presuppositions, and then proceeded to strip away the facade of the Gospel accounts and theorize about what Jesus must really have been like. Not surprisingly, the Jesus they found corresponded very closely to whatever philosophical presuppositions they had brought with them into their studies. The fact that Schleiermacher concluded that Jesus was a man totally dependent upon God and Ritschl discovered that Jesus was a man of unusual moral fiber told us more about Schleiermacher and Ritschl than it did about Jesus. Schweitzer was determined to let the Gospel accounts speak for themselves, but his acceptance of the destructive criticism of the earlier liberals meant that he recognized very little in the Gospel accounts as being genuine. He therefore concluded that the genuine portions of the Gospels must be those elements that were difficult to explain, or that tended to cast Jesus in a negative light (after all, who would have made such things up?). He focused in on those passages in which Jesus spoke about the coming judgment, and professed ignorance of the time of the coming of the Kingdom. Schweitzer then argued that the historical Jesus was a man convinced that the world was soon to end. On the basis of this false belief, Jesus had thrust himself into the role of the Messiah, even to the point of sacrificing himself in the hope of bringing the Kingdom more quickly into the world. The result is hardly comforting. Instead of a man of deep emotion or sterling morality, we are left with a noble but deluded fool who failed to accomplish what he set out to do. Schweitzer, like the others before him, was unwilling to reject this Jesus that he had debunked, however. He still saw him as a man whose example of self-sacrifice was worth emulating, and put his beliefs into practice in decades of service among the natives of Africa.

KIERKEGAARD AND THE EXISTENTIALISTS

Although the purpose of this chapter is to discuss the development of German liberalism, we must pause to include a paragraph or two about the Danish philosopher and theologian Søren Kierkegaard (1813-1855). Kierkegaard had considerable influence in his native Denmark during his lifetime, but his work remained unknown throughout much of Europe and America until the twentieth century. Kierkegaard's work consisted largely of a reaction against two elements of Danish Christianity. The first was the philosophy of Hegel, which had permeated the thought of his era. The second was the established Lutheran Church, which he considered to be no more Christian than the religion of the most benighted pagan. While Hegel's teaching led to the assumption that the Absolute Spirit permeated all of life and the established church led people to believe that all one had to do to be a good Christian was to be a good Dane, Kierkegaard insisted that Christianity was demanding - the religion of the narrow way. He believed that only through personal suffering could one know what it means to know God. This suffering need not be physical in nature. In fact, true suffering consists of despair - a sense of being alone in the universe, with no guide and no place to turn. Only in such a position of alienation may a person understand the meaning of faith. To

Kierkegaard, faith was a leap into the dark. He illustrated his point with the example of Abraham, who was told by God to sacrifice his son Isaac. God's command did not make sense; in fact, it contradicted everything Abraham knew about God. Abraham's obedience to God's command was thus an act of true faith, because he obeyed in a situation in which he knew and understood nothing.

Kierkegaard is generally considered the father of Existentialism. His teachings were brought to the attention of many through the work of Karl Barth, though Barth did not consider himself an existentialist. Unlike the secular existentialists of the twentieth century who believe that man achieves meaning in a meaningless world only by a naked act of the will which is the moral equivalent of jumping voluntarily into an ocean with no shores and no bottom, the "Christian existentialists" who followed Kierkegaard taught that the leap into the darkness brought one into contact with God - though they were not willing to assert anything about the God they were likely to meet in the process. Among these "Christian existentialists" are two influential twentieth-century Germans, Rudolf Bultmann (1884-1976) and Paul Tillich (1886-1965).

Bultmann was a New Testament scholar who, like Strauss, believed that the New Testament was written in the language of myth. The true meaning of the New Testament documents could only be discovered, therefore, by "demythologizing" them. As we should by now anticipate, Bultmann "discovered" that behind the mythology of the New Testament was teaching that was very similar in content to existential philosophy.

Tillich, who fled Germany when the Nazis came to power and spent the remainder of his career teaching in liberal American seminaries, reached the logical conclusion toward which liberalism had been moving for over a century. For Tillich, God was simply the Ground of Being, and faith consisted of whatever a person's Ultimate Concern in life happened to be. Any references to Scripture in Tillich's works are for obvious reasons purely incidental.

KARL BARTH AND THE THEOLOGY OF CRISIS

The old liberalism of the nineteenth century was essentially optimistic. Whether rooted in the historical optimism of Hegel, the social optimism of the Ritschlians, or the biological optimism of evolutionary theory, the men of the nineteenth century believed that things would continue to get better. Then came World War I, and the optimism of the preceding age drowned in a sea of blood. Suddenly the glib answers of the liberals were no longer good enough. People were no longer convinced that the men and women of the earth, through their shared religious experience, were in the process of bringing in the Kingdom of God. Kierkegaard's writings found a new and appreciative audience in the early decades of the twentieth century, as the leap of faith in the face of a meaningless and impotent church and society began to appeal to many who struggled with the overpowering implications of the war.

In 1918, in the midst of this confusion, with the foundations of liberalism crumbling on every side, a young Reformed pastor in German Switzerland published a commentary on the book of Romans. Karl Barth (1886-1968) had been trained in the liberal tradition of Ritschl, but had found the social gospel empty and devoid of significance for a world in crisis. The last thing people needed to be told was that they had within themselves the resources to change the world. Their own resources had already been stretched beyond endurance and found wanting. They needed a word from God.

Barth's system of theology, variously referred to as the theology of crisis, dialectical theology, and neo-orthodoxy, repudiated much of the old liberalism, borrowed heavily from Kierkegaard, and sought a return to a God who speaks and is active in the lives of His people. Barth's break with liberalism was not total, however. He still retained the conclusions of the liberal critics of Scripture. Whatever may be said of Barth - and his system is certainly a vast improvement over the virtually godless liberalism of the nineteenth century - one must realize that he did not in any sense return to the orthodox teaching of the infallibility and authority of the Bible as the Word of God.

Barth followed Kierkegaard in affirming the need for an encounter with God. Such an encounter came by means of a leap of faith in a time of crisis, when all other resources had failed. Unlike Kierkegaard, however, Barth emphasized Scripture as the medium through which man may meet God. Barth accepted the liberal teaching that the Bible was a human book that witnessed to the encounters with God experienced by various men. As such, it contained factual errors, but these were secondary to its fundamental message. Barth believed that the Bible became the living Word of God in the life of an individual as God spoke through it. Though his approach was praised by many as bringing the hope of God back to men who had been stranded by the liberals, he also drew strong criticism from theologians on both sides. Liberals saw his supernaturalism as a throwback to old superstitions, while evangelicals recognized that his view of Scripture remained highly subjective, allowing no room for propositional revelation. After all, the Bible may become God's Word to me as I read it today, but what about tomorrow? Will it say the same thing? Will it speak to me in the same voice with which it speaks to my neighbor? Clearly there was no more room for absolute truth in the theology of Barth than there had been among the Kantians and Hegelians of the nineteenth century.

Not only did Barth deny that the Bible could be the source of objective authority or propositional truth, he also put an unusual twist on the classical Reformed doctrine of salvation. Reformed theology, following Calvin, had always stressed the sovereignty of God in salvation. Salvation is completely the work of God. Man can do nothing to save himself. When Jesus died on the cross, He did all that needed to be done to accomplish the work of salvation. Along with this, Reformed theologians also taught that the death of Christ accomplished salvation for particular people - the elect. Barth followed Calvin in teaching that salvation was entirely the work of God, but also believed that Christ had died on the cross for the sins of all men. The inevitable conclusion he reached was that all men were saved.

The defeat of Germany at the end of World War I did not end the crisis in Europe. After the war, Barth spent about fifteen years teaching in various German universities. When Hitler came to power in 1933, Barth was among those who spoke out against his attempts to manipulate the church for political ends. Many of the German Protestants had given in to Hitler's bullying, forming a church body called the German Christians that attempted to cooperate with National Socialism (Nazism). The German Christians structured the church along the same lines as the state, appointing a führer as their leader who was one of Hitler's henchmen. They also incorporated into their organization the infamous Aryan Paragraph, which prohibited anyone of Jewish ancestry from holding office in the church. Some Germans found this high-handed manipulation of the church too much to stomach, however, and formed the Confessing Church, which sought to retain independence from the state (though they at all times professed total loyalty to Hitler in political matters). In 1934, the Confessing Church published the Barmen Declaration. This document, largely written by Barth, stated in no uncertain terms that the church was not an arm of the state, and owed its primary loyalty to God. Soon after, the Confessing Church was forced underground, and Barth left Germany to teach in his native Switzerland, where he remained for the rest of his life.

The leaders of the Confessing Church suffered much at the hands of Hitler. Martin Niemöller, who had fought as a German U-boat commander during World War I, went to prison for his outspoken opposition to Hitler and the German Christians. Dietrich Bonhoeffer (1906-1945), a young pastor whose devotional classic *The Cost of Discipleship* is valued by many today for its repudiation of cheap grace and exhortation to live a life of total commitment to Christ, was sent to a concentration camp after being implicated in a plot to assassinate Hitler, and eventually was hanged weeks before the allied invasion of Germany. For him, discipleship was costly indeed.

Since the end of World War II, Germany has continued to produce liberal theologians. For the most part, these men have propounded new twists on the older liberal, neo-orthodox, and existential schemes. Jurgen Moltmann's Theology of Hope emphasizes a "realized eschatology" in which the future hope of the Christian has already been revealed in Christ and is being worked out in the present age as Christians live as pilgrims, identifying with the poor and oppressed, while Wolfhart Pannenberg has proclaimed a Theology of Liberation that pictures God at work in history through the transformation of sinful social structures. The latter has been particularly influential in Latin American circles, where Liberation Theology has been adapted to support revolutionary movements of various kinds.

MAKING DRY BONES LIVE

"By their fruit you will recognize them." Ideas have consequences, both in the lives of those who teach them and in the lives of their followers. Modern critics of rock music often point to the lifestyles of the musicians as proof of the sinfulness of their music. Is this conclusion valid? When a musician who glorifies the use of drugs dies of a drug overdose, it would certainly seem so.

Yet we must show considerable caution when relating a person's life to his teachings. If the immoral life of a rock star leads to the conclusion that his music is evil, what are we to conclude when a preacher of the Gospel is found to be practicing immorality? Do we therefore reject Christianity as false? Surely we must recognize that the sinfulness of a teacher does not automatically invalidate his teaching.

In the same way, there are many people whose lives are far better than their teachings would indicate. Certainly this is true of many of the men covered in this chapter. While some of those mentioned above lived lives that fit their teachings - Kierkegaard was considered peculiar, Strauss was ostracized by his contemporaries, and Nietzsche spent the last decade of his life in an asylum - others were pious, dedicated, godly men who showed great courage in the face of enormous trials. Who would dare criticize the sacrificial service of Schweitzer or the courageous stand taken by Bonhoeffer against Nazi oppression? Karl Barth was known throughout Europe and America not only as a man of deep conviction, but also as a godly and humble man who truly loved Jesus Christ. While only God knows the spiritual condition of these men, their public lives certainly were above reproach. This does not mean that their teachings were right or even good, however.

Students tend to be influenced more by the lives of their teachers than by what those teachers say. In the early part of the twentieth century, many American theological students went to German universities to study. Because they were impressed by the godliness of their teachers, they accepted the ideas being propounded by those teachers, and in the process brought back to America liberal theological notions that effectively undermined the basis of the Christian faith. It is therefore important for all who profess to be Christians to evaluate the things they are taught carefully in the light of Scripture. In the same way that Satan may appear as an angel of light, the most destructive and unbiblical ideas may often be taught by men whose attractive personalities and evident godliness disguise the poison they disseminate.

God's Orphans

FOR REVIEW AND FURTHER THOUGHT

1. In what sense did the German liberals complete what the rationalists of the Enlightenment had begun?

2. Why is it possible to group all liberals together despite the significant differences in their teachings?

3. How did Kant describe the process whereby human beings gain knowledge?

4. Why did Kant's approach rule out the possibility of absolute knowledge?

5. How did God and the Bible fit into Kant's scheme of knowledge?

6. Why did Kant call his theory of knowledge a Copernican revolution?

7. What was the Categorical Imperative, and how did Kant use it to derive moral values?

8. How did the Categorical Imperative lead Kant to conclude that God must exist?

9. How did Hegel's teachings differ from pantheism?

10. What is dialectic, and how did Hegel apply the concept to God and history?

11. How did Feuerbach's teaching contribute to the development of Marxism?

12. How did Darwin's theory of evolution contribute to the philosophy of Nietzsche?

13. Why did Nietzsche believe that traditional Christian morality was harmful to the human race?

14. How did Hitler pervert the philosophy of Nietzsche in Nazi Germany?

15. How did Schleiermacher define the essence of true religion?

16. Why did he believe Christianity was the highest religion?

17. In what way does the theology of Schleiermacher illustrate the dangers inherent in Pietism?

18. How did Baur use Hegelian philosophy to reconstruct the history of the New Testament?

19. Briefly describe the view of the Pentateuch proposed by Wellhausen's Documentary Hypothesis.

20. Why did Wellhausen believe that the Books of Moses had been written in their present form during the Intertestamental Period?

21. What do the Documentary Hypothesis and the theory of evolution have in common?

22. Why did Ritschl teach that it was legitimate to refer to Jesus as God?

23. What did Ritschl mean by the Kingdom of God?

24. Why did the influence of Harnack decline following the First World War?

25. Why did Schweitzer consider the nineteenth-century liberal studies of the life of Jesus to be inadequate?

26. How did Schweitzer himself view Jesus? What led him to this conclusion?

27. Against what elements of Danish religion did Kierkegaard react?

28. How did Kierkegaard define true faith?

29. In what way did Kierkegaard and other "Christian existentialists" differ from the secular existentialists of the twentieth century?

30. Identify the following in one sentence each: Rudolf Bultmann, Paul Tillich, Dietrich Bonhoeffer, Jurgen Moltmann, Wolfhart Pannenberg.

31. In what way did World War I contribute to the downfall of nineteenth-century liberal theology?

32. Why is "neo-orthodoxy" an appropriate name for Karl Barth's theological system?

33. How did Barth's view of Scripture differ from that of evangelical Christianity?

34. On what basis did Barth conclude that all men were saved?

35. Who were the German Christians, and what did they attempt to do?

36. What was the Confessing Church, and why did they separate themselves from the rest of the Protestant church in Germany?

37. What was the Barmen Declaration?

38. To what extent is a person's lifestyle a valid indicator of the truth of what that person believes and teaches?

39. How is it possible for a person who denies God's Word by what he teaches to live a life that to all appearances is a fine example of true Christianity?

40. Make a chart showing how the theologians discussed in this chapter relate to the philosophers covered in the first section.

ESTABLISHMENT AND DISESTABLISHMENT

A school child who wants to impress his peers with his spelling prowess will often rattle off, as quickly as possible, the correct spelling of *antidisestablishmentarianism*. Needless to say, many more children know how to spell this word than know what it means. For Englishmen in the nineteenth century, however, antidisestablishmentarianism was more than a word - it was a conflict that cut to the heart of life as they had known it in the British Isles. Shortly after the death of John Wesley, the Methodist Church had declared its independence from the Church of England. Adding the Methodists to the other long-standing dissenting groups such as the Baptists, Presbyterians, and Congregationalists meant that the Dissenters now claimed as many church members as the Anglicans. Only Anglicans, however, could receive university degrees or hold public office. Furthermore, members of dissenting groups still had to pay tithes to support the Anglican Church and its ministers - despite the fact that many of those ministers didn't even live in their parishes, and simply collected fat stipends while some poorly-paid and overworked curates did their pastoral work for them. Reform was in the air, and the type of reform favored by many (especially the Dissenters) was disestablishment - the total severing of ties between the Church of England and the government. Those within the Church of England who wanted to maintain the existing church-state ties were thus said to be antidisestablishmentarians.

The churches of Victorian England also faced a whole complex of problems generated by the Industrial Revolution. Factory towns were booming all over England, and the population in these towns was growing so fast that the churches couldn't possibly keep up. There simply weren't enough churches to house all the people. Worse yet, it required an act of Parliament to form a new parish - a lengthy process at best. In addition, the people of nineteenth-century England were extremely class-conscious. The Church of England, with most of its leading clergy drawn from the aristocracy, was identified in the minds of the people with the upper class. The factory workers in the cities wouldn't have gone to an Anglican church even had there been one available.

How did the Anglicans respond to the threatened loss of their privileged status? What resulted from the Dissenter agitation for disestablishment? How did Anglicans and Dissenters alike respond to the challenges of the Industrial Revolution? The chapter before us will attempt to address these questions.

THE ANGLICANS

The Church of England accommodated a wide variety of viewpoints almost from the time of its inception - royalists and parliamentarians, Puritans and Latitudinarians, Calvinists and Arminians, sacramentarians and evangelicals. The major factions within the Church of England in the nineteenth century are generally classified under the headings of the High Church, the Low Church, and the Broad Church. While this classification has certain weaknesses and not everyone in the Victorian Church fits neatly into one category, the system is nonetheless useful for understanding the Church of England in the nineteenth century.

A. THE LOW CHURCH

The eighteenth-century Methodist revival had not only produced the Methodist Church, it had breathed new life into the Anglican Church as well. The evangelical Anglicans, known as the Low Church because of their lack of concern with ritual and tradition and their emphasis on preaching and evangelism, included among their ranks such notable pastors as John Newton and Charles Simeon. Inspired by the example of the Methodists, the evangelicals also devoted a great deal of attention to social reform. William Wilberforce and the members of the Clapham Sect, of whom we have already spoken in chapter thirty, spearheaded evangelical efforts in the early years of the nineteenth century. Though they are best known for giving impetus to the anti-slavery movement in Britain, they also worked to improve the conditions of the poor.

The dominant figure in evangelical social action in the middle part of the nineteenth century was A.A. Cooper, the Seventh Earl of Shaftesbury (1801-1885). Lord Shaftesbury was raised in an aristocratic home where his parents were too busy helping the poor to pay any attention to their children. His upbringing was supervised by a godly nurse who introduced him to evangelical Christianity. As an adult, there were few social abuses that failed to gain his attention. He fought for restrictions on female and child labor, introduced legislation to prevent the abuse of children used as chimney sweeps, advocated humane treatment of the insane, forced town after town throughout England to install public sanitation facilities, and formed "ragged schools" for the education of poor children. For Lord Shaftesbury and other nineteenth-century evangelicals, there could be no dichotomy between evangelism and social action. Christian compassion required attention to both the physical and the spiritual needs of men, women, and children.

Though the Anglican evangelicals did not share the desire of the Dissenters for disestablishment, they freely cooperated with the Dissenters in efforts aimed toward evangelism and social reform. Most of these cooperative efforts were channeled through voluntary societies such as interdenominational mission boards and social service organizations. The growth of these voluntary societies not only gave Christians a way to work together across denominational lines, but also to a significant extent separated the social applications of Christianity from the churches. These voluntary societies, sometimes referred to today as parachurch organizations, were often led by laymen, and provided a Christian witness in areas where the churches were frequently silent.

The nineteenth-century evangelicals are viewed today as having shown little concern for theology or biblical scholarship. To some extent, this was because they were too busy changing society to worry about theological questions. More frequently, though, the evangelicals rejected the theology of the day because of its liberal orientation. The teachings of the German liberals gradually made their way across the English Channel, and evangelicals were appalled at the flagrant attacks being made against the Bible and the historic Christian faith. Because they stood firmly upon the historic teachings of the Christian Church and refused to accept the conclusions of the liberals, they were accused of being "unscholarly." This was neither the first nor the last time that such a charge would be leveled against those who accepted the Bible as the inerrant Word of God.

B. THE BROAD CHURCH

If British evangelicals comprised the Low Church movement, the Broad Church movement was made up of England's liberals. The man who is often considered the founder of the Broad Church movement is Samuel Taylor Coleridge (1772-1834), perhaps best known for his poem, *The Rime of the Ancient Mariner*. Coleridge studied in Germany, and was strongly influenced by the idealism of Kant and the work of the German Romanticists. He accepted the liberal criticism of the Bible, and became convinced that the Bible's authority lay, not in a collection of infallible propositions, but in its impact upon the human heart.

It was through the Broad Church movement that critical scholarship first penetrated the English church. Two key books brought the destructive criticism of German biblical scholarship to the attention of the British public. *Essays and Reviews* (1860) and *Lux Mundi* (1889) both included collections of essays by respected British scholars in which the traditional views of the Bible and Christian doctrine were openly challenged. The essays denied everything from the inspiration of Scripture to the Mosaic authorship of the Pentateuch to the miracles of Jesus to the Resurrection to the reality of eternal punishment. Many called for the authors of the essays to be disciplined, but nothing ever came of it, and it quickly became clear that it was possible for a member in good standing of the Church of England to believe or teach just about anything.

This, of course, was precisely what the members of the Broad Church movement had in mind. They viewed the Church of England almost as a department of state, and argued that the church and state should be coextensive as much as possible. In order for this to occur, virtually all doctrinal standards would have to be removed. The advocates of the Broad Church would have liked nothing better than to see the Church of England absorb the various dissenting groups, while allowing each person and each congregation to continue to believe and worship however they desired. They drew the line at incorporating Catholics and Jews, though why they should have done so is difficult to imagine.

The Broad Church movement was liberal in politics as well as in theology. The Christian Socialists, often associated with the Broad Church movement, came to prominence near the middle of the nineteenth century under the leadership of F.D. Maurice (1805-1872), the son of a Unitarian minister. For arguing that hell was a present condition of separation from God rather than a state of eternal punishment, he lost his teaching job at King's College. He also viewed the Kingdom of God as potentially a present reality, and sought with his fellow Socialists to bring about that Kingdom through legislation and relief efforts that would make all men equal in this life. Needless to say, his brand of socialism differed significantly from the atheistic variety being worked out at about the same time by Karl Marx (1818-1883) in his *Communist Manifesto* (1848).

C. THE HIGH CHURCH

There were many in the Church of England who were appalled by both the evangelicals and the Broad Churchmen, however. To them, both groups represented a loss of continuity with the past. They were afraid that the Church of England was losing its moorings, and was about to drift out into an uncharted sea. The political situation did nothing to ameliorate their fears. In 1828, the laws against Dissenters were repealed, allowing them to hold office for the first time since the Cromwell era. Catholics received the same right the following year. Then, in 1832, the Tory government fell from power, and the Whigs passed a Reform Bill that not only expanded the franchise to a much larger segment of the English population, but also gave representation in Parliament to many of the new industrial cities and towns. While all of these changes seem from the perspective of the present to be no more than simple justice, they struck fear into the hearts of many devout Anglicans. After all, the Church of England was a state church, under the control of Parliament. What was to become of the church if Parliament fell into the hands of Dissenters, papists, and infidels? How could such people make wise decisions about church matters? Alarmists among the Anglicans foresaw destruction, or at the very least disestablishment. Such threats to the traditional privileges of the Church of England were not to be tolerated without a fight.

The final straw came in 1833 when Parliament voted to reorganize the Church of Ireland by eliminating ten bishops. The move was hardly a radical one, since most Irish were Catholic, and many Church of Ireland pastors had no Protestants in their parishes! The practicality of the move was not the issue, however. What was objectionable was the fact that a Whig Parliament would have the temerity to lay hands upon the sacred organization of the Anglican Church. Shortly after the passage of the Irish Church Act, John Keble, a professor at Oxford University, preached a sermon on *The National Apostasy*. While he had the reorganization of the Irish Church specifically in mind, it soon became apparent that his objections to the direction of the English Church were much more deep-seated. In fact, the true apostasy was nothing other than the Protestant Reformation. Keble's sermon crystallized feelings of protest that had been building among High Church Anglicans for several decades, and spawned what is variously known as the Oxford Movement (since most of its leaders were professors at Oxford University) or the Tractarian Movement (after the ninety tracts published by the group between 1833 and 1841).

The major leaders of the Tractarians were Keble, John Henry Newman, and Old Testament scholar Edward B. Pusey. They believed that the Church of England needed to get back to its roots - not the roots of the sixteenth century, but the roots of the early centuries of the church. For them, the Old Catholic Church of the first five centuries was the ideal. Tradition was an important part of safeguarding that ideal, and ritual was far more useful in communicating Christian truth than a rational analysis of Scripture ever could be. Above all, they rejected the idea that the state could exercise authority over the church. To uphold the church's authority, they were even willing to accept disestablishment.

A major break in the Tractarian Movement occurred in 1841 with the publication of the ninetieth and last of the tracts, which came from the pen of John Henry Newman. In this tract, Newman argued that the Thirty-Nine Articles were not really anti-Catholic, but could be interpreted in a way that conformed to the teachings of the Catholic Church. In the resulting uproar, Newman was forced to resign his post, and four years later completed his journey by joining the Roman Catholic Church, where he eventually became a cardinal, though many Catholics were never willing to trust him completely (more because of his suspected sympathies with liberalism than because of his Protestant background). Over eight hundred clergy followed Newman into the arms of Rome over the next twenty years. Ironically, the Catholic Church struck a mortal blow to the Oxford Movement when it proclaimed the dogma of papal infallibility in 1870. From this point on, it was impossible for the Tractarians who remained within the Church of England to pretend unity with the universal catholic church.

Most of the Tractarians, including Keble and Pusey, did remain within the Church of England, however. In the long run, their major impact was to bring about a greater emphasis on ritual in the worship of the church. They also helped mount a conservative challenge to the incursions of liberalism through the Broad Church movement. Pusey in particular opposed liberal criticism in his commentaries on Daniel and the Minor Prophets, while other High Church leaders took strong stands against Darwinism. Ultimately, though, their emphasis on tradition and ritual made them powerless to stop the broad-minded Broad Church liberals.

THE DISSENTERS

The nineteenth century was the heyday of the British dissenting churches. Like the Church of England, the Baptists and Congregationalists were stimulated to greater activity by the Methodist revival. In addition, several new dissenting groups arose that were to have a significant impact on the history of the church.

A. THE BAPTISTS

We have already seen that in the eighteenth century, the General Baptists moved toward Unitarianism while the Particular Baptists tended toward hypercalvinism. Both derived new energy from the Methodist revival. For the Particular Baptists, the revival stimulated an involvement in missions about which we will learn more in chapter thirty-four. Both General and Particular Baptists developed a greater interest in reaching the lost and helping the needy, and pooled their efforts with the formation of the Baptist Union, which was formed by the Particular Baptists in 1812 and was opened up to General Baptists twenty years later. By the end of the century, the two groups had merged completely.

By far the most influential Baptist in the nineteenth century was Charles Haddon Spurgeon (1834-1892), the famed pastor of the Metropolitan Tabernacle in London. The son of an Independent minister, Spurgeon was converted at the age of sixteen when he wandered into a Primitive Methodist chapel on a cold and snowy winter night. The pastor was not present, so one of the laymen presented a simple Gospel message, and Spurgeon responded. Within a year he was preaching, and at the age of nineteen was called to pastor the Park Street Chapel, an old but somewhat run-down Baptist church in London. Spurgeon proved to be a great preacher, and soon the old building couldn't hold the crowds who came to hear him. Thousands came to Christ through his ministry. For several years, he was forced to hold services in music halls while the Metropolitan Tabernacle was being built for his congregation. When the 6000-seat Tabernacle was ready for occupancy, it too was almost immediately filled to capacity. Week after week, Spurgeon would preach to a packed house. Visitors to London would always want to include a trip to hear Spurgeon as part of their itinerary. Often, the members of the church were asked to attend other churches on Sunday evenings to leave some seats for the multitude of visitors. Spurgeon's sermons were printed and sold on the streets, selling out almost as quickly as they came off the presses. In fact, the weekly publication and sale of his sermons on the streets of London continued for over thirty years after his death.

In addition to his preaching, Spurgeon wrote a voluminous commentary on the Psalms (*The Treasury of David*) and a book of daily devotions (*Morning and Evening*). The Metropolitan Tabernacle sponsored a Colportage Society for the publication of Christian literature, and Spurgeon edited a monthly magazine called *The Sword and the Trowel* (the name came from the book of Nehemiah, where the builders of the wall worked with a sword in one hand and a trowel in the other). He also operated an orphanage and a school for pastors. Though Spurgeon was a Calvinist, he was willing to cooperate with other evangelicals. Communion services at the Metropolitan Tabernacle were open to all Christians, and Spurgeon openly supported the evangelistic crusades of D.L. Moody. He refused to tolerate liberalism, however. He opposed Darwinism and German criticism, and left the Baptist Union in 1887 when many of its members proved themselves open to liberal views of Scripture (the "Down Grade Controversy").

B. THE IRVINGITES

Edward Irving (1792-1834) was a Church of Scotland minister who had notable success in the early years of his preaching career, first in Glasgow and later in London. He grew increasingly interested in the prophecies concerning the Second Coming of Christ, especially after translating a work on the subject by a Spanish Jesuit in 1827. When congregants at his meetings began speaking in tongues in 1831, he became convinced that the time of Christ's return was near. His followers came to believe that, prior to the Second Coming, the true church would be restored, complete with Pentecostal gifts and the apostolic office. Like the Tractarians, they placed great stock in the ritual associated with the sacraments, and believed that they were means by which the saving grace of God was conveyed to man. Shortly before Irving's death, they formed the Catholic Apostolic Church, which combined the High Church ritual and sacramental emphasis with tongues-speaking and other gifts of the Apostolic Age.

The Irvingites, who never grew to prominence, would hardly deserve mention in an account of this nature except for the fact that their teachings presaged two widely divergent groups that were to have a significant impact on the Christianity of the twentieth century. The first group, obviously, is the Pentecostals, who have left their mark on the American church, and will come under consideration in chapter forty-five. The second is the dispensationalists. Though dispensationalism traces its roots to the teachings of John Nelson Darby (see below), it was among the Irvingites that the doctrine of the pretribulational rapture, which is such an important part of dispensational teaching, first made its appearance. Irving and his followers were the first ones in the 1800-year history of the church to teach that Christ would remove His followers from the world prior to a seven-year period of tribulation. This teaching, in fact, was said to have been given to the Irvingites through tongues-speaking. Though there is no evidence that Darby derived his teaching from the Irvingites, or even that he was aware of what they taught, it is nonetheless instructive to note that a teaching so familiar in many evangelical circles in America made its first appearance at so late a date in the history of the church.

C. THE PLYMOUTH BRETHREN

John Nelson Darby (1800-1882) was a Church of Ireland minister who became dissatisfied with what he perceived as deadness in the church. In his late twenties he was bedridden with a serious illness for almost a year. During this time, he studied the Bible intensively, and became convinced that the popular understanding of the church was completely mistaken. He noted that Paul, in the book of Ephesians, repeatedly refers to Christians as being "in heavenly places in Christ Jesus." From this emphasis of the Apostle's, Darby drew two conclusions that were to become the basis of his theological system. The first was that, since Christians were already in heavenly places in Christ, they needed no mediator to deal with Him. Consequently, the whole notion of a priesthood was a perversion that had been imported by the early church from the Old Testament. Christians were to acknowledge no head on earth but Christ, and were to deal with one another in perfect equality, as brethren.

He also concluded that the present status of Christians as dwelling in heavenly places in Christ would have been impossible prior to the resurrection and ascension of Christ and the coming of the Holy Spirit. Consequently, the Church stands in a unique relationship to Christ that was never enjoyed by Old Testament Israel. This radical distinction between Israel and the Church became the foundation out of which grew the entire dispensational system, with history divided into periods of time during which God dealt differently with men, with the Church Age pictured as a sort of parenthesis between the Old Testament age and the Millennium, during which God would again deal with national Israel. Since the Great Tribulation is prophesied in the Old Testament in relation to Israel, the Church must not be present during that time, which led Darby to adopt the teaching of the pretribulational rapture that has come to be so widely associated with dispensationalism.

Darby's studies led him to leave the Church of Ireland, after which he began to meet with a small group for prayer and Bible study. They refused to take on any denominational identification, preferring to be called simply Brethren. As his teachings spread, other groups of Brethren appeared. The most famous of these groups met in Plymouth, England. It was from this group that Darby and his followers came to be called Plymouth Brethren. The Brethren recognized no clergy, came to practice baptism by immersion (despite the fact that Darby had originally been a paedobaptist), and adopted Darby's dispensational eschatology. Their services were simple and loosely structured, and any man who was led by the Lord to do so could get up during the service and preach. Darby believed that no formal leadership was necessary in the church because the Holy Spirit would give unity to the brethren who gathered in Christ's name. Disagreement inevitably arose, of course, but Darby taught that when such occurred, the person or persons in the minority should leave the group, since they clearly were opposing the leading of the Spirit. B.W. Newton, the leader of the Plymouth fellowship, eventually accused Darby of trying to set himself up as an authority in the church, and Darby in turn accused Newton of heresy. This led to the first of many splits in the group, with Darby becoming the leader of the Exclusive Brethren while Newton became a leader in the Open Brethren.

Later in his life, Darby made a number of trips to America, where he spread his teachings. While a few Brethren assemblies were established in America as a result of his work, by far the greatest impact of his preaching came through the wide dissemination of dispensational eschatology. While dispensationalism spread through many of

America's evangelical denominations, Darby could never understand why Americans accepted his eschatology so readily while at the same time rejecting his vision of the church.

The Open Brethren, meanwhile, became very active in missions, social services, and voluntary societies. One of the best-known of these was the orphanage operated in Bristol by George Müller, who saw God miraculously provide for thousands of orphans despite the fact that he never publicized the financial needs of the orphanage.

D. THE SALVATION ARMY

Another group that had an enormous impact in the area of social reform was the Salvation Army, founded by Methodist minister William Booth (1829-1912). Booth became disillusioned with the Methodists because they were not effectively meeting the needs of London's slum-dwellers. He opened his Christian Mission in a tent in Whitechapel in 1865 to feed and clothe the poverty-stricken inhabitants, while at the same time opening their hearts to the message of the Gospel. The Christian Mission gradually evolved into the Salvation Army, complete with military officers, marching songs, and a magazine called *The War Cry*. Booth and his wife Catherine ministered to London's beggars and prostitutes, going where many in the established church feared to tread. He publicized the cause of home missions with his 1890 book, *In Darkest England and the Way Out*, in which he compared the condition of London slum-dwellers to that of the natives in Africa.

By the time of Booth's death, the Salvation Army had spread to major cities all over the world. His son succeeded him as General of the Army, while his daughter Evangeline for many years headed up the branch in the United States (from the very beginning, the Army had practiced equality between men and women; many claimed that Catherine Booth was a better preacher than her husband!). Early in its history the Salvation Army developed many of its characteristic practices - the trained musicians using rousing popular songs to gather a crowd for preaching, the pseudo-military uniforms, and the wide variety of social services. From the beginning the Salvation Army has refused to practice any sacraments, believing that they are divisive and detract from the true goals of Christianity.

SCHOLARS AND WRITERS

England also produced a number of men who contributed significantly to the life of the church, yet may not easily be fit into any one of the categories we have yet discussed. These include both noted Bible scholars and Christian writers.

A. THE CAMBRIDGE COMMENTATORS

In the late nineteenth century, three professors of New Testament at Cambridge University decided to collaborate on a set of New Testament commentaries. Brooke Foss Westcott (1825-1901), J.B. Lightfoot (1828-1889), and F.J.A. Hort (1828-1892) decided which of them would write on which books, then began to work. While the project was never completed - Hort was so methodical that he never was able to complete much of what he started - Lightfoot's work on several of the Pauline epistles and Westcott's commentaries on John and Hebrews have since become classics. These scholars took the thinking and methods of the liberal critics seriously, but generally arrived at conclusions that were quite in line with historic Christianity (Hort was less evangelical than the others, since he declared himself open to the theory of evolution).

Perhaps the greatest contribution of the Cambridge scholars, however, was not their commentaries, but their work on the text of the New Testament. During the nineteenth century, many manuscript discoveries pushed back our knowledge of the text of the New Testament hundreds of years beyond the manuscripts that had been used to translate such familiar classics as the King James Version of the Bible. Westcott and Hort devoted decades to the study of these newly-discovered manuscripts, demonstrating relationships that existed between families of manuscripts and devising a sort of "family tree" that illustrated the transmission of the text of the New Testament. They also devised principles for determining what readings were most likely to be accurate in cases where the manuscripts showed minor deviations. The result of their work was a Greek text of the New Testament that combined the information from all available manuscripts and allowed scholars to draw much closer to the original words written by the authors of the New Testament books than had previously been possible. Their work provided the foundation for most of the modern English translations of the New Testament, including the New American Standard Bible and the New International Version.

B. THE INKLINGS AND THEIR FRIENDS

Another group of Christians who contributed much to the life of the church were British writers who lived in the late nineteenth and early twentieth centuries. Their most popular work is fictional, including everything from drama and poetry to fantasies, science fiction, and children's books. The forerunner of this group was Scottish minister George MacDonald (1824-1905), whose children's books, fantasies, and short stories have enthralled readers and inspired writers for more than a century. A later contributor was the Catholic author and apologist G.K. Chesterton (1874-1936), who is perhaps best known for his Father Brown murder mysteries, which use Christian insights into human nature to solve mysteries that the "professionals" seem unable to fathom.

Perhaps the best-known Christian writers of the era were a group of men who belonged to a writers' club called the Inklings, which met at Cambridge University weekly for thirty years beginning in 1933. These writers, many of whom were Christians, critiqued one another's works in progress, and also spent much time discussing literature in general and the affairs of the world. Foremost among these men was C.S. Lewis (1898-1963), whose mind-boggling array of writings included everything from apologetics (*Mere Christianity*, *God in the Dock*) to science fiction (the space trilogy consisting of *Out of the Silent Planet*, *Perelandra*, and *That Hideous Strength*) to children's stories (*The Chronicles of Narnia*). The group also included J.R.R. Tolkien (1892-1973), author of *The Hobbit* and *The Lord of the Rings*, and Charles Williams (1886-1945), who wrote "metaphysical thrillers" such as *The Place of the Lion*. Mention should also be made of Dorothy L. Sayers (1893-1957), a friend of Lewis who is best known for her murder mysteries featuring Lord Peter Wimsey, though she also wrote serious religious drama and poetry.

These Christian writers have reached and influenced many people for Christ who would never have listened to a conventional Gospel presentation. Their works are permeated with a Christian view of the world and Christian principles that speak to people whose minds would close at the very thought of preaching.

MAKING DRY BONES LIVE

Ever since the destruction of united Christendom and the formation of denominations, Christians have longed for unity. History has shown, however, that such unity is very difficult to achieve. In this chapter, we have seen a number of very different approaches to Christian unity. The Plymouth Brethren sought unity on the basis of consensus - all should agree, since all are under the influence of the same Spirit. Unfortunately, sinful men in a sinful world do not always listen to the Spirit, and disagreements are inevitable, as the Brethren found out to their dismay after numerous divisions among their ranks.

The members of the Broad Church movement sought unity through discarding all theological standards. Surely men could live as one if they were free to believe anything they wished. The open approach of the Broad Church was no more capable of achieving unity than the narrow method of the Brethren, however. Men who have no standard of belief inevitably use their own minds as the final authority, which produces even less agreement than overt reliance on the Spirit of God.

Another approach is the one attempted by the Tractarians, who sought to find a basis for Christian unity in the traditions of the early church. If everyone could only return to the beliefs and practices of the first five centuries, before the introduction of all the factors that divide modern Christians, then surely God's people could live as one. The problem with the approach taken by the Tractarians was that they had an overly naive picture of the early church. As the readers of this book hopefully realize by now, the early years of the church were marked by anything but harmony over matters of doctrine and practice.

Or perhaps the Salvation Army had the right idea. Doctrines and sacraments are divisive. What is really important is that Christians work together to change society and meet the needs of the poor. The Salvation Army soon discovered, however, that people working together with no doctrinal foundation soon find that their message becomes purely social, with little or no distinctive Christian content. Such unity can hardly be called Christian, and it is doubtful whether unity of that kind is worth having.

What about the Inklings? Anglicans and Catholics with widely divergent views of Christian doctrine and practice, they succeeded in communicating a Christian world view to a world that had forgotten the roots of Western civilization. Is this where Christian unity must ultimately lie - in a unified view of the world that transcends doctrine and specific religious practices? But if so, how should Christians worship, and what message should they preach to the world that so desperately needs the transforming power of the Gospel?

In short, unity is much easier to long for than it is to achieve. Paul wisely told the Ephesians to "make every effort to keep the unity of the Spirit through the bond of peace" without specifying how it should be done. Jesus perhaps said it best when He gave His disciples a simple yet difficult command: "Love one another."

FOR REVIEW AND FURTHER THOUGHT

1. Define the following: establishment, disestablishment, antidisestablishmentarianism.

2. What led many of the Dissenters in nineteenth-century England to call for disestablishment of the state church?

3. What challenges faced the churches of England as a result of the Industrial Revolution?

4. Why was the term "Low Church" used to describe Anglican evangelicals?

5. How did the growth of voluntary societies expand the application of Christianity to society? How did it help to divorce this application from the churches?

6. Why were the British evangelicals considered unscholarly by their peers as well as by modern historians?

7. Why was the name "Broad Church" appropriate for England's liberal churchmen?

8. On what basis did F.D. Maurice argue against the biblical doctrine of hell?

9. How did the socialism of Maurice differ from that of his contemporary Karl Marx?

10. What changes in the early part of the nineteenth century caused apprehension among traditional Anglicans?

11. Why is High Church Anglicanism in the nineteenth century sometimes called the Oxford Movement or the Tractarian Movement?

12. What led many of the Tractarians into the Catholic Church in the middle of the nineteenth century?

13. How did the Catholic Church effectively undermine the position of the Tractarians?

14. What long-range impact did the Tractarians have on the Church of England?

15. What changes occurred in England's Baptist churches in the nineteenth century?

16. What was the Down Grade Controversy?

17. What were the distinctive teachings and practices of the Catholic Apostolic Church?

18. How did the doctrine of the pretribulational rapture first enter the annals of church history?

19. How did Darby reach his conclusions concerning the nature of the church?

20. How did Darby's eschatology grow out of his view of the church?

21. What factors led to numerous schisms in the early history of the Plymouth Brethren?

22. What were some of the distinctive characteristics of the Salvation Army?

23. How did the work of Westcott and Hort advance the cause of New Testament scholarship and Bible translation?

24. How is it possible for literature to communicate Christian truth to those who might never be open to Gospel preaching?

25. Why is the ideal of Christian unity so difficult to achieve? How did various groups studied in this chapter try and fail to provide a basis for Christian unity?

THE REFORMED CHURCHES OF EUROPE

In the nation of France today, there are more Muslims than evangelical Protestants. While the Catholic heritage of France and the extensive immigration from France's former colonies in North Africa may partially explain this situation, it does not explain why there are also more Mormons than evangelical Christians - a clear indication of the sorry state of French Protestantism. The homes of the other great European Reformed churches - Switzerland and the Netherlands - are in somewhat better shape, but not by much. What has become of the homelands of the Huguenots, of Calvin and Beza, of the noble Dutch Protestants who withstood the murderous persecution of the Spanish Inquisition? After giving our attention to the modern history of the Church of England and the Lutheran Church in Germany, it is now time to consider the development of the Reformed churches of Europe since the time of the Reformation.

FRANCE

When we last visited France, the Huguenots had just been granted a reprieve after decades of bitter religious warfare by the turncoat king Henry IV, who had converted to Catholicism in order to secure the French crown for himself and the House of Bourbon. In 1598, Henry had issued the Edict of Nantes, granting official toleration to the French Protestants, allowing them freedom of worship in certain designated areas, and permitting them to maintain a number of fortified cities throughout France.

Though Henry IV was cut down by the knife of the assassin Ravaillac in 1610, the Huguenots continued to prosper, growing to the point where they became almost a state within a state in France. Not only did the industrious Protestants, who represented the bulk of France's growing middle class, wield enormous economic power, but the Huguenots also had their own troops, along with a navy superior to that of the king.

Such a situation would have been politically intolerable had it not been for the fact that the Huguenots were the most committed royalists in the realm. They were unquestioningly loyal to the king. The royal advisors who dominated the French political scene in the middle of the seventeenth century, however, wanted more than loyalty. Cardinal Richelieu and his successor, Mazarin, would accept nothing short of royal absolutism, which to them could occur only when the French people were united fully behind the king. Richelieu started the process by systematically reducing the military power of the Huguenots, culminating in the siege and fall of the Huguenot fortress of La Rochelle in 1629. The cardinal had no religious ax to grind, however, and allowed the Huguenots to retain their religious liberties. Mazarin continued the policy, and it paid off handsomely, not only through the fierce loyalty of the Huguenots to the crown, but also through the growing prosperity of France. All during this time, however, the Jesuits, backed by the popes, were agitating for the destruction of the Huguenots. They were soon to get their wish.

A. THE AGE OF LOUIS XIV

Shortly before the death of Mazarin in 1661, the young king Louis XIV assumed control of his own foreign and internal affairs. The quintessential royal absolutist, Louis not only identified himself with the state (*L'etat, c'est moi!*), but also insisted that France be completely unified on all levels - one king, one law, one faith (*Un roi, une loi, une foi*). As far as he was concerned, this required the destruction of the Huguenots, despite the fact that they had never given the king any reason to question their devotion to him.

In 1659, a group of Jesuits in the Huguenot stronghold of Montauban set up a stage in the courtyard of the Huguenot academy in order to put on a play - something certain to offend the clean-living Protestants. Several enraged Huguenots destroyed the stage, eliciting a protest from the local Catholic bishop. This was all the justification Louis needed to put his plan into action. The academy was closed and the buildings turned over to the Jesuits, the Huguenots who were involved, either directly or indirectly, were either executed or sent to the galleys, and the Protestant churches were demolished or given to the Catholics. Louis was determined from this point on to interpret the Edict of Nantes in the strictest possible way. Any liberty not specifically promised in the Edict was removed, and the king instituted policies that harassed the Protestants in the exercise of the very freedoms he himself had guaranteed when he confirmed the Edict of Nantes in 1652.

Between 1660 and 1685, Louis turned the screws progressively tighter on the Huguenot population. They were excluded from public office. Certain occupations were closed to them, and they found it almost impossible to advance even in those trades in which they were permitted to engage. Egged on by the Jesuits, Louis confiscated the property of Huguenot churches and schools all over France, then gave the buildings to the Catholics - even in towns where almost the entire population was Protestant. Such strictures produced some conversions to Catholicism, but matters were moving too slowly for the king. Louis then established a fund for the purpose of bribing Huguenots to convert to Catholicism. At the same time, conversion to Protestantism became punishable by confinement to the galleys. Given the enormous economic pressure already faced by the Huguenots, many professed conversion in order to ensure financial survival for themselves and their families.

The king's next target was the Protestant family. Not satisfied with producing Huguenot conversions by bribery, he now declared that Protestant children as young as twelve (the age was later lowered to seven) would be permitted to deny the heresy in which they had been raised and convert to Catholicism. Those who did so would be removed from the baneful influence of their parents and placed with Catholic families, where they could attend the best schools and rise to their proper station in society. Needless to say, numerous overzealous local officials used this edict as a pretext to seize the children of Protestants and thereby force the conversion of the parents. Despite all this, many Huguenots still remained faithful to their convictions. But the worst was yet to come.

Louis next instituted the dreaded Dragonnade. It had been common practice for many years for French soldiers (dragoons) to live in the homes of the French people where they were stationed when they were not abroad fighting for the glory of France. When the king chose to do so, however, the quartering of troops could become a formidable weapon against internal enemies. When Louis imposed the Dragonnade upon the Huguenots, he ordered that French troops be quartered in Protestant homes - especially those of the rich and influential among them. These soldiers were encouraged to do all they could to contribute to the conversion of the benighted heretics - everything short of murder and rape, that is (though these too were occasionally overlooked). The result was a reign of terror to which many Protestants probably would have preferred the guillotine. Huguenots were impoverished, beaten, tortured, humiliated, and practically enslaved by the troops who invaded their homes. Since conversion to Catholicism was the only escape, thousands became Catholics to rid themselves of the dragoons. Thousands of others fled the country, despite edicts condemning all who were caught to the galleys.

Finally, in 1685, Louis' advisors convinced him that he had achieved his goal - that for all practical purposes, no Protestants remained in France, and he now ruled a unified and Catholic population. Since there were no Protestants left, the Edict of Nantes was now an anachronism, so Louis formally revoked it. Protestantism was now illegal in France. Despite the king's belief that none remained, well over a hundred thousand Huguenots fled the country when their religion was outlawed. Some estimate that in the second half of the seventeenth century, almost a half million Protestants - industrious, loyal people representing the bulk of France's middle class - emigrated to England, Germany, Switzerland, the Netherlands, the American colonies, and even to South Africa. The economic loss was one from which France never recovered. Politically, as well, the Bourbons lost an important buffer against radicalism. Had the Huguenots remained as a viable force in France, the agitation for reform in the eighteenth century might have driven the dissatisfied into Protestantism rather than into the arms of the revolutionaries. In addition, those Protestants who were forced to convert to Catholicism tended to be more susceptible to the skepticism of the eighteenth century than they otherwise might have been had they been permitted to retain their religious roots.

After the Edict of Nantes was revoked, a few Protestants remained, but they were hounded mercilessly, never being allowed to live in peace. Most of those who stayed in France were forced to hide out in the mountains, where they formed small communities, concealing themselves during the daylight hours and gathering at night for times of worship. These communities often had no seasoned leadership, since most of the pastors had been exiled, imprisoned, sent to the galleys, or executed. The result was undisciplined radicalism. Some of the groups fell into various excesses in their worship, claiming visions and revelations and exercising miraculous gifts. Others turned to violence. The Camisards, small bands of peasants who wore white robes to enable them to identify one another at night, lived in the caves of the Cevennes mountains and carried on guerilla warfare against the Catholic population of the region. They assassinated Catholic leaders, burned buildings and crops, and attacked small military detachments. In the first decade of the eighteenth century, many of these bands were hunted down and mercilessly slaughtered - men, women, and children - by French troops.

B. THE REVOLUTION, NAPOLEON, AND BEYOND

Throughout most of the eighteenth century, the Protestant church in France operated underground, while the French authorities turned their attention to eradicating the Jansenists, who had been condemned by the papal bull *Unigenitus* in 1713. Having lost all legal standing and living in constant fear of their lives, the few remaining Huguenots formed the *Church of the Desert* (*desert* means "wilderness" in French), which met in hiding places all over France, particularly in the mountainous regions. The leading lights of the Church of the Desert were Antoine Court (1696-1760) and Paul Rabaut (1718-1794). Court did much to put an end to the radicalism of the Huguenot communities in the Cevennes, and by his restraint brought new respect to the Protestant cause. He also established a theological seminary in Lausanne, Switzerland in order to train pastors for the Huguenot churches. These young men, having received training in Switzerland, crossed the border into France knowing that they were putting their lives in jeopardy. In fact, many of the graduates of the Lausanne seminary "graduated" into the presence of the Lord within a year of their passage into France.

Paul Rabaut was one of these young pastors, but he found that the increasing skepticism of the French Enlightenment was working to the advantage of the persecuted Huguenots. During the half-century in which he ministered in France, he worked to gain toleration for the French Protestants. The philosophes of the Enlightenment proved to be surprising allies in his battle. Though many of the leading French skeptics hated Christianity with a passion and mocked it mercilessly, they were equally passionate in their love of freedom of thought and expression. Consequently, men such as Voltaire and the Marquis de Lafayette, the hero of the American Revolution, were more than willing to speak out on behalf of the persecuted Huguenots. The ultimate result of the increasing respectability of the Huguenots themselves and the liberalizing spirit of the Enlightenment was the passage in 1787 of the Edict of Toleration, which formally ended the persecution of the French Protestants.

The sons of Court and Rabaut, Court de Gebellin and Rabaut St. Etienne, both played major roles in gaining recognition for the Huguenots. Both rose to high office - Court de Gebellin as royal censor and Rabaut St. Etienne as president of the revolutionary National Assembly. The latter eventually became one of the victims of the Reign of Terror.

Protestants and Catholics alike suffered during the early years of the French Revolution. The heady days of freedom were followed quickly by the folly of skepticism run amok, as the radicals of the Revolution first outlawed Christianity and instituted the worship of the Goddess Reason (complete with an actress decked out in classical fashion enthroned on the altar of the cathedral of Notre Dame in Paris), then instituted a new calendar that included a ten-day "week," eliminated Christian holidays, saints' days and the sabbath, and instituted days of rest that could profitably be used for edifying philosophical lectures and discussions. The new calendar was in use for ten years, though it was widely ignored by the population at large. The worship of Reason was later replaced by the deistic Cult of the Supreme Being, which was not much of an improvement, though it did open the door just a crack for Christian belief.

By the time Napoleon came to power and reinstituted religious toleration, there was not much religion left to tolerate. With few notable exceptions, such as the revival in the French Protestant church under the leadership of Adolphe and Frederick Monod in the early years of the nineteenth century, France has been marked by religious skepticism. Today, few Frenchmen attend a church of any kind, though most are professing Catholics, while evangelical Protestants make up only a fraction of one percent of the population.

SWITZERLAND

When last we looked at Switzerland, John Calvin had transformed Geneva into the model Protestant city, and his work was being carried on by his friend and successor Theodore Beza. In the years following the death of Beza, the Swiss Protestants became preoccupied with fighting theological battles, some more worthwhile than others. Francis Turretin, professor of theology at Geneva, defended Calvinist orthodoxy against the growing liberalism and rationalism of his day and wrote a theological textbook, the *Institutes*, which was the standard in Reformed seminaries for the next two centuries. He also helped to draft the Helvetic Consensus (1675), which condemned the teachings of the Amyraldians at the University of Saumur across the border in France (see chapter twenty-two). Meanwhile, four members of the Buxtorf family were defending orthodox Christianity as professors of theology at Basel. One of these, Johann Buxtorf, sought to uphold the authority of Scripture by arguing that the Hebrew vowel points (introduced into the text of the Old Testament several hundred years after the time of Christ by a group of Jewish scholars called the Masoretes) were divinely inspired!

Like the rest of Europe, Switzerland rushed headlong into rationalism in the eighteenth century. One of the leaders of this movement was J.A. Turretin, the son of the great theologian. His Enlightenment philosophy not only led him to seek the union of the Lutheran and Reformed churches in Switzerland, but also to seek repeal of the Helvetic Consensus. The Swiss church declined rapidly thereafter, as Socinianism, Unitarianism, and Latitudinarianism infiltrated from England and Germany.

God injected new life into the Protestant church in Switzerland by means of a revival led by the Scottish preacher Robert Haldane (1764-1842) in the early years of the nineteenth century. Haldane, a Baptist, had originally intended to pursue missionary service, but could find no support in Scotland. He then turned to itinerant evangelism, traveling around Europe and the British Isles to preach the Gospel. In 1816 he arrived in Geneva, and began leading a Bible study on the book of Romans. Young men from the university and the surrounding community attended these studies, and many were converted, some of whom went on to become leaders in forming a new Evangelical Church in Switzerland. Among these men were J.H. Merle D'Aubigne (1794-1872), the great historian of the Reformation; César Malan (1787-1864), a powerful preacher whose staunch Calvinism led to his removal from his pulpit in Switzerland, after which he became a traveling evangelist; François Gaussen (1790-1863), the author of *Theopneustia*, a defense of the inspiration of Scripture; and Adolphe Monod (1802-1856), who with his brother Frederick went on to spur revival among French Protestants.

Though today there remains in Switzerland more evangelical Christianity than may be found in France, the land of Zwingli and Calvin for the most part knows little of the teachings of those great men of the faith. Like Germany, it has come to be dominated by the man-centered skepticism of the liberal critics.

THE NETHERLANDS

The modern history of Dutch Protestantism is remarkably similar to what we have just seen in Switzerland. In the early seventeenth century, the defenders of Calvinist orthodoxy, many of whom went considerably beyond Calvin in their teachings, condemned Arminius and his followers, the Remonstrants, at the Synod of Dordt (1618-19). The ensuing persecution was in large part politically motivated, and in any case was short-lived. The Arminians soon returned, establishing churches, schools, and a theological seminary. The major theological dispute of the seventeenth century was between Johannes Cocceius (1603-1669), an Arminian who is considered the originator of Covenant Theology, and Gisbert Voetius (1588-1676), a staunch defender of the Calvinism of the Synod of Dordt who exercised a significant influence on the English Puritans. The two differed not only in their understanding of the doctrine of salvation, but also in their interpretation of biblical teaching regarding the Sabbath. Cocceius believed that the Sabbath was an Old Covenant ordinance fulfilled in Christ, and therefore concluded that Sabbath observance constituted legalistic bondage, while Voetius argued for strict Sabbath observance on the ground that the Sabbath command was a creation ordinance. The view of Cocceius eventually became popular in many of the European Protestant churches, while the English Puritans and their American cousins followed the position of Voetius.

As was true in Switzerland, the eighteenth century brought skepticism to the Dutch church, but the nineteenth century saw the dawn of revival. When the poet Willem Bilderdijk (1756-1831) began teaching a course on the history of Christianity, some of his students became interested in orthodox Christianity, including a converted Jew named Isaak da Costa (1798-1860). Under the leadership of these men, the Dutch Reformed Church experienced a renewed interest in theological orthodoxy.

In the years that followed, some Christians became concerned about the liberalism of the state church. Under the leadership of Gröen van Prinsterer (d.1867), they moved to use the mechanism of the state to bring about change in the church. In order to accomplish this, they formed a Christian political party. One of the earliest parliamentary representatives of this party was a young pastor named Abraham Kuyper (1837-1920). Kuyper had received the typical liberal theological training of the day, but was caught by surprise when the parishioners in his first church, by no means educated people, displayed a much greater knowledge of the Bible than he was able to muster. This drove him to study the Scriptures for himself, and he became an ardent evangelical. When Van Prinsterer approached him with his idea for a Christian political party, Kuyper expressed his willingness to serve. The country pastor soon became one of the most outspoken advocates of orthodox Christianity in the Netherlands. While his attempts to reform the state church failed, he eventually led a secession from the state church, forming not only an independent evangelical Dutch Reformed Church (unfortunately, the names of the state church and the independent church translate the same way into English), but also the Free University of Amsterdam, for many years one of the leading evangelical schools in the world.

In fact, it was the issue of education that eventually brought Kuyper to the forefront of Dutch politics. The liberalism of the nineteenth century had led to the elimination of religious instruction from the state schools. This concerned not only the evangelical Protestants, but the Catholics as well, both of whom sought state support for the schools they operated in order to provide religious education for their children. Kuyper galvanized the two groups into a powerful political coalition that eventually gained a majority in the Dutch parliament. The result was that Kuyper, as the head of the coalition, served as Prime Minister of the Netherlands from 1901 to 1905.

Today, the evangelical church has little influence in the Netherlands. Like much of northern and western Europe, the Dutch now have a pluralistic and permissive society where many show no concern for religious matters, and few speak out for the truth of the Gospel.

MAKING DRY BONES LIVE

Ichabod - "the glory has departed" - was the name the wife of Phineas gave to her newborn son when she heard that the Ark of the Covenant had fallen into the hands of the Philistines. In our study of church history, we have seen, time and again, the word "Ichabod" scrawled in bold letters across churches where at one time the message of the Gospel prospered. The lands of North Africa, which were once a stronghold of the Christian faith, are now practically devoid of Christian witness. Dominated by Islam, the Christian churches that remain are steeped in dead tradition, while missionaries work on the fringes to communicate the Gospel through literature and radio ministries.

Western Europe is not much better. The homelands of the Reformation are uniformly characterized by dead churches, pitifully low church attendance, and an evangelical witness that amounts to little more than a voice in the wilderness. In the place properly occupied by Jesus Christ, we find instead the enthronement of the Goddess Reason and her kin. One of the greatest misnomers in history occurred when the humanism and rationalism of the eighteenth century was labeled "the Enlightenment." Instead of bringing the professed light, it proved nothing more than that men love darkness rather than light.

Though the study of history can be discouraging, we must also realize that the Enlightenment philosophers were wrong when they asserted that man was the master of his own destiny. Despite their denials, God is still in control of this world and its inhabitants. His sovereignty overrules men's paltry designs. Though the revivals in France, Switzerland, and the Netherlands in the nineteenth century are now little more than a dim memory, God is equally able to generate revival in the spiritual darkness of modern Europe. In the same way that the elevation of the Goddess Reason collapsed from the weight of its own folly during the French Revolution, so today we see one of the most godless philosophies in all of human history, communism, crumbling to the ground. Who knows what God will bring about in those European countries where for the better part of this century the truth has been suppressed?

The Reformed Churches of Europe

FOR REVIEW AND FURTHER THOUGHT

1. What privileges were granted to the Huguenots under the Edict of Nantes?

2. Why did Richelieu consider the Huguenots to be a threat to the crown?

3. After the siege of La Rochelle, why were the Huguenots still permitted to worship freely?

4. Why did Louis XIV seek to destroy the Huguenots?

5. What techniques did Louis XIV use to convince the Huguenots to convert to Catholicism? To what extent were these techniques successful?

6. What was the Dragonnade, and how did Louis XIV use it to oppress Protestants in his realm?

7. Why did Louis XIV revoke the Edict of Nantes in 1685?

8. What was the effect of the revocation of the Edict of Nantes on the French economy?

9. In what sense did the flight of the Huguenots from France and the forced conversion of most who remained contribute to the French Revolution a century later?

10. Who were the Camisards?

11. What was the bull *Unigenitus*?

12. What was the *Church of the Desert*, and how did it preserve French Protestantism?

13. How did Antoine Court and Paul Rabaut contribute to the restoration of Protestantism in France?

14. What roles were played by the sons of Court and Rabaut in the restoration of Protestantism?

15. Describe the French Enlightenment's idea of humanistic religion.

16. How are the histories of the Protestant churches in Switzerland and the Netherlands since the Reformation similar?

17. Identify the following in one sentence each: Francis Turretin, Johann Buxtorf, J.A. Turretin, Willem Bilderdijk, Isaak da Costa, Robert Haldane, J.H. Merle D'Aubigne, César Malan, François Gaussen, Gröen van Prinsterer.

18. Besides the Swiss revival under Haldane, what other incidents from church history can you recall that were sparked by the book of Romans?

19. On what key issues did Cocceius and Voetius disagree? What groups did each influence?

20. What was the intention of the men who formed a Christian political party in the Netherlands?

21. Do you think it would be a good idea to have a Christian political party in the United States? Why or why not?

22. What was the key issue that propelled Abraham Kuyper to the office of Prime Minister of the Netherlands?

23. Why can the study of history sometimes be depressing? Why should it also provide hope?

THE WORLD IN THEIR HANDS

In 1783, a twenty-two year old English cobbler sat at his bench and prayed. On the wall behind him was a crude map, on which he had written bits of information about the religions, languages, cultures, and flora and fauna of the countries of the world. In his hands he held a leather globe stitched together from the scraps of his trade. As he prayed, he would rotate the globe in his hands, pleading with God for the salvation of the lost souls in the distant continents and far-flung islands of the seas. Ten years later, that cobbler, whose name was William Carey, would travel to India in the vanguard of the greatest missionary movement since the initial expansion of the church throughout the Roman Empire in the first century, and thus earn for himself the title of the Father of Modern Protestant Missions.

WHY SO LONG?

It seems peculiar, to say the least, that a man who lived two and a half centuries after the beginning of the Protestant Reformation should be known as the Father of Modern Protestant Missions. Carey was not the first Protestant missionary, of course. A few had gone before, but they concentrated their efforts largely on European colonists, and saw little fruit among native populations. A number of factors, both political and religious, delayed the full-scale involvement of Protestants in foreign missions, while others set the stage for the enormous expansion of the church throughout the world in the nineteenth century.

A. POLITICAL FACTORS

When the Protestant Reformation began, Spain was the dominant force in European politics. Her explorers girdled the globe, followed by conquistadors who in turn were followed by Jesuits. Missionaries brought Catholicism to the lands of Latin America and established outposts in parts of Asia and Africa. Spanish dominance ended with the defeat of the Spanish Armada in 1588, and control of the seas passed to England.

The English, later joined by the Dutch, did not use their sea power for the spread of Christianity, however. While the Spanish had conquered and colonized the lands of the New World, the British and Dutch wanted trade rather than colonies. Even in the British colonies in North America, scant attention was paid to evangelizing the Indians. Those "missionaries" who came to the New World, like John Wesley in Georgia, restricted their ministries largely to the English settlers.

Even when the British changed their strategy and began accumulating the colonies that were to become the British Empire, the trading companies such as the British East India Company that played a major role in administering the colonies were often hostile to missionary endeavor. Missionaries were meddlesome fools whether they succeeded or failed. Missionaries who failed to convert the native peoples often stirred them up to indignation by challenging their long-cherished religious beliefs and practices. Those who succeeded in their efforts to spread the life-changing message of the Gospel often hindered the exploitation of the native population in the process, not only by fighting for the rights of the indigenous peoples, but also by teaching them skills, such as reading, that made them more difficult to exploit. Besides, the men who ran the trading companies somehow found it easier on their consciences to abuse heathen rather than exploiting "fellow Christians."

The other major Protestant nations had little desire or opportunity to engage in missionary effort. Both Germany and Switzerland were seriously divided along religious lines, and the Protestant churches spent the early years after the beginning of the Reformation fighting for their existence. The whole state church mentality often worked against missions. The Protestant rulers naturally gave their primary attention to their own people, and had little interest in the religious welfare of people in other countries. The few who did expressed their interest by sending soldiers rather than missionaries. After all, if the religion of the prince is the religion of the people, the best way to get the people to change their religion is to conquer them and give them a new prince! The only notable exception to this lack of enthusiasm for missions among the Protestant state churches was Denmark, which was willing to finance the missionaries who went out from the University of Halle.

B. RELIGIOUS FACTORS

The lack of Protestant involvement in missions in the centuries following the Reformation cannot be blamed entirely on the political situation, however. There were also religious factors that kept Protestants from looking outward to the lost peoples of the world. One of the most important of these factors was the theological controversy to which the Protestants gave so much of their time and energy. Whether Lutheran versus Reformed, both of them against the Anabaptists, Calvinists versus Arminians, or any number of less significant theological disputes, the Protestants involved themselves so deeply in the doctrines of the faith that they had little time left to give to spreading that faith. Their vision rarely extended beyond the boundaries of their own small world, and those whose eyes may have strayed to the regions beyond were usually so fragmented that the cooperative effort needed to marshal the resources for such an enormous task was unthinkable.

The Enlightenment only made matters worse, of course. Rationalism drove many Protestant churches toward Unitarianism, which clearly gave little motivation for missionary work. Those who remained orthodox were also influenced by the rationalism of the age - an influence that often manifested itself in the form of hypercalvinism. To many in the eighteenth century, missionary effort would be a futile repudiation of the sovereignty of God. They argued that the Great Commission had not been given to the church of all ages, but to the apostles, and that they had carried out the last command of the Savior. If the heathen were in spiritual darkness, did not this represent the judgment of the sovereign God against their wickedness and idolatry? Certainly it is important for Christians everywhere to pray for the conversion of the heathen, but the initiative belongs to God. If men were to take such a matter into their own hands, they would be fighting God, and their effort would be doomed to failure. Thus the eighteenth century presents the ironic picture of prayer groups all over England meeting to pray for the evangelism of the lost, but refusing to take action as a matter of theological principle.

C. AIDS TO MISSIONARY EXPANSION

The greatest single factor in changing the thinking of Protestants on the subject of missions was the evangelical revival of the eighteenth century, spurred by the Pietists in Germany and later by the Methodists in England. The Pietist emphasis on evangelizing those at home who professed to be Christians could not help but be transferred to a vision for the unsaved multitudes abroad. As we have already seen in an earlier chapter, the Pietists set an example in the field of foreign missions that others eventually followed.

While the state churches continued to drag their heels in the area of missions, the rise of voluntary societies contributed greatly to the missionary cause. The Baptist Missionary Society founded by Carey in 1792 was the first of many such organizations, some affiliated with denominations and some independent. These voluntary societies became the greatest source of missionary workers in the modern era. Finally, Protestants had discovered a way to overcome minor theological differences and work together for the advancement of the Kingdom of God, though as we will see, theological differences were not always successfully kept in the background.

Politically speaking, the Pax Britannica did as much to further missionary expansion in the nineteenth century as the Pax Romana had done in the first. The sun never set on the British Empire, and the peace and ease of travel associated with that global network benefitted missionaries enormously. Though British officials and missionaries often were at odds with one another, the Empire continued to provide a stable and relatively safe environment in which missionaries could operate. The invention of the steamship allowed for faster and safer travel almost anywhere in the world, while the technological advances connected with the Industrial Revolution helped open the door for missionaries to native peoples eager for Western goods.

EARLY PROTESTANT MISSIONS

Brief attention should be given to those pioneer Protestant missionaries who preceded Carey. One of the earliest Protestant attempts to spread the Gospel abroad was organized in 1555 by John Calvin and Gaspard de Coligny. The intention of the organizers was to send a party of Huguenots to establish a settlement on the coast of Brazil, which could then serve as a base for an evangelistic effort among the natives. The whole endeavor came to nothing, however, when the head of the colony, Nicholas de Villegagnon, converted to Catholicism and betrayed the colonists to the Portuguese. Most of the colonists were slaughtered, many died at sea attempting to return to France, and the few who did survive were put on trial for heresy when they arrived home.

In the seventeenth century, a few in the British colonies of North America dedicated their lives to the evangelization of the American Indians. Perhaps the most notable of these was John Eliot (1604-1690), a pastor at Roxbury in the Massachusetts Bay Colony. He took the time to master the language of the Indians, preached to them and taught them in their own tongue, and saw many come to Christ through his efforts. He translated the Bible, along with other Christian books, into the tribal language, established churches, gathered the Indians into "praying villages" where they would be safe from the temptations and harassments of their unconverted brethren, and arranged to have several Indians trained for the ministry at Harvard. At about the same time, Thomas Mayhew, the first of four generations of missionaries from his family, was beginning a work among the Indians of Martha's Vineyard.

Most of the missionary efforts at this time were directed at European colonists, however. Anglican pastor Thomas Bray (1656-1730) founded two organizations (the Society for Promoting Christian Knowledge, which provided books for colonial pastors and published literature for use by the colonists, and the Society for the Propagation of the Gospel, which sent ministers to the colonies) that eventually turned their attention to the evangelization of the heathen, though they were concerned initially with the plight of the European colonists. While many of the colonists were a godless lot who sorely needed evangelizing, most European Christians remained blind to the needs of the world outside Europe.

The Pietists and Moravians were the exception to this trend, and of them we have already spoken in chapter twenty-nine. They had no state church ties and, with the exception of the Danish-Halle mission, received no state support in their efforts. Caring little for national boundaries, they preached the Gospel wherever they went, and in their desire to spread the Word of God became the forerunners of the Golden Age of European Missions.

THE FATHER OF MODERN MISSIONS

We are ready now to turn our attention to the life and ministry of William Carey (1761-1834). Carey was born in the village of Paulerspury, Northamptonshire, to the local schoolmaster and his wife. From childhood he loved books. From hours spent wandering the fields around his home and studying the plant life there, he developed an ambition to become a gardener. Pollen allergies soon made that course of action impractical, however. He apprenticed himself to a shoemaker at age fourteen, and four years later was converted through the influence of a fellow apprentice. After marrying his master's sister-in-law, an illiterate woman five years his senior, he set up his own cobbler shop. As he worked, he would read voraciously. Carey was particularly interested in stories about other lands, such as the narrative of the voyages of Captain Cook in the South Pacific. Languages fascinated him, and he managed to teach himself Latin, Greek, Hebrew, Italian, French, and Dutch - all of this by a young man with minimal formal education. It was at this time, too, with the map on his wall and the globe in his hands, that he began praying for the people in the lands about which he had been learning.

At about this time Carey became a Baptist, and soon began spending some of his time teaching local children and serving as lay preacher in a Baptist congregation. In 1786, he was ordained to the Baptist ministry, and for the next six years pastored several Baptist churches. His heart longed to preach the Gospel abroad, but he found little support among his fellow pastors (though the famous incident where Carey was told by a fellow minister to sit down and stop talking about foreign missions because "when God pleases to converse with heathen He'll do it without consulting you or me" is probably apocryphal, it accurately reflects the hypercalvinism of many of the Particular Baptists of Carey's day).

Carey persevered in his vision for missions, however, and in 1792 he published *An Enquiry into the Obligation of Christians to Use Means for the Conversion of the Heathen* (the actual title was much longer; in those days book titles were almost as long as some modern books), in which he not only defended the necessity of evangelism among the unbelieving peoples of the world, but also set out a strategy to fulfill the requirements of the Great Commission and answered a variety of practical objections often raised against the effort. That same year, he preached a sermon on Isaiah 54:2-3 entitled, *Expect Great Things from God, Attempt Great Things for God*. By this time, a number of the younger Baptist ministers were convinced that Carey was right, and fourteen of them banded together to form the Particular Baptist Society for Propagating the Gospel among the Heathen.

In 1793, Carey left for India as the society's first missionary. Before leaving, he had to overcome the objections of his wife, his father, and his congregation, but he finally was able to set sail on a Danish ship bound for India, since no ship of the British East India Company was willing to transport a missionary. Carey and his family arrived in India in December of 1793 - without money, without a job (the East India Company had refused to give Carey a work permit), without a place to stay, and with no knowledge of the local language. They faced incredible hardships in the early years in India. Moving inland to avoid deportation, Carey carved a small clearing out of a tiger-infested swamp and built a home for his family. He finally obtained a job as foreman of an indigo factory where he worked while learning the Bengali language. Meanwhile, his family suffered much illness from the tropical climate and the unfamiliar diet, and one of his sons died. His wife, who had never really wanted to come to India in the first place, had a mental breakdown, and was reduced to helpless lunacy until her death in 1807. Carey made his first attempt at Bible translation, rendering the entire Bible into Bengali, but found that the natives, while they understood the words, could make no sense out of what he had written, because it completely lacked the idiom of Bengali speech. Up to this time, Carey had not seen a single Indian convert.

The turning point in Carey's ministry came in 1799, when he was joined by a new group of volunteers from England. These recruits included the printer William Ward, Joshua Marshman, a schoolteacher, and his wife Hannah. When the British East India Company refused to let the ship bearing the volunteers land, Carey and his new associates decided to settle in the little Danish colony of Serampore, up the coast from Calcutta. Here they established a little church and a printing press.

Later a school was added to train native pastors (Serampore College). From these small beginnings, the ministry of Carey in India blossomed. Carey, Marshman, and Ward came to be known as the Serampore Trio, and the pattern of their work inspired countless others to follow their example.

Carey and his co-workers mounted a five-pronged attack in their efforts to spread the Gospel in India. In addition to the obvious ministry of preaching, they sought to translate the Bible into the native languages, provide education for the people to whom they ministered, train indigenous leaders who could then go out and evangelize their own people and establish churches, familiarize themselves with the culture of India, and have an impact on that culture by working against social abuses.

In all of these areas, Carey enjoyed amazing success. The linguistic skills Carey had shown in his early studies at the cobbler's bench served him well in India. By the time of his death, he had translated the entire Bible into six different Indian tongues and the New Testament into twenty-three others, in addition to ten other partial translations. While most of these translations were rough, and have been improved upon in the years that followed, Carey not only was able to expose thousands to the Word of God in their own language for the first time, but also showed others the value of Bible translation as a tool of missionary work.

Carey's educational work included not only Serampore College, but also over forty primary and secondary schools in the surrounding territories. Carey also taught Indian languages at Fort William College, established by the British East India Company to train their own employees and their families. Ironically, Carey's work at Fort William College supported the ministry of the entire Serampore colony for years, allowing them to devote much more of their resources to printing and disseminating Bibles and other Christian literature.

The graduates of Serampore College established native churches all over India, so that Carey's work continued to have an impact on the country long after his death in 1834. As many missionaries have discovered since, education has the potential for enormous influence.

Indigenous churches remain even when missionaries are no longer permitted access to a country, and children who are trained in missionary schools often go on to become leaders in their own nations.

Carey's efforts to learn the culture of India drew much criticism from his supporters at home. He even took the time to translate the Indian epic poem *Ramayana* into English, exposing many Englishmen to Hindu thought for the first time. The effort to understand the culture of the people paid great dividends, however, when Carey was able to use that knowledge to reach members of the upper classes for Christ. Traditionally, Christian missionaries have had much greater success among the lower classes and primitive peoples of regions to which they have taken the Gospel. Few have successfully made inroads into the "establishment" of non-Christian religions to the extent that Carey was able to do.

His knowledge of the culture also enabled Carey to influence that culture. He worked for years to get the British government to put a stop to the ritual burning of widows, and finally succeeded when he proved to the local Hindu authorities that the practice was not taught in the holy books of Hinduism!

THE GOLDEN AGE

By the time of William Carey's death in 1834, dozens of missionary societies had been established to carry out the work of foreign missions, and the Golden Age of Protestant Missions had begun. It would be futile to attempt to summarize even the major figures of the era, which is filled with inspiring stories of men and women who dedicated their lives to the work of the Gospel and saw God work through them to change the religious complexion of the world. Instead, we will look briefly at five examples of missionaries who put into practice the fundamental principles incorporated by Carey into his work in Serampore.

Unquestionably one of the greatest Bible translators of the era was Henry Martyn (1781-1812). After a brilliant academic career at Cambridge in which he earned the rank of Senior Wrangler (equivalent to our valedictorian) in his class, he spent a few years working under Charles Simeon in London, then turned to the work of foreign missions. He went to India as a chaplain for the British East India Company, but refused to limit himself to working with British colonists. After several transfers designed to keep him away from the Indians, he finally went to Persia, where in a few years he translated the Bible into Urdu before his death at the age of thirty-one. The translation was of such a marvelous quality that it remains the standard Urdu Bible to the present day.

One of the most notable missionary educators of the nineteenth century was Alexander Duff (1806-1878), the first missionary sent to India by the Church of Scotland. He spent much time with Carey in the great pioneer's final years, then turned to the task of educating the children of upper-class Indians with the hope of bringing them to Christ and seeing them change their own country. Many educated Hindus wanted a Western education for their children, so Duff's schools were well-received and well-attended (one of his institutions eventually became the University of Calcutta). Though in his years in India Duff saw only thirty-three Hindus converted to Christianity, these thirty-three men almost all went on to positions of leadership and influence in Indian society.

Perhaps the most ambitious attempt to develop indigenous Christian leadership was the Sierra Leone Mission organized by the Church of England under the leadership of Samuel A. Crowther (c.1806-1891). Crowther grew up in West Africa and had been captured and sold into slavery early in life. When Wilberforce succeeded in ending slavery in the British Empire, Crowther was freed and received his education in the colony for freed slaves founded by the Clapham Sect in Sierra Leone. He traveled to England to be ordained to the Anglican priesthood, after which he returned to West Africa to head up a missionary effort among his own tribesmen in Nigeria. Though Crowther had become very "British" as a result of the years spent among educated Englishmen, he was able to gain the sort of access to the tribesmen of Nigeria that never would have been possible for a white man. He founded many churches, and eventually became the first black bishop in the Church of England. Despite much criticism from jealous white missionaries, Crowther left behind a fine example of what can be accomplished by a man who is committed to bringing the message of Jesus Christ to his own people.

No man did more to help Christians appreciate the value of cultural adaptation than Hudson Taylor (1832-1905), the founder of the China Inland Mission. Not only did he insist that his missionaries adopt Chinese dress, eat Chinese food, and practice Chinese customs except where they violated Scriptural teaching, but he also introduced many other innovations into the operation of his mission. Unlike most missions, he accepted committed Christians from a variety of denominational backgrounds, and did not require that his candidates have a college education. The China Inland Mission solicited no financial support, but, as George Müller did for his orphanages, trusted God to meet the needs of the mission. Taylor also demanded that policy decisions be made by the missionaries in the field rather than by a board of men at home who had no direct knowledge of conditions in China. At one point in his long career, the China Inland Mission was the largest missionary organization in the world, with over six hundred missionaries scattered through every region of China.

In the realm of social impact, the name that stands out is that of David Livingstone (1813-1873), the great Scottish medical missionary and explorer. After working for almost a decade with Robert Moffatt in South Africa, he set out for the interior, where he longed to reach the thousands of villages of men and women who had never heard the name of Jesus. He went where no white man had gone before, mapping the interior of Africa as he traveled. His kindness and gentleness earned him the respect of Africans wherever he went. By the time he returned to England he was an international celebrity. He then went back to Africa as an agent of the British government, though he continued to preach the Gospel in his travels. He was determined above all else to put a stop to the slave trade that had for years been destroying and demoralizing Africa. Though the British Empire had outlawed slavery, it was still being practiced in America, as well as by Arab traders in East Africa. Livingstone discovered that the Africans themselves were profiting from the trade, preying on weaker neighboring tribes and selling their captives to the traders. He made every effort to introduce legitimate commerce to Africa so that slavery would lose its financial appeal. Though his efforts to turn the Africans themselves in other directions produced mixed results, the publicity he gave to the horrors of the slave trade produced a worldwide reaction and contributed significantly to the disappearance of the practice.

MISSIONS IN THE MODERN ERA

The twentieth century has been an age of global conflicts among the great Western powers and growing nationalistic spirit among the emerging nations who formerly had been under the control of Western empire-builders. It has also been an age that has witnessed the colossal rise, and in recent years the beginnings of the fall, of worldwide communism, and a great resurgence among the practitioners of Islam. While the world wars of the first half of the twentieth century did much to disrupt missionary activity, the emergence of new nations in Asia and Africa and the growth of communism and Islam have had a much greater impact. Communism succeeded in completely closing large sections of Europe and Asia to missionary activity, while at the same time generating hostility toward Western missionaries in many nations of Africa. Islamic missionaries have also been active in sub-Saharan Africa, and the aggressiveness of their efforts has not only put Christians to shame, but has closed the ears of large segments of people to the message of the Gospel. The new nations that have gained their independence since World War II have tended to be ambivalent in their attitude toward missionary work among their people. While some have, in their nationalistic fervor, rejected missionaries as just one more example of hated Western influence, others have sought the help of the West in developing their economies, and have at the same time welcomed the efforts of Western missionaries, who are appreciated for their educational and social services. At the same time, there has been a much greater emphasis on partnership among Christians of the West and those in the Third World, rather than the paternalistic attitude that had often characterized earlier missionary efforts.

In the churches of the West, the enthusiasm for missions is no longer what it once was. Much of this is due to the growing conviction, especially among churches involved in the ecumenical movement, that evangelism is not necessary because God accepts all men as His children. In these churches, the resources formerly directed toward evangelism and church planting now are put to other uses, as we shall see in chapter forty-four.

Perhaps the greatest measure of the success of the missionary movement of the nineteenth century is the fact that the fastest-growing churches in the world are now to be found, not in Europe or America, but in the countries of the Third World - in Latin America, Africa, and Asia. In the same way that the early center of Christianity in the Eastern Mediterranean shifted later to Western Europe to such an extent that Europeans sent missionaries to evangelize the formerly Christian lands of the Middle East and North Africa, so today we are seeing the beginnings of what may eventually become a major trend - the nations of Africa and Asia are sending missionaries to Europe and America. Like the early European missionaries, they are presently concentrating their efforts largely among their own people - immigrants who have come from Africa and Asia to the "Christian" lands of Europe and the United States. It shouldn't be too long, though, before God places a burden on their hearts to send evangelists to fight the new paganism that has settled like a great shroud over the civilizations of the West.

MAKING DRY BONES LIVE

At the beginning of the nineteenth century, Protestant Christianity was almost exclusively a white man's religion. On the eve of World War I, Jesus Christ was being worshipped by men and women of virtually every "tribe and tongue and nation" on the face of the earth. While the missionaries of the nineteenth century have often been criticized in recent years as "cultural imperialists," and while it must be acknowledged that they did not always successfully distinguish between Christian truth and Western culture, the contributions of these faithful men and women should never be minimized. Many of the peoples to whom the missionaries went hungrily seized the fruits of Western culture; the missionaries themselves did not Westernize those to whom they ministered - that would have happened in any case. Instead, they ensured that with Western culture came the Christian church and Christian morality. Furthermore, we should not fail to note that many of those who criticize the "imperialistic" missionaries of Europe and America do so from the perspective of a liberal world view that equates all cultures and all religions. The work of the nineteenth-century missionaries is only praiseworthy, or indeed justifiable, if one shares their conviction that those who die without Christ are doomed to an eternity in hell.

Many have attempted to explain the great missionary expansion of the nineteenth century in terms of political and economic factors. What they forget is that Christ is the Lord of His Church and the sovereign Ruler of the world He brought into being. He uses political and economic factors to accomplish His purposes in the same way that He uses people. What we must remember is that He is able to use people who are committed to Him today to change the world in the same way He used the great missionaries of the nineteenth century. The words of William Carey in his *Enquiry* are as true today as they were two centuries ago: "Surely it is worth while to lay ourselves out with all our might, in promoting the cause, and kingdom of Christ."

The World in Their Hands

FOR REVIEW AND FURTHER THOUGHT

1. How did the colonial policies of the Protestant countries of Europe differ from those of the Catholic countries?

2. Why did the British and Dutch trading companies oppose the work of missionaries?

3. Why was there little interest in missions among the state churches of Germany and Switzerland?

4. What characteristics of the Protestant churches themselves hindered the development of concern for foreign missions?

5. What is hypercalvinism, and how did it work against the progress of missions?

6. How did Pietism and the Methodist revival contribute to the missionary movement?

7. What is a "voluntary society," and how did they help to spark missionary activity?

8. In what ways did the British Empire help and in what ways did it hinder the missionary expansion of the church?

9. Identify the contributions of the following to early Protestant missionary efforts: John Calvin, Nicholas de Villegagnon, John Eliot, Thomas Mayhew, Thomas Bray.

10. What traits did William Carey display early in life that later helped him in his missionary work?

11. What were some of the obstacles faced by Carey in the early years of his work in India?

12. What does Carey's life say to you about the validity of using circumstances as an indicator of the will of God for your life?

13. What were the five major emphases of the work of the Serampore Trio in India?

14. Why is Bible translation such an important part of missionary work?

15. What good results came from the effort made by Carey to familiarize himself with the culture of India?

16. Summarize briefly the contributions to missions made by the following: Henry Martyn, Alexander Duff, Samuel Crowther, Hudson Taylor, David Livingstone.

17. How has the modern growth of Islam hindered missionary work?

18. What impact has Third World nationalism had on missions in the twentieth century?

19. How has communism affected the spread of the Gospel?

20. How have the attitudes of Protestant churches in the twentieth century dampened the enthusiasm for missions?

21. What evidence exists that the Third World may in the near future become the center of world Christianity?

22. Why were the missionaries of the nineteenth century sometimes accused of cultural imperialism? To what extent was this charge true, and to what extent was it unjustified?

23. What assumptions lie behind much of the modern criticism of the missionaries of the nineteenth century?

Part Five

THE AMERICAN CHURCH
(from 1607)

35

A CITY SET ON A HILL

The newly-established colony in the wilds of North America took its religion seriously. Part of the legal code reads as follows:

"No man shall speak any word, or do any act which may tend to the derision or despite of God's holy Word, upon pain of death. Nor shall any man unworthily demean himself unto any preacher or minister of the same, but generally hold them in all reverent regard and dutiful intreaty; otherwise he, the offender, shall openly be whipped three times, and ask public forgiveness in the assembly of the congregation three several Sabbath days. Every man and woman duly twice a day, upon the first tolling of the bell, shall upon the working days repair unto the church to hear divine service, upon pain of losing his or her day's allowance for the first omission; for the second to be whipped; and for the third to be condemned to the galleys for six months. Also every man and woman shall repair in the morning to divine service, and sermon preached upon the Sabbath day, and in the afternoon to divine service and catechising; upon pain for the first fault to lose their provision and allowance for the whole week following; for the second, to lose the said allowance, and also to be whipped; and for the third to suffer death."

Undoubtedly most people, upon reading such a harsh religious code, would immediately conclude that it must have been produced by the solemn Puritans of Massachusetts Bay. In fact, the preceding excerpt came from the legal code in use in the Jamestown colony in Virginia from 1610 to 1619. While it is in many ways true that the colonies of New England were largely settled for religious purposes while the colonies of the south had more of an economic focus, such a distinction should not be stretched too far. The seventeenth century was a religious age, and the men and women who colonized the New World during that age were for the most part religious people. As we survey the founding of the Thirteen Colonies in this chapter, it is important to remember that even those settlements that seemed secular in comparison to the Puritans were strongly religious by modern standards.

VIRGINIA AND THE SOUTHERN COLONIES

When the London Company sent three shiploads of settlers to Jamestown in 1607, they may have been seeking profits, but they also were concerned for the spiritual welfare, not only of the English colonists, but also of the Indians. The first colonists brought a minister, Robert Hunt, with them, and thus planted the Church of England on American soil at the same time they planted the English flag. After all, if the Spanish could accumulate incredible wealth while at the same time bringing the good news of Christianity to the Indians, could not the English hope for the same success?

What the English colonists discovered in North America, however, was a far cry from what the Spanish had encountered in the south. There was simply no gold to be found, and the Indians seemed to be no more than ignorant savages. Dreams of wealth were quickly shattered by the harsh realities of life in the New World. The young colony struggled terribly at first; according to one estimate, 13,000 of the first 14,000 settlers to come to Jamestown succumbed to disease, starvation, or Indian attack. After twelve years of clinging to life, the

Jamestown colony finally achieved a measure of stability in 1619. In that year, three events dramatically altered the colony's fortunes. First of all, the London Company came under new management. Edwin Sandys, a capable man with Puritan leanings, took a firm grip on the affairs of the colony. He promptly repealed the code quoted at the beginning of the chapter, which had never really been enforced anyway, and ordered the colonists to establish a House of Burgesses as a representative governing body. In the same year, tobacco growing was introduced to the region from the British colonies in the Caribbean. The new cash crop provided enough revenue to assure the colony's future survival and prosperity. Tobacco-growing was not the only thing imported from the Caribbean, however. At the same time, African slaves were brought in to help work the tobacco plantations. While the use of slaves also enhanced the economic condition of the colony, it laid the groundwork for the bitter dispute over slavery that would eventually result in the American Civil War.

As far as the religious condition of Virginia was concerned, the high ideals of the founders were never realized. Not only were the religious laws intended to sustain the spiritual commitment of the community never enforced, but the noble effort to win the Indians to Christ soon ended in failure. Despite early successes such as the conversion of the Indian princess Pocohontas, Indian attacks in the first two decades of the colony's existence turned most of the colonists against the Indians, so that some even went so far as to say that the only way the Indians could ever become Christians was if all of their chiefs and medicine men were to be killed first. From this time on, the colonists of Virginia were more inclined to use force against the Indians than preach the message of the Gospel to them.

The spiritual condition of the church in Virginia was generally quite low. One of the main reasons for this was the lack of adequate spiritual leadership. With a few exceptions, such as Alexander Whitaker, "the Apostle to the Indians," who had been instrumental in the conversion of Pocohontas, the ministers who came to the New World were incompetent, immoral, or worse. Unlike the Puritans and others who were fleeing persecution, and thus were willing and able to send their best men to America, the Anglicans were comfortably in power, and only those who couldn't make it in England were willing to take the risk of moving to the American colonies. As a result, Virginia faced both a chronic shortage of ministers and an almost total absence of capable ones. Consequently, the lofty notions of the colony's founders soon withered and died under the intense heat of reality. The Anglican Church in Virginia only developed some stability with the founding of the Society for the Propagation of the Gospel. James Blair, who served as the Society's representative in Virginia for many years, recognized the need for qualified ministers, and was instrumental in founding the College of William and Mary in 1693 for the purpose of training pastors for the colony.

The state of the Anglican Church in the other southern colonies was even worse. Though Virginia, the Carolinas, and eventually Georgia all recognized the Church of England as the established church of the colony, establishment ultimately meant relatively little. Centralized control was virtually impossible in the American wilderness. Parishes extended for dozens of miles along rivers and through forests, so that even those parishes that had ministers rarely saw them. Discipline was virtually impossible, since the Church of England steadfastly refused to send a bishop to America despite the frequent pleas of the colonists. Furthermore, England had the annoying habit of encouraging people to settle in America who would not be tolerated at home. Whether the immigrants were religious dissenters from England or elsewhere in Europe or refugees from debtor's prisons who settled in Georgia under the benevolent oversight of James Oglethorpe, the colonists tended to inherit people unwanted in the mother country. This did not make for a great deal of religious stability.

Probably the best way to summarize the religious condition of the southern colonies during the colonial period is to note that they were in many ways distorted mirrors of England itself. The Anglicans in the south sided with the

Royalists during the English Civil War, harried Puritans and Quakers during the later years of the Stuart monarchy, accepted the tolerant attitudes of William and Mary and Anne, and eagerly espoused the Deism popular during the reigns of the early Hanoverians. While much that happened in the New England and Middle Atlantic colonies was in reaction against events in England and the rest of Europe, the southern colonies for the most part mimicked the trends of the mother country.

MASSACHUSETTS BAY AND THE NEW ENGLAND COLONIES

A. THE PLYMOUTH COLONY

As we saw in chapter twenty-four, James I did not like Dissenters. The little congregation at Scrooby, under the leadership of their pastor, John Robinson, had become convinced that the Church of England would never be willing to practice biblical religion, and had separated themselves from that church. The ensuing persecution drove them to the friendlier confines of the Netherlands, where in Leyden they faced other kinds of struggles. The men of the congregation had a great deal of trouble supporting their families, often finding it necessary to take low-paying jobs for which they had no training. Even worse, the tolerant spirit of the Netherlands encouraged the sort of loose living that was bound to have a negative influence on children. A minority of families in the congregation decided that the only alternative left to them was to risk resettlement in the New World. They joined a group of like-minded people from England, gained permission from the London Company to settle in Virginia, arranged for financial backing, and set sail for America. Less than precise navigation landed them a bit north of their intended destination - Massachusetts, where they established the Plymouth Plantation.

If the Jamestown settlers included religious concerns among their reasons for migrating to the New World, the Pilgrims of Plymouth unquestionably viewed religion as their major purpose. They expressed their objectives in the Mayflower Compact, which became the foundational document of the new colony. They quickly founded a congregational church upon landing in 1620, though for the first few years they could not practice the sacraments because they had no ordained pastor among their number (Pastor Robinson died before he was able to join the Plymouth settlers). William Brewster, an elder from the Leyden congregation, served as their preacher, and held the church together until a pastor could be obtained from England. From the very beginning, the able leadership of William Bradford, governor of the colony, gave stability to the struggling settlers. Despite many obstacles, the settlement expanded in the years that followed, though it never became very large in population. Ultimately the Plymouth colony was absorbed by their bigger and more prosperous neighbors in Massachusetts Bay, with whom they merged in 1691.

The religious impact of the Plymouth colony on the history of the American church is really rather limited. The principles of congregationalism undoubtedly influenced the development of American democracy, though that influence was mediated more by the Puritans than by the Pilgrims. We also remember the Pilgrims in our celebration of Thanksgiving, of course, though our self-indulgent excess bears little resemblance to their heartfelt praise to God for survival through a bitter winter.

B. THE MASSACHUSETTS BAY COLONY

The Puritans of Massachusetts Bay, unlike the Pilgrims of Plymouth, were not separatists. Like those Puritans who remained in England, they wanted to finish the Reformation. They were convinced, however, that they could only do so out of range of the long arm of Archbishop Laud. In order to put their religious ideas into practice, they formed a trading company, the Massachusetts Bay Company, and obtained a royal charter. Unlike other trading companies, however, they then bought out all stockholders who wanted to remain in England, and moved the entire company, charter and all, to the New World, where both they and their charter were safe from royal interference. There they proceeded to set up a purified Church of England, in a holy commonwealth that had much in common with Calvin's community of the saints in Geneva less than a century earlier.

1. THE RELIGION OF THE PURITANS

In chapter twenty-four we saw that, while the English Puritans agreed that the Reformation in England had not gone far enough, they disagreed among themselves as to the shape the fully-reformed church should take. While a minority continued to support the episcopal form of government by which the Anglican Church operated, most Puritans favored either the congregational or presbyterian models of church government. It should not surprise us, then, to find that the Puritans who migrated to New England set up a church that combined aspects of congregational and presbyterian polity. Internally, the churches followed the presbyterian model developed by Calvin in Geneva, with each church being ruled by a pastor ("teaching elder") and a group of "ruling elders." Externally, they were congregational in the sense that each assembly operated independently of the others, with the members of the individual congregation establishing their own covenant, calling their own pastor, and exercising their own discipline. Despite the protestations of the Puritans that they were remaining faithful to the Church of England in an effort to purify it from within, their church structure differed so little from that of the separatist Pilgrims in Plymouth that the four early New England colonies of Plymouth, Massachusetts Bay, Connecticut, and New Haven were able to agree in 1648 on the church order defined in the Cambridge Platform, which enunciated the fundamental principles of American Congregationalism.

In addition to the church government of the Puritans, we should also take note of their use of the "gathered church" concept. In England, as in much of Europe, the basic unit of church life was the parish. All the citizens of a given region were considered members of the local state church (except for Catholics, Jews, and Dissenters, of course). The Puritans, though they continued to establish parishes in New England, believed in the necessity of a conversion experience. A person was not a Christian until he or she had been transformed by the inner working of the Holy Spirit. The church, therefore, though it may be defined in terms of geographical boundaries, does not include everyone in the parish. Only those who have experienced conversion are included in the community of saints, the "gathered church," along with their children (for the Puritans, infant baptism incorporated a child of believing parents into the covenant community).

2. CHURCH AND STATE IN MASSACHUSETTS BAY

The Puritan colony in Massachusetts Bay has often been described as a theocracy. Such a description can easily be misleading unless it is carefully defined. If by a theocracy is meant rule by priests or religious leaders (the ministers of the colony), then Massachusetts Bay certainly does not qualify. The pastors in Boston, Salem, and other Massachusetts towns wielded no power and had no voice in the government of the colony. Like Calvin in Geneva, their influence was purely moral, derived entirely from the high esteem in which they were held by the people and their rulers. Massachusetts Bay also does not qualify as a theocracy if by that is meant that the church dominates the state and dictates matters of policy. The Puritans believed that the church and state each had its proper realm of authority. While both acted according to biblical precepts and each supported the other, neither should intrude on the domain of the other.

In short, Massachusetts Bay may only be called a theocracy in the sense that it was designed to be a holy commonwealth in which church and state alike operated on the basis of God's Word. The state did not inflict civil penalties for Sabbath-breaking because the church said it should; the state exercised that authority because the Puritans wanted a society in which God's Word was law.

At this point, we should also say a word about the Puritan reputation for intolerance. Many historians puzzle over the fact that the Puritans sought religious freedom in America and then proceeded to deny it to those who disagreed with them. To secular historians, and to some Christians as well, such an attitude is terribly inconsistent. To the Puritans, however, the logic was clear. They had come to America to build a society on the foundation of God's Word. The Puritans simply did not want a pluralistic society. Their whole way of life depended upon uniformity and voluntary submission to the standards of the community. No one was forced to live in Massachusetts Bay. Those who settled in the colony were voluntarily choosing to submit themselves to the colony's standards and chosen way of life. Those who subsequently were unable to live up to this commitment were free to live elsewhere - after all, America had plenty of land.

Some of the most troublesome disturbers of the peace in Massachusetts turned out to be the Quakers. While dissenters like Roger Williams and Anne Hutchinson reluctantly accepted exile from the colony when they could no longer submit to the standards of the Puritans, the Quakers stubbornly insisted on intruding where they were not wanted. Quakers made a habit of disrupting church services - in one celebrated case, a young woman walked into a church in the middle of the sermon wearing only the clothing with which she had been born, and crying out against the naked sinfulness of the community - and took opposition as a call to greater effort. After repeatedly ejecting a number of Quakers from the colony because of their disruptive behavior, the Puritans finally passed a law that Quakers who returned after being ejected would be subject to the death penalty. In the months that followed, four Quakers deliberately sought martyrdom, and the Puritan fathers obliged them, hanging them on Boston Common. Such harsh measures not only did no good, but were repulsive to the Puritans themselves, and were soon discontinued.

3. THE PURITAN VIEW OF EDUCATION

Unlike the adventurers who settled in Virginia and the refugees in Plymouth, the Puritans were a highly-educated group of people. Some estimate that as many as twenty percent of the early colonists of Massachusetts Bay were university graduates. Unlike some of the other colonies, they suffered no shortage of ministers. While as educated men they considered education of great importance, they did not value it simply for its own sake. For the Puritans, education was essential for the future stability of the holy commonwealth. If decisions about the future of the colony were to be made according to biblical principles, those who made the decisions must know the Bible. In order for them to know the Bible, they must be able to read. Therefore education was essential. Illiterate people were easy prey for demagogues. Largely for this reason, the Puritans established a system of compulsory education that became the model for educational systems all over America in the years that followed. Every town of substantial size was required to maintain a school for the education of the young. Textbooks taught biblical truths as they taught the three R's. The *New England Primer*, for instance, taught the alphabet with brief verses such as "A - In *A*dam's fall, we died all." The fact that the first public education in America was Christian education should not escape our attention in an era when public education and Christian education are often thought to be fundamentally incompatible.

Ministerial education was also a matter of concern. The English universities were not only inaccessible because of the difficulties involved in a voyage across the ocean, but were untrustworthy because of the way in which the Church of England routinely compromised biblical truth. The Puritans therefore determined at a very early date to start a college in which to prepare men for the pulpits of Massachusetts. Such a college was founded in 1636 in Cambridge, Massachusetts, as a result of a generous gift of money and books donated in his will by a young clergyman, John Harvard, after whom the school was subsequently named.

4. PROSPERITY AND DECLINE

More than any other group of colonists, the Puritans of Massachusetts Bay prospered. The persecution directed against the Puritans by Charles I and Archbishop Laud assured that a steady stream of reinforcements would make the journey across the Atlantic to Massachusetts. By the outbreak of the English Civil War in the 1640's, Massachusetts Bay had a population of over 20,000. Prosperity, however, brought its share of problems. Since the original intention of the founders of the colony was to establish a biblical commonwealth, only adult male landowning church members were permitted to vote (even at that, the franchise in Massachusetts was broader than that in England). The more the population grew, however, the more it came to be dominated numerically by those who did not meet the qualifications for voting. The new immigrants put increasing pressure on the fathers of the colony to broaden the franchise. The authorities resisted, knowing that to give the vote to those who would not affirm the covenant of the church would be to compromise the very principles on which the colony had been founded. The Cambridge Platform of 1648 reaffirmed the commitment of the churches of New England to a standard of church membership tied to a clear experience of conversion and evidence of the fruits of repentance in a person's life.

The picture was complicated even more, however, by a threat to the holy commonwealth that came from within the covenant community - the children of the saints. Because the Puritans believed that infant baptism incorporated the children of believers into the covenant and brought them under the care and authority of the church, these "covenant children" inherited the franchise when they came of age. Unless they themselves experienced conversion, however, they were not accorded the privileges of full church membership, nor were they permitted to take communion. The entire system, therefore, was gradually undermining the original commitment of the founders of the colony by giving the vote to unconverted children of Christian parents. The authorities felt that they could live with this as long as the chain stopped there. Baptized but unconverted church members may be able to vote, but they could not perpetuate the chain by having their children baptized.

As the original founders of the colony began to die out, however, it soon became apparent that Massachusetts Bay was going to wind up being governed by an increasingly small minority of the population. The unrest that was sure to accompany such a situation had the potential to destroy the colony completely. As a result, some of the ministers proposed a compromise called the Half-Way Covenant. Adopted in 1662 over considerable opposition, it allowed the children of baptized but unconverted church members to be baptized, while retaining the requirement of church membership for voting in the commonwealth. The result was a dilution of the concept of church membership that produced a noticeable religious decline in the community. Soon people were arguing that if clean-living (but unconverted) members of the community were good enough to have their children baptized, why weren't they good enough to take communion? Solomon Stoddard, a pastor in Northampton, Massachusetts, and the grandfather of Jonathan Edwards, even went so far as to argue that unconverted members of the covenant community should be admitted to the Lord's Supper because the ordinance might have a "converting influence" on them. When the succeeding years brought wars with the Indians, diseases, and the disastrous reign of James II during which the Puritans lost their charter, conservative ministers such as Increase Mather, the president of Harvard and an opponent of the Half-Way Covenant, were convinced that God was judging His people for their unfaithfulness. Finally, in 1691, Massachusetts came under a new royal charter in a merger with the Plymouth colony, and the franchise was given to all adult male landowners who lived respectable lives in the community. The holy commonwealth was dead.

Given the no-win proposition of choosing between expanding the franchise beyond the limits of church membership or weakening the definition of church membership to include more people, it is easy to see from our perspective that a growing population doomed the Puritan commonwealth. What may not be so easy to see is the damage done by the choice that they made. While the Half-Way Covenant clearly demolished the Puritan theocracy, it also did irreparable damage to the Congregational Church of New England. When church membership became a matter of respectable living rather than being defined by a life-changing encounter with Jesus Christ, the church began a decline that has not been reversed to the present day. As we will see in the chapters to come, the Half-Way Covenant started the churches of New England down the path to Unitarianism and a spiritual deadness so profound that, even with the intervention of the Great Awakening in the eighteenth century, to this day there are fewer evangelical churches in New England than in any other region of the United States.

5. THE WITCHES OF SALEM VILLAGE

We cannot leave our consideration of the Puritans without at least a brief mention of the infamous Salem witch trials of 1692. Disproportionate attention is often given to this incident in the same way that people tend to direct a morbid focus at the death of Servetus when studying the life and ministry of John Calvin. In the same way that the Inquisition was burning thousands while Calvin was guilty of complicity in the death of a single heretic, the nations of Europe were trying and executing thousands of purported witches, but it is the nineteen who were hanged by the Puritans in Salem who get all the publicity.

In the same way that most people take an unduly negative view of Calvin's attitude toward Servetus because they do not take heresy seriously, most who criticize the Salem incident do not believe in Satan, demons, or witches. The Puritans, however, did believe in these things, and considered it their responsibility to do battle against the devil whenever and wherever he put in an appearance. Having noted the legitimacy of the Puritan concern for evil supernatural forces, however, we must honestly conclude that the Salem witch trials were a tragically misguided miscarriage of justice.

The incident began when a daughter and niece of the village pastor, Samuel Parris, became ill, and upon being questioned, confessed to participating with some of their friends in Satanic revels in the woods outside Salem under the guidance of a servant from Barbados named Tituba. Tituba eventually confessed to witchcraft, incriminating other women of questionable reputation in the process. The girls, however, were enjoying the attention by this time, and began accusing one person after another of coming to them in spectral form and tormenting them. As the number of the accused mounted, a special court was convened. Two misjudgments marred the proceedings of this court - the fact that they accepted "spectral evidence" without question, and their somewhat peculiar decision to release those who confessed to witchcraft and repented while imprisoning and even executing those who steadfastly maintained their innocence. The result was that over a hundred citizens were tried and imprisoned, while nineteen were hanged as witches. As the trials progressed, it became increasingly obvious that, if the devil was at work, he was occupying himself in the accusers more than in the accused. Finally, as more and more clearly blameless citizens were named by the girls, voices of reason interrupted the proceedings. Increase Mather of Boston and his son Cotton Mather, both of whom had written treatises on witchcraft that had provided useful instruction for the magistrates, first argued that the condemned witches should be counseled rather than executed, with the goal of saving their souls, then spoke out strongly against the use of spectral evidence in such a criminal court. The devil, they said, could certainly appear in the form of an innocent person as well as the form of one who had sold himself into Satan's service. Ultimately those who had been imprisoned were released, and the chief magistrate in the trials gave a public apology for his role in the tragedy. Needless to say, the Salem witch trials have been a blot on the reputation of the Puritans ever since.

C. RHODE ISLAND AND PROVIDENCE PLANTATIONS

Every closed society needs a safety valve to control dissent. In twentieth-century Russia, that safety valve was the Gulag, where dissenters were sent to keep them from infecting the rest of society. In seventeenth-century England, the American colonies provided the outlet for dissent. Those who were not welcome in England could come to America, where they could put their peculiar ideas into practice without threatening the stability of the realm. Massachusetts Bay was also a closed society; for the Puritans, the safety valve was the little colony of Rhode Island and Providence Plantations. Established initially by the disgruntled Puritan Roger Williams in 1636, Rhode Island eventually became the home to Baptists, Quakers, and various other minorities who were not welcomed in most of the British colonies (the tolerant Pennsylvania colony was not founded until forty-five years later). In fact, one of the more ironic results of Rhode Island's reputation for religious toleration is that it remains even today the state with the highest percentage of Roman Catholics in America.

Roger Williams (c.1603-c.1683) was one of those unsettled souls who could only be content when he was opposing the system. He came to New England in 1631 seeking religious freedom, and was warmly welcomed in Boston. He settled in Salem, but his radical views quickly stirred up controversy. He was a separatist, and loudly proclaimed that he would have nothing to do with the churches of Boston until they renounced all ties with the apostate Church of England. He also argued that the magistrates had no right to enforce religious practices such as Sabbath observance, and furthermore insisted that the charter of the Massachusetts Bay Company was illegal, since the land belonged to the Indians, and Charles I had no right to give it to anybody! It is easy to understand how someone who insisted on undermining the religious, civil, and legal foundations of the entire colony would be less than popular. The authorities strongly suggested that Williams might be happier elsewhere, so he left Massachusetts Bay and settled in Plymouth with the Pilgrims, who shared his separatist views. His outspokenness soon got him into trouble with them, too, at which time he returned to Salem. Upon his return to Massachusetts Bay, he continued the earlier controversies, and was finally told in 1635 that he must leave the colony. The magistrates told him that he could remain until the following spring if he would agree to keep quiet. He refused to do so, with the result that the authorities arranged to put him on a ship bound for England. Before this could be done, Williams fled the colony, trekking through the snow of winter until he was rescued by a friendly band of Indians. He then purchased some land from them and established the settlement of Providence, for which he later obtained a colonial charter. Here he became convinced of the need for believer's baptism and established the first Baptist church in America, though he left it a few years later when his views grew closer to those of the Quakers. By the time he died, he had become one of those tragic figures whose circle of fellowship had narrowed to himself alone, since his views agreed with no one else. His legacy to America was his writing in defense of religious freedom.

Another dissenter who wound up in Rhode Island was Anne Hutchinson, an educated and eloquent woman who belonged to the congregation of the famous Puritan preacher John Cotton (1584-1652). She followed him to America from England, and soon organized a group of friends who met together on Sunday afternoons to discuss the sermon of the day. She firmly believed that Cotton was the only truly biblical preacher in Massachusetts. Like many a great preacher, Cotton soon came to the place where he wished fervently that God would deliver him from his followers.

According to her, all others preached law rather than grace because they taught that a person could prepare himself to receive the grace of God by reading Scripture, praying, and attending church, and that holy living after a profession of faith was a sign of the genuineness

RELIGION IN THE THIRTEEN COLONIES

COLONY	CHARTER DATE	CHARTER RECIPIENT	FIRST SETTLED	SETTLERS	MAIN REASON FOR COMING	RELIGIOUS ORIENTATION	ESTABLISHED CHURCH
VIRGINIA	1606	Virginia Company	1607	English	Economic gain	Anglican	Church of England
	1624	Royal Colony					
MASSACHUSETTS	1619	Pilgrims	1620	Pilgrims	Religious freedom	Separatist	Congregationalist
	1629	Massachusetts Bay Company		Puritans	Establish theocracy	Congregationalist	
	1684	Royal Colony					
NEW HAMPSHIRE	1679	Royal Colony	1623	Puritans	Expansion from Massachusetts Bay	Congregationalist	Congregationalist
NEW YORK	1664	Royal Colony	1624	Dutch	Economic gain	Dutch Reformed	Church of England (1692)
MARYLAND	1632	Lord Baltimore	1634	English	Refuge for Roman Catholics Personal empire for Calverts	Roman Catholic and others	Church of England (1691)
	1691	Royal Colony					
CONNECTICUT	1662	John Winthrop, Jr. (Royal Colony)	1634	Puritans	Expansion from Massachusetts Bay	Congregationalist	Congregationalist
RHODE ISLAND	1644	Roger Williams	1636	English	Radicals fleeing Massachusetts Bay	Congregationalist	None
	1663	Renewed					
NEW JERSEY	1664	John Berkeley, George Carteret	1638	Swedish	Economic gain	Lutheran	None
	1702	Royal Colony		Dutch	Expansion from New York	Dutch Reformed	
				English	Religious freedom	Quaker	
DELAWARE	1683	Duke of York	1638	Swedish	Economic gain	Lutheran	None
	1693	Part of Pennsylvania		Dutch		Dutch Reformed	
	1704	Separate government		English		Anglican	
NORTH CAROLINA	1712	Separate government from SC	1653	English	Economic gain	Anglican	Church of England
	1729	Royal Colony					
SOUTH CAROLINA	1663	Carolina Company	1670	English	Economic gain	Anglican	Church of England (1704)
				French	Religious freedom	Huguenots	
PENNSYLVANIA	1681	William Penn	1681	English	Religious freedom	Quaker	None
				German	Fleeing Thirty Years' War	Lutheran	
					Religious freedom	Mennonite, Brethren, Amish, Schwenkfelder, Moravian	
GEORGIA	1732	James Oglethorpe	1733	English	Relief for those in debtors' prison	Anglican	Church of England (1758)
	1752	Royal Colony		German	Religious freedom	Moravian	

of that profession. Her emphasis on the grace of God led to a teaching called antinomianism, which denies that works have anything to do with a person's spiritual standing, either as a precondition or as a test of genuineness. The Puritans, of course, realized that such a view would eliminate the possibility of enforcing any kind of religious or moral behavior, or even exercising church discipline. The last straw came when Mrs. Hutchinson asserted that her teachings were true because she had received them by direct revelation from God. Shortly thereafter, she was exiled from Boston and settled in Rhode Island along with a group of her followers.

THE MIDDLE ATLANTIC COLONIES

A. THE DUTCH REFORMED SETTLEMENTS

Not all of the settlers in the American colonies were English, of course. Swedish Lutherans settled in what is now Wilmington, Delaware. French Huguenots fled to the colonies after the revocation of the Edict of Nantes in 1685, with many making their homes in the Carolinas. German Protestants came over after the debacle of the Thirty Years' War and later troubles in the Palatinate, many settling in Pennsylvania. But the largest and earliest non-English settlement was New Amsterdam, established by the Dutch in 1624. A Dutch trading settlement grew up on the land purchased by Peter Minuit from the Indians and became a thriving commercial venture. Religion in the colony was most notable by its absence; in its early years, the entire colony had only one Dutch Reformed minister. When the British took over the colony and renamed it New York in 1664 (part of the Dutch possessions eventually became New Jersey), they agreed to allow freedom of religion to the Dutch, though the religion of the colony never amounted to much until the revival sparked by Theodore J. Frelinghuysen as part of the Great Awakening in the eighteenth century.

B. MARYLAND

Protestant dissenters were not the only people who found the England of the seventeenth century an uncomfortable place. Catholics, too, faced certain disabilities, despite the tendency toward Catholicism in the later Stuart monarchs. In 1632, a Roman Catholic nobleman named George Calvert, whose title was Lord Baltimore, obtained a charter for a colony in the New World. It was his intention to found a sort of medieval fiefdom with himself as the lord and master. He died before he could act on his charter, however, and the claim passed to his son Cecil, the second Lord Baltimore. He named his colony Maryland, in honor of the Virgin (and also England's last Catholic queen), and began to recruit settlers. He quickly found that the colony would never succeed if he depended entirely on Roman Catholics. There simply were not enough Catholics who wanted to move to America. He therefore determined to allow freedom of religion in Maryland, both to protect the Catholics who did settle there and also to insure a steady enough flow of colonists to bring prosperity to his settlement. He even went so far as to invite Puritans to come down from Massachusetts. The colony did succeed, although the open settlement policy caused Calvert many headaches - dissenters generally do not tend to make for cooperative and placid citizens, especially when they live in a mixed society. Eventually, the charter reverted to the crown in 1691, at which time the Church of England was established and Catholicism again faced legal disadvantages.

C. WILLIAM PENN'S GREAT EXPERIMENT

While the Maryland colony allowed religious freedom as a matter of practical necessity, the colony founded by William Penn in 1681 practiced it as a matter of principle. William Penn, a Quaker, received the land grant that became the Pennsylvania colony from Charles II in repayment of a debt incurred by the king from Penn's father. Penn's ideal was to establish a settlement based on religious toleration and fair treatment of the Indians, and he recruited, not only Quakers, but also other persecuted minorities from all over Europe. The Quakers were dominant in the early years, but soon were joined by Anabaptists (Mennonites and Amish) and Lutherans from Germany (the "Pennsylvania Dutch"), Scotch-Irish Presbyterians from Ulster, and a variety of others. Penn's ideal of toleration became a reality, but other aspects of his vision failed. The Quakers soon became the colony's aristocracy, and many turned from their simple lifestyles to seek the comforts of wealth. Others abandoned their pacifism in the face of pressures on the frontier, and many treated the Indians with far less than the respect that Penn had envisioned. Though Pennsylvania prospered and Philadelphia became, along with Boston, Williamsburg, and New York, one of the chief cities of the colonial era, Penn died in 1718 a frustrated and disappointed man.

MAKING DRY BONES LIVE

The early colonial period raises a very important question: Is it possible to build a Christian society? The Puritans of Massachusetts Bay tried to construct a Christian society by restricting control to those in accord with the principles of the founders, while William Penn thought Christianity would be better served by tolerating all religious opinions and encouraging men to live in peace with one another. Neither approach worked - in fact, both were sabotaged from within.

William Penn found that toleration must have certain limits if harmony is to be attained - even he had no use for atheists. Complete toleration implies abandonment of any standard of truth. Such a society cannot in any sense of the word be Christian. Even within the limited definition of toleration espoused by Penn, however, it soon became clear that those who care passionately about what they believe find it hard to put up with those who believe differently.

Both lack of convictions and strong convictions can quickly lead to the destruction of a "great experiment."

Massachusetts Bay was sabotaged from within in a different way - by their own children. The entire history of the church makes it clear that the second generation, knowing the struggles of their parents by word of mouth but not by experience, rarely possess the zeal of their forebears. In the case of the Puritans, the problem was even greater than lack of zeal. The fact of the matter is that many of their children simply were not Christians, never having experienced the saving power of the Holy Spirit in their lives. Even if the first generation of Puritans had been completely united in purpose and all committed to Christ, which they were not, their Christian society was doomed to failure. Had they succeeded in completely excluding all settlers who were not of one mind with the Puritan fathers, they still would have failed to build a theocracy. No matter how strong their faith, they simply had no way of guaranteeing that their children would become Christians. Though their practice of infant baptism and their belief in the covenant family brought their children under the influence and discipline of the church, the fact of the matter is that nothing they could do would secure the conversion of their offspring.

The inevitable conclusion is that a Christian society is impossible today. In Old Testament Israel, the children automatically became part of the covenant community by circumcision. God's people were identified by a physical sign. Since the coming of Christ, however, God's people have been identified by a spiritual mark - the presence of the Holy Spirit - which cannot be passed on from generation to generation. Creating a Christian society even for a brief period of time is difficult, as the Puritans discovered. Maintaining one for longer than a single generation is simply impossible, and those who dream of someday making America a Christian nation are deceiving themselves.

FOR REVIEW AND FURTHER THOUGHT

1. Why would it be inaccurate to describe the Jamestown colony as secular?

2. What three important changes in 1619 helped bring prosperity to the Jamestown colony?

3. Identify the following in one sentence each: Robert Hunt, Edwin Sandys, Alexander Whitaker, James Blair, James Oglethorpe.

4. What factors prevented the Anglican Church in Virginia from attaining the strength hoped for by the founders of the colony?

5. Why was it difficult for the Virginia colonists to obtain capable ministers in the seventeenth century?

6. What were the first two colleges founded in America, and what was the purpose for which they were founded?

7. In what sense was it true that the Anglican Church in the southern colonies was like the Anglican Church in England?

8. Identify the following in one sentence each: John Robinson, William Brewster, William Bradford, John Harvard, Solomon Stoddard.

9. Why did the Scrooby congregation move to the Netherlands, and why didn't they want to stay there?

10. What influence did the Pilgrims have on the history of America and the American church?

11. In what important ways did the Pilgrims and Puritans differ from one another? What did they have in common?

12. What clever piece of strategy gave the Massachusetts Bay colony virtual independence from England for the first sixty years of its history?

13. What form of church government was adopted by the Puritans of Massachusetts Bay?

14. What was the Cambridge Platform of 1648?

15. In what sense is it true that Massachusetts Bay was a theocracy? In what sense is such a statement inaccurate?

16. What was a "gathered church," and why did the Puritans use this approach within their parishes?

17. Why did the Puritans see no inconsistency in wanting religious freedom for themselves while denying it to others?

18. Why were the Quakers persecuted by the Puritans?

19. Why did the Puritans value education so highly?

A City Set on a Hill

20. How did prosperity make it difficult for the Massachusetts Bay colony to maintain the ideals of its founders?

21. How did the concept of the covenant family contribute to the disintegration of the Puritan commonwealth?

22. What was the Half-Way Covenant? What factors led to its adoption? How did it destroy the Puritan theocracy?

23. What, in your opinion, would have been the best way for the Massachusetts Bay colony to satisfy the desire of the majority of the population to participate in self-government?

24. How did the Half-Way Covenant damage the Congregational Church?

25. Why do many people have such a difficult time understanding the motivations behind those who conducted the Salem witch trials?

26. What errors in judgment led to the execution of nineteen alleged witches at Salem?

27. What finally brought an end to the witch trials in Salem?

28. Why did the Puritans consider Roger Williams a threat to the commonwealth? Do you think they were right?

29. What were the major contributions of Roger Williams to the history of the American church?

30. What is antinomianism?

31. Why did the Puritans see Anne Hutchinson's teachings as a threat? Do you think they were right?

32. Identify the following in one sentence each: Peter Minuit, George Calvert, Cecil Calvert, William Penn.

33. From what countries other than England did colonists come to North America, and where did they settle?

34. In what ways did the Pennsylvania colony fall short of its founder's expectations?

35. Why is it impossible to perpetuate a Christian society?

THE SURPRISING WORK OF GOD

Any student of elementary chemistry would recognize the reaction produced by heating a mixture of potassium chlorate and manganese dioxide. The end products of this reaction are potassium chloride, oxygen, and - manganese dioxide! While the manganese dioxide does not actually enter into the chemical reaction, it serves as a catalyst, speeding up the reaction and making it more efficient.

As we saw in the last chapter, the Puritan dream of a holy commonwealth was destroyed by the second generation and the ensuing Half-Way Covenant. The southern colonies, meanwhile, had little religious fervor to begin with, while the middle colonies were religiously diverse. The seventeen twenties and thirties, however, witnessed numerous spontaneous outbreaks of revival in the American colonies. But the fires of revival began burning much more brightly in 1739 when a catalyst arrived in the person of George Whitefield. As we shall see in our examination of the revival known as the First Great Awakening in this chapter, Whitefield through his itinerant preaching brought together the various manifestations of spiritual renewal to produce a unified phenomenon which left an indelible mark on the character of American Christianity.

THE RARITAN VALLEY REVIVAL

As we noted in the last chapter, the Dutch Reformed colonists in New York and New Jersey were not a particularly religious lot. Their religion was formal at best, with very little notable spiritual fervor. In 1720, however, a man arrived on the scene who was soon to change that situation dramatically. Theodore J. Frelinghuysen (1691-1748), a German-born and Dutch-educated Pietist, came to the New World to minister to the Dutch colonists. After serving briefly in New York, he accepted the call to pastor four churches in the Raritan Valley in New Jersey. He was appalled by the spiritual deadness he found in the churches, and determined that the situation called for drastic measures. Frelinghuysen immediately began preaching about the need for an experience of conversion, and refused to admit those church members who were not converted to the Lord's Supper. Since those he adjudged as unconverted included several of the elders in the church, his preaching produced an immediate negative response. Members of his congregations began writing letters of protest to leading pastors in New York. Their objections to Frelinghuysen's tactics accomplished little, however - the fiery Dutchman simply accused his ministerial critics of being unconverted themselves. After an initial drop in church attendance and church membership, however, people in the Raritan Valley began to respond to Frelinghuysen's preaching. Many committed their lives to Christ, and the revival soon spread into neighboring towns in New Jersey. Frelinghuysen soon took under his wing a young Presbyterian minister in nearby New Brunswick named Gilbert Tennent, of whom we will hear more later. When George Whitefield visited Frelinghuysen shortly before the Dutchman's death, he acknowledged that his preaching had produced the earliest sparks of what was to become America's greatest revival. Frelinghuysen was able to consolidate the gains made by the revival by winning a measure of independence from the church authorities in Holland for the Dutch Reformed Church in America, and his followers later established Queen's College (now Rutgers University) in

1764 for the training of ministers in the revival tradition.

PRESBYTERIANISM IN THE MIDDLE COLONIES

Presbyterians were relative latecomers to the American colonies. Troubles in Ulster led to the migration of numerous Irish Presbyterians of Scottish descent in the latter part of the seventeenth century, but it was not until the arrival of Francis Makemie (1658-1708) that American Presbyterianism took on organized form. Makemie was a tireless itinerant who planted congregations throughout the middle colonies from Maryland to New York. At one point, he was arrested and imprisoned in New York for preaching without a license, though he was ultimately acquitted. Makemie was the motivating force behind the formation in 1706 of the Philadelphia Presbytery, the first presbytery in the New World.

Ten years after the founding of the first American presbytery by Makemie, an Irishman named William Tennent (1673-1746) arrived in New York. After pastoring several churches in the middle colonies, he came in 1726 to Neshaminy, Pennsylvania, where he lived for the rest of his life. Recognizing the need for trained ministers for the growing number of Scotch-Irish immigrants, and having already tutored his oldest son Gilbert, he built a rough log cabin on his property north of Philadelphia and invited promising young men to study with him for the ministry. In the twenty years between the establishment of the "Log College" and Tennent's death, he prepared eighteen men for the Presbyterian ministry, including three more of his own sons. These men went out with such a zeal for the Gospel that they turned the Presbyterian Church upside down, and the middle colonies along with it.

By far the most outspoken of the Presbyterian revivalists was Gilbert Tennent (1703-1764). Shortly after accepting a call to the Presbyterian church in New Brunswick, New Jersey in 1726, Tennent came under the influence of Frelinghuysen. The zeal of the older man inspired Tennent to follow his example, and soon stern denunciations of unconverted church members boomed from his pulpit. Two of Tennent's younger brothers took churches in the area, and before long all of central New Jersey was on fire with revival. Like Frelinghuysen, the Tennents faced opposition from those who were scandalized by the informal style of the revivalists, as well as from those who were the targets of their constant denunciations. When Gilbert Tennent preached a sermon on *The Danger of An Unconverted Ministry* (1740) in which he named some of those he deemed to be blind leaders of the blind, his opponents concluded that he had gone too far. Using the excuse that the graduates of the Log College lacked proper theological training (i.e., a university education), the Philadelphia Presbytery voted to exclude the churches headed by the revivalists. The result was a schism in the Presbyterian Church that lasted from 1741 to 1758. While the split lasted, the anti-revival group ("Old Side") declined in numbers, while the "New Side" revivalists increased greatly. It is an indication of how much he had mellowed with age to note that Gilbert Tennent, by then the pastor of the Second Presbyterian Church in Philadelphia, was the main mover in the reconciliation of the two groups in 1758.

The concern for sound theological education that had first driven William Tennent to found the Log College continued to be a matter of importance to the ministers of the New Side. In 1746, a group of men, most of them Log College graduates, organized a college for training ministers that came to be called the College of New Jersey (now Princeton University). Yale graduate Jonathan Dickenson (1698-1747) became the first president of the college. Dickenson had already shown his wisdom by moderating the highly divisive subscription controversy among Presbyterians in 1729 (the issue was over whether or not ministers should be required to affirm every detail of the Westminster Confession of Faith; Dickenson argued that the Confession required substantial agreement, but that flexibility should be permitted with regard to certain non-essential sections). Dickenson died a year later, and was succeeded by Aaron Burr (son-in-law of Jonathan Edwards and father of the politician), who was succeeded by Edwards himself, then by Samuel

Davies, who had received his ministerial training under Log College graduate Samuel Blair. In the years that followed, the College of New Jersey produced some of the greatest religious and political leaders in America.

NEW LIGHT IN NEW ENGLAND

The "good old days" were gone forever in New England. The holy commonwealth of the Puritans had suffered a painful death at the hands of the Half-Way Covenant. Harvard had departed so far from the Puritan ideal that the trustees felt compelled to ask staunch Puritan Increase Mather to resign the presidency of the college, and Yale, which had been founded in 1701 to compensate for the decline at Harvard, was fast moving in the same direction. Meanwhile, in Northampton, Massachusetts, old warrior Solomon Stoddard, who had seen many revivals of spiritual life in his day, was trying to generate another one by opening the communion table to unbelievers, hoping that the ordinance would bring them to the Savior it commemorated. In general, however, the corpse of New England Puritanism showed little sign of coming back to life.

In 1727, however, Stoddard's grandson, Jonathan Edwards (1703-1758), joined him in the ministry in Northampton. Edwards was a brilliant scholar who had entered Yale before his thirteenth birthday. He already was skilled in Hebrew, Greek, and Latin before he entered college, and was writing philosophical treatises by the time he was sixteen. After completing his theological studies, he spent several years as a tutor, then briefly pastored a Presbyterian church before returning to Northampton to assist his grandfather. When Stoddard died two years later, Edwards became the church's senior pastor. By all accounts, there was nothing remarkable about the preaching of Jonathan Edwards. His sermons were orderly, well-reasoned, and scrupulously biblical, but his style was colorless at best. He read his sermons verbatim from a written manuscript, gestured only rarely, and never raised his voice. He was a far cry from the picture of the hellfire-and-brimstone rabble-rousing pulpit-pounder most people associate with revival preachers. In fact, for the first seven years of Edwards' ministry, there was little discernible response to his preaching. In 1734, however, he preached a series of sermons on justification by faith. The response was incredible. Suddenly, everyone in Northampton was talking about little other than the state of their souls. Sinners filled with distress became Christians filled with joy. The revival continued for about a year, then died down as quickly as it had begun. Edwards knew better than anyone that the response of the people could not be attributed to his preaching. When he wrote an account of the revival in 1737, he called it *A Narrative of the Surprising Work of God in New England*. Edwards was a firm believer in the sovereignty of God in salvation, and knew that the revival in Northampton had been the work of the Holy Spirit rather than the product of his preaching prowess.

In the years that followed, other towns in New England experienced similar revivals. When George Whitefield arrived for his second visit to America in 1739, however, he served as the catalyst who brought the various manifestations of the revival together. He started in Philadelphia, where he impressed Benjamin Franklin, among others (see chapter thirty). In fact, Franklin and Whitefield became lifelong friends, though the famous statesman remained a crusty reprobate to the time of his death. Franklin was so impressed with Whitefield's ministry that he helped raise funds to erect a building in Philadelphia where Whitefield could preach when he was in town, since most of the churches refused to let him use their buildings. That structure was later used by Gilbert Tennent's Second Presbyterian Church, then became a charity school, and finally served as the location of the fledgling University of Pennsylvania.

On his way north, Whitefield met with William Tennent, Theodore Frelinghuysen, and Gilbert Tennent, whom he encouraged to take his revival ministry beyond the boundaries of his New Brunswick parish. The younger Tennent subsequently traveled with Whitefield, and had great success as a revivalist as far north as New England. When Whitefield arrived in New England in 1740, he sparked another outbreak of revival. He met with and encouraged Edwards in Northampton, and had the opportunity to speak to the student bodies of both Harvard and Yale (though both schools later closed their doors to him).

The revival in New England lasted until about 1743. While Jonathan Edwards was not surprised that the same God who could of His own will choose to bring revival could just as easily put an end to that revival, his parishioners lacked his equanimity. Many tired of revival preaching, while others became jealous of the attention being given to their now famous pastor. When Edwards, ignoring the provisions of the Half-Way Covenant and reversing the policy of his grandfather, insisted that no one in the congregation could take communion who had not been converted, the church asked for his resignation. The great revivalist, in his late forties with a wife and numerous children to support, was suddenly unemployed. In 1750, he accepted a call to pastor the church in Stockbridge, on the western frontier of Massachusetts. While there, he ministered to the settlers and the Indians, and wrote his most profound works, including his *Treatise on Religious Affections* and his discussion of *The Freedom of the Will*. In 1758, Edwards was invited to assume the presidency of the College of New Jersey, but he died of a smallpox inoculation shortly after arriving in Princeton. To this day he is considered by many to be the greatest philosopher and religious thinker America has ever produced.

The revival in New England had a wide variety of consequences, including stimulating evangelism and missions, producing a few radical extremists, generating opposition, and dividing the churches. Revival preachers traveled to the newly-settled regions of the south, while others brought the Gospel to the Indians. Perhaps the most notable among the latter was David Brainerd (1718-1747). Converted during the revival, he entered Yale to prepare for the ministry. He proved an excellent scholar, but his support for the revival was unpopular among the college professors. When another student overheard him making a disparaging remark about one of his professors, he was expelled from the college. He went on to serve as a missionary to the Indians in Pennsylvania, until illness brought him down at the age of twenty-nine. He died in the home of Jonathan Edwards, to whose daughter Jerusha he was engaged to be married. Edwards edited and published the young missionary's diary, which inspired many in later years to give their lives to missions. Another notable missionary to the Indians was Eleazar Wheelock (1711-1779), whose mission school to prepare Indians to minister to their own people eventually became Dartmouth College.

Any popular movement tends to produce some highly colorful characters who bring discredit to the movement, and the Great Awakening was no exception. Among the most colorful was the emotionally unstable revival preacher James Davenport (1716-1757). Davenport's wild style of preaching produced highly emotional responses among his listeners, but also provided considerable ammunition to the critics of the Awakening, who were more than ready to believe that it was all emotion and no substance. When Davenport responded by accusing his critics of being unbelieving agents of the devil, he brought little credit to the cause of Christ.

Critics of the Awakening did not restrict their criticism to preachers like Davenport, however. While anti-revival spokesmen like Charles Chauncy of Boston focused on the emotional aspects of the revival in their criticism, they also were very uncomfortable with the emphasis placed by the revival on conscious conversion experiences. They wanted the church to incorporate all of society, and despised anything that smacked of exclusiveness. Furthermore, the critics hated the strict Calvinism of the revivalists. They had imbibed much of the rationalism that had already gained popularity in Europe, and they preferred the Arminian view that salvation was a cooperative effort between God and man. In fact, many of the critics of the revival, Chauncy among them, went on to become Unitarians.

Before long, the Congregationalists of New England were divided into pro-revival ("New Lights") and anti-revival ("Old Lights") factions like the Presbyterians in the middle colonies. The Old Lights dominated Harvard, Yale, and the great churches of Boston. The New Lights, meanwhile, were busy founding new schools, and found most of their support in the more sparsely populated frontier areas. In many cases, the New Lights were forced out of the Congregational churches and formed "Separate" congregations. Many of these churches, which like the revival emphasized conversion as a precondition for church membership, eventually recognized the incompatibility of infant baptism with such a stance and became Baptist churches. Thus the Baptists, who had very little direct involvement with the early stages of the Awakening, benefited from it by gaining a large number of churches in New England.

LUTHERAN PIETISM IN PENNSYLVANIA

As we saw in the last chapter, troubles in Germany brought a great influx of German Lutherans to Pennsylvania in the early part of the eighteenth century. These German settlers for the most part lacked any sort of religious organization, and Count von Zinzendorf attempted to incorporate them into a Protestant union with his Moravians. In 1742, however, a man arrived in America whose impact on these disorganized German settlers gave him the title of the Father of American Lutheranism. Henry Melchior Muhlenberg (1711-1787), a Halle-trained Pietist, formed the German settlers into congregations and breathed new spiritual life into the fledgling churches. He traveled tirelessly as he cared for his young churches, often finding it necessary to preach three sermons in three different languages (German, Dutch, and English) on the same day. While Muhlenberg was not a revival preacher in the strict sense of the word, he had great sympathy with the Awakening, and maintained friendly contact with revivalists like the Tennents.

REVIVAL ON THE SOUTHERN FRONTIER

The Awakening came late to the southern colonies, and made less impact there than in Pennsylvania, New Jersey, and New England. Though George Whitefield's whirlwind colonial tours occasionally took him through the southern colonies, he found the same kind of resistance among the Anglicans in Virginia and the Carolinas that his friend John Wesley was encountering at home in England. The first revivalists to turn their attention southward did so as a result of encouragement by the graduates of the Log College. The most notable of these was Samuel Davies (1723-1761), later to become president of the College of New Jersey, who founded numerous Presbyterian churches on the frontier and organized the Hanover Presbytery in Virginia, despite considerable opposition from the Anglicans. Davies extended his revival preaching to the Indians and Negro slaves as well as working among the white settlers of the region.

Davies was followed by the Regular (Particular or Calvinistic) Baptists, who set up churches in the region. Later, the Separate (Arminian) Baptists entered the southern colonies through the preaching of Shubal Stearns (1706-1771), who had been converted under the preaching of Whitefield in Boston, and his brother-in-law Daniel Marshall (1706-1784). Facing opposition from Anglicans and Regular Baptists alike, Stearns and Marshall passed through Virginia and settled in North Carolina, where they founded the Sandy Creek Baptist Association. In the years before the Revolution, the Baptists experienced phenomenal growth on the southern frontier, though nothing like the growth that would come during the Second Great Awakening in the early part of the nineteenth century. The informal style of the Baptist preachers, along with their disparagement of formal education, made them popular with the rugged frontiersmen.

The revival had little impact on the Anglicans in the southern colonies. A few Anglicans, such as Devereux Jarratt (1733-1801), attempted to rouse the churches, but gained little positive response. The Methodists, of course, were represented by Whitefield's itinerant ministry, but he planted no churches, and by the time of the Revolution, there were only a few thousand Methodists in the colonies.

A discussion of the major contributions made by the Methodists to American church life must await the chapter on the Second Great Awakening.

THE RESULTS OF THE GREAT AWAKENING

As is true with all revivals, the Great Awakening had a relatively short lifespan. In a variety of ways, however, it made a lasting impact on both the American churches and society at large. As far as the churches were concerned, the Awakening served to a large extent to define American evangelicalism. The New Light Congregationalists and the New Side Presbyterians quickly found that they had more in common with one another despite their doctrinal distinctives than they did with the anti-revival factions within their own churches. From the time of the Great Awakening on, American evangelicalism has been characterized as a religion of the heart, and American evangelism by an appeal to the will. Though evangelical Congregationalists, Presbyterians, Baptists, and Methodists may differ from one another in many ways, they have always had these basic approaches in common.

The Awakening also had significant political implications, however. More than any other single factor, the revival in the middle of the eighteenth century served to unite the people of the Thirteen Colonies. The Awakening touched almost every colonist in some way, and the resulting commonality of experience produced a new tendency among the colonists to think of themselves as American Christians rather than Massachusetts Congregationalists, New Jersey Presbyterians, or Pennsylvania Lutherans. The unifying effect of the Awakening later played a key role in the struggle of the colonies for independence from Great Britain.

In addition, the leaders of the Revolution borrowed heavily from the methods of the revivalists to stir up support for independence. In the same way that abolitionists and prohibitionists later made use of the revival techniques of the Second Awakening to propagate their agendas for social change, the patriot agitators adapted both the language of Scripture and the emotion-stirring aura of the revival meeting to elicit the support of a population that had become accustomed to moving pulpit oratory.

MAKING DRY BONES LIVE

Secular historians have a notoriously difficult time explaining religious revivals. Whether dealing with the Protestant Reformation, the Methodist Revival in England, or the Great Awakening in the American colonies, a long list of political, economic, and social factors never quite seems adequate to explain the magnitude of the change that revival brings to a society. Such must always be the case with those who leave God out of the picture. In the same way that secular science will never be able to give a satisfactory explanation for the mystery of life, secular psychology will never be able to understand or explain the workings of God in the human soul, nor will secular historians be able to comprehend the awakening of an entire people to God through the moving of the Holy Spirit.

Jonathan Edwards, who more than any other man was at the heart of the Great Awakening, knew better than to try to explain it. He knew from his own experience that the revival could never be attributed to his preaching. Both the style and content of his pulpit ministry varied little during his thirty-year preaching career. Yet that same preaching brought little response until 1734, produced great fruit for the next eight years, and then finally resulted in Edwards' dismissal from his church in 1750. The only way Edwards could explain what had happened was to ascribe it to the mysterious working of the Holy Spirit in the lives of men, women, and children. Unlike many who followed him, Edwards was not so foolish as to believe that revival could be manufactured by creating the proper environment or setting the proper mood. He knew that those who manipulate people to the point of conversion produce hypocrites, not true Christians. Only when the change is brought about by God is that change true and lasting.

The Surprising Work of God

FOR REVIEW AND FURTHER THOUGHT

1. What is a catalyst, and why may the term appropriately be applied to the role played by George Whitefield in the First Great Awakening?

2. Summarize briefly the role played by each of the following preachers in the Great Awakening: Theodore J. Frelinghuysen, Francis Makemie, William Tennent, Gilbert Tennent, Jonathan Dickenson.

3. Whitefield once remarked that the churches of America were dead because they had dead men preaching to them. What other revivalists shared Whitefield's concern for spiritual deadness among ministers, and how was that concern reflected?

4. Why were the revivalists of the Awakening concerned about quality education? What schools did they start to meet the needs they perceived?

5. What were the similarities and differences between the Old Side/New Side and Old Light/New Light schisms?

6. Why was Jonathan Edwards' work describing the revival in New England appropriately titled?

7. In what ways was Edwards different from the stereotype created by anthologies that picture him only as the man who preached *Sinners in the Hands of an Angry God*?

8. Describe briefly the role played by the following preachers in the Great Awakening: David Brainerd, James Davenport, Charles Chauncy, Eleazar Wheelock, Henry Melchior Muhlenberg.

9. In what way did the Baptists benefit from the Awakening in New England?

10. What did the ministries of Makemie and Muhlenberg have in common?

11. What role did each of the following play in the revival in the southern colonies: Samuel Davies, Shubal Stearns, Daniel Marshall, Devereux Jarratt?

12. How did the Great Awakening help to shape the character of American evangelicalism?

13. How did the Great Awakening help to prepare the way for the American Revolution?

14. Why do secular historians have trouble explaining religious revivals?

15. Why is it foolish for preachers to attempt to manufacture a revival by creating certain conditions or manipulating people into making decisions?

37

BROTHER AGAINST BROTHER

When Paul wrote his letter to the Christians in Rome, he spoke to them in the following words about their duty to submit to those in authority over them:

"Everyone must submit himself to the governing authorities, for there is no authority except that which God has established. The authorities that exist have been established by God. Consequently, he who rebels against the authority is rebelling against what God has instituted, and those who do so will bring judgment on themselves. For rulers hold no terror for those who do right, but for those who do wrong. Do you want to be free from fear of the one in authority? Then do what is right and he will commend you. For he is God's servant to do you good. But if you do wrong, be afraid, for he does not bear the sword for nothing. He is God's servant, an agent of wrath to bring punishment on the wrongdoer. Therefore, it is necessary to submit to the authorities, not only because of possible punishment but also because of conscience."

These famous words from Romans 13:1-5 seem on the surface to rule out completely any attempt by Christians to overthrow the government under which God has placed them. When we look at the history of the United States, however, we see a different picture. The same people who loudly proclaim that America was founded as a Christian country also glorify the heroes of the war of independence. How can such a stance be reconciled with Paul's teaching?

The Christians who lived in the American colonies in the closing decades of the eighteenth century had to struggle with the same question, of course. The variety of ways in which they came to terms with the morality or immorality of rebellion helped to shape, not only the course of the Revolutionary War, but also the future character of both the American nation and the American church.

The interrelationships between the American churches and the events of the Revolutionary era are very complex, and any attempt to summarize those interrelationships runs the risk of oversimplification. The fact of the matter is that political loyalties of the period may not be divided neatly along geographical, denominational, or theological lines. Consequently, when we attempt in this chapter to make generalizations about the attitudes of various religious groups in the colonies, it is necessary to realize that such statements are merely generalizations, and that numerous exceptions could be cited for each one. Generalizations have their value, however, and hopefully by the time this chapter reaches its conclusion, the reader will have a clearer picture of the variety of Christian impulses that motivated the colonists who rebelled against England, as well as those who remained loyal.

CHRISTIANS WHO SUPPORTED THE WAR OF INDEPENDENCE

Throughout most of the eighteenth century, the American colonists were quite content with their place in the growing British Empire. The colonies were prospering, and the colonists enjoyed a greater degree of freedom than did most Englishmen. The height of good feeling toward the Mother Country was reached during the French and Indian War, in which British troops and colonists fought side by side to defeat the Indian tribes who had been stirred up to violence by their French allies. When the war ended in 1763, however, the situation changed dramatically. England had incurred a large debt as a result of the seven years of fighting in the colonies and elsewhere, and felt it only fair that the prosperous colonists, who had benefitted the most from the victory, should bear some of the costs of the war. The result was a series of new taxes that the colonists were not eager to pay. In addition, the philosophy of mercantilism was coming to the fore in England. As far as Parliament was concerned, the colonies existed for the benefit of the Mother Country; they were an economic asset, and all policies were devised in order to take full advantage of that asset.

The colonists responded with the predictable outrage of any constituency whose ox is being gored. Because of the strongly religious nature of many of the colonies, however, that outrage was often expressed in Christian terms. In this section, we want to look at some of the religious justifications given by those who supported the War of Independence.

A. SECULARIZING THE PURITAN IDEAL

As is the case with any powerful influence in society, the forms of Puritanism continued to shape American thinking long after the substance had been largely discarded. Certainly one of the dominant modes of thinking among the Puritans had been the concept of the covenant. As far as the Puritans were concerned, the entire Bible pictured a covenant between God and man. God's people were bound by the terms of that covenant, both as a church and as a Christian society. Though the Puritan theocratic ideal had long been dead by the time of the American Revolution, many Americans, particularly in New England, continued to think of themselves as God's covenant people. When the British Parliament broke faith with the colonies by trying to take away some of their cherished liberties (by unilaterally changing the terms of a colonial charter, for instance), the villains were guilty of violating God's covenant. Could anything but judgment follow? Besides, the king and Parliament were clearly claiming absolute authority for themselves. Such authority belongs only to God, and those who fear God ought to oppose those who usurp His prerogatives.

The Puritans were not the only ones who saw in the concept of the covenant adequate justification for rebellion against England, however. If anything, the growing population of Scotch-Irish immigrants in the middle colonies took the notion of the covenant even more seriously than the Puritans did (see chapter twenty-seven). The outstanding Scottish preacher of the Revolutionary era, John Witherspoon (1723-1794), who became president of Princeton College in 1768, later went on to serve in the Continental Congress, and was the only clergyman to sign the Declaration of Independence, constantly used the concept of the covenant to stir up support for the Revolution among both his parishioners and his students.

Another aspect of the Puritan ideal that helped fuel the revolutionary fires was the Puritan concept of the Millennium. The seventeenth-century Puritans such as Increase and Cotton Mather had been premillennialists, teaching that the world would go through a period of decline before the glorious return of Christ to establish His Kingdom on earth. In fact, they were convinced that the disasters associated with the Half-Way Covenant, and the succeeding setbacks in society that to them were clear marks of divine judgment, showed that the time of Christ's Kingdom was drawing near indeed. With the arrival of the Great Awakening, the emphasis shifted to a view known as postmillennialism, espoused by Jonathan Edwards. Postmillennialists believed that God would work through His Church to usher in a Golden Age in which society would achieve the Christian ideal for which the Puritans sought. Edwards and others thought that the Awakening might be the early stages of this coming Golden Age. In addition, many were convinced that America had been chosen by God as the site of His holy work. To many Christians of the eighteenth century, England had been a chosen vessel, but England's day of blessing had passed. The English church was becoming increasingly rationalistic, while the British government and English society in general were becoming more corrupt every day. Clearly,

America was God's new Israel, and Americans were His Chosen People. This sense of destiny made many Americans impatient with the corruptions of Parliament, and eager to help God build His Kingdom by throwing off the shackles of British tyranny. Somewhat surprisingly, this mindset was common even among those who spurned the revival and showed little interest in a thorough application of Christianity to society. The Millennium became a secular hope in much the same way that the concept of the covenant was secularized for political purposes.

If the Puritans wanted a justification for revolution, they didn't have far to look. John Calvin, who more than any single man influenced the Puritan view of life, gave such a justification in the final chapter of his *Institutes of the Christian Religion*. In the section on Civil Government, Calvin asserted that Christians, as private citizens, had the obligation to obey their rulers, even when those rulers were tyrants, unless such obedience required direct violation of God's Word. When speaking of magistrates, however, Calvin painted a different picture:

"So far am I from forbidding these officially to check the undue license of kings, that if they connive at kings when they tyrannize and insult over the humbler of the people, I affirm that their dissimulation is not free from nefarious perfidy, because they fraudulently betray the liberty of the people, while knowing that, by the ordinance of God, they are its appointed guardians."

In other words, Calvin taught that those in legitimate places of authority had not only the right, but also the duty, to oppose tyrants. The obvious conclusion to such an argument is that the Christian who is ruled by competing authorities, one tyrannical and the other seeking to oppose that tyranny, must support the legitimate authority that is most nearly biblical in its stance. Clearly, many Christians in the colonies had little trouble seeing the British king and Parliament as tyrants who were being justly opposed by the legally constituted colonial legislatures and Continental Congress. This enabled them to picture support of the Revolution as divinely sanctioned obedience to authority rather than rebellion against it.

B. DEISTS IN THE SOUTHERN COLONIES

The revolutionary cause in the American colonies revolved around two centers. While Massachusetts may have been the hotbed of revolutionary agitation, Virginia ultimately provided most of the key leaders of the emerging nation. The spokesmen for independence in the south - men like George Washington, Patrick Henry, and Thomas Jefferson - were for the most part Anglicans. We have already noted that the Anglicanism of the southern colonies bore much the same character as that back in England, and in the eighteenth century that meant Deism.

The Deists, with their optimistic view of man, naturally tended to favor the cause of independence. As far as they were concerned, God had made man with an inherent dignity that should be reflected in the organization of society. Governments, as Locke had said, existed only by the consent of the governed, through a sort of social compact. Any government that violated the compact by which it existed forfeited its right to continue in power. The rights of men were not benefits graciously given by kings and Parliaments, but were an inalienable part of what it means to be a human being. With such an understanding of man and society, democracy was not an option - it was the only form of government suited to the full dignity of man.

Perhaps Thomas Jefferson provides the best example of how the Deistic brand of Christianity that dominated southern Anglicanism left its impact on the Revolutionary era. Jefferson's understanding of Christianity was almost purely moral. He compiled his own version of the Scriptures, sometimes called the *Jefferson Bible*, which amounted to little more than the sayings of Jesus. He considered the Old Testament outdated and the New Testament epistles overly doctrinal, so he included only the Gospels in his Bible. He then removed from the Gospels any mention of supernatural occurrences - the birth narratives, the miracles of Jesus, and of course the Resurrection. The result may have been the Deist ideal of true religion, but it was not Christianity by any stretch of the imagination.

It should not then surprise us to find that Jefferson was one of the most outspoken champions of religious freedom in the colonies. He believed that doctrinal divisions were foolish and destructive, and was convinced that allowing every man to worship as he saw fit would enhance the Christian morality that was the backbone of any stable society. We should note that he also championed separation of church and state (that infamous statement about the "wall of separation" that has caused so much controversy in our own day came from his pen) - not just to keep the government out of church affairs, but also to keep the church out of politics.

Anyone who has the least familiarity with the founding documents of the United States can see the impact of Deist thought on those documents. They are permeated with talk of "natural law" and "inalienable rights" that flows from a Deist view of man and his world. Thus the Anglicans in the south also had religious reasons to support the Revolution, though those reasons had little to do with orthodox Christianity.

C. THE FEAR OF ANGLICAN ESTABLISHMENT

One religious factor that motivated a wide variety of people to support the Revolution is one that often gets little attention, largely because it is difficult for people today to understand or appreciate. In the years preceding the Revolution, the possibility of the British sending an Anglican bishop to America was a source of great controversy. On the surface, the issue seemed simple enough. For over a century, any young man who sought ordination to the Anglican priesthood had to undertake the dangerous and costly journey to England in order to be ordained. Furthermore, the Anglican churches in the colonies suffered organizationally because there was no bishop in America to supervise their activities, though the representatives of the Society for the Propagation of the Gospel fulfilled some of the organizational functions of bishops in an informal way. The Anglican priests were therefore constantly asking that a bishop be appointed for the American colonies. The authorities back in England were reluctant to do so, largely because they wanted to keep control of the church in the colonies in their own hands. Ironically, however, it was not the refusal to send a bishop, but rather the possibility that one might finally be sent, that appeared to many of the colonists of all religious persuasions to be a threat to their liberties.

The reasons why people viewed the possible appointment of an Anglican bishop for the colonies as a threat varied widely. The Anglican laymen, many of whom were Deists, opposed their own pastors because they had no desire to see a bishop meddle in their grand political experiment. They had seen enough of meddlesome bishops in England. The New England Congregationalists, though they had declined considerably from the religious ideals of the early Puritans, nonetheless had no desire to see a bishop come to the colonies. For them, episcopacy would be a step backward, and they feared that the sending of a bishop would be merely the first step in establishing episcopacy throughout the American colonies. Other Christians, such as the Presbyterians and Lutherans, had no inherent objection to church-state ties, but would have preferred to see their own churches established. Certainly they had no desire to see the Anglican Church in such a position of power. Many of the smaller groups, on the other hand, such as the Quakers, Mennonites, and Baptists, opposed church-state ties on principle, and with some justification feared a renewal of the sort of persecution many of them had come to America to avoid.

The controversy over this issue was so great that by the time the Church of England decided that a bishop was needed, feelings in the colonies were so volatile that sending one was out of the question. Someone even had the bright idea of offering the job to George Whitefield, figuring that he was so popular that no one could object to making him an American bishop, but he wisely declined the honor and went on with his itinerant ministry. The American Anglicans never did get a bishop until after the Revolution, when bishops were appointed for the newly-established and independent Protestant Episcopal Church.

CHRISTIANS WHO OPPOSED THE WAR OF INDEPENDENCE

When American students cover the Revolutionary War era in school, their studies are often very one-sided. The Patriots are always assumed to be heroes, while the Tories are selfish, disloyal, and generally disagreeable. Clearly no self-respecting Christian could have supported England when God was obviously on the side of the colonies. In fact, however, many sincere Christians sided with England during the conflict. We usually think of the Civil War as pitting brother against brother, but such a picture is equally true of the American Revolution. Brothers in Christ stood on both sides of this conflict. Approximately twenty percent of the American colonists sided with England, many for religious reasons, and their decision proved to be a very costly one in many cases.

Probably those whose position was the most clear-cut were the Anglican clergy. As priests in a state church, their ordination vow included an affirmation of loyalty to the king. Furthermore, the Anglican liturgy incorporated prayers for the king. When Anglican clergy in the colonies were required to omit these prayers from the liturgy, they felt that to do so would be a violation of their ordination vows. Since the Bible has some very strong things to say about people who break oaths they have made, most refused to do so. The result was a major decline in the Anglican Church, so that even after the war was over, many Anglicans were considered suspect by their fellow Americans.

While the Anglican laymen in the southern colonies were largely Deists, and as such supported the Revolution, the Anglicans in the middle and New England colonies tended to be much more theologically and politically conservative. Besides using Romans 13 as a basis for opposing rebellion, these Anglican laymen argued that monarchy was a form of government ordained by God. Democracy, on the other hand, was untried and unproven, and if those radicals in Boston were any indication, it was probably better off remaining that way. They feared that the stability of the realm would be threatened by turning it over to the whims of an unruly mob. Once the Revolutionary War actually began, they were convinced more than ever of the folly of the rebels. How could these men be claiming to fight for the cause of Christ when they formed an alliance with papist France, who two decades earlier had tried to incite the Indians to take their scalps, against the greatest Protestant nation in human history?

Besides the Anglican laymen of the middle and northern colonies, another group who generally stood opposed to the Revolution were the Methodists. At this point, of course, Methodism had not yet separated from the Church of England, but it was nonetheless a recognizably distinct movement within that church. By the time of the American Revolution, there were only a few thousand Methodists in the colonies. John Wesley had sent Thomas Coke and Francis Asbury over to organize societies in America, but their work was still in its infancy. When the Revolution began to occupy everyone's attention, Wesley spoke out on the subject. Though he sympathized with some of the grievances of the colonists, he simply did not believe their problems were sufficient to justify rebellion. He noted, for instance, that the complaint of taxation without representation was absurd, since he himself, because he owned no land, could not vote in English Parliamentary elections. Wesley's attitude immediately brought all Methodists in the colonies under a cloud of suspicion. Many chose to return to England rather than face the opposition of ardent patriots who were willing to act on any rumor of disloyalty to the colonial cause. Asbury, however, spoke out openly for the American cause, and continued to preach and work throughout the years of the Revolution. As a result of his itinerant ministry, Methodism actually grew during the war, particularly in the south. By the time the Methodist Church was formed after the war with Asbury as its head, it was in a great position to take advantage of the expanding western frontier.

CHRISTIANS WHO OCCUPIED THE MIDDLE GROUND

Sitting down while straddling a fence can be a rather uncomfortable experience. This is particularly true if the fence separates warring parties - in that case, the fence-sitter often becomes a target for both sets of combatants. In the same way that Christians fought on both sides of the American Revolution to fulfill what they believed to be their Christian duty, some Christians remained neutral. Their stance may have been the most courageous of all, since they did in fact suffer at the hands of both sides.

The most notable of the neutrals were the pacifists, including Quakers, Mennonites, and Moravians. Though many of them sympathized with the aspirations of the colonists, they strongly believed that Christians should not use force, and certainly should not be involved in taking human life. The members of these groups participated in the events of the Revolutionary era as their consciences permitted. Some served in the colonial militias in non-combatant capacities. Others willingly hired others to take their places in the army. Some could not bring themselves to support the war effort in any way, and instead opened their homes to care for the wounded on both sides. This last group often faced persecution when they were accused by zealots on both sides of aiding and abetting the enemy. Quakers in Philadelphia were in a particularly difficult position because the city changed hands so many times during the war. With each change in the status of the city came a new set of accusations based on the aid given by the Quakers to the previous administration.

The German immigrants were not all pacifists, but many remained neutral during the war simply because they could not manage to work up sufficient outrage against British tyranny. Those colonists who had come from Britain were alive to the slightest threat to their traditional liberties. The Germans, on the other hand, had trouble seeing what everybody was getting so worked up about. To them, the freedom accorded them in the American colonies was enormous compared to what they had left behind in Germany. How could anyone quibble over such a minor annoyance as a Stamp Tax? This was essentially the position taken by the patriarch of American Lutheranism, Henry Melchior Muhlenberg. He remained aloof from the war, though his sons were actively involved in it (one son, John Peter Gabriel Muhlenberg, dramatically announced his intention to fight for the colonies from the pulpit of his Lutheran church, after which he went into a back room, removed his clerical robes, and reappeared in the uniform of a colonel of the militia; he later went on to become a general in Washington's army).

Another group of fence-sitters were those who criticized the movement for independence from within. While supporting the Revolution, they were not afraid to speak out against certain injustices they perceived in the drive for liberty. Among the most notable in this group were the opponents of slavery. Throughout the Revolutionary era, critics denounced the notion that men could speak of liberty for themselves without being willing to grant the same liberty to others. The injustice against which the colonists were rebelling was far less than that being experienced by the African slaves who by the time of the Revolution made up at least ten percent of the population. The Quakers were early leaders in the movement to abolish slavery. They were aided by a number of the more prominent New Divinity theologians in New England, especially Samuel Hopkins (1721-1803), a friend and follower of Jonathan Edwards.

Other critics concerned themselves largely with the question of religious freedom. At the time of the Revolution, many of the colonies had established churches (in fact, Massachusetts and Connecticut continued to support the Congregational Church until the early part of the nineteenth century). The Baptists in the colonies were particularly outspoken about the need to couple political and religious freedom. Led by Isaac Backus (1724-1806), they argued that if taxation without representation were reprehensible, how could the colonies themselves continue taxing people for the support of churches to which they did not belong? While their argument for religious freedom was based on a completely different line of thinking than that of Jefferson and the Deists, the two groups found they could readily agree on the consummation devoutly to be wished, even though their reasons for advocating it differed.

THE EFFECTS OF THE WAR OF INDEPENDENCE ON THE CHURCHES

As one might anticipate, the Revolutionary War had both positive and negative effects on the churches in the former British colonies. One of the most obvious and long-lasting was that the advocates of religious freedom carried the day. Though the citizens of the new nation favored religious freedom for a variety of reasons, most did indeed favor it, and the first paragraph of the Bill of Rights - the first amendment to the Constitution - stipulated that the federal government could neither establish religion nor interfere with its free exercise. We should note, of course, that the first amendment was written to serve a far narrower purpose than it is being made to serve today. In short, it institutionalized freedom of religion while prohibiting the formation of a national church (Connecticut and Massachusetts continued to have state-supported Congregational churches, with Massachusetts maintaining an established church until 1833). The thought that the first amendment could be used as a weapon against all sorts of public exercises of religion, from manger scenes in public squares to morning prayers in public schools, would have been totally foreign to the drafters of the Bill of Rights. In any case, the Bill of Rights ensured that the churches would have to depend upon their own resources for survival in a religious "open market." No church could count on a privileged position. Furthermore, the religious freedom guaranteed by the new Constitution institutionalized the concept of religious voluntarism - in America, people would involve themselves with churches as a matter of choice, not simply birth or geographical location.

Secondly, the Revolutionary War brought about a serious decline in the churches of America. The disruptions of the war were a major factor in this, with churches being taken over for use as hospitals, men being killed in battle, and many pastors leaving their pulpits to participate in the Revolution as chaplains or even soldiers. More importantly, though, the war pushed religion into the background as a matter of public concern. During the Great Awakening, religion had been the hot topic of conversation in every town in the colonies, and men knew the names of George Whitefield and Jonathan Edwards far better than those of George Washington and Benjamin Franklin. By the time the war was over, however, everyone was intensely immersed in political issues; religion took a back seat, and has never again come to the forefront of the American consciousness. Worse yet, the rationalism of the Deists increasingly dominated the popular thought of the day, so that religion became unfashionable as well as of secondary importance. As we will see in the next chapter, the Second Great Awakening brought about a renewed interest in religion - largely, however, among the rough pioneers on the western frontier rather than the intellectual leaders of the nation.

The Revolution also marked a change in the theological orientation of the American churches. The Puritan influence in the colonial period guaranteed that Calvinism would be the dominant American theology. While the Revolution did not in itself bring about the shift to an Arminian emphasis, the concept of liberty that for many was the driving force behind the fight for independence certainly favored an Arminian understanding of Christianity. Perhaps a brief review of the Five Points of Calvinism would help convey the incompatibility of these teachings with the American mindset in the Revolutionary era and beyond.

While Calvinists taught total depravity - that man in himself was capable of doing nothing to please God - the Americans of the Revolutionary era were convinced that man was a noble creature, entrusted by God with his own destiny. Calvinists also taught unconditional election - that God had determined before time began who would be saved, and that such a choice was completely independent of the merits of the one chosen. Arminians, on the other hand, taught that God chose those whom He knew would believe - surely a view more congenial to the democratic ideal that men should be permitted to choose their own way of life. If the doctrine of election became obnoxious because it denied human freedom, how much more the idea of limited atonement? Irresistible grace was no better, since it implied that God exercised His power arbitrarily - was not such tyranny evil, as the war against the tyrant George III had just demonstrated? As far as perseverance of the saints is concerned, Americans have continued to cherish the notion, but in a form that Calvin never envisioned. Instead of viewing the doctrine as teaching that God through His unmerited grace keeps and sustains those who belong to Him apart from meritorious effort on their part, many Americans view it as teaching that a person's own commitment to God guarantees his permanent standing. This American form of Arminianism, though not as extreme as that taught by Arminius himself, became dominant in the American church, especially in the fast-growing Baptist and Methodist churches on the frontier. Calvinism has continued throughout the more than two centuries of American national history to be a minority voice among the churches.

MAKING DRY BONES LIVE

Today in the evangelical community, many voices cry out for a return to America's roots as a "Christian nation." Hopefully, this chapter has helped the reader to see the futility of such a call. While the America of the Revolutionary era was unquestionably religious, it would be very difficult to pin down a set of teachings or even a point of view that defined "Christian America." Sincere Christians differed with one another radically on the Revolution itself, while most of those who ultimately shaped the emerging nation were motivated only tangentially by religious considerations, while holding to a Deist view of man and the world that was hardly congenial to Christianity in any serious sense of the word.

It is much better to view the religious pronouncements of the Founding Fathers with the same sort of skepticism with which we listen to politicians today, who often make religious-sounding pronouncements in circumstances where they have determined that such statements will earn voter support. George Washington made numerous public statements that today have a strongly Christian ring to them. While there is no reason to question his sincerity, the fact remains that his private morality fell far short of biblical standards. Such has been the case throughout American history. "Civil religion" is the term often given to these public pronouncements, vague though they inevitably are, which have little connection with the private lives of the individuals who speak them. We must therefore conclude that America may be called a "Christian nation" only in two senses - first, because the majority of Americans profess some form of Christianity, as opposed to Hinduism or Islam, and second, because the public rhetoric of American politicians has since the beginning of the nation been sprinkled with Christian language. Is a return to the open but largely empty civil religion of the past what American evangelicals really want for their country?

FOR REVIEW AND FURTHER THOUGHT

1. If you had been alive in 1776, what would have been your position with regard to the American Revolution, and why?

2. Why did the aftermath of the French and Indian War help stir up revolutionary sentiments in the American colonies?

3. What is mercantilism, and how did it contribute to the outbreak of the War of Independence?

4. How did the covenant theology of the Puritans contribute to support for the American Revolution?

5. Who was John Witherspoon, and what role did he play in the pre-Revolutionary era?

6. What is the difference between premillennialism and postmillennialism? How did the latter lead some to support the Revolutionary War?

7. What did John Calvin teach about the question of revolution, and how did his teachings influence the Patriot cause?

8. What features of Deism caused the Deists to favor independence?

9. What was the *Jefferson Bible*, and how does it illustrate the Deist view of religion?

10. List the various groups that opposed the appointment of an Anglican bishop for the colonies, and indicate why each group opposed such an appointment.

11. Why did the Anglican clergy in the southern colonies generally oppose the Revolution while the laymen in their churches often favored it?

12. Why did the more theologically conservative Anglican laymen in the middle and New England colonies generally oppose the Revolution?

13. Why did John Wesley oppose the American Revolution, and what effect did his opposition have on American Methodists?

14. Why did groups such as the Quakers and Mennonites refuse to participate in the American Revolution?

15. Why did many non-pacifist German immigrants remain aloof from the war effort?

16. How did men like Samuel Hopkins and Isaac Backus use the rhetoric of the Revolutionary War to criticize what they perceived as social ills in the emerging nation?

17. How did the institutionalizing of freedom of religion in the United States affect the character of the American churches?

18. What was the original intention of the religion clause in the first amendment to the Constitution, and how is it being used differently today?

19. Why did the American Revolution bring about a decline in church life in America?

20. Why was Calvinism incompatible with the spirit of Revolutionary America?

21. To what extent is it fair to refer to America as a Christian nation?

22. What is "civil religion," and how can it distract people from the true condition of American Christianity?

FIRE ON THE MOUNTAINS

Peter Cartwright, a Methodist preacher, was traveling through Kentucky in 1820, and found it necessary to take lodging in a place where a dance was being held that very night. He was determined to find some way of preaching the Gospel to the benighted heathen there. He described what happened as he sat at the edge of the room where the dance was being held:

"A beautiful, ruddy young lady walked very gracefully up to me, dropped a handsome courtesy, and pleasantly, with winning smiles, invited me out to take a dance with her.... I can hardly describe my thoughts or feelings on that occasion. However, in a moment I resolved on a desperate experiment. I rose as gracefully as I could.... We walked on the floor.... I then spoke to the fiddler to hold a moment, and added that for several years I had not undertaken any matter of importance without first asking the blessing of God upon it, and I now desired to ask the blessing of God upon this beautiful young lady and the whole company, that had shown such an act of politeness to a total stranger.

"Here I grasped the young lady's hand tightly ..., and then instantly dropped on my knees, and commenced praying with all the power of soul and body that I could command. The young lady tried to get loose from me, and I held her tight. Presently she fell on her knees. Some of the company kneeled, some stood, some fled, some sat still, all looked curious....

"While I prayed, some wept, and wept aloud, and some cried for mercy. I rose from my knees and commenced an exhortation, after which I sang a hymn. The young lady who invited me on the floor lay prostrate, crying earnestly for mercy. I exhorted again, I sang and prayed nearly all night. About fifteen of that company professed religion, and one meeting lasted next day and next night, and as many more were peacefully converted. I organized a society, took thirty-two into the church, and sent them a preacher."

Here was revival, American style. The nineteenth century in America was an age of almost continual revival activity. Millions professed faith in Christ in a movement almost unprecedented in the history of the church. While some historians distinguish second, third, and even fourth Great Awakenings, it is preferable to see the revival activity of the nineteenth century as being all of one piece - a revival that in a sense continues even today through the activity of mass evangelists such as Billy Graham. To a large extent, the history of evangelical Christianity in America is the history of revivals. In this chapter, we will examine the phenomenon of revivalism as it developed in the nineteenth century, while noting its continuing impact on American Christianity. In the chapters to come, we will see some of the effects, both positive and negative, that the revivals of the nineteenth century had on American society and its churches.

FRONTIER REVIVALS AND REVIVALISTS

American historian Frederick Jackson Turner has asserted that the existence of the frontier is the controlling element in American history. The ability to move westward, to seek one's fortune, to live one's life as one chooses, to start all over again, has shaped American individualism, American democracy, and American religion. While any such explanation may be overly simplistic, there is certainly a large amount of truth to the assertion that the frontier has helped to shape the character of America as a nation.

With the signing of the Treaty of Paris with England in 1783 and the Louisiana Purchase from France in 1804, the vast central portion of the continent was opened for settlement. Thousands from the original thirteen colonies migrated westward, and the population west of the Appalachians mushroomed accordingly. The westward migration presented a unique challenge for the churches. The frontier settlers were notoriously wild and lawless. They lived in scattered towns and villages, and many were constantly on the move in search of better land. Frontier life was hard, and the ever-present danger posed by nature and the Indians who were being displaced frightened off all but the hardiest souls. Those who braved the dangers, however, often found fertile soil for their crops and fertile souls for their preaching. Different denominations approached the problem of bringing religion to the frontier in different ways, and the methods they chose had a great deal to do with their success or failure, as well as with the character of the religion that resulted. The fact that the region in question continues even today to be described as the Bible Belt says a great deal about the impact of nineteenth-century revivalism.

A. BACKWOODSMEN IN THE SOUTH

The big winners in the battle for the souls of the men and women of the Appalachian frontier regions of Kentucky and Tennessee were the Methodists and the Baptists. By the middle of the nineteenth century, these two churches were by far America's largest. Both seemed ideally suited for the enormous task of conquering the wild frontier for Christ and His Kingdom.

The Methodists, under the leadership of the indefatigable Francis Asbury (1745-1816), continued to follow the precedent established by Wesley and Whitefield in England of bringing the Gospel to the people wherever they were. For the widely-scattered people of Kentucky and Tennessee, this meant circuit riding. Asbury established circuits and assigned preachers to travel them. Each preacher would thus have charge of several congregations, and would visit each on a regular basis as he traveled through the countryside, dealing with such necessary matters as marriages and baptisms. During his absence, lay preachers would conduct the services. In this way, a relatively small number of pastors could minister to a widely dispersed population. While Asbury was the great organizing genius of American Methodism, he was no remote desk jockey. He himself carried on an itinerant ministry, traveling throughout America to visit his congregations and establish new ones. His circuit riders may have had numerous churches to visit, but the whole country was Asbury's circuit. By the time of his death, Methodist churches had been established throughout the original thirteen states as well as on the western frontier.

The Methodist preachers, like the people to whom they preached, were often uneducated, and their sermons were straightforward, to the point, and often highly emotional. Peter Cartwright (1785-1872), with whom we began the chapter, was one of the most outstanding of these frontier revivalists. Anecdotes about his unusual (and unusually successful) tactics for spreading the Gospel abound. A big, strapping man who stood well over six feet in height, Cartwright was not afraid to challenge the hecklers who often attended his religious meetings. More than a few changed their minds about the Gospel after the big preacher administered a sound licking or threw them bodily from the building where the meeting was taking place.

On one occasion, Cartwright became concerned that the Baptists in a certain area were "stealing his sheep." He quickly hurried back to the region lest the Baptists should "run my converts into the water before I could come round," and professed his desire to join the Baptist church. The Baptist preachers were delighted, of course, and readily agreed to baptize him along with the other Methodists who had already made a similar decision. When he went down into the creek, however, he asserted that he still believed in infant baptism (Methodists are extremely flexible about such things; most permit either infant or adult baptism, while the mode varies considerably). The Baptists were then forced to turn him down, and the sight of their preacher being rejected as a candidate for baptism caused all the other Methodists to refuse it as well. Cartwright's church was saved.

In 1824, Cartwright requested a transfer to the north because he could no longer abide the institution of slavery. He settled down in Illinois, where he continued to preach and provide leadership for the Methodists. He also got involved in politics, serving several terms in the Illinois legislature. His only defeat came in 1846, when he lost to a gangly young lawyer from Springfield by the name of Abe Lincoln.

The frontier Baptists were like the Methodists in many ways. While they did not advocate circuit-riding, they spread over the frontier through the work of farmer-preachers, laymen who would support themselves by working their farms, while at the same time gathering and ministering to a church in the community. When the members of the community felt the itch to have more "elbow-room," the preacher would move westward right along with them. Such farmer-preachers were almost boastful of their lack of education; after all, what had education done for those liberals in the churches back East? The Baptists and Methodists also attracted the simple frontier folk with their simple preaching of a simple Gospel. Unlike the Presbyterians and Congregationalists, who required that a person assent to a complex doctrinal formula like the Westminster Confession of Faith, the Methodists and Baptists required only that a person be saved. Furthermore, they preached an Arminian view of salvation that was very appealing to the self-reliant backwoodsmen to whom they ministered.

The one evangelistic method, however, that more than any other has come to be associated with the frontier revival was the campmeeting. While circuit-riding and farmer-preachers were designed to bring the preachers to the people, the campmeeting was a way of bringing the people to the preachers. The technique was originated by Presbyterian James McGready (c.1758-1817) in 1800, but the Presbyterians never really developed the practice on any significant scale. The Baptists and Methodists seized on it eagerly, though it eventually came to be identified almost exclusively with the Methodists.

The campmeeting involved people coming from many miles around to spend close to a week camped out in a clearing in the woods or a farmer's field. They would bring their own food and set up tents around the central meeting area. During the campmeeting, numerous preachers would hold forth, often several at the same time at different locations around the camp. The greatest campmeeting of all was held in Cane Ridge, Bourbon County, Kentucky, in August of 1801 under the leadership of Presbyterian preacher Barton W. Stone (1772-1844). Varying accounts set the attendance at between 10,000 and 25,000 people, with dozens of preachers ministering to their needs. The preaching was loud, long, and simple, and often produced strong emotional reactions in the listeners. Some would stiffen up and fall on the ground (the "falling exercise"), remaining in a trance or prophesying from a prone position. Others would suddenly lose control of a part of the body (the "jerking exercise"), which would twitch rapidly back and forth (Peter Cartwright noted that when a person got the jerks in his head, it would twitch back and forth so quickly that the individual's facial features could not be distinguished). Sometimes the jerks would be accompanied by quick, uncontrolled emissions of breath ("the barking exercise"). These emotional and physical responses could befall saints and sinners alike, and were believed to be a sign of the activity of the Holy Spirit. Though the preachers tried to limit some of the more excessive responses, it is not surprising that frontier believers soon came to be called "holy rollers" by those who disdained their extreme forms of religious expression.

Like other spontaneous forms of religion, the campmeeting eventually became institutionalized. Soon the campsites were donated to the churches, buildings were set up to replace the tents, and meetings were scheduled, usually for several weeks during the summer. Many of the old campmeeting sites became Bible conference centers or resorts. The emotional responses, too, died down, though certain aspects of campmeeting religion still characterize the Christianity of Appalachia today.

B. THE MIDWEST

While the Methodists and Baptists were winning the southern frontier, the Presbyterians and Congregationalists were hatching plans of their own to meet the needs of the thousands who were following the westward call. Many of those who were moving out from the established settlements into western Pennsylvania, Ohio, and Indiana had come from New England Puritan or Scotch-Irish Presbyterian backgrounds, so these churches naturally were concerned with ministering in these newly-settled regions. The Presbyterians and Congregationalists were unwilling to follow the pattern established by the Methodists and Baptists. They had no desire to simplify their doctrine, and continued to insist on an educated ministry (in fact, the Presbyterian Church in Kentucky split over these issues when the Transylvania Presbytery appointed preachers who had no theological education and were blatantly Arminian in their doctrine; the resulting Cumberland Presbyterian Church adopted many of the techniques of the Methodists and Baptists). They faced a major problem, however, in that there simply were not enough educated ministers to serve the far-flung western population. As a result, in 1801, the Presbyterian and Congregational churches drafted a Plan of Union. By the provisions of this plan, Congregationalists and Presbyterians on the frontier would form joint congregations, which would then be free to call a minister from either denomination. The church government of the individual congregation would be established by majority vote. The Plan of Union also set up rather complicated procedures to deal with grievances and disputes.

For the most part, the Plan of Union was not terribly successful. Though it did permit more effective ministry to the Presbyterians and Congregationalists who migrated westward, it did little to win the unchurched to Christ. Furthermore, when it became apparent that the majority of churches were moving in the direction of Presbyterianism, the Congregationalists became disenchanted, and bickering between the two groups broke out again. Though the Plan of Union was in effect until the Presbyterians withdrew in 1837, it served only to antagonize the westerners concerning doctrinal issues in general.

One of the more extreme reactions to the doctrinal disputes engendered by the Plan of Union developed under the leadership of the Scotch-Irish Presbyterian preacher Thomas Campbell (1763-1854) and his son Alexander (1788-1866). Like many before him, Thomas Campbell hated the doctrinal disputes that so often turned Christians against one another. He was convinced that the basis for Christian unity could only be found in the primitive church of the New Testament. He resigned from the Presbyterian Church and established an independent congregation in Brush Run, Pennsylvania. When his outspoken son Alexander joined him from Scotland, the son quickly adopted the views of the father, and soon became the most vocal exponent of those views. For a few years, the Campbells and their followers joined the Baptists, but they soon parted ways over a number of issues. While the Campbellites agreed with the Baptists about the need for congregational autonomy and believer's baptism, they asserted that baptism was necessary for salvation, which was a bit more than the Baptists were willing to affirm. Furthermore, the Campbellites excluded instrumental music from the worship of the church, since no such practice is mentioned in the New Testament. Alexander Campbell eventually discovered that his ideas had much in common with those of southern revivalist Barton W. Stone, who had also left the Presbyterian Church to found a "back to the basics" movement. The two groups merged by combining their churches in regions where both existed together. Though the Campbells disdained denominational labels, preferring to call themselves simply "Christians" or "Disciples," those names soon became labels in themselves, and the churches they founded became a denomination, known today as the Christian Church or the Disciples of Christ.

C. NEW ENGLAND PUSHES WESTWARD

The Great Awakening in New England under Jonathan Edwards provided only a temporary roadblock in the downward path of Puritanism. In the decades following the American Revolution, the pastors in the leading churches of Boston, such as William Ellery Channing (1780-1842) of the Federal Street Church, began openly preaching the humanized Gospel of Unitarianism. When Unitarian Henry Ware (1764-1845) was appointed Hollis Professor of Divinity at Harvard in 1805 over the strong objections of many orthodox Congregationalists, it was obvious that Puritanism had strayed far from its roots. The demise of Puritanism became even clearer in 1820, when the Connecticut Supreme Court, in the Dedham Decision, determined that all taxpayers, whether they belonged to the church or not, could vote in pastoral elections because they helped to support the church by their taxes. It is easy to see why Unitarianism quickly took over Congregational churches where unbelievers were permitted to vote for the pastors. Even Samuel Hopkins and the New Divinity theologians, who purported to be followers of Jonathan Edwards and opposed the liberalism of the Unitarians, departed in several significant ways from the staunch Calvinism that had marked Edwards' theology, including denying original sin and denying that Christ suffered the penalty of God's wrath as a substitute for the elect when He died on the cross.

Meanwhile, revival was breaking out at Yale. The spiritual condition of the student body at the beginning of the nineteenth century was pitiful. Most of the students were open scoffers, enamored of the skepticism of the French Revolution. When Timothy Dwight (1752-1817), a grandson of Jonathan Edwards, was appointed president of Yale in 1802, he preached a series of chapel messages defending orthodox Christianity against the popular skepticism of his students. Through his preaching, a third of the student body was converted, and many went on to enter the Christian ministry. The revival soon spread to other New England campuses, including Williams College, where the famous Haystack Prayer Meeting provided the stimulus for the formation of the American Board of Commissioners for Foreign Missions and sparked the missionary labors of Adoniram Judson in Burma. One of the men converted under Dwight's preaching, Lyman Beecher (1775-1863), went on to become New England's leading revival preacher in the first half of the nineteenth century, while also spearheading Christian efforts against slavery and liquor. Two of his children were Harriet Beecher Stowe, the author of *Uncle Tom's Cabin*, and Henry Ward Beecher, preacher and social activist.

The New England branch of the Second Great Awakening was sedate in comparison to what was happening in Kentucky and Tennessee. The leading itinerant evangelist in New England, Asahel Nettleton (1783-1844), very much followed the pattern of the earlier New England revival in that his preaching was restrained, his services were orderly, and his theology was strictly Calvinistic. Such was not the case on New England's version of the frontier, however. While adventurers from Virginia and the Carolinas moved westward to Kentucky and Tennessee and those from the Middle Atlantic states headed for western Pennsylvania and Ohio, New Englanders who sought greener pastures generally headed for western New York. This region came to be known as the Burned-Over District because of all the revival activity that took place there, and while the revivals in the Burned-Over District were a bit more controlled than the frontier campmeetings in the south, they were considerably more lively than the sedate awakenings in the towns and villages of New England.

No preacher exemplifies the revival spirit of the Burned-Over District, or indeed that of the Second Great Awakening as a whole, more than Charles Grandison Finney (1792-1875). Born in Warren, Connecticut, Finney soon moved with his family to upstate New York. Though he attended church regularly as a young man, he was not converted, and enjoyed nothing more than debating the doctrines of Christianity with his pastor. His liking for debate led him to the legal profession. After working for several years as a lawyer, he was saved at the age of twenty-nine, and immediately gave up his law practice to preach the Gospel. He was licensed to preach by the Presbyterian Church, though he later admitted he had never read the Westminster Confession, and disagreed strongly with the Calvinistic doctrines espoused by the Presbyterians. He later left the Presbyterian Church and became a Congregationalist.

Finney began his revival preaching in the small towns of upstate New York in 1824. From the very beginning, people responded to his straightforward, informal preaching style and powerful delivery. Compared to what these transplanted New Englanders had been used to, Finney's approach was radical indeed. Rather than waiting for the Holy Spirit to send a revival (like Jonathan Edwards' "surprising work of God"), Finney was convinced that God wanted revival, and had equipped His servants to bring it about by the use of the means He had ordained. During his years of itinerant evangelism, he developed what he called the New Measures - techniques for stimulating revival that to a large extent have become standard practice among American evangelists. Perhaps the most notable of these was the "anxious bench" - a pew in the front of the church where those under conviction of sin could come forward to receive prayer and counsel. He also stimulated the consciences of his listeners by addressing them directly (and occasionally by name) from the pulpit, praying by name for specific sinners (and their specific sins) in the congregation, and encouraging those who had been saved to give testimony of their conversion experiences in the service (the real shocker here was that Finney included women in this). In fact, in one of Finney's early revival meetings, he learned the effectiveness of such tactics in an unexpected way. He was preaching in a little town called Sodom, and could not resist the temptation to preach on Genesis 19. Unbeknownst to him, one of the more prominent members of the congregation was a certain Mr. Lot, who was less than pleased with the sermon presented by the evangelist. The ensuing uproar led to a revival in the town, however, and Finney learned a lesson he was to apply in various ways in many of the places he visited.

Finney's tactics generated opposition among more orthodox Congregationalists, who disliked his emphasis on man's ability to respond to the call of God, and strongly opposed his assertion that revival was a human work. Asahel Nettleton and Lyman Beecher were among his chief opponents, but his ministry was so successful that few could stand against him - Nettleton finally gave up trying to oppose him, while Beecher eventually came to favor Finney's methods. The high point of Finney's career as a revivalist came in Rochester from September of 1830 to March of 1831. This six-month crusade produced thousands of professions of faith and secured Finney's reputation as the greatest revivalist of the era. The next year, he left itinerant ministry to become the pastor of a church in New York City. In 1837, he was invited to become professor of theology at Oberlin College in Ohio. He remained there until his death, serving as president of the college from 1851-1866. He still traveled periodically to conduct revivals, but much of his time was now devoted to teaching and writing. The most notable aspect of Finney's later years was his development of the doctrine of entire sanctification. Like Wesley before him, he taught that sinless perfection was attainable for the Christian in this life.

Finney also exercised a significant impact on the social issues of his day. He himself was an ardent opponent of slavery, and one of his converts, Theodore Weld, became a leading abolitionist. His New Measures also were used by social crusaders to generate support for a variety of issues, including abolitionism and temperance. He also did much for the rights of women. Oberlin admitted men and women (and also blacks and whites) on an equal basis, and was the first college in the country to grant a bachelor's degree to a black woman (Mary Jane Patterson, in 1862).

REVIVAL COMES TO THE CITY

The later work of Charles Finney marks the transition of American revivalism from the frontier settlements, farms, villages, and small towns to the urban centers of America. In the years prior to the Civil War, revivalists more and more focused their attention on America's great cities and their unchurched multitudes. One of the more remarkable revivals of the prewar period occurred in 1857-1859. In these years, large numbers of businessmen began meeting at local YMCA's during their lunch hours for times of prayer and testimony. These meetings were interdenominational, no one was permitted to discuss controversial matters, and prayers and testimonies were restricted to five minutes in length in order to keep any one individual from dominating the available time. The revival began in New York City and spread to other large cities around the country, and many were converted through the witness of fellow businessmen.

The greatest urban evangelist of the postwar era was Dwight Lyman Moody (1837-1899). Raised in a Unitarian family in Northfield, Massachusetts, and converted in his teens through the influence of his Sunday School teacher, Moody became a shoe salesman in his uncle's business in Boston. Later he moved to Chicago, where he continued working in the shoe business, and developed a growing concern for the poor children of the city who had never heard the Good News of Jesus Christ. He started a Sunday School in an abandoned railway car to reach these children, and became increasingly involved in a variety of urban ministries. By 1860, the Sunday School was attracting 1500 students; eventually, it developed into what is now Moody Memorial Church. During the Civil War, a prison camp for Confederate soldiers was located near Chicago, and Moody would spend hours among the prisoners, trying to win them to Jesus Christ (it is worth noting that at the same time the Confederate army itself was experiencing a major revival; thousands were converted through worship services and prayer meetings encouraged by such Confederate leaders as Robert E. Lee and Stonewall Jackson). Later, he traveled with a division of the Union army and held revival meetings.

After the war, Moody worked for the Chicago YMCA. At a YMCA convention in 1870, he met Ira D. Sankey (1840-1908), who was to become the song leader and vocal soloist in Moody's evangelistic crusades. Sankey also wrote many hymns, the best-known of which is *The Ninety and Nine*. Moody and Sankey established their international reputation for evangelistic work on a trip to England from 1873-1875. They drew huge crowds to their meetings, and thousands professed faith in Christ. Among those converted were the Cambridge Seven, a group of wealthy young men (including all-England cricketer C.T. Studd) who dedicated their lives to foreign missions and soon set off for China to work with Hudson Taylor's China Inland Mission.

By the time Moody and Sankey returned to the United States in 1875, they were famous men. For the remainder of the century, they traveled the length and breadth of the country, holding evangelistic crusades in major cities all over America. Moody never did seek ordination, but his own lack of education taught him the value of learning. During his career, he made an enormous amount of money, but poured almost all of it into charitable causes, including the schools he founded - Northfield Seminary and Mount Hermon School, private secondary schools for girls and boys, respectively, in his home town, and the Chicago Evangelization Society, a school established to train laymen to preach the Gospel, which is now known as Moody Bible Institute.

Like other revivalists of the nineteenth century, Moody was deeply involved in some of the social issues of his day. He supported the temperance movement, and often invited Frances Willard, the founder of the Women's Christian Temperance Union, to appear on the platform at his crusades. He, like Billy Graham in our own day, was criticized for cooperating with men and churches that were far from evangelical, though he himself never deviated from biblical orthodoxy.

In the years following Moody's crusades, other men continued the work that he had begun. Among these were the scholarly Reuben A. Torrey (1856-1928), who also served as the first president of Moody Bible Institute, J. Wilbur Chapman (1859-1918), and the colorful former professional baseball player Billy Sunday (1862-1935). Billy Graham today continues the line begun by these great evangelists of the last century.

MAKING DRY BONES LIVE

The Second Great Awakening and the revivals of the nineteenth century unquestionably made a major impact on American Christianity. The revivals gave the Methodists and Baptists their dominant position in American Protestantism, and created a moral consensus that some have called "Methodist Puritanism" - the traditional evangelical Protestant aversion to such practices as drinking, smoking, dancing, card-playing, and other similar recreational activities that have developed in more recent years. Nineteenth-century Christians also left their mark on the major social controversies of their day - slavery, temperance, and women's rights - as we will see in the next chapter.

But the Second Great Awakening also had its share of harmful effects on American religion. Nowhere may these effects be seen more clearly than in the Burned-Over District - that region where Charles Finney and others like him carried on their work. How did this area come to be "burned over"? When a revivalist came to a town, he would hold a protracted series of meetings, often lasting weeks or even months. During these meetings, emotions in the town would be stirred to a fever pitch, and many would profess conversion. Such a successful crusade would earn an invitation to return at a later date. When the evangelist returned, the same pattern would be repeated, and again many would come forward to put their faith in Christ; unfortunately, this would include many of the same ones who had gotten "saved" the first time. As the cycle continued, it would take more and more dramatic emotional appeals to stir the people. Finally, they became hardened to any sort of preaching.

As Paul warned Timothy in I Timothy 4:1, such people "abandon the faith and follow deceiving spirits and things taught by demons." They are able to be moved only by the truly bizarre, and fall prey to "hypocritical liars, whose consciences have been seared as with a hot iron." It should come as no surprise, then, to discover that the four major American cults that appeared in the nineteenth century all grew out of the soil of the Burned-Over District and its surrounding regions. Both Mormonism and Seventh-Day Adventism had their roots in western New York (along with the Spiritist hoax perpetrated by the Fox sisters), while Christian Science appeared in southern New England and the Jehovah's Witnesses originated in western Pennsylvania. Finney himself, toward the end of his life, realizing that many who had been "converted" through his preaching had turned away from the faith, questioned the effectiveness of his revival ministry. A revival in which the preacher stirs the emotions does nothing but give false security to lost sinners unless the Holy Spirit also changes the heart.

FOR REVIEW AND FURTHER THOUGHT

1. How did the existence of the frontier help to shape the character of the American people and the American church?

2. What unique challenges did the churches face with the expansion of America into the western frontier regions?

3. What methods used by Baptists and Methodists contributed to their success on the frontier?

4. How did the Baptists differ from the Methodists in their approach to the problems of the frontier?

5. What was a campmeeting, and why was it particularly suited to frontier conditions?

6. How did frontier Christians come to be called "holy rollers"?

7. How did the approach of the Presbyterians and Congregationalists in the West differ from that of the Baptists and Methodists?

8. What was the Plan of Union, and why did it fail?

9. How did the Disciples of Christ originate, and what were the distinctives of their brand of Christianity?

10. Most efforts in recent centuries to get back to the primitive church of the first century have been motivated by disgust over denominational divisions. Why do you think these movements have generally succeeded only in producing new denominations?

11. What was the Dedham Decision, and how did it contribute to the decline of New England Congregationalism?

12. What role did the following play in the Second Great Awakening in New England: Timothy Dwight, Lyman Beecher, Adoniram Judson, Asahel Nettleton, Charles G. Finney?

13. What were the New Measures, and how did they differ from earlier approaches to evangelism?

14. What aspects of the New Measures have continued to be used by modern evangelists?

15. How did Finney influence the major social controversies of his day?

16. In what way does D.L. Moody serve as a transitional figure between the evangelism of Charles Finney and that of Billy Graham?

17. Who were the Cambridge Seven, and for what were they famous?

18. What impact did Moody have upon the field of education?

19. What is "Methodist Puritanism," and how did the Second Great Awakening help to cultivate it?

20. How did the Burned-Over District get its name?

21. How did the revivalism of the nineteenth century contribute to the birth and growth of the American cults?

22. What are the dangers associated with overly-emotional evangelistic preaching?

ONWARD, CHRISTIAN SOLDIERS

The blood of crusaders courses through the veins of American Christians. Those who came to the New World brought with them the fundamental conviction that society could be changed for the better, and that no effort should be spared in order to bring such change to pass. In the nineteenth century, that crusading impulse flowed from varied elements of American society to generate a great river of idealism that swept an entire nation forward into countless areas of social improvement.

What forces in American society produced these soldiers for Christ who dedicated their lives to bringing God's Kingdom to earth? Certainly the Puritan view of society contributed to the reforming spirit. The Puritans believed that every area of life was to be brought into submission to the Lordship of Christ. Even though the theology of the Puritans had grown unfashionable by the beginning of the nineteenth century, their idea that society should be Christian had been firmly implanted in their descendants, whether those descendants included the New Divinity theologians like Samuel Hopkins or Unitarians like William Ellery Channing.

The revivalism of the Second Great Awakening also contributed significantly to the reforming spirit. The preachers of the Awakening stirred up a vision of a Christian America that would lead the entire world into the millennial age. Spurred by the Methodist interest in social conditions, the revivalists and those converted through their ministry took an interest in social causes ranging from the abolition of slavery to the observance of the Sabbath. To men like Charles G. Finney, "holiness" was to be the goal of both the individual and the nation.

Even the rationalists had cause to seek reform. The Deists who dominated the leadership of the nation in its formative years believed firmly in the dignity and perfectibility of man. For them, as with the Unitarians in New England, the essence of Christianity, and indeed of all religion, lay in its moral precepts. Man could only realize his destiny when those moral precepts were incorporated into society as a whole.

The crusading spirit of the nineteenth century gave impetus to countless societies dedicated to a wide variety of causes. Some were focused on narrow concerns, such as New York's Society for Poor and Infirm Aged Widows and Single Women of Good Character, Who Have Seen Better Days. Others, like Bronson Alcott's Friends of Universal Reform, reflected broader interests. Crusaders put an end to the practice of dueling, changed the face of American public education, agitated for reforms in the laws governing labor, and encouraged the states to pass Blue Laws regulating commerce on Sunday. In all of these crusades, American Christians played an important role, though often from a variety of perspectives.

There were also crusaders who worked against social change, of course. The massive waves of immigration that flowed into the United States in the era between the Civil War and the First World War frightened many. The Protestant Christian consensus under which America had been operating since its inception was now being challenged by immigrants of a variety of ethnic and religious backgrounds. To others, the threat from within posed by the emancipation of the slaves was an even greater problem. In the face of such perceived threats, the dark underside of the crusading spirit found expression. In a variety of ways extending from the legal drive to limit immigration from certain "undesirable" parts of the world to the violent pseudo-patriotism of the Ku Klux Klan, reformers sought to mold their ideal society by excluding all who were unlike themselves. It is one of the great tragedies of American Christianity that many Christians lent their support to such efforts.

It is not the purpose of this chapter to examine the negative side of nineteenth-century reform, however. In order to gain some understanding of the role played by the churches in changing the face of America, we will focus on three of the more significant reform movements of the nineteenth century - abolitionism, temperance, and women's rights.

SETTING THE CAPTIVES FREE

The year 1619 may have been notable because of the establishment of the first representative assembly in the New World (the Virginia House of Burgesses), but it also marked the beginning of two activities that would cast long, dark shadows over the centuries of American history that followed. In that year, tobacco was first introduced into Virginia. It saved the economy of the Jamestown colony and has been an economic boon to the region ever since, but it has also cost the lives of millions of Americans in the intervening centuries. At the same time, the Virginia colonists imported slaves to work the tobacco plantations. From this small beginning has grown the tragedy of slavery and racism that has plagued the United States, and shaped much of its history, up to the present time.

By the time of the American Revolution, slaves made up about one-fifth of the population of the country. Slavery was widely viewed as an evil institution, but the practical problems associated with bringing it to an end intimidated the Founding Fathers. Despite agitation on the part of some, the Constitution said nothing about slavery. The general attitude of the population is reflected in the fact that slavery was prohibited in the northwest territories by the Ordinance of 1787, and provisions were made for outlawing the slave trade by 1808. As far as the churches were concerned, it was generally agreed that slavery should gradually be eliminated while provisions were being made to educate and evangelize the slaves in preparation for their full participation in society.

The whole picture changed, however, when Eli Whitney invented the cotton gin in 1793. The new invention suddenly made cotton an enormously profitable crop. With the growing demand for raw materials to feed the textile mills of England, southern plantation owners realized that there were fortunes to be made. The key to those fortunes lay in obtaining cheap labor to harvest the cotton and prepare it for sale. Slaves thus became an essential part of the southern economy. Instead of a tragic institution that all agreed should be phased out, slavery now came to be viewed in the south as necessary for economic survival.

In the first three decades of the nineteenth century, the voices most frequently heard were those counseling moderation. When President James Monroe, Senators Daniel Webster and Henry Clay, and other prominent political leaders formed the American Colonization Society in 1817, many churches followed their lead. The American Colonization Society sought to raise funds in order to purchase the freedom of black slaves and transport them back to their homes in Africa. Congress obtained some land in Africa for this purpose, which became the country of Liberia. During a span of fifty years, the society was responsible for settling over 30,000 blacks in Liberia. Though the American Colonization Society may have been motivated by a genuine desire to help those blacks who had been enslaved, their approach was totally impractical. It would have been impossible for the society to have raised enough money to liberate all three million slaves in the United States. Besides, most southern plantation owners had no intention of getting rid of their slaves, with or without compensation.

The slaves themselves were not consulted about any of this, of course. The fact of the matter is that many of the slaves had come from generations of slaves. They had no more desire to return to Africa than their owners had to return to England, France, or wherever their families had come from. Worse yet, the American Colonization Society also wanted to send free blacks back to Africa. Many of these had, through enormous efforts and sacrifices, built stable lives for themselves in America, and understandably had no desire to suffer what they viewed as little better than exile. Though their intentions were undoubtedly benevolent, the American Colonization Society failed, both because their mediating position satisfied neither slaveholders nor abolitionists and because their assumptions of white superiority insulted the very people they were trying to help.

Beginning about 1830, however, the militant advocates of immediate emancipation and the vocal defenders of slavery as a legitimate economic system and a positive moral good gradually forced the voices of moderation into the background. In both of these efforts, the churches were in the forefront. Religious leaders played a major role in polarizing the country to the point where war was the only solution.

In the north, William Lloyd Garrison (1805-1879) may have stirred up a great deal of heat through his newspaper *The Liberator*, but it was Christian reformers who drummed up the grass-roots support that made abolitionism an irresistible political force. Most notable among these Christian reformers was Theodore Dwight Weld (1803-1895). Weld was converted under the preaching of Charles Finney, and later spent two years assisting in Finney's crusades. While studying at the Oneida Institute, Weld met the Christian philanthropist Lewis Tappan, and became convinced of the sinfulness of slavery and the need for immediate abolition of the institution. When Weld moved on to Lane Seminary in Cincinnati, where Lyman Beecher was the president, he soon turned the school into a hotbed of abolitionist sentiment. When the board of directors objected and banned any further abolitionist activity on campus, Weld and fifty other students left the school and moved to Oberlin College, where they were instrumental in convincing Finney to take on the post of professor of theology. Thereafter Oberlin became the center of abolitionist activity in the midwest.

While at Lane Seminary, Weld had spent a great deal of time with professor of Hebrew Calvin Stowe and his wife, Harriet Beecher Stowe. Harriet became an enthusiastic abolitionist, and her novel, *Uncle Tom's Cabin*, became a best-seller. The anti-slavery propaganda of the novel was so effective that Abraham Lincoln later spoke of Harriet Beecher Stowe as "the little lady who made this big war."

Weld also helped to found the American Anti-Slavery Society in 1833, and traveled all over the country drumming up support for the abolitionist cause. As he moved from town to town, he made use of the lessons he had learned in his years as one of Finney's assistants. His abolitionist lectures were like revival meetings, and when he gave a call at the end of the meeting for those who were willing to commit themselves to the abolitionist cause to rise and come forward, the sounds and smells of the sawdust trail filled the building. For Theodore Weld, the cause of Christ and the cause of abolitionism were one and the same.

Not all Christians in the north were abolitionists, of course, but as the debate heated up, it became more and more difficult for moderates to gain a hearing. Men such as Charles Hodge, the great Presbyterian theologian at Princeton Seminary, continued to argue that slavery in itself could not be called sinful, though many of the practices associated with it clearly violated the teachings of Scripture. Their cries for gradual reform fell on deaf ears, however, and they were vilified as compromisers who were too cowardly to speak up against evils in society. How could careful biblical exegesis stand up against the question, "Could you imagine Jesus owning slaves?"

Meanwhile, in the south, fear generated extremism in the other direction. When abolitionists called for an immediate end to slavery, southerners saw a threat to their way of life. They feared that the violent rhetoric of the northern abolitionists could not help but produce actual deeds of violence. When Nat Turner led a bloody slave revolt in Virginia in 1831 that cost the lives of dozens of whites and hundreds of blacks, their fears were realized. Like the white minority during apartheid in South Africa, they came to equate liberation with wholesale slaughter and social chaos. The myth of the benevolent slaveholder and the grateful Negro could no longer bear the scrutiny of reality.

In the same way that Christians in the north eagerly lent their support to the abolitionist cause, many southern pastors became apologists for slavery. They used the examples of Abraham and others in the Old Testament to show that slavery was accepted in Scripture. They cited the laws of the Old Testament to justify the practice of holding slaves. They noted that Paul had advised slaves to obey their masters, and argued that neither Jesus nor Paul had ever spoken against slavery as a practice. They also used passages such as Genesis 9 (the so-called curse of Ham) to argue for the inferiority of the Negroes as a race, while maintaining that the enslavement of the black man was justified because it was the mark of God's judgment upon him. Even after the Civil War and the emancipation of the slaves, many southerners, such as Presbyterian theologian Robert G. Dabney (1820-1898), continued to use similar arguments to support the southern practice of racial segregation.

Others, while not holding quite such a blatantly racist position, argued that slavery was a positive good. Church leaders such as James H. Thornwell (1812-1862), one of the founders of the Southern Presbyterian Church, maintained that God had ordained slavery as an institution whereby the black man could be brought from his heathen condition in Africa and introduced to the saving grace of Jesus Christ. Though he recognized that much about the slave system was evil, he argued that what was needed was not abolition, but reform. If slaves and slaveholders alike followed the admonitions of Paul in Ephesians and Colossians, the blessings of God would be showered upon all, and upon the nation as a whole.

With church leaders speaking out so strongly in favor of opposing positions, it was inevitable that the churches would split over the issue of slavery. Not surprisingly, the churches affected the most by the dispute were those that had a significant number of congregations on both sides of the Mason-Dixon Line. When the Presbyterians divided into Old School and New School groups in 1837, the issue was revivalism, but slavery lay not far below the surface. In general, the revivalists of the New School were strongly abolitionist, while the Old School Presbyterians ranged from cautious moderates to overt defenders of slavery as an institution. Both Old School and New School Presbyterians divided over slavery shortly after the beginning of the Civil War, with the southern bodies merging to form the Presbyterian Church in the United States (PCUS) after the war ended, while the northern groups reunited to form the Presbyterian Church in the United States of America (PCUSA) in 1870. The two regional Presbyterian denominations remained estranged until their merger in 1983.

Though an outspoken abolitionist contingent had pulled out to form the Wesleyan Methodist Church in 1843, the major division in the Methodist Church occurred in 1844. It was sparked by the issue of whether a slaveholder could serve as a Methodist bishop. The Methodists had long taken a strong stand against slavery, beginning with a pamphlet written by John Wesley condemning the institution. The Methodist Church in the United States had gradually relaxed its stance in the early decades of the nineteenth century, but matters came to a head when a Methodist bishop from Georgia, James O. Andrew, married into a slave-owning family. When the Annual Conference voted to suspend him from his duties until such time as he should divest himself of his slaves, the southern churches seceded to form the Methodist Episcopal Church, South. The two branches of Methodism remained apart until 1939.

The third major denomination to divide over the slavery issue was the Baptists, who split in 1845. Given the strong Baptist belief in the autonomy of the local congregation, one might not think that Baptist churches worked together often enough to split over anything. They did cooperate in one endeavor, however - missionary work. Baptist societies for home and foreign missions met every three years in a Triennial Convention. At the 1841 convention, partisans on both sides agitated for definite action on the slavery question. Abolitionists wanted the body to take a strong stand against slavery, while the southerners wanted the abolitionists to stop meddling in their affairs. Moderates won out, however, and the convention closed with no definitive statement on the issue. At the next Triennial in 1844, however, the southerners forced the issue by presenting for approval as a missionary a man who was known to hold slaves. The moderates again attempted to duck the issue, but when it finally came to a vote, the societies decided that they could not possibly support a missionary who owned slaves. At that, the southern delegates pulled out, and in 1845 formed the Southern Baptist Convention. Unlike the other denominations that divided over slavery, the Baptists have never reunited, and the Southern Baptist Convention is today the largest Protestant church body in the United States.

The other large denominations in the country for a variety of reasons felt the impact of the slavery controversy to a much lesser extent than the three groups that experienced major splits. The Congregationalists were generally strong abolitionists, but they suffered no disturbance over the issue because almost all of their churches were in the north. The Episcopalians divided during the Civil War, and for a time functioned as separate churches within the worldwide Episcopal communion, but quickly came together again once the war was over. Because of the nature of its hierarchy, the Roman Catholic Church could not divide, though some parishes took strong stands on one side of the issue or the other. The Disciples of Christ, like the Baptists strongly congregational, did not divide because, unlike the Baptists, they had no kind of national organization that was in a position to split.

Once the war was over, the crusading zeal that had been directed against slavery was turned in other directions. For some, the issue now was how to help the newly-freed slaves to adjust to their altered status. The failure of the churches in this regard contributed greatly to the formation of the black churches, which even today make the Christian church the most segregated organization in American society (see chapter forty). Others turned their attention to other social problems, such as alcoholic beverages and the rights of women.

DEMON RUM

Unlike the slavery issue, which had been simmering just under the surface of the American consciousness throughout much of the eighteenth century, alcoholic beverages were not really viewed as a significant social problem before the nineteenth century. The Puritans had taken the attitude toward alcohol common both in England and on the European continent - that alcoholic beverages were not wrong in themselves, but rather should be viewed as one of God's good gifts. It was the abuse, not the use, of alcohol that was to be condemned by Christians. When America expanded into the frontier beyond the Appalachians, however, drink became a significant social problem. Drunkenness not only contributed to the legendary lawlessness and violence of the frontier, but also was associated with other social problems such as prostitution. Crusaders soon began speaking out against the evils of drink, and forming organizations to fight the problem. One of the earliest of these organizations was the American Society for the Promotion of Temperance (one of the ironies of the anti-liquor movement was that organization after organization used the word *temperance* when they really meant *abstinence*), founded in 1826 by that man of many interests, Lyman Beecher. Frontier preachers during the Second Great Awakening spoke out against liquor, and soon a national movement arose to oppose the traffic in what Shakespeare called "an enemy in [men's] mouths to steal away their brains." In 1846, Maine passed the first state-wide ordinance prohibiting the manufacture, distribution, and sale of alcoholic beverages, and within the next ten years, thirteen other states followed suit.

As has always been true with wars, the end of the Civil War was accompanied by a relaxation of standards of all kinds, and most of the states repealed their prohibition legislation. The great waves of immigrants who entered the United States in the latter half of the nineteenth century caused renewed interest in the subject, however. The immigrants, whether German, Irish, or Italian, brought with them European attitudes toward wine, beer, and liquor. The immigrants settled in the burgeoning cities, and brought their drink with them. Now it was no longer just the frontier regions that faced major alcohol problems.

Motivated partly by the seriousness of the social problems associated with alcohol abuse and partly by a fear of millions of immigrants who seemed to be threatening the familiar American way of life, the temperance movement reappeared with greater force than ever. The great postwar temperance organizations included the National Prohibition Party (1869), which tried to get anti-liquor candidates elected to local, state, and national offices; the Women's Christian Temperance Union (1874), which under the leadership of Frances Willard mobilized thousands of women for the temperance cause; and the Anti-Saloon League (1893), which became the major political force behind the Prohibition Amendment of 1919. The National Prohibition Party, like most third parties in American history, produced more publicity than concrete results. The WCTU became a potent force for reform, while at the same time advancing the cause of women in American society. Frances Willard (1839-1898), who headed the organization from 1879 until her death, was one of the most energetic women in American history. She traveled all over the country, organizing rallies and WCTU chapters and speaking out for the abolition of the liquor trade and the enfranchisement of women. She contributed as much through her speaking to the causes of temperance and woman suffrage as Harriet Beecher Stowe had done for abolitionism through her writing. After her death, the Anti-Saloon League took up the crusade and, aided by evangelists such as Billy Sunday, mobilized evangelical support behind the great political effort that culminated in the National Prohibition Amendment in 1919. The First World War gave the temperance forces the momentum they needed to get the constitutional amendment passed because it generated great fear and hatred of Germans, and made it quite easy to picture the German brewers as part of some great anti-American conspiracy. Though Prohibition failed because it proved to be unenforceable and because it spawned greater evils in the form of organized crime, it nonetheless stands as the high water mark of evangelical influence in American society.

While most of the evangelical churches in America supported the temperance movement, none stood behind it as firmly as did the Methodists. This hymn, entitled *When the Drink is Swept Away*, appeared in the 1921 edition of the *Primitive Methodist Church Hymnal*, and gives some idea of the fervor with which the Methodists espoused the temperance cause.

> Fight on, comrades, don't give over,
> For we're surely gaining ground,
> In the ranks of our blest army
> Some, once drunkards, now are found;
> Don't grow weary or faint-hearted,
> Keep on fighting every day,
> Till the pubs are closed forever,
> And the drink is swept away.
>
> All the little hungry children
> Will have quite enough to eat,
> No more shoeless nippers
> Will be found upon the street;
> And the poor, degraded drunkard
> Will be sober every day,
> When the pubs are closed forever,
> And the drink is swept away.
>
> Our asylums will be fewer,
> Our police have less to do,
> All our jails will nigh be empty,
> And the poorhouse empty, too;
> And instead of homes of sorrow
> We'll have homes that sing and pray,
> When the pubs are closed forever,
> And the drink is swept away.

CHORUS:
> Swept away, O swept away,
> When the drink is swept away;
> There'll be work for everybody,
> And we'll all get better pay,
> When the pubs are closed forever,
> And the drink is swept away.

ONE WOMAN, ONE VOTE

Like the modern feminist movement, the crusade for women's rights in the nineteenth century garnered far less evangelical support than the other major social issues of the day. Most of the chief leaders of the movement, such as Elizabeth Cady Stanton and Susan B. Anthony, came from among the Quakers, who had always given women an equal place in their societies. Evangelicals did contribute to the growing educational opportunities for women in the nineteenth century, however. The Tappan brothers used their fortune to keep Oberlin College afloat while that institution educated men and women on an equal footing, even to the point of granting a degree in theology to a woman, while Baptist philanthropist Matthew Vassar founded the women's college that bears his name.

The movement for women's rights gained considerable impetus from the two reform movements we have already discussed. Women looked at the gains made by former slaves and noted that if blacks deserved full rights as citizens, so did women. The temperance movement, in turn, became the proving ground where many leaders of the drive for woman suffrage cut their teeth and honed their leadership skills. When it came to full equality for women, however, evangelicals were much more reluctant to lend their support. Because of the admonitions given by Paul in the New Testament forbidding women to speak or exercise leadership in the church, many conservative Christians believed that the same strictures should apply in society at large. Thus, when the Woman Suffrage Amendment was adopted in 1920, it was a victory, not for evangelical Christians, but for the radical feminists who have tended to dominate the women's rights crusade ever since.

MAKING DRY BONES LIVE

Evangelical Christians made an enormous impact for good on nineteenth-century American society. Our country changed for the better because Christians believed that the principles of the Word of God should be applied to the life of the nation. As a result, slaves gained their freedom, America's educational system became the best in the world, and conditions for workers improved drastically. Yet by the early decades of the twentieth century, the women's movement had left many Christians far behind by seeking goals that could not claim biblical support, while Prohibition, which represented the high water mark of evangelical social influence, was by all accounts an almost unmitigated disaster.

The history of Christian social reform in the nineteenth century raises a question: Is Christian social reform possible in the twenty-first century? Some have suggested that the only reason Christians were able to accomplish so much in the nineteenth century is because of the relative uniformity of American culture. Americans were overwhelmingly Christian in their religious profession; most of those Christians were Protestants, and most of those Protestants were evangelicals.

Today, however, we live in a different world. Christian values are no longer the common heritage of the American people. In fact, those who still hold to the kinds of values that made the social reforms of the nineteenth century possible are fast becoming a minority. Can Christians at the beginning of the twenty-first century hope to impress their values upon a nation that has espoused a secularism that is in many ways the antithesis of biblical Christianity? Even if it were possible, should Christians attempt to do so?

The obvious social issue to which such questions must be directed in our own day is abortion. In earlier years, the shared Christian values of the nation prevented such a practice from ever becoming an issue. More recently, abortion has taken a terrible toll in human lives. Will future generations be able to look back on some date near the beginning of the twenty-first century on which abortion was outlawed with the same satisfaction that people today associate with the Emancipation Proclamation? Will future Americans shake their heads in sorrow at the barbarism of those who would take the lives of their own children in their mother's wombs, or will they live in an age where the "termination of a pregnancy" requires no more than a simple pill? If twenty-first-century evangelicals are to leave their mark on the social consciousness of the nation, it will require men and women who are as dedicated to seeing America conform to God's Word as any nineteenth-century abolitionist or temperance worker.

FOR REVIEW AND FURTHER THOUGHT

1. What different factors motivated different groups of Americans to seek social reform in the nineteenth century?

2. In what sense did some crusaders pervert the reforming spirit and use it to try to prevent change?

3. What was the prevailing attitude toward slavery at the end of the Revolutionary War?

4. How did the development of the cotton gin help to polarize and harden people's views on slavery?

5. What was the main goal of the American Colonization Society?

6. Why did the American Colonization Society fail to achieve its goal?

7. What were some of the contributions of Theodore Weld to the abolitionist cause?

8. Why were moderate voices gradually silenced on both sides of the Mason-Dixon Line as the Civil War approached?

9. On what basis did theologians in the south argue that slavery was biblical?

10. Do you think that the arguments used to support slavery by southern theologians were legitimate? Why or why not?

11. On what basis did James H. Thornwell argue that slavery was a good thing?

12. What major denominations in America split over the issue of slavery? How were these splits brought about?

13. What denominations remained intact through the period of the Civil War? Why didn't they divide like the others?

14. What attitude toward alcoholic beverages prevailed during the colonial period?

15. How did the settlement of the frontier contribute to the alcohol problem in America?

16. How did the waves of immigrants who came to America in the latter half of the nineteenth century contribute to the country's liquor problem?

17. What were the distinctive emphases of the great temperance organizations mentioned in the chapter?

18. Why did Prohibition fail?

19. Based on the words to *When the Drink is Swept Away*, do you think that the hopes of Christians who supported the temperance movement were realistic? Why or why not?

20. In what sense did the movement for women's rights grow out of the crusades that had preceded it?

21. In what ways did evangelical Christians contribute to the movement for women's rights?

22. Why did many Christians shy away from pushing for women's rights in society? Are these reasons the same as those used by Christians today who oppose feminism?

23. Do you believe that American society has changed so much that Christians can no longer bring about social change?

24. What can Christians today learn about implementing social change from the reformers of the nineteenth century?

25. In what ways is the modern abortion issue like the reform questions of the nineteenth century, and in what ways is it different?

THE INVISIBLE CHURCH

On August 28, 1963, Martin Luther King stood in front of the Lincoln Memorial in Washington, D.C., and spoke these memorable words:

"I have a dream that one day, on the red hills of Georgia, sons of former slaves and the sons of former slaveowners will be able to sit down together at the table of brotherhood. I have a dream that one day even the state of Mississippi, a state sweltering with the heat of injustice, sweltering with the heat of oppression, will be transformed into an oasis of freedom and justice. I have a dream that my little children will one day live in a nation where they will not be judged by the color of their skin but by the content of their character...."

After centuries of slavery, discrimination, segregation, and injustice, Dr. King hoped that the civil rights movement for which he was providing such vocal leadership would bring about a color-blind society in America. Yet not all blacks who sought equal rights agreed with King's assessment of the ultimate goal of their efforts. While some sought a world where people would be oblivious to the color of a man's skin, others believed that the path to equality for the black man required an emphasis on black distinctiveness. They trumpeted slogans such as "Black is Beautiful," and some even taught doctrines of racial superiority. Throughout the history of the civil rights movement, there has been conflict between those who strive for the removal of all racial distinctions and those who favor racial affirmation.

This dilemma is particularly acute for the Christian church in America. After all, the Body of Christ is supposed to be one. How can Christians claim to represent a Savior who breaks down the artificial barriers imposed by human sin and prejudice when 11:00 A.M. Sunday morning continues to be the most segregated hour of the week throughout America? If blacks and whites can work together, go to school together, and play together, why can't they worship together? What does such stark separation do to the testimony of Jesus Christ in our country? Is segregated worship something that we should deplore and seek to bring to an end, or is it instead unavoidable, necessary, or even healthy? The answers to these questions are complex, and we will only be able to scratch the surface of the issue in this chapter, but one thing is certain - no answer to these questions may even be attempted apart from some understanding of the history and importance of the black church in America.

During the centuries of slavery, black worship was often conducted in the woods or by the riverbank, away from the eyes of prying whites. Some historians refer to the black church in the days of slavery as "the invisible institution." Since the end of the Civil War, the black church has played a major role in the life of the black segment of our population, yet to a large extent it has remained invisible - because blacks worship in their own churches, few in the white majority know anything about those churches, nor can begin to understand their importance. In earlier years, black churches were often ignored by the historians of the church as well, though that oversight (deliberate or otherwise) has to a significant degree been overcome in the latter part of the twentieth century.

BLACK RELIGION BEFORE THE CIVIL WAR

When slaves were first imported into the American colonies in the seventeenth century, little effort was made to introduce the Africans to Christianity. One of the major reasons for this was the common fear among white settlers that conversion to Christianity would render the Africans unsuitable for service as slaves. After all, the Israelites in the Old Testament were permitted to enslave outsiders, but were not allowed to keep fellow Jews in permanent bondage. There are even a few early examples of slaves being released after converting to Christianity. Toward the end of the seventeenth century, however, Virginia, the largest slaveholding colony at the time, decided that the religion of the slave had no bearing on his condition before the law. Breathing great sighs of relief, plantation owners then became much more willing to allow preachers access to their slaves. Some even came to believe that Christian slaves were more obedient and docile than pagan ones, and on that basis encouraged their slaves to adopt Christianity.

The great awakenings of the eighteenth and early nineteenth centuries made enormous inroads into the slave population of the south. Presbyterians, Baptists, and Methodists were particularly active among slaves, with the latter two groups attracting many black converts for the same reasons they attracted many frontier whites - the simplicity of their message and the lack of educational requirements for pastoral ministry (slaves, of course, had little opportunity for education, and many slaveholders even prevented their slaves from learning to read and write).

In the decades preceding the Civil War, religion among blacks took on several different forms. Perhaps the most common situation in the south was where slaves attended the churches of their masters. In the white churches, slaves could participate in all aspects of worship, though they usually were required to sit in a separate section of the church - either in the balcony or in the rear of the sanctuary, often behind a screen. It was not unusual for black preachers to speak in such churches, though always under the authority of white pastors. In fact, as the Civil War approached, concern of the slaveowners for the spiritual welfare of their slaves actually increased, both because of the impact of the Second Great Awakening on evangelistic zeal in general, and because the slaveowners of the south felt the need to respond to the criticisms of abolitionists that they were ignoring the spiritual needs of their slaves.

Sometimes when there were a large number of slaves in a particular area, the slaves were permitted to form their own church under the care and supervision of the local white congregation. The slaves could choose their own pastor and leaders and exercise their own discipline, but always under the ultimate control of the white church with which they were affiliated. Most of these churches broke away from their parent congregations after the Civil War and either remained independent or affiliated themselves with the emerging black denominations.

A third form of slave religion in the south was the "invisible institution" referred to above. Slaves on large plantations would often gather for worship on their own, and it was in these times of emotional release, where the slaves could be themselves, that the deep feelings of the Negro spirituals took shape. The distinctives that even today set black religion apart from the worship found in most white churches grew out of these days of slave religion. Though in its broad outlines the worship of the slaves differed little from that of the southern whites, the themes of freedom and heavenly bliss that continue to play such a prominent role in black religion today came to the fore through the deep agonies suffered in centuries of bondage.

Not all people of African descent were slaves before the Civil War, of course. The black church has its roots, not only in the religion of the slaves, but also in the free black churches founded decades prior to the Civil War. Baptists early showed themselves willing to license promising black converts to preach, and many of these black preachers formed independent Baptist churches, both in the north and in the south. Some even ministered to mixed congregations, though the majority of black Baptist pastors led churches made up exclusively of other blacks. As the Civil War approached, it became increasingly difficult for such churches to function in the south. The slave revolts under Denmark Vesey and Nat Turner, both of which had religious overtones, frightened southern whites to the extent that they would not permit their slaves to attend services led by free blacks.

The most notable free black churches before the Civil War, however, were founded by the Methodists. In 1787, in a Methodist church in Philadelphia, a young black man named Richard Allen, along with several other blacks, was interrupted during a time of congregational prayer and asked by the ushers to move to an area of segregated seating in the rear of the church. Allen replied that he would move once he had finished praying. The ushers insisted, however, and Allen then led the other blacks out of the doors of the church, never to return. Richard Allen went on to become the founding bishop of the first black denomination in the United States, the African Methodist Episcopal Church.

Richard Allen (1760-1831) had been born into slavery in the household of a prominent Philadelphia lawyer, Benjamin Chew. When he was eight years old, he was sold, along with his parents and siblings, to a farmer in Dover, Delaware. At the age of seventeen, Allen was converted through the preaching of an itinerant Methodist, and in turn was instrumental in the conversion of his master. His master then offered him the opportunity of purchasing his freedom, and after working at odd jobs and saving up $2000, Allen became a free man. He went on to become a Methodist preacher, and was eventually invited back to his home town of Philadelphia to preach. He soon joined St. George's Methodist Episcopal Church, where he worshipped and led early-morning services for the black members of the congregation. It was at St. George's that the momentous event occurred that led to the formation of an independent black Methodist denomination. Even the tolerant Methodists clearly harbored a great deal of prejudice, and Allen could not reconcile such behavior with the teachings of Christ. After leaving St. George's, he first formed a benevolent association, then in 1794 formed Bethel African Methodist Episcopal Church, which was dedicated by Allen's friend and supporter, Francis Asbury. Allen not only pastored the church that is now known as Mother Bethel, but also encouraged the formation of black churches in other cities. In 1816, a group of these churches met in Philadelphia to form the African Methodist Episcopal Church, with Allen as its first bishop. Five years later, a group of black Methodists in New York City formed the African Methodist Episcopal Zion Church, and these two quickly became (and remain today) the two largest black Methodist denominations.

RECONSTRUCTION AND BEYOND

The black church as it exists today came into being for the most part during the period of Reconstruction following the Civil War. It is difficult to determine whether the whites or blacks were more eager to see the establishment of separate black churches. While the southern whites were unquestionably eager to see the former slaves leave their churches, it is also true that the newly freed blacks wanted to form their own organizations and develop their own leadership apart from the inevitably paternalistic oversight of the white churches. While some of the instances of black departures from white-dominated congregations carry some of the same overtones of racism seen in the founding of the independent black denominations in the north before the Civil War, some divisions were very amicable. The Southern Methodists, for instance, not only helped the former slaves to organize their congregations, but also drew up a plan for dividing church property so that blacks would have buildings in which to worship. The black and white Methodists in the south were thus able to work together in peace and harmony for many years after the formation of the Colored Methodist Episcopal Church (now the Christian Methodist Episcopal Church) in 1870.

Meanwhile, the "invisible institution" from the days of slavery came out into the open during Reconstruction. Many of the black congregations that had met secretly on plantations now organized formally, often as independent Baptist churches. As Baptist congregations multiplied among blacks in both the north and south, talk of cooperation grew, and black Baptists finally joined to form the National Baptist Convention in 1895. Despite schisms in 1915 and 1961, the National Baptist Convention, U.S.A., Inc. is today the largest black denomination in the country, and the third largest Baptist group of any kind.

The black Methodist denominations that had been formed in the north before the Civil War were also active in the south during Reconstruction. They sent evangelists and church planters into the south, and these men organized the newly-freed slaves into Methodist congregations. Both the African Methodist Episcopal Church and the African Methodist Episcopal Zion Church grew significantly during the years following the Civil War. By the end of the Reconstruction period, both were considerably more numerous than the Colored Methodists who had broken off from the Methodist Episcopal Church, South.

When Congress voted to withdraw federal troops from the southern states in 1877, thus bringing an end to Reconstruction, the plight of the black man in the south quickly worsened. While blacks had been able to gain political office during Reconstruction, with some serving in the U.S. House of Representatives and many sitting in state legislatures, the withdrawal of federal troops brought the full weight of southern rage down on the heads of the black population. Blacks were quickly disenfranchised in a large number of creative ways, the most popular of which were literacy tests and poll taxes that were used to keep blacks from registering or voting. If these tactics didn't work, of course, there was always the Ku Klux Klan. The closing quarter of the nineteenth century thus marks the worst era of black powerlessness since the Emancipation Proclamation.

During this time, the church took on enormous importance in the life of American blacks, particularly in the south (at the end of the nineteenth century, ninety percent of American blacks still lived in the south, and the vast majority of those lived in rural areas). Because blacks were excluded from the political arena by discriminatory practices, the church was their only outlet for political activity. They therefore entered enthusiastically into church politics, whether the issues involved the election of church leaders or the exercise of church discipline. In addition, many of the most capable black men were drawn toward the ministry, since the pastorate was for the most part the only profession open to blacks. Black preachers thus became leaders in their communities; even today, a large number of prominent black politicians entered public life from the Christian ministry.

The First World War brought about a major change in the black community and in the black church. Despite the burdens of segregation in the south, most blacks had little alternative but to remain there. As sharecroppers, they were perpetually in debt with little hope of gaining economic independence. With the coming of the First World War, however, the picture changed dramatically. The war brought a sudden need for unskilled workers in the northern industrial cities, and blacks moved northward to take advantage of the available jobs. The result was an enormous shift in the demographics of America in general and blacks in particular. In the twentieth century, American blacks became to a large extent an urban people.

When southern blacks moved to the cities of the north, they brought their churches with them. But the sense of community that had become so important to rural blacks was lost in the rootless cities of the north, and the large churches that quickly grew up in the cities did little to compensate for the resulting sense of loss. Consequently, the burgeoning cities witnessed not only the growth of large black churches, but also the planting of thousands of small congregations that met in homes and abandoned storefronts. These small churches were often led by uneducated and unordained men (or women) who felt a call from God and on that basis set out to organize a church. For many uprooted blacks in the city, these churches provided a stability that the city could never give.

The urban black churches have in recent years developed in a way that distinguishes them from the categories that are usually applied to churches in the white community. It is not always easy, for instance, to pin a label of "liberal" or "evangelical" on a black church. While most black churches have retained an evangelical theology that distinguishes them from liberal churches in the white community, they have at the same time taken a liberal stand on social issues that sets them apart from white evangelicals. Involvement in politics by the black church is nothing new, of course, and the black urban churches have been at the forefront of efforts to deal with the persistent problems of the inner city. Furthermore, since the days of slavery in the south, black worship has had an otherworldly thrust, so that evangelical worship, with its emotional expression and traditional black musical styles, continues alongside political and social programs that may or may not be rooted in or motivated by Scripture.

For instance, the black church has played a major role in the civil rights movement in the twentieth century. Black preachers have at times taken stances that obviously derive their roots from the Word of God, while others, such as Martin Luther King, have looked more to Mahatma Gandhi for their inspiration. Other black leaders, such as Black Power theologian James Cone, have shown a willingness to take advantage of the Marxist-oriented Theology of Liberation in order to picture Jesus as a revolutionary.

Like the white churches, the black churches produced their share of bizarre movements and heretical cults. Among the more notable of these are the movements that grew up under the leadership of "Sweet Daddy" Grace and Father Divine, both of whom blasphemously claimed to be God. Charles M. Grace (1882-1960) organized the United House of Prayer for All People, into which he baptized hundreds of people at a time using a fire hose. George Baker (1876-1965), otherwise known as Father Divine, founded the Father Divine Peace Mission. He had earlier been associated with two other black preachers who had also believed themselves to be God, Samuel Morris and St. John the Divine Hickerson, but the three eventually separated over disagreements as to the appropriate role each should play in the Trinity! Cults such as the Jehovah's Witnesses have also made significant inroads into the black community, largely because of their opposition to racial discrimination, voiced long before it became fashionable in white society in general.

The latter part of the twentieth century has also witnessed an alarming growth of non-Christian religions among urban blacks. By far the most significant of these has been Islam. The Islamic religion first gained entrance into the black community through a black supremacy movement originated in the early part of the century by Wallace D. Fard and Elijah Poole, who later changed his name to Elijah Muhammad. This "Nation of Islam" grew from the roots of an earlier black nationalist movement started by Marcus Garvey, and taught that white men were of the devil, while encouraging blacks to take charge of their own lives. In reality, it had little to do with Islam, and Muslims in the Middle East refused to acknowledge the movement. The Black Muslims opposed the push for integration led by civil rights advocates like Dr. King, instead encouraging blacks to separate themselves from their white oppressors and seize control of their own lives, and then of society as a whole. While most of the Black Muslim leaders spoke of blacks gaining economic self-determination, there were some who spoke of violence against the oppressors, and these prophets of confrontation helped contribute to the atmosphere that produced the urban race riots of the late sixties. A split in the movement occurred when Malcolm X (1925-1965), who had become Elijah Muhammad's chief assistant, became disillusioned with what he viewed as hypocrisy on the part of his leader (the head of the Nation of Islam had been carrying on affairs with several of his secretaries while preaching a message of sexual purity). Malcolm X became increasingly interested in mainstream Islam, and was eventually ejected from the Nation of Islam, and later assassinated. When Elijah Muhammad died in 1975, his son Wallace Muhammad became the leader of the Nation of Islam. He quickly shifted the emphasis of the movement away from black supremacy and more in the direction of mainstream Islam (it is now called the American Muslim Mission), though some broke away in order to continue to preach the separatist Gospel under the leadership of Louis Farrakhan. Islam has made such progress among inner-city blacks that my black students today tell me that they know more Muslims than Catholics - even though the Catholic Church has made great gains among blacks in recent years.

Another non-Christian movement that has made great progress among inner-city blacks is a Japanese form of Buddhism known as Nichiren Shoshu Buddhism. In addition to the normal trappings of Buddhism, Nichiren Shoshu incorporates a very materialistic focus that, like the "Prosperity Gospel," has appealed to and misled many who both lack and covet the goods this world always seems to provide to others.

THE BLACK CHURCH AND BLACK CULTURE

In the years following the Emancipation Proclamation, the black church became the focal point of black society. There was little alternative - much of society was closed to the black man, and he could find both acceptance and an outlet for his skills and ambitions in the church. It is no surprise that a large number of the leaders produced by the black community have first learned to use their skills in the churches.

With the shift to the cities of the north, the black churches were confronted with enormous problems. They continued to provide a social focus, but the disruptions accompanying rapid population shifts, poverty, and unemployment were too much for the black churches to handle. After all, why should they be expected to succeed where numerous government efforts have failed, though they have made an heroic effort and seen success on a small scale in many neighborhoods?

Two of the greatest problems facing the black church today involve the family and secularization. American blacks have always had to struggle to maintain a stable family life. During the centuries of slavery, men and women were routinely coupled by their owners for breeding purposes, often without benefit of any formal marriage. Furthermore, slave families were often separated when husbands, wives, or children were sold, never to see one another again. Thus, after the end of the Civil War, family stability was something that had to be *learned*. The black churches sought to inculcate morality and stability into the family lives of their people, but the job was not an easy one. In the cities of the north, the problem became even more difficult to solve. Poverty produced rootlessness, and when welfare programs were introduced to help those in need, they often were set up in a way that encouraged families to break apart for the sake of financial survival. Thus urban black society has become largely matriarchal, though for different reasons than during the years of slavery. Black churches face the problems of providing male role models and encouraging young men to take responsibility for themselves and their families.

The migration to the cities also contributed to the problem of secularization. The city unquestionably provided more options than rural life. Religion became less the focus of life than it had been in the rural south, and black churches were faced with a dilemma. If they continued to preach an other-worldly Gospel, they would quickly become irrelevant and lose all influence in the black community. On the other hand, if they addressed all the concerns of society, they soon would have no time for the fundamental task of the church - preaching the Gospel. Black churches have approached this problem in different ways, though almost all have sought to strike some sort of balance between the needs of the society around them and their responsibility to proclaim God's Word. While some, like liberal white churches, seem to have abandoned the message of individual salvation in favor of functioning as some sort of combination social service agency/political action committee, others view themselves as putting the Gospel of Jesus Christ into practice in the lives of the people of their communities through meeting the needs of those around them.

Before we conclude this section, a word must be said about black music. There is probably no way in which black churches have had a greater impact on the nation as a whole than through music. The Negro spirituals, transplanted into the urban environment, produced new forms of music - Gospel music and jazz - that have in turn influenced many modern musical forms, including the ubiquitous rock and roll. While one's own musical tastes will determine his evaluation of this contribution, there can be no question that the black churches have made a significant impact on the American musical scene.

MAKING DRY BONES LIVE

We must turn now to the question of the unity of the Body of Christ. While Jesus may not have had organizational unity in mind when He prayed in John 17 that all His disciples might be one, the segregation of Christian worship in America speaks eloquently against the existence of the unity for which the Savior prayed. In seeking an explanation for the segregation of the American church, we must consider both how that segregation came about and why it persists so stubbornly.

When racially segregated churches originated in the northern states in the early years of the nineteenth century, there can be little question that the primary cause was white bigotry. Richard Allen and others like him would have been quite content to worship in the company of their white brothers and sisters had not those same brothers and sisters made it clear that they considered him to be a second-class citizen. Thus the black churches originated from the violation by white Americans of the teaching found in James 2. In the south, those black churches that were formed before the Civil War also came into existence because of white racism. The slaves were only free to worship in ways that their masters would permit, and many of the early black churches in the south came into existence because southern whites encouraged blacks to form their own congregations - usually when whites were afraid of being outnumbered.

After the Civil War, matters became a bit more complex. Continuing racism on the part of the white population was now mixed with a desire on the part of blacks to run their own lives. The black churches enabled them to do this. Had they remained in predominantly white churches, they would have been in no position to develop leadership or influence decisions. In addition, some white Christians who sympathized with black Christians' desire for self-determination encouraged them and helped them in establishing independent churches. Thus, in the years following the Civil War, white fear and racism combined with a desire among blacks to conduct their own affairs without interference from the white man to produce segregated churches with which blacks and whites were equally content.

In the century following the Civil War, cultural developments in many ways drove the churches farther apart. The black churches developed distinctive styles of preaching and worship that set them apart, even from those white churches that shared their general theological perspective. In addition, the generally segregated nature of housing patterns in the United States meant that blacks and whites rarely attended one another's churches because they rarely lived in the same neighborhoods.

With the growth of the civil rights movement in the middle of the twentieth century, the situation became increasingly complex. Blacks began to fight aggressively for equality in American society, and, as the 1954 Supreme Court decision in Brown vs. Board of Education (Topeka, Kansas) made clear, "separate but equal" was not good enough. What is true for schools is not necessarily true for churches, of course. Schools are run by the government for the benefit of its citizens, and it is blatantly unfair for one segment of society to enjoy the benefits of government-run schools that are far superior to those operated for another segment of society. Churches, on the other hand, are voluntary societies that receive no government support, and no one could seriously argue that white churches are inherently "superior" to black churches, or vice versa.

Why, then, can't black and white Christians manage to get together? As far as whites are concerned, a number of factors are involved. In the first place, no serious observer of the American scene could doubt that racism persists in many quarters. Some white Christians simply do not want black people in their churches. Others take the somewhat hypocritical position of being willing to support missionary efforts in Africa and even inner-city missions to help needy blacks, but resisting strenuously any effort by blacks to enter their neighborhoods or their churches. Still others have made a legitimate effort to welcome black families into their churches, and have found that, for a variety of reasons, those black families simply are not comfortable, whether because of the more sedate style of worship or because of the natural discomfort that comes from being a rather obvious minority.

Among blacks, the problem also has many dimensions. Unquestionably, the distinctive style of worship that characterizes black churches is part of the reason why blacks attend such churches in preference to those that are predominantly white. In addition, the liberal theology and bland preaching of many white churches is singularly unattractive to blacks. We should also note, however, that the civil rights movement has emphasized black pride as well as racial equality. As indicated at the beginning of the chapter, many blacks wish to retain their distinctives as a matter of racial pride rather than seeing those distinctives lost through assimilation into the "melting pot" of American society. As with any minority, assimilation in a certain sense means loss of power. In black churches, black preferences and cultural distinctives are dominant; if blacks were to mix in with the white churches, those distinctives and preferences would largely be lost because of the minority status of black people.

In the last analysis, however, we must admit that all of these considerations are secondary. If the Body of Christ is truly one, that oneness must have some visible manifestation. A segregated church does not communicate to a race-conscious society that Christians worship a God who breaks down the artificial barriers set up by sinful men to divide one group from another. The American church simply *must* find a way to display the unity of Christ's church to the unbelieving world if we are to have a credible witness before that world.

The Invisible Church

FOR REVIEW AND FURTHER THOUGHT

1. Why was the black church before the Civil War called "the invisible institution"?

2. Why were seventeenth-century slaveholders often reluctant to introduce their slaves to Christianity?

3. What factors led to the growth of Baptist and Methodist churches among the slave population?

4. List and describe the four forms of black religion that existed prior to the Civil War.

5. Why did the concern of slaveowners for the spiritual welfare of their slaves increase as the Civil War approached?

6. Why was it difficult for independent black churches to function in the south as the Civil War approached?

7. Who was Richard Allen, and why is he important in the history of the black church in America?

8. What forces led to the formation of separate black churches after the Civil War?

9. Why were blacks as eager for separation as whites were?

10. How did the end of Reconstruction affect the black churches in the south?

11. What important change in the country occurred as a result of World War I, and what effect did it have on the black church?

12. What factors led to the growth of storefront churches in the cities?

13. Why is it difficult to classify black churches as "evangelical" or "liberal"?

14. Who were "Sweet Daddy" Grace and Father Divine?

15. Why did many refuse to recognize the Black Muslims as being followers of Islam?

16. What role did the Black Muslims play in the civil rights movement?

17. What is Nichiren Shoshu Buddhism, and why has it become popular in the black community?

18. How did slavery and the discrimination that followed it contribute to the breakdown of black families?

19. How did the urbanization of black culture contribute to its secularization?

20. In what different ways have black churches responded to the problem of secularism?

21. In what way has the black church influenced the development of American music?

22. In what ways were whites responsible for the segregation of the Christian church in America?

23. In what ways did blacks contribute to the segregation of the American church?

24. What factors prevent the integration of the church in modern America?

25. Do you believe that churches should be integrated, or should they remain segregated as they are today? Why? If you favor integration, how would you bring it about?

WEEDS IN FERTILE GROUND

The fertile soil of the American continent produced far more than abundant crops. From the early colonists to the pioneers on the frontier, the open spaces of America encouraged religious experiments of all kinds. Though these experiments varied considerably both in style and content, they shared certain common features, many of which stemmed from the revivals of the Second Great Awakening. The first of these common features was a belief in the perfectibility of man. Whether stemming from the optimism of the transcendentalists or the perfectionist doctrines of revivalists like Charles Finney, the innovators believed that man could raise himself up to the heights under the proper set of circumstances. Furthermore, all agreed that the heady air of freedom provided in the United States was the ideal condition for the perfecting of the human race. Thus the old Puritan idea of America as the Promised Land was reincarnated in a variety of new American gospels that purported to know what was required in order to usher in the Kingdom of God.

Perfectionism was not the only contribution made by the revival to the religious experiments of the nineteenth century, however. The Second Great Awakening had produced a religious renewal in many, but others were hardened by the perpetual emotional appeals of the revivalists. When people have been "burned over" by manipulative preaching, they often are eager to hear something new - the more bizarre, the better. Thus the Second Awakening spawned numerous aberrant forms of Christianity that are usually referred to as sects or cults. Many of the movements that grew in the soil prepared by the revivals of the nineteenth century were like weeds that grew quickly and died out just as fast. Others have proven to be more like the ubiquitous kudzu vine that threatens to overwhelm some portions of our countryside - they have grown to the point where they have become permanent fixtures on the American landscape.

UTOPIAN COMMUNITIES

When Thomas More published a description of an ideal society in 1516, he called it *Utopia*, which is Latin for "nowhere." More used his fictional community as a vehicle to take satirical jabs at the very real society in which he lived. He was wise enough to realize, however, that such a society could never exist in reality. Nineteenth-century Americans, however, entertained no such defeatist thoughts. Many were convinced that the perfect society was attainable, and some attempted to put their ideas into practice. While most were ephemeral, a few managed to outlive their founders, though not without significant changes along the way.

Some of the earliest utopian communities were transplanted from Europe. The most notable of these was the United Society of Believers in Christ's Second Appearing, better known as the Shakers. Ann Lee Stanley (1736-1784) came to America from England with a small group of followers in 1774. Part of a small sect called Shaking Quakers, they engaged in a variety of agitated movements during worship under the supposed influence of the Holy Spirit. In America, Mother Ann Lee began falling into trances in which she would receive revelations from God. The most notable of these revelations indicated that the sex act was the root of all evil, and that therefore God's children were to be celibate like the angels in heaven. Since they were living in the last days, procreation would no longer be necessary. Mother Ann also taught that she was the Second Coming of Christ - the feminine manifestation of God in the same way that Jesus had been the masculine one. After her death, former Baptist Joseph Meacham took over leadership of the movement, and under his direction the Shakers made enormous gains among the converts of the Second Awakening on both the northern and southern frontiers. For many, their message seemed the logical path to the sinless perfection promised by the revivalists. By the middle of the nineteenth century, the Shakers numbered about six thousand members in nineteen communities scattered throughout the United States. It is very difficult for a celibate society to perpetuate itself, however, and like the Manichaeans in the ancient church, the Shakers could not gain enough converts to replenish their ranks as members left the community or died. By the middle of the twentieth century, the Shakers had been reduced to a handful of elderly women seeking vainly to carry on a dying tradition.

Other communitarian groups had their origins in German Pietism. Among these were the Order of the Solitary, founded by Conrad Beissel (1690-1768) and later led by John Peter Miller (1710-1796), who established a sort of Protestant monastery in Pennsylvania known as the Ephrata Cloister; the Harmony Society or Rappites, led by George Rapp (1757-1847), who established communal farms at Harmony, Pennsylvania, New Harmony, Indiana, and Economy, Pennsylvania; and the Community of True Inspiration, which settled first in Ebenezer, New York, and later moved to Amana, Iowa, where their communal sect evolved into a prosperous corporation that now manufactures quality kitchen appliances.

Not all of the utopian communities came from Europe, however. America produced its share of home-grown idealists. Some of these gathered around a single charismatic personality, like the Society of the Public Universal Friend. Jemima Wilkinson (1752-1819), a Quaker who had been excommunicated because of her revivalist leanings, had a vision during a serious illness that led her to believe that she had died and had been reborn as the Public Universal Friend, the Publisher of Truth. Her teachings were very similar to those of the Shakers, though she seems to have had no contact with the followers of Mother Ann Lee. Like the Shakers, the Society of the Public Universal Friend slowly disappeared as the members aged; the last member died in 1874.

Perhaps the most notorious of the utopian experiments of the nineteenth century was the Oneida Community, founded by John Humphrey Noyes (1811-1886). Noyes was a convert of Finney, and was encouraged by the great revivalist to study for the ministry. After studying theology at Andover and Yale and receiving a license to preach, however, he came to the conclusion that the Second Coming had occurred with the destruction of Jerusalem in 70 A.D., which had brought the Jewish era to a close. Furthermore, he went beyond his mentor and decided that the transforming power of Christ completely separated the believer from sin - he believed himself to be sinlessly perfect. Because of these convictions, he lost his license to preach. This didn't stop him, however, and he went on to gather together a group of followers with whom he settled down in Putney, Vermont in 1838 to pursue a life of Christian perfection. Noyes soon became convinced, like the Shakers, that marriage was the root of all evil. The solution, however, was not celibacy, but what he called "complex marriage." In order to avoid the jealousies and barriers erected by exclusive marital relationships, Noyes taught that Christians should hold their wives in common as well as their possessions. Thus every woman in the community was considered to be the wife of every man, and every man was the husband of every woman. The neighbors were not amused, though Noyes couldn't understand why such a mutually loving arrangement should be viewed as promiscuous by outsiders. Growing opposition forced Noyes to move his community to the wilds of western New York, where they settled at Oneida in 1848. Despite what one might expect from a community practicing "complex marriage," few children were born at Oneida until Noyes suggested an experiment in eugenics. Thereafter, children were produced through unions planned and discussed by the community as a whole, with quite a few of them fathered by Noyes himself. Meanwhile, the community grew through an influx of outsiders (for some reason they found it easier to gain converts than the Shakers had), and became prosperous through the manufacture, first of animal traps, and later of their famous Community Plate silver-plated dinnerware. As the population of the region increased, however, the community again faced pressure from neighbors who frowned on their sexual practices, and in 1879 Noyes was forced to abandon the practice of complex marriage. A year later the community disbanded and formed a joint stock company, which like the Amana community has grown into a very prosperous corporation.

We should also note in passing a few utopian efforts that had nothing to do with either Pietism or the Second Great Awakening. The great transcendentalist Ralph Waldo Emerson once noted sardonically that every man of letters in America walked around with the plan for a communal society in his waistcoat pocket. This may have been an exaggeration, but among the transcendentalists themselves, it was close to the truth. Attempts to put these perfectionist theories into practice failed miserably, as the communities collapsed under the weight of their own misconceptions about human nature and human sinfulness. Some, like the Hopedale community (1841-1856) founded by Universalist preacher Adin Ballou and transcendentalist George Ripley's Brook Farm (1841-1847), made a go of it for a while, but others, such as the Fruitlands experiment organized by Bronson Alcott (father of novelist Louisa May Alcott) in Massachusetts in 1843, didn't even last a year.

AMERICAN CULTS

Not all of the extremist groups spawned by the Second Great Awakening failed, of course. Some, energized by leaders who trumpeted a new revelation for a new day, have continued to the present as peculiarly American contributions to the history of Christian heterodoxy. We could include in this category the Spiritist craze generated by the Fox sisters in Hydesville, New York, and publicized by P.T. Barnum, which took on a life of its own despite the later admission by Margaret Fox that the "rappings" had been produced by the girls cracking their toes! We shall concentrate our attention, however, on the four heterodox groups that went on to establish permanent organizations that have become a recognized part of the American religious scene.

A. THE CHURCH OF JESUS CHRIST OF LATTER-DAY SAINTS

No cult illustrates more clearly the dark side of revivalism in the Burned-Over District than the Church of Jesus Christ of Latter-Day Saints, commonly known as the Mormons. Joseph Smith (1805-1844), the founder of the church, was born in Sharon, Vermont, but moved at an early age with his family to Palmyra, New York, in the heart of the Burned-Over District. In Smith's own account of the experiences surrounding the beginning of the Mormons, written years after the events occurred, he speaks of "an unusual excitement on the subject of religion" in 1820 that "became general among all the sects in that region" so that "the whole district seemed affected by it, and great multitudes united themselves to different religious parties, which created no small stir and division amongst the people." Smith's family seems to have been caught up in the excitement of the revival, though the competing factions left young Joseph himself in a state of confusion. The fifteen-year-old boy decided that the only way to resolve the issue was to ask God for help, so he went out into the woods to pray. While praying, according to his account, there appeared to him two men in shining garments, standing above him in the air. They introduced themselves as God the Father and God the Son, and told him that he was to join none of the competing denominations because they were all wrong. When he returned home and began telling others about his vision, they were less than receptive; this was especially true of the local preachers.

Three years later, Smith claimed that he received a visit from an angel named Moroni, who told him of the existence of a book inscribed on golden plates and buried in the hill Cumorah, which was conveniently located just outside the town of Palmyra. Moroni did not allow him to take the plates until four years later, however. When Smith finally obtained the plates, he was given the responsibility of translating them. They were written in "Reformed Egyptian hieroglyphics," but Smith was able to translate them with the aid of gigantic spectacles containing the Urim and Thummim, the stones from the breastplate of the High Priest of ancient Israel that were used for divining purposes. Over the next year and a half, Smith periodically went behind a curtain and read the translation to an amanuensis who would then write down the words as he spoke. After the translation was completed, Moroni reclaimed the plates, though the Mormon Church claims that they were seen by numerous witnesses (it is worth noting that those who saw the plates did so in a vision, and that half of them later left the church and repudiated their testimonies).

In 1830, the translation was published as *The Book of Mormon*, and in the same year Smith organized the Church of Jesus Christ of Latter-Day Saints. He continued to claim visions that established his authority over the church, including visits from John the Baptist giving him the authority to remit sins by baptism and from Peter, James, and John giving him the power to bestow the Holy Spirit by the laying on of hands. Meanwhile, Mormon missionaries were having some success on the frontier, including enlisting former Baptist and Campbellite leader Sidney Rigdon for the cause. In 1831, Smith and his followers joined Rigdon in Kirtland, Ohio, and established a communal settlement there. When the state government refused to allow them to start a bank, Smith organized a financial institution that he called an "anti-bank," in which many invested. When it failed and all the investors lost their money in the Panic of 1837, Smith was tarred and feathered and ridden out of town on a rail. The Prophet and his followers then moved to Independence, Missouri, where another group of Mormons had settled earlier. Here they did no better, especially when Smith organized a private militia known as the Danites to protect Mormons from persecution. Fighting broke out between the Mormons and their neighbors (the "Mormon War"), and Smith fled across the border just in time to avoid being arrested for treason.

The Mormons now moved to the upper reaches of the Mississippi and established a settlement called Nauvoo (Smith claimed this was the Hebrew word for "beautiful place," though no Hebrew lexicon seems to concur). By this time they numbered about fifteen thousand, and represented the largest voting block in the sparsely-populated territory. Politicians from both parties courted them assiduously, and Smith was able to wrench from the government incredibly favorable laws that allowed Nauvoo to function almost as an independent entity, subject only to its own internal law. The settlement prospered, and by 1844 was the largest city in Illinois - even bigger than Chicago. But the Mormon militia and the peculiar ways of the citizens of Nauvoo were generating increasing fear in the non-Mormon inhabitants, a fear fueled even more by rumors of sexual irregularities among the Mormon leaders (polygamy did not become official Mormon policy until after they reached Utah, but according to the testimony of some of the women in Nauvoo, it was practiced by Smith and others even at this early date).

The extent to which absolute power had corrupted Smith's mind is illustrated by the fact that in 1844, he declared himself a candidate for the Presidency of the United States. When a newspaper published in Nauvoo criticized Smith for his ambition, the newspaper office burned to the ground the following night. In the ensuing uproar, Smith and his brother were arrested and confined in the jail in nearby Carthage, Illinois. Before they could come to trial, however, an angry mob stormed the jail and shot the two Mormon leaders.

After a brief power struggle, Brigham Young (1801-1877) gained control of the church, and led the majority of Mormons on a long and dangerous trek out of United States territory to the borders of what was then controlled by Mexico - the basin of the Great Salt Lake. In that barren land, they settled, worked hard, and prospered, away from the fears of non-Mormons who seemed unable to appreciate their peculiar faith. When the United States gained control of Utah as a result of the Mexican War, however, conflict began all over again. This time, the major problem was the Mormon practice of polygamy, which by now had become official teaching in the church. Though Brigham Young, an avowed polygamist, served as the first territorial governor of Utah, laws passed by Congress prohibited Utah from becoming a state until they repudiated plural marriage. Interestingly enough, shortly after the Supreme Court ruled that Congress indeed had the right to legislate against plural marriage, the head of the Mormon Church had a new revelation stating that polygamy was not to be practiced in the present age. The way was then clear for Utah to achieve statehood.

The Mormon Church today continues to dominate the state of Utah and portions of Nevada, Arizona, and California. They have amassed enormous wealth and wield considerable political power. In addition, the aggressive missionary policy of the Mormon Church has contributed to worldwide growth, especially in the countries of the Third World.

While it is not the purpose of this chapter to discuss the teachings of these aberrant sects, we should at least note in passing that the Book of Mormon was very much a tract for the times. It addresses and purports to give divine revelation concerning almost every major doctrinal controversy raised by the Second Great Awakening, from the role of baptism to the free will of man. Though recent evidence indicates that Smith may have borrowed the "plot" of the book, which concerns the early history of the Western Hemisphere (and teaches that American Indians are descended from Jewish stock), from an unpublished novel by Presbyterian preacher Solomon Spaulding, he clearly used the framework to give "inspired" answers to the questions troubling the people of his day. Other bizarre Mormon teachings, such as polygamy and the notion that God was once a man and that men can become gods, came later, and are found nowhere in the *Book of Mormon*.

B. THE SEVENTH-DAY ADVENTISTS

The Seventh-Day Adventists evolved out of the millennial excitement that accompanied the Second Awakening in some quarters. While the transcendentalists were convinced that the Kingdom of God would be brought to earth by human effort, others taught that only the Second Coming of Christ could save the world from its pitiful condition. One of the most remarkable preachers of this message in the first half of the nineteenth century was a Baptist farmer and lay preacher named William Miller (1782-1849). In his early years, Miller had adopted some of the rationalistic thinking popular in his day, but was converted during a revival in 1816 (not long before the "religious excitement" to which Joseph Smith referred in his testimony). Like Smith, he was confused by the contradictory claims of the various churches, and he determined to study the matter out for himself. For a period of two years after his conversion, Miller spent all his spare time studying alone in his barn, with no help except for a battered copy of *Cruden's Concordance*. His studies led him to the conclusion that Christ would return "about the year 1843." He remained quiet about his findings until 1831, when he began to spread his teachings among a few friends and local congregations. In 1833, he was licensed to preach by the Baptists. In 1838, he published his calculations in a little book called *Evidence from Scripture and History of the Second Coming of Christ, About the Year 1843*. His timing couldn't have been better. The book came out shortly after the Panic of 1837. The ensuing financial crisis convinced many that only Christ's coming could cure the world's ills. A year after the publication of his book, Miller encountered Joshua V. Himes, a creative publicist who took Miller under his wing. Soon Miller was traveling all over the country preaching to packed houses in the world's largest portable tent. By the time 1843 rolled around, over fifty thousand "Millerites" eagerly awaited the coming of Christ. Miller's followers pressed him for a specific date for the Second Coming, but he was reluctant to oblige.

MAJOR NINETEENTH-CENTURY AMERICAN CULTS

	MORMONS	ADVENTISTS		CHRISTIAN SCIENCE	JEHOVAH'S WITNESSES
OFFICIAL NAME	Church of Jesus Christ of Latter-Day Saints	Seventh-Day Adventists		Church of Christ, Scientist	Zion's Watchtower Bible and Tract Society
FOUNDER(S)	Joseph Smith, Jr. (1805-1844)	William Miller (1782-1849) [movement]	Former followers of Miller [church]	Mary Baker Glover Patterson Eddy (1821-1910)	Charles Taze Russell (1852-1916)
DATE	1830	1844	1860	1879	1884
PLACE	Harmony, PA	Upstate NY	Battle Creek, MI	Boston, MA	Pittsburgh, PA
OTHER MAJOR FIGURES	Brigham Young (1801-1877) Sidney Rigdon (1793-1876)	Hiram Edson (1806-1892) Joseph Bates (1792-1872) Ellen G. White (1827-1915)		Phineas P. Quimby (1802-1866)	Joseph F. Rutherford (1869-1942) Nathan H. Knorr (1905-1977) Frederick Franz (1895-1992)
EXTRABIBLICAL SOURCES OF AUTHORITY	*Book of Mormon* *Doctrine and Covenants* *Pearl of Great Price* Ongoing divine revelation through president of church	Writings of Ellen G. White Continuing gift of prophecy within the church		*Science and Health with Key to the Scriptures*	*New World Translation of the Holy Scriptures* Writings produced by Brooklyn, NY headquarters
DOCTRINE OF GOD	Polytheism - God was once man, man becomes god. God has a body.	Orthodox.		Pantheism - all is God. Matter does not exist.	Monotheism - doctrine of the Trinity denied.
PERSON OF CHRIST	Christ is divine, but not unique.	Orthodox.		Distinguish between Jesus (a man) and Christ (a divine idea) cf. Gnosticism.	Arian - Christ is unique but not divine, identified with Michael the Archangel, the first created being.
WORK OF CHRIST	Death of Christ erased effect of Adam's sin, thus providing for the resurrection of all people.	Atonement is substitutionary but not finished; Investigative Judgment is now determining whose sins are to be blotted out.		Christ was the great example of a scientific healing practitioner.	Ransom removes original sin from all "good and faithful" people, providing them with opportunity for everlasting life.

MAJOR NINETEENTH-CENTURY AMERICAN CULTS

	MORMONS	ADVENTISTS	CHRISTIAN SCIENCE	JEHOVAH'S WITNESSES
HOLY SPIRIT	Impersonal force.	Orthodox.	Not distinguished from God.	Impersonal force.
MAN	Man was preexistent and has innate goodness.	Orthodox (dichotomist).	Man is coeternal with God. Bodies are non-existent. Sin is imaginary.	Sin is not pervasive, merely an imperfection.
SALVATION	Comes through faith, repentance, baptism, laying on of hands, keeping commandments.	Comes through faith, keeping Mosaic law (especially Sabbath commandment).	Comes through realizing that sin and evil do not exist.	Comes through faith plus works to gain God's approval.
CHURCH	Exclusivist - after Apostle John died, church ceased to exist until 1830; only their sacraments valid.	Formerly exclusivist; now teach that all true believers will eventually keep the Ten Commandments.	Exclusivist.	Exclusivist - all others will be annihilated.
INDIVIDUAL ESCHATOLOGY	There is a second chance after death; no eternal punishment; man eventually advances to godhood.	Soul sleep and annihilation of wicked are taught.	There is probation after death, allowing growth into truth; otherwise, annihilation.	Soul sleep and annihilation of wicked are taught.
GENERAL ESCHATOLOGY	Israel (American Indians) will be restored. Millennial reign of Christ will take place from Jerusalem and Independence, MO. All people will be assigned to one of three kingdoms, according to degree of spiritual advancement.	Hold premillennial, posttribulational views. Righteous will spend eternity on renewed earth.		Christ returned in 1914. Millennial Kingdom was to begin after Armageddon in 1975. The 144,000 will spend eternity in heaven; all other Witnesses in earthly Paradise.
PRACTICE	Practice abstinence from liquor, tobacco, coffee, tea. Fasting, tithing, Sabbath-keeping required. Marriage is for time and eternity. Encourage baptism for dead relatives.	Adhere to Old Testament dietary laws. Practice Sabbath-keeping, believers' baptism by immersion, foot-washing.	Have no sacraments. Church government and teaching cannot be changed without written permission from Mrs. Eddy. All churches are linked to the Mother Church in Boston.	Teach total pacifism. Refuse to participate in government (voting, holding office, saluting flag, taking oaths, national holidays, etc.). No blood transfusions are permitted.

He originally had believed that Christ would return between March 21, 1843 and March 21, 1844 (we don't have room to go into his calculations here, but the Jews used a lunar calendar that started in the spring). When March 21, 1844 passed without incident, some of Miller's followers concluded that the correct day must be October 22, 1844 - the Jewish Day of Atonement. As the great day approached, anticipation grew; some Millerites were reported to have sold their possessions and dressed themselves in white "ascension robes" in order to be prepared for the big event. Unfortunately for Miller, the Great Day turned into the Great Disappointment. Miller's following quickly dissipated, and he died five years later, a lonely and forgotten man.

Not all of his followers gave up so easily, however. One Hiram Edson claimed to have seen a vision on the night of the Great Disappointment that showed Christ entering the Holy of Holies in the Heavenly Sanctuary. He concluded from this vision that Miller had the right date, but the wrong event. Adventists to this day believe that October 22, 1844 marked the beginning of what they call the Investigative Judgment, in which Christ is "cleansing the heavenly sanctuary" by examining the books to determine which of the dead are worthy to participate in the resurrection of the body (Adventists teach that unbelievers will be annihilated rather than going to hell). Another Millerite, Joseph Bates, published a tract in 1847 in which he argued that the two beasts of Revelation 13 were the Catholic Church and the United States government, and that the infamous "mark of the beast" was Sunday worship (apparently he was convinced that the Catholic Church was responsible for changing the day of worship from Saturday to Sunday, and blamed the U.S. government for enforcing Sunday worship through "blue laws" and other Sabbath legislation).

The various Millerite groups were finally brought together, however, through the influence of Ellen G. Harmon (1827-1915), whose family had been excommunicated from the Methodist Church because of their involvement with the Millerites. Shortly after the Great Disappointment, this teenage girl began seeing visions that she believed to be revelations from God. After marrying Adventist preacher James White in 1846, she began spreading her teaching in Millerite circles. She soon gained recognition as a prophetess, and for the rest of her life she wrote prolifically on a wide variety of subjects, religious and otherwise. Her leadership played an important role in the formation of the Seventh-Day Adventist Church in 1860, and her prophetic utterances continue today to be the basis for many of the doctrinal peculiarities associated with Seventh-Day Adventists (though they are far more orthodox than the other groups we are considering in this chapter).

One of the more interesting subjects with which Mrs. White concerned herself was the matter of health. She opposed the eating of meat, and favored many of the dietary restrictions of the Old Testament. In fact, the town of Battle Creek, Michigan, where she lived for much of her life, became the headquarters for the breakfast cereal empire of the Kellogg family - Adventists who made a fortune by encouraging people to follow Ellen G. White's advice about healthful eating (though what the company produces today is rarely considered health food). It is worth noting that the Post cereal empire also had Adventist roots.

Adventists today have spread to nations all over the world, and are noted particularly for their educational institutions and publications. The orthodoxy of many of their teachings has led some evangelicals to question whether they should still be considered a cult, or whether it might not be more appropriate to recognize them as an evangelical denomination. The fact of the matter is that Adventists themselves are seriously divided between traditionalists who are wedded firmly to Mrs. White's distinctive teachings and younger leaders who are seeking to move more into the evangelical mainstream. As long as those young leaders continue to be disciplined or even excommunicated for offenses such as teaching justification by faith alone or questioning the validity of Mrs. White's "gift of prophecy," however, it is hard to imagine how Adventists could be considered part of orthodox evangelicalism.

C. THE CHURCH OF CHRIST, SCIENTIST

The Idealism and Romanticism that characterized the early nineteenth century in both Europe and America manifested themselves in many ways, from the philosophy of Kant and Hegel to the poetry of Keats and Shelley to the music of Wagner. They also appeared in a variety of more unusual forms. In Austria, Franz Mesmer was making fantastic claims for the practice of "animal magnetism" (hypnosis) as a way of getting in touch with the ultimate reality of the universe. In Sweden, scientist and philosopher Emmanuel Swedenborg was postulating a spirit world parallel to our own and claiming to be able to communicate with its inhabitants. In America, the Spiritist craze grew from the same interests, as did the increased concern with the practice of faith healing. Phineas P. Quimby (1802-1866) became convinced that Mesmer's teachings held the key to human health. He believed that through hypnosis a person could get in touch with his inner self and discover and eradicate the corrupt thinking that led to his illness. It was not Quimby, however, but his most famous pupil, who spread the gospel of mental healing across the land.

Mary Baker (1821-1910) was born in New Hampshire, and from her youth suffered a variety of physical problems, including a painful spinal condition and some sort of nervous disorder. She married George Glover at the age of twenty-two, but he died within a year. Ten years later she married an itinerant dentist named Daniel Patterson. Their marriage was not a pleasant one, and he eventually deserted and later divorced her. It was during her marriage to Patterson, however, that she heard about Quimby and his healing techniques. She traveled to Maine to study under him, and was clearly impressed by what she heard (though she later shrugged off Quimby and his "animal magnetism" as a fraud, her teachings bear a strong resemblance to some of Quimby's own writings).

The year 1866 was a crucial year in the life of Mrs. Patterson - one in which she faced tragedy after tragedy. First, her husband left her; then she received word that her mentor Quimby had died. Finally, she fell on the ice (she claimed later that her injury was diagnosed as fatal, but the attending physician denied it). While recuperating from her fall, she occupied herself by reading the Bible. According to her account, on the third day after her fall, she read Matthew 9:1-8, was convinced that sickness and disease were as much a product of the deceitful human mind as was sin itself, and rose immediately from her bed, completely healed (again, her doctor begged to differ - she apparently remained bedridden for months after the incident in question). She then began to travel around spreading her gospel of mental healing, though at first with little success. In 1875, she published the first of hundreds of editions (many significantly revised) of *Science and Health with Key to the Scriptures*, which according to the author gives the true sense of the teachings of the Bible. In 1875, she and a few followers (including her third husband, Asa G. Eddy) formed the Church of Christ, Scientist, with Mary as founder and pastor. Two years later, she established the Massachusetts Metaphysical College in Boston to spread her teachings. In the last two decades of the nineteenth century, the sect grew quickly, though it has always been smaller than the other cults discussed in this chapter. It had a broad appeal among upper-class women, more because of its mental healing techniques than because of its doctrine, which is an almost nonsensical mysticism that denies the reality of matter, sin, disease, and even death.

In her latter years, Mary Baker Eddy became increasingly reclusive, confining herself to her stately home and visiting her church and college only rarely. Her physical condition worsened to the point that she had to take regular doses of non-existent morphine to kill the non-existent pain in her non-existent body! She kept a group of followers around her constantly to ward off the attacks of her enemies, who she believed assaulted her with Malicious Animal Magnetism (when her third husband died in 1882, she claimed he had been "mentally murdered with arsenic," and at her own death in

1910 she instructed her followers to spread the word that she had been mentally murdered).

After her death, Christian Science settled down to become a small but "respectable" movement among the American upper class. It has never grown very large, but has exerted significant influence through its publications, including the widely-respected *Christian Science Monitor*. The dead hand of Mrs. Eddy still controls the church she founded. Worship services do not include preaching, which might lead to innovation, but only the reading of the Bible, *Science and Health*, and other edifying literature. Meanwhile, the doctrines and practices of the church may not be changed without the founder's written permission.

D. ZION'S WATCHTOWER BIBLE AND TRACT SOCIETY

Unlike Christian Science, which appealed largely to upper-class New Englanders, the last of the major nineteenth-century cults has had its greatest impact among the dispossessed in the cities and towns of America. The Zion's Watchtower Bible and Tract Society, better known as the Jehovah's Witnesses, first appeared in the midst of another burst of millennial excitement similar to that which had spawned the Adventist movement a generation earlier. In fact, Charles Taze Russell (1852-1916), the founder of the cult, was influenced by a group of Adventists early in his career. Russell grew up with a terrible fear of hell, but was greatly relieved when he attended an Adventist Bible study and discovered that hell did not exist. In 1872, he started a Bible study group in Pittsburgh, Pennsylvania, and shortly thereafter proclaimed that the return of Christ would occur in 1874. This was not the last time that the founder of the Jehovah's Witnesses (or his successors) would engage in date-setting. Russell later amended his prediction of the date of the Second Coming to 1914 - a date to which Jehovah's Witnesses continue to hold today (they believe Christ's coming was secret and "spiritual"). In 1879, he began publishing a magazine called *Zion's Watchtower*, and in 1884 he incorporated his group as the Zion's Watchtower Bible and Tract Society. Russell was a prolific writer, and published a number of works, including the six-volume *Studies in the Scriptures*, which contain many of the peculiar teachings of the Jehovah's Witnesses. He also introduced the practices of house-to-house witnessing and home Bible studies for which the group would later become notorious.

During the period of Russell's leadership, the group remained relatively small, partly because of the repeated scandals in which Russell became involved. He went through a messy divorce in 1903. In 1913, he generated quite a bit of money by selling Miracle Wheat and Millennial Beans, which were supposedly superior to the everyday garden variety. When the scam was exposed by a newspaper, Russell sued, but lost the case. Later that same year, he filed suit against a Toronto pastor, J.J. Ross, who had criticized Russell's teachings in a published pamphlet. Ross, who had accused Russell of making false statements about the wording and meaning of the Greek New Testament, won the case when his attorney was able to prove that Russell's claim to know New Testament Greek was patently false.

When Russell died in 1916, Joseph F. ("Judge") Rutherford (1869-1942), Russell's attorney during his legal troubles, assumed leadership of the cult. Rutherford brought new stability to the group, though it was still essentially a personality cult. The Judge's writings now became the authoritative teaching of the group. He even provided Witnesses with portable phonographs that they could carry around with them as they went door-to-door, enabling them to play one of Rutherford's lectures to any who would listen. It was Judge Rutherford who changed the name of the group to Jehovah's Witnesses in 1931. Since "Zion's Watchtower Bible and Tract Society" is rather unwieldy, most people referred to the cult simply as "Russellites" - an identification that Rutherford wanted to remove as quickly as possible. Rutherford's greatest contribution to the group came through his perpetual legal efforts on their behalf. During his career he won over two hundred court cases that gained for the Witnesses the right to exercise their freedom of speech and freedom of religion by spreading their peculiar gospel from door to door without interference from police.

With Rutherford's death in 1942, the cult entered its greatest period of growth under the unassuming leadership of Nathan H. Knorr (1903-1977). Knorr ended the emphasis on personality, instituting a policy by which all publications coming out of the group's Brooklyn headquarters would be anonymous. He also replaced the phonographs with a series of intensive training sessions that prepared all Witnesses to answer the vast majority of questions they might face while going door to door. Knorr was also responsible, along with his long-time associate Frederick Franz (who became president of the group when Knorr died in 1977), for the *New World Translation of the Holy Scriptures* (1955, revised 1961), which incorporates the distinctive teachings of the Jehovah's Witnesses into an incredibly wooden translation of the Bible.

Today, Jehovah's Witnesses continue their aggressive evangelism in America and in countries all over the world. They are strongly anti-authoritarian in their message, teaching that governments and churches are of the devil (though the teachings of the cult are to be accepted without question). They also preach an egalitarian gospel - they have long opposed racism of any kind, and all male members are considered ministers. In recent years, they have made significant inroads among the blacks in the American inner cities, while growing to alarming proportions in many countries of the Third World.

As far as their doctrine is concerned, the Witnesses have borrowed most of their distinctives from other groups. Their teachings of soul sleep and annihilation of the wicked come directly from Seventh-Day Adventism, while their denial of the deity of Christ (they teach instead that He was the first of God's creatures) merely repeats the Arian heresy from the early years of church history. They have persisted in setting dates, the most recent of which involved a long-standing prediction that the world would end in a nuclear holocaust in 1975.

MAKING DRY BONES LIVE

Despite P.T. Barnum's assertion that "There's a sucker born every minute," it is in some ways difficult to understand the growth of movements like those we have examined in this chapter. The difficulty becomes even more acute after examining their teachings in any detail. How, one asks, could anyone possibly believe such transparent drivel? Such a question misses the point, however. In general, people do not join cults as a result of a rational evaluation of their teachings. Instead, their involvement usually stems from some emotional need or personal experience.

The most obvious example of this sort of thing may be found in Christian Science. Their doctrine, despite its pseudo-intellectual aura, is complete nonsense; those who turn to Christian Science do so because in it they have found relief from pain and sickness. Doctors now realize that a great deal of physical suffering is closely tied to a person's mental and emotional state. For some, the Christian Science teaching that "disease is all in your head" is true, and after they are "healed" through reorienting their thinking, they become "true believers." For such people, nonsensical theology is no deterrent.

Other groups, such as Jehovah's Witnesses and Mormons (and more recently the members of Sun Myung Moon's Unification Church) offer acceptance within a caring community to those who feel estranged from society. A person who finds people who are willing to love him as he is will believe almost anything those people tell him. In this sense, the cults exist as both a rebuke to the church for its failure to reach out to society's disenfranchised millions and a Satanic counterfeit of what the church is intended to be.

Lastly, the cults succeed for the reason false religions have always succeeded - they convince lost sinners that their salvation is in their own hands. Whether that salvation may be attained through Sabbath-keeping, literature distribution, baptism, plural marriage, or right thinking, it is something I am able to do for myself. Thus the devil's lie continues to turn millions of men and women away from their only hope of salvation - the grace of God that may be found only in Jesus Christ.

FOR REVIEW AND FURTHER THOUGHT

1. What aspects of the Second Great Awakening contributed to the growth of cults in the nineteenth century?

2. What was the relationship between the Shakers and the Quakers?

3. What were the distinctive doctrines of the Shakers?

4. What was the major factor in the decline of the Shaker movement?

5. How did Pietism influence the communitarian movement in nineteenth-century America?

6. What did Ann Lee Stanley and Jemima Wilkinson have in common?

7. Describe John Humphrey Noyes' doctrine of "complex marriage."

8. Why do you think so many bizarre religious groups have unusual teachings about sex?

9. What was the major cause of the failure of the transcendentalist-sponsored communal experiments?

10. What misunderstanding about man do all groups that hope to create a perfect society have in common?

11. What are the more common names of the Church of Jesus Christ of Latter-Day Saints, the Church of Christ, Scientist, and the Watchtower Bible and Tract Society?

12. Identify the following in one sentence each: Moroni, Cumorah, Urim and Thummim, Sidney Rigdon, Danites.

13. What aspects of Mormon life generated opposition among their neighbors?

14. What function did the *Book of Mormon* play in the development of the Mormon Church?

15. Was William Miller right to try to understand the Bible without human help? Why or why not?

16. What is the Adventist doctrine of the Investigative Judgment?

17. What was the source of the Adventists' "seventh-day" doctrine?

18. How did Ellen G. White contribute to the American way of eating breakfast?

19. What elements separate Adventists from the mainstream of evangelical Christianity?

20. How did Franz Mesmer and Emmanuel Swedenborg influence American movements like Spiritism and Christian Science?

21. What is animal magnetism?

Weeds in Fertile Ground

22. What were some of the circumstances that led Mary Baker Eddy to "discover" the principles of Christian Science?

23. What aspect of Christian Science is most responsible for its ability to attract followers?

24. What were the major contributions made to the development of the Jehovah's Witnesses by their first three presidents?

25. What scandals involving the founder brought disrepute to the Jehovah's Witnesses?

26. What aspects of Jehovah's Witnesses' teaching have made them popular among the poor and downtrodden?

27. What Jehovah's Witness teachings were borrowed from other groups we have studied?

28. What factors lead people to join bizarre cults?

29. In what sense may cults be viewed as Satanic counterfeits of the true church?

30. In what sense does the existence of cults demonstrate an area of failure on the part of the church?

31. Why do people find the doctrine of salvation by works attractive?

ROOTS OF AMERICAN FUNDAMENTALISM

By all accounts, the nineteenth century in America was not an era of profound theological discourse. The great religious movements of the nineteenth century, such as the Second Great Awakening and the revivalism it spawned, had a decidedly experiential slant and often devoted little or no serious attention to theological issues. By the end of the century, however, the great theological controversy of our own age - that between liberalism and fundamentalism - was beginning to emerge. In this chapter, we want to devote our attention to the two lines of theological thought that were to have the greatest impact on American fundamentalism - the Princeton theology and dispensational premillennialism.

THE PRINCETON THEOLOGY

The nineteenth century was an age of great educational advances in America, and witnessed the founding of many colleges and seminaries. None had a greater impact on the American religious scene, however, than the theological seminary opened by the General Assembly of the Presbyterian Church in Princeton, New Jersey in 1812. With the opening of the frontier, the shortage of qualified pastors became acute for denominations like the Presbyterians and Congregationalists that required candidates for the ministry to have a theological education. Princeton University simply was not producing enough trained pastors. When Andover Seminary, founded by Congregationalists, began generating a steady stream of pastors for the frontier, the Presbyterians decided that they needed a seminary of their own. The General Assembly then invited Archibald Alexander (1772-1851), a Philadelphia pastor who had previously served as president of Hampden-Sydney College in Virginia, to become the new school's first professor. Alexander was joined in 1813 by Samuel Miller, and in 1820 by one of the school's first graduates, Charles Hodge (1797-1878), who more than any other single man was responsible for the theology that came to be associated with Princeton Seminary.

It is important to note that what has come to be known as the Princeton Theology was not an innovation of any kind. In fact, what made it remarkable was the very fact that it was *not* new. While the successors of Jonathan Edwards in New England were spreading the New Divinity and Charles G. Finney was trumpeting his revivalistic New Measures, Charles Hodge and the other Princeton theologians adhered stubbornly to classical Calvinism, especially in the form expounded in the Westminster Standards and in the systematic theology of Francis Turretin, a seventeenth-century Swiss defender of Calvinist orthodoxy. When Charles Hodge published his own three-volume *Systematic Theology* near the end of his fifty-year teaching career, it followed closely the format of Turretin's text, which Hodge had used to instruct over three thousand students in the doctrines of the Christian faith. Thus when Hodge asserted that, in fifty years at Princeton, he had never once taught a new idea, he was simply proclaiming his faithfulness to historic Christian orthodoxy - a faithfulness that more than anything else is the hallmark of the Princeton Theology.

What, then, makes the Princeton Theology so significant? The refusal of the

Princeton theologians to modify or compromise the traditional doctrines of evangelical Christianity brought them into constant conflict with those who sought change in the church. In the early years of the seminary's existence, the chief enemies of orthodoxy were Unitarian rationalism, New Divinity "Arminianism," and the perfectionism and man-centered emphases of the revivalists of the Second Great Awakening. By the end of the nineteenth century, new challenges to the faith had emerged, including the theory of evolution, liberal criticism of Scripture, and the Social Gospel. It was the effectiveness of the Princeton theologians in developing intelligent, thoughtful, biblical responses to these challenges that more than anything else gave them their place of prominence in the history of the American church.

Who, then, were these Princeton theologians, and what were the battles in which they fought to defend the historic Christian faith? Archibald Alexander was the guiding light of the seminary in its early years, and he not only shaped the school's curriculum, but also endowed the seminary with something of his own gentleness of character. Particularly in the years of strife between Old School and New School Presbyterians, the men of Princeton, though sympathizing fully with the Old School's theological position, sought to moderate the harshness with which the members of the New School were often treated by their Old School brethren.

Charles Hodge, too, was deeply involved in the controversy between the Old School and the New School. Though he spoke with a voice of moderation both at the time of the dissolution of the Plan of Union in 1837 and throughout the controversy over slavery, his defense of traditional Calvinism brought him into constant conflict with the advocates of revivalism in the New School. He was particularly critical of Finney and his "New Measures," arguing that they were Arminian at best and Pelagian at worst. When Hodge published his three-volume *Systematic Theology* near the end of his career, it showed the influence, not only of Turretin and the Westminster Confession of Faith, but also of a philosophy known as Scottish Common Sense Realism, which led him to support each doctrine he discussed with parallel biblical and rational arguments. Two of Hodge's sons, Caspar Wistar Hodge (1830-1891) and Archibald Alexander Hodge (1823-1886), followed him at Princeton, with the latter succeeding his father as Professor of Theology.

One of the more remarkable disputes to arise in the Presbyterian Church during Hodge's tenure at Princeton was that surrounding revival preacher, commentator, and abolitionist Albert Barnes (1798-1870). Barnes grew up in the Methodist Church, but became a Presbyterian while attending Princeton Seminary. After graduation, he became the pastor of a Presbyterian church in Morristown, New Jersey, where he soon stirred up considerable controversy with his revival preaching and his denial of original sin. When he moved to a prominent church in Philadelphia, opposition to his preaching intensified, and he was charged with heresy. He was acquitted, but immediately got himself into deeper trouble by publishing a commentary on the book of Romans (the first volume of the famous *Barnes' Notes*), which clearly contradicted the church's confessional stance in a number of areas. His opponents again charged him with heresy, and his case contributed directly to the schism between the Old School and the New School in 1837. Albert Barnes illustrated clearly the connection between the revivalism of the nineteenth century and a theology that emphasized man's ability and duty to respond to the free offer of the Gospel.

If during Charles Hodge's day, Arminianism was the great enemy of orthodoxy, his successors faced a far more formidable foe in the form of liberal theology, which was gradually working its way westward from Germany. It was left to A.A. Hodge and his successor, Benjamin Breckinridge Warfield (1851-1921), to uphold the standard of Princeton orthodoxy against this latest onslaught. Warfield is best known for his defense of the inspiration and inerrancy of Scripture against the attacks of the liberal critics, though he also wrote a well-known critique of Pentecostalism in which he argued that speaking in tongues was a gift reserved for the apostolic age. His wide-ranging writings, added to those of his predecessors, helped put the fundamentalist movement on a firm intellectual footing as the great battles of the twentieth century approached. In the long run, however, Princeton Seminary became a casualty in that battle. As we will see in the next chapter, the seminary quickly collapsed into liberalism after the death of Warfield.

If the case of Albert Barnes best illustrates the watered-down theology of revivalism against which Charles Hodge struggled, the heresy trials of Charles Augustus Briggs (1841-1913), Henry Preserved Smith (1847-1927), and Arthur C. McGiffert (1861-1933) reveal the forces of liberalism arrayed against the Princeton theologians during the Warfield era. Briggs was a professor of Old Testament at Union Theological Seminary in New York, a school with ties to the Presbyterian Church. He established an international reputation for Hebrew scholarship with his work with Francis Brown and S.R. Driver on the *Hebrew and English Lexicon of the Old Testament*. In 1891, however, he was appointed to the chair of Biblical Theology at Union Seminary. In his inaugural address, he attacked the inspiration and inerrancy of Scripture and advocated the methods and conclusions of higher criticism (see chapter thirty-one). Conservatives in the denomination promptly charged him with heresy, but both Union Seminary and the New York presbytery defended him. Finally the case was appealed to the General Assembly, where in 1893 Briggs was condemned of heresy and deprived of his ministerial credentials. The fact that Union Seminary broke its ties with the Presbyterian Church rather than lose a scholar of Briggs' caliber indicates something about the state of Union; that Briggs was ordained by the Episcopal Church after losing his Presbyterian ordination says something about the condition of the Episcopal Church.

The Smith and McGiffert cases were similar, though less spectacular. Smith, a professor at Lane Seminary in Cincinnati, spoke out in support of Briggs and his teachings. He, too, was ousted from the Presbyterian ministry, but received support from his colleagues at the seminary, and was later ordained by the Congregationalists. McGiffert, a professor of Church History, moved from Lane to Union shortly after the Briggs fiasco. A few years later, he published a history of the early church in which he denied the authenticity of certain books of the New Testament. Conservatives again objected, but McGiffert resigned from the Presbyterian ministry in order to avoid a heresy trial. He remained at Union Seminary, however, and eventually became the president of that institution.

In response to these struggles with theological liberalism, the Presbyterian Church adopted a series of statements reaffirming its belief in the foundational doctrines of orthodox Christianity. These included the Portland Deliverance of 1892, which required ministerial candidates to believe and preach the inerrancy of the original manuscripts of the Bible, and the declaration of the General Assembly in 1910 that a man must affirm five fundamental doctrines (the inerrancy of Scripture, the Virgin Birth, the bodily resurrection of Christ, the substitutionary atonement, and the reality of the miracles recorded in Scripture) in order to serve as a Presbyterian pastor. These official declarations of the Presbyterian Church contributed directly to the movement known as Fundamentalism, which we will examine in the next chapter.

DISPENSATIONALISM IN AMERICA

We have already mentioned the origins of dispensationalism in chapter thirty-two, where we looked briefly at John Nelson Darby and the Plymouth Brethren. We saw that Darby made numerous trips to America, where to his considerable dismay, his eschatology caught on while his ecclesiology did not. That eschatology was to become one of the most identifiable aspects of twentieth-century fundamentalism.

As we saw earlier, dispensationalism divided history into periods of time (seven is the number used most often, though the number of dispensations varies among those who teach the system), each of which begins with and is defined by the terms of a covenant between God and man. This covenant sets forth the requirements by which man is to live in that particular dispensation (some examples would be the dispensation of human government under the covenant with Noah, the dispensation of promise under the covenant with Abraham, and the dispensation of law under the covenant given to Moses at Mount Sinai). Each dispensation ends with man's failure to keep God's covenant, and God's resulting judgment. The present age, the age of the church, is also doomed to failure. Dispensationalists take a very pessimistic view of both the world and the church in these "Last Days," and believe that both will continue to get worse until the return of Christ at the end of the present dispensation. When Christ returns, He will take His people out of this world, and this Rapture of the Church will initiate the Great Tribulation, a period of intense suffering during which the world will fall into the hands of the Antichrist, but which will also witness a full-scale conversion of the Jewish people. The Tribulation will end in the great Battle of Armageddon, after which Christ will reign on earth with His saints for a thousand years - the Millennium, the last of earth's dispensations. This, too, will end in failure, as Satan will mount a final rebellion, which will be put down immediately prior to the Last Judgment and the inauguration of the New Heavens and the New Earth.

How did these teachings become such an important part of American evangelicalism? While Darby's visits to America played a significant part in disseminating his ideas, the man who played the most prominent early role was Presbyterian pastor James H. Brookes (1830-1897), who was the moving force behind the Niagara Bible Conferences, which did much to spread dispensational views of prophecy in the closing decades of the nineteenth century. Brookes wrote many books, including *Maranatha*, one of the most popular early explanations of dispensationalism. Other prominent early dispensationalists included William J. Erdman (1834-1923), hymn-writers Philip P. Bliss (1838-1876) and Daniel W. Whittle (1840-1901), Adoniram Judson Gordon (1836-1895), the founder of the school for missionaries that later bore his name, Jewish evangelists William E. Blackstone (1841-1935) and Arno C. Gaebelein (1861-1945), and Reuben A. Torrey (1856-1928).

The early dispensationalists also spread their ideas through Bible schools and institutes, such as Moody Bible Institute (founded in 1886), the Bible Institute of Los Angeles (BIOLA - 1907), and the Philadelphia College of the Bible (1914), all of which continue today to be bastions of dispensational teaching. The greatest of the dispensational schools, of course, is Dallas Theological Seminary, founded in 1924 by Lewis Sperry Chafer (1871-1952). Chafer provided the most extensive exposition of dispensationalism to date in his eight-volume *Systematic Theology*, while also serving as editor of Dallas Seminary's theological journal, *Bibliotheca Sacra*.

By far the greatest popularizer of dispensationalism, however, was Cyrus Ingerson Scofield (1843-1921). Scofield grew up in Tennessee and served under Robert E. Lee in the Civil War. He studied law after the war, served briefly in the Kansas House of Representatives, and was later U.S. attorney in St. Louis, Missouri. He was converted in 1879 under the ministry of James H. Brookes in St. Louis, after which he gave up his law practice in order to pastor churches in Dallas and Northfield, Massachusetts. While speaking at a Bible conference at Sea Cliff, Long Island (the successor of the Niagara Conference), he was encouraged by Arno C. Gaebelein to prepare an annotated Reference Bible. Scofield agreed that such a tool was needed, and began to work on a set of explanatory notes. These notes were first published as the Scofield Reference Bible in 1909 (revised 1917). The work was an immediate success, and quickly came into widespread use among fundamentalists. The notes, of course, taught dispensationalism, and through the Scofield Reference Bible the dispensational interpretation of biblical prophecy spread throughout the evangelical community. The notes did contain some problems, including the notorious comment implying that Old Testament saints were saved by works, but these were largely corrected with the publication of the New Scofield Reference Bible in 1967.

A COMPARISON OF HISTORIC COVENANT AND HISTORIC DISPENSATIONAL THEOLOGY

ISSUE	COVENANT POSITION	DISPENSATIONAL POSITION
PATTERN OF HISTORY	Covenant of Works with Adam; Covenant of Grace with Christ on behalf of the elect (some distinguish between Covenant of Redemption with Christ and Covenant of Grace with the elect).	Divided into dispensations (usually seven); e.g., Innocence (pre-Fall), Conscience (Adam), Human Government (Noah); Promise (Abraham), Law (Moses), Grace (Christ's First Coming), Kingdom (Christ's Second Coming).
VIEW OF HISTORY	Optimistic; God is extending His kingdom.	Pessimistic; the Last Days are marked by increasingly worse wickedness in the world and by apostasy in the church.
GOD'S PURPOSE IN HISTORY	There is a unified redemptive purpose.	There are two distinct purposes, one earthly (Israel), one heavenly (Church).
VIEW OF THE BIBLICAL COVENANTS	They are different administrations of the Covenant of Grace.	They mark off periods of time during which God's specific demands of man differ.
RELATIONSHIP OF OLD TESTAMENT TO NEW TESTAMENT	Acceptance of Old Testament teaching required unless specifically abrogated by New Testament.	Old Testament prescriptions are not binding unless reaffirmed in New Testament.
RELATIONSHIP BETWEEN ISRAEL AND THE CHURCH	The church is spiritual Israel, in continuity with true Israel of Old Testament.	The church is the spiritual people of God, distinct from Israel, the physical people of God.
OLD TESTAMENT PROPHECY	Refers to God's people, the church.	Refers to ethnic Israel.
CHURCH AGE	God's redemptive purpose continued to unfold.	There is a parenthesis between past and future manifestations of the kingdom.
ROLE OF THE HOLY SPIRIT	The Holy Spirit indwells God's people throughout history.	The Holy Spirit indwells God's people only from Pentecost to the Rapture.
BAPTISM	Unified covenant generally used to support infant baptism by analogy with circumcision.	Israel/Church distinction often (but not always) used to support believers' baptism.
SOCIAL IMPLICATIONS	Emphasized "Cultural Mandate."	The only way to save the world is to save individuals, therefore evangelism takes precedence over "social action."
ESCHATOLOGY	Usually amillennial; rarely postmillennial; occasionally premillennial.	Premillennial, usually pretribulational.
MILLENNIUM	Symbolic, often identified with present age.	Literal, earthly 1000-year reign after Second Coming.

MAKING DRY BONES LIVE

If the Princeton Theology provided fundamentalism with its link to the orthodox Christianity of centuries past, dispensationalism gave that orthodoxy a new twist. For many Americans today who have been raised in fundamentalist circles, the dispensationalist picture of the future is very familiar - in fact, they may never have heard any other ideas on the subject, and often assume that all true Christians believe these things. Few realize the extent to which this teaching is a novelty, and fewer still recognize its implications for the church and its role in society.

In the first place, dispensational eschatology is a novelty because of its teaching of the pretribulational rapture. As noted in chapter thirty-two, this teaching was completely unknown in the church prior to the nineteenth century. Newness does not make the doctrine wrong or even unbiblical, of course, but one might at least have reason to examine a doctrine more carefully if no student of God's Word had been able to discern it for almost two millennia of Christian history. The reason I take time to emphasize the novelty of the doctrine of the pretribulational rapture is that many fundamentalists today continue to make it a test of fellowship, refusing to acknowledge the orthodoxy of those who view the future of the church differently. If truly orthodox believers must accept the doctrine of the pretribulational rapture, what are we to think of all the great Christians who lived before 1800?

Secondly, it is important to recognize the novelty of dispensational eschatology because of the universal nature of the church. Too many American Christians assume that all evangelicals are dispensationalists. The truth of the matter is quite different. The fact is that dispensationalism, while popular in America, is virtually unknown outside of our country except among the Plymouth Brethren, and in those places in the world where it has been transplanted by American missionaries. Most Christians throughout the world have never even heard of those issues to which many American fundamentalists devote so much time and attention, and which they all too often use to define the orthodoxy of others.

It is also important to recognize the implications of the pessimistic view of the church and the world produced by dispensationalist teaching. Dispensationalist pessimism about the course of world events - the idea that sin will increase and the world will get increasingly worse in the days before the Great Tribulation - has often produced among devotees of the system a lack of concern for social problems. If society is destined to irreversible decline, efforts to improve society cannot succeed, and are a waste of the church's precious resources. Besides, if we are truly living in the Last Days, all of the church's efforts should be directed toward evangelism. Saving men's souls is what really counts. In many cases such an attitude has produced a false dichotomy between the spiritual and physical needs of the lost, and led to a situation where Christians isolate themselves from society and its needs.

Dispensationalists are pessimistic about the church as well as the world. According to dispensationalist teaching, the church will become increasingly corrupt in the Last Days, with false teaching dominating to the point that the church will actually contribute to the coming to power of the Antichrist. This teaching is not in itself new - the Protestant Reformers identified the Catholic Church as Babylon the Great, and thought that the Pope was the Antichrist. In addition, the growth of liberalism in the twentieth century has provided considerable evidence of the church's decline. Yet pessimism about the church should not lead Christians to abandon the church in favor of an individualistic brand of Christianity that rejects all authority. After all, the church is still under the control of its Head, Jesus Christ, and He has promised that the gates of Hell will not prevail against it. What God is accomplishing in this world, He is doing through His Church, not in spite of it.

FOR REVIEW AND FURTHER THOUGHT

1. Why is the nineteenth century in America not known as a period of great theological discourse?

2. What were the major contributions to the history of Princeton Theological Seminary made by Archibald Alexander, Charles Hodge, and B.B. Warfield?

3. What was the Princeton Theology, and why was it important?

4. What did Charles Hodge mean when he said that he had never taught anything new in his years at Princeton? How do you think his critics interpreted his statement?

5. What were the main challenges to orthodoxy faced by the Princeton theologians in the Hodge era? the Warfield era?

6. What were the heresies with which Barnes and Briggs were charged? Which do you consider to be more serious, and why?

7. What do the heresy trials of Barnes and Briggs indicate about the changes that occurred on the American religious scene during the nineteenth century?

8. How did the Princeton Theology contribute to the eventual development of Fundamentalism?

9. What was the Portland Deliverance, and how do you suspect it might have been used in the heresy trial of Charles A. Briggs?

10. Summarize briefly in your own words the eschatology of dispensationalism.

11. In what ways did James H. Brookes play an important role in the spread of dispensationalism in America?

12. Many dispensationalists have been active in Jewish evangelism. Why do you think this is true?

13. What were the most important contributions of Lewis Sperry Chafer to the spread of dispensationalism?

14. How did the Scofield Reference Bible contribute to the dissemination of dispensational views?

15. In what sense is dispensationalism a new teaching in the history of the church?

16. Do you think it is appropriate to make a single doctrine a test of fellowship? If so, what must be true of that doctrine? If not, why not?

17. Where in the church today is dispensational teaching prevalent?

18. How does the pessimistic view of the world associated with dispensationalism influence a person's definition of the role of the church?

19. How does pessimism about the future of society tend to isolate Christians from the world in which they live?

20. How does dispensationalist pessimism about the church itself tend to downplay the importance of the church in the ongoing work of God in the world?

43

THE BATTLE FOR THE BIBLE

In 1907, German Baptist pastor Walter Rauschenbusch wrote a book entitled *Christianity and the Social Crisis*, in which he identified the true aim of the Christian church as the revitalization of society by means of the principles of the Kingdom of God.

"As we have seen, the industrial and commercial life to-day is dominated by principles antagonistic to the fundamental principles of Christianity, and it is so difficult to live a Christian life in the midst of it that few men even try. If production could be organized on a basis of cooperative fraternity; if distribution could at least approximately be determined by justice; if all men could be conscious that their labor contributed to the welfare of all and that their personal well-being was dependent on the prosperity of the Commonwealth; if predatory business and parasitic wealth ceased and all men lived only by their labor; if the luxury of unearned wealth no longer made us all feverish with covetousness and a simpler life became the fashion; if our time and strength were not used up either in getting a bare living or in amassing unusable wealth and we had more leisure for the higher pursuits of the mind and the soul - then there might be a chance to live such a life of gentleness and brotherly kindness and tranquility of heart as Jesus desired for men. It may be that the cooperative Commonwealth would give us the first chance in history to live a really Christian life without retiring from the world, and would make the Sermon on the Mount a philosophy of life feasible for all who care to try."

Such a reduction of Christianity to ethical living was common among the liberals of the late nineteenth and early twentieth centuries, though not all advocated the radical form of socialism espoused by Rauschenbusch. Quite naturally, evangelical Christians reacted against liberal attempts to truncate the faith. The resulting conflict, between liberals (or modernists) and fundamentalists, tore many denominations and other Christian organizations apart, and did much to determine the character of the American church and the direction of American church history in the twentieth century.

LIBERALISM AND THE SOCIAL GOSPEL

The evangelical revivalism that dominated the American churches of the nineteenth century faced four severe challenges as that century drew to a close. The first of these challenges came from Darwinism. When Darwin wrote *The Origin of Species* in 1859, it drew little attention in America because everyone was preoccupied with the impending Civil War. Once the war was over, however, people began to recognize that Darwin's theory directly contradicted the biblical picture of Creation. While evangelicals like Princeton's Charles Hodge spoke out strongly against the theory of evolution, other prominent Christian spokesmen, such as Henry Ward Beecher (son of Lyman Beecher and brother of Harriet Beecher Stowe), a leading Congregational pastor in New York, were willing to adopt the new scientific view of biological development as a description of the way God did His work. They argued that the real significance of the Bible - its moral teaching

- was not at all compromised by the discovery that its pages reflected a primitive, prescientific view of the world. If Darwin undermined the historicity of the Fall, they sensed no great loss, since such preachers had long ago rejected the doctrine of original sin. Darwinism even gave scientific support to their optimistic belief in human perfectibility, and they enthusiastically glorified man as the pinnacle of evolution. What they failed to recognize, of course, was that Darwinism undermined the biblical teaching of the uniqueness of man. In our own day, we can clearly see, in the absence of moral standards in our society, the effects of the belief that man is no more than an animal.

The second major challenge to the revivalistic Christianity of the nineteenth century came from the higher criticism of the Bible. We saw in chapter thirty-one the development of biblical criticism in Germany. By the end of the nineteenth century, these teachings had made their way to America, largely through theological students who had received their training in German universities. If Darwin taught that man was just like any other animal, the liberal critics taught that the Bible was just like any other book. They undermined the authority of Scripture by questioning first the authorship of certain books (the Pentateuch, part of Isaiah, and Daniel were among the earliest to be questioned), then the historicity of certain biblical narratives (by the time we reach the middle of the twentieth century, it is a rarity when a liberal critic is willing to admit that *anything* in the Bible is historical).

The assault of the liberal critics posed a major threat to Protestants. Since the time of the Reformation, Protestants had taught that each man is capable of interpreting the Bible for himself, under the guidance of the Holy Spirit. By denying the mediatorial role of either church or clergy, Protestantism left the Bible as the only visible, earthly link between man and God. An attack on the reliability of Scripture, therefore, was a strike against the very foundations of orthodox Protestantism. Liberals did not view their actions in this light, however. Instead of seeing themselves as destroyers of the faith, they viewed themselves as liberators who were crusading to free the church from the bonds of tradition so that it could fulfill its true purpose - the elevation of man and society. For the liberal critics, the church could only be effective in this world if it shook off its preoccupation with the world to come.

A third assault came from the social sciences. Auguste Comte and Sigmund Freud, with their pioneering work in sociology and psychology respectively, undermined evangelical Christianity by giving alternative explanations for religious behavior. After all, if conversion experiences may be explained in terms of psychological forces operating within a person's mind, why do we need to speak any longer of the work of the Holy Spirit? If the gathering of people into churches may be explained in terms of the social needs of the human organism, why should we continue to speak of Christ as the head of the church in any more than a figurative sense?

The fourth and final challenge that faced the church at the end of the nineteenth century was the changing social situation. The growth of cities and the rapid industrialization of the country produced a new set of problems with which the church was in many ways unequipped to deal. Revivalism had been very effective at dealing with moral issues relating to individuals, such as slavery and alcohol, but social sins were a bit more elusive. The pro-business conservatism of the Gilded Age had spawned poverty, slums, and misery that seemed beyond the scope of church and state alike.

Some in the churches responded to these challenges by following the path of liberalism. These Christians chose to embrace the findings of biblical scholars and natural and social scientists with enthusiasm, and approached eagerly what they saw as the opportunity to remold the church in a way that addressed the needs of modern society. In order to do so, they were more than willing to relegate doctrinal considerations to a secondary status. They really believed that such an approach was the only way to save the church from destruction at the hands of cynical skeptics such as Robert G. Ingersoll (1833-1899), an agnostic who lectured widely and made a handsome living by ridiculing religion in general and Christianity in particular.

By the end of the nineteenth century, liberalism dominated most of the theological schools founded in the early years of the Second Great Awakening. From the Congregational school of theology at Andover to the Presbyterian schools in Cincinnati (Lane) and New York (Union) to the great Baptist seminary in Chicago (University of Chicago Divinity School), the voice of liberalism filled the pulpits and bookstores throughout the land. Among the established seminaries in the north and midwest, only Princeton held out against the liberal tide, though, unfortunately, not for long.

Though many theological liberals were also social conservatives, preaching a Gospel of Wealth and supporting Herbert Spencer's Social Darwinism (a sort of economic "survival of the fittest" that encouraged a free market that would allow the best to prosper, while the unfit would justly suffer the poverty produced by their own laziness), one particular group of liberals became known as advocates of radical social reform. These men preached what came to be called the Social Gospel. The fundamental goal of the Social Gospel movement was the conversion of society and its institutions. They believed that applying the principles of the Sermon on the Mount to the problems of business, labor, and government would usher in the Kingdom of God. The Social Gospel preachers tended to reject capitalism in favor of socialism, and sought with a fervor equal to that of the Puritans to turn America into the Promised Land.

The Social Gospel movement was never large, but gained widespread attention through the efforts of some of its most influential advocates. Among these were Congregational pastor Washington Gladden (1836-1918), who ministered in Columbus, Ohio, and wrote many books advocating the Social Gospel; Walter Rauschenbusch (1861-1918), German Baptist pastor and professor at Rochester Theological Seminary, whose words formed the introduction to this chapter; and Charles M. Sheldon (1857-1946), Congregational pastor and editor of *Christian Herald*. Gladden had in some ways the most direct impact on his own day, largely through his efforts in support of unions in Columbus and his attempts to give his denomination a social conscience (he once encouraged the Congregationalists to turn down a large donation from Standard Oil because he considered it to be "tainted money"). Rauschenbusch was the theologian of the movement, and had perhaps the greatest influence of any of the Social Gospellers beyond his own lifetime. His books on *Christianizing the Social Order* and *A Theology for the Social Gospel* had a great influence on a more recent Baptist social reformer named Martin Luther King. Sheldon, the greatest disseminator of the Social Gospel on the popular level, is best known for a novel he wrote in 1897 called *In His Steps*. The book, which became a best-seller, described a small-town congregation where the people were challenged by their pastor to make all their decisions by asking themselves the question, "What would Jesus do?" While such a question undoubtedly can be a valuable guide for Christian living, there is great danger when ethical behavior becomes the standard by which Christianity is defined. A person who tries to follow the example of Jesus is not necessarily a Christian. Such a blatant advocacy of salvation by works, along with its naively rosy view of man and society, doomed the Social Gospel to failure. The death blow to the unwarranted optimism of the liberals was delivered by the bloody horror known as the First World War.

FUNDAMENTALISM

Not all Christians were willing to follow the liberals down the path to secularism and socialism, however. Many stood firmly for the historic Christian faith, and opposed the incursions of Darwinism, biblical criticism, and the social sciences. These people have come to be known as fundamentalists. Like the liberals, they drew support from a variety of denominations. Fundamentalism was essentially a reaction to the liberal departures from the faith, but was not initially reactionary in the sense in which it is often viewed today. Fundamentalists asserted rightly that the foundations of the

Christian religion were not subject to change because they were established by God through His Son and His Word. Anyone who rejected these foundations might be practicing religion, but he should have the integrity to call his religion something other than Christianity.

The name "fundamentalism" originated in a series of incidents in the decades surrounding the turn of the century. In the closing decades of the nineteenth century, the Niagara Bible Conferences, while focusing attention on biblical prophecy and dispensational teaching, also served to emphasize the doctrines of historic Christianity that were being so widely challenged in the intellectual world of that day. The Niagara Creed of 1878 effectively summarized these foundational doctrines, though the format is somewhat more extensive than those that appeared later. In 1892, the General Assembly of the Presbyterian Church issued the Portland Deliverance, which upheld the inspiration and authority of Scripture and the historic doctrines of the church; in 1910, the General Assembly expanded and supported the Portland Deliverance with a five-point declaration of doctrines that are essential to true Christianity. The five "fundamental" doctrines enumerated in 1910 included the inerrancy of the original manuscripts of Scripture, the Virgin Birth of Christ, the substitutionary atonement, the bodily resurrection of Christ, and the historical reality of the miracles recorded in the Bible.

In the same year, two California oilmen, Lyman and Milton Stewart, financed the publication and distribution of twelve paperback volumes entitled *The Fundamentals*. The books, edited by Amzi C. Dixon and Reuben A. Torrey of Moody Bible Institute, contained ninety articles written by some of the most prominent evangelical scholars in the United States, Canada, and Great Britain. These articles ranged in subject matter from personal testimonies to Bible prophecy, but the authors devoted most of their attention to specific issues about which the liberals were challenging the Christian faith, and to the fundamental doctrines of that faith. The Stewarts saw to it that copies of these books were mailed free of charge to every pastor, missionary, and Christian worker whose addresses they were able to obtain. Though *The Fundamentals* did not succeed in stemming the tide of modernism, the books effectively increased American Christians' awareness of the attacks that were being directed against their faith.

They also gave a name to a movement. In many ways this is rather unfortunate, since it has become very easy for people today to view fundamentalism as a recent aberration. Quite the opposite is true. Fundamentalism is simply another name for historic Christianity; it is the liberals who have departed from the faith.

THE SCOPES TRIAL

If the twelve volumes published by the Stewart brothers gave fundamentalism a name in the popular culture, the Scopes trial defined its character in the public mind. The famous Scopes "Monkey Trial" of 1925 involved far more than the abortive conviction of a first-year high school biology teacher on charges of promulgating the theory of evolution in the classroom. It became the stage on which large egos struggled over large issues, and its outcome extended far beyond the precincts of Dayton, Tennessee.

By the early nineteen twenties, liberalism had gained a firm foothold in the northeast and midwest, but traditional Christianity continued to dominate most of the southern and western states. In an attempt to stave off the encroachment of liberal ideas, several southern states had passed laws against the teaching of evolution in the public schools. The American Civil Liberties Union, then as now a crusader for liberal causes, was determined to challenge these laws. They found someone willing to serve as a test case in the person of John T. Scopes, who was in his first year of teaching biology in Dayton, Tennessee. When Scopes introduced the theory of evolution into his biology classroom, he was arrested by the local authorities. The ACLU then announced that it had obtained the services of the great Clarence Darrow (1857-1938), trial lawyer and notorious freethinker who had already established his reputation in cases such as the Leopold-Loeb murder trial of 1924. Upon hearing that the defense had enlisted the aid of the Great Infidel, William Jennings Bryan

(1860-1925) entered the fray on the side of the prosecution. Bryan, spellbinding orator, champion of the common man, three-time Democratic Presidential candidate, and Secretary of State under Woodrow Wilson, was also an ardent fundamentalist. The trial soon became a three-ring circus. In the clash of the titans, Scopes was soon lost in the shuffle. He may have been on trial for violating the law of the state of Tennessee, but as far as the rest of the country was concerned, the law itself was on trial, and fundamentalism along with it. The press contributed to the circus, led by the acerbic wit of H.L. Mencken of the *Baltimore Sun*. Millions of words poured from Dayton into the newspapers of people all over the country, most of them designed to make the fundamentalists look like ignorant hicks and anti-intellectual bigots.

Bryan did not help the cause. He was a great orator and fine Christian man, but he was not by any stretch of the imagination a Bible scholar. When he made the mistake of allowing Darrow to put him on the witness stand, the wily defense attorney made him look like a fool. When Bryan fell, fundamentalism fell with him - at least in the minds of millions of Americans. Scopes was convicted, but was only given a token fine, and the sentence was overturned on appeal by a higher court. Bryan died five days after the end of the trial, a great man who should be remembered for finer things than his final appearance on the public stage.

The Scopes Trial is important on a number of levels. To begin with, it provided the first link in the chain of legal decisions that have brought us to the point where today, laws that *allow* the teaching of the biblical view of Creation in science classrooms are routinely struck down as unconstitutional. Secondly, and even more importantly, the Scopes Trial played a major role in shaping the public perception of evangelical Christianity. The image of fundamentalist as buffoon has been indelibly imprinted on the popular mind, and has created an environment in which Christians simply are not taken seriously. When a superb scholar such as Francis Schaeffer is described in his obituary as a "fundamentalist pastor," it is a form of dismissal. The term "fundamentalist" has taken its place alongside "puritan" as a put-down of a way of thinking that is considered hopelessly behind the times.

A third development to which the Scopes Trial at least contributed was the increasing defensiveness of fundamentalists themselves. In the five decades that occupied the middle of the twentieth century, fundamentalists tended to define themselves primarily in terms of what they opposed - evolutionism, liberalism, communism, and on a lesser level, things like smoking, drinking, dancing, movies, and mixed bathing. Such negativism served to isolate fundamentalists from American culture, and convinced the majority to an even greater extent of the irrelevance of biblical religion. Only with the advent of organizations such as the Moral Majority and the struggle against abortion did fundamentalism begin to emerge from its partially self-imposed isolation to enter once again the mainstream of American political and social discourse.

DENOMINATIONAL SCHISMS

Like the struggle over slavery in the nineteenth century, the dispute between modernists and fundamentalists cut across denominational lines and divided many churches. Unlike the wounds caused by slavery, however, those caused by the advent of modernism have never been healed. Denominations with a large majority of liberals or conservatives remained largely unaffected by the dispute. Groups like the Methodists and Congregationalists, both dominated by liberalism, remained basically untouched by the furor. Southern Baptists breezed through it for the opposite reason - fundamentalism so controlled the conference that few tremors were felt. Lutherans also maintained a generally conservative stance in the early twentieth century, though it would not be quite appropriate to refer to them as fundamentalists. [NOTE: The apparent calm in these two large Protestant groups was really nothing more than a delayed reaction. The most conservative of the large Lutheran bodies, the Lutheran Church, Missouri Synod, fought a major battle over the authority of Scripture and related issues in the 1970's, while the Southern

Baptists continue to this day to struggle against the incursions of liberalism. Conservatives in the LCMS drove the liberals from the denomination, while fundamentalists continue to hold tenuous control over the leadership of the Southern Baptist Convention, though they long ago lost their grip on most of the seminary faculties.] The denominations that were fairly evenly divided between liberals and fundamentalists, however, experienced bitter schisms. The most notable of these were the northern Presbyterians and the northern Baptists.

A. THE NORTHERN PRESBYTERIANS

We saw in the last chapter the attempts by evangelical Presbyterians to oppose the incursions of liberalism in their denomination, especially through the heresy trials of Briggs, Smith, and McGiffert. Yet liberalism continued to progress, even on the faculty of that bastion of biblical orthodoxy, Princeton Theological Seminary. With the death of B.B. Warfield in 1921, the mantle of conservative leadership at Princeton fell upon the shoulders of J. Gresham Machen (1881-1937), professor of New Testament. Machen was a staunch opponent of liberal criticism of the Bible, and his books remain today among the classic responses to liberal teaching. In *Christianity and Liberalism*, Machen argued that liberalism was not Christianity at all, but an entirely different religion, a religion of man, which had simply borrowed traditional Christian terminology with which to express its anti-Christian ideas. In *The Virgin Birth* and *The Origin of Paul's Religion*, he defended the historicity of the Virgin Birth and argued that Paul's Gospel was divinely revealed rather than being a mere compilation of current Greek philosophies. Despite Machen's leadership, however, the evangelicals on the Princeton faculty were unable to prevent the eventual domination of the seminary by the growing liberal segment of the northern Presbyterian church.

Liberals continued to chafe at the restrictions established by the Portland Deliverance of 1892 and the General Assembly's recognition of the five doctrines that gave fundamentalism its name in 1910. In the 1920's, they became increasingly aggressive under the leadership of Harry Emerson Fosdick (1878-1969). Fosdick was not even a Presbyterian - he was a liberal Baptist - but he had been invited to occupy the pulpit of the First Presbyterian Church in New York City as a "guest preacher." In 1922, he preached a sermon entitled *Shall the Fundamentalists Win?* which was later published in the liberal magazine *The Christian Century*. In the following year, a group of 149 liberal Presbyterian ministers drafted a document known as the Auburn Affirmation. In this document, they asserted that the denomination had no right to require adherence to the five fundamentals. Furthermore, they claimed that inerrancy was not taught either by the creeds of the church or by the Bible itself, and that the other doctrines included in the fundamentals, such as the virgin birth and bodily resurrection of Christ, were no more than theological hypotheses. Within less than six months, over twelve hundred Presbyterian clergymen had affixed their names to the Auburn Affirmation. For the first time, it was obvious to all that the liberals had the support necessary to defeat fundamentalist efforts in the Presbyterian Church.

In 1929, liberals succeeded in implementing a reorganization of Princeton Theological Seminary that took control of the curriculum out of the hands of the predominantly conservative Board of Directors and placed it in the hands of a Board of Control dominated by liberals, including two signers of the Auburn Affirmation. At this point, Machen led an exodus of evangelical Princeton faculty, who left to form Westminster Theological Seminary, which has perpetuated the Princeton theology (i.e., orthodox Christianity) throughout the twentieth century. Joining Machen on the Westminster faculty in its early years were men such as Old Testament scholars Robert Dick Wilson and Oswald T. Allis (whose *Five Books of Moses* remains the definitive refutation of Wellhausen's Documentary Hypothesis); New Testament professor Ned B. Stonehouse, the first editor of the *New International Commentary* series; Church History professor Paul Woolley;

John Murray in Systematic Theology; and a young man who was to become the greatest Christian apologist of the twentieth century, Cornelius Van Til.

Now that the machinery of the denomination was unquestionably under liberal control, the conservatives became concerned about the church's missionary program. How could evangelical churches, of which there were still many in the denomination, send money to a mission board that was commissioning missionaries who were spreading the Social Gospel rather than the Good News of Jesus Christ? Machen and other evangelicals addressed the issue by forming an Independent Board of Presbyterian Foreign Missions in 1931. The liberals who now controlled the denomination had not been concerned about the formation of Westminster Theological Seminary because they wrongly believed that it would never survive. The new mission board was quite another matter, however. As evangelical Presbyterian churches began funneling their missionary giving through the Independent Board rather than the denominational mission board, the latter experienced a noticeable decline in financial support. While the liberals clearly did not consider doctrinal deviation to be an offense worthy of discipline, they felt otherwise about insubordination - especially when going against the authority of the denomination generated a loss in income. The result was that Machen and the others involved in the Independent Board were defrocked in 1935, at which time they and other evangelicals left the Presbyterian Church, U.S.A. (the official name of the northern Presbyterians) and formed the Orthodox Presbyterian Church (1936). As is often the case with people who care deeply about doctrine, the evangelical Presbyterians continued throughout the middle of the century to suffer schisms, most of which were associated in one way or another with rambunctious separatist Carl McIntire.

B.   THE NORTHERN BAPTISTS

If conservative Presbyterians were unable to hold the line in a denomination that historically has shown a great deal of concern for doctrinal matters, how much harder was the task faced by the evangelicals within the Northern Baptist Convention? Here, too, liberalism had made deep inroads by the second decade of the twentieth century, particularly in Baptist seminaries such as Rochester Theological Seminary, Crozer Theological Seminary in Philadelphia, and of course the University of Chicago Divinity School. How were evangelicals to advocate or enforce doctrinal conformity in a church that historically had opposed creeds of any kind? Throughout the twenties, fundamentalists within the Northern Baptist Convention attempted to fight liberalism on several fronts. They formed organizations such as the Fundamentalist Fellowship (1920) and the Baptist Bible Union (1923), but these organizations rarely were able to gain a serious hearing in convention meetings. They attempted to gain passage of simple doctrinal statements, but though the ones they advocated were even less specific than the five fundamentals passed by the Presbyterians in 1910, the liberals defeated their passage with endless palaver about "Baptist liberty." Efforts to screen missionary candidates for doctrinal orthodoxy proved even less successful here than they had been among the Presbyterians.

The reputation of the fundamentalist movement among the Baptists was also damaged by two scandals in the late twenties. J. Frank Norris (1877-1952), pastor of the First Baptist Church in Fort Worth, Texas, and a leader among fundamentalists, used his church's publication to attack the Democratic Party in general as the party of "Rum and Romanism" (they opposed Prohibition and were on the verge of nominating the Catholic governor of New York, Al Smith, for the presidency). He saved his most vivid assaults, however, for the Catholic mayor of Fort Worth. The mayor promptly fired six members of Norris' congregation from a store he owned. When Norris exposed the retaliatory firings, a supporter of the mayor visited the pastor in his study. An argument ensued, the mayor's friend was shot and killed, and Norris found himself on trial for murder.

DENOMINATIONAL DIVISIONS OVER THE MODERNIST-FUNDAMENTALIST CONTROVERSY

DENOMINATION	YEAR OF DIVISION	SECEDING GROUP	NATURE OF SECEDING GROUP	KEY FIGURES	
				CONSERVATIVE	LIBERAL
DISCIPLES OF CHRIST	1927	Christian Churches; Churches of Christ	Conservative	John W. McGarvey R.C. Foster P.H. Welshimer	James H. Garrison Herbert L. Willett C.C. Morrison
NORTHERN BAPTIST CONVENTION (now American Baptist Convention)	1932	General Association of Regular Baptists	Conservative	John Roach Straton Jasper C. Massee Amzi C. Dixon William Bell Riley Chester Tulga Robert Ketcham	Walter Rauschenbusch Harry Emerson Fosdick
	1947	Conservative Baptist Association	Conservative		
PRESBYTERIAN CHURCH IN THE UNITED STATES OF AMERICA	1936	Orthodox Presbyterian Church	Conservative	J. Gresham Machen Paul Woolley	J. Ross Stevenson Henry Sloan Coffin
PRESBYTERIAN CHURCH IN THE UNITED STATES	1973	Presbyterian Church in America	Conservative	G. Aiken Taylor	
LUTHERAN CHURCH, MISSOURI SYNOD	1976	Association of Evangelical Lutherans	Liberal	Jacob A.O. Preus Ralph Bohlmann	John Tietjen Arlis Ehlen

Though he was eventually acquitted, the incident destroyed his ministry.

Three years later, T.T. Shields (1873-1955), a Baptist fundamentalist, pastor of the Jarvis Street Baptist Church and head of the Toronto Baptist Seminary, arranged the purchase of the financially ailing Des Moines University and attempted to turn it into a fundamentalist school. Since many of the same students and teachers remained from the previous regime, however, his efforts met with strong resistance. Finally, the students rioted and began pelting the administration building with rocks. Shields escaped with his life, but the school was closed down never to reopen, and newspapers around the country were emblazoned with headlines that brought further embarrassment to the fundamentalist cause.

By the advent of the Depression in 1929, it was becoming increasingly clear to many Baptist fundamentalists that the Northern Baptist Convention had moved into the liberal camp beyond recall. In 1932, many seceded under the leadership of Robert T. Ketcham (1889-1978) to form the General Association of Regular Baptists. Other evangelicals who were less inclined toward separatism continued to work within the denomination, but as liberal control became more deeply entrenched, they, too, pulled out, forming the Conservative Baptist Association in 1947. Meanwhile, the Northern Baptist Convention became the American Baptist Convention in 1950, and continues to be a voice for liberalism among Baptists in the United States.

MAKING DRY BONES LIVE

In Harry Emerson Fosdick's famous sermon *Shall the Fundamentalists Win?* he makes the following distinction between fundamentalists and liberals:

"It is interesting to note where the Fundamentalists are driving in their stakes to mark out the deadline of doctrine around the Church, across which no one is to pass except on terms of agreement. They insist that we must all believe in the historicity of certain special miracles, pre-eminently the virgin birth of our Lord; that we must believe in a special theory of inspiration - that the original documents of the Scripture, which of course we no longer possess, were inerrantly dictated to men a good deal as a man might dictate to a stenographer; that we must believe in a special theory of the atonement - that the blood of our Lord, shed in a substitutionary death, placates an alienated Deity and makes possible welcome for the returning sinner; and that we must believe in the second coming of our Lord upon the clouds of heaven to set up a millennium here, as the only way in which God can bring history to a worthy denouement. Such are some of the stakes which are being driven to mark a deadline of doctrine around the Church.

"If the man is a genuine liberal, his primary protest is not against holding these opinions, although he may well protest against their being considered the fundamentals of Christianity.... The question is, Has anybody a right to deny the Christian name to those who differ with him on such points and to shut against them the doors of the Christian fellowship? The Fundamentalists say that this must be done. In this country and on the foreign field they are trying to do it. They have actually endeavored to put on the statute books of a whole State binding laws against teaching modern biology. If they had their way, within the Church, they would set up in Protestantism a doctrinal tribunal more rigid than the Pope's. In such an hour, delicate and dangerous, when feelings are bound to run high, I plead this morning the cause of magnanimity and liberality and tolerance of spirit...."

To put the matter bluntly, fundamentalists are those who rather inconsiderately require that a person should commit himself to the teachings of the Bible in order to deserve the name of Christian. Liberals, on the other hand, see tolerance as the greatest virtue, and view with disdain any who would have the audacity to claim that a person must actually believe certain specific doctrines in order to fall within the pale of the Church. Liberals have thus for more than a century claimed for themselves the moral high ground. After all, they are willing to allow fundamentalists to continue holding their (outdated, antiquated, unscholarly, foolish) beliefs; why should fundamentalists be so narrow-minded as to refuse to extend to liberals the same courtesy?

For those who adhere to the historic Christian faith, now as earlier in this century, the bottom line is truth. If God's Word is truth, that which denies it must be branded as falsehood. Christians indeed must be tolerant in matters of uncertainty such as eschatology and church polity, but toleration of deviations from the fundamental teachings of the Bible is not Christian charity, but the first step toward apostasy.

FOR REVIEW AND FURTHER THOUGHT

1. What were the four major attacks leveled against evangelical Christianity in the latter part of the nineteenth century?

2. How did the theory of evolution undermine biblical teachings about the uniqueness and sinfulness of man?

3. Why was the liberal criticism of Scripture more of a threat to Protestants than it was to Catholics?

4. How did the growth of the social sciences serve to undermine belief in the supernatural aspects of the Christian religion?

5. In what way did the liberals believe themselves to be saving Christianity from the assaults of the infidels?

6. What was the Social Gospel, and what did its advocates seek?

7. What did the preachers of the Social Gospel have in common with the early Puritans, and in what important ways did they differ?

8. What contributions were made by Washington Gladden, Walter Rauschenbusch, and Charles M. Sheldon to the Social Gospel movement?

9. Why is the question "What would Jesus do?" a good guide for Christians, but a poor one for unbelievers?

10. What is fundamentalism, and where did the fundamentalists get their name?

11. In what sense was fundamentalism a reaction against liberalism, and in what sense has it existed as long as the church itself?

12. What were the five fundamental doctrines of the fundamentalist movement?

13. What contribution did the Stewart brothers make to the fundamentalist movement?

14. Describe the respective reputations enjoyed by Clarence Darrow and William Jennings Bryan in the early twenties.

15. What decision at the Scopes Trial by William Jennings Bryan did the most to damage the reputation of fundamentalists?

16. How did the Scopes Trial influence the public perception of fundamentalism?

17. What impact did the Scopes Trial and other events of the same period have on the fundamentalists themselves?

18. What major Protestant denominations were unaffected by the conflict between modernists and fundamentalists, and why?

19. Who was J. Gresham Machen, and what were his contributions to the fundamentalist movement?

20. What role did Harry Emerson Fosdick play in the liberal takeover of the northern Presbyterian Church?

21. What was the Auburn Affirmation, and why was it important?

22. Why did Machen and others form the Independent Board of Presbyterian Foreign Missions?

23. How did the Orthodox Presbyterian Church come into being?

24. Why was it even more difficult for Baptists to enforce doctrinal orthodoxy than it was for Presbyterians?

25. What scandals damaged the fundamentalist cause among Northern Baptists in the twenties?

26. What did Machen mean when he said that liberalism was an entirely different religion from Christianity? Do you think he was right?

27. Under what circumstances is tolerance praiseworthy, and when is it destructive?

THAT THEY MAY BE ONE

In 1810, William Carey proposed the convening of a missionary conference in the Cape of Good Hope at the southern tip of Africa. The great pioneer missionary wanted to invite representatives of all Protestant missions to attend, with the intention of increasing cooperation among them. He and other missionaries had quickly recognized the futility of importing western denominational distinctives into newly-opened mission fields. The distinctions were often cultural as well as theological, and European cultural differences clearly meant nothing to people in Asia, Africa, and Latin America. In addition, Carey was concerned about time, money, and material being wasted through duplication of effort. Why should three denominational missions set up three schools in the same town, when one school operated by the three in conjunction would be much more efficient? Furthermore, Carey realized the damage being done to the cause of Christ by the open competition in which many of the missions engaged. Lack of unity among Christians did not enhance the reputation of Christianity among those the missionaries were trying to reach.

Carey's proposed general missionary conference never occurred. The divisions that separated the missions from one another in their work were so strong that most had no desire to cooperate with others, or even talk together. Such an attitude did not continue forever, however. Gradually, the churches began to realize the truth of Benjamin Franklin's aphorism, spoken in the context of the American Revolution: "If we do not hang together, then we shall surely hang separately." Yet the road to unity has not been a smooth one. As we will see in this chapter, those who have pursued unity most successfully have done so at an appalling cost - the cost of the Gospel itself.

FORERUNNERS OF THE ECUMENICAL MOVEMENT

The movement for unity and cooperative effort among Christians has come to be called the Ecumenical Movement. The word *ecumenical* means "worldwide," and is used to indicate the universal nature of the Church of Jesus Christ. While many today use the term in reference to attempts to bring about denominational mergers, it may also refer to organizations and programs in which many denominations participate.

When Carey issued his call for an interdenominational missionary conference, his intention was to promote cooperation rather than organizational unity. Despite the failure of his effort, many organizations did arise in the nineteenth century that practiced the very sort of cooperation that Carey had visualized. Fifteen years before Carey's attempt to organize a conference, his earlier efforts had borne fruit in the formation of the interdenominational London Missionary Society. Later, in America, the United Foreign Missionary Society (1817) pooled the resources of several denominations, and in 1826 this organization merged with the (Congregational) American Board of Commissioners of Foreign Missions. Similar interdenominational mission boards were organized in many of the Protestant nations of Europe. Later, missions such as Hudson Taylor's China Inland Mission operated without any direct church connection, but accepted candidates from a wide variety of evangelical churches.

Other cooperative organizations formed for purposes other than missionary work. Among these were a large number of Bible societies, such as the British and Foreign Bible Society (1804) and the American Bible Society (1816); youth organizations such as the Young Men's Christian Association (1844) and the Young Women's Christian Association (1855); and the Evangelical Alliance (1846). All cut across denominational lines for the purpose of cooperating in the cause of the Gospel.

By far the greatest advocate of Christian cooperative effort in the early years of the ecumenical movement was Methodist layman John R. Mott (1865-1955). After serving for many years as secretary of the YMCA, Mott assumed leadership of the Student Volunteer Movement, which had been organized many years before for the purpose of recruiting missionary candidates. Under Mott's leadership (1888-1920), the SVM sent over 20,000 American and European missionaries overseas, bearing with them their battle cry, "the evangelization of the world in our generation." He also helped to form the World's Student Christian Federation in 1895, which united student organizations from countries all over the world. Most of the leaders of the ecumenical movement in the early years of the twentieth century were influenced by Mott, and his global efforts earned him the Nobel Peace Prize in 1946.

THE NATIONAL COUNCIL OF CHURCHES

In America, Christians had been cooperating for many years in matters of social reform, whether in connection with the abolition of slavery or the elimination of the curse of demon rum. With the rise of the Social Gospel movement near the end of the nineteenth century, however, cooperative effort to reform society took a new direction. The earlier efforts had involved cooperation of theologically conservative churches who could agree about and work together on the basis of the historic teachings of the Christian faith. Social Gospel advocates, however, operated on the basis of liberal assumptions conditioned by the higher criticism of the Bible and the destructive effects of the theory of evolution. Thus the essential difference between the social reform movements of the nineteenth century and the ecumenical efforts to address society's problems in the twentieth century are the common beliefs around which those efforts united.

Led by the advocates of the Social Gospel, delegates from a variety of American denominations met in Philadelphia in 1908 to form the Federal Council of Churches of Christ in America. The organization sought cooperation rather than unity, and established for itself the following purposes:

I. To express the fellowship and catholic unity of the Christian Church.

II. To bring the Christian bodies of America into united service for Christ and the world.

III. To encourage devotional fellowship and mutual counsel concerning the spiritual life and religious activities of the churches.

IV. To secure a larger combined influence for the churches of Christ in all matters affecting the moral and social condition of the people, so as to promote the application of the law of Christ in every relation of human life.

V. To assist in the organization of local branches of the Federal Council to promote its aims in their communities.

The FCCCA also published a document called *The Social Creed of the Churches*, which listed humanitarian goals that were dear to the hearts of most of the social reformers of the day (fair labor practices, labor laws for women, the abolition of child labor, etc.). Since evangelicals could concur with the social goals of the organization, some became involved with it despite its theological deficiencies. They soon found, however, that goals would not long coincide when people were operating on the basis of significantly different assumptions.

Many of the advocates of the Social Gospel had socialist leanings to begin with, and the politics of the Federal Council did not improve with time. Beginning with the peace movement in the decades following World War I, the FCCCA increasingly took up the support of leftist political causes, while at the same time giving less and less lipservice to biblical justification for the positions they took. Most evangelicals responded by severing connections with the organization. Those who attempted to work within it for change were largely stymied, especially as the power structures of the major denominations were taken over by liberals.

In 1950, the Federal Council of Churches joined with other cooperative agencies to form the National Council of Churches in the United States of America. Despite early (and futile) efforts by evangelical United Presbyterian layman J. Howard Pew, the chairman of the board of Sun Oil, to place evangelicals on the board of the National Council, the NCC has been almost totally unresponsive to evangelical concerns. When speaking out on controversial social issues ranging from racism to feminism to homosexuality to environmentalism, the National Council has consistently taken positions that would correspond roughly to those of the left wing of the Democratic Party, while showing little interest in establishing a biblical foundation for those positions. Meanwhile, Church World Service, the relief agency of the NCC, has funded African Marxist revolutionary groups. Even when the NCC has turned its attention to Scripture, the results have not been laudable. It sponsored the preparation and publication of the Revised Standard Version of the Bible (1952), which incorporated the results of liberal textual criticism, even to the point of incorporating unsupported textual emendations into the translation of some of the poetic passages in the Old Testament. More recently, the *Inclusive Language Lectionary* (1983), issued to provide Scripture readings for use in worship services, showed the council's support for the feminist movement by replacing all references to God as male with gender-neutral terminology. With such obvious lack of regard for the inspired Word of God, it is no wonder that the National Council of Churches has almost totally alienated evangelicals, despite repeated pleas for their support and cooperation.

THE WORLD COUNCIL OF CHURCHES

Exactly one century after Carey originally proposed the idea, an international conference of missionaries came to pass. The World Missionary Conference met in Edinburgh, Scotland in 1910 amid great optimism and enthusiasm about the future of world missions. Delegates agreed that they should foster greater cooperation in an attempt to bring about "the evangelization of the world in this generation." The conference established a Continuation Committee in order to implement their desire for cooperative effort. The Edinburgh meeting was the most important in the history of the ecumenical movement, since it stimulated the formation of the three organizations that eventually joined forces to form the World Council of Churches. Those three organizations were the International Missionary Council, Life and Work, and Faith and Order.

The International Missionary Council (IMC) evolved directly from the Continuation Committee of the Edinburgh conference. It was formally organized at Lake Mohonk, New York in 1921. By that time, the events of the preceding decade had tempered the optimism of the World Missionary Conference. The practical difficulties involved in cooperative effort had already surfaced at Edinburgh. For instance, when the Anglican representatives suggested that Latin America had already been evangelized because it was Roman Catholic, and therefore was not in need of missionaries, delegates from the evangelical missions were appalled. When the IMC met for the first time in 1928 in Jerusalem, matters quickly worsened. Many of the liberal delegates were by this time beginning to doubt the uniqueness of Christianity, and favored instead a "comparative religions" approach that viewed the Christian religion as one among many ways to God. They advocated cooperation with members of other religions instead of attempts to convert such people to Christianity. Evangelicals objected loudly to such a betrayal of the missionary cause. The conferees attained a somewhat uneasy peace when William Temple, the Archbishop of Canterbury, proposed a slogan around which liberals and conservatives alike could rally: "Our message is Jesus Christ - we cannot give less, we dare not give more." Though all could cheerfully affirm their support of this slogan, there is no question that liberals and conservatives interpreted it differently. While evangelicals saw it as an affirmation of the full Gospel of Jesus Christ, liberals read it as signifying the need to share the moral values of Jesus with the world without including the excess "theological baggage" of traditional Christianity.

As the International Missionary Council moved toward merger with the World Council of Churches in 1961, the universalism implicit in the Jerusalem meeting became more overt. In conferences in Madras, India (1938), Whitby, Ontario, Canada (1947), Willingen, the Netherlands (1952), and Ghana (1958), the IMC progressively redefined the missionary task to the point where it would have been unrecognizable to most of the delegates at the Edinburgh convention in 1910. At Madras, the subjective universalism of Karl Barth's neo-orthodoxy dominated the discussion of the delegates. If all men are truly accepted by God in Christ, what then is the task of the missionary? The Willingen conference answered that question by affirming that the missionary was to bear witness *with* the world rather than bearing witness *to* the world. The Christian must show his oneness with all men, particularly by taking a stand of solidarity with the oppressed in opposition to their oppressors.

The second organization spawned by the Edinburgh conference was Life and Work, which was largely the brainchild of Swedish archbishop Nathan Söderblom (1866-1931). Söderblom believed that the mission of the church was to have an impact on society for good. He identified closely with the aims of the Social Gospel movement in America, and believed that the churches could accomplish much if they could put their differences behind them and work together for the improvement of society around the world. He convened the first meeting of the Life and Work movement in Stockholm, Sweden in 1925, choosing as a theme "Theology Divides, Service Unites." Following the debacle of World War I, the conferees spent most of their time developing strategies for ensuring world peace. By the time they met again in 1937, however, at Oxford, England, to make plans for the formation of the World Council of Churches, the peace movement was dead, largely because of the enormous Führer-shaped cloud hanging like a pall over Europe.

While Life and Work concerned itself with the social responsibility of the church, Faith and Order, under the leadership of Episcopalian bishop Charles H. Brent (1862-1929) of the United States, met head-on the knotty issues of doctrine and church government that divided Christians one from another. At least, that was their intention. When Faith and Order met for the first time in Lausanne, Switzerland in 1927, they concluded that it was necessary for the churches to understand one another's positions before they could legitimately seek accord on the issues that divided them. Consequently, the entire conference was given over to an enumeration of the varieties of doctrine and church government espoused by the churches represented, with no attempt made to pass judgment on any of these beliefs or practices, or even to establish criteria by which such judgments might be made. By the time of their second meeting in Edinburgh in 1937, the differences listed a decade before had been rendered irrelevant by the movement's espousal of universalism. After all, if everyone is saved, aren't doctrine and church government simply matters of tradition and personal taste? They certainly should not be considered barriers that divide one portion of God's people from another.

After an enforced postponement of their merger plans because of World War II, Life and Work and Faith and Order came together in Amsterdam, the Netherlands in 1948 to form the World Council of Churches. The WCC defined itself as "a fellowship of churches which accept Jesus Christ as our God and Savior," though the terms of this statement have never been defined or enforced. When many of the participants in the World Council of Churches accept Jesus as God only in the sense that there is a spark of divinity within every man, it is easy to see that J.

Gresham Machen was right when he charged that liberalism was a distinct religion that merely borrowed Christian terminology for its own purposes.

Since 1948, Life and Work (Department of Church and Society) and Faith and Order (Commission on Faith and Order) have continued to function as divisions within the WCC. In 1961, the International Missionary Council joined the WCC and became the Commission on World Mission and Evangelism. The assumption of universal salvation and the consequent redefining of the mission of the church have caused the WCC to focus the large majority of its time, money and influence on social issues. A quick survey of some of the meetings since 1948 will help paint a more complete picture of the activity of the World Council.

The 1952 Faith and Order meeting in Lund, Sweden encouraged the churches to lay their differences aside and work together wherever conscience permitted. The assembly also witnessed the greatest success story in the history of the WCC when several major Protestant denominations in India (Congregationalists, Presbyterians, Methodists, and Anglicans) announced their intention to join forces to form the Church of South India. The churches agreed to get around the problem of apostolic succession, which had been the greatest barrier to union on the part of the Anglicans, by tabling the subject for thirty years. During that time, all ministers who were ordained by the new church would receive their ordination with the participation of a bishop within the apostolic succession. At the end of thirty years, the issue would be a moot one, since all those ordained before the merger would by then have retired or died.

When the WCC met again in 1954 in Evanston, Illinois, under the theme "Christ, the Hope of the World," the theme of universalism was again prominent. In response to a question about what makes a Christian different from others if everyone is God's child, the council affirmed that a Christian is unique because he *knows* that everyone is saved.

The 1961 meeting of the WCC in New Delhi, India was important for several reasons. In the first place, it marked the entrance of the International Missionary Council into the World Council of Churches. Secondly, the conference expanded the subscription to read, "The World Council of Churches is a fellowship of churches which confess the Lord Jesus Christ as God and Savior according to the Holy Scriptures and therefore seek to fulfill their common calling to the glory of the one God, Father, Son, and Holy Spirit." The new statement provides a classic example of the verbal gymnastics in which the representatives of the WCC habitually engage. On the surface, it may seem to be considerably more evangelical than the 1948 statement, since it includes references to the Bible and the Trinity. To the liberal mind, however, the new statement was actually less restrictive than the old one because of the change in the main verb. According to the liberal doublespeak in which the WCC frequently engages, one may "confess" something without "accepting" or "believing" it. In other words, the Bible and the doctrine of the Trinity may have subjective value without being in any objective sense *true*. Such use of language suits Big Brother far more than the church of Jesus Christ, who said that His followers were to let their "yes" be "yes" and their "no" be "no."

The third important development at the New Delhi meeting was the participation for the first time of representatives from churches in the Communist Bloc, including the Russian Orthodox Church. The Russians immediately gained significant representation on WCC committees and boards because of the highly inflated membership figures they gave for their churches (somewhat ironic for a regime that officially repressed all religious expression). Since at that time the Soviet Union only gave travel permits to those deemed ideologically sound, it was not at all surprising that the Russian representatives to the WCC toed the party line and strenuously supported the communist agenda on the social and political issues addressed by the Council. The result was a body quite vocal about racial repression in South Africa but strangely silent about religious persecution in the Soviet Union. One delicious irony connected with Russian participation in the WCC is that, though the

Russians have continually taken positions at the left wing of a leftist organization, they are actually among the most theologically conservative groups in the World Council.

Meetings over the next decade followed a somewhat predictable pattern. In the 1963 meeting of Faith and Order in Montreal, Canada, the delegates came to the conclusion that pluralism in the New Testament justifies pluralism in the church today - in other words, if Peter and Paul couldn't agree about doctrine, why should we? The Commission on World Mission and Evangelism met in Mexico City in the same year, and decided that the mission of the church could best be defined in terms of political action. When the Department of Church and Society met in Geneva, Switzerland in 1966, they went even further, announcing that the work of God involves tearing down sinful social structures, and that man may come to know God by participating in His work of revolution. For good measure, they also put their stamp of approval on situation ethics. When evangelicals within the WCC member churches tried to respond to these radical positions at the general meeting in Uppsala, Sweden in 1968, they were listened to politely, but ignored.

The betrayal of Christian teaching and ministry became even more overt in the seventies. When the Commission on World Missions and Evangelism met in Bangkok, Thailand in 1972, they adopted the theme "Salvation Today," but defined their mission as a concern "with the salvation of human spirituality, with man's right choices in the realm of self-transcendence, and with structures of ultimate meaning and sacredness ... in relation to and expressed within the material, social, and cultural revolutions of our time." In other words, the mission of the church is to enhance the humanity of man in society through the liberation of the human spirit. When the entire WCC met in Nairobi, Kenya in 1975, the real attitude of the Council toward missionary work became clear when they supported the call for a missionary moratorium - an end to western missionary efforts in the countries of the Third World for a period of five years. Missionary work was painted as a form of cultural imperialism for which the western churches needed to repent.

The remainder of the seventies and eighties saw the World Council supporting Marxism more openly than ever, in addition to the Liberation Theology that grew from a merger of Christian and Marxist thought among the theologians of Latin America. The WCC also sponsored the controversial Program to Combat Racism, which contributed tens of thousands of dollars to Marxist revolutionary movements in southern Africa.

EVANGELICAL ECUMENISM

Evangelicals in general have remained on the outside of the ecumenical movement. The major denominations who dominate the movement are largely liberal, with relatively few evangelicals among their members. The smaller evangelical churches, on the other hand, have no desire to become involved in a common endeavor with those who deny the faith while claiming to speak in the name of Christ (the same is also true of larger predominantly evangelical denominations like the Southern Baptists and Missouri Synod Lutherans). Furthermore, evangelicals generally recognize the importance of doctrine, and will not easily lay aside their distinctives in an effort to cooperate, even with other evangelicals.

As a result, evangelical cooperation has developed on a smaller scale and in more limited areas than what exists among the liberal churches. Three types of evangelical cooperation are visible in the church today. The first of these is through parachurch organizations, which, like the faith missions started in the nineteenth century, accept workers from a variety of evangelical churches. In addition to the faith missions and Bible societies, these include groups like InterVarsity Christian Fellowship, Campus Crusade for Christ, and the Navigators.

A second area of cooperation is the negative focus of those who unite in opposition to a common enemy. The most notable example of this kind of cooperation is Carl McIntire, the maverick Presbyterian who formed the American Council of Christian Churches in opposition to the National Council of Churches and the International Council of Christian Churches in opposition to the World Council of Churches. These groups, made up largely of small fundamentalist churches, emphasize their separation from the corruption of Christianity found in the ecumenical movement. This emphasis was brought out most clearly in the founding meeting of the ICCC, which occurred at the same time as the founding meeting of the WCC in Amsterdam. McIntire's forces met in a hotel across the street, and spent a considerable amount of their time picketing the hotel being used by the World Council.

A third type of evangelical cooperation is found in organizations that bring together churches and individual Christians for the purpose of serving one another in specifically defined and limited areas. Such groups as the National Sunday School Association and the National Association of Religious Broadcasters provide mutual support in specific ministries in which evangelicals are involved. Many of these groups have been brought together under the umbrella of the National Association of Evangelicals, formed in 1942 to provide an evangelical voice in a nation that had become increasingly deaf to the Word of God. Fundamentalist churches with a more separatist orientation have a similar organization in the Independent Fundamental Churches of America, founded in 1930.

DENOMINATIONAL MERGERS

The ecumenical movement has stimulated many Christians to look more carefully at the scandal of divisions in the Body of Christ. For some churches, this has led them to join hands in a formal organizational way. The most notable, though thus far unsuccessful, of these merger attempts in the United States is the Consultation on Church Union (COCU), initiated in 1960 by Presbyterian ecumenist Eugene Carson Blake and Episcopal bishop James A. Pike. Blake, who had earlier headed the National Council of Churches and would in succeeding years serve as General Secretary of the World Council of Churches, preached a sermon in Pike's church in San Francisco in which he proposed a merger of four large liberal denominations - the United Presbyterian Church, the Methodist Church, the Protestant Episcopal Church, and the United Church of Christ. By 1966, these four had been joined in their deliberations by six other denominations - the Disciples of Christ, the Evangelical United Brethren, the Presbyterian Church in the United States (Southern Presbyterians), the African Methodist Episcopal Church, the African Methodist Episcopal Zion Church, and the Christian Methodist Episcopal Church. The representatives of the churches prepared a document that they believed could serve as the basis for organizational union in 1970, but found that the churches were lukewarm to the whole idea. In 1973, COCU became the Churches of Christ Uniting, but the plan of union has gained little ground in the decades since it was originally proposed.

Several liberal denominations have successfully concluded mergers in the twentieth century, however. The Evangelical and Reformed Church merged with the Congregational Christian Churches in 1957 to form the United Church of Christ. Unitarians and Universalists linked arms to become the Unitarian Universalist Association in 1961. Two COCU churches, the Methodist Church and the Evangelical United Brethren, joined to form the United Methodist Church in 1968. The Presbyterian Church in the United States (Southern Presbyterians) and the United Presbyterian Church in the United States of America (Northern Presbyterians) ended the schism caused by the slavery issue over a century before when they joined to form the Presbyterian Church in the United States of America in 1983. The large liberal Lutheran denominations, the Lutheran Church in America and the American Lutheran Church (both of which were the results of mergers of smaller ethnic Lutheran bodies in the early sixties), merged with the Association of Evangelical Lutherans (a somewhat inappropriately named offshoot of the conservative Lutheran Church, Missouri Synod) in 1988 to form the Evangelical Lutheran Church in America.

Needless to say, evangelical bodies have been much less active on the unity front, largely because of the emphasis they place on matters of doctrine and church polity. Two notable mergers have occurred among small evangelical denominations, however. The Wesleyan Methodist Church and the Pilgrim Holiness Church merged to form the Wesleyan Church in 1968, and the Presbyterian Church in America, an evangelical offshoot of the Southern Presbyterians, absorbed the Reformed Presbyterian Church, Evangelical Synod (a third-generation schism from the Northern Presbyterians) in 1982.

MAKING DRY BONES LIVE

One of the original goals of the ecumenical movement was to produce through united effort an influence for good upon society. In the early years of the movement, and increasingly through its peak decade in the sixties, organizations like the National Council of Churches and the World Council of Churches spoke with voices that were heard, if not always heeded. Council meetings and council pronouncements made front-page news and earned extensive media coverage. At the beginning of the twenty-first century, however, we find that media coverage of the ecumenical organizations is both scarce and scanty. The only time the National Council of Churches makes the news anymore is when it goes through a financial scandal or throws its support behind the Moonies in a court case.

Why has the ecumenical movement seemingly lost its voice? The major reason for this lies in the fact that a prophetic voice must come from outside the society to which that voice is addressed. When the liberal ecumenical organizations decided that it was the duty of Christians to bear witness with the world rather than bearing witness to the world, the church (or at least that branch of it) lost its distinctiveness. Without its distinctive message that Jesus Christ came into the world to save lost sinners through His death and resurrection, the church becomes just another Political Action Committee or Rotary Club. Christians need to take note of the fact that Jesus, in the same chapter where He prayed that His disciples might be one, also described them as being in the world, but not of it.

That They May Be One 487

FOR REVIEW AND FURTHER THOUGHT

1. Why were missionaries the first to show an interest in cooperative effort among churches?

2. How had church divisions hindered the work of foreign missions?

3. What is the meaning of the term "ecumenical movement"?

4. What were some of the ways in which John R. Mott inspired the ecumenical movement?

5. How did the Social Gospel differ from earlier social reform efforts such as abolitionism?

6. What was the basic purpose for which the Federal Council of Churches was formed?

7. Why were evangelicals able to participate in the Federal Council in its early years? What changes later drove them away?

8. In what ways has the National Council of Churches shown its disregard for the Bible as the inspired Word of God?

9. In what way was the 1910 Edinburgh conference a springboard for the ecumenical movement?

10. What incident at the Edinburgh conference indicated that missionary cooperation would not be an easy goal to attain?

11. In what way did the "comparative religions" approach to missions undermine the entire purpose of missionary work?

12. Give examples from this chapter of the ambiguous use of language by the representatives of the ecumenical movement.

13. What is universalism, and why is it deadening to the work of missions?

14. What contributions did Nathan Söderblom and Charles H. Brent make to the ecumenical movement?

15. What were the main purposes for which Life and Work and Faith and Order were formed?

16. How did the ecumenical movement render differences in doctrine and church government irrelevant?

17. How does the World Council of Churches illustrate the truth of Machen's assertion that liberalism is really a different religion that simply uses Christian language?

18. How did the Church of South India succeed in overcoming the problem of apostolic succession? Do you think their solution was a good one? Why or why not?

19. What three major changes occurred in connection with the 1961 WCC meeting in New Delhi?

20. What influence have the Russian Orthodox representatives to the World Council of Churches had on political and theological issues?

21. Describe some of the liberal political causes embraced by the World Council of Churches. What is their idea of the mission of the church?

22. Why have evangelicals generally shied away from the ecumenical movement?

23. In what ways have evangelicals been able to cooperate with one another without compromising their beliefs?

24. What is COCU?

25. Why has the ecumenical movement lost its voice in recent years?

26. What lessons should evangelical Christians learn from the experience of the ecumenical movement?

45

TODAY'S NEWS, TOMORROW'S HISTORY

The last chapter of a history book like this is always the hardest to write. In the early chapters, it is relatively easy to isolate important people and events. History has already rendered its verdict, and we are able to look backward and see what individuals and movements were transitory and which had a lasting impact on the church. When writing about our own time, however, we lack the perspective of history. Who is to say what events of the last half of the twentieth century will stick out in the minds of historians at the end of the twenty-first? What unknown writer laboring in obscurity will develop applications of biblical truth that alter the direction of the church in the years following his death? It is therefore with considerable trepidation that I undertake the task of penning this closing chapter, in which we will examine the American evangelical church at the end of the twentieth century. Which of the issues addressed in this chapter will be seen a century from now as having had a lasting impact on the church, only God can say.

THE PROBLEM OF DEFINITION

One of the things that makes any discussion of contemporary American evangelicalism difficult is the challenge of defining exactly what constitutes an evangelical. When *Time* magazine dubbed 1976 "The Year of the Evangelical" on the strength of the election of vaguely liberal but outspoken Southern Baptist Jimmy Carter as President of the United States, it underscored the uncertainty with which the term is used. The fact that almost two-thirds of American Christians would call themselves evangelicals does not help matters at all.

One attempt to clarify what it means to be an evangelical Christian centers around the concept of biblical inerrancy. Apologist Francis Schaeffer once described inerrancy as "the watershed of evangelicalism," by which he meant that it served as the dividing line between those who were evangelical and those who were not. In the last half of this century, however, many who call themselves evangelical have questioned the doctrine of inerrancy, especially in the form expounded by Hodge and Warfield at Princeton a hundred years ago. Harold Lindsell, then the editor of *Christianity Today*, warned in *The Battle for the Bible* (1976) that such a watered-down view of Scripture would undermine its authority in the life of the church and ultimately lead to the repudiation of other doctrines central to the Christian faith. In a theological version of the "domino theory," Lindsell traced the progressive betrayal of orthodox Christianity in individuals and institutions who had left the door open to heterodoxy through the denial of inerrancy. Denominational struggles over inerrancy have recently been fought among Southern Baptists, where the outcome remains inconclusive, and Missouri Synod Lutherans, where for the only time in this century those who denied inerrancy were routed in the face of staunch conservative opposition. Evangelicals from many denominations formed the International Council on Biblical Inerrancy, which met four times between 1977 and 1987 to formulate statements and present papers geared to strengthen the confidence of Christians in the Bible as God's infallible Word.

While some who would call themselves evangelical reject the doctrine of inerrancy as too restrictive, other Christians eschew the "evangelical" label as too inclusive, while demanding a standard for Christian fellowship that goes beyond an affirmation of the inerrancy of Scripture. Such Christians continue proudly to refer to themselves as "fundamentalists," and define their number on the basis of what they consider to be the biblical doctrine of separation. Refusing to be "unequally yoked together with unbelievers," and taking seriously Paul's admonition to "come out from among them, and be ye separate," these Christians view cooperation with liberals as sinful compromise, and advocate separation from both liberals and those who would cooperate with them. They speak pejoratively of those who cooperate with liberals as "neo-evangelicals," while those who cooperate with neo-evangelicals are called "neo-fundamentalists," which also is not intended to be a compliment.

The fundamentalist movement of the early years of the twentieth century has thus generated a variety of offspring. On the left wing are those who repudiate inerrancy while retaining the evangelical label. This group, those attacked by Lindsell in his book, includes schools such as Fuller Theological Seminary in California and many of the Southern Baptist institutions. Those stigmatized by hardcore fundamentalists as "neo-evangelicals" would affirm inerrancy but take modern scholarship seriously, while being willing to work with liberal Christians in certain areas. This group is represented by evangelist Billy Graham, scholars such as Carl F.H. Henry, and most of the Bible colleges and conservative seminaries in the country. *Christianity Today* is the leading organ for this segment of evangelicalism. "Neo-fundamentalists" include those who speak loudly and often of separation from liberalism, but have shown increasing willingness to work with other evangelicals. Perhaps the best example of this stance is television preacher Jerry Falwell, former head of the Moral Majority, pastor of Thomas Road Baptist Church, and founder of Liberty University in Lynchburg, Virginia. The strict fundamentalists are best represented by the work of Bob Jones University in Greenville, South Carolina. Their stance of isolation from all who differ is unfortunately the one latched onto by the media to paint evangelical Christians as anti-intellectual obscurantists, though such a picture ignores completely the positive contributions made by even the strictest fundamentalists.

STIRRINGS OF THE SPIRIT

As the century drew to a close, the most important development in American evangelicalism in the twentieth century may well have been one that does not fit conveniently into any of the above categories. In fact, the various outpourings of the Spirit associated with the terms "Pentecostal" and "charismatic" were originally repudiated by most of those in the mainstream of American evangelicalism as fraudulent or even demonically-inspired.

The roots of Pentecostalism lie in the Holiness Movement in the last half of the nineteenth century. In response to a liberal lethargy that was already drawing Methodism far from its roots, some in the church sought a renewal of the emphasis on holy living and Christian perfectionism that had been so central to the teaching and preaching of John Wesley. Many of these wound up leaving the Methodist Church and founding groups such as the Wesleyan Methodists, the Free Methodists, and the Church of the Nazarene. The Holiness Movement in Methodism was thus the equivalent of fundamentalism among the Presbyterians and Baptists. While the doctrinally-oriented churches responded to liberalism by stressing the fundamental doctrines of the faith, the Methodists, who have always emphasized Christian experience over doctrine, fought liberalism with a renewed concern for holy living.

It was through the ministry of holiness preacher Charles F. Parham that Pentecostalism began. The miraculous gifts of the Spirit have appeared at numerous other times in church history, of course, usually in fringe groups such as the Montanists, the Camisards, and the Irvingites. The modern manifestation of these gifts began on December 31, 1900, in Parham's Bethel Bible College in Topeka, Kansas, at a faculty-student Watchnight service. As the new year came in, Agnes Ozman, a student in the school, began to speak in tongues. Soon other students and teachers received the gift, and the Pentecostal revival was under way. Parham, who became one of the chief agents in spreading the revival, soon received the gift of healing as well. When Parham moved to Houston, Texas, one of those touched by Pentecostalism was a young black man named William J. Seymour. Shortly thereafter, Seymour moved to Los Angeles, where the Azusa Street Mission became the center from which Pentecostalism radiated throughout the region and ultimately the nation.

Initially, Pentecostals, like their Pietist and Methodist predecessors, sought to purify and enliven the churches from within. Like the Methodists in earlier years, however, they were rejected by their churches as super-spiritual fanatics, and eventually formed their own churches. From the beginning, Pentecostalism was a lower-class movement, finding its greatest reception among the urban poor in storefront churches and in the rural regions of Appalachia. Most Pentecostal churches are either independent or are part of small denominations. Among the largest Pentecostal bodies is the Assemblies of God, which was formed in 1914 through the merger of a number of smaller Pentecostal organizations. Pentecostals are clearly evangelical in doctrine, though they follow their holiness antecedents in placing more emphasis on experience than on doctrine. They tend toward legalism in their approach to moral questions, and often stress tongues-speaking as the sign of the baptism of the Holy Spirit, which they view as the second blessing, the post-salvation experience of entire sanctification.

Pentecostalism remained on the fringes of American Christianity until 1960. In that year, Episcopal priest Dennis Bennett claimed to have received the Pentecostal gift of tongues, and in the process initiated what came to be called the Charismatic Movement. The Charismatic Movement initially had no connection with Pentecostalism. It spread largely among main-line liberal churches such as the Episcopalians, Lutherans, and Presbyterians. It had no distinctive doctrine, but found its identity in the experience of speaking in tongues. The Charismatic Movement spread to the Roman Catholic Church in 1967 through Duquesne and Notre Dame Universities, where it received wary acceptance from the hierarchy. Most of those who responded to the charismatic renewal were people in liberal churches who longed for an experience of God that had been denied them by the sterile religion of man proclaimed from their pulpits. To a large extent, these people remained in their churches, though some formed independent congregations, and in recent years many have gradually found their way into more traditional evangelical bodies.

The Charismatic Movement also deeply affected the countercultural rebellion of the late sixties and early seventies. Many young people who dropped out of society to seek answers in Eastern mysticism, free sex, and drugs found that those avenues were in reality dead-end streets. In the late sixties, they began to turn to Jesus in droves. The so-called "Jesus People" or "Jesus Freaks" found a spiritual high in Christ that satisfied them like drugs or sex never could. From the streets of San Francisco to the campuses of universities all over the country, young people discovered the meaning of life in Christianity. Not surprisingly, the brand of Christianity espoused by many of these students was highly experiential, and focused on the same charismatic gifts that were changing the face of many middle-class liberal congregations.

In the decade of the eighties, the three forms of Holy Spirit renewal (lower-class Pentecostalism, the middle-class Charismatic Movement, and the radical Jesus Movement of the students and street people) coalesced to a large extent. Pentecostalism gained a new aura of respectability as it gained additional middle-class adherents, while student radicals grew up and entered the mainstream of society, at the same time joining established churches. While the traditional evangelicals did not initially respond well to Pentecostalism (B.B. Warfield wrote *Counterfeit Miracles* in an effort to debunk the movement, asserting that the gift of tongues was restricted to the Apostolic Age) or the Charismatic Movement (some openly spoke of tongues as a demonic trick to lead the unwary astray), these renewals have in recent years enriched the evangelical church through their emphasis on worship and holy living. Pentecostals have been even more influential outside the United States. The charismatic renewal has spread throughout many of the nations of the Third World, especially in Latin America and Africa, and has attracted large numbers of Catholics and Protestants alike.

PROPAGATING THE FAITH

As always, the modern evangelical church in America is concerned with spreading the Gospel of Jesus Christ to those who are not Christians. Today there is little agreement, however, on how that task should be carried out. A survey of the most popular methods in use in our day will give some idea of the variety that exists.

Ever since the First Great Awakening, mass evangelism has been an important tool for spreading the Gospel in America. From George Whitefield to Charles G. Finney to Dwight L. Moody to Billy Sunday, crowds have gathered to hear the preaching of the Gospel, and many have been won to Christ as a result. Their modern successor, and perhaps the greatest mass evangelist in history, is William Franklin Graham (b.1918). Graham began his preaching career while in college, and later served as the first full-time evangelist for the newly-formed Youth for Christ. The turning point in his career came in 1949. While conducting a tent crusade in Los Angeles, Graham received extensive publicity from the Hearst chain of newspapers (William Randolph Hearst's terse order to his reporters to "puff Graham" apparently stemmed from the evangelist's strong anti-communism) and became a national celebrity. Later, he left Youth for Christ to form the Billy Graham Evangelistic Association, which has organized over 250 crusades all over the world in the last thirty-five years, in which Graham has preached to more than a hundred million people. No evangelist in history has had such an extensive ministry. In addition to his evangelistic crusades, Graham communicates the Gospel through the *Hour of Decision* radio broadcast, *Decision* magazine, televised versions of his crusades, and over a hundred films produced by the BGEA. He also played an important role in founding *Christianity Today*, and has sponsored global missionary conferences in Berlin in 1966 and Lausanne in 1974 and one for itinerant evangelists in Amsterdam in 1983. Though soundly evangelical in his doctrine and preaching, Graham has received criticism from evangelicals on both the right and the left. Fundamentalists have been extremely critical of his willingness to work with liberals, Catholics, and Orthodox Christians in order to gain a hearing for his message. Even when he became the first evangelist to break through the Iron Curtain to hold crusades in Eastern Europe, conservatives criticized him for working with communist sympathizers. Evangelicals on the left, on the other hand, have criticized him for remaining silent on social issues. Graham has steadfastly refused to be drawn into controversies on such matters, insisting that to do so would detract attention from the Gospel, which he considers to be his primary responsibility. Despite his success, Graham appears to be the last of a dying breed. Though men such as Luis Palau continue to hold successful evangelistic crusades in countries of the Third World, the United States seems to be increasingly unresponsive to the mass appeals of urban evangelism that have played such an important role in her history, particularly in the last century. Many churches are therefore turning to other methods to win their communities to Christ.

The most popular methods in use today may be classified according to the ground on which those who use them believe the Gospel may be most fruitfully presented. Some, for instance, believe that the Gospel is most effectively communicated in the church. It is important, therefore, to get people into the church in order for them to hear the Gospel. One of the more popular strategies associated with this philosophy of evangelism is the bus ministry. Churches reason that far more people would come to church if transportation were made available to them, so they purchase buses and send them on routes stretching out from the church in all directions, hoping to attract unbelievers to the services. Some of the country's largest Sunday Schools have been built in this way, including Jerry Falwell's Thomas Road Baptist Church in Lynchburg, Virginia.

The problem with such an approach, of course, is that it tends to attract mostly children whose parents want them in Sunday School, but have no desire to come themselves. While the method has achieved some success in evangelism, it often does little to build the church by incorporating families into its membership.

Others believe that evangelism can most fruitfully be carried out on an individual level in the unbeliever's home. Some churches therefore prepare teams of canvassers to go through their neighborhoods, knocking on doors and presenting the Gospel to those who will listen. The best known of these strategies is the Evangelism Explosion method pioneered by Presbyterian pastor D. James Kennedy of Coral Ridge, Florida. Church members receive initial training, then go out in pairs, with a trainee accompanying an experienced evangelist in order to learn and gain confidence. When a person responds to the Gospel, he or she is incorporated into a Bible study and discipleship group, and later trained to witness to others.

Some churches feel that even such an individually-oriented approach as Evangelism Explosion is too confrontational and relies too much on "cold turkey" contacts. They argue that communication of the Gospel occurs most effectively in the context of relationships. Many churches therefore encourage their members to get involved in "friendship evangelism," which requires building informal relationships with unbelievers in order to gain a hearing for the Gospel.

Evangelicals today are also concerned about communicating the faith to their own children. For over a century, the Sunday School has provided religious instruction to the children of Christian parents. Such instruction was believed adequate, since it was supplemented by moral instruction at home and in the public schools. Our century, however, has been one in which the Christian tone of the public schools has virtually disappeared. Beginning with the controversy over the teaching of evolution, continuing with the humanistic educational philosophies of John Dewey, and culminating in the school prayer and Bible reading decisions of the early sixties, Christians have found that the public schools can no longer be counted upon to support the Christian instruction given in homes and churches. Furthermore, the increasing breakdown of families since the moral chaos of the sixties has placed a burden on the Sunday Schools that simply cannot be borne effectively in one hour per week. As a result, the second half of the twentieth century has witnessed an enormous growth in private Christian primary and secondary schools. Catholics have operated parochial schools for years, of course, along with the ethnically-oriented Lutherans and Christian Reformed, but evangelical Protestants did not really begin to get involved in private education until after the Second World War. The formation of Christian schools greatly accelerated in the sixties and seventies because of the school prayer and Bible reading decisions, and also (shamefully) to some extent because of racial desegregation in the public schools. There are today thousands of Christian schools throughout America, represented by such organizations as the National Association of Christian Schools (affiliated with the National Association of Evangelicals), the American Association of Christian Schools (with more of a fundamentalist orientation), and the Association of Christian Schools International. Though some of the smaller schools have been forced to close, many are becoming established and gaining respect and formal accreditation. Bob Jones University Press has been a leader in producing educational materials for Christian schools, along with A Beka Books, associated with Pensacola Christian College.

A newer trend in the field of Christian education is the home schooling movement. An increasing number of parents are choosing to educate their children at home, often because of continuing distrust of the public schools combined with an inability to bear the financial burden connected with private education. Home school support groups are appearing all over the country, providing materials and practical and legal advice, though few parents have the time or ability to educate their children beyond the elementary grades.

CHALLENGING THE CULTURE

While the Gospel and human nature do not change from decade to decade or century to century, the challenges faced by the church are changing constantly. The church must therefore apply the changeless principles of Scripture to a society in a constant state of flux. What are the major issues with which society has been preoccupied, and that the church has been forced to address?

In the first place, the second half of the twentieth century has been dominated by the concern for rights. Blacks, other ethnic minorities, women, and even homosexuals have loudly demanded what they consider to be their rightful place in American society. The civil rights movement in the sixties was succeeded by the feminism of the seventies, and both helped to generate an environment in the eighties in which minorities of all kinds demanded equality, not only under law, but also in terms of public acceptance of their views and behavior. Liberal churches were very active in the civil rights movement, while evangelical churches generally remained on the sidelines because of an aversion to "social action" that had carried over from the earlier liberal-fundamentalist conflicts. Despite the substantial gains made by blacks as a result, the church remains America's most segregated institution. Much more needs to be done in this area.

As far as feminism is concerned, most of the liberal churches, believing that the Bible's directives against women in ministry are culturally conditioned, responded to the demands of women for equal recognition by ordaining women to the pastoral ministry. Evangelical churches, because of their conviction that the New Testament restricts official church leadership roles to men, have largely resisted this trend thus far, though some smaller denominations (notably Pentecostals) have ordained women for years. Most evangelical seminaries, however, have expanded their offerings in recent years to include courses designed to prepare women for non-pastoral ministries in the church. Some of the main-line denominations have also ordained practicing homosexuals, though the majority of churches continue to view what is claimed to be an "alternative sexual preference" as sin.

The prevalence of homosexuality is only a small part of the breakdown of the family with which the church has been forced to contend in the closing years of the twentieth century. Enormous increases in divorce, couples living together without benefit of marriage, pregnancies among unmarried women, particularly teenagers, in epidemic proportions, and single parents by the millions for all of these reasons pose a gigantic challenge to the churches. Many churches have responded by placing greater emphasis on ministries to singles, as well as by providing such services as day care and counseling.

The great moral issue of our day, however, is abortion. Long generally recognized as the murder of a human being, abortion on demand was legalized by the United States Supreme Court in the *Roe vs. Wade* decision on January 22, 1973. Since that time, over forty-five million legal abortions have been performed in the United States - a death toll that far exceeds all the casualties the United States has suffered in all the wars throughout its history combined. Evangelical Christians have joined forces with Roman Catholics to put a stop to the carnage, and in the process have gained political power unmatched since the passage of the Prohibition amendment in 1919. Conservative presidents and a conservative court have slowly been chipping away at abortion "rights," though at the present time those who favor abortion seem to be regaining the upper hand in many states.

Some have compared abortion to the earlier prohibition of alcoholic beverages. Are the issues comparable? Is the fight against abortion an exercise in futility, one where even success would result in failure because of the widespread flouting of the law that it would produce? While there are certain legitimate comparisons between the fight against alcohol and the fight against abortion, there is also a major difference that must be noted. Christian opposition to abortion stands on firmer biblical ground than any other crusade in which the church has engaged in the history of our country.

The Bible clearly permits the use of alcohol, though it condemns its abuse; even slavery is condoned in Scripture, though no one could legitimately claim biblical support for the racially-oriented practice in the American South. But abortion is different - it is the willful taking of an innocent human life, and as such is prohibited by God's Word. Whether or not the opponents of abortion succeed, the endeavor is a worthy one, and one in which Christians ought to make their voices heard.

We ought not conclude this chapter without mentioning another important development in Christian thinking about the way in which the church ought to confront the secular culture in which it exists. At various times in this book, we have examined the Christian approach to apologetics - the defense of the faith. To a large extent, such efforts have focused on meeting the world at the point of conflict, whether that point of conflict involved the arguments for God's existence advanced by Thomas Aquinas, the evidences presented by Joseph Butler in opposition to Deism, or the responses of modern creation scientists to the theory of evolution.

In recent years, however, a new style of apologetics has appeared in the church. Cornelius Van Til (1895-1987), long-time professor of apologetics at Westminster Theological Seminary, argued that unbelief must be challenged, not on the level of its conclusions, but on the level of its assumptions. His "presuppositional apologetics" grew out of the belief that the unregenerate man is unable to understand spiritual things, and thus is blinded to the truth in even his most fundamental assumptions about the nature of reality, the nature of man, and the nature of truth. Christians thus must not assume that evidence from nature of God's creative activity could ever by itself convince the unbeliever of God's existence, since the unbeliever evaluates that evidence on the basis of a mind that is in rebellion against God. Instead, the Christian must challenge that fundamental attitude of unbelief, and rely on the Holy Spirit to change the eyes with which the sinner perceives his world. Van Til's teachings were popularized by Presbyterian pastor and missionary Francis A. Schaeffer (1912-1985), who wrote more than twenty books in the last twenty years of his ministry, during which he traveled widely, speaking in churches and on college campuses, in addition to his work at L'Abri Fellowship in Switzerland, where he ministered to students from all over the world who struggled with the intellectual dilemmas of a fallen humanity. In a nation and world in which the Christian worldview no longer dominates society, it is vital that Christians and unbelievers alike understand the radical discontinuity between biblical thinking and that practiced by those outside the family of God.

MAKING DRY BONES LIVE

What does the future hold for the Christian church? Being neither a prophet nor the son of a prophet, I am reluctant even to hazard a guess. Whatever the direction in which the church may move, however, it is apparent that the beginning of the twenty-first century is a period of transition. The evangelical church in the United States faces the paradox of having larger numbers and greater influence on the political process than at any time in recent memory, while at the same time exercising seemingly little influence on the moral state of the nation. Are these things signs that the voice of the church is getting louder, or is it fading into obscurity? Do they mean that evangelical Christianity is coming to be recognized as a legitimate special interest group whose voice deserves to be heard, but that Christian values will never again gain the general acceptance required to influence public and private morality? In any case, it seems clear that the concept of America as the embodiment of the Kingdom of God is dead. If the United States was ever a Christian nation - a dubious proposition to begin with - it certainly is not one today.

On a global scale, we may be witnessing another of the great geographical shifts that have characterized the history of Christianity. In the first chapter, we saw a tale of three cities, as the center of Christian activity shifted from Jerusalem to Antioch to Rome. Later Constantinople and Moscow gained importance for Orthodox Christians, while Rome continued to serve as the center of Catholicism. With the advent of the Protestant Reformation, Geneva played a major role, and Western Europe in general became the center of world Christianity. The nineteenth century witnessed a period of British leadership, while the twentieth century was dominated by the United States. With the decline of Christianity as a determinative force in America, the end of the twentieth century has witnessed an accompanying growth and maturation in the churches of the Third World where the Gospel had been planted by western missionaries in earlier years. The fastest-growing churches are no longer in the United States, but in Asia, Latin America, and especially Africa. Where will the center of Christian activity be in the twenty-first century? Seoul? Nairobi? Sao Paulo?

Whatever the direction in which the church moves in the twenty-first century, we can be confident that God will continue to carry out His work through His ordained institution. Our study has shown us many areas where the church has failed, but we have also seen God do marvelous things through His earthly people. The bottom line here is that, despite the sinfulness of men, Jesus Christ is the Head of His church, and He has promised that "the gates of Hell will not overcome it."

FOR REVIEW AND FURTHER THOUGHT

1. Why is modern history harder to write than ancient history?

2. What factors in modern American history have made the term "evangelical" a difficult one to define?

3. What are "neo-evangelicals" and "neo-fundamentalists"?

4. What did Francis Schaeffer mean when he said that the inerrancy of Scripture was "the watershed of evangelicalism"? Do you think he was right?

5. What are the advantages and dangers associated with a strong doctrine of separation?

6. What was the Holiness Movement?

7. In what sense was Pentecostalism a product of the Holiness Movement?

8. What roles did Charles F. Parham and William J. Seymour play in the origin of Pentecostalism?

9. In what ways are Pentecostal teachings similar to those of Methodism? In what ways are they different?

10. In what ways did the Charismatic Movement differ from Pentecostalism?

11. Who were the "Jesus People," and what was their relationship to the Charismatic Movement?

12. What factors caused the lessening of the distinctions among the three branches of the charismatic renewal toward the end of the century?

13. Why did evangelicals respond negatively to the various forms of the charismatic renewal? Why do you think they have become less negative in recent years?

14. What are some of the ways in which Billy Graham has been involved in the work of spreading the Gospel throughout his long career?

15. For what reasons has Billy Graham received criticism from other Christians?

16. What differing philosophies underlie the most popular evangelistic techniques in the modern American church?

17. How do bus ministries, Evangelism Explosion, and "friendship evangelism" differ? What are the strengths and weaknesses of each?

18. What factors in modern America contributed to the growth of the Christian school movement in the second half of the twentieth century?

19. What factors have fueled the growth of the home school movement?

20. Why were liberals more active than evangelicals in the civil rights movement?

21. Why have liberal and evangelical churches reacted differently to feminism?

22. What religious groups provide the greatest opposition to abortion in America today?

23. What similarities exist between the anti-abortion movement and Prohibition? What are the key differences between the two?

24. What is presuppositional apologetics, and how does it differ from most of the apologetic methods used throughout the history of the church?

25. In what ways does the evangelical church in America today exert great influence? In what area is its influence lacking?

26. What signs exist today that indicate that the focus of global Christianity may be shifting to the Third World?

APPENDIX - THE POPES RECOGNIZED BY THE ROMAN CATHOLIC CHURCH

Peter (30-67)
Linus (67-76)
Anacletus (76-88)
Clement I (88-97)
Evaristus (97-105)
Alexander I (105-115)
Sixtus I (115-125)
Telesphorus (125-136)
Hyginus (136-140)
Pius I (140-155)
Anicetus (155-166)
Soter (166-175)
Eleutherius (175-189)
Victor I (189-199)
Zephyrinus (199-217)
Callistus I (217-222)
Urban I (222-230)
Pontianus (230-235)
Anterus (235-236)
Fabian (236-250)
Cornelius (251-253)
Lucius I (253-254)
Stephen I (254-257)
Sixtus II (257-258)
Dionysius (259-268)
Felix I (269-274)
Eutychianus (275-283)
Caius (283-296)
Marcellinus (296-304)
Marcellus I (308-309)
Eusebius (310)
Melchiadus (311-314)
Sylvester I (314-335)
Mark (336)
Julius I (337-352)
Liberius (352-366)
Damasus I (366-384)
Siricius (384-399)
Anastasius I (399-401)
Innocent I (401-417)
Zozimus (417-418)
Boniface I (418-422)
Celestine I (422-432)
Sixtus III (432-440)
Leo I (440-461)
Hilarus (461-468)
Simplicius (468-483)
Felix II (483-492)
Gelasius I (492-496)
Anastasius II (496-498)

Symmachus (498-514)
Hormisdas (514-523)
John I (523-526)
Felix III (526-530)
Boniface II (530-532)
John II (533-535)
Agapitus I (535-536)
Silverius (536-537)
Vigilius (537-555)
Pelagius I (556-561)
John III (561-574)
Benedict I (575-579)
Pelagius II (579-590)
Gregory I (590-604)
Sabinianus (604-606)
Boniface III (607)
Boniface IV (608-615)
Adeodatus I (615-618)
Boniface V (619-625)
Honorius I (625-638)
Severinus (640)
John IV (640-642)
Theodore I (642-649)
Martin I (649-655)
Eugene I (655-657)
Vitalian (657-672)
Adeodatus II (672-676)
Donus (676-678)
Agatho (678-681)
Leo II (682-683)
Benedict II (684-685)
John V (685-686)
Cono (686-687)
Sergius I (687-701)
John VI (701-705)
John VII (705-707)
Sisinnius (708)
Constantine (708-715)
Gregory II (715-731)
Gregory III (731-741)
Zachary (741-752)
Stephen II (752)
Stephen III (752-757)
Paul I (757-767)
Stephen IV (768-772)
Adrian I (772-795)
Leo III (795-816)
Stephen V (816-817)
Paschal I (817-824)
Eugene II (824-827)

Valentine (827)
Gregory IV (827-844)
Sergius II (844-847)
Leo IV (847-855)
Benedict III (855-858)
Nicholas I (858-867)
Adrian II (867-872)
John VIII (872-882)
Marinus I (882-884)
Adrian III (884-885)
Stephen VI (885-891)
Formosus (891-896)
Boniface VI (896)
Stephen VII (896-897)
Romanus (897)
Theodore II (897)
John IX (898-900)
Benedict IV (900-903)
Leo V (903)
Sergius III (904-911)
Anastasius III (911-913)
Lando (913-914)
John X (914-928)
Leo VI (928)
Stephen VIII (928-931)
John XI (931-935)
Leo VII (936-939)
Stephen IX (939-942)
Marinus II (942-946)
Agapitus II (946-955)
John XII (955-963)
Leo VIII (963-964)
Benedict V (964)
John XIII (965-972)
Benedict VI (973-974)
Benedict VII (974-983)
John XIV (983-984)
John XV (985-996)
Gregory V (996-999)
Sylvester II (999-1003)
John XVII (1003)
John XVIII (1004-1009)
Sergius IV (1009-1012)
Benedict VIII (1012-24)
John XIX (1024-1032)
Benedict IX (1032-1044)
Sylvester III (1045)
Benedict IX (1045)
Gregory VI (1045-1046)
Clement II (1046-1047)

Benedict X (1047-1048)
Damasus II (1048)
Leo IX (1049-1054)
Victor II (1055-1057)
Stephen X (1057-1058)
Nicholas II (1059-1061)
Alexander II (1061-1073)
Gregory VII (1073-1085)
Victor III (1086-1087)
Urban II (1088-1099)
Paschal II (1099-1118)
Gelasius II (1118-1119)
Callistus II (1119-1124)
Honorius II (1124-1130)
Innocent II (1130-1143)
Celestine II (1143-1144)
Lucius II (1144-1145)
Eugene III (1145-1153)
Anastasius IV (1153-1154)
Adrian IV (1154-1159)
Alexander III (1159-1181)
Lucius III (1181-1185)
Urban III (1185-1187)
Gregory VIII (1187)
Clement III (1187-1191)
Celestine III (1191-1198)
Innocent III (1198-1216)
Honorius III (1216-1227)
Gregory IX (1227-1241)
Celestine IV (1241)
Innocent IV (1243-1254)
Alexander IV (1254-1261)
Urban IV (1261-1264)
Clement IV (1265-1268)
Gregory X (1272-1276)
Innocent V (1276)
Adrian V (1276)
John XXI (1276-1277)
Nicholas III (1277-1280)
Martin IV (1281-1285)
Honorius IV (1285-1287)
Nicholas IV (1288-1292)
Celestine V (1294)
Boniface VIII (1294-1303)
Benedict XI (1303-1304)
Clement V (1304-1314)
John XXII (1316-1334)
Benedict XII (1334-1342)
Clement VI (1342-1352)
Innocent VI (1352-1362)

Urban V (1362-1370)
Gregory XI (1370-1378)
Urban VI (1378-1389)
Boniface IX (1389-1404)
Innocent VII (1404-1406)
Gregory XII (1406-1415)
Martin V (1417-1431)
Eugene IV (1431-1447)
Nicholas V (1447-1455)
Callistus III (1455-1458)
Pius II (1458-1464)
Paul II (1464-1471)
Sixtus IV (1471-1484)
Innocent VIII (1484-1492)
Alexander VI (1492-1503)
Pius III (1503)
Julius II (1503-1513)
Leo X (1513-1521)
Adrian VI (1522-1523)
Clement VII (1523-1534)
Paul III (1534-1549)
Julius III (1550-1555)
Marcellus II (1555)
Paul IV (1555-1559)
Pius IV (1559-1565)
Pius V (1566-1572)
Gregory XIII (1572-85)
Sixtus V (1585-1590)
Urban VII (1590)
Gregory XIV (1590-1591)
Innocent IX (1591)
Clement VIII (1592-1605)
Leo XI (1605)
Paul V (1605-1621)
Gregory XV (1621-1623)
Urban VIII (1623-1644)
Innocent X (1644-1655)
Alexander VII (1655-67)
Clement IX (1667-1669)
Clement X (1670-1676)
Innocent XI (1676-1689)
Alexander VIII (1689-91)
Innocent XII (1691-1700)
Clement XI (1700-1721)
Innocent XIII (1721-1724)
Benedict XIII (1724-1730)
Clement XII (1730-1740)
Benedict XIV (1740-1758)
Clement XIII (1758-1769)
Clement XIV (1769-1774)
Pius VI (1775-1799)
Pius VII (1800-1823)
Leo XII (1823-1829)
Pius VIII (1829-1830)
Gregory XVI (1831-46)
Pius IX (1846-1878)
Leo XIII (1878-1903)
Pius X (1903-1914)
Benedict XV (1914-1922)
Pius XI (1922-1939)
Pius XII (1939-1958)
John XXIII (1958-1963)
Paul VI (1963-1978)
John Paul I (1978)
John Paul II (1978-2005)
Benedict XVI (2005-   )

BIBLIOGRAPHY

Ahlstrom, Sydney E. *A Religious History of the American People*. Garden City, New York: Doubleday, 1975.

Ahlstrom, Sydney E., ed. *Theology in America*. New York: Bobbs-Merrill, 1967.

Alexander, Archibald. *The Log College*. London: Banner of Truth, 1968.

Arnold, Eberhard, ed. *The Early Christians*. Rifton, New York: Plough, 1970.

Arnold, Eberhard. *History of the Baptizers Movement*. Rifton, New York: Plough, 1970.

Austin, Bill. *Austin's Topical History of Christianity*. Wheaton: Tyndale, 1983.

Bainton, Roland H. *Here I Stand*. New York: Mentor, 1950.

- *The Horizon History of Christianity*. New York: Avon, n.d.
- *The Reformation of the Sixteenth Century*. Boston: Beacon, 1952.

Bangs, Carl. *Arminius*. Grand Rapids: Zondervan, 1985.

Banks, William L. *The Black Church in the U.S.* Shelbyville, TN: Bible and Literature Missionary Foundation, 1983.

Beale, David O. *In Pursuit of Purity*. Greenville, South Carolina: Unusual Publications, 1986.

Beaver, R. Pierce, et. al., eds. *Eerdmans' Handbook to the World's Religions*. Grand Rapids: Eerdmans, 1982.

Bedell, George C., Leo Sanden, Jr., and Charles T. Wellborn. *Religion in America*. New York: Macmillan, 1975.

Berkhof, Louis. *The History of Christian Doctrines*. Grand Rapids: Baker, 1975.

Berry, W. Grinton, ed. *Foxe's Book of Martyrs*. Grand Rapids: Baker, 1978.

Bettenson, Henry, ed. *Documents of the Christian Church*. London: Oxford University Press, 1976.

Bilhartz, Terry D., ed. *Francis Asbury's America*. Grand Rapids: Asbury, 1984.

Bishop, Morris. *The Middle Ages*. New York: American Heritage, 1968.

Boer, Harry R. *A Short History of the Early Church*. Grand Rapids: Eerdmans, 1976.

Boettner, Loraine. *Roman Catholicism*. Philadelphia: Presbyterian and Reformed, 1962.

Bratt, John H., ed. *The Rise and Development of Calvinism*. Grand Rapids: Eerdmans, 1964.

Brauer, Jerald C. *Protestantism in America*. Philadelphia: Westminster, 1953.

Brauer, Jerald C., ed. *The Westminster Dictionary of Church History*. Philadelphia: Westminster, 1971.

Bricknell, W. Simcox. *The Judgment of the Bishops Upon Tractarian Theology*. Oxford: J. Vincent, 1845.

Bromiley, Geoffrey W. *Historical Theology*. Grand Rapids: Eerdmans, 1978.

Brown, John. *The Pilgrim Fathers of New England*. Pasadena, Texas: Pilgrim, 1970.

Bruce, F.F. *New Testament History*. Garden City, New York: Doubleday, 1972.

- *The Spreading Flame*. Grand Rapids: Eerdmans, 1979.

Buckley, James M. *A History of Methodism in the United States*. New York: Christian Literature Co., 1897.

Budgen, Victor. *On Fire for God*. Welwyn, Hertfordshire, England: Evangelical Press, 1983.

Butterfield, Herbert. *The Origins of Modern Science*. New York: Macmillan, 1961.

Cairns, Earle E. *Christianity Through the Centuries*. Grand Rapids: Zondervan, 1981.

- *An Endless Line of Splendor*. Wheaton, Illinois: Tyndale, 1986.

Cantor, Norman F., ed. *The Medieval World: 300-1300*. New York: Macmillan, 1963.

Chadwick, Henry. *The Early Church*. Harmondsworth, Middlesex, England: Penguin, 1967.

Chadwick, Henry, and G.R. Evans, eds. *Atlas of the Christian Church*. New York: Facts on File, 1987.

Chadwick, Owen. *The Reformation*. Harmondsworth, Middlesex, England: Penguin, 1964.

Chamberlin, E.R. *The Bad Popes*. New York: Dial, 1969.

Clark, Gordon H. *Thales to Dewey*. Boston: Houghton Mifflin, 1957.

Conforti, Joseph A. *Samuel Hopkins and the New Divinity Movement*. Grand Rapids: Christian University Press, 1981.

Cook, Harold R. *Highlights of Christian Missions*. Chicago: Moody, 1967.
Corbett, James A. *The Papacy*. Princeton, New Jersey: Van Nostrand, 1956.
Coulson, John, ed. *The Saints*. New York: Guild Press, 1958.
Cragg, Gerald R. *The Church and the Age of Reason 1648-1789*. Harmondsworth, Middlesex, England: Penguin, 1960.
Cruse, Christian Frederick, tr. *The Ecclesiastical History of Eusebius Pamphilus*. Grand Rapids: Baker, 1955.
Cunningham, William. *The Reformers and the Theology of the Reformation*. London: Banner of Truth, 1967.
Dallimore, Arnold A. *George Whitefield*. Westchester, Illinois: Cornerstone Books, 1979.
Dampier, Sir William Cecil. *A History of Science*. New York: Macmillan, 1942.
Dannenfeldt, Karl H. *The Church of the Renaissance and Reformation*. St. Louis: Concordia, 1970.
D'Aubigne, J.H. Merle. *History of the Reformation of the Sixteenth Century*. Grand Rapids: Baker, 1976.
 - *The Life and Times of Martin Luther*. Chicago: Moody, 1978.
Dickens, A.G. *The Counter Reformation*. Norwich, England: Harcourt, Brace, and World, 1969.
 - *Reformation and Society in Sixteenth-Century Europe*. Norwich, England: Harcourt, Brace, and World, 1966.
Dolan, John P. *History of the Reformation*. New York: Mentor, 1965.
Douglas, J.D. *Light in the North*. Grand Rapids: Eerdmans, 1964.
Douglas, J.D., ed. *The New International Dictionary of the Christian Church*. Grand Rapids: Zondervan, 1974.
Dowley, Tim, ed. *Eerdmans' Handbook to the History of Christianity*. Grand Rapids: Eerdmans, 1977.
Dunn, Samuel, ed. *The Best of John Calvin*. Grand Rapids: Baker, 1981.
Durant, Will. *The Age of Faith*. New York: Simon and Schuster, 1950.
 - *Caesar and Christ*. New York: Simon and Schuster, 1944.
 - *The Reformation*. New York: Simon and Schuster, 1957.
 - *The Renaissance*. New York: Simon and Schuster, 1953.
 - *The Story of Philosophy*. New York: Simon and Schuster, 1953.
Durant, Will and Ariel. *The Age of Louis XIV*. New York: Simon and Schuster, 1963.
 - *The Age of Reason Begins*. New York: Simon and Schuster, 1961.
 - *The Age of Voltaire*. New York: Simon and Schuster, 1965.
Edman, V. Raymond. *The Light in Dark Ages*. Wheaton, Illinois: Van Kampen, 1949.
Edwards, David L. *Christian England*. Grand Rapids: Eerdmans, 1983.
Edwards, Paul, and Arthur Pap, eds. *A Modern Introduction to Philosophy*. New York: Free Press, 1965.
Elton, G.R., ed. *Renaissance and Reformation: 1300-1648*. New York: Macmillan, 1963.
Estep, William R. *The Anabaptist Story*. Grand Rapids: Eerdmans, 1975.
Fountain, David G. *The Mayflower Pilgrims and their Pastor*. Worthing, England: Henry E. Walter, 1970.
Fremantle, Anne, ed. *A Treasury of Early Christianity*. New York: New American Library, 1953.
 - *The Age of Belief*. New York: New American Library, 1954.
Friedrich, Carl J. *The Age of the Baroque: 1610-1660*. New York: Harper and Row, 1962.
Gaustad, Edwin Scott. *A Religious History of America*. New York: Harper and Row, 1974.
Gibbon, Edward. *Christianity and the Decline of Rome*. New York: Collier, 1962.
Gillespie, Paul F., ed. *Foxfire 7*. Garden City, New York: Anchor, 1982.
Gillies, John. *Historical Collections of Accounts of Revival*. Fairfield, PA: Banner of Truth, 1981.
Glover, Robert H., and J. Herbert Kane. *The Progress of World-Wide Missions*. New York: Harper and Row, 1960.
Gonzalez, Justo L. *A History of Christian Thought*. Nashville: Abingdon, 1975.
Gray, Janet Glenn. *The French Huguenots*. Grand Rapids: Baker, 1981.
Hall, A.R. *The Scientific Revolution 1500-1800*. Boston: Beacon Press, 1962.

Hay, Denis. *The Medieval Centuries*. New York: Harper and Row, 1964.
Herlihy, David, ed. *Medieval Culture and Society*. New York: Harper and Row, 1968.
Heron, James. *A Short History of Puritanism*. Edinburgh: T. & T. Clark, 1908.
Hillerbrand, Hans, ed. *The Reformation*. Grand Rapids: Baker, 1978.
Hoad, Jack. *The Baptist*. London: Grace Publications, 1986.
Houghton, S.M. *Sketches From Church History*. Edinburgh: Banner of Truth, 1980.
House, H. Wayne. *Chronological and Background Charts of the New Testament*. Grand Rapids: Zondervan, 1981.
Hudson, Winthrop S. *Religion in America*. New York: Charles Scribner's Sons, 1965.
Hughes, Philip. *A Popular History of the Reformation*. Garden City, NY: Doubleday, 1960.
Hunnex, Milton D. *Chronological and Thematic Charts of Philosophies and Philosophers*. Grand Rapids: Zondervan, 1986.
Jackson, Jeremy C. *No Other Foundation*. Westchester, Illinois: Cornerstone Books, 1980.
Kelly, J.N.D. *Early Christian Doctrines*. San Francisco: Harper and Row, 1978.
Kittler, Glenn D. *The Papal Princes*. New York: Dell, 1960.
Knox, John. *The History of the Reformation in Scotland*. Edinburgh: Banner of Truth Trust, 1982.
Latourette, Kenneth Scott. *A History of Christianity*. New York: Harper and Row, 1953.
 - *A History of the Expansion of Christianity*. Grand Rapids: Zondervan, 1970.
Lebreton, Jules, and Jacques Zeiller. *The Triumph of Christianity*. New York: Collier, 1962.
Loane, Marcus L. *Makers of Puritan History*. Grand Rapids: Baker, 1980.
Lovelace, Richard F. *The American Pietism of Cotton Mather*. Grand Rapids: Christian University Press, 1979.
Luccock, Halford E. *Endless Line of Splendor*. Chicago: Advance for Christ and His Church, 1950.
Lumpkin, William L. *Baptist Confessions of Faith*. Philadelphia: Judson, 1959.
Manschreck, Clyde L., ed. *A History of Christianity*. Grand Rapids: Baker, 1981.
Marks, Claude. *Pilgrims, Heretics, and Lovers*. New York: Macmillan, 1975.
Mather, Cotton. *The Great Works of Christ in America*. Edinburgh: Banner of Truth, 1979.
McBirnie, William Steuart. *The Search for the Twelve Apostles*. Wheaton: Tyndale, 1973.
McConnell, S.D. *History of the American Episcopal Church*. New York: Thomas Whittaker, 1890.
Meyer, Carl S. *The Church from Pentecost to the Present*. Chicago: Moody, 1969.
Miller, Basil. *William Carey*. Minneapolis: Bethany House, 1980.
Miller, Perry, ed. *The American Puritans*. Garden City, New York: Anchor, 1956.
Morgan, Edmund S. *The Puritan Family*. New York: Harper and Row, 1966.
Moyer, Elgin S. *Great Leaders of the Christian Church*. Chicago: Moody, 1951.
Moyer, Elgin S. and Earle E. Cairns. *The Wycliffe Biographical Dictionary of the Church*. Chicago: Moody, 1982.
Neill, Stephen. *A History of Christian Missions*. Harmondsworth, Middlesex, England: Penguin, 1964.
Newman, Albert Henry. *A Manual of Church History*. Philadelphia: American Baptist Publication Society, 1931.
Noll, Mark A. *Christians in the American Revolution*. Grand Rapids: Christian University Press, 1977.
Noll, Mark A., and Nathan O. Hatch, George M. Marsden, David F.Wells, and John D. Woodbridge, eds. *Eerdmans' Handbook to Christianity in America*. Grand Rapids: Eerdmans, 1983.
Nussbaum, Frederick L. *The Triumph of Science and Reason:1660-1685*. New York: Harper and Row, 1962.
Olin, John C., ed. *A Reformation Debate*. New York: Harper and Row, 1966.
Panofsky, Erwin. *Gothic Architecture and Scholasticism*. New York: World, 1951.
Parker, Percy Livingstone, ed. *The Journal of John Wesley*. Chicago: Moody, n.d.
Parker, T.H.L. *John Calvin*. Herts, England: Lion, 1975.
Parry, J.H. *The Age of Reconnaissance*. New York: New American Library, 1963.
Pledge, H.T. *Science Since 1500*. New York: Harper and Row, 1959.

Pollock, John. *Wilberforce*. Herts, England: Lion, 1977.
Pusey, Edward B., tr. *The Confessions of Saint Augustine*. New York: Collier, 1978.
Reid, W. Stanford, ed. *John Calvin: His Influence in the Western World*. Grand Rapids: Zondervan, 1982.
Renwick, A.M. *The Story of the Church*. Leicester, England: InterVarsity, 1958.
Ryle, J.C. *Christian Leaders of the 18th Century*. Edinburgh: Banner of Truth, 1978.
Schaff, Philip. *History of the Christian Church*. Grand Rapids: Eerdmans, 1973.
Schiller, Frederick. *The History of the Thirty Years' War in Germany*. New York: A.L. Burt, n.d.
Sheldon, Henry C. *History of the Christian Church*. Peabody, MA: Hendrickson, 1895.
Shelley, Bruce L. *Church History in Plain Language*. Waco, Texas: Word, 1982.
Simonson, Harold. *Jonathan Edwards: Theologian of the Heart*. Grand Rapids: Eerdmans, 1974.
Smith, Huston. *The Religions of Man*. New York: New American Library, 1958.
Smith, M.A. *The Church Under Siege*. Downers Grove, IL: InterVarsity, 1976.
   - *From Christ to Constantine*. Downers Grove, IL: InterVarsity, 1971.
Southern, R.W. *Western Society and the Church in the Middle Ages*. Harmondsworth, Middlesex, England: Penguin, 1970.
Sparks, Jack, ed. *The Apostolic Fathers*. Nashville: Thomas Nelson, 1978.
Spitz, Lewis W., ed. *The Protestant Reformation*. Englewood Cliffs, NJ: Prentice-Hall, 1966.
Sticco, Maria. *The Peace of St. Francis*. New York: Hawthorne, 1962.
Stoeffler, F. Ernest. *Continental Pietism and Early American Christianity*. Grand Rapids: Eerdmans, 1976.
Sweet, William W. *The Story of Religion in America*. Grand Rapids: Baker, 1973.
Thompson, Robert Ellis. *A History of the Presbyterian Churches in the United States*. New York: Scribners, 1907.
Torbet, Robert G. *A History of the Baptists*. Valley Forge, Pennsylvania: Judson Press, 1963.
Vaughan, Alden T., ed. *The Puritan Tradition in America 1620-1730*. Columbia, South Carolina: University of South Carolina Press, 1972.
Vidler, Alec R. *The Church in an Age of Revolution*. Harmondsworth, Middlesex, England: Penguin, 1961.
Vos, Howard F. *Highlights of Church History*. Chicago: Moody, 1960.
Walton, Robert C. *Chronological and Background Charts of Church History*. Grand Rapids: Zondervan, 1986.
Westcott, Brooke Foss. *A General Survey of the History of the Canon of the New Testament*. Grand Rapids: Baker, 1980.
Wightman, W.P.D. *The Growth of Scientific Ideas*. New Haven: Yale University Press, 1953.
Willison, George F. *Saints and Strangers*. New York: Time, 1964.

INDEX OF NAMES

Abdallah 97
Abelard, Peter 155-158, 162, 167
Abu Bakr 101, 103
Adrian IV 127
Adrian VI 210, 211, 215, 280
Al Tarik 101, 103
Alaric 77, 105
Alban 33
Albertus Magnus 171
Albrecht of Mainz 207
Albret, Jeanne d' 242, 243, 251
Alcott, Bronson 425, 447
Alcott, Louisa May 447
Alcuin of York 110, 115
Alexander 56, 57, 65, 71, 72, 75
Alexander III 145, 187
Alexander V 183-185, 187, 191
Alexander VI 188, 191, 200
Alexander, Archibald 459, 460, 465
Alexander of Jerusalem 33
Alexander Severus 36
Alexander the Great 4, 6, 7, 121, 342
Alexius 146
Allen, Richard 437, 441, 443
Allen, William 260
Allis, Oswald T. 472
Alva, Duke of 247, 251, 277
Ambrose 50, 55, 59, 60, 63, 65, 87, 90
Amina 97, 103
Amyraut, Moses 249, 250
Anacletus II 187
Ananias 4
Andelot, François d' 242
Andrew, James O. 428
Angelus, Isaac 144, 146
Anne 304, 385
Anne of Bohemia 197
Anne of Cleves 256
Anne of Denmark 266
Anselm 126, 155, 156, 158-160, 162, 163, 294
Anthony of Thebes 57, 65, 86, 87
Anthony, Susan B. 431
Anthusa 57, 65
Antoninus Pius 33, 35
Apollinarius 71, 73, 75
Aquinas, Thomas 155, 158-163, 171, 282, 291, 311, 495
Arcadius 58, 59, 65
Argyle, Marquis of 303
Aristotle 153, 154, 157, 159-162, 291, 292, 339
Arius 56, 57, 65, 71, 72, 75, 80, 157

Arminius, James 115, 225, 248-250, 252, 333, 367, 412
Arndt, Johann 318, 325
Arnold of Brescia 167
Arthur 254
Asbury, Francis 329, 333, 337, 409, 416, 437
Astrolabe 156, 162
Athanasius 55-57, 65, 69-73, 75, 80, 86, 87, 92
Athenagoras 137, 138
Attila the Hun 48, 105
Augustine of Canterbury 106, 108, 112
Augustine of Hippo 16, 26, 55, 59, 62, 63, 65, 70, 71, 76-78, 80, 87, 90, 91, 110, 115-117, 120, 124, 132, 138, 141, 150, 155, 158, 167, 168, 171, 176, 205, 211, 226, 248, 282, 308
Augustus 7
Aurelian 33, 37
Averröes 153, 154, 160
Avicenna 160
Ayesha 100, 103

Backus, Isaac 410, 413
Bacon, Francis 294, 309
Bacon, Roger 171
Bainton, Roland 110, 256
Baker, George 439, 443
Baldwin of Flanders 145
Ballou, Adin 447
Bancroft, Richard 266, 273
Barnabas 5
Barnabas of Alexandria 12
Barnes, Albert 460, 461, 465
Barnes, Robert 254
Barnum, P.T. 447, 455
Baronius, Caesar 279
Barth, Karl 346-348, 350, 482
Basil the Great 55, 71, 72, 87, 88
Basilides 35, 40
Bates, Joseph 450, 452
Baur, F.C. 342-345, 349
Beaton, David 244, 245, 251
Beaton, James 244
Beecher, Henry Ward 419, 467
Beecher, Lyman 419, 420, 423, 427, 429, 467
Beissel, Conrad 446
Belisarius 107
Benedict VIII 124, 134, 138
Benedict IX 124
Benedict XI 180
Benedict XIII 183-185, 187, 191
Benedict XIV 168

Benedict of Nursia 88, 166
Bengel, J.A. 329
Bennett, Dennis 491
Berengar 117, 120
Berengar II 123
Berkeley, John 391
Bernard of Clairvaux 141, 143, 145, 155, 157, 158, 162, 167
Bernardone, Pietro 170
Bertha 106
Berthold 168
Beza, Theodore 225, 243, 248, 251, 363, 366
Bilderdijk, Willem 367, 369
Bilney, Thomas 254
Blackstone, William E. 462
Blair, James 384, 394
Blair, Samuel 399
Blake, Eugene Carson 485
Blandina 33, 35, 40
Blaurock, Georg 235
Bliss, Philip P. 462
Boehler, Peter 329, 330, 332, 337
Boehm, Jacob 237
Boethius 105, 153, 155
Bohlmann, Ralph 474
Boleyn, Anne 246, 254, 255, 257, 259
Bonaparte, Napoleon 296, 342, 366
Bonaventure, John 171
Bonhoeffer, Dietrich 347, 348, 350
Boniface 106, 107, 109, 112, 115
Boniface VIII 179, 180, 190, 191
Boniface IX 183
Booth, Catherine 357
Booth, Evangeline 357
Booth, William 357
Bora, Katherine von 211
Borgia, Cesare 188, 191
Borgia, Lucrezia 188
Bothwell, James 246
Botticelli 199
Bourg, Anne du 242, 251
Boyle, Robert 293
Bradford, William 385, 394
Bradwardine, Thomas 195, 226, 248
Brainerd, David 400, 403
Bray, Thomas 373, 379
Brent, Charles 482, 487
Bres, Guido de 247, 251
Brewster, William 385, 394
Briggs, Charles A. 461, 465, 472
Brigitta of Sweden 181, 190
Brookes, James 462, 465
Brown, Francis 461
Bruno of Cologne 168

Bryan, William Jennings 470, 471, 476
Bucer, Martin 213, 221-223, 257, 280
Buddha 25, 26
Bullinger, Heinrich 221, 222
Bultmann, Rudolf 346, 350
Bunyan, John 271, 274, 307
Bure, Idelette de 223
Burr, Aaron 398
Burrus 7
Butler, Joseph 310, 311, 315, 495
Buxtorf, Johann 366, 369

Caecilian 71, 76, 80
Caesarius of Arles 71
Cajetan 208
Caligula 7, 10
Calixtus, George 317, 325
Callistus II 187
Calvert, Cecil 391, 392, 396
Calvert, George 391, 392, 396
Calvin, John 63, 78, 115, 158, 222-233, 238, 239, 240-242, 245-252, 257, 263, 269, 277, 282, 308, 314, 333, 334, 338, 347, 363, 366, 367, 373, 379, 386, 389, 407, 412, 413
Cameron, John 249
Cameron, Richard 303, 306
Campbell, Alexander 418
Campbell, Thomas 418
Campeggio 255
Canisius, Peter 279
Carey, William 335, 371-376, 378, 379, 479, 481
Carlstadt, Andreas von 210
Carter, Jimmy 489
Carteret, George 391
Cartwright, Peter 415-417
Cassian, John 71, 78, 81
Cassiodorus 88, 93, 105
Catherine de Medici 242, 243, 251
Catherine of Aragon 254, 255, 257-259, 263
Catherine of Siena 181, 190
Celestine III 127
Cerdo 25, 29
Cerinthus 8, 10, 68
Cerularius, Michael 131, 133, 135, 137, 138
Cesarini, Julian 187
Chafer, Lewis Sperry 462, 465
Channing, William Ellery 419, 425
Chapman, J. Wilbur 421
Charlemagne 101, 110, 111, 115, 118, 120, 121, 129, 132, 133, 138
Charles I 266-271, 273, 301, 308, 388, 390
Charles II 270, 271, 274, 301-303, 305-308, 392
Charles V 209-213, 215, 247, 255, 258, 280, 287
Charles VIII 200

Index of Names

Charles IX 242, 243, 251
Charles of Lorraine 242
Charles the Bald 118, 121
Chatillon, Odet of 242
Chaucer, Geoffrey 253
Chauncy, Charles 400, 403
Chemnitz, Martin 213
Cherbury, Herbert of 310, 314
Chesterton, G.K. 358
Chew, Benjamin 437
Clara 170
Claudius 7
Clay, Henry 426
Clement V 180, 187, 191
Clement VII 182, 183, 191, 280
Clement of Alexandria 16, 17, 35, 57, 73
Clement of Rome 11, 16, 23, 33, 34, 42, 45
Clothilde 109
Clovis 109, 112
Cocceius, Johannes 367, 369
Coelestius 71, 77, 81
Coffin, Henry Sloan 474
Coke, Thomas 329, 333, 409
Coleridge, Samuel Taylor 352
Coligny, Gaspard de 242, 243, 251, 373
Collins, Anthony 310
Columba 106, 112
Columbanus 106, 112
Comenius, J.A. 320, 325
Comnenus, Alexius 140, 142
Comte, Auguste 468
Conde, Louis Prince of 242
Cone, James 439
Constantine 22, 35, 37, 38, 49, 50, 55-57, 60, 70-72, 75, 76, 80, 85, 109, 110, 112, 122, 124, 188
Constantine IV 75
Constantine V 114, 115, 120
Constantine VI 75, 115
Constantius 72
Constantius Chlorus 37, 38
Contarini, Gasparo 280
Cook, James 374
Cop, Nicholas 222
Copernicus, Nicholas 292, 293, 299, 340
Cornelius 5, 343
Cornelius of Rome 76, 80
Cotton, John 390
Court de Gebellin 366, 369
Court, Antoine 365, 366, 369
Coverdale, Miles 254, 257
Cowper, William 335, 337
Cranmer, Thomas 254-257, 259, 261-264, 308
Crescens 35

Crescentius 123
Cromwell, Oliver 269-271, 273, 301, 306-308, 353
Cromwell, Richard 270
Cromwell, Thomas 256
Crowther, Samuel 376, 379
Cyprian 16, 18, 19, 33, 36, 40, 43, 44, 46, 49, 52, 59, 75, 76, 80, 83
Cyril of Alexandria 55, 71, 73-75, 80

D'Ailly, Peter 184, 187, 191, 195, 198
D'Aubigne, J.H. Merle 367, 369
Dabney, Robert 428
Da Costa, Isaak 367, 369
Damasus 46, 52, 61, 65
Dandolo, Enrico 145, 146, 150
Darby, John Nelson 355, 356, 360, 461, 462
Darnley, Henry 246, 265
Darrow, Clarence 470, 471, 476
Darwin, Charles 295, 296, 299, 341, 342, 344, 349, 354, 355, 467, 468
Davenport, James 400, 403
David, Christian 320, 321, 325
Davies, Samuel 399, 401, 403
Decius 16, 19, 33, 36, 40, 46, 74, 76, 85
Denck, Hans 237
Descartes, René 294, 295, 297-299, 310
Dewey, John 493
Dickens, A.G. 241
Dickenson, Jonathan 398, 403
Diocletian 33, 37, 38, 40, 48, 76, 86
Dioscurus 74, 75, 80
Diotrephes 8, 10, 42
Dixon, Amzi 470, 474
Dober, Leonard 321
Domitian 8, 10, 33, 34
Donatus 71, 76, 80
Driver, S.R. 461
Duff, Alexander 376, 379
Dupanloup, Felix 284
Durant, Will 22, 160, 163
Dwight, Timothy 419, 423

Eck, Johann 208, 209, 215
Eck, John 214
Eddy, Asa 453
Eddy, Mary Baker 450, 451, 453, 454, 457
Edson, Hiram 450, 452
Edward I 180, 190
Edward VI 245, 257, 258, 260, 261, 263
Edwards, Jerusha 400
Edwards, Jonathan 388, 398-400, 402, 403, 406, 410, 411, 419, 420, 459
Ehlen, Arlis 474
Einstein, Albert 297

Eleanor of Aquitaine 143
Eliot, John 373, 379
Eliot, T.S. 105
Elizabeth I 245-247, 251, 253, 255, 257-261, 264, 265, 308
Emerson, Ralph Waldo 447
Episcopius, Simon 248
Erasmus, Desiderius 201, 202, 204, 210, 211, 218, 247, 254, 282
Erdman, William J. 462
Erigena, John Scotus 113, 118, 120, 155
Erret, Isaac 474
Erskine, Ebenezer 304, 306
Ethelbert 106, 112
Eudoxia 58, 59, 65
Eugene III 143, 145, 167
Eugene IV 186, 187, 191
Eusebius of Caesarea 12, 17, 19, 34, 35, 42, 55, 56, 65, 69, 72, 75
Eusebius of Nicomedia 71, 72, 75
Eutyches 71, 74, 75
Eutychius 75

Fabianus 33
Falstaff, John 197
Falwell, Jerry 490, 492
Fard, Wallace D. 439
Farel, Guillaume 221, 223, 228, 229
Farrakhan, Louis 440
Fatima 97, 103
Fawkes, Guy 266, 273
Felicitas 35
Felix V 186, 188, 191
Felix of Aptunga 76, 80
Ferdinand of Aragon 101, 174, 209, 254, 255, 276, 277, 286
Feti, Domenico 317
Feuerbach, Ludwig 341, 349
Finney, Charles 419, 420, 422, 423, 425, 427, 445, 446, 459, 460, 492
Flacius, Matthias 213
Flavian 58, 65, 74, 80
Flavius Clemens 34, 40
Formosus 121
Fosdick, Harry Emerson 472, 474, 475, 477
Fox, George 270, 274
Fox, Margaret 422, 447
Foxe, John 259
Francis I 209, 221, 223, 242, 251, 280, 287
Francis II 242, 243, 245, 246
Francis of Assisi 149, 165, 170, 171, 173, 176
Francke, A.H. 319-321, 323, 325, 329, 342
Franklin, Benjamin 331, 399, 411, 479
Franz, Frederick 455

Frederick II 127, 145, 148, 187
Frederick IV 321, 325
Frederick Barbarossa 127, 144, 145
Frederick the Wise 206, 208-210, 215
Frelinghuysen, Theodore 392, 397-399, 403
Freud, Sigmund 468
Frith, John 254
Froschauer, Christoph 217
Fulbert 156, 162

Gaebelein, A.C. 462
Galerius 33, 37, 38
Galilei, Galileo 161, 291-293, 298, 300
Gallio 6, 7, 10
Gamaliel 4, 10
Gandhi, Mahatma 439
Gansfort, Wessel 201
Garibaldi, Giuseppe 283
Garrick, David 330
Garrison, James H. 474
Garrison, William Lloyd 427
Garvey, Marcus 439
Gaussen, François 367, 369
Geddes, Jenny 268, 273, 301
Gelasius I 48, 52
George III 412
Gerhardt, Paul 318, 325
Gerson, John 184, 187, 191, 195, 198
Gladden, Washington 469, 476
Glover, George 453
Godfrey 145
Gomarus, Francis 248
Gordon, A.J. 462
Gottschalk 115, 116, 120, 122, 226, 248
Grace, Charles M. 439, 443
Graham, Billy 415, 421, 423, 490, 492, 497
Gratian 60, 65
Grebel, Conrad 235
Gregory I 47, 88, 105-110, 112, 115
Gregory II 106
Gregory III 114, 120
Gregory V 124
Gregory VI 124
Gregory VII 85, 122, 124-127, 129, 134, 138, 139, 155, 165-167, 176, 179
Gregory IX 171
Gregory X 187
Gregory XI 182, 183, 191, 196
Gregory XII 183-185, 187, 191, 197
Gregory XIII 243
Gregory of Nazianzus 55, 71, 72, 75, 83
Gregory of Nyssa 55, 71, 72, 75
Gregory of Rimini 195, 226
Grey, Jane 257-259, 261, 263

Index of Names

Groote, Gerhard 201
Gui, Bernardo 171
Guiscard, Robert 126
Guise, Henry Duke of 242
Gustavus Adolphus 214
Guthrie, James 303, 306
Guzman, Dominic 168, 171

Hadrian 33, 35
Haldane, Robert 366, 367, 369
Hamilton, Patrick 244, 251
Harnack, Adolf von 344, 345, 350
Harris, Howell 331, 337
Harvard, John 387, 388, 394
Hastings, Selina 329, 331, 337
Hearst, William Randolph 492
Hefele, Karl 284
Hegel, G.W.F. 341-347, 349, 453
Helena 24, 29
Heloïse 156
Helwys, Thomas 267, 273
Henderson, Alexander 301, 306
Henrietta Maria 266
Henry II 126, 143, 144, 242, 245
Henry III 124, 242
Henry IV 125, 126, 129, 139, 242-244, 250-252, 363
Henry IV of England 197
Henry V 196, 197
Henry VII 246, 254, 260, 267
Henry VIII 128, 212, 242, 244-246, 253-261, 263, 266, 276, 280, 286
Henry, Carl F.H. 490
Henry, Patrick 407
Hereford, Nicholas 196
Hermas 12
Herod Agrippa I 5
Herod the Great 6, 34
Hickerson, St. John the Divine 439
Hilary of Poitiers 55
Himes, Joshua 449
Hincmar 116, 120, 122
Hippolytus 33
Hitler, Adolf 296, 342, 347, 349
Hodge, A.A. 460
Hodge, C.W. 460
Hodge, Charles 427, 459, 460, 461, 465, 467, 489
Hoffmann, Melchior 236, 239
Hogarth, William 327
Honorius 75
Honorius II 145
Honorius III 171
Hooper, John 259
Hopkey, Sophia 328
Hopkins, Samuel 410, 413, 419, 425

Hort, F.J.A. 357, 358, 361
Hosius 71, 75
Howard, John 335, 337
Hubmaier, Balthasar 231, 235
Hugo the Iron 146
Humbert 131, 135, 138
Hume, David 310, 311, 313-315, 339, 340
Hunt, Robert 383, 394
Huss, John 185, 187, 195, 197-204, 209, 214
Hutchinson, Anne 387, 390, 392, 395
Hutter, Jacob 235, 239

Ignatius of Antioch 11-13, 33, 35, 39, 40, 42, 43, 45
Ignatius of Constantinople 122, 134
Ingersoll, Robert 468
Innocent I 46, 52
Innocent II 145, 187
Innocent III 116, 117, 120, 122, 127-129, 140, 141, 144, 146, 147, 150, 165, 170-172, 179, 187, 189, 190, 196
Innocent IV 187
Innocent VII 183
Irenaeus 8, 15, 19, 24, 33, 43-45, 51, 52, 68
Irene 115, 120
Irving, Edward 355, 356
Isabella of Castile 101, 174, 209, 254, 255, 276, 277, 286
Isidore of Seville 113

Jackson, Stonewall 421
Jacob, Henry 267, 273
James, brother of Jesus 5, 23, 184
James, son of Zebedee 4, 448
James I 246, 265-267, 270, 273, 308, 385
James II 271, 272, 303, 388
James V 244
Jan of Leyden 236, 237, 239
Jarratt, Devereux 401, 403
Jefferson, Thomas 302, 407, 408, 411, 413
Jerome 55, 60-62, 65, 70, 71, 77, 81, 83, 87, 90
Joan 123
John 8, 12, 15, 33, 34, 44, 50, 68, 72, 172, 448, 451
John I 127-129, 143, 144, 196
John VII 136
John X 123
John XI 123
John XII 123, 124
John XIX 124
John XXII 160, 168, 181, 191
John XXIII 185, 283, 284
John XXIII (antipope) 183, 185, 187, 190, 191, 197, 198

John Chrysostom 55, 57-61, 65, 73, 132
John Mark 6, 10, 68
John of Antioch 74, 80
John of Brienne 145
John of Damascus 113, 114, 120
John of Gaunt 196
John of Wesel 201
John Paul II 211
John the Baptist 25, 83, 146, 201, 448
Judson, Adoniram 419, 423
Julian the Apostate 57, 72
Julius 46, 52
Julius II 188, 191, 207
Julius III 284
Justin Martyr 13, 15, 33, 35, 40, 45, 49
Justina 83, 93
Justina (Empress) 60, 65
Justinian 75, 107, 112

Kaiser, Jacob 220
Kant, Immanuel 339-344, 347, 349, 352, 453
Keats, John 453
Keble, John 353, 354
Kempis, Thomas à 201
Kennedy, D. James 493
Ketcham, Robert 474
Khadija 97, 98, 101, 103
Kierkegaard, Søren 345-348, 350
King, Martin Luther 435, 439, 469
Knorr, Nathan 450, 455
Knox, John 217, 245, 246, 251, 257, 260
Konrad III 143, 145
Küng, Hans 284
Kuyper, Abraham 367, 368, 370

Lafayette, Marquis de 366
Lanfranc 117, 120, 126
Langton, Stephen 127
Las Casas, Bartolomeo de 171
Lasco, John à 257
Latimer, Hugh 254, 257, 259, 263, 308
Laud, William 267-269, 273, 308, 385, 388
Law, William 311, 315, 329
Laynez, James 278, 282, 284, 286
Lee, Robert E. 421, 462
Lefevre d'Etaples, Jacques 221, 222, 242, 251
Leo I 41, 43, 46-48, 52, 71, 74, 75, 80, 101, 105, 108
Leo III 111
Leo IV 115
Leo IX 124, 131, 133, 135, 137
Leo X 188, 191, 198, 205, 207-210, 280
Leo XIII 159
Leo of Ochrida 135, 138

Leo the Isaurian 113, 114, 120, 131, 135, 138
Leonidas 17, 19, 33, 35, 40
Lewis, C.S. 313, 358
Libanius 57, 65
Licinius 38
Lightfoot, J.B. 357
Lincoln, Abraham 417, 427
Lindsell, Harold 489, 490
Lindsey, Theophilus 312, 315
Livingstone, David 376, 377, 379
Locke, John 302, 309, 314, 407
Lothair 121
Lothair II 122
Louis VII 143, 145
Louis IX 143, 145, 148, 151, 158
Louis XIV 244, 271, 274, 364, 365, 369
Louis of Bavaria 160
Louis of Blois 145
Louis the German 121
Louis the Pious 121
Loyola, Ignatius 275, 277, 278, 286
Luke 25, 68
Lull, Raymond 149
Luther, Hans 206
Luther, Margaret 206
Luther, Martin 51, 63, 78, 115, 160, 168, 169, 186, 188, 198, 199, 201, 202, 205-220, 225, 229, 232, 235, 241, 244, 247, 254, 255, 257, 275, 279, 280, 282, 292, 308, 317, 318, 330, 333, 337

McCullough, William 331
MacDonald, George 358
McGarvey, John W. 474
McGiffert, Arthur 461, 472
McGready, James 417
Machen, J. Gresham 472-474, 477, 483, 487
Machiavelli, Niccolo 188, 191, 254
McIntire, Carl 473, 484, 485
Mack, Alexander 329
Maillesec, Guy de 187
Majorinus 76, 80
Makemie, Francis 398, 403
Malan, César 367, 369
Malcolm X 439
Mani 24-26
Manning, Henry 284
Manz, Felix 231, 235
Map, Walter 173
Marcian 75
Marcion 24, 25, 27, 68, 69
Marcus Aurelius 13, 19, 33, 35, 37, 40
Margaret of Valois 243
Margaret of York 254

Index of Names

Marozia 123
Marshall, Daniel 401, 403
Marshman, Hannah 374
Marshman, Joshua 374, 375
Marsilius of Padua 184, 190
Martel, Charles 101, 103, 109, 112
Martin V 183, 185-187, 191, 197, 198
Martin of Tours 87, 88, 93, 206
Martyn, Henry 375, 376, 379
Marx, Karl 296, 300, 341, 349, 353, 360
Mary 17, 63, 70, 71, 73, 83, 90-92, 99, 114, 117, 158, 159, 168, 205, 219, 237, 284
Mary of Guise 244, 245
Mary Stuart 245, 246, 251, 260, 265
Mary Tudor 245, 247, 253-255, 257-261, 263, 264, 266, 280
Massee, Jasper C. 474
Mather, Cotton 389, 406
Mather, Increase 388, 389, 399
Matthew 12, 23
Matthys, Jan 236, 237, 239
Maurice, F.D. 353, 360
Mauritius 33
Maurus, Rabanus 116, 120
Maxentius 38
Maximian 38
Maximilla 27, 29, 68
Maximin Daia 38
Maximinus the Thracian 33, 36, 40
Mazarin, Jules 363, 364
Meacham, Joseph 446
Medici, Lorenzo de 199, 200
Melanchthon, Philip 210-213, 215, 216, 225, 244, 280
Meletius 75, 76
Melville, Andrew 246, 251
Mencken, H.L. 471
Mesmer, Franz 453, 456
Methodius 115, 120
Michelangelo 188, 199
Miller, John Peter 446
Miller, Samuel 459
Miller, William 449, 450, 452, 456
Miltitz, Karl von 208
Milton, John 269, 271
Minucius Felix 31, 40
Minuit, Peter 392, 395
Mirandola, Pico della 199
Moffatt, Robert 376
Moltmann, Jurgen 348, 350
Monica 62, 63, 65
Monod, Adolphe 366, 367
Monod, Frederick 366, 367
Monroe, James 426

Montanus 26, 27, 68
Montfort, Simon de 145, 172
Moody, D.L. 355, 421, 423, 492
Moon, Sun Myung 455
More, Thomas 255, 445
Morone, Giovanni 284
Moroni 447, 448, 456
Morris, Samuel 439
Mott, John R. 480, 487
Muhammad 97-101, 103, 144, 147
Muhammad, Elijah 439
Muhammad, Wallace 439
Muhlenberg, Henry Melchior 317, 321, 325, 401, 403, 410
Muhlenberg, John Peter Gabriel 410
Müller, George 357, 376
Münzer, Thomas 210, 211
Murray, Earl of 246
Murray, John 472

Nero 7, 8, 10, 32-34, 45, 47
Nestorius 71, 73, 75, 157
Nettleton, Asahel 419, 420, 423
Newman, John Henry 354
Newton, B.W. 356
Newton, Isaac 292-297, 299, 309
Newton, John 334, 335, 337, 352
Nicholas I 122, 129, 134, 138
Nicholas II 124
Nicholas V 188, 191
Nicholas of Cologne 145, 147
Nicholas of Cusa 184, 187, 191, 195, 201
Niemöller, Martin 347
Nietzsche, Friedrich 296, 341, 342, 348, 349
Nitschmann, David 321
Norbert 168
Norris, J. Frank 473
Northumberland, Duke of 257, 258, 263
Novatian 76, 80
Novatus 76, 80
Noyes, John Humphrey 446, 447, 456

Odovacar 105, 112
Oecolampadius, John 221
Oglethorpe, James 328, 384, 391, 394
Oldcastle, John 196, 197
Olevianus, Caspar 213
Origen 16, 17, 33, 35, 55, 57, 58, 69, 73
Oswy 106
Otto I 123, 129
Otto II 123
Otto III 123, 124
Owen, John 271, 307
Ozman, Agnes 490

Pachomius 87, 88
Palaeologus, Manuel 136
Palaeologus, Michael 136, 138
Palau, Luis 492
Paley, William 311, 315
Pamphilus 55, 65
Pannenberg, Wolfhart 348, 350
Pantaenus 16
Papias 12
Parham, Charles F. 490, 491, 497
Parr, Catherine 257
Parris, Samuel 389
Pascal, Blaise 294
Patricius 62
Patrick 88, 93, 106
Patterson, Daniel 453
Patterson, Mary Jane 420
Paul 4-6, 8, 10-12, 18, 19, 21, 23, 25, 33, 34, 40, 45, 47, 49, 65, 67-69, 83, 84, 90, 91, 114, 119, 137, 205, 278, 324, 343, 356, 357, 359, 405, 422, 428, 431, 472, 484, 490
Paul III 280, 282, 284, 287
Paul IV 277
Paul VI 137, 284
Pelagius 71, 75, 77, 89, 91, 115, 157
Pelagius II 108
Penn, William 270, 271, 274, 391-393, 395
Pepin the Short 109, 110, 112
Perpetua 33, 35
Peter 3-6, 8, 10, 12, 23, 24, 33, 34, 38, 40, 41, 43, 45-48, 63, 67-69, 106, 107, 114, 121, 127, 179, 180, 184, 205, 343, 448, 484
Peter of Castelnau 172
Peter the Hermit 142, 145, 150
Pew, J. Howard 481
Philargi, Peter 187
Philip 4
Philip II 243, 247, 251, 258-260, 263
Philip Augustus 127, 144-146
Philip of Hesse 211-213, 216, 220
Philip the Arabian 36
Philip the Fair 169, 180, 190, 241
Philo 73
Photius 122, 134, 138
Pierce, James 312
Pike, James A. 485
Pilate, Pontius 3, 149
Pius II 188, 191
Pius IV 284
Pius V 243
Pius IX 284
Pius XII 283
Placaeus 249
Plato 14-16, 72, 73, 154, 155, 162, 291

Pliny the Younger 34
Plutschau, Heinrich 321, 325
Pocohontas 384
Poe, Edgar Allen 174
Pole, Reginald 258, 280
Polycarp 11-13, 15, 33, 35, 40, 42, 44
Potamiaena 35, 40
Pothinus 33, 35, 40
Preus, Jacob 474
Priestley, Joseph 312
Priscilla 27, 29, 68
Ptolemy 292, 340
Purvey, John 196
Pusey, Edward 354

Quimby, Phineas P. 453

Rabaut St. Etienne 366, 369
Rabaut, Paul 365, 366, 369
Radbertus, Paschasius 117, 118, 120
Rahner, Karl 284
Raikes, Robert 334, 335, 337
Raphael 188
Rapp, George 446
Ratramnus 117, 120
Rauschenbusch, Walter 467, 469, 474, 476
Ravaillac 363
Raymund of Toulouse 145
Reginald of Chatillon 143, 144, 150
Richard I 127, 143-145, 169
Richard II 197
Richelieu, Armand de 214, 244, 363, 369
Ridley, Nicholas 254, 257, 259, 263, 308
Rigdon, Sidney 448, 456
Riley, William Bell 474
Ripley, George 447
Ritschl, Albrecht 342, 344-346, 349
Rizzio, David 246
Robert of Molesme 166, 176
Robert of Normandy 145
Robinson, John 267, 273, 385, 394
Romulus Augustulus 105
Roscelin 156, 162
Ross, J.J. 454
Rothad 122
Rothmann, Bernard 236, 239
Rousseau, Jean-Jacques 302
Rowland, Daniel 331
Rudolf 126
Rufus 33
Russell, Charles Taze 450, 454
Rutherford, Joseph F. 450, 454, 455
Rutherford, Samuel 301, 302, 306

Index of Names

Sabellius 70
Sadoleto, Jacopo 223, 230, 277
Saladin 143-145, 150, 169
Salmeron, Alfonso 278, 282
Samson, Bernard 219
Sandys, Edwin 384, 394
Sankey, Ira 421
Sapphira 4
Sattler, Michael 232
Savonarola, Girolamo 188, 195, 199-203
Savoy, Duke of 221, 241
Sayers, Dorothy 358
Schaeffer, Francis 471, 489, 495, 497
Schaff, Philip 115
Schleiermacher, Friedrich 342, 343, 345, 349
Schwartz, C.F. 321, 325
Schweitzer, Albert 345, 348, 350
Schwenkfeld, Caspar 237
Scofield, C.I. 462, 465
Scopes, John 470, 471, 476
Scotus, John Duns 155, 159, 160, 163, 171
Seneca 7
Septimus Severus 33, 35
Sergius III 123
Servetus, Michael 222, 226-228, 230, 237, 389
Seymour, Jane 257
Seymour, William J. 491, 497
Shaftesbury, Seventh Earl of 352
Shakespeare, William 197, 244, 429
Sharp, Archbishop 303
Sharp, Granville 335
Sheldon, Charles M. 469, 476
Shelley, Percy 453
Shields, T.T. 474
Sigismund 185, 187, 190, 198
Simeon, Charles 352, 376
Simeon the Stylite 86, 93
Simon Magus 24, 29
Simons, Menno 237
Sixtus II 33, 36, 40
Sixtus IV 188, 191, 201
Smith, Al 473
Smith, Henry P. 461, 472
Smith, Joseph 447-450
Smyth, John 267, 273
Socinus, Faustus 237, 312, 315
Socinus, Laelius 237, 312, 315
Söderblom, Nathan 482, 487
Somerset, Duke of 257
Spangenberg, August 321, 325, 329, 332
Spaulding, Solomon 449
Spencer, Herbert 469
Spener, Philip Jacob 318-320, 325, 329, 342
Spurgeon, Charles 354, 355

Stanley, Ann Lee 445, 446, 456
Stanton, Elizabeth Cady 431
Staupitz, Johann von 206
Stearns, Shubal 401, 403
Stephen 4
Stephen I 46, 52
Stephen III 109
Stephen VII 121
Stephen of Cloyes 145, 146
Stevenson, J. Ross 474
Stewart, Lyman 470, 476
Stewart, Milton 470, 476
Stoddard, Solomon 388, 394, 399
Stone, Barton 417, 418
Stonehouse, Ned 472
Storch, Nicholas 210
Stowe, Calvin 427
Stowe, Harriet Beecher 419, 427, 430, 467
Straton, John Roach 474
Strauss, David 343, 345, 346, 348
Stübner, Marcus 210
Studd, C.T. 421
Sunday, Billy 421, 430, 492
Swedenborg, Emmanuel 453, 456
Sylvester I 110
Sylvester II 124
Sylvester III 124, 129
Symeon 33

Tancred 145
Tappan, Lewis 427, 431
Tatian 14, 15, 19
Taylor, G. Aiken 474
Taylor, Hudson 376, 379, 421, 479
Telesphorus 33
Temple, William 482
Tennent, Gilbert 397-399, 401, 403
Tennent, William 398, 399, 401, 403
Tertullian 16, 24, 27, 29, 32, 40, 43, 44, 51, 52, 68, 70, 71, 74, 204
Tetzel, Johann 207, 208, 215, 219
Teutberga 122
Thaddaeus 6, 10
Theodora 115, 120
Theodora, wife of Theophylact 123
Theodore of Mopsuestia 55, 57, 65, 73
Theodoret 71
Theodoric 105, 112
Theodosius 44, 60, 65, 75
Theodosius II 75
Theophilus 115
Theophilus of Alexandria 58, 65
Theresa of Avila 168
Thibaut of Champagne 145

Thomas 6, 10, 146
Thomas à Becket 126
Thornwell, James 428, 433
Tietjen, John 474
Tillich, Paul 346, 350
Tillotson, John 309
Timothy 18, 84, 422
Tindal, Matthew 309, 314
Tituba 389
Titus 34
Toland, John 309, 314
Tolkien, J.R.R. 358
Toplady, Augustus 333, 337
Torquemada, Tomas de 171, 276, 286
Torrey, Reuben A. 421, 462, 470
Trajan 33-35, 40
Tulga, Chester 474
Turner, Frederick Jackson 415
Turner, Nat 427, 437
Turretin, Francis 366, 369, 459, 460
Turretin, J.A. 366, 369
Tyndale, William 196, 244, 254, 256, 257, 263, 266

Ugolino 171
Ulfilas 107, 112
Urban II 139-142, 145, 166, 181
Urban VI 182, 183, 191
Ursinus, Zacharius 213
Ursula 33

Valens 72, 105
Valentinian II 60
Valentinian III 41
Valentinus 24, 25
Valerian 33, 36, 37, 40, 48, 85
Valla, Lorenzo 110, 188, 191
Van Prinsterer, Gröen 367, 369
Van Til, Cornelius 473, 495
Vassar, Matthew 431
Vesey, Denmark 437
Victor I 45, 46, 50, 52
Villegagnon, Nicholas de 373, 379
Vladimir 136, 138
Voetius, Gisbert 367, 369
Voltaire 366

Wagner, Richard 453
Waldo, Peter 173
Walter the Penniless 142, 145, 150
Warburton, William 311, 315
Ward, William 374, 375
Ware, Henry 419
Warfield, B.B. 460, 461, 465, 472, 489, 491
Washington, George 407, 410-412

Webster, Daniel 426
Weld, Theodore 420, 427, 433
Wellhausen, Julius 343, 344, 349, 472
Wenceslaus IV 197, 198
Wesley, Charles 318, 327-330, 335, 337
Wesley, John 115, 309, 311, 312, 318, 322, 327-335, 337, 338, 351, 371, 401, 409, 413, 416, 420, 428, 490
Wesley, Samuel 327, 328
Wesley, Susanna 327, 331, 332
Westcott, B.F. 357, 358, 361
Wheelock, Eleazar 400, 403
Whitaker, Alexander 384, 394
White, Ellen G. 450, 452, 456
White, James 452
Whitefield, Elizabeth 331
Whitefield, George 115, 309, 312, 322, 328-337, 397, 399, 401, 403, 408, 411, 416, 492
Whitney, Eli 426
Whittle, Daniel W. 462
Wibert 126
Wilberforce, William 335-337, 352, 376
Wilkinson, Jemima 446, 456
Willard, Frances 421, 430
Willett, Herbert L. 474
William of Aquitaine 166
William of Champeaux 156, 162
William of Holland 145
William of Nogaret 180
William of Ockham 155, 159, 160, 163, 171, 184, 190, 195
William of Orange 272, 274, 304, 385
William the Pig 146
William the Silent 247, 251
Williams, Charles 358
Williams, Roger 387, 390, 391, 395
Williams, William 335
Willibrord 106, 112
Wilson, Robert Dick 472
Wilson, Woodrow 471
Winthrop, John 391
Wishart, George 244, 245, 251
Witherspoon, John 406, 413
Wolsey, Thomas 253-255
Woolley, Paul 472, 474
Woolston, Thomas 310
Wycliffe, John 195-200, 202-204, 214, 253, 256

Xavier, Francis 278, 279, 286
Ximenes, Francisco 277, 286

Young, Brigham 448-450

Index of Names

Zarathustra 22, 29
Zeisberger, David 321, 325
Ziegenbalg, Bartholomew 321, 325
Zinzendorf, Nikolaus von 199, 317, 319-322, 325, 329, 332, 334, 401

Zizka, John 198
Zozimus 33
Zwingli, Ulrich 63, 78, 188, 212, 217-222, 225, 228, 229, 231, 232, 235, 236, 367

INDEX OF PLACES

Aachen 110
Achaia 91
Acre 144, 145, 147, 148, 169
Adrianople 105
Aix-la-Chapelle 110
Albi 172
Alcala 277
Aldersgate Street 330, 331, 337
Alexandria 5, 6, 12, 13, 16, 17, 24, 35, 42-44, 47, 55-58, 70-75, 80, 86, 101, 114
Alsace 122
Alva 247, 251, 277
Amana 446, 447
Amboise 243, 251
Amsterdam 237, 482, 485, 492
Anagni 180, 191
Andover 446, 459, 469
Antioch 3-5, 8, 11, 42-44, 46, 47, 56-58, 61, 65, 73, 74, 80, 101, 114, 142-145, 495
Anwoth 302
Appalachians 416, 418, 429, 491
Aptunga 76, 80
Aquino 158
Aquitaine 143, 166
Aragon 254, 255, 257, 263, 276
Argyle 303
Arizona 449
Arles 71, 76, 81
Armenia 26, 58, 74
Assisi 149, 165, 170, 171, 173, 176
Athens 21
Auburn 472, 477
Augsburg 126, 207, 212, 213, 216, 317
Austria 144, 145, 199, 214, 220, 221, 231, 232, 237, 282, 453
Avignon 180-185, 187, 190, 195, 196, 203, 241
Avila 168

Babel 307, 313, 314
Balkans 26
Baltimore 333, 471
Bangkok 484
Barbados 389
Basel 184, 186-188, 191, 198, 203, 218, 220, 221, 223, 366
Battle Creek 450, 452
Bavaria 160, 214
Bedford 271
Belgium 247, 257, 260, 264, 282
Berea 91
Berlin 318, 319, 341, 492
Bern 218, 220, 241

Berthelsdorf 320
Bethlehem 61, 62
Bethlehem, PA 321
Beziers 173
Bithynia 34
Blois 145
Bohemia 197-199, 203, 209, 213, 320
Bologna 127, 188
Bordeaux 180
Boston 386, 387, 389, 390, 392, 393, 400, 401, 409, 419, 421, 450, 451, 453
Bourges 222, 241
Brandenburg 319
Brazil 373
Breda 271, 274, 302
Brescia 167
Brienne 145
Bristol 330, 337, 357
Brittany 156
Brixen 126
Brooklyn 450, 455
Brush Run 418
Bulgaria 26, 135, 142
Burgundy 109, 166
Burma 419
Burned-Over District 419, 422, 423, 447

Caesarea 55, 56, 72, 75
Calcutta 374, 376
California 449, 470, 490
Callinicum 60
Cambridge 254-257, 357, 358, 375, 388, 421, 423
Cambridge, MA 387
Cambuslang 331, 337
Cane Ridge 417
Canossa 126
Canterbury 106, 108, 126, 127, 155, 195, 196, 255, 256, 259, 261, 266, 267, 273, 277, 308, 309, 482
Cape of Good Hope 479
Capernaum 25
Cappadocia 55, 72, 83, 87, 143
Carolinas 384, 392, 401, 419
Carthage 16, 18, 35, 36, 44, 46, 62, 69, 70, 75-77, 81, 101
Carthage, IL 448
Castelnau 172
Castile 276
Cevennes 365
Chalcedon 43, 45, 48, 52, 71, 72, 74, 75, 81, 86, 132, 133, 136
Champagne 145

Champeaux 156, 162
Chartreuse 168
Chatillon 143, 150, 242
Chicago 421, 448, 469, 473
China 74, 279, 376, 421, 479
Cilicia 144
Cincinnati 427, 461, 469
Citeaux 166, 167
Clairvaux 141, 143, 145, 155, 157, 158, 162, 167
Clapham 335, 338, 352, 376
Clermont 139, 141, 147
Cleves 256
Cloyes 145, 146
Cluny 166
Cologne 145, 147, 159, 168
Colosse 8
Columbus 469
Connecticut 386, 391, 410, 411, 419
Constance 183, 185-187, 190, 191, 196-198, 203, 209
Constantinople 17, 19, 43, 45-48, 52, 57, 58, 65, 71-75, 81, 100, 101, 108, 109, 114, 115, 122, 131, 133-137, 142-146, 148, 150, 151, 153, 186, 188, 495
Coral Ridge 493
Corbie 117
Corinth 6, 8, 11, 42, 45, 231, 278
Crete 184
Ctesiphon 25, 29
Cumorah 447, 456
Cusa 184, 187, 191, 195, 201
Cyprus 144, 169

Dakotas 235
Dallas 462
Damascus 113, 114, 120, 143, 145
Damietta 145, 148
Danube 231
Dayton 470, 471
Delaware 391, 392, 437
Denmark 236, 266, 321, 325, 345, 350, 372-374
Des Moines 474
Dordt 225, 226, 248, 249, 252, 367
Douai 260, 264
Dover 437
Dresden 318, 320
Durham 310
Dusseldorf 317, 320

Ebenezer 446
Economy 446
Ecuador 295
Edessa 6, 143, 145
Edinburgh 245, 268, 481, 482, 487

Egypt 22, 24, 72, 74, 76, 85-87, 92, 101, 144-149, 170, 171, 292
Einsiedeln 219
Eisleben 206
Ephesus 8, 15, 41, 71, 73-75, 77, 81, 86, 90, 91, 99, 119, 324, 359
Ephrata 446
Epworth 327, 328, 331, 337
Erfurt 201, 206, 319
Evanston 483
Exeter 312

Ferrara 136, 186, 187, 191
Flanders 145
Florence 186, 188, 199, 200, 203
Florida 493
Fort Worth 473, 474
Frankfurt 115, 245, 318
Freiburg 241
Frisia 106, 107, 112
Fulda 115

Galapagos Islands 295
Gaul 15, 35, 41, 43, 48, 59, 72, 78, 87, 88, 100, 101, 109
Geneva 217, 221-230, 234, 238, 239, 241-243, 245-248, 251, 257, 260, 263, 266, 269, 277, 308, 334, 366, 367, 386, 484, 496
Genoa 147
Georgia 321, 328, 329, 331, 332, 337, 371, 384, 391, 428, 435
Ghana 482
Gibraltar 101
Glarus 218
Glasgow 355
Gloucester 328, 330, 331, 334, 337
Great Salt Lake 449
Greenland 321
Greenville 490

Haarlem 236
Halle 319, 321, 325, 329, 342, 372, 373, 401
Hampton Court 265, 273
Harmony 446, 450
Heidelberg 247
Helmstadt 317
Hesse 211-213, 216, 220
Hierapolis 12
Hippo 55, 62, 63, 71, 106, 115, 167
Houston 491
Hungary 110, 142, 146, 214, 217, 225
Hydesville 447

Index of Places

Illinois 417, 448, 483
Independence 448, 451
India 6, 25, 279, 321, 322, 371, 374-376, 379, 482, 483, 487
Indiana 418, 446
Ingolstadt 208, 231
Iona 106
Iowa 446
Ireland 88, 106, 118, 268, 270, 293, 301, 303, 304, 331, 353, 356, 393, 398, 406, 418, 429

Jamestown 383-385, 394, 426
Japan 279, 440
Jericho 142
Jerusalem 3-5, 7, 8, 10, 14, 23, 33, 43, 45, 47, 50, 101, 114, 139-145, 148, 169, 187, 320, 324, 343, 446, 451, 481, 482, 495
Joppa 145

Kansas 441, 462, 490
Kent 106
Kentucky 415-419
Kenya 484
Kirtland 448
Königsberg 339

La Rochelle 244, 363, 369
Lake Mohonk 481
Lancaster 196
Laodicea 73
Lausanne 365, 482, 492
Leipzig 197, 209, 214, 215, 319, 325
Leyden 236, 237, 239, 247, 248, 385
Liberia 426
Limmat 231, 235
London 136, 196, 255, 257, 265, 267, 268, 270, 312, 329-332, 334, 335, 354, 355, 357, 376, 383-385
Lorraine 122, 242
Los Angeles 462, 491, 492
Louisiana 416
Lund 483
Lutterworth 196
Lynchburg 490, 492
Lyons 15, 35, 136, 173, 187

Macedonia 91
Madaura 62
Madras 482
Maine 429, 453
Mainz 116, 207
Malta 169
Manitoba 235

Mansura 148
Manzikert 140
Marburg 212, 216, 220, 244
Marseilles 146
Martha's Vineyard 373
Maryland 333, 391, 392, 398
Masada 7
Massachusetts 247, 268, 373, 383, 385-395, 399, 400, 402, 407, 410, 411, 421, 447, 450, 453, 462
Mecca 97-100, 103, 144
Medina 98, 103, 144
Mexico 448
Mexico City 484
Michigan 450, 452
Milan 26, 38, 40, 45-50, 59, 60, 63, 85, 172
Mississippi 435, 448
Missouri 448, 451, 462, 471, 474, 484, 485, 489
Molesme 166, 176
Montauban 364
Monte Cassino 88, 93, 158
Montreal 484
Mopsuestia 55, 57, 65, 73
Moravia 235, 237, 239, 320
Morristown 460
Moscow 136, 495
Mount Carmel 168
Mount Hira 98, 103
Mount Sinai 462
Münster 234, 236, 237, 239
Murray 246

Nag Hammadi 24, 29
Nairobi 484, 496
Nantes 244, 250, 251, 363-365, 369, 392
Naples 180, 182, 185, 197
Nauvoo 448
Navarre 242, 243, 250-252, 276
Nazareth 3, 91
Nazareth, PA 321
Nazianzus 55, 71, 72, 75, 83
Neshaminy 398
Neuchatel 223
Nevada 449
New Amsterdam 392
New Brunswick 397-399
New Delhi 483, 487
New Hampshire 391, 453
New Harmony 446
New Haven 386
New Jersey 304, 391, 392, 397-402, 459, 460
New York 391-393, 397, 398, 419-422, 425, 437, 446, 447, 450, 461, 467, 469, 472, 473, 481

Niagara 462, 470
Nicea 43, 44, 52, 55-57, 71, 72, 75, 81, 110, 115, 132, 142, 145
Nicomedia 71, 72, 75
Nigeria 376
Nogaret 180
Normandy 145
North Carolina 391, 401
Northampton 388, 399, 400
Northamptonshire 373
Northfield 421, 462
Northumberland 257, 258, 263
Northumbria 106
Noyon 222
Nursia 88, 166
Nyssa 55, 71, 72, 75

Oberlin 420, 427, 431
Ochrida 135, 138
Ohio 418-420, 448, 469
Oneida 427, 446
Ontario 482
Orange 71, 78, 81, 108, 115
Orleans 222
Oxford 159, 195-197, 203, 328-332, 353, 354, 360, 482

Padua 184, 190
Palmyra 447, 448
Pamplona 275
Papal States 110, 182, 283
Paris 136, 156, 159, 184, 190, 221, 222, 242, 243, 250, 277, 278, 366, 416
Patmos 8, 33, 34
Paulerspury 373
Pennsylvania 237, 271, 304, 312, 321, 390-393, 395, 398-402, 418, 419, 422, 446, 450, 454
Pensacola 493
Pepuza 26, 27, 29
Persia 22, 25, 36, 37, 47, 73, 100, 101, 376
Philadelphia 301, 331, 393, 398, 399, 410, 437, 459, 460, 462, 473, 480
Philippi 12, 42
Phrygia 26, 27
Pisa 183-187, 190
Pittsburgh 450, 454
Pityus 58
Plymouth 356, 358, 360, 461, 464
Plymouth, MA 247, 385-388, 390
Poissy 243, 251
Poitiers 55
Poland 169, 211, 282, 292, 312
Portland 461, 465, 470, 472
Portugal 182, 276, 282, 373

Prague 197, 203, 213, 216
Premontre 168
Princeton 398, 400, 406, 427, 459-461, 464, 465, 467, 469, 472, 489
Providence 390
Prussia 169
Putney 446

Raritan 397
Ratisbon 280, 287
Ravenna 46, 107, 126
Rheims 116, 122, 260
Rhode Island 390-392
Rhodes 169
Rimini 195, 226
Rochester 245
Rochester, NY 420, 469, 473
Rome 3, 5, 7, 8, 11-13, 15, 16, 21-25, 27, 31-36, 38, 41-48, 50, 52, 55, 56, 59-63, 69, 70, 72-74, 76, 77, 84, 88, 100, 105-112, 121-126, 128, 131-133, 135, 136, 142, 143, 148, 170, 171, 173, 180-188, 190, 191, 197, 199-201, 205, 206, 208, 210, 215, 219, 231, 234, 241, 243, 254, 255, 259, 271, 275-278, 280, 283, 405, 495
Roxbury 373
Russia 136, 237, 390, 483, 484, 488

St. Andrews 244, 245, 302
St. Gall 218
St. Louis 462
St. Thomas 321
Salem 386, 389, 390, 395
Samaria 24
San Francisco 485, 491
Sao Paulo 496
Sardica 46, 52
Sardinia 146
Saumur 249, 252, 366
Savoy 221, 241, 268
Saxony 198, 206, 208, 320, 321, 332
Schleitheim 232, 233
Schwyz 220
Scotland 106, 182, 217, 224, 225, 241, 244-246, 249-251, 260, 265, 266, 268-271, 273, 301-308, 310, 331, 334, 355, 358, 367, 376, 393, 398, 406, 418, 460, 481
Scrooby 267, 385, 394
Sea Cliff 462
Sens 157
Seoul 496
Serampore 374, 375, 379
Seville 113
Sharon 447
Shinar 307

Index of Places

Siena 123, 181, 190
Sierra Leone 335, 338, 376
Sinope 25
Smyrna 11, 12, 15
Sodom 420
Soissons 157
Somerset 257
South Africa 365, 376, 427, 483
South Carolina 391, 490
Southwark 267
Speier 211, 212, 216
Springfield 417
Stockbridge 400
Stockholm 482
Strasbourg 221, 223, 224, 236
Surrey 270
Sutri 124
Sweden 181, 190, 214, 236, 391, 392, 453, 482-484

Tabennisi 87, 93
Tagaste 62, 63
Tarsus 4
Tennessee 416, 419, 462, 470, 471
Texas 473, 491
Thailand 484
Thebes 57, 65, 86
Thessalonica 60, 91
Toledo 133, 277
Topeka 441, 490
Toronto 454, 474
Toulouse 145, 174, 175, 180
Tours 87, 88, 93, 101, 110, 147, 206
Trent 70, 202, 212, 275, 278, 280, 282-285, 287
Trier 59
Tübingen 339, 343, 344
Tunis 148
Tusculum 123

Tyre 55, 72

Ulster 393, 398
Uppsala 484
Utah 448, 449

Vatican 201, 282-285, 287
Venice 144-146, 150
Verdun 121, 122, 129
Vermont 446, 447
Vienna 218, 231
Vienne 35, 187
Virginia 383-385, 387, 391, 394, 401, 407, 419, 426, 427, 436, 459, 490, 492

Wales 331, 334
Warren 419
Wartburg 210, 220
Washington, D.C. 435
Westphalia 214, 236, 247
Whitby 106, 482
Whitechapel 357
Wildhaus 218
Williamsburg 393
Willingen 482
Wilmington 392
Wittenberg 205-210, 212, 213, 220, 235, 239, 244, 318, 320
Worms 126, 187, 209, 210, 214, 215, 256

York 110, 115, 253, 391

Zara 145, 146
Zug 220
Zurich 217-221, 229, 231, 232, 235, 239, 260
Zwickau 210, 215, 235

INDEX OF EVENTS, MOVEMENTS, ORGANIZATIONS, BOOKS, AND TERMS

Abolitionism 402, 420, 425-430, 432, 433, 436, 460, 480, 487
Abortion 305, 336, 431, 434, 471, 494, 495, 498
Act of Uniformity 271
Address to the German Nobility 209
Adoptionism 70, 133
Aeterni Patris 284
Adventists 422, 449-452, 454-456
African Methodist Episcopal Church 437, 438, 485
African Methodist Episcopal Zion Church 437, 438, 485
Against Celsus 17
Against Heresies 15
Against the Thieving and Murdering Hordes of Peasants 211
Agape 49, 53
Age of Reason 283, 293, 307, 313
Aggiornamento 284
Albigensians 26, 29, 128, 149, 171, 172, 180, 234, 276
Amalekites 243
American Anti-Slavery Society 427
American Association of Christian Schools 493
American Baptist Convention 474
American Bible Society 480
American Board of Commissioners for Foreign Missions 419, 479
American Civil Liberties Union 470
American Colonization Society 426, 427, 433
American Council of Christian Churches 485
American Muslim Mission 439
American Revolution 241, 301, 305, 306, 309, 366, 401-403, 405-414, 419, 426, 433, 479
American Society for the Promotion of Temperance 429
Amish 233, 237, 238, 391, 393
Amyraldianism 249, 250, 366
Anabaptists 210, 220, 223, 231-240, 247, 261, 270, 317, 322, 372, 393
Analogy of Religion 310
Anchorites 85-87, 92
Andover Theological Seminary 446, 459, 469
Anglicans 259, 260, 266, 269-272, 308, 310, 312, 327-335, 337, 351-354, 359, 360, 373, 376, 384, 386, 391, 394, 401, 407-409, 413, 481, 483
Animal magnetism 453, 456
Annates 181, 190
Anti-burghers 304
Anti-Saloon League 430
Antidisestablishmentarianism 351, 360

Antinomianism 333, 334, 338, 392, 395
Apocalypse of Peter, The 68, 69
Apocrypha 62, 70, 78, 80, 281, 282, 284
Apollinarianism 71, 73, 75, 80
Apology 32
Apostles' Creed 49
Arianism 56, 59, 60, 65, 71, 72, 75, 80, 86, 97, 106-108, 112, 450, 455
Arminian, The 333
Arminianism 225, 248-250, 252, 267, 308, 314, 331, 333, 351, 367, 372, 400, 401, 411, 412, 417, 418, 460
Aryan Paragraph 347
Assemblies of God 491
Association of Christian Schools International 493
Assumption of Mary 91
Athanasian Creed 234
Auburn Affirmation 472, 477
Augsburg Confession 212, 317
Augustinianism 78, 80, 115, 132, 138, 195, 205, 211, 226, 248, 282
Augustinians 167, 168, 171, 176, 195, 205, 206
Authorised Version 266
Auto-da-fé 276, 286
Azusa Street Mission 491

Babylonian Captivity 180-183, 188, 190, 241
Babylonian Captivity of the Church, The 209
Baltimore Sun 471
Baptist Bible Union 473
Baptist Missionary Society 372, 374
Baptist Union 354, 355
Baptists 267-269, 271, 273, 307, 308, 312, 314, 332, 351, 354, 355, 360, 366, 374, 390, 401-403, 408, 410, 412, 416-418, 422, 423, 428, 429, 431, 436-438, 443, 446, 448, 449, 467, 469, 471-475, 477, 484, 489, 490, 492
Barmen Declaration 347, 350
Barnabas, Epistle of 12, 68
Barnes' Notes 460
Battle of Manzikert 140
Battle of Milvian Bridge 38
Battle of Tours 101, 147
Battle for the Bible, The 489
Beauty of Holiness 267
Beghards 170, 187
Beguines 170, 187
Belgic Confession 247, 248
Benedictines 88, 106, 108, 158, 166-168, 176, 232
Bethel Bible College 490
Bible Institute of Los Angeles 462

Bibliotheca Sacra 462
Bill of Attainder 269
Bill of Rights 411
Billy Graham Evangelistic Association 492
Blue Laws 425, 452
Board of Triers 270, 273
Bob Jones University 490, 493
Bogomils 26, 172
Bohemian Brethren 197, 199, 203, 320
Bondage of the Will, The 211
Bonfire of the Vanities 200
Book of Common Prayer 257, 258, 268
Book of Martyrs 259
Book of Mormon, The 448-450, 456
Book of Sports 267, 273
Brethren of the Common Life 201, 202, 204, 206, 247
British and Foreign Bible Society 480
British East India Company 371, 374-376, 379
Broad Church 351-354, 358, 360
Brook Farm 447
Brown vs. Board of Education 441
Buddhism 25, 26, 83, 440
Burghers 304

Caesaropapism 107, 110, 112, 114, 131, 136
Calvinism 213, 225, 230, 248, 249-252, 258, 266, 267, 293, 299, 308, 312, 314, 329, 331, 333-335, 338, 347, 351, 355, 366, 367, 372, 400, 401, 411, 412, 414, 419, 420, 459, 460
Cambridge Platform 386, 388, 394
Cambridge University 254-256, 357, 358, 375, 421, 423
Cameronians 303
Camisards 365, 369, 490
Campbellites 418, 448
Campmeeting 417-419, 423
Campus Crusade for Christ 484
Canaanites 22, 141, 236
Canterbury Tales 253
Carmelites 168, 176
Caroline Books 115
Carolinum 220
Carthusians 168, 176, 277
Case of Reason, The 311
Catabaptists 231, 239
Catechumens 49, 50, 53
Categorical Imperative 340, 349
Cathari 26, 172-174, 176, 187, 190, 195
Catholic Apostolic Church 355, 360
Cavaliers 269
Celibacy 26, 84, 85, 90, 93, 125, 133-135, 156, 167-170, 201, 219, 280, 445, 446

Charismatics 27, 285, 287, 490-492, 497
Chicago Evangelization Society 421
Children's Crusades 145-147, 151
China Inland Mission 376, 421, 479
Chorepiscopi 43
Christian Century, The 472
Christian Church 418
Christian Herald 469
Christian Methodist Episcopal Church 437, 485
Christian Reformed Church 493
Christian Science 422, 450, 451, 453-457
Christian Science Monitor 454
Christian Socialists 353
Christianity and Liberalism 472
Christianity and the Social Crisis 467
Christianity Today 489, 490, 492
Christianizing the Social Order 469
Christmas Conference 333
Chronicles of Narnia 358
Church of England 249, 253-255, 257-260, 263, 265, 268, 272, 273, 304, 306-309, 312, 314, 315, 330-334, 337, 338, 351, 353, 354, 360, 363, 376, 383-387, 390-392, 408, 409
Church of Ireland 268, 353, 356
Church of Scotland 245, 268, 271, 301, 303, 304, 306, 355, 376
Church of South India 483, 487
Church of the Desert 365, 369
Church of the Nazarene 490
Church World Service 481
Cistercians 158, 166-168, 176
City of God 110
Civil War 384, 409, 421, 425, 428, 429, 433, 435-438, 440, 441, 443, 462, 467
Clapham Sect 335, 338, 352, 376
Clarendon Code 271, 274, 303, 307
Clericis laicos 180, 190
Cluniacs 166, 167, 176
Coenobites 85, 87, 92
Cogito ergo sum 294, 310
College of Cardinals 124, 126, 127, 129, 181-185, 187, 188, 207, 211, 280, 283
College of New Jersey 398-401
College of William and Mary 384
Collegia pietatis 318, 325
Collegium Philobiblicum 319, 325
Colloquy of Poissy 243, 251
Communist Manifesto 353
Community of True Inspiration 446
Complutensian Polyglot 277, 286
Conceptualism 154, 157, 158, 160, 162
Concordat of Worms 126, 187
Confessing Church 347, 350
Confessions 62, 65, 77

Index of Events, Movements, Organizations, Books, and Terms

Congregationalists 351, 354, 385, 386, 389, 391, 395, 400-402, 408, 410, 411, 417-420, 423, 429, 459, 461, 467, 469, 471, 479, 483, 485
Conservative Baptist Association 474
Consolamentum 172, 176
Consolation of Philosophy, The 105
Consubstantiation 212
Consultation on Church Union 485, 488
Continental Congress 406, 407
Conventicle Act 271
Conventicles 318, 320, 322, 323, 329, 332
Cost of Discipleship, The 347
Council of Arles 71, 76, 81
Council of Basel 184, 186-188, 191, 198, 203
Council of Carthage 46, 77, 81
Council of Chalcedon 43, 45, 48, 52, 71, 72, 74, 75, 81, 86, 132, 133, 136
Council of Clermont 139, 141, 147
Council of Constance 183, 185-187, 190, 191, 196-198, 203, 209
Council of Constantinople (381) 43, 45, 46, 52, 57, 71-73, 75, 81
Council of Constantinople (553) 75
Council of Constantinople (681) 74, 75, 81
Council of Constantinople (754) 114, 115
Council of Ephesus (431) 71, 73, 75, 77, 81, 86, 91
Council of Ephesus ("Robber Synod") (449) 71, 74, 81
Council of Ferrara 136, 186, 187, 191
Council of Lyons (1245) 187
Council of Lyons (1274) 136, 187
Council of Nicea (325) 43, 44, 52, 55-57, 71, 72, 75, 81
Council of Nicea (787) 75, 110, 115, 132
Council of Orange 71, 78, 81, 108, 115
Council of Pisa 183-187, 190
Council of Sardica 46, 52
Council of Sens 157
Council of Soissons 157
Council of Toulouse 174, 175
Council of Trent 70, 202, 212, 275, 278, 280, 282-285, 287
Council of Vienne 187
Counterfeit Miracles 491
Countess of Huntingdon's Connexion 329
Covenant Theology 367, 406, 407, 413, 463
Covenanters 301-306
Crozer Theological Seminary 473
Critique of Practical Reason 340
Critique of Pure Reason 340
Cruden's Concordance 449
Crusades 101, 103, 121, 127, 136, 139-151, 153, 158, 162, 167-170, 172-174, 179, 181, 187, 188, 190, 291

Cuius regio, eius religio 213, 216
Cult of the Supreme Being 366
Cultural Mandate 225, 230, 293, 299, 463
Cumberland Presbyterian Church 418
Cur Deus Homo 155

Dallas Theological Seminary 462
Danger of An Unconverted Ministry, The 398
Danites 448, 456
Dartmouth College 400
De ecclesia 198
Dead Sea Scrolls 23, 83
Decision 492
Declaration of Breda 271, 274, 302
Declaration of Independence 406
Declaration of Sentiments 248
Dedham Decision 419, 423
Deed of Declaration 333, 338
Defender of the Faith 255
Defenestration of Prague 213, 216
Deism 294, 295, 299, 304, 309-312, 314, 315, 322, 327, 329, 339, 366, 385, 407-409, 411-413, 425, 495
Depression 474
Des Moines University 474
Descent of Man, The 295
Dialogue with Trypho the Jew 15
Diatessaron 14, 15, 19
Didache 13, 19, 42, 48, 69
Diet of Augsburg 212, 216
Diet of Speier (1526) 211, 216
Diet of Speier (1529) 212, 216
Diet of Worms 209, 214, 215
Diggers 270
Disciples of Christ 418, 423, 429, 474, 485
Disestablishment 351-354, 360
Dispensationalism 355, 356, 459, 461-466, 470
Divine Right of Kings 246, 265, 267, 302
Docetism 11, 19
Doctrine and Covenants 450
Documentary Hypothesis 343, 349, 472
Dominicans 158, 159, 165, 168, 169, 171, 174, 176, 177, 199, 200, 207, 277
Donation of Constantine 110, 112, 122, 188
Donation of Pepin 110, 112
Donatism 16, 38, 63, 71, 74-77, 80, 100, 131
Down Grade Controversy 355, 360
Dragonnade 364, 369
Drunken Parliament 303
Duquesne University 491
Dutch Reformed 247, 367, 368, 391, 392, 397

Earthquake Synod 196
Ebionism 23, 26, 29, 70
Ecce Homo 317
Ecclesiastical History 56
Ecumenism 345, 377, 479-481, 484-488
Edict of Milan 26, 38, 40, 45-49, 85
Edict of Nantes 244, 250, 251, 363-365, 369, 392
Edict of Toleration 366
Elizabethan Settlement 260
Emancipation Proclamation 431, 438, 440
Empiricism 339, 340
Enlightenment 283, 287, 307, 309, 313-315, 322, 339, 349, 365, 366, 368, 369, 372
Enquiry 374, 378
Ephrata Cloister 446
Epicureanism 22
Epiphany 50, 53
Episcopalians 409, 429, 461, 482, 485, 491
Essays and Reviews 353
Essenes 23, 83, 93
Eutychianism 71, 74, 75, 80
Evangelical Alliance 480
Evangelical United Brethren 485
Evangelism Explosion 493, 497
Evidence from Scripture and History of the Second Coming of Christ, About the Year 1843 449
Evolution 291, 295, 296, 299, 300, 341, 342, 344, 346, 349, 354, 355, 357, 460, 467, 468, 470, 471, 476, 480, 493, 495
Ex cathedra 283, 284
Ex opere operato 281, 284
Exclusive Brethren 356
Execrabilis 188, 190
Existentialism 283, 339, 345, 346, 348, 350
Expect Great Things from God, Attempt Great Things for God 374
Exsurge domini 205, 209

Faith and Order 481-484, 487
Father Divine Peace Mission 439
Federal Council of Churches of Christ in America 480, 481, 487
Feminism 431, 434, 481, 494, 498
Fifth Monarchy Men 270
Filioque Controversy 132-134, 138, 187
First Blast of the Trumpet Against the Monstrous Regiment of Women 245
First Great Awakening 304, 331, 389, 392, 397, 400-403, 406, 411, 419, 436, 492
First Kappel War 220, 241
First Lateran Council 187
Five Books of Moses 472
Five Mile Act 271
Five Points of Calvinism 225, 226, 230, 249, 411
Formula of Concord 213

Fort William College 375
Forty-Two Articles 257, 258
Fourth Lateran Council 128, 147, 165, 171, 187
Franciscans 128, 159, 163, 165, 169-171, 173, 176, 187, 188, 200, 277
Fraticelli 171
Free Methodists 490
Free University of Amsterdam 368
Freedom of the Christian Man, The 209
Freedom of the Will, The 211
Freethinkers 310, 314
French and Indian War 405, 413
French Revolution 244, 276, 312, 313, 327, 366, 368, 369, 419
Friends of Universal Reform 425
Fruitlands 447
Fuller Theological Seminary 490
Fundamentalism 459, 461, 462, 464, 465, 467, 469-477, 485, 490, 492-494, 497
Fundamentalist Fellowship 473
Fundamentals, The 470

Gallican Confession 242, 251
General Association of Regular Baptists 474
Geneva Bible 257, 266
Geocentrism 298
German Christians 347, 350
Gilded Age 468
Glorious Revolution 272, 274, 302-304, 306, 309
Gnosticism 8, 15, 17, 23-29, 43-45, 60, 68, 69, 73, 80, 83, 84, 89, 97, 131, 450
God in the Dock 358
God-fearer 5, 10
Gospel of Truth, The 24, 29, 69
Grand Remonstrance 268
Great Bible 257
Great Papal Schism 182-187, 190, 191, 195, 196, 203
Great Schism 121, 131-138, 140, 284
Gunpowder Plot 266, 273

Hadith 99
Half-Way Covenant 388, 389, 395, 397, 399, 400, 406
Halley's Comet 221, 229
Hampden-Sydney College 459
Hampton Court Conference 265, 273
Hanover Presbytery 401
Hare Krishna 297
Harmony Society 446
Harvard University 373, 387, 388, 399-401, 419
Haystack Prayer Meeting 419
Hebrew and English Lexicon of the Old Testament 461
Hegira 98, 103

Heidelberg Catechism 247
Heliocentrism 291-293, 299
Helvetic Consensus 250, 366
Herrnhut 320, 321, 325, 329, 332
High Church 328, 330, 351, 353-355, 360
Hinduism 83, 321, 375, 376, 412
Hobbit, The 358
Holiness Movement 490, 497
Hollow Men, The 105
Holy Club 328, 330, 332, 337
Homoousios 75
Hopedale 447
Hospitallers 169
House of Burgesses 384, 426
Huguenots 220, 221, 225, 241-244, 250, 363-366, 369, 373, 391, 392
Humanae Salutis 284
Humiliati 170
Hundred Years' War 195
Hussites 149, 174, 187, 198, 199, 202, 203, 235, 320
Hutterites 233, 235, 238, 239
Hypercalvinism 308, 314, 354, 372, 374, 379

Icons 75, 101, 109, 110, 113-115, 120, 132, 133, 135
Idealism 341, 352, 453
Ijma 99
Imitation of Christ, The 201
Immaculate Conception 91, 93, 159
In Darkest England and the Way Out 357
In His Steps 469
In Praise of Folly 202
Inclusive Language Lectionary 481
Independent Board of Presbyterian Foreign Missions 473, 477
Independent Fundamental Churches of America 485
Index 175, 202, 282, 284, 292
Indulgences 141, 147, 148, 172, 180, 181, 187, 188, 190, 197, 199, 201, 203, 207, 208, 215, 219, 280
Industrial Revolution 327, 351, 360, 373
Infralapsarianism 248, 251
Inklings 358, 359
Inner Light 270
Inquisition 128, 154, 165, 171-174, 177, 187, 188, 201, 209, 226, 243, 247, 267, 275-277, 280, 285, 286, 291, 295, 363, 389
Institutes 366
Institutes of the Christian Religion 222, 223, 225, 227, 241, 242, 407
Interdict 127-129, 148, 179, 197, 200
International Council of Christian Churches 485
International Council on Biblical Inerrancy 489

International Missionary Council 481-484
InterVarsity Christian Fellowship 484
Investigative Judgment 450, 452, 456
Irvingites 27, 355, 356, 490
Islam 46, 47, 77, 97-103, 105, 109, 113-115, 120, 131, 133, 135, 136, 138-144, 147-151, 153, 158, 160, 170, 171, 179, 199, 276, 278, 286, 321, 363, 368, 377, 379, 412, 439, 440, 443

Jansenists 282, 294, 365
Jefferson Bible 407, 413
Jehovah's Witnesses 80, 422, 439, 450, 451, 454, 455, 457
Jerusalem Council 5, 10, 343
Jesuits 168, 186, 199, 202, 212, 214, 250, 260, 266, 275, 277-279, 282, 285, 286, 294, 355, 363, 364, 371
"Jesus Freaks" 491, 497
Jihad 100, 147
Jinn 97, 103
Judaizers 6, 7, 10, 23

Ka'aba 97-99, 103, 144
Killing Time 303
King James Version 202, 210, 257, 260, 266, 357
King's College 353
Know Thyself 157
Ku Klux Klan 426, 438

L'Abri Fellowship 495
Laetare Hierusalem 284
Lane Theological Seminary 427, 461, 469
Latitudinarians 309, 311, 312, 314, 315, 327, 351, 366
Laura 86, 92
Lay investiture 125, 126, 129, 139, 141, 155, 306
Lay patronage 304, 306
League of Smalcald 212, 213, 216
Lent 50, 53, 86, 115, 134, 200, 217, 219
Levellers 270
Lex Rex 302, 306
Libellus 36, 40, 74
Liberator, The 427
Libertines 224, 228, 230, 246
Liberty University 490
Life and Work 481-484, 487
Life of Jesus 343
Loci Communes 210
Log College 398, 399, 401
Logos 16, 19, 72, 73
Lollards 174, 185, 196, 197, 199, 202, 203, 253
London Company 383-385
London Confession 268, 308

London Missionary Society 479
Long Parliament 268, 269
Lord of the Rings, The 358
Louisiana Purchase 416
Low Church 351, 352, 360
Lutherans 196, 210-218, 220, 225, 227, 229, 231,
 233, 236, 239, 247, 280, 317-323, 325, 329,
 345, 363, 366, 372, 391-393, 401, 402, 408,
 410, 471, 474, 484, 485, 489, 491, 493
Lux Mundi 353

Magdeburg Centuries 279
Magi 25
Magna Carta 128, 129, 187
Magna Mater 22, 29
Mandaeans 25, 29
Manichaeism 25, 26, 62, 89, 158, 172, 446
Maranatha 462
Marburg Colloquy 212, 216, 220
Marrow of Modern Divinity, The 304
Marrowmen 304, 306
Marxism 296, 300, 341, 349, 439, 481, 484
Masoretes 366
Massachusetts Metaphysical College 453
Mayflower Compact 385
Mennonites 233, 237, 267, 391, 393, 408, 410, 413
Mental reservation 278, 279, 286
Mercantilism 406, 413
Mere Christianity 358
Methodist Revival 327, 330, 334, 335, 338, 352,
 354, 379, 402
Methodists 27, 327-338, 351, 352, 354, 355, 357,
 372, 379, 401, 402, 409, 412, 413, 415-418,
 422, 423, 425, 428, 430, 436-438, 443, 452,
 460, 471, 480, 483, 485, 486, 490, 491, 497
Mexican War 449
Mile Act 303, 306
Millenary Petition 265, 273
Millerites 27, 449, 452
Miracle Wheat 454
Missouri Synod Lutherans 471, 472, 474, 484, 485, 489
Mithraism 22, 29, 97
Modalism 70, 71, 80
Monarchianism 70, 80
Monophysitism 74, 75, 80, 99
Monothelitism 74, 75, 80
Montanism 16, 23, 26-29, 35, 43, 68, 70, 77, 80,
 84, 89, 490
Moody Bible Institute 421, 462, 470
Moral Majority 471, 490
Moravians 27, 199, 320, 321, 325, 328-330, 332,
 334, 337, 338, 342, 373, 391, 401, 410

Mormon War 448
Mormons 363, 422, 447-451, 455, 456
Morning and Evening 355
Mount Hermon School 421
Muggletonians 270
Muratorian Canon 68, 69
Mystery cults 22, 23, 25, 26, 29

Napoleonic Wars 296
*Narrative of the Surprising Work of God in New
 England, A* 399
Nation of Islam 439
National Apostasy, The 353
National Assembly 366
National Association of Christian Schools 493
National Association of Evangelicals 485, 493
National Association of Religious Broadcasters 485
National Baptist Convention 438
National Council of Churches 480, 481, 485-487
National Covenant 268, 273, 301-303, 306
National Prohibition Party 430
National Sunday School Association 485
Navigators 484
Nazirites 83
Nazism 347-349
Neo-Orthodoxy 339, 346, 348, 350, 482
Neoplatonism 62, 63, 83, 118
Nestorianism 73, 75, 80, 91, 99
New Age 297
New Divinity 410, 419, 425, 459, 460
New England Primer 387
New Lights 400-403
New Measures 420, 423, 459, 460
New Model Army 269
New School 428, 460
New Side 398, 402, 403
New World Translation of the Holy Scriptures 450, 455
New York Presbytery 461
Niagara Bible Conferences 462, 470
Nicene Creed 72, 75, 132-134, 138, 234
Nichiren Shoshu Buddhism 440, 443
Nicolaitanism 125, 129, 134
Ninety-Five Theses 208, 215, 219, 275
Nominalism 154, 156, 157, 159, 160, 162, 195, 198
Northern Baptist Convention 473, 474, 477
Northfield Seminary 421

Oberlin College 420, 427, 431
Ockham's Razor 160, 163
Octavius 31
Old Lights 400, 401, 403
Old School 428, 460
Old Side 398, 403

Index of Events, Movements, Organizations, Books, and Terms 529

On Fasting 27
Oneida Community 446
Oneida Institute 427
Ontological Argument 155, 159, 162, 294
Open Brethren 356
Oratory of Divine Love 277, 280, 286
Order of the Grain of Mustard Seed 319, 325
Ordinance of 1787 426
Origin of Paul's Religion, The 472
Origin of Species, The 295, 467
Orthodox Presbyterian Church 473, 474, 477
Out of the Silent Planet 358
Oxford Movement 354, 360
Oxford University 159, 195-197, 203, 328-332, 353, 354, 360

Panic of 1837 448, 449
Patarenes 172
Patriarchs 43-48, 52, 56, 101, 108, 109, 114, 115, 122, 131, 133-137, 142, 146
Patripassionism 70
Paulicians 26, 172
Pax Britannica 373
Pax Romana 6, 10, 205, 373
Peace of Augsburg 213
Peace of Westphalia 214, 247
Pearl of Great Price 450
Peasants' Revolt 211, 216, 241
Pelagianism 46, 63, 71, 75, 77, 78, 80, 81, 89, 115, 157, 195, 460
Pensacola Christian College 493
Pentecost 3, 26, 50, 463
Pentecostalism 27, 29, 334, 355, 460, 490-492, 494, 497
Pentland Rising 303
Perelandra 358
Perfectionism 333, 334, 338, 420, 425, 445, 447, 460, 490
Pharisees 3, 51
Philadelphia College of Bible 462
Philadelphia Presbytery 398
Pia desideria 318, 329
Pietism 27, 317-326, 329, 331, 332, 335, 337, 342, 349, 372, 373, 379, 397, 401, 446, 447, 456, 491
Pilgrim Holiness Church 486
Pilgrim's Progress 271
Pilgrims 267, 385, 386, 390, 391, 394
Pit and the Pendulum, The 174
Place of the Lion, The 358
Plan of Union 418, 423, 460
Platonism 72, 73, 155, 339
Pleroma 24, 25, 29
Plymouth Brethren 356, 358, 360, 461, 464
Poor Clares 170

Pornocracy 123, 129, 179
Portland Deliverance 461, 465, 470, 472
Praemunire 255, 263
Pragmatic Sanction of Bourges 241
Premonstrants 168, 176
Presbyterian Church in America 474, 486
Presbyterians 224, 225, 229, 245, 246, 265, 266, 268, 269, 301-308, 312, 332, 351, 386, 393, 397-402, 408, 417, 418, 420, 423, 427, 428, 436, 449, 459-462, 469, 470, 472-474, 477, 481, 483, 485, 486, 490, 491, 493, 495
Presuppositionalism 495, 498
Prince, The 188, 254
Princeton Theological Seminary 427, 459-461, 464, 465, 467, 469, 472, 489
Princeton University 398, 406, 459
Principia Mathematica 293, 299
Probabilism 278, 279, 286
Program to Combat Racism 484
Prohibition 402, 429-431, 433, 473, 494, 498
Protectorate 270, 271
Pseudo-Isidorean Decretals 122, 129
Puritans 225, 241, 260, 261, 264-269, 271-274, 301, 302, 307, 308, 314, 317, 329, 334, 351, 367, 383-395, 397, 399, 406-408, 411, 413, 418, 419, 422, 423, 425, 429, 445, 469, 471, 476

Quakers 270, 273, 332, 334, 385, 387, 390-394, 408, 410, 413, 431, 445, 446, 456
Quartodeciman Controversy 45, 50, 53
Queen's College 397
Quest of the Historical Jesus, The 345
Quintomonarchists 270
Qur'an 98-100, 103

Ramadan 99, 103
Ramayana 375
Rappites 446
Rationalism 308, 312, 318, 322, 324, 329, 339, 340, 349, 366, 368, 372, 400, 406, 411, 425, 449, 460
Realism 154-157, 162, 195, 198, 203
Reasonableness of Christianity, The 309
Reconstruction 437, 438, 443
Reform Bill 353
Reformed 196, 211-217, 220, 221, 225, 227, 231, 233, 239, 244, 245, 247, 248, 250, 260, 268, 293, 320, 346, 347, 363, 366, 372
Reformed Presbyterian Church, Evangelical Synod 486
Reign of Terror 366
Relativity 297
Relics 37, 83, 90, 92, 93, 108, 140, 142, 144, 146, 150, 198, 201, 210, 219
Remanence 197

Remonstrance 248, 249
Remonstrants 248, 249, 252, 333, 367
Renaissance 102, 103, 136, 148, 151, 160, 161, 163, 188, 189, 195, 199-201, 203-205, 218-220, 247, 253-255, 276, 277, 292, 299
Reservations 181, 190
Restoration 271, 274, 302, 307, 308, 314, 333
Rime of the Ancient Mariner, The 352
Rochester Theological Seminary 469, 473
Roe vs. Wade 494
Romanticism 342, 352, 453
Roundheads 269
Rump Parliament 269
Russellites 454
Russian Orthodox Church 483, 488
Rutgers University 397

Sabellianism 70
Sadducees 3
St. Bartholomew's Day Massacre 243, 251
Salters' Hall 312
Salvation Army 357, 359, 361
Sandy Creek Baptist Association 401
Sanhedrin 3, 4, 6, 10, 195
Saturnalia 50, 53
Savoy Confession 268
Scapulary 168, 176
Schleitheim Confession 232, 233
Scholasticism 102, 103, 105, 121, 153-163, 175, 195, 202, 282, 291, 318, 339
Schwenkfelders 391
Science and Health with Key to the Scriptures 450, 453, 454
Scopes Trial 470, 471, 476
Scottish Common Sense Realism 460
Scriptoria 89, 93
Sea Beggars 247, 251
Second Great Awakening 401, 402, 411, 415, 419, 422, 423, 425, 429, 436, 445-447, 449, 456, 459, 460, 469
Second Helvetic Confession 221
Second Kappel War 221, 241
Second Lateran Council 187
Semi-Arianism 72
Semi-Augustinianism 71, 78, 80, 108, 115, 331
Semi-Pelagianism 78, 80
Separatists 247, 261, 385, 386, 390, 391
Septuagint 6, 10, 70
Serampore College 375
Serampore Trio 375, 379
Serious Call to a Devout and Holy Life, A 329
Shakers 445-447, 456
Shall the Fundamentalists Win? 472, 475

Shepherd, The 12, 19, 68, 69
Short Parliament 268
Shrine of the Black Madonna 219
Sic et Non 157, 162
Sierra Leone Mission 376
Simony 125, 126, 129, 195
Sinners in the Hands of an Angry God 403
Six Articles 256
Six Discourses on the Miracles of Our Saviour 310
Social Creed of the Churches, The 480
Social Darwinism 296, 300, 469
Social Gospel 339, 345, 346, 460, 469, 473, 476, 480-482, 487
Society of Friends 270
Society of Jesus 275, 277-279
Society for Poor and Infirm Aged Widows and Single Women of Good Character, Who Have Seen Better Days 425
Society for Promoting Christian Knowledge 373
Society for the Propagation of the Gospel 373, 384, 408
Society of the Public Universal Friend 446
Socinianism 312, 315, 366
Sola Scriptura 51, 275, 281
Solemn League and Covenant 268, 273, 301, 306
Southern Baptist Convention 429, 471, 472, 484, 489, 490
Spanish Armada 247, 260, 371
Spiritism 422, 447, 453, 456
Spiritual Exercises 277
Star Chamber 267, 273
Stigmata 171
Stoicism 22, 33, 35
Student Volunteer Movement 480
Studies in the Scriptures 454
Summa Contra Gentiles 158
Summa Theologica 158, 159
Sunday School 334, 338, 421, 485, 492, 493
Supralapsarianism 248, 251
Supremacy Oath 271
Suras 99, 103
Sword and the Trowel, The 355
Synagogue 25, 48, 52, 60, 142, 148
Synod of Carthage 69, 70
Synod of Constantinople 17, 19
Synod of Dordt 225, 226, 248, 249, 252, 367
Synod of Frankfurt 115
Synod of Mainz 116
Synod of Rome 69, 70
Synod of Toledo 133
Synod of Whitby 106
Systematic Theology 459, 460

Index of Events, Movements, Organizations, Books, and Terms 531

Table Talk 211
Taborites 199, 203
Talmud 99
Taurobolium 22, 29
Teaching of the Twelve Apostles, The 13, 68
Temperance 420-422, 426, 429-433, 480
Templars 169, 187
Test Act 271, 274, 303, 306
Teutonic Knights 169
Textus Receptus 202
That Hideous Strength 313, 358
Theocracy 200, 225, 228, 386, 389, 391, 393-395
Theology for the Social Gospel, A 469
Theology of Crisis 346
Theology of Hope 348
Theology of Liberation 348, 439, 484
Theology of Moral Value 344
Theopneustia 367
Third Lateran Council 171, 187
Thirty Years' War 213, 216, 235, 266, 267, 317, 320, 325, 391, 392
Thirty-Nine Articles 308, 312, 315, 354
Time 489
Tome 74
Toronto Baptist Seminary 474
Tractarians 354, 355, 358-360
Transcendental Meditation 297
Transcendentalism 445, 447, 449, 456
Transubstantiation 16, 19, 49, 116-118, 120, 128, 172, 173, 187, 196, 197, 201, 209, 271, 280-282, 284
Transylvania Presbytery 418
Treasury of David, The 355
Treatise on Religious Affections 400
Treaty of Paris 416
Treaty of Verdun 121, 122, 129
True Christianity 318
Tumult of Amboise 243, 251

Unam sanctam 179, 180, 190
Uncle Tom's Cabin 419, 427
Unification Church 455, 486
Unigenitus 365, 369
Union Theological Seminary 461, 469

Unitarianism 237, 304, 308, 311, 312, 315, 353, 354, 366, 372, 389, 400, 419, 421, 425, 460, 485
Unitas Fratrum 199, 320, 325
United Church of Christ 485
United Foreign Missionary Society 479
United House of Prayer for All People 439
Universalists 447, 485
University of Alcala 277

University of Basel 218, 366
University of Berlin 341
University of Bourges 222
University of Calcutta 376
University of Chicago Divinity School 469, 473
University of Erfurt 201, 206
University of Geneva 224
University of Halle 319, 321, 325, 329, 342, 372, 373, 401
University of Ingolstadt 208, 231
University of Leipzig 197, 319, 325
University of Leyden 248
University of Notre Dame 491
University of Orleans 222
University of Paris 156, 159, 184, 190, 221, 222, 242, 277, 278
University of Pennsylvania 399
University of Prague 197
University of St. Andrews 302
University of Saumur 249, 252, 366
University of Tübingen 339, 343, 344
University of Vienna 218
University of Wittenberg 206-210, 212, 213, 244, 318, 320
Urim and Thummim 448, 456
Ursulines 277
Utopia 445
Utraquists 199, 203

Vatican I 283, 284, 287
Vatican II 135, 185, 283-285, 287
Vedas 279
Virgin Birth, The 472
Vulgate 61, 62, 65, 70, 110, 196, 256, 282, 284

Waldensians 128, 170, 172-177, 187, 195, 196, 199, 202, 218, 234, 237, 242, 276
War Cry, The 357
Wars of the Roses 254
Wesleyan Methodist Church 428, 486, 490
Westminster Assembly 268, 269, 273, 302, 307
Westminster Confession 268, 308, 398, 417, 420, 460
Westminster Standards 268, 269, 273, 459
Westminster Theological Seminary 472, 473, 495
What Is Christianity? 345
White Horse Inn 254
Williams College 419
Women's Christian Temperance Union 421, 430
World Council of Churches 481-488
World Missionary Conference 481
World War I 344, 346, 347, 350, 377, 425, 430, 438, 443, 469, 481, 482

World War II 348, 377, 482, 493
World's Student Christian Federation 480

Yale University 398-401, 419, 446
Young Men's Christian Association 421, 480
Young Women's Christian Association 480

Youth for Christ 492

Zealots 6, 7, 10
Zion's Watchtower 454
Zoroastrianism 22, 25, 100

www.ingramcontent.com/pod-product-compliance
Lightning Source LLC
Chambersburg PA
CBHW080526170426
43195CB00016B/2486